MOON HANDBOOKS®

GUADALAJARA

A Tequila *agavero* (agave worker) begins the harvest process by cutting away the first leaves of a mature blue agave plant.

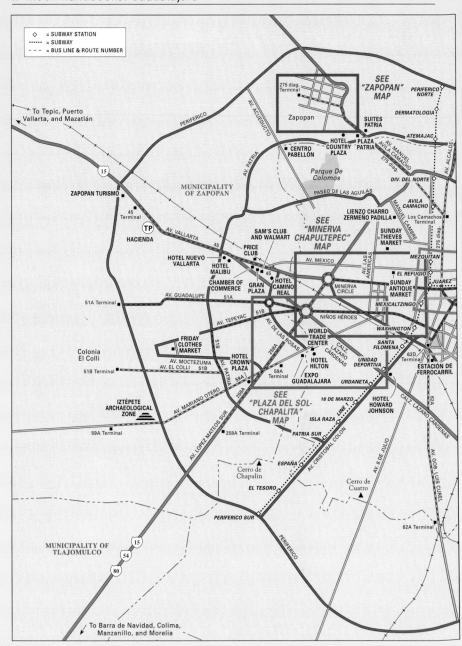

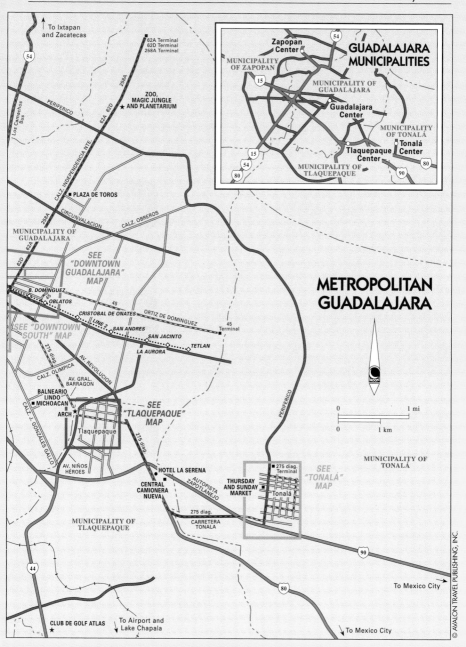

Petalillo is laboriously hand-painted.

MOON HANDBOOKS®
GUADALAJARA

FIRST EDITION

BRUCE WHIPPERMAN

AVALON
TRAVEL

Moon Handbooks: Guadalajara
First Edition

Bruce Whipperman

Published by
Avalon Travel Publishing
1400 65th Street, Suite 250
Emeryville, CA 94608 USA

Please send all comments, corrections,
additions, amendments, and critiques to:

Moon Handbooks: Guadalajara
AVALON TRAVEL PUBLISHING
1400 65TH STREET, SUITE 250
EMERYVILLE, CA 94608, USA
email: atpfeedback@avalonpub.com
www.moon.com

Printing History
1st edition—October 2002
5 4 3 2 1

ISBN: 1-56691-419-1
ISSN: 1541-3012

Editor: Jeff Lupo
Series Manager: Erin Van Rheenen
Copy Editor: Gina Wilson Birtcil
Graphics Coordinator: Melissa Sherowski, Erika Howsare
Production Coordinator: Darren Alessi
Cover Designer: Kari Gim
Interior Designers: Amber Pirker, Alvaro Villanueva, Kelly Pendragon
Map Editor: Olivia Solís
Cartographers: Mike Morgenfeld, Bart Wright, Annette Olson, Kat Kalamaras
Proofreader: Kristina Malsberger
Indexer: Laura Welcome

Front cover photo: © Bruce Whipperman

Distributed by Publishers Group West

Printed in the United States by Worzalla

ABOUT THE AUTHOR
Bruce Whipperman

In the early 1980s, the lure of travel drew Bruce Whipperman away from a 20-year career of teaching physics. The occasion was a trip to Kenya, which included a total solar eclipse and a safari. He hasn't stopped traveling since.

With his family grown, he has been free to let the world's wild, beautiful corners draw him on: to the ice-clawed Karakoram; the Gobi Desert's trellised oases; the pink palaces of Rajasthan; Japan's green wine country; Bali's emerald terraces; and the Puerto Vallarta region's golden beaches, wildlife-rich mangrove wetlands, and flower-festooned mountain valleys.

Bruce has always pursued his travel career for the fun of it. He started with slide shows and photo gifts for friends. Others wanted his photos, so he began selling them. Once, stranded in Ethiopia, he began to write. A dozen years later, after scores of magazine and newspaper feature stories, *Pacific Mexico Handbook* became his first book. For him, travel writing heightens his awareness and focuses his own travel experiences. He always remembers what a Nepali Sherpa once said: "Many people come, looking, looking; few people come, see."

Travel, after all, is for returning home, and that coziest of journeys always brings a tired but happy Bruce back to his friends, family, and wife, Linda, in Oakland, California.

Bruce invites *Moon Handbooks: Guadalajara*'s readers likewise to "come see"—and discover and enjoy—Guadalajara's delights with a fresh eye and renewed compassion.

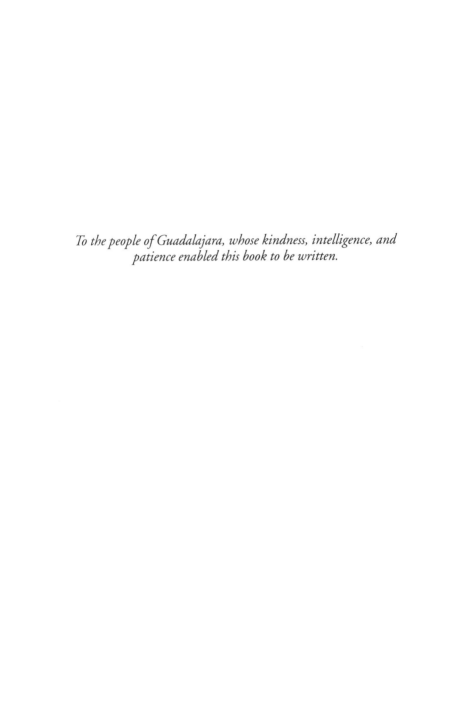

To the people of Guadalajara, whose kindness, intelligence, and patience enabled this book to be written.

Contents

THE HEART OF THE CITY 97

CITY: WEST AND NORTH OF DOWNTOWN 131

SPECIAL TOPICS

CITY: EAST AND SOUTH OF DOWNTOWN 181

HISTORY 182
TLAQUEPAQUE 182
Sights; Accommodations; Food; Entertainment and Events; Sports and
Recreation; Shopping; Services; Communications and Information; Health,
Emergencies, and Getting There
TONALÁ 200
Sights; Accommodations; Food; Entertainment and Events; Sports and
Recreation; Shopping; Services; Communications and Information; Health,
Emergencies, and Getting There

SPECIAL TOPICS

LAKE CHAPALA AND VICINITY 214

History; Sights; Accommodations; Food; Entertainment and Events; Sports and
Recreation; Shopping; Services; Information; Getting There and Away

SPECIAL TOPICS

GUADALAJARA GETAWAYS 240

SAN JUAN DE LOS LAGOS: A SHRINE FOR ALL SEASONS 241
History; Sights; Accommodations; Food; Entertainment and Events; Services and
Information; Medical and Emergencies; Getting There
MAZAMITLA: INTO THE SIERRA DEL TIGRE 247
History; Sights; Accommodations; Food; Entertainment and Events; Shopping
and Services; Information and Communications; Medical and Emergencies;
Getting There

SPECIAL TOPICS

RESOURCES 275

Maps

MAP SYMBOLS

═══ Divided Highway	◉ State Capital	⛪ Church
═══ Primary Road	○ City/Town	▲ Mountain/Volcano
═══ Secondary Road	★ Point of Interest	ⓉⓅ Trailer Park
------ Unpaved Road	• Accommodation	⛽ Gas Station
▓▓▓ Pedestrian Street	▾ Restaurant/Bar	🯌 Waterfall
	▪ Other Location	⛰ Archaeological Site

© AVALON TRAVEL PUBLISHING, INC.

Abbreviations

a/c—air-conditioning
Av.—*avenida* (avenue)
Blv.—*bulevar* (boulevard)
C—Celsius
Calz.—*calzada* (thoroughfare, main road)
d—double occupancy
Fco.—Francisco (proper name, as in "Fco. Villa")
Fracc.—*Fraccionamiento* (subdivision)
Hwy.—Highway

Km—kilometer marker
kph—kilometers per hour
km—kilometers
Nte.—*norte* (north)
Ote.—*oriente* (east)
Pte.—*poniente* (west)
s—single occupancy
s/n—*sin número* (no street number)
t—triple occupancy

Keeping Current

We're especially interested in hearing from female travelers, handicapped travelers, people who've traveled with children, RVers, seniors, hikers, campers, and residents, both foreign and Mexican. We welcome the comments of business and professional people—hotel and restaurant owners, travel agents, government tourism staff—who serve Guadalajara travelers.

We welcome submissions of unusually good photos and drawings for possible use in future editions. If photos, send duplicate slides or slides from negatives; if drawings, send clear photocopies. Please include a self-addressed stamped envelope if you'd like your material returned. If we use it, we'll cite your contribution and give you a free new edition. Please address your responses to:

Moon Handbooks: Guadalajara
Avalon Travel Publishing
1400 65th Street, Suite 250
Emeryville, CA 94608 USA
email: atpfeedback@avalonpub.com

Preface

Manifold motivations propel the millions of foreign arrivees who visit Guadalajara every year. Many of them come to bask in its year-round springlike weather, so beautiful that anytime is the best time to go. Others come for Guadalajara's wonderful handicrafts: from papier-mâché so fine that it resembles bright sculpture; to opals by the handful; to fetching pottery animals and designer resort wear.

The list goes on. An army of businesspersons come to sell and to buy the products of Guadalajara's burgeoning "Silicon Valley of the South," a label that has gone far past a slogan. A list of Guadalajara's giant electronics plants—Sony, Hewlitt-Packard, NEC, Motorola, Intel—reads like a who's who of the computer revolution.

Others come to Guadalajara seeking a quiet retirement. Many folks, after selling their U.S. or Canadian homes, settle in Guadalajara or along the shores of Lake Chapala. Many of them find much more luxurious homes than they had in Palo Alto or Winnipeg—often for half the price, with servants—and there's enough left over to live on the interest.

Plenty more come simply because they've heard the buzz: Guadalajara (the "Most Mexican of Cities") and its environs abound with culture—venerated monuments, beloved old churches, world-class folkloric performances, renowned murals, quiet country hot springs resorts, adored pilgrimage shrines, picturesque colonial mountain towns, historic haciendas, world-class restaurants, and much more. It's simply enough to write a book about.

Introduction

The Land

Guadalajara (pop. 3.5 million), Western Mexico's grand capital, is blessed with a sunny, spring-like climate and fertile soils, born from the host of ancient volcanoes that dot its region. Go to any high place in the city on a clear day and you'll see these volcanoes as humps and hillocks rising from the broad Atemajac Valley (Place Where the Waters Divide Among the Rocks) that surrounds the metropolis.

One of the most prominent of these is the still-active **Volcán Colli** (Volcano of the Gods, approx. 7,500 feet, 2,300 meters) jutting up beyond the city's southwest suburb. Shift your view westward to the far horizon, and on a clear day you'll see the rugged mass of **Volcán Tequila,** (9,580 feet, 2,920 meters), with the unique rounded plug topping its summit.

Continue your survey by reversing your view to the opposite horizon and look for the dark, brooding massif of **Cerro Gordo** (Fat Mountain, 8,760 feet, 2,670 meters), on the eastern horizon, and the same for **Cerro las Gallinas** (Mountain of the Hens, 8,301 feet, 2,530 meters) to the far southeast.

Rivers and lakes likewise feature prominently in Guadalajara's list of geographical surprises. Hidden south of the city, beyond the ridge, marked on its western side by high peak **Cerro Bela del Viejo** (9,710 feet, 2,960 meters), spreads the broad expanse of **Lake Chapala,** Mexico's largest lake. Hidden to the west of Lake Chapala, a number of lesser lakes, including **Laguna de Sayula, Laguna San Marcos,** and **Laguna Atotonilco** decorate the landscape. At this writing, Lake Chapala has receded to it lowest level in memory—hopefully, though, authorities will prevent it from suffering the same fate as very shallow lakes Sayula and San Marcos, now nearly always dry.

© BRUCE WHIPPERMAN

The tropical, deciduous forest of the Barranca del Río Grande de Santiago grows right into the north edge of urban Guadalajara.

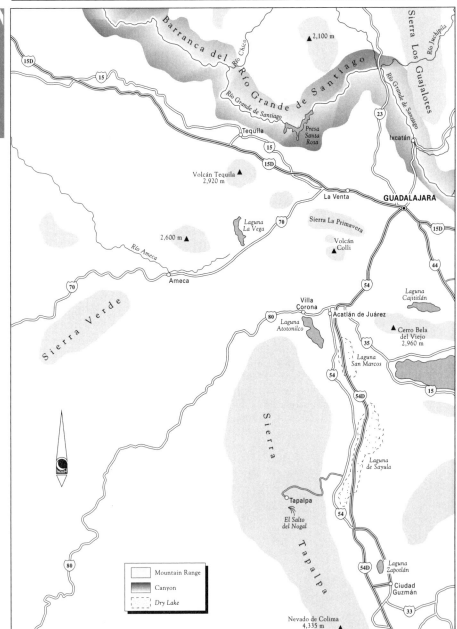

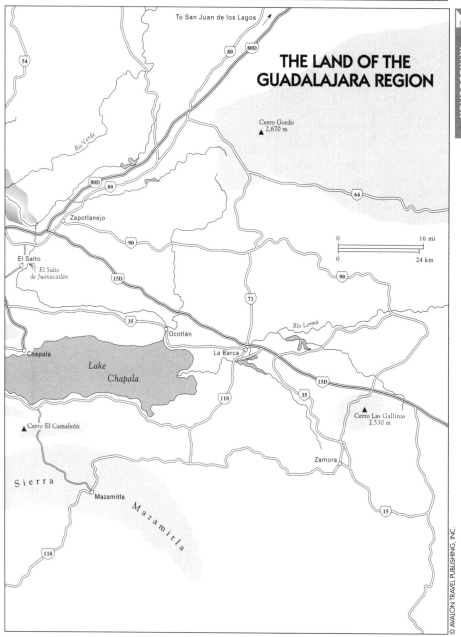

THE LAND OF THE
GUADALAJARA REGION

To San Juan de los Lagos

Cerro Gordo
▲ 2,670 m

Río Verde

Zapotlanejo

El Salto
El Salto
de Juanacatlán

Río Lerma

Ocotlán

La Barca

Chapala

Lake
Chapala

Cerro Las Gallinas
▲ 2,530 m

▲ Cerro El Camaleón

Zamora

Sierra

Mazamitla

Mazamitla

0   16 mi
0   24 km

© AVALON TRAVEL PUBLISHING, INC.

(See the special topic Of Whitefish and Water Hyacinths in the Lake Chapala chapter.)

The fate of Lake Chapala is strongly tied to that of another of Guadalajara's natural wonders, the **Río Lerma–Santiago.** Mexico's longest river, the Lerma-Santiago rises in the mountains west of Mexico City and flows westward through eight states—Mexico, Michoacán, Aguascalientes, Queretaro, Guanajuato, Zacatecas, Jalisco, and Nayarit—finally emptying into the Pacific Ocean, north of San Blas.

Despite its long meandering journey, the Lerma-Santiago's crucial juncture is in Jalisco not far southeast of Guadalajara, where, known as the Lerma upstream, and appearing as a mere drainage canal at La Barca town, it empties into Lake Chapala. Then, at Ocotlán, only about 15 miles to the northwest, the river, thenceforth known as the Santiago downstream, flows out of the lake and meanders northwest through the Atemajac Valley.

In the southeast city outskirts, at **El Salto** (The Jump), the river drops in rainy years as a foaming, brown waterfall. El Salto also marks the beginning of another of the river's episodes: the **Barranca,** or more formally, the **Grand Canyon of the Río Santiago.** The river's channel, starting as a mere crease in the Atemajac Valley at El Salto, quickly grows to a magnificent verdant gorge. It's conveniently viewable from points (like the Guadalajara Zoo) on the north edge of town, a district locally known as Huentitán. Here, the viewer's eye follows an airy panorama down the canyon slope, dropping steeply to the tropical river bottom far below, then rising on the far north side to towering ramparts topped by high oak- and pine-studded ridges.

GUADALAJARA TEMPERATURE AND RAINFALL

Average high and low temperatures (in degrees Fahrenheit and Celsius) and the monthly average rainfall (in inches and centimeters):

Month	High and Low Temperatures (°F and °C)	Rainfall (in. and cm)
January	72, 22 and 45, 7	.49, 1.24
February	76, 24 and 46, 8	.20, .52
March	86, 30 and 45, 7	.17, .43
April	90, 32 and 45, 7	.25, .64
May	92, 33 and 51,11	.98, 2.5
June	88, 31 and 58,14	6.6, 16.8
July	83, 28 and 55,13	10.6, 26.9
August	83, 28 and 56,13	8.5, 21.6
September	83, 28 and 52,11	5.7, 14.4
October	82, 28 and 48, 9	2.3, 6.0
November	81, 27 and 43, 6	.62, 1.6
December	81, 27 and 41, 5	.47, 1.2

Total Yearly Rainfall: 37 inches, 94 centimeters

Data Source: University of Guadalajara Institute of Astronomy and Meteorology

Even more spectacular is the descent (easiest by car or bus via Saltillo Hwy. 54—see the Zapopan section in the City: West and North of Downtown chapter) into the canyon itself. As the elevation diminishes, the air becomes warmer and noticeably more humid; hanging vines and riots of tropical verdure cover the slope. The experience climaxes with the bountiful green mango, banana, and citrus groves that carpet both sides of the river at canyon bottom.

Climate

Historical evidence indicates that Spanish colonial authorities encouraged settlement in Guadalajara for both its easy access and its dry, temperate climate. A legion of latter-day visitors and residents still enjoy Guadalajara's famously balmy two-season climate, with the rainy season coming in summer and early fall, and the dry season in winter and spring (see the chart Guadalajara Temperature and Rainfall).

Guadalajara's winter (December–February) days will usually be mild and springlike, climbing to around 75°F (24°C) by noon, with nights dropping to a temperate 45°F (5°C). Winter visitors should pack a sweater or light jacket: During cold snaps, Guadalajara's nighttime temperatures occasionally drop to near-freezing.

April, May, and June, before the rains, are customarily Guadalajara's warmest months, with highs around 90°F (32°C). July, August, and September temperatures are moderated by the rains. Mornings are typically bright, warming to the low 80s (28°C). By afternoon, clouds sometimes gather and bring short, occasionally heavy thundershowers. Later the clouds usually part, the sun dries the pavements, and the temperature cools to a balmy 70°F (21°C)—perfect for strolling.

Moreover, the Guadalajara region is blessed by a diversity of microclimates. As most everywhere in Mexico, elevation rules the climate. If, on a Guadalajara winter day, you hanker for some warmth, simply travel 30 minutes downhill along Hwy. 54 north to the tropical canyon bottom of the Barranca and bask in the heat of perpetual summer—or get the same effect three hours south in Colima or Manzanillo, or four hours west in Puerto Vallarta.

Conversely, if on a warm June day you crave a spell of cool mountain breezes, simply travel two hours south to Jalisco's high mountain country—here you'll enjoy the fresh, pine-scented air and warm glow of an evening wood fire. (See the Mazamitla and Tapalpa sections in the Guadalajara Getaways chapter.)

Flora and Fauna

The Guadalajara region's strongly distinct two-season (dry-wet) climate has fostered a highly diverse and tenacious array of native animal and plant species. In the metropolitan zone, however, benign conditions—including human hands and abundant year-round irrigation water—have nurtured nonnative plants that otherwise could not survive the region's November–May drought. Thus, many neighborhoods—especially in the leafy suburbs west of the downtown center—comprise a de facto botanical garden of exotics from all over the world. In a single afternoon stroll in a suburban neighborhood, a plant lover might recognize dozens of tropical and temperate varieties, such as sago palm, coconut, bamboo, orchids, roses, elms, maples, firs, California red-

wood, eucalyptus, ginkgo, bananas, begonias, azaleas, and more.

NATURAL VEGETATION ZONES

Outside of urban and agricultural districts, plants have evolved on their own. Eons of adaptation to wet and dry, sun and shade, and competition from animals and other plants have nurtured the natural cover of the Guadalajara region. Botanists recognize at least 14 major vegetation zones in Mexico, five of which lie within the Guadalajara region. Most often, travelers pass by long stretches of these zones, seeing only thickets, forests, and fields, without understanding what they're seeing. However, a little advance knowledge of

INTRODUCTION

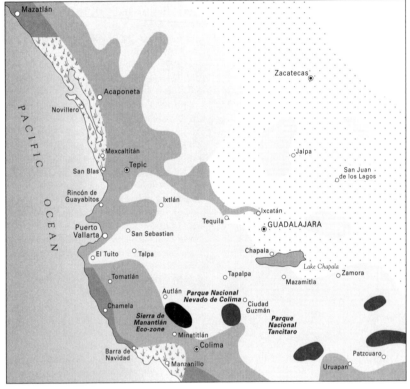

VEGETATION ZONES OF THE GUADALAJARA REGION

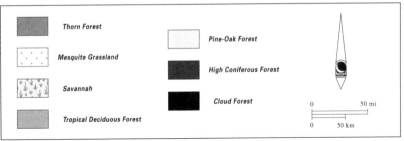

Thorn Forest

Mesquite Grassland

Savannah

Tropical Deciduous Forest

Pine-Oak Forest

High Coniferous Forest

Cloud Forest

0   50 mi

0   50 km

© AVALON TRAVEL PUBLISHING, INC.

what to expect can blossom into recognition and discovery, transforming the humdrum into the extraordinary.

Directly along the Guadalajara regional highways, travelers often pass long sections of the three most common vegetation zones: pine-oak forest, mesquite grassland, and tropical deciduous forest, each detailed below.

Pine-Oak Forest

Along the mountain highways (notably west of Guadalajara along the old, non-toll, two-lane Hwy. 15 toward Tequila and Magdalena, and south along Hwy. 80 toward Barra de Navidad), agricultural land gives way to temperate pine-oak forest, the Guadalajara region's most extensive vegetation zone. Here, many of Mexico's 112 oak and 39 pine species thrive. Oval two-inch cones and foot-long drooping needles (three to a cluster) make the *pino triste,* or sad pine *(Pinus lumholtzii),* appear in severe need of water. Unlike many of Mexico's pines, it produces neither good lumber nor much turpentine, although it *is* prized by guitar makers for its wood.

Much more regal in bearing and commer-cially important are the tall **Chihuahua pine** *(Pinus chihuahuana)* and **Chinese pine** *(Pinus leiophylla).* Both reddish-barked with yellow wood, they resemble the ponderosa pine of the Western United States. You can tell them apart by their needles: the *pino prieto* (Chihuahua pine) has three to a cluster, while the *pino Chino* (Chinese pine) has five.

Pines often grow in stands mixed with **oaks,** which fall into two broad classifications—*encino* (evergreen, small-leafed) and *roble* (deciduous, large-leafed)—both much like the oaks that dot California hills and valleys. Clustered on their branches and scattered in the shade, *bellota* (acorns) distinctly mark them as oaks. The **Bosque de Primavera** is the most accessible and diverse pine-oak forest preserve in the Guadalajara region (see the Guadalajara Getways chapter).

Mesquite Grassland

Although many outlying districts have been tamed into farmland, much of the country northeast of Guadalajara (notably along Hwy. 80 between Tepatitlán and San Juan de los Lagos) exhibits the landscape of the mesquite grassland

© RÍO CALIENTE SPA

The pine-oak forest of the Bosque de Primavera coats the hills west of the Guadalajara metropolis.

vegetation zone, similar to the semiarid plateauland of the U.S. Southwest.

Despite its sometimes monotonous roadside aspect, the mesquite grassland nurtures surprisingly exotic and unusual plants. Among the most interesting is the **maguey** (mah-GAY), or century plant, so-called because it's said to bloom once, then die, after 100 years of growth—although its life span is usually closer to 50 years. The maguey and its cactuslike (but not true cacti) *Agave* relatives (**mescal,** *lechugilla,* and **sisal**) each grow as a roselike cluster of leathery, long, pointed, gray-green leaves, from which a single flower stalk eventually blooms.

Century plants themselves, which can grow as large as several feet tall and wide, thrive either wild or in cultivated fields in rank and file like a botanical army on parade. These fields, of the **blue agave** subspecies, are prominently visible from National Hwy. 15 west of Guadalajara. They are eventually harvested, crushed, fermented, and distilled into fiery 80-proof tequila, the most renowned of which comes from the town of Tequila on old Hwy. 15.

Watch for the mesquite grassland's *candelilla (Euphorbia antisyphillitica),* an odd cousin of the poinsettia, also a Mexico native. In contrast to the poinsettia, the *candelilla* resembles a tall (two- to three-foot) candle, with small white flowers scattered upward along its single vertical stem. Abundant wax on the many pencil-sized stalks that curve upward from the base is useful for anything from polishing your shoes to lubricating your car's distributor.

Equally exotic is the *sangre de drago*—"blood of the dragon"—*(Jatropha dioica),* which also grows in a single meaty stem, but with two-inch-long lobed leaves and small white flowers. Break off a stem and out oozes a clear sap, which soon turns blood-red.

Tropical Deciduous Forest

In well-watered lower-altitude areas, the pine-oak forest grades into tropical deciduous forest. This is the "friendly" or "short-tree" forest, blanketed by a tangle of summer-green leaves that fall in the dry winter to reveal thickets of branches.

© BRUCE WHIPPERMAN

The spiny bromeliad, a cousin of the pineapple, flourishes in the tropical deciduous forest of the Barranca of the Río Santiago.

Excursions by jeep or foot along shaded, off-highway tracks through the tropical deciduous forest can bestow delightful jungle scenes. During the rainy summer in the tropical deciduous forest's most verdant reaches, you might see vine-strewn thickets overhanging your path like a scene from some lost prehistoric world, where at any moment you expect a dinosaur to rear up.

Actually, the biological realities here are nearly as exotic. A four-foot-long, green iguana, looking every bit as primitive as a dinosaur, sunbathes on a rock. Nearby, a spreading, solitary **strangler fig** *(Ficus padifolia)* stands, draped with hairy, hanging air roots (which in time plant themselves in the ground to support the branches). Its Mexican name, *matapalo* (killer tree), is gruesomely accurate: strangler figs often entwine themselves in death embraces with less aggressive tree-victims.

Other, more benign trees show bright fall reds and yellows, which during the late winter blossom with brilliant flowers—spider lily, cardinal sage, pink trumpet, poppylike yellowsilk *(pomposhuti)*, and mouse-killer *(mala ratón)*, which swirl in the spring wind like cherry-blossom blizzards.

Nevertheless, unwary travelers must watch out for the poison-oaklike *mala mujer* (evil woman) tree. The oil on its large five-fingered leaves can cause an itchy rash.

Travelers can reach stretches of tropical deciduous forest easily, either along Hwy. 54 downhill north of town or south two hours toward Colima, or along Hwy. 80, past Autlán downhill.

Cloud Forest

Adventurous visitors who travel to certain remote, dewy mountainsides above 7,000 feet can explore the plant and wildlife community of the cloud forest. The Sierra Manantlán, a roadless de facto wilderness southeast of Autlán, Jalisco, and west of Colima city, preserves such a habitat. There, abundant cool fog nourishes forests of glacial-epoch remnant flora: tree ferns and lichen-draped pines and oaks, above a mossy carpet of orchids, bromeliads, and begonias.

High Coniferous Forest

The Guadalajara region's rarest, least accessible vegetation zone is the high coniferous forest, which swathes the slopes of lofty peaks, notably, the Nevado de Colima, elev. 14,220 feet (4,335 meters), on the Jalisco-Colima border. This pristine alpine island, accessible only on horseback or by foot, nurtures stands of pines and spruce, laced by grassy meadows, similar to the higher Rocky Mountain slopes in the United States and Canada. Reigning over the lesser species is the regal **Montezuma pine** *(Pinus montezumae),* distinguished by its long, pendulous cones and rough, ruddy bark, reminiscent of the sugar pine of the Western United States.

For many more details of Mexico's feast of roadside plants, see M. Walter Pesman's delightful *Meet Flora Mexicana* (unfortunately out of print, but major libraries may have copies). Also informative is the popular paperback *Handbook of Mexican Roadside Flora,* by Charles T. Mason Jr. and Patricia B. Mason.

WILDLIFE

Despite continued habitat destruction—forests are logged, wetlands filled, rivers are dammed—great swaths of the Guadalajara region still abound with wildlife. Common in the temperate pine-oak forest highlands are mammals familiar to U.S. residents: mountain lion (puma), coyote, fox *(zorro),* rabbit *(conejo),* and badger *(tejón).*

However, the tropical deciduous forests are home to fascinating species normally seen only in zoos north of the border. The reality of this dawns on travelers when they glimpse something exotic, such as raucous, screeching swarms of small green parrots rising from the roadside, or an armadillo or coati crossing the road in front of their car or bus.

Population pressures have nevertheless decreased wild habitats, endangering many previously abundant animal species. If you are lucky (and quiet) as you hike a remote forest trail, you may get a view of the endangered striped cat, the **ocelot** *(tigrillo)* or its smaller relative, the **margay.** On such an excursion, if you are really fortunate, you may hear the chesty roar or catch a glimpse of a jaguar, the fabled *el tigre.*

El Tigre

Each hill has its own *tigre,* says a Mexican proverb. With black spots spread over a yellow-tan coat, stretching five feet (1.5 meters) and weighing 200 pounds (90 kg), the typical jaguar resembles a muscular spotted leopard. Although hunted since prehistory, and now endangered, the jaguar lives on in the Guadalajara region. It hunts along thickly forested stream bottoms and foothills. Unlike the mountain lion, the jaguar will eat any game. Jaguars have even been known to wait patiently for fish in rivers and to stalk beaches for turtle and egg dinners. If they have a favorite food, it is probably the piglike wild peccary, *jabalí.* Experienced hunters agree that no two jaguars will have the same prey in their stomachs.

Although humans have died of wounds inflicted by cornered jaguars, there is little or no hard evidence that they eat humans, despite legends to the contrary.

Armadillos, Coatis, and Bats

The cat-sized **armadillos** are mammals that act and look like opossums, but carry reptilianlike shells. If you see one, remain still, and it may walk right up and sniff your foot before it recognizes you and scuttles back into the woods.

A common inhabitant of the tropical deciduous forest is the raccoonlike **coati** *(tejón, pisote)*. In the wild, coatis like shady stream banks, often congregating in large troops of 15–30 individuals. They are identified by their short brown or tan fur, small round ears, long nose, and straight, vertically held tail. They make endearing pets; the first coati you see may be one on a string offered for sale at a local market.

Mexican **bats** *(murciélagos)* are widespread, with at least 126 species compared to 37 in the United States. In Mexico, as everywhere, bats are feared and misunderstood. As sunset approaches, many bat species come out of their hiding places and flit through the air in search of insects. Most people, sitting outside enjoying the early evening, will mistake their darting silhouettes for those of birds, who, except for owls, do not generally fly at night.

Bats are often locally called *vampiros,* even though only three relatively rare Mexican species actually feed on the blood of mammals (nearly always cattle) and birds.

The many nonvampire Mexican bats carry their vampire cousins' odious reputation with forbearance. They go about their good works, pollinating flowers, clearing the air of pesky gnats and mosquitoes, ridding cornfields of mice, and dropping seeds, thereby restoring forests.

BIRDS

Despite the city environment, plenty of birds make the Guadalajara metropolitan area their home. Lots of these are kin to the familiar temperate species—busy woodpeckers *(pájaro carpintero),* soaring turkey vultures *(zopilotes)* and hawks *(halcones),* scurrying banded quail *(codorniz),* solitary mottled owls *(tecolotes),* and lots of hummingbirds *(colibris).*

Reservoirs and marshy ground in suburban and adjacent agricultural areas provide habitats for water birds, such as egrets and herons *(garzas),* especially the large, long-necked snowy egret and its even larger cousin, the majestic great blue heron. Other familiar waterborne residents—black cormorants and their cousins, the snake-necked anhingas—and also the dark brown lily-walkers *(jacanas),* stalk, nest, and preen in local lagoons and wetlands.

In forest zones, especially in semitropical lower-altitude habitats, the choices include most of the above plus exotic species seen only in U.S. and Canadian zoos. These include several varieties of small parrots, such as the lilac-crowned parrot and the Mexican parrotlet, and a number of spectacular species, such as the mountain trogon *(Trogon mexicanus),* sometimes known as the *pájaro bandera* (flag bird) for its red, white, and green coloration, identical to the Mexican flag. Nearly as spectacular is the yellow-breasted kiskadee flycatcher *(Pitangus sulpuratus),* known locally as the "Luis" bird because it seems to call this name (with a Spanish accent, of course) repeatedly.

REPTILES AND AMPHIBIANS

Snakes and Gila Monsters

Mexico has 460-odd snake species, the vast majority shy and nonpoisonous; they will get out of your way if you give plenty of warning. In Mexico, as everywhere, poisonous snakes have been largely eradicated in city and tourist areas. In brush or forest habitats, carry a stick or a machete and beat the bushes ahead of you while watching where you put your feet. When hiking or rock-climbing in the country, don't put your hand in niches you can't see into.

The most venomous of Mexican snakes is the **coral snake** *(coralillo),* which occurs as about two dozen species, all with multicolored bright bands that always include red. Although relatively rare, small, and shy, coral snakes occasionally inflict serious, sometimes fatal bites.

More aggressive and generally more dangerous is the Mexican **rattlesnake** *(cascabel)* and its viper relative, the **fer-de-lance** *(Bothrops atrox).* About the same in size (up to six feet) and appearance as the rattlesnake, the fer-de-lance (which confines itself to tropical forest habitats) is known by various local names, such as *nauyaca, cuatro narices, palanca,* and *barba amarilla.* It is potentially more hazardous than the rattlesnake because it lacks a warning rattle.

The Gila monster (confined in Mexico to northern Sonora) and its southern tropical rela-tive, the yellow-spotted, black ***escorpión** (Helo-derma horridum),* are the world's only poisonous lizards. Despite its beaded skin and menacing, fleshy appearance, the *escorpión* only bites when severely provoked. Even then, its venom is rarely fatal.

History

Once upon a time, perhaps as early as 40,000 years ago, the first bands of hunters, perhaps paddling kayaks or canoes along the coastline or trudging overland following the great game herds, crossed from Siberia to the American continent. They drifted southward, many of them eventually settling in the lush highland valleys of Mexico.

The earliest human remains found in the Guadalajara region are 10,000-year-old arrow-heads in the seminal Clovis style (of the earlier re-mains, found at Clovis, New Mexico). Much later, perhaps around 5000 B.C., these early peo-ple began gathering and grinding the seeds of a hardy grass that required only the summer rains to thrive. After generations of selective breed-ing, *teocentli* (sacred seed), the grain that we call maize or corn, led to prosperity.

Early local residents left evidence of their grow-ing sophistication. Ceramic jugs with handles, artfully decorated vases, and animal-, plant-, and human-motif figurines, between 2,500 and 1,500 years old, have been unearthed near Cerro El Tecolote, San Marcos, and Zacoalco, not far west of Guadalajara.

EARLY MEXICAN CIVILIZATIONS

With abundant food, settlements grew and leisure classes arose—artists, architects, warriors, and ruler-priests—all of whom had time to think and create. Using a calendar, they harnessed the constant wheel of the firmament to life on earth, defining the days to plant, harvest, feast, travel, and trade. Eventually, grand cities arose.

Teotihuacán

Teotihuacán, with a population of perhaps 250,000 around the time of Christ, was one of the world's great metropolises. Its epic monu-ments still stand not far north of Mexico City: the towering Pyramid of the Sun at the terminal of a grand, 150-foot-wide ceremonial avenue facing a great Pyramid of the Moon. Along the avenue sprawls a monumental temple-court surrounded by scowling, ruby-eyed effigies of Quetzalcoatl, the feathered serpent god of gods.

Its inhabitants gradually abandoned Teoti-huacán mysteriously around A.D. 650, leaving a host of former vassal states to tussle among themselves. The Guadalajara region's people—notably the Tecuejes and Cocas, but also the Huicholes, Nahuas, and Purépechas—were among these. Iztepete, their most monumental construction yet uncovered, stands at Guadala-jara's southwest edge. Recent excavations indi-cate that it was an early ceremonial site with distinct Teotihuacán architectural influence, built in several stages, beginning around the Christian era.

The Aztecs

Among the several civilizations that flowered in Mexico following the fall of Teotihuacán were the Aztecs, a collection of seven aggressive sub-tribes that migrated around A.D. 1350 from a mysterious western land of Aztlán (Place of the Herons) into the lake-filled valley that Mexico City now occupies.

The Aztecs survived by being forced to fight for every piece of ground they occupied. Within a century, the Aztecs' dominant tribe, whose members called themselves the "Méxica," had clawed its way to dominion over the Valley of Mexico. With the tribute labor that their em-perors extracted from local vassal tribes, the Méxica built a magnificent capital, Tenochtitlán, on an island in the middle of the valley-lake. From there, Aztec armies, not unlike Roman legions, marched out and subdued kingdoms for hundreds of miles in all directions. They returned with the spoils of conquest: gold, brilliant feathers, precious jewels, and captives, whom they sacrificed by the thousands as food for their gods.

Among those gods they feared was Quetzalcoatl—tradition held that he was bearded and fair-skinned. This turned out to be a remarkable, fateful coincidence. When the bearded, fair-skinned Castilian, **Hernán Cortés,** landed on Mexico's eastern coast on April 22, 1519, it happened to be the very year that legends said Quetzalcoatl would return.

The Aztecs survived by being forced to fight for every piece of ground they occupied. Within a century, the Aztecs' dominant tribe, whose members called themselves the "México," had clawed its way to dominion over the Valley of Mexico.

THE CONQUEST

Although a generation had elapsed since Columbus founded Spain's West Indian colonies, returns had been meager. Scarcity of gold and of native workers, most of whom fell victim to European diseases, turned adventurous Spanish eyes westward once again, toward rumored riches beyond the setting sun.

Preliminary excursions piqued Spanish interest, and Cortés was commissioned by Spanish Governor Diego Velázquez to explore further. Cortés, then only 34, had left his Cuban base in February 1519 with an expedition of 11 small ships, 550 men, 16 horses, and a few small cannons. By the time he landed in Mexico, he was burdened by a murderous crew. His men, mostly soldiers of fortune hearing stories of the great Aztec empire west beyond the mountains, had realized the impossible odds they faced and became restive.

Cortés, however, cut short any thoughts of mutiny by burning his ships. As he led his grumbling but resigned band of adventurers toward the Aztec capital of Tenochtitlán, Cortés played Quetzalcoatl to the hilt, awing local chiefs. Coaxed by **Doña Marina** (Malinche), Cortés' native translator-mistress, local chiefs began to add their warrior-armies to Cortés' march against their Aztec overlords.

Moctezuma, Lord of Tenochtitlán

Once inside the walls of Tenochtitlán, the Aztecs' Venicelike island-city, the Spaniards were dazzled by gardens, animals, gold and palaces, and a great pyramid-enclosed square where tens of thousands of people bartered goods gathered from all over the empire. Tenochtitlán, with perhaps a quarter of a million people, was the grand

MALINCHE

If it hadn't been for Doña Marina (whom he received as a gift from a local chief), Cortés may have become a mere historical footnote. Doña Marina, speaking both Spanish and native tongues, soon became Cortés' interpreter/go-between, and negotiator. She persuaded a number of important chiefs to ally themselves with Cortés against the Aztecs. Clever and opportunistic, Doña Marina was a crucial strategist in Cortés' deadly game of divide and conquer. She eventually bore Cortés a son and lived in honor and riches for many years, profiting greatly from the Spaniards' exploitation of the Mexicans.

Latter-day Mexicans do not honor her by the gentle title of Doña Marina, however. They call her Malinche, after the volcano—the ugly, treacherous scar on the Mexican landscape—and curse her as the female Judas who betrayed her country to the Spanish. *Malinchismo* has become known as the tendency to love things foreign and hate things Mexican.

capital of an empire more than equal to any in Europe at the time.

But Moctezuma, the lord of the empire, was unsure if Cortés was really the returned Quetzalcoatl—he was frozen by fear and foreboding. He quickly found himself hostage to Cortés, then died a few months later, during a riot against Spanish greed and brutality. On July 1, 1520, on what came to be called *el noche triste* (the sad night), the besieged Cortés and his men broke out, fleeing for their lives along a lake causeway from Tenochtitlán, carrying Moctezuma's treasure. Many of them drowned beneath their burdens of gold booty, while the survivors hacked a bloody retreat through thousands of screaming Aztec warriors, finally reaching the safety of the lakeshore.

A year later, reinforced by a small fleet of armed sailboats and 100,000 native warrior-allies, Cortés retook Tenochtitlán. The stubborn defenders, led by Cuauhtémoc, Moctezuma's nephew, fell by the tens of thousands beneath a smoking hail of Spanish grapeshot. But the Aztecs refused to surrender, forcing Cortés to destroy the city in order to take it.

The triumphant conquistador soon rebuilt the city in the Spanish image; Cortés' cathedral and main public buildings—the present *zócalo* or central square of Mexico City—still rest upon the foundations of Moctezuma's pyramids.

NEW SPAIN

With the Valley of Mexico firmly in his grip, Cortés sent his lieutenants south, north, and west to extend the limits of his domain. Alonso de Ávalos commanded the first expedition to the present region of Guadalajara; later, in 1524, Cortés sent his cousin, Francisco Cortés de Buenaventura, in charge of a company of soldiers and cavalry, to pacify the chiefdom of Xalisco, west of Guadalajara (in the present state of Nayarit). The Spanish later converted the name to Jalisco (Place Built on the Surface of Sand), which later became the name of the present-day Mexican state.

Within a few years, most of Mexico—a realm several times the size and population of old Spain—was under Cortés' control. His conquest now consolidated, Cortés, in a letter to King Charles V, christened his empire "New Spain of the Ocean Sea."

The Missionaries

While Cortés and his conquistador officers subjugated the native people, missionaries began arriving to teach, heal, and baptize them. A dozen Franciscan brothers impressed the natives and conquistadors alike by trekking the entire 300-mile stony path from Veracruz to Mexico City in 1523. Missionary authorities generally enjoyed a sympathetic ear from Charles V and his successors, who earnestly pursued Spain's Christian mission, especially when it dovetailed with its political and economic goals.

Trouble in New Spain

Increasingly after 1525, the crown, through the Council of the Indies, began to wrest power away from Cortés and his lieutenants, many of whom had been granted rights of *encomienda:*

A visit to view the miniature Bible scenes at the Tlaquepaque parish church is a high point of many a parishoner's day.

taxes and labor of an indigenous district. From the king's point of view, tribute pesos collected by *encomenderos* from their indigenous serfs reduced the gold that would otherwise flow to the crown. Moreover, many *encomenderos* callously enslaved and sold their native wards for quick profit. Such abuses, coupled with European-introduced diseases, began to reduce the native population at an alarming rate.

No region of New Spain suffered more from Spanish depredations than the West. In the latter 1520s, with New Spain seemingly secure, Cortés returned to Europe for three years, leaving one of his senior officers, **Nuño Beltrán de Guzmán,** in charge in Mexico City.

It quickly turned out that Guzmán had plans of his own. He wasted no time aggrandizing himself and his friends by attacking and burning villages and selling the natives into slavery. Alarmed by word of Guzmán's excesses, the King dispatched a new royal *audiencia* (executive-judicial panel) to take control from Guzmán. Seeing the writing on the wall, Guzmán cleared out beforehand, three days before Christmas in 1529. He was in command of a small renegade army of adventurers bent upon finding new riches in Western Mexico.

Guzmán first encountered the natives of the Valley of Atemajac and their Queen, **Cihualpilli,** at Tonalá, in the eastern suburb of present-day Guadalajara. Though Cihualpilli and her subjects resisted Guzmán's brutality with a stiff armed resistance from their hilltop stronghold —now called Cerro de la Reina (Hill of the Queen) at the north edge of Tonalá—they were no match for Spanish armor and cannons. They surrendered after a bloody siege. Guzmán and his men celebrated their victory at Guadalajara's first mass, on March 25, 1530.

The Many Guadalajaras

As soon as he had pacified the Valley of Atemajac, Guzmán began looking for a settlement site to name after his old hometown, Guadalajara, back in Spain. The first settlement called Guadalajara was founded on January 5, 1532, about 55 miles (90 km) to the north, near Nochistlán, in present-day Zacatecas state.

But the local natives, the seminomadic Caxcanes, refused to work and rebelled. With no labor, the ragged band of Spanish settlers and their military escort returned back south across the Río Santiago canyon to Tonalá in 1533.

Guzmán, however, wanted Tonalá, the richest town in the valley, for himself, and sent the colonists back north across the river, to Tlacotlán, where their refounded Guadalajara lasted until 1541. Although the settlers didn't know it at the time, the crown, on November 8, 1539, granted Guadalajara the rank of city, complete with the coat of arms that the city retains to the present day.

By 1541, however, Guzmán was gone, having been arrested in the mid-1530s by a powerful and incorruptible new viceroy, **Antonio de Mendoza,** and sent back to prison in Spain. Rebellious natives again sent Guadalajara's mere 200 tattered settlers fleeing Tlacotlán, back to the Valley of Atemajac, where, near the exact center of modern Guadalajara, they founded their city for the final time on February 14, 1542.

The Mixtón War

Although Nuño de Guzmán was gone, his cruel legacy remained in the hatred and resentment that his brutality had raised among the native peoples of Western Mexico. Deadly rebellion, led by Caxcane chief Tenamaxtli, broke out in 1540 and lead to slaughter, pillage, and retribution on both sides. The uprising radiated from the Cerro de Mixtón, an impenetrable maze of ridges and deep canyons, in the present municipality of Apozol, about 60 miles (100 km) north of Guadalajara. From there, native guerrilla bands attacked Spanish settlers and garrisons, retiring to their Mixtón hideaways with impunity, leaving terror and destruction in their wake.

Viceroy Mendoza, alarmed at the death in battle of Pedro de Alvarado (the conqueror of Guatemala), took personal command of Spanish forces in January 1541. Mendoza, arguably the best viceroy that New Spain ever had, managed to secure a truce within a year. He was greatly aided by the apparition of the Virgin of the Pacification, a mysterious figure swathed in a brilliant light, witnessed by a throng of rebellious natives who were so awestruck that they laid down their arms. The very same miraculous figure, now called the Virgin of Zapopan is feted in a grand procession of many hundreds of thousands of Guadalajarans every October 12.

COLONIAL GUADALAJARA

In 1542, the Council of the Indies, through Viceroy Mendoza, promulgated its liberal New Laws of the Indies. They rested on high moral ground: The only Christian justification for New Spain was the souls and welfare of the native Mexicans. Slavery was outlawed, and the colonists' *encomienda* rights over land and the native peoples were to eventually revert to the crown.

Despite near-rebellion by angry colonists, Mendoza and his successors kept the lid on New Spain. Although some *encomenderos* held their privileges into the 18th century, chattel slavery of native Mexicans was abolished in New Spain 300 years before Lincoln's Emancipation Proclamation.

Meanwhile, with peace established, colonists and missionaries streamed west from Mexico City to found new settlements around Guadalajara and Zacatecas. Others continued west, to Santiago de Compostela (in present-day Nayarit), north to Culiacán, and south to Colima.

In 1548, recognizing Western Mexico's growing importance, colonial authorities created **Nueva Galicia** a domain that encompassed a vast western territory, including the present-day states of Jalisco, Nayarit, Colima, Aguascalientes, and parts of Zacatecas, San Luis Potosí, Sinaloa,

and Durango. Nueva Galicia's governing *audiencia,* originally headquartered in Compostela, was shifted to Guadalajara in 1560.

Although peace reigned, sleepy Guadalajara grew only slowly at first. *Audiencias* came, served, and went; newcomers put down roots; friars built country churches; and the original settlers' rich heirs played while their indigenous charges labored.

Expansion to the Californias

In the 1700s, exploration and expansion accelerated Nueva Galicia's growth. Missionaries pushed north; Jesuit fathers Kino and Salvatierra established a string of missions on both coasts of the Gulf of California. Guadalajara's merchants benefited as their town, no longer the end of the road to nowhere, became a supply hub for a burgeoning western domain.

Propelled by British, French, and Russian pressure in the north Pacific, the Spanish established a new port and Pacific naval headquarters in 1768 at San Blas, on the coast west of Guadalajara. After the King expelled the Jesuits in 1767, Spanish colonial authorities asked the Franciscans, led by **Padre Junipero Serra,** to revitalize the Jesuit mission. They answered the call, using Guadalajara as their supply center, and San Blas as their jumping-off point, sailing north to found dozens of mission settlements as far north as San Francisco, in Alta California, by 1800.

Guadalajara's growing population demanded more and better goods; entrepreneurs responded with dozens of small new factories to supply textiles, leather, soap, and liquor. Increased commerce led to construction of better roads and bridges to connect Guadalajara with Colima,

POPULATION CHANGES IN NEW SPAIN

	Early Colonial (1570)	Late Colonial (1810)
peninsulares	6,600	15,000
criollos	11,000	1,100,000
mestizos	2,400	704,000
indígenas	3,340,000	3,700,000
negros	22,000	630,000

THE VIRGIN OF GUADALUPE

Conversion of the *indígenas* was sparked by the vision of Juan Diego, a humble farmer. On the hill of Tepayac north of Mexico City in 1531, Juan Diego saw a brown-skinned version of the Virgin Mary enclosed in a dazzling aura of light. She told him to build a shrine in her memory on that spot, where the Aztecs had long worshipped their "earth mother," Tonantzín. Juan Diego's brown virgin told him to go to the cathedral and relay her instruction to Archbishop Zumárraga.

The archbishop, as expected, turned his nose up at Juan Diego's story. The vision returned, however, and this time Juan Diego's brown virgin realized that a miracle was necessary. She ordered him to pick some roses at the spot where she had first appeared to him (a true miracle, since roses had been previously unknown in the vicinity) and take them to the archbishop. Juan Diego wrapped the roses in his rude fiber cape, returned to the cathedral, and placed the wrapped roses at the archbishop's feet. When he opened the offering, Zumárraga gasped: Imprinted on the cape was an image of the brown virgin herself—proof positive of a genuine miracle.

In the centuries since Juan Diego, the brown virgin—La Virgen Morena, or Nuestra Señora La Virgen de Guadalupe—has blended native and Catholic elements into something uniquely Mexican. In doing so, she has become the virtual patroness of Mexico, the beloved symbol of Mexico for *indígenas*, mestizos, *negros*, and criollos alike.

Virtually every Guadalajara region town and village celebrates the cherished memory of their Virgin of Guadalupe on December 12. This celebration, however joyful, is but one of the many fiestas that Mexicans, especially the *indígenas*, live for. Each village holds its local fiesta in honor of their patron saint, who is often a thinly veiled sit-in for a local pre-Conquest deity. Themes appear Spanish—Christian vs. Moors, devils vs. priests—but the native element is strong, sometimes dominant.

San Blas, and Mexico City. The ferment raised Guadalajara from a backwater of 6,000 souls in 1703 to a bustling city of 35,000 a century later.

The immigration influx overtaxed existing facilities and led to the construction of two of Guadalajara's most distinguished institutions: the **Hospital of Belén,** and the **Hospicio Cabañas,** respectively promoted by Bishops Antonio Alcalde and Juan Cruz Ruíz de Cabañas. (Both institutions, now known as the Hospital Civil and the Centro Cultural Cabañas, continue their benevolent missions.)

The Church

Religious activity in colonial Mexico was rigorously confined to Catholic rites. An active Inquisition watched vigilantly for any straying brethren, be they errant Protestants or Jews, or native Mexicans covertly worshipping their old gods.

Nevertheless, the church had carried out its original compassionate Christian mission. It had protected the native Mexicans from the colonists' excesses, taught them useful trades, and moderated their toil. As a result, the native population, which by 1600 had sunk to a mere 10 percent of the original numbers, had doubled by 1800. Moderate prosperity even allowed for a few luxuries. Indigenous folks looked forward to feast days, when they would dress up, parade their patron saint, drink *pulque,* dance in the plaza, and ooh and aah at the fireworks.

The church profited from the rosy status quo. The biblical tithe—one-tenth of everything earned—filled clerical coffers. By 1800, the church owned half of Mexico.

Furthermore, both the clergy and the military were doubly privileged. They enjoyed the right of *fuero* (exemption from civil law) and could only be prosecuted by ecclesiastical or military courts.

Despite its faults, Spain's Mexican Empire, by most contemporary measures, was prospering in

1800. The Indian labor force was both docile and growing, and the galleons carried increasing tonnage of silver and gold across the Atlantic to Spain. The authorities, however, failed to recognize that Mexico had changed over 300 years.

Criollos, the New Mexicans

Nearly three centuries of colonial rule gave rise to a burgeoning population of more than a million criollos—Mexican-born, pure European descendants of Spanish colonists, many rich and educated—to whom power was denied.

High government, church, and military office had always been the preserve of a tiny minority of *peninsulares*—whites born in Spain. Criollos could only watch in disgust as unlettered, unskilled *peninsulares,* derisively called *gachupines,* "wearers of spurs," were boosted to authority over them.

Mestizo, *Indígena,* and *Negro* Classes

Upperclass luxury existed by virtue of the sweat of Mexico's mestizo (mixed), *indígena* (native), and *negro* laborers and servants. African slaves were imported in large numbers during the 17th century after typhus, smallpox, and measles epidemics wiped out most of the *indígena* population. Although the Afro-Mexicans contributed significantly (crafts, healing arts, dance, music, drums, and marimba), they had arrived last and experienced discrimination from everyone.

INDEPENDENCE

Although the criollos stood high above the mestizo, *indígena,* and *negro* underclasses, that seemed little compensation for the false smiles, deep bows, and costly bribes that *gachupines* demanded. By 1800 the republican revolutions in the United States and France had spilled over all the way to Guadalajara. Revolutionary ferment had led to higher aspirations, notably by rich criollo merchants and professionals, who were ripe for rebellion.

The chance for change came during the aftermath of the French invasion of Spain in 1808, when Napoléon Bonaparte replaced Spain's King Ferdinand VII with his brother Joseph. Most *peninsulares* backed King Ferdinand VII; most criollos, however, talked and dreamed of independence. One such group, urged on by a firebrand parish priest, acted.

El Grito de Dolores

"¡Viva México! Death to the gachupines!" cried **Father Miguel Hidalgo** passionately from the church balcony in the Guanajuato town of Dolores on September 16, 1810, igniting action. A mostly *indígena,* machete-wielding army of 20,000 coalesced around Hidalgo and his compatriots, Ignacio Allende and Juan Aldama. Their ragtag force raged out of control around Guanajuato, massacring hated *gachupines* and pillaging their homes.

The insurgency quickly spread to Guadalajara, where, on November 11, 1810, an irregular force led by Hidalgo's compatriots, Manuel Hidobro and José "El Amo" Antonio Torres, over-

Miguel Hidalgo, father of the Mexican Republic

whelmed the small royalist garrison. Hidalgo arrived two weeks later and pushed his insurgency by organizing a revolutionary local government, eliminating royal taxes, reiterating the abolition of slavery, and urging the publication of Latin America's first revolutionary newspaper, *El Depertador Americano,* by Francisco Severo Maldonado, on December 20, 1810.

Emboldened, Hidalgo (now "Generalisimo") But he was unnerved by stiff royalist resistance, and they instead retreated and regrouped east of Guadalajara. Although its numbers had swollen to 80,000, Hidalgo's army was no match for the disciplined 6,000-strong pursuing force of royalist General Felix Calleja. After suffering a disastrous defeat at Calderon Bridge on the banks of the Río Santiago on January 17, 1811, Hidalgo fled north toward the United States—he was soon apprehended, defrocked, and executed. His head and those of his comrades hung from the walls of the Guanajuato granary for 10 years in compensation for the slaughter of 138 *gachupines* by Hidalgo's army.

Meanwhile, as Calleja pacified the Guadalajara region, his lieutenant, General José de la Cruz, marched north and retook Zacatecas; Calleja captured and executed "El Amo" Torres. Later, Cruz's forces erased the last pockets of resistance around Lake Chapala.

The Ten-Year Struggle

Other *insurgentes* carried on the fight. A mestizo former student of Hidalgo, **José María Morelos,** led a revolutionary shadow government in the present states of Guerrero and Oaxaca for four years until he was apprehended and executed in December 1815.

As Morelos' compatriot, **Vicente Guerrero,** continued a war of attrition, a new government in Spain approved a new, liberal constitution that radically reduced the King's authority. Mexican conservatives, with the royal rug thus pulled out from beneath their feet, began linking with the Mexican insurgents. In February 1820, Guerrero and criollo royalist Brigadier Agustín de Iturbide announced the Plan de Iguala, promising the renowned Trigarantes (Three Guarantees)—Independence,

Catholicism, and Equality—which their united army would enforce.

As royalist resistance gradually melted away, Nueva Galicia became independent before New Spain, when, on June 13, 1821, royalist Brigadier Pedro Celestino Negrete, with the influential backing of Bishop Cabañas, signed on to the Plan de Iguala in Tlaquepaque. Nueva Galicia's military commander, General de la Cruz, fled and local authorities formally declared independence. On September 21, 1821, Iturbide rode triumphantly into Mexico City at the head of his army of Trigarantes. Mexico was independent at last.

The Rise and Fall of Agustín I

Iturbide, crowned Emperor Agustín I by the bishop of Guadalajara on July 21, 1822, soon lost his charisma. In a pattern that became sadly predictable for generations of topsy-turvy Mexican politics, an ambitious garrison commander issued a *pronunciamiento* or declaration of rebellion against him; old revolutionary heroes endorsed a plan to install a republic. Iturbide, his braid tattered and brass tarnished, abdicated in February 1823.

Guadalajarans, led by businessman Luis Quintanar, became the first to declare statehood—"the free and sovereign state of Xalisco"—on June 16,1823, before the federal republic was even formed. Finally, on January 31, 1824, the new national congress in Mexico City followed with the act of Mexican federation that conferred statehood upon "Jalisco."

Prisciliano Sanchéz became Jalisco's first constitutional governor. He and his immediate successors initiated liberal programs to broaden political and religious freedoms, lower taxes, stimulate commerce, limit church and military special privileges and create Guadalajara's first public institution of higher education, the Instituto de Ciencias del Estado (State Scientific Institute).

The Disastrous Era of Santa Anna

Despite good-intentioned attempts at reform, independence had solved little except to expel the *peninsulares.* With an illiterate populace and no experience in self-government, Mexicans began a tragic 40-year love affair with a fantasy: the general on the white horse, the gold-braided hero who could save them from themselves.

Antonio López de Santa Anna, the eager 28-year-old military commander of Veracruz whose *pronunciamiento* had pushed Iturbide from his white horse, maneuvered to gradually replace him. Meanwhile, throughout the late 1820s the federal government teetered on the edge of disaster as the presidency bounced between liberal and conservative hands six times in three years. During the last of these upheavals, Santa Anna jumped to prominence by defeating an abortive Spanish attempt at counterrevolution in Tampico in 1829. Santa Anna was called the "The Victor of Tampico."

In 1833, the government was bankrupt; mobs demanded the ouster of conservative President Anastasio Bustamante, who had executed the rebellious old revolutionary hero, Vicente Guerrero. Santa Anna issued a *pronunciamiento* against Bustamante; Congress obliged, elevating Santa Anna to "Liberator of the Republic" and naming him president in March 1833.

Santa Anna would pop in and out of the presidency like a jack-in-the-box 10 more times before 1855. First, he foolishly lost Texas to rebellious Anglo settlers in 1836; then he lost his leg (which was buried with full military honors) fighting the emperor of France.

Santa Anna's greatest debacle, however, was to declare war on the United States with just 1,839 pesos in the treasury. With his forces poised to defend Mexico City against a relatively small 10,000-man American invasion force, Santa Anna inexplicably withdrew. United States marines surged into the "Halls of Montezuma," Chapultepec Castle, where Mexico's six beloved Niños Héroes cadets fell in the losing cause on September 13, 1847.

In the subsequent treaty of Guadalupe Hidalgo, Mexico lost two-fifths of its territory—the present states of New Mexico, Arizona, California, Nevada, Utah, and Colorado—to the United States. Mexicans have never forgotten; they have looked upon gringos with a combination of awe, envy, admiration, and disgust ever since.

For Santa Anna, however, enough was not enough. Called back as "His Most Serene Highness" and elevated to president for the 11th and last time in 1853, Santa Anna financed his final extravagances by selling off a slice of what later became southern New Mexico and Arizona for $10 million: the Gadsden Purchase.

Jalisco liberals, however, had seen enough. They formulated the "Plan of Ayutla" to remove Santa Anna, preparing to storm Guadalajara in August 1855. Santa Anna, however, pre-empted their plan and cleared out forever. Guadalajara federal authorities gave up without a fight, opening the door for a liberal sweep that vaulted Santos Degollado into the Jalisco governorship.

Fortunately for Guadalajarans, the turbulence and destruction of the Santa Anna years had largely spared Guadalajara. Since Independence, the city had finished important public works, added new factories and businesses, and grown from a population of 47,000 in 1822 to 68,000 by 1856.

REFORM, CIVIL WAR, AND INTERVENTION

Despite the demise of Santa Anna, Mexico still suffered from a severe political split. While conservatives searched for a king to replace Santa Anna, liberals plunged ahead with three controversial reform laws: the **Ley Juárez, Ley Lerdo,** and **Ley Iglesias.** These *reformas,* augmented by a new Constitution of 1857, directly attacked the privilege and power of Mexico's landlords, clergy, and generals. The reforms abolished *fueros* (the separate military and church courts), reduced huge landed estates, and stripped the church of its excess property and power.

Conservative generals, priests, *hacendados* (landholders), and their mestizo and *indígena* followers revolted. Conservative President Comonfort attempted a coup d'état; in response, liberals elevated Vice President **Benito Juárez** to the presidency, but conservative forces sent Juárez and his government fleeing to Guanajuato, then Guadalajara.

Guadalajara, teetering between liberal and conservative control, turned out to be an insecure perch for Juarez's government. Thanks to the help of his ministers and his liberal Guadalajara friends, Juárez barely escaped assassination, then arrest, by fleeing with his ministers to Manzanillo, then on to safe haven in Veracruz. There, Juárez ran the government while the War of the Reform (not unlike the U.S. Civil War) raged in the countryside. Finally, Juárez's victorious liberal armies captured Guadalajara for the last time, on November 3, 1860, then paraded triumphantly in Mexico City on New Year's Day, 1861.

Juárez and Maximilian

Benito Juárez, the leading *reformista,* had won the day. Like his contemporary, Abraham Lincoln, Juárez—of pure Zapotec Indian blood—overcame his humble origins to become a lawyer, a champion of justice, and the president who held his country together during a terrible civil war. Also like Lincoln, Juárez had little time to savor his triumph.

After President Juárez suspended debt payment, Imperial France invaded Mexico in January 1862. At the end of two costly years of fighting, the French pushed Juárez's liberal army into the hills, occupying Guadalajara from January 1864 until December 1866. In Mexico City, the French installed the king whom Mexican conservatives thought the country needed. Austrian Archduke Maximilian and his wife Carlota, the very models of modern Catholic monarchs, were crowned emperor and empress of Mexico in June 1864.

The well-meaning but naive Emperor Maximilian I was surprised that some of his subjects resented his presence. Meanwhile, Juárez refused to yield, stubbornly performing his constitutional duties in a somber black carriage one jump ahead of the French occupying army. The climax came in May 1867, when Juarez's forces besieged and defeated Maximilian's army at Querétaro. Juárez, giving no quarter, sternly ordered Maximilian's execution by firing squad on June 19, 1867.

Peace reigned in Jalisco, but not for long. A native rebellion—not unlike the colonial-era Mixtón War—led by indigenous leader Manuel Lozada (the "Tigre de Alica"), spread from Nayarit to Jalisco. It was finally stopped at the outskirts of Guadalajara by General Ramón Corona on January 28, 1873.

THE PORFIRIATO, REVOLUTION, AND STABILIZATION

Juárez worked day and night at the double task of reconstruction and reform. He won reelection but died, exhausted, in July 1872.

The death of Juárez, the stoic partisan of reform, signaled hope to Mexico's conservatives. They soon got their wish: General **Don Porfirio Díaz,** the "Coming Man," was elected president in 1876.

Pax Porfiriana

Don Porfirio is often remembered wistfully, as old Italians remember Mussolini: "He was a bit rough, but, dammit, at least he made the trains run on time."

Although Porfirio Díaz's humble Oaxaca mestizo origins were not unlike Juárez's, Díaz was not a democrat. When he was a general, his officers took no captives; when he was president, his country police, the *rurales,* shot prisoners in the act of "trying to escape."

"Order and Progress," in that sequence, ruled Mexico for 34 years. Foreign investment flowed into the country; new railroads brought the products of shiny factories, mines, and farms to modernized Gulf and Pacific ports. Mexico balanced its budget, repaid foreign debt, and became a respected member of the family of nations.

Most Guadalajarans united around Díaz's policies. The city enjoyed a long-deserved rest. Telephone service arrived in 1882, electric lights in 1884, and streetcars in 1907. Presidential aspirant Ramón Corona, elected Jalisco's governor in 1887, promoted the railroad, which arrived from Mexico City in 1888 (and was finally completed, via Colima, to Manzanillo in 1909). Corona's liberal social agenda, which included universal public elementary education, was cut short by his assassination in 1889. Nevertheless, Guadalajara continued booming, reaching a population of 100,000 by 1900.

In retrospect, President Diaz's "Order and Progress" had come at a high human price. He allowed more than a hundred million acres— one-fifth of Mexico's land area (including most of the arable land)—to fall into the hands of his friends and foreigners. Poor Mexicans suffered the most. By 1910, 90 percent of the *indígenas* had lost their traditional communal land. In the spring of 1910, a smug, now-cultured and elderly Don Porfirio Díaz anticipated with relish the centennial of Hidalgo's Grito de Dolores.

¡No Reelección!

Porfirio Díaz himself had first campaigned on this slogan. It expressed the idea that the president should step down after one term. Although Díaz had stepped down once in 1880, he had gotten himself reelected for 26 consecutive years. In 1910, **Francisco I. Madero,** a short, squeaky-voiced son of rich landowners opposed Díaz under the same banner.

Madero campaigned in Guadalajara twice before Díaz had him jailed before the balloting. But even after Díaz had been declared the winner, Madero refused to quit. From a safe platform in the United States, he called for a revolution to begin on November 20, 1910.

Villa and Zapata

Not much happened, but soon the millions of poor Mexicans who had been going to bed hungry began to stir. In Jalisco, *maderistas* Enrique Estrada, Luis Moza, and Domingo Arriega organized guerrilla bands that harassed federal troops. In Chihuahua, followers of **Francisco (Pancho) Villa,** an erstwhile ranch hand, miner, peddler, and cattle rustler, began attacking the *rurales,* dynamiting railroads, and raiding towns. Meanwhile, in the south, horse trader, farmer, and minor official **Emiliano Zapata** and his *indígena* guerrillas were terrorizing rich *hacendados* and forcibly recovering stolen ancestral village lands. Zapata's movement gained steam and by May had taken the Morelos state capital, Cuernavaca. Meanwhile, Madero crossed the Rio Grande and joined with Villa's forces, who took Ciudad Juárez.

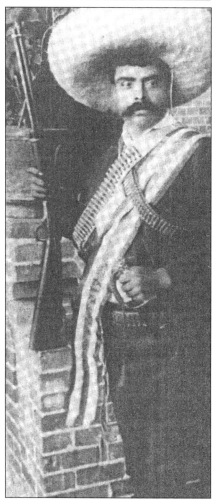

Emiliano Zapata, incorruptible revolutionary and defender of "Land and Liberty," assassinated 1919

The *federales* (government army troops) began deserting in droves, and on May 25, 1911, Díaz submitted his resignation.

As General Victoriano Huerta (Madero's deputy) put Díaz on his ship of exile in Veracruz, Díaz confided, "Madero has unleashed a tiger. Now let's see if he can control it."

The Fighting Continues

Emiliano Zapata, it turned out, was the tiger Madero had unleashed. Meeting with Madero in Mexico City, Zapata fumed over Madero's go-slow approach to the "agrarian problem," as Madero termed it. Madero tried to negotiate with Zapata, but government forces, led by Huerta, attacked Zapata's guerillas as they were getting ready to lay down their arms. By November, Zapata had denounced Madero. *"¡Tierra y Libertad!"* (Land and Liberty!) the Zapatistas cried, as they renewed their fiery rebellion in the south. During 1912, a number of serious anti-Madero revolts broke out, which Madero appointed Huerta to quell. But in February 1913, Huerta switched sides. Backed by his troops, Huerta forced Madero to resign on February 18, 1913, immediately got himself appointed president, then ordered Madero murdered four days later.

The rum-swilling Huerta ruled like a Chicago mobster; general rebellion, led by the "Big Four"—Villa, Álvaro Obregón, Venustiano Carranza in the north, and Zapata in the south—soon broke out. Although not occupied by revolutionary forces until mid-1914, increasing numbers of radicals and homeless refugees began living in the Guadalajara streets, forcing rich residents to flee to their west-side suburban homes.

Eventually, on July 8, 1914, forces of Generals Obregón, Rafael Buelna, Lucio Blanco, and Manuel M. Dieguez decisively defeated Huerta's forces north of Guadalajara and entered the city in triumph. Pressed by the rebels on all sides and refused U.S. recognition, Huerta fled into exile in late July 1914. Dieguez, installed as governor for the second time, immediately declared state support for secondary education, fixed minimum wages and work standards, and required a Sunday work holiday and cash payment of wages.

Fighting sputtered on for three more years as authority seesawed between Obregón and Carranza's Constitutionalist faction on one hand and Zapata and Villa on the other. Finally Carranza, who ended up controlling most of the country by 1917, got a convention together in Querétaro to formulate political and social goals. The resulting Constitution of 1917, while re-stating most ideas of the Reformistas' 1857 constitution, additionally prescribed a single four-year presidential term, advocated labor reform, and subordinated private ownership to public interest. Every village had a right to communal *ejido* land, and subsoil wealth could never be sold away to the highest bidder.

The Constitution of 1917 was a revolutionary expression of national aspirations and, in retrospect, represented a social and political agenda for the entire 20th century. In modified form, it has lasted to the present day.

Obregón Stabilizes Mexico

On December 1, 1920, General Álvaro Obregón legally assumed the presidency of a Mexico still bleeding from 10 years of civil war. Although a seasoned revolutionary, Obregón was also a pragmatist who recognized peace was necessary to implement the goals of the revolution. In four years, Obregón managed to put down a number of rebellions (one of which included Jalisco governor Dieguez), disarmed a swarm of warlords, executed hundreds of *bandidos,* obtained U.S. diplomatic recognition, assuaged the worst fears of the clergy and landowners, and began land reform.

All this set the stage for the work of **Plutarco Elías Calles,** Obregón's Minister of Gobernación

The "Constitutionalists," 1917; Álvaro Obregón is on the left.

(Interior) and handpicked successor, who won the 1924 election. Aided by peace, Mexico returned to a semblance of prosperity. Calles brought the army under civilian control, balanced the budget, and shifted Mexico's revolution into high gear. New clinics vaccinated millions against smallpox, new dams irrigated thousands of previously dry acres, and campesinos received millions of acres of redistributed land.

Meanwhile, Guadalajara was solidifying its position as Mexico's second city. In 1927, crews completed the Guadalajara rail link with the U.S. California and Arizona border. Built by Americans, it was later nationalized and named the Ferrocarril del Pacífico (Pacific Railroad.) It opened the gate for the burgeoning Guadalajara–United States trade that continues today.

The Cristero War

By single-mindedly enforcing the agrarian, pro-labor, and anticlerical articles of the 1917 constitution, Calles made many influential enemies. The clergy, infuriated by the government's confiscation of church property, closing of monasteries, and deportation of hundreds of foreign priests and nuns, issued a pastoral letter in July 1926, refusing to perform marriages, baptisms, and last rites. Riots broke out, especially in Guadalajara, where a violent confrontation erupted when soldiers tried to evict a group of Catholic rebels—"Cristeros"—who had barricaded themselves in the downtown Sanctuary of Guadalupe.

The Cristero rebellion climaxed most violently in Jalisco's conservative upland "Los Altos" region around Tepatitlán, San Juan de los Lagos, and Lagos de Moreno, not far northeast of Guadalajara. One of the leading Cristeros was Victoriano Ramírez ("El Catorce"), whose followers began to wage a deadly effective shoot-and-run guerilla war upon federal troops. After a series of bloody skirmishes, federal troops initiated a ruthless scorched-earth policy, forcing rural populations to concentrate in towns, burning crops and farms, and killing and confiscating livestock.

Eventually the Cristero guerillas, weak from hunger and without ammunition, surrendered. In mid-1929, church officials and federal authorities were able to negotiate a peace settlement.

Calles, who started out brimming with revolutionary fervor and populist zeal, became increasingly conservative and dictatorial. Although he bowed out peaceably in favor of Oregón (the constitution had been amended to allow one six-year nonsuccessive term), Obregón was assassinated two weeks after his election in 1928. Calles continued to rule for six more years through three puppet-presidents: Emilio Portes Gil (1928–30), Pascual Ortíz Rubio (1930–32), and Abelardo Rodríguez (1932–34).

For 14 years since 1920, the revolution had first waxed, then waned. With a cash surplus in 1930, Mexico skidded into debt as the Great Depression deepened and Calles and his cronies lined their pockets. In blessing his minister of war, General Lázaro Cárdenas, for the 1934 presidential election, Calles expected more of the same.

Lázaro Cárdenas, President of the People

The 40-year-old Cárdenas, former governor of Michoacán, immediately set his own agenda, however. He worked tirelessly to fulfill the social prescriptions of the revolution. As morning-coated diplomats fretted, waiting in his outer office, Cárdenas ushered in delegations of campesinos and factory workers and sympathetically listened to their petitions.

In his six years of rule, Cárdenas moved public education and health forward on a broad front, supported strong labor unions, and redistributed 49 million acres of farmland, more than any president before or since.

Cárdenas' resolute enforcement of the constitution's Artículo 123 brought him the most renown. Under this pro-labor law, the government turned over a host of private companies to employee ownership and, on March 18, 1938, expropriated all foreign oil corporations.

In retrospect the oil corporations, most of which were British, were not blameless. They had sorely neglected the wages, health, and welfare of their workers while ruthlessly taking the law into their own hands with private police forces. Although Standard Oil cried foul, U.S.

President Franklin Roosevelt did not intervene. Through negotiation and due process, the U.S. companies eventually were compensated with $24 million, plus interest. In the wake of the expropriation, President Cárdenas created Petróleos Mexicanos (Pemex), the national oil corporation that today continues to run all Mexican oil and gas operations.

Although the 1930s were by and large a time of rebuilding, Guadalajara still suffered from the ideological split aggravated by the Cristero War. The dispute broke out at the state-financed University of Guadalajara, where leftists demanded that socialist philosophy should rule university policies and curriculum. Governor Sebastián Allende took office in April 1932, facing a violent student strike that forced him to close the university for a year.

Meanwhile, he and his successor, Evarardo Topete, continued an ambitious road-building plan to connect Guadalajara with paved highways south, west, and east, with Barra de Navidad, Tequila, and the state of Michoacán.

Manuel Ávila Camacho, the "Believer."

Manuel Ávila Camacho, elected in 1940, was the last general to be president of Mexico. His administration ushered in a gradual shift of Mexican politics, government, and foreign policy as Mexico allied itself with the U.S. cause during World War II. Foreign tourism, initially promoted by the Cárdenas administration, ballooned. Good feelings surged as Franklin Roosevelt became the first U.S. president to officially cross the Río Grande when he met with Camacho in Monterrey in April 1943.

In both word and deed, moderation and evolution guided President Camacho's policies. *"Soy creente"* ("I am a believer"), he declared to the Catholics of Mexico as he worked earnestly to bridge Mexico's serious church-state schism. Land policy emphasis shifted from redistribution to utilization as new dams and canals irrigated hundreds of thousands of previously arid acres. On one hand, Camacho established IMSS (Instituto Mexicano de Seguro Social) and on the other, trimmed the power of labor unions.

As WW II moved toward its 1945 conclusion, both the United States and Mexico were enjoying the benefits of four years of governmental and military cooperation and mutual trade in the form of a mountain of strategic minerals which had moved north in exchange for a similar mountain of U.S. manufactures that moved south.

Meanwhile, in Guadalajara, a pair of progessive governors, Marcelino Garcia Barragan (1943–47) and Jesùs González Gallo (1947–53) pushed the modernization of Guadalajara: a westside industrial park (including the now-renowned Guadalajara Arch) and widening east-west Av. Vallarta–Juárez and north-south Av. 16 Septiembre–Alcalde.

CONTEMPORARY MEXICO AND GUADALAJARA
The Mature Revolution

During the decades after WW II, beginning with moderate President **Miguel Alemán** (1946–52), Mexican politicians gradually honed their skills of consensus and compromise as their middle-aged revolution bubbled along under liberal presidents and sputtered haltingly under conservatives. Doctrine required that all politicians, regardless of stripe, be "revolutionary" enough to be included beneath the banner of the PRI (Partido Revolucionario Institucional), Mexico's dominant political party.

To date, Mexico's revolution hadn't been very revolutionary about women's rights. The PRI didn't get around to giving Mexican women, millions of whom fought and died during the revolution, the right to vote until 1953.

Adolfo Ruíz Cortínes, Alemán's secretary of the interior, was elected overwhelmingly in 1952. He fought the corruption that had crept into government under his predecessor, continued land reform, increased agricultural production, built new ports, eradicated malaria, and opened a dozen automobile assembly plants.

Women, voting for the first time in a national election, kept the PRI in power by electing liberal **Adolfo López Mateos** in 1958. Resembling Lázaro Cárdenas in social policy, López Mateos redistributed 40 million acres of farmland, forced automakers to use 60 percent domestic components, built thousands of new schools, and distributed hundreds of millions of new textbooks. *"La electricidad es nuestra"* ("Electricity is ours"), Mateos declared as he nationalized foreign power companies in 1962.

Despite his left-leaning social agenda, unions were restive under López Mateos. Protesting inflation, workers struck; the government retaliated, arresting Demetrios Vallejo, the railway union head, and renowned muralist David Siqueiros, former communist party secretary.

Despite the troubles, López Mateos climaxed his presidency gracefully in 1964 as he opened the celebrated National Museum of Anthropology, appropriately located in Chapultepec Park, where the Aztecs had first settled 20 generations earlier.

During the decade of the 1950s, Guadalajara doubled its population, to about 850,000 as waves of migrants from the countryside flocked to new factory jobs in the city. Guadalajara's new metropolitan status was underlined by the appointment of Guadalajara's archbishop, José Garibi Rivera, as Mexico's first cardinal. Meanwhile, a handful of conservation-conscious citizens in 1955, worried that Lake Chapala had sunk to its lowest level in memory, breathed a sigh of relief when the lake recovered a few years later.

Elected in 1964, dour, conservative President **Gustavo Díaz Ordaz** immediately clashed with liberals, labor, and students. The pot boiled over just before the 1968 Mexico City Olympics. Reacting to a student rebellion, the army occupied the National University; shortly afterwards, on October 2, government forces opened fire with machine guns on a downtown protest, killing or wounding hundreds of demonstrators.

Guadalajarans were fortunate to escape much of the violent social ferment of the 1960s. As the city's population passed the 1,000,000 mark, optimistic investors pushed up Guadalajara's first two skyscrapers, the Hilton Hotel and Condominios Guadalajara, planned to anchor a shiny new financial center on the south edge of downtown. Concurrently, confident developers promoted and built Latin America's first U.S.–style mall, Plaza del Sol, in Guadalajara's westside suburb. Although the downtown financial center never prospered, Plaza del Sol was (and still is) a huge success.

Maquiladoras

Despite its serious internal troubles, Mexico's relations with the United States were cordial. President Lyndon Johnson visited and unveiled a statue of Abraham Lincoln in Mexico City. Later, Díaz Ordaz met with President Richard Nixon in Puerto Vallarta.

Meanwhile, bilateral negotiations produced the **Border Industrialization Program.** Within a 12-mile strip south of the United States–Mexico border, foreign companies could assemble duty-free parts into finished goods and export them without any duties on either side. Within a dozen years, a swarm of such plants, called *maquiladoras,* were humming as hundreds of thousands of Mexican workers assembled and exported billions of dollars worth of shiny consumer goods—electronics, clothes, furniture, pharmaceuticals, and toys—worldwide.

In the 1970s, following Mexico's improved transportation network, *maquiladora* construction shifted to Mexico's interior, arriving in Guadalajara in 1975. The first four plants—harbingers of things to come—were all electronics: Motorola, General Instruments, Unisys, and TRW.

The 1974 discovery of gigantic new oil and gas reserves along Mexico's Gulf Coast added fuel to Mexico's already rapid industrial expansion. During the late 1970s and early 1980s, billions in foreign investment financed other major developments—factories, hotels, power plants, roads, airports—all over the country.

Economic Trouble of the 1980s

The negative side of Mexico's industrial expansion was the huge dollar debt required to finance it. President **Luis Echeverría Alvarez** (1970–76), diverted by his interest in international affairs, passed Mexico's burgeoning financial deficit to his successor, **José López Portillo.** As feared by some experts, a world petroleum glut during the early 1980s burst Mexico's ballooning oil bubble and plunged the country into financial crisis. When the 1982 interest came due on its foreign debt,

Mexico's largest holding company couldn't pay the $2.3 billion owed. The peso plummeted more than fivefold, to 150 per U.S. dollar. At the same time, prices doubled every year.

But by the mid-1980s, President **Miguel de la Madrid** (1982–88) was working hard to get Mexico's economic house in order. He sliced government and raised taxes, asking rich and poor alike to tighten their belts. Despite getting foreign bankers to reschedule Mexico's debt, de la Madrid couldn't stop inflation. Prices skyrocketed as the peso deflated to 2,500 per U.S. dollar, becoming one of the world's most devalued currencies by 1988.

Despite the economic trouble, optimism still reined in Guadalajara. Having seen the population of their metropolis double again to more than 2,000,000 in the previous decade, Guadalajarans initiated a civic construction project of visionary proportions—Plaza Tapatía—which architect Ignacio Díaz Morales conceived to unify the downtown into a grand strolling ground. But there was bad news that developers tried to minimize: Upwards of 10 square commercial blocks, including dozens of noteworthy historic buildings (including the popular bullring), had to be torn down despite the protests of Guadalajarans.

Salinas de Gortari and NAFTA

Public disgust with official corruption led to significant opposition during the 1988 presidential election. Billionaire PAN candidate Michael Clothier and liberal National Democratic Front candidate Cuauhtémoc Cárdenas ran against the PRI's Harvard-educated technocrat Carlos Salinas de Gortari. The vote was split so evenly that all three candidates claimed victory. Although Salinas eventually won the election, his showing, barely half of the vote, was the worst ever for a PRI president.

Salinas, however, became Mexico's "Coming Man" of the 1990s. His major achievement—despite significant national opposition—was the North American Free Trade Agreement (NAFTA), negotiated in 1992 by him, U.S. President George Bush, and Canadian Prime Minister Brian Mulrooney.

Crisis in Chiapas; Disaster in Guadalajara

On the very day in early January 1994 that NAFTA took effect, rebellion broke out in the poor, remote state of Chiapas. A small but well-disciplined campesino force, calling itself Ejército Zapatista Liberación Nacional (Zapatista National Liberation Army—EZLN—or "Zapatistas") captured a number of provincial towns and held the former governor of Chiapas hostage.

Earlier, back in Guadalajara, the 1990s had started off on a positive note, with the Ibero-American summit of 19 Latin American heads of state, plus Portugal and Spain in July, 1991.

Soon, however, a pair of tragedies struck the city. On April 22, 1992, gasoline leaking into the street drains ignited a horrific explosion that blew six miles of city pavements, cars, buildings, and people into the air, killing 200 and injuring thousands. Scarcely a year later, assailants gunned down Guadalajara's cardinal, Juan Jesùs Posada Ocampo, along with four other victims, at the Guadalajara airport. Although the streets have been repaired and city officials swear such an explosion will never occur again, Cardinal Posada Ocampo's killers have never been brought to justice.

To further complicate matters, Mexico's already tense 1994 drama veered toward tragedy. While Salinas de Gortari's chief negotiator, Manuel Camacho Solis, was attempting to iron out a settlement with the Zapatista rebels, PRI presidential candidate Luis Donaldo Colosio, Salinas' handpicked successor, was gunned down just months before the August balloting. However, instead of disintegrating, the nation united in grief; opposition candidates eulogized their fallen former opponent and later earnestly engaged his replacement, stolid technocrat **Ernesto Zedillo,** in Mexico's first presidential election debate.

In a closely watched election unmarred by irregularities, Zedillo piled up a solid plurality against his PAN and PRD opponents. By perpetuating the PRI's 65-year hold on the presidency, the electorate had again opted for the PRI's familiar although imperfect middle-aged revolution.

New Crisis, New Recovery

Zedillo, however, had little time to savor his victory. Right away he had to face the consequences of his predecessor's shabby fiscal policies. Less than a month after he took office, the peso crashed, losing a third of its value just before Christmas 1994. A month later, Mexican financial institutions, their dollar debt having nearly doubled in a month, were in danger of defaulting on their obligations to international investors. To stave off a worldwide financial panic, U.S. President Clinton, in February 1995, secured an unprecedented multibillion dollar loan package for Mexico, guaranteed by U.S. and international institutions.

Although disaster was temporarily averted, the cure for the country's ills was another painful round of inflation and belt-tightening for poor Mexicans. During 1995, inflation soared; more and more families became unable to purchase staple foods and basic medicines. Malnutrition, and a resurgence of Third World diseases, such as cholera and dengue fever, menaced the countryside.

At the same time, Mexico's equally serious political ills seemed to defy cure. Raul Salinas de Gortari, an important PRI party official and the former president's brother, was arrested for money laundering and political assassination. As popular sentiment began to implicate Carlos Salinas de Gortari himself, the former president fled Mexico to an undisclosed location.

Meanwhile, as negotiations with the rebel Zapatistas sputtered on and off in Chiapas, a new, well-armed revolutionary group, **Ejército Popular Revolucionario** (People's Revolutionary Army, or EPR), killed two dozen police and soldiers at several locations, mostly in southwestern Mexico.

Mexican democracy got a much-needed boost when notorious Guerrero governor Ruben Figueroa, who had tried to cover up the Aguas Blancas massacre with a bogus videotape, was forced from office. At the same time, the Zedillo government gained momentum in addressing the Zapatistas' grievances in Chiapas, even as it decreased federal military presence, built new rural electrification networks, and refurbished health clinics. Moreover, Mexico's economy

began to improve. By mid-1996, inflation had slowed to a 20 percent annual rate, investment dollars were flowing back into Mexico, the peso had stabilized at about 7.5 to the U.S. dollar, and Mexico had paid back half the borrowed U.S. bailout money.

Zedillo's Political Reforms

In the political arena, although the justice system generally left much to be desired, a pair of unprecedented events signaled an increasingly open political system. In the 1997 congressional elections, voters elected a host of opposition candidates, depriving the PRI of an absolute congressional majority for the first time since 1929. A year later, in early 1998, Mexicans were participating in their country's first primary elections—in which voters, instead of politicians, chose party candidates.

Although President Zedillo had had a rough ride, he entered the twilight of his 1994–2000 term able to take credit for an improved economy, some genuine political reforms, and relative peace in the countryside. The election of 2000 revealed, however, that the Mexican people were not satisfied.

End of an Era: Vicente Fox Unseats the PRI

During 1998 and 1999 the focal point of opposition to the PRI's three-generation rule had been shifting from lackluster left-of-center Cuauhtémoc Cárdenas to relative newcomer Vicente Fox, former President of Coca-Cola Mexico and clean former PAN governor of Guanajuato.

Fox, who had announced his presidential candidacy two years before the election, seemed an unlikely challenger. After all, the minority PAN had always been the party of wealthy businessmen and the conservative Catholic right. But blunt-talking, six-foot-five Fox, who sometimes campaigned in *vaquero* boots and a ten-gallon cowboy hat, preached populist themes of coalition building and "inclusion." He backed up his talk by carrying his campaign to hardscrabble city *barrios,* dirt-poor country villages, and traditional outsider groups, such as Jews.

Meanwhile, as the campaign heated up in

early 2000, PRI candidate Francisco Labastida, suave, ex–Interior Secretary and governor of the drug-plagued state of Sinaloa, sounded the usual PRI themes to gatherings of party loyalists. At the same time, dour PRD liberal Cuauhtémoc Cárdenas, resigning from a mediocre term as mayor of Mexico City, faded to a weak third place. On the eve of the election, polls predicted a dead heat of about 40 percent of the vote each for Fox and Labastida.

In a closely monitored election, on July 2, 2000, Fox decisively defeated Labastida, 42 percent to 38 percent, while Cárdenas received only 17 percent. Fox's win also swept a PAN plurality (223/209/57) into the 500-seat Chamber of Deputies lower house (although the Senate remained PRI-dominated).

Nevertheless, in removing the PRI from the all-powerful presidency after 71 consecutive years of domination, Fox had ushered Mexico into a new, more democratic era.

Despite stinging criticism from his own ranks, President Zedillo, whom historians were already judging as the real hero behind the new democratic era, made an unprecedented, early appeal, less than a week after the election, for all Mexicans to unite behind Fox.

On the eve of his December 1 inauguration, Mexicans awaited Fox's speech with hopeful anticipation. He did not disappoint them. Although acknowledging that he can't reverse 71 years of PRI entrenchment in one six-year term, he vowed to ride the crest of reform, revamping the tax system, and reduce poverty by 30 percent, by creating a million new jobs a year through new private investment in electricity and oil production and a forming a new common market with Latin America, the United States, and Canada.

He promised, moreover, to secure justice for all by a much-needed reform of police, the federal attorney general, and the army. Perhaps most difficult of all, Fox called for the formation of an unprecedented congressional "Transparency Commission" to investigate a generation of past grievances, including the 1968 massacre of student demonstrators and assassinations of, among others, Cardinal Posada Ocampo in 1993 and presidential candidate Donaldo Colosio in 1994.

Vicente Fox, President of Mexico

Wasting little time getting started, President Fox first headed to Chiapas to confer with indigenous community leaders. Along the way, he shut down some Chiapas military bases and removed dozens of roadblocks. Back in Mexico City, he sent the long-delayed peace plan, including the indigenous bill of rights, to Congress. Zapatista rebels responded by journeying en masse from Chiapas to Mexico City where, in their black masks, they addressed Congress, arguing for indigenous rights. Although by mid-July 2001, Congress had passed a modified version of the negotiated settlement and a majority of states had ratified the required constitutional amendment, indigenous leaders condemned the legislation plan as watered down and unacceptable—proponents, however, claimed it was the best possible compromise between the Zapatistas demands and the existing Mexican constitution.

On July 2, 2001, the first anniversary of his election, Vicente Fox celebrated by marrying his spokeswoman and confidante, Martha Sahagun, in a private civil ceremony.

The news on that day, however, was not all good. Although Fox had pushed a peace settlement through Congress, it was doubtful whether it would satisfy the Zapatistas. Moreover, Mexico's economy had soured in 2001, eliminating half a million jobs, instead of creating the million jobs that Fox had promised. Furthermore, Fox's promised "Transparency Commission" was not yet producing results. And a so-called "Towelgate" furor (in which aides had purchased dozens of $400 towels for the presidential mansion) had weakened Fox's squeaky-clean image.

On the positive side during his first six months, Fox did put major drug lords on the defensive, negotiated a major immigration agreement with the United States, and attracted a record pile of foreign investment dollars into Mexico. On balance, critics were writing that "Fox still has time" to accomplish what he promised.

More significantly, the Mexican person in the street, who eventually will judge Fox's success or failure in the voting booth, is by and large still cheering for Fox. It's important not to forget July 2, 2000: On that day, when Mexicans pushed out the PRI after 71 years and cleanly elected an opposition president, the country took a crucial, irreversible step in its long journey toward democracy and justice for all.

Economy and Government

THE ECONOMY

Post-Revolutionary Gains

By many measures, Mexico's 20th-century revolution appears to have succeeded. Since 1910, illiteracy has plunged from 80 percent to 10 percent, life expectancy has risen from 30 years to nearly 70, infant mortality has dropped from a whopping 40 percent to about 2 percent, and, in terms of caloric intake, Mexicans are eating about twice as much as their forebears at the turn of the 20th century.

Decades of near-continuous economic growth account for rising Mexican living stan-

© BRUCE WHIPPERMAN

Toilet paper is such a dear commodity in Mexico that it's sometimes measured out into small packages at the entrance to *el baño*.

dards. The Mexican economy has rebounded from its last two recessions due to several factors: plentiful natural resources, notably oil and metals; diversified manufacturing, such as cars, steel, petrochemicals, and electronics; steadily increasing tourism; exports of fruits, vegetables, and cattle; and its large, willing, low-wage workforce.

Recent governments, moreover, have skillfully exploited Mexico's economic strengths. The Border Industrialization Program has led to millions of jobs in thousands of *maquiladora* factories, from Tijuana to the mouth of the Rio Grande to Mexico City and Guadalajara. Dependency on oil exports, which led to the 1980s peso collapse, has been reduced from 75 percent in 1982 to less than 15 percent in 2000. Foreign trade, a strong source for new Mexican jobs, has burgeoned since the 1980s, due to liberalized tariffs as Mexico joined General Agreement on Tariffs and Trade (GATT) in 1986 and NAFTA in 1994. As a result, Mexico has become a net exporter of goods and services to the United States, its largest trading partner. Belt-tightening measures brought inflation down and foreign investment has been flowing into Mexico—especially Guadalajara—since 1996. And benefits from the devalued peso, such as increased tourism and burgeoning exports, have contributed to a generally improving economy since 1997 (although a slowdown, beginning in 2001, reflects the U.S. economic downturn).

Guadalajara remains one of the stars of the Mexican economy, especially in electronics. From 1994 to 2000, electronics exports from Guadalajara skyrocketed from $1.6 billion to $8 billion, adding strong credence to the claim that Guadalajara has become the "Silicon Valley of Mexico." By 2000, scores of big electronics factories, with heavyweight names such as Hewlitt-Packard, NEC, Texas Instruments, Intel, Kodak, SCI, and IBM, dotted Guadalajara's industrial landscape.

Contemporary Economic Challenges

Despite huge gains, Mexico's Revolution of 1910 is nevertheless incomplete. Improved public health, education, income, and opportunity have barely outdistanced Mexico's population, which has increased nearly sevenfold—from 15 million to 101 million—between 1910 and 2000. For example, although the literacy rate has increased, the actual number of Mexican people who can't read, some 10 million, has remained about constant since 1910.

Moreover, the land reform program, once thought to be a Mexican cure-all, has long been a disappointment. The *ejidos* of which Emiliano Zapata dreamed have become mostly symbolic. The communal fields are typically small and unirrigated. *Ejido* land, constitutionally prohibited from being sold, cannot serve as collateral for bank loans, (except under special circumstances). Capital for irrigation networks, fertilizers, and harvesting machines is consequently lacking. Communal farms are typically inefficient; the average Mexican field produces about *one-quarter* as much corn per acre as a U.S. farm. Mexico must accordingly use its precious oil dollar surplus to import millions of tons of corn—originally indigenous to Mexico—annually.

The triple scourge of overpopulation, lack of arable land, and low farm and factory income has driven millions of campesino families to seek better lives in Mexico's cities and young men to seek work north of the border. Since 1910, Mexico has evolved from a largely rural country, where 70 percent of the population lived on farms, to an urban nation where 70 percent of the population lives in cities. Fully one-fifth of Mexico's people now live in Mexico City.

Nevertheless, the future appears bright for many privately owned and managed Mexican farms, concentrated largely in the northern border states. Exceptionally productive, they typically work hundreds or thousands of irrigated acres of crops, such as tomatoes, lettuce, chilies, wheat, corn, tobacco, cotton, fruits, alfalfa, chickens, and cattle, just like their counterparts across the border in California, New Mexico, Arizona, and Texas.

Staples—wheat for bread, corn for tortillas, milk, and cooking oil—are all imported and consequently expensive for the typical working-class Mexican family, which must spend half or more of its income (typically $500 per month) for food. Recent inflation has compounded the problem, particularly for the millions of families on the bottom half of Mexico's economic ladder.

Although average gross domestic product figures—about $9,000 per capita—place Mexico above nearly all other Third World countries' averages, in reality the numbers have little socioeconomic relevance. Historically, the richest one-fifth of Mexican families earns about 10 times the income of the poorest one-fifth. A relative handful of people own a large hunk of Mexico, and they don't seem inclined to share any of it with the less fortunate. As for the poor, the typical Mexican family in the bottom one-third income bracket often owns neither car nor refrigerator; nor do the children finish elementary school.

GOVERNMENT AND POLITICS
The Constitution of 1917

Mexico's governmental system is rooted in the Constitution of 1917, which incorporated many of the features of its reformist predecessor of 1857. The 1917 document, with amendments, remains in force. Although drafted at the behest of conservative revolutionary Venustiano Carranza by his handpicked Querétaro "Constitucionalista" congress, it was greatly influenced by Álvaro Obregón and generally ignored by Carranza during his subsequent three-year presidential term.

Although many articles resemble those of its United States model, the Constitution of 1917 contains provisions developed directly from Mexican experience. Article 27 addresses the question of land. Private property rights are qualified by societal need; subsoil rights are public property, and foreigners and corporations are severely restricted in land ownership. Although the 1917 constitution declared *ejido* (communal) land inviolate, 1994 amendments allow, under certain circumstances, the sale or use of communal land as loan security.

Article 23 severely restricts church powers. In declaring that "places of worship are the property of the nation," it stripped churches of all title to real estate, without compensation. Article 5 and Article 130 banned religious orders, expelled foreign clergy, and denied priests and ministers all political rights, including voting, holding office, and even criticizing the government.

Article 123 establishes the rights of labor: to organize, bargain collectively, strike, work a maximum eight-hour day, and receive a minimum wage. Women are to receive equal pay for equal work and be given a month's paid leave for childbearing. Article 123 also establishes social security plans for sickness, unemployment, pensions, and death.

On paper, Mexico's constitutional government structures appear much like their U.S. prototypes: a federal presidency, a two-house congress, and a supreme court, with their counterparts in each of the 32 states. Political parties field candidates, and all citizens vote by secret ballot.

Mexico's presidents, however, enjoy greater powers than their U.S. counterparts. They can suspend constitutional rights under a state of siege, can initiate legislation, veto all or parts of bills, refuse to execute laws, and replace state officers. The federal government, moreover, retains nearly all taxing authority, relegating the states to a role of merely administering federal programs.

Although ideally providing for separation of powers, the Constitution of 1917 subordinates both the legislative and judicial branches, with the courts being the weakest of all. The supreme court, for example, can only, with repeated deliberation, decide upon the constitutionality of legislation. Five separate individuals must file successful petitions for writs *amparo* (protection) on a single point of law in order to affect constitutional precedent.

Jalisco's government reflects the federal model. By secret ballot, voters in 20 state electoral districts elect the governor, several of the governor's cabinet, and the 40 deputies of the unicameral legislature. Legislative candidates must be a minimum 21 years of age, not hold executive or judicial office and have been a Jalisco resident for two years.

© BRUCE WHIPPERMAN

Peaceful political protest, a measure of Mexican democratization, is increasingly common. Here, children and parents march in a right-to-life procession in Tlaquepaque.

Democratizing Mexican Politics

Reforms in Mexico's stable but top-heavy "Institutional Revolution" came only gradually. Characteristically, street protests were brutally put down at first, with officials only later working to address grievances. Dominance by the PRI led to widespread cynicism and citizen apathy.

Change began slowly in the late 1980s and picked up steam with the election of PRI presidential candidate Ernesto Zedillo. Following his 1994 inaugural address, in which he called loudly and clearly for more reforms, President Zedillo quickly began to produce results. He immediately appointed a respected member of the PAN opposition party as attorney general—the first non-PRI cabinet appointment in Mexican history. Other Zedillo firsts were federal senate confirmation of both supreme court nominees and the attorney general, multiparty participation in the Chiapas peace negotiations, and congressional approval of the 1995 financial assistance package received from the United States. Zedillo, moreover, organized a series of precedent-setting meetings with opposition leaders that led to a written pact for political reform and the establishment of permanent working groups to discuss political and economic questions.

Perhaps most important was Zedillo's campaign and inaugural vow to separate both his government and himself from PRI decision-making. He kept his promise, becoming the first Mexican president in as long as anyone could remember who did not choose his successor.

Guadalajara's end-of-millennium politics led the national trend, with a succession of three PAN governors, Alberto Cárdenas (1988–1994,

1994–2000), and Ramírez Acuña (2000–2006). Meanwhile, opposition PRD and Green parties gained significant minorities in the state legislature, with PAN and PRI about equally divided by 2000.

A New Mexican Revolution

Finally, in 2000, like a Mexican Gorbachev, Ernesto Zedillo—the man most responsible for Mexico's recent democratic reforms—watched as PAN opposition reformer Vicente Fox swept his PRI from the presidency after a 71-year rule. Despite severe criticism from within his own party, Zedillo quickly called for the country to close ranks behind Fox. Millions of Mexicans, still dazed but buoyed by Zedillo's statesmanship and Fox's epoch-making victory, eagerly awaited Fox's inauguration address on December 1, 2000.

He promised nothing less than a new revolution for Mexico and backed it up with concrete proposals: Reduce poverty by 30 percent with a million new jobs a year from revitalized new electricity and oil production; a Mexican Silicon Valley in Guadalajara; and free trade between Mexico, all of Latin America, and the United States and Canada. He promised justice for all, through a reformed police, army, and the judiciary. He promised conciliation and an agreement with the Zapatista rebel movement in the south, including a bill of rights for Mexico's native peoples. With all of Mexico listening, Fox brought his speech to a hopeful conclusion: "If I had to summarize my message today in one sentence, I would say: Today Mexico has a future, but we have lost much time and wasted many resources. Mexico has a future, and we must build that future starting today."

People

Let a broad wooden chopping block represent Mexico; imagine hacking it with a sharp cleaver until it is grooved and pocked. That fractured surface resembles Mexico's central highlands, where most Mexicans, divided from each other by high mountains and yawning *barrancas,* have lived since before history.

The Mexicans' deep divisions, in large measure, led to their downfall at the hands of the Spanish conquistadors. The Aztec empire that Hernán Cortés conquered was a vast but fragmented collection of tribes. Speaking more than a hundred mutually alien languages, those original Mexicans viewed each other suspiciously, as barely human barbarians from strange lands beyond the mountains. Even today the lines Mexicans draw between themselves—of caste, class, race, wealth—are mostly the result of the realities of their mutual isolation.

POPULATION

The Spanish colonial government and the Roman Catholic religion provided the glue that over 400 years has welded Mexico's fragmented people into a burgeoning nation-state. Although Mexico's population in recent years has increased steadily, this has not always been so. Historians estimate that European diseases, largely measles and small-pox, wiped out as many as 25 million—perhaps

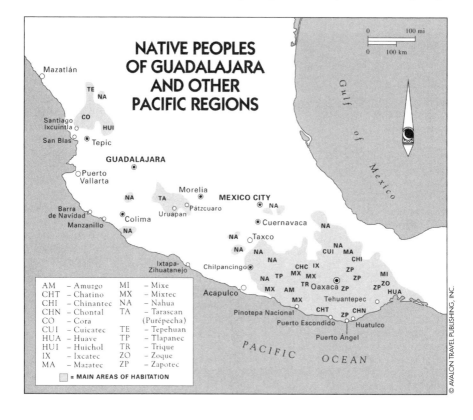

NATIVE PEOPLES OF GUADALAJARA AND OTHER PACIFIC REGIONS

AM	– Amuzgo	MI	– Mixe
CHT	– Chatino	MX	– Mixtec
CHI	– Chinantec	NA	– Nahua
CHN	– Chontal	TA	– Tarascan
CO	– Cora		(Purépecha)
CUI	– Cuicatec	TE	– Tepehuan
HUA	– Huave	TP	– Tlapanec
HUI	– Huichol	TR	– Trique
IX	– Ixcatec	ZO	– Zoque
MA	– Mazatec	ZP	– Zapotec

= MAIN AREAS OF HABITATION

INDIGENOUS POPULATIONS OF GUADALAJARA AND OTHER IMPORTANT PACIFIC REGIONS

For the Guadalajara region states of Nayarit and Jalisco and the significant Pacific states of (north to south) Sinaloa, Colima, Michoacán, Guerrero, and Oaxaca, the 2000 government census totals were:

State	Indigenous Population (Over Five Years of Age)	Total Population (Over Five Years of Age)	Percent of Total
Guadalajara Region:			
Nayarit	37,200	769,000	4.8 percent
Jalisco	39,300	5,323,000	0.7 percent
Other Pacific States and Regions:			
Sinaloa	49,700	2,130,000	2.3 percent
Colima	2,900	421,000	0.7 percent
Michoacán	121,800	3,342,000	3.6 percent
Guerrero	367,100	2,572,000	14.3 percent
Oaxaca	1,120,300	2,924,000	38.3 percent

The same government sources tabulate indigenous peoples by language groupings. Although such figures are probably low, the 2000 figures revealed significant populations in many areas:

Language	Group Population(2000)	Important Centers
Guadalajara Region:		
Cora	15,600	Nayarit (Acaponeta)
Huichol	27,900	Nayarit-Jalisco (Santiago Ixcuintla, Huejuqilla)
Nahua	8,100	Jalisco (Ciudad Guzmán)
Purèpecha	3,000	Southern Jalisco (Zamora)
Neighboring Pacific States and Regions (From North to South):		
Tepuan	17,000	Sinaloa-Durango
Tarasco	111,000	Michoacán (Pátzcuaro)

Language	Group Population(2000)	Important Centers
Nahua	160,000	Guerrero (Taxco and Chilpancingo)
Mixtec	363,000	Western Oaxaca (Huajuapan, Tlaxiaco, and Santiago Jamíltepec)
Tlapanec	93,000	East Guerrero (Tlapa de Comonfort)
Amusgo	40,000	Oaxaca-Guerrero (San Pedro Amusgos and Xochistlahuaca)
Chinantec	107,000	Northern Oaxaca (Valle Nacional)
Chatino	40,000	Southern Oaxaca (Santos Reyes Nopala)
Zapotec	380,000	Central, East, and South Oaxaca (Tlacolula, Ocotlán, Tehuántepec)
Chontal	5,000	Southeast Oaxaca (Santiago Astata)
Triqui	16,000	West Oaxaca (Juxtlahuaca)
Chocho	1,000	Northwest Oaxaca (Coixtlahuaca)
Cuicatec	12,000	Northern Oaxaca (Cuicatlán)
Huave	14,000	Southeast Oaxaca (San Mateo del Mar)
Mazatec	175,000	North Oaxaca (Huatla de Jiménez)
Mixe	106,000	Northeast Oaxaca (Ayutla)
Zoque	5,000	Southeast Oaxaca (San Miguel Chimalapa)
Ixcatec	1,000	Northwest Oaxaca (Ixcatlán)

Guadalajara street vendors are often indigenous people from poorer parts of Mexico, such as Michoacán, Guerrero, and Oaxaca, seeking a better life.

95 percent—of the *indígena* population within a few generations after Cortés stepped ashore in 1519. Consequently, the Mexican population dwindled to a mere one million inhabitants by 1600. It wasn't until 1950, four centuries after Cortés, that Mexico's population had recovered to its preconquest level of 20 million.

After 1950, reflecting a typical Third World birthrate of seven or eight children per woman, Mexico's population zoomed upward, more than quadrupling, to around 90 million by 1990. But during the decade of the 1990s, increased education, affluence, and greater political and social freedom for women reduced the birth rate to 2–3 children per woman. Consequently Mexico's population, which managed to reach 101 million in 2000, is increasing at a moderate pace of about 1 percent annually.

Guadalajara's population, by contrast, increased from about 2.65 million in 1990 to around 3.5 million in 2000, and continues to grow about 3 percent per year. While this growth rate is about triple the national average, it mostly reflects an influx from the country to the city, rather than a high birthrate.

Mestizos, *Indígenas,* Criollos, and *Negros*

Although by 1950 Mexico's population had recovered, it was completely transformed. The mestizo, a Spanish-speaking person of mixed blood, had replaced the pure Native American, the *indígena* (een-DEE-hay-nah), as the typical Mexican.

The trend continues. Perhaps three of four Mexicans (and Guadalajarans) would identify themselves as mestizo: that class whose part-European blood elevates them, in the Mexican mind, to the level of *gente de razón*—people of "reason" or "right." And there's the rub: The *indígenas* (or, mistakenly but much more commonly, Indians), by the usual measurements of income, health, or education, squat at the bottom of the Mexican social ladder.

The typical *indígena* family lives in a small adobe house in a remote valley, subsisting on corn, beans, and vegetables from their small, unirrigated *milpa* (cornfield). They usually have chickens, a few pigs, and sometimes a cow, but no electricity; their few hundred dollars a year in cash income isn't enough to buy even a small refrigerator, much less a truck.

MACHISMO

I once met an Acapulco man who wore five gold wristwatches and became angry when I quietly refused his repeated invitations to get drunk with him. Another time, on the beach near San Blas, two drunk campesinos nearly attacked me because I was helping my girlfriend cook a picnic dinner. Outside Taxco I once spent an endless hour in the seat behind a bus driver who insisted on speeding down the middle of the two-laned highway, honking aside oncoming automobiles.

Despite their wide differences (the first was a rich criollo, the campesinos were *indígenas*, and the bus driver, mestizo), the common affliction shared by all four men was machismo, a disease that seems to possess many Mexican men. Machismo is a sometimes reckless obsession to prove one's masculinity, to show how macho you are. Men of many nationalities share the instinct to prove themselves. Japan's *bushido* samurai code is one example. Mexican men, however, often seem to try the hardest.

When confronted by a Mexican braggart, male visitors should remain careful and controlled. If your opponent is yelling, stay cool, speak softly, and withdraw as soon as possible. On the highway, be courteous and unprovoking—don't use your car to spar with a macho driver. Drinking often leads to problems. It's best to stay out of bars or cantinas unless you're prepared to deal with the macho consequences. Polite refusal of a drink may be taken as a challenge. If you visit a bar with Mexican friends or acquaintances, you may be heading for a no-win choice of a drunken all-night *borrachera* (binge) or an insult to the honor of your friends by refusing.

For women, machismo requires even more cautious behavior. In Mexico, women's liberation is long in coming. Few women hold positions of power in business or politics. One woman, Rosa Luz Alegría, did attain the rank of minister of tourism during the former Portillo administration; she was the president's mistress.

Machismo requires that female visitors obey the rules or suffer the consequences. Keep a low profile; wear bathing suits and brief shorts only at the beach. Follow the example of your Mexican sisters: Make a habit of going out, especially at night, in the company of friends or acquaintances. Mexican men believe an unaccompanied woman wants to be picked up. Ignore such offers; any response, even refusal, might be taken as a "maybe." If, on the other hand, there is a Mexican man whom you'd genuinely like to meet, the traditional way is an arranged introduction through family or friends.

Mexican families, as a source of protection and friendship, should not be overlooked—especially on the beach or in the park, where, among the gaggle of kids, grandparents, aunts, and cousins, there's room for one more.

The typical mestizo family, on the other hand, enjoys most of the benefits of the 20th century. They usually own a modest concrete house in town. Their furnishings, simple by developed-world standards, will often include an electric refrigerator, washing machine, propane stove, television, and old car or truck. The children go to school every day, and the eldest son sometimes looks forward to college.

Sizable *negro* communities, descendants of 18th-century African slaves, live in the Gulf states and along the Guerrero-Oaxaca Pacific coastline. Last to arrive, the *negros* experience discrimination at the hands of everyone else and are integrating very slowly into the mestizo mainstream.

Above the mestizos, a tiny criollo (Mexican-born white) minority, a few percent of the total population, inherits the privileges—wealth, education, and political power—of their colonial Spanish ancestors.

Indígena Language Groups

The Maya speakers of Yucatán and the aggregate of the Nahuatl (Aztec language) speakers of the central plateau are Mexico's most numerous *indígena* groups, totaling about two and a half million (one million Maya, a million and a half Nahua).

Official figures, which show that the Guadalajara region's indigenous population amounts to a mere 1 percent of the total, are misleading. Official counts do not measure the droves of transient folks—migrants and new arrivals—who sleep in vehicles, shanty towns, behind their crafts stalls, and with friends and relatives. Although they are officially invisible, you will see them in Guadalajara, especially around the Libertad Market downtown, laden with their for-sale fruit or handicrafts: men in sombreros and scruffy jeans, women in homemade full-skirted dresses with aprons much like your great-great-grandmother may have worn.

Immigrants in their own country, they flock to cities and tourist resorts from hardscrabble rural areas of the poorest states, often Michoacán, Guerrero, and Oaxaca. Although of pure native blood, they will not acknowledge it or will even be insulted if you ask them if they are *indígenas*. It would be more polite to ask them where they're from. If from Michoacán, they'll often speak Tarasco (more courteously, say Purépecha: poo-RAY-pay-chah); if from Guerrero, the answer will usually be Nahuatl. Oaxaca folks, on the other hand, will probably be fluent in a dialect of either Zapotec or Mixtec. If not one of these, then it might be Chinantec, Mazatec, Mixe (MEE-shay), Chatino or any one of a dozen others from Oaxaca's crazy-quilt of language.

As immigrants always have, they come seeking opportunity. If you're interested in what they're selling, bargain with humor. And if you err, let it be on the generous side: Like anyone, they'd prefer to walk away from a sale rather than lose their dignity.

The Huichol and Cora

In contrast to the migrants from the south, the Huichol and their northerly neighbors, the Cora, are native to the Guadalajara region. Isolated and resistant to Mexicanization, about 30,000 Huichol (and about half as many Cora) farm, raise cattle, and hunt high in their Sierra Madre mountain homeland, which extends northerly and easterly from the foothills northwest of Guadalajara. Although the Cora's traditional territory intermixes with the Huichol's at its southern limit, it also spreads northward, between the foothills and the 6,000-foot-high Sierra Madre Occidental valleys, to the Nayarit-Durango border.

The Huichol, more so than all *indígena* groups, have preserved their colorful dress and religious practices. Huichol religious use of hallucinogenic peyote and the men's rainbow-tinted feathered hats and clothes are renowned. (Be sure to visit the excellent Huichol cultural museum in Zapopan; see the City: West and North of Downtown chapter.)

Dress

Country markets are where you're most likely to see people in traditional dress. And although virtually no men in the Guadalajara region wear the white cottons of yesteryear, nearly all men throughout Mexico wear the Spanish-origin straw sombrero (literally, "shade-maker") on their heads.

Country women's dress, by contrast, is more colorful. It can include a *huipil* (long, sleeveless dress) embroidered in bright floral and animal motifs and a handwoven *enredo* (wraparound skirt that identifies the wearer with a locality). A *faja* (waist sash) and, in winter, a *quechquemitl* (shoulder cape) complete the ensemble.

RELIGION

"God and Gold" was the two-pronged mission of the conquistadors. Most of them concentrated on gold, while missionaries tried to shift the emphasis to God. They were hugely successful; about 90 percent of Mexicans profess to be Catholics.

Catholicism, spreading its doctrine of equality of all persons before God and incorporating native gods into church rituals, eventually brought the *indígenas* into the fold. Within a hundred years, nearly all native Mexicans had accepted the new religion, which raised the universal God of humankind over local tribal deities.

On the Road

This section covers transportation *to* Guadalajara by various means, including by bus and by car. For more information on transportation *within* Guadalajara once you've arrived, refer to the Getting Around section, later in this chapter. It has further information regarding (among others) bus, car, and taxi transportation in and around the city.

BY AIR
From the United States and Canada

Most foreign visitors reach Guadalajara by air. Flights are frequent and reasonably priced. Competition sometimes shaves tariffs down as low as $250 for a Guadalajara round-trip from one of the Guadalajara departure gateways of Sacramento, San Francisco, Oakland, San Jose, Los Angeles, Las Vegas, Phoenix, Tucson, Dallas, Houston, Chicago, and New York.

Air travelers can save lots of money by shopping around. Don't be bashful about asking for the cheapest price. Make it clear to the airline or travel agent you're interested in a bargain. Ask the right questions: Are there special-incentive, advance-payment, night, midweek, business, senior, tour package, or charter fares? Peruse the ads in the Sunday newspaper travel section for bargain-oriented travel agencies.

Alternatively, log on to airlines' websites or Web ticket agencies such as www.travelocity.com or www.expedia.com (see the Internet Resources section at the end of this book) and look for promotions. Although some agents charge booking fees and don't

Feeding pigeons is the ideal Sunday relaxation in the downtown Plaza de la Liberación.

AIRLINES

The air carriers with the greatest number of scheduled direct connections between North American gateways and the Guadalajara region are (in approximate descending order of activity): Aeroméxico, Mexicana, Delta, American, Aerocalifornia, America West, and Continental. Canadian World of Vacations winter–spring charters connect with Puerto Vallarta.

(GD=Guadalajara, PV=Puerto Vallarta, MX=Mexico City)

Airline	Origin	Destinations
Aeroméxico		
tel. 800/237-6639	Los Angeles	GD, PV, MX
www.aeromexico.com	Tijuana	MX
	New York	GD, MX
	Miami	MX
	Houston	MX
	San Diego	MX,
	Atlanta	GD, MX
	Phoenix	GD, MX
	Dallas	MX
Mexicana		
tel. 800/531-7921	Los Angeles	GD, MX
www.mexicana.com.mx	Sacramento	GD
	San Francisco	GD, MX
	San Jose	GD
	Oakland	GD
	Las Vegas	GD
	Tijuana	GD, MX
	Denver	MX
	Chicago	GD, PV
Delta		
tel. 800/221-1212	Los Angeles	PV, GD, MX
www.delta.com	Dallas	MX
	Atlanta	GD, MX
	Orlando	MX
	New York	MX
	Miami	MX

Airline	Origin	Destinations
American		
tel. 800/433-7300	Dallas	GD, PV, MX
www.aa.com	Los Angeles	GD
	Chicago	MX
	Miami	MX
Aerocalifornia		
tel. 800/237-6225	Los Angeles	GD, MX
	Tijuana	MX
	Tucson	GD
America West		
tel. 800/363-2597	Phoenix	GD, PV, MX
www.americawest.com		
Continental		
tel. 800/231-0856	Houston	GD, PV, MX
www.continental.com		
Canadian World of Vacations		
winter–spring charter	Toronto	PV
tel. 800/661-8881	Winnepeg	PV
www.worldofvacations.com	Regina	PV
	Saskatoon	PV
	Vancouver	PV

ON THE ROAD

like discounted tickets because their fee depends on a percentage of ticket prices. Many will nevertheless work hard to get you a bargain, especially if you book an entire air-hotel package with them.

Although few airlines fly directly to Guadalajara from the northern United States and Canada, some **charters flights** do. In locales near Vancouver, Calgary, Ottawa, Toronto, Montreal, Minneapolis, Detroit and Cleveland, consult a travel agent for charter flight options. Be aware that charter reservations, which often require fixed departure and return dates and provide minimal cancellation refunds, decrease your flexibility.

If available charter choices are unsatisfactory, then you might choose to begin your trip with a connecting flight to one of the Guadalajara gateways of Sacramento, San Francisco, Oakland, San Jose, Los Angeles, Las Vegas, Phoenix, Tucson, Dallas, Houston, Chicago, or New York.

You may be able to save money by booking an air/hotel package through one of the airlines that routinely offer them from certain Guadalajara gateway cities:

Mexicana: from Sacramento, San Francisco Los Angeles, Denver, and Chicago; tel. 800/531-7921

America West: from Phoenix; tel. 800/356-6611

American: from Dallas; tel. 800/321-2121

Aeroméxico: from Los Angeles and San Diego; tel. 800/245-8585

Continental: from Houston; tel. 888/898-9255

Delta: from Los Angeles; tel. 800/872-7786

From Europe, Australasia, and Latin America

A few airlines fly across the Atlantic directly to Mexico; they usually include Air France, KLM, and Lufthansa, all of which fly to Mexico City, where travelers can catch a connecting flight to Guadalajara.

Few, if any, airlines fly directly to Mexico from Australasia; transpacific travelers usually transfer at Los Angeles to a Guadalajara-bound flight.

A number of Latin American flag carriers fly directly to Mexico City. From there, easy connections are available via Mexicana, Aeroméxico, or Aerocalifornia airlines to Guadalajara. For more information, consult a travel agent, or log on to a airline ticketing website such as www.travelocity.com or www.expedia.com.

For many more arrival and departure details specific to the Guadalajara airport, see the Heart of the City chapter (Getting There and Away).

Baggage, Insurance, "Bumping," and In-Flight Meals

Balmy Guadalajara makes it easy to pack light (see the Packing Checklist at the end of this chapter). Veteran travelers often condense their luggage to carry-ons only. Airlines routinely allow a carry-on (not exceeding 45 inches in combined length, width, and girth), and a purse. Thus relieved of heavy burdens, your trip will become much simpler. You'll avoid possible luggage loss and long baggage-check-in lines by being able to check in directly at the boarding gate.

Even if you can't avoid checking luggage, loss of it needn't ruin your trip. Always carry your irreplaceable items in the cabin with you. These should include all money, credit cards, traveler's checks, keys, tickets, cameras, passport, prescription drugs, and eyeglasses.

At the X-ray security check, calmly insist **that your film and cameras be hand-inspected.** Regardless of what attendants claim, repeated X-ray scanning will fog any undeveloped film, especially the sensitive ASA 400 and 1,000 high-speed varieties. The cleverest (although weighty) film option is to use one or two lead-lined film bags, which X-rays cannot penetrate. This, of course, forces hand-inspection.

Travelers packing lots of expensive baggage, or those who may have to cancel a nonrefundable flight or tour (because of illness, for example), might consider buying **travel insurance.** Travel agents routinely sell packages that include baggage, trip cancellation, and default insurance. Baggage insurance covers you beyond the conventional liability limits (typically about $1,000 domestic, $400 international); check with your carrier. **Trip cancellation insurance** pays if you must cancel your prepaid trip, while **default insurance** protects you if your carrier or tour agent does not perform as agreed. Travel insurance, however, can be expensive. **Travel Insurance Services,** for example, offers $3,000 of baggage insurance per person for two weeks for about $65. Weigh your options and the cost against benefits carefully before putting your money down. For more information, call toll-free 800/937-1387 or log on the Travel Insurance Services website: www.travelinsure.com. Or contact World Travel Center, website: www.worldtravelcenter.com, tel. 800/786-5566; ask for the travel department.

It's wise to **reconfirm** both departure and return flight reservations, especially during the busy Christmas and Easter seasons. This is a useful strategy, as is prompt arrival at check-in, against getting "bumped" (losing your seat) by the tendency of airlines to overbook the rush of high-season vacationers. For further protection, always get your seat assignment and boarding pass included with your ticket when possible.

Airlines generally try hard to accommodate travelers with dietary or other special needs. When booking your flight, inform your travel agent or carrier of the necessity of a low-sodium, low-cholesterol, vegetarian, lactose-reduced, or other meal requirements. Seniors, handicapped persons, and parents traveling with children should refer to Specialty Travel under Other Practicalities, later in this chapter, for more information.

BY BUS

Just as air travel rules in the United States, bus travel rules in Mexico. Hundreds of sleek, first-class bus lines with names such as Elite, Turistar, Futura, Transportes Pacífico, and White Star (Estrella Blanca) depart the border daily, headed for the Guadalajara region.

Since North American bus lines ordinarily terminate just north of the Mexican border, you must usually disembark, collect your things, and, after having filled out the necessary but very simple paperwork at the Mexican immigration office, proceed on foot across the border to Mexico, where you can bargain with one of the local taxis to drive you the few miles to the *camionera central* (central bus station).

First- and luxury-class bus service in Mexico is much cheaper and often better than in the United States. Tickets for comparable trips in Mexico cost a fraction (as little as $50 for the Guadalajara trip, compared to $100 for a similar-length trip in the United States)

In Mexico, as on U.S. buses, you often have to take it like you find it. *Asientos reservados* (seat reservations), *boletos* (tickets), and information must generally be obtained in person at the bus station, and credit cards and traveler's checks are usually not accepted. Neither are reserved bus tickets usually refundable, so don't miss the bus. On the other hand, plenty of buses roll south almost continuously.

Request a reserved seat, if possible, with numbers 1–25 in the front *(delante)* to middle *(medio)* of the bus. Sometimes, the rear seats are occupied by smokers, drunks, and rowdies. At night, you will sleep better on the right side *(lado derecho)* away from the glare of oncoming traffic lights.

Baggage is generally secure on Mexican buses. Label it, however. Overhead racks are sometimes too cramped to accommodate airline-sized carryons. Carry a small bag with your money and irreplaceables on your person; pack clothes and nonessentials in your checked luggage. For peace of mind, watch the handler put your checked baggage on the bus and watch to make sure it is not mistakenly taken off the bus at intermediate stops.

If your baggage gets misplaced, remain calm. Bus employees are generally competent and conscientious. If you are patient, recovering your luggage will become a matter of honor for many of them. Baggage handlers are at the bottom of the pay scale; a tip for their mostly thankless job is very much appreciated.

Bus Routes to Guadalajara

From California and the West, cross the border to Tijuana, Mexicali, or Nogales, where you can ride one of at least three bus lines along the Pacific coast route (National Hwy. 15) south to Guadalajara by Estrella Blanca (via its subsidiaries, Elite, Transportes Norte de Sonora, or Turistar) or independent Transportes del Pacífico).

A few Estrella Blanca and Transportes del Pacífico departures go all the way from the border to Guadalajara. Otherwise, you will have to change buses at Mazatlán or Tepic, depending on your connection. Allow a full day and a bit more (about 30 hours), depending upon connections, for the trip. Carry liquids and food (which might only be minimally available en route) with you.

From the Midwest, cross the border from El Paso to Juárez and head south by way of Chihuahua and Durango by either Estrella Blanca (via subsidiaries Transportes Chihuahuenses, or luxury-class Turistar) or independent Omnibus de Mexico. Similarly, from the U.S. Southeast and East, cross the border at Laredo to Nuevo Laredo and ride Transportes del Norte or Turistar direct (or transfer at Monterrey) to Guadalajara.

BY CAR OR RV

If you're adventurous and like going to out-of-the-way places, but still want to have all the comforts of home, you may enjoy driving your car or RV to Guadalajara. On the other hand, cost, risk, wear on both you and your vehicle, and congestion hassles in towns may change your mind.

DRIVING AND BUSING TO THE GUADALAJARA REGION

UNITED STATES

From Eastern U.S.

From Central U.S.

From Western U.S.

Gulf of Mexico

GUATEMALA

San Diego
Tijuana
Calexico
Mexicali
159/193
3:15
Sonoyta
165/266
3:45
Nogales
Tucson
173/279
3:15
Hermosillo
282/422
5:30
Ciudad Obregon
161/260
3:00
169/431
5:00
Juarez
El Paso
233/375
5:00
Chihuahua
284/457
6:30
Torreon
157/253
3:30
Durango
168/318
6:00
Culiacan
139/224
2:30
Mazatlan
182/293
4:00
Tepic
141/227
3:00
198/317
4:30
Laredo
Nuevo Laredo
McAllen
Reynosa
1:00
Monterrey
143/230
2:30
Saltillo
53/85
1:00
174/280
3:45
Zacatecas
230/370
Ciudad Victoria
180/290
4:15
Tampico
197/317
GUADALAJARA
224/361
5:45
Morelia
154/248
4:30
Toluca
74/119
2:15
40/64
1:00
227/366
5:15
MEXICO CITY
350/564
8:00
Taxco
150/242
4:00
259/417
5:15
Oaxaca
148/238
6:15
291/469
8:15
Acapulco
Puerto Ángel
199/318
Playa Azul
Ixtapa-Zihuatanejo
195/314
8:15
76/122
2:30
Manzanillo
172/276
4:30
Puerto Vallarta
104/167
3:00

PACIFIC OCEAN

Sea of Cortez

California

Baja

La Paz
Cabo San Lucas

150 mi
0

150 km
0

NOTE: DISTANCES ARE SHOWN AS MILES/KILOMETERS.
APPROXIMATE DRIVING TIMES ARE SHOWN AS HOURS:MINUTES

© AVALON TRAVEL PUBLISHING, INC.

© BRUCE WHIPPERMAN

The common Mexican warning sign *"Se ponchan llantas gratis"* (Tires punctured free of charge) isn't usually taken literally.

Mexican Car Insurance

Mexico does not recognize foreign insurance. When you drive into Mexico, Mexican auto insurance is at least as important as your passport. At the busier crossings, you can get it at insurance "drive-ins" just north of the border. The many Mexican auto insurance companies are government-regulated; their numbers keep prices and services competitive. Alternatively, if you want to get insurance ahead of time, consult your own auto insurance agent.

One of the best known agencies is the well-known Sanborn's Mexico insurance, which certainly seems to be trying hardest. Besides insurance, it offers a number of books and services, including a guide to RV campgrounds, road map, *Travel With Health* book, "smile-by-mile" *Travelog* guide to "every highway in Mexico," hotel discounts, and more. All of the above is available to members of Sanborn's "Sombrero" Club. You can buy insurance, sign up for membership (at moderate additional cost), or order books through its toll-free number, 800/222-0158. For other queries, call 956/682-7433 or write Sanborn's Mexico, P.O. Box 310, McAllen, TX 78502.

Mexican car insurance runs from a bare-bones rate of about $5 a day to a more typical $10 a day for more complete coverage ($50,000/$40,000/$80,000 public liability/property damage/medical payments) on a vehicle worth $10,000–15,000. On the same scale, insurance for a $50,000 RV and equipment runs about $30 a day. These daily rates decrease sharply for six-month or one-year policies, which run from about $200 for the minimum to $400–1,600 for complete coverage.

If you get broken glass, personal effects, and legal expenses coverage with these rates, you're lucky. Mexican policies don't usually cover them.

You should get something for your money, however. The deductibles should be no more than $300–500, the public liability/medical payments should be about double the ($25,000/$25,000/$50,000) legal minimum, and you should be able to get your car fixed in the United States and receive payment in U.S. dollars for losses. If not, shop around.

A Sinaloa Note of Caution

Although *bandidos* no longer menace Mexican roads (though loose burros, horses, and cattle still do), be cautious in the infamous marijuana- and opium-growing region of Sinaloa state, north of Mazatlán. Best not stray from Hwy. 15 between Culiacán and Mazatlán or from Hwy. 40 between Mazatlán and Durango. Curious tourists have been assaulted in the hinterlands adjacent to these roads.

The Green Angels

The Green Angels have answered many motoring tourists' prayers in Mexico. Bilingual teams of two, trained in auto repair and first aid, help distressed tourists along main highways. They patrol fixed stretches of road twice daily by truck. To make sure they stop to help, pull completely off the highway and raise your hood. You may want to hail a passing trucker to call them for you (toll-free tel. 01-800/903-9200 for the tourism hotline, who might alert the Green Angels for you).

If, for some reason, you have to leave your ve-

ON THE ROAD

hicle on the roadside, don't leave it unattended. Hire a local teenager or adult to watch it for you. Unattended vehicles on Mexican highways are quickly stricken by a "mysterious disease," the symptoms of which are rapid loss of vital parts.

Mexican Gasoline

Pemex, short for Petróleos Mexicanos, the government oil monopoly, markets diesel fuel and two grades of unleaded gasoline: 92-octane premium and 89-octane **Magna.** Magna is good gas, yielding performance similar to that of U.S.–style "regular" or "super-unleaded" gasoline. (My car, whose manufacturer recommended 91-octane, ran well on Magna.) Depending on the dollar-peso exchange rate, Magna runs $2 or more per gallon ($.55 per liter). The premium grade, although yielding even better performance, is more expensive.

On main highways, Pemex makes sure that major stations (spaced typically about 30 miles apart) stock both grades plus diesel.

Gas Station Thievery

Although the problem has abated considerably in recent years, boys who hang around gas stations to wash windows are notoriously light-fingered. When stopping at the *gasolinera,* make sure that your cameras, purses, and other movable items are out of reach. Also, make sure that your car has a locking gas cap. If not, insist on pumping the gas yourself, or be super-watchful as you pull up to the gas pump: Be certain that the pump reads zero before the attendant pumps the gas.

A Healthy Car

Preventative measures spell good health for both you and your car. Get that tune-up (or that long-delayed overhaul) *before,* rather than after, you embark.

Carry a stock of spare parts, which will be more difficult to get and more expensive in Mexico than at home. Carry an extra tire or two, a few cans of motor oil and octane enhancer, oil and gas filters, fan belts, spark plugs, tune-up kit, points, and fuses. Be prepared with basic tools and supplies, such as screwdrivers, pliers (including Vice-Grip), lug wrench, jack, adjustable wrenches, tire pump and patches, tire pressure gauge, steel wire, and electrical tape. For breakdowns and emergencies, carry a folding shovel, a husky rope or chain, a gasoline can, and flares.

Car Repairs in Mexico

The American big three—General Motors, Ford, and Chrysler—as well as Nissan and Volkswagen, are well represented by extensive dealer networks in Mexico. Latecomer Honda has a few widely scattered agencies. Getting your car or truck serviced at such agencies is straightforward. While parts will probably be higher in price, shop rates run about half U.S. prices, so repairs will generally come out cheaper than back home.

The same is not true for repairing other makes, however. Mexico has few, if any, Toyota or other Japanese car or truck dealers; and other than Mercedes-Benz, which has some truck agencies, it is difficult to find officially certified mechanics for Japanese, British, and European makes other than Volkswagen and Nissan.

Many clever Mexican independent mechanics, however, can fix any car that comes their way. Small *talleres mecánicos* (tah-YER-ays may-KAH-nee-kohs), or repair shops, dot town and village roadsides everywhere.

Although most mechanics are honest, beware of unscrupulous operators who try to collect double or triple their original estimate. If you don't speak Spanish, find someone who can assist you in negotiations. *Always* get a cost estimate, including needed parts and labor, in writing, even if you have to write it yourself. Make sure the mechanic understands, then ask him to sign it before he starts work. Although this may be a hassle, it might save you a much nastier hassle later. Shop labor at small, independent repair shops should run about $10–20 per hour. For much more information, and for entertaining

The Green Angels have answered many motoring tourists' prayers in Mexico. Bilingual teams of two, trained in auto repair and first aid, help distressed tourists along main highways.

anecdotes of car and RV travel in Mexico, consult Carl Franz's *The People's Guide to Mexico.*

Bribes *(Mordidas)*

A common meeting point of the typical foreign visitor and Mexican police is at the visitor's car on a highway or downtown street. To the tourist, such an encounter may seem mild harassment by the police, accompanied by vague threats of going to the police station or impounding the car for such-and-such a violation. The tourist often goes on to say, "It was all right, though. . . we paid him $10 and he went away. . . Mexican cops sure are crooked, aren't they?"

And, I suppose, if people want to go bribing their way through Mexico, that's their business. But calling Mexican cops crooked isn't exactly fair. Police, like most everyone else in Mexico, have to scratch for a living, and they have found that many tourists are willing to slip them a $10 bill for nothing. Rather than crooked, I would call them hungry and opportunistic.

Instead of paying a bribe, do what I've done a dozen times: Remain cool, and if you're really guilty of an infraction, calmly say, "Ticket, please." *("Boleto, por favor.")* After a minute or two of stalling, and no cash appearing, the officer most likely will not bother with a ticket, but will wave you on with only a warning. If, on the other hand, the officer does write you a ticket, he will probably keep your driver's license, which you will be able to retrieve at the *presidencia municipal* (city hall) the next day in exchange for paying your fine.

Highway Routes from the United States

Four main routes head south from U.S. border crossings to Guadalajara. At safe highway speeds, each of these routes requires a minimum of about 24 hours driving time. For comfort and safety, many folks allow three or four full south-of-the-border driving days to Guadalajara.

All of these routes follow **toll** *(cuota)* expressways, which often parallel the original two-lane non-toll *(libre)* routes. You can avoid some of the tolls (around $40–60 total to Guadalajara) for a passenger car, about double that for big, mul-

tiple-wheeled RVs, by sticking to the old *libre* route. However, the one or two days of extra travel time, with the associated hotel and food costs, and the significantly increased road hazards—pedestrians, roadside carts, stray animals, noisy, smoky trucks, and congestion—will, in most cases, not be worth the $20–30 savings.

From the U.S. Pacific Coast and points west, follow National Hwy. 15 (or 15D when it's a four-lane expressway) from the border at Nogales, Sonora, an hour's drive south of Tucson, Arizona. Highway 15D continues southward smoothly, leading you through cactus-studded mountains and valleys, that turn into green, to lush farmland and tropical coastal plain and forest by the time you arrive in Mazatlán. Watch for the peripheral bypasses *(periféricos)* and truck routes that route you past the congested downtowns of Hermosillo, Guaymas, Ciudad Obregón, Los Mochis, and Culiacán. Between these centers, you can cruise along, via *cuota* (toll) expressways, virtually all the way to Mazatlán.

From Mazatlán, continue along the narrow (but soon to be replaced) two-lane route to Tepic, where the route forks left (east) as *cuota autopista* (toll expressway) 15D, continuing to Guadalajara.

If, however, you're driving to Guadalajara from the central United States, cross the border at El Paso to **Ciudad Juárez,** Chihuahua. There, National Highway 45D, the *cuota* (toll) multi-lane expressway, leads you southward through high, dry plains past the cities of Chihuahua and Jiménez. From here, you'll continue, by combined Hwys. 45 and 49, to just north of Gómez Palacio–Torreón. There, bypass the downtown (toward Durango-Fresnillo-Zacatecas) and proceed about 60 miles (100 km) southwest, where you fork south (toward Fresnillo-Zacatecas), continuing along Hwys. 45 and 49. Bypass Fresnillo (via Zacatecas direction) and continue south along Hwys. 45 and 49 to Zacatecas where you connect to Hwy. 54 south (toward Guadalajara), which leads the rest of the way to Guadalajara.

Folks heading to Guadalajara from the eastern and southeastern United States should cross the border from McAllen, Texas, to **Reynosa,**

Tamaulipas. From there, follow either the National Hwy. 40 non-toll *(libre)* route or the new toll *(cuota)* expressway Hwy. 40D southwest, which continues to the eastern outskirts of Monterrey. Bypass Monterrey (toward Saltillo, west) via expressway Hwy. 40. At Saltillo, connect to two-lane Hwy. 54 south via Zacatecas, continuing all the way to Guadalajara.

BY TRAIN

Privatization is rapidly putting an end to most passenger train service in Mexico, with the exception of the **Copper Canyon** scenic route. One of the few remaining passenger train rides in Mexico begins with a bus trip or flight south to Chihuahua, where you board the Chihuahua-Pacific Railway train and ride west along the renowned Copper Canyon (Barranca del Cobre) route to the Pacific. Only finished during the early 1960s, this route traverses the spectacular canyonland home of the Tarahumara people. At times along the winding 406-mile (654-km) route, your rail car seems to teeter at the very edge of the labyrinthine Barranca del Cobre, a canyon so deep that its climate varies from Canadian at the top to tropical jungle at the bottom.

The railway-stop village of Creel, with a few stores and hotels and a Tarahumara mission, is the major jumping-off point for trips into the canyon. For a treat, reserve a stay en route to Guadalajara at the Copper Canyon Lodge in Creel. From there, the canyon beckons: Explore the village, enjoy panoramic views, observe mountain wildlife, and breathe pine-scented mountain air. Farther afield, you can hike to a hot spring or spend a few days exploring the canyon-bottom itself. For more information, tel. 800/776-3942 or 248/340-7230; write Copper Canyon Hiking Lodges, 2741 Paldan St., Auburn Hills, MI 48326; website: www.coppercanyonlodges.com.

Copper Canyon Tours

Some agencies arrange unusually good Copper Canyon rail tours. Among the best is **Columbus Travel** (900 Ridge Creek Lane, Bulverde, TX 78163-2872; tel. 800/843-1060, website: www.canyontravel.com), which employs its own

resident, ecologically sensitive guides. Trips range from small-group, rail-based sight-seeing and birding/natural history tours to customized wilderness rail-jeep-backpacking adventures.

Elderhostel has long provided some of the best-buy Copper Canyon options, designed for seniors. Participants customarily fly to Los Mochis on the Pacific coast, then transfer to the first-class Mexican Chihuahua-Pacific train for a four-day canyonland adventure. Highlights include nature walks, visits to native missions, and cultural sites in Cerrocahui village and Creel, the frontier outpost in the Tarahumara heartland. The return includes a comfortable overnight at Posada Barranca, at the canyon's dizzying edge. For more information and reservations, contact 75 Federal St., 3rd Fl., Boston MA 02110-1941; tel. 877/426-8056; website: www.elderhostel.org.

Another noteworthy tour provider is the **Mexican American Railway Company,** which specializes in luxury Copper Canyon rail sight-seeing tours. Trips begin at either Chihuahua or Los Mochis, at opposite ends of the Copper Canyon Line. Participants can enjoy the amenities of either restored 1940s-era first-class cars or the "South Orient Express," super-deluxe European-class cars that are added to the regular train. In addition to onboard sight-seeing, the four- to six-day itineraries include short tours to points of interest such as Creel and the Tarahumara Mission, Mennonite settlements at Cuauhtémoc, and the colonial town of El Fuerte.

The South Orient Express service features gourmet fare in opulent dining cars and expansive mountain vistas from deluxe-view dome rail coaches. Evenings, participants enjoy meals and comfortable accommodations in first-class hotels and mountain lodges. Tariffs run roughly $1,600 per person double occupancy, all-inclusive for the usual super-deluxe five-day tour. For details, tel. 800/659-7602 or write the Mexican American Railway Company, 14359-A Torrey Chase Blvd., Houston TX 77014; email: info@thetraincollection.com; website: www.thetraincollection.com. In Mexico, contact the company at Cortés de Monroy 2514, Colonia San Felipe, Chihuahua, Chih. 31240; tel. 14/107-570.

BY FERRY

The ferries *(transbordadores)* from La Paz at the tip of Baja California across the Gulf of California to Mazatlán or Topolobampo in Sinaloa provide a tempting route to Guadalajara, especially for travelers without cars. However, if you try to take your car during busy times, especially Christmas and Easter holidays, you may get "bumped" by the large volume of commercial traffic, despite your reservation.

The ferry system, privatized in the early 1990s, has greatly improved service, at the expense of steeply increased fares. Tickets and reservations (apply early) are available at the terminals and may be available through certain travel agents in La Paz, Los Mochis, and Mazatlán.

Passengers are not allowed to remain in their vehicles during the crossing but must purchase a passenger ticket. Options include *salón* (reclining coach seats), *turista* (shared cabin with bunks), *cabina* (private cabin with toilet), and *especial* (deluxe private cabin). La Paz–Mazatlán tariffs range from about $15 to $60 per person. Additional vehicle fees run about $60 for a motorcycle, about $270 for an automobile or light RV, and more for a larger RV. Charges for the shorter La Paz–Topolobampo run are about half these.

The La Paz–Mazatlán ferries usually depart in the mid-afternoon daily, arriving at the opposite shores the following morning. The La Paz–Topolobampo crossing is shorter; ferries depart from either end at around 10 A.M. daily and arrive on the opposite shores around 6 P.M.

For more information and reservations, usually available in either English or Spanish, contact the ferry headquarters direct from outside Mexico; La Paz tel. 112/538-33; Mazatlán tel. 69/817-020; and Topolobambo tel. 686/201-41. Within Mexico, dial the same numbers or, better yet, tel. 800/696-9600.

SPECIAL TOURS AND STUDY OPTIONS

Some tour programs include in-depth activities centered around arts and crafts, language and culture, wildlife-viewing, or off-the-beaten-track adventuring.

Elderhostel's rich offering includes a pair of cultural programs in Guadalajara. One focuses on the arts and crafts of colonial Mexico and includes visits to the venerable monuments of downtown Guadalajara, especially Hospicio Cabañas for viewing and discussions of the Diego Rivera murals. The tour continues on to Uruapan and Pátzcuaro, in Michoacán, where the focus shifts to native and colonial arts and crafts traditions. Another Guadalajara program includes intensive intermediate-level Spanish language instruction, combined with cultural experiences. For details, request the international catalog: Elderhostel, 75 Federal St., 3rd Fl., Boston, MA 02110-1941, tel. 877/426-8056, website: www.elderhostel.org.

Naturalists should consider the excellent **Field Guides** birding tour, centered in wildlife-rich Jalisco and Colima backcountry. For more information, tel. toll-free 800/728-4953, fax 512/263-0117; email: fieldguides@field guides.com; website: www.fieldguides.com.

The remote lagoons and islands of Baja California, about 200 miles (300 km) due west of Mazatlán, nurture a trove of marine and onshore wildlife. Such sanctuaries are ongoing destinations of winter **Oceanic Society** expedition-tours from La Paz, Baja California. Tours customarily cost about $1,400, cover several islands, and include a week of marine mammal watching, snorkeling, birding, and eco-exploring, both on- and offshore. For details, contact the Oceanic Society, Fort Mason Center, Building E, San Francisco, CA 94123; tel. 800/326-7491 or 415/441-1106, fax 474-3395; website: www.oceanic-society.org.

This trip might make an exciting overture or finale to your Guadalajara adventure. You can connect with the Oceanic Society's Baja California (La Paz–Los Cabos) jumping-off-points via Mexican airlines' (Mexicana, Aéromexico, or Aerocalifornia) mainland (Mazatlán/Guadalajara/Puerto Vallarta) destinations.

ON THE ROAD

Accommodations

The Guadalajara region has hundreds of lodgings to suit every style and pocketbook: luxury resort and business hotels, moderate-to-inexpensive hotels, apartments and condominiums, and bed-and-breakfasts and *casas de huéspedes* (guesthouses), trailer parks, and even some unofficial places to camp.

The dozens of accommodations detailed in this book are positive recommendations—checked out in detail—solid options from which you can pick according to your taste and purse. (For specific accommodation descriptions, refer to the relevant destination chapter.)

Accommodation Rates

The rates listed in this book are U.S. dollar equivalents of peso prices, taxes included, as quoted by the lodging management at the time of writing. They are intended as a general guide only and probably will only approximate the asking rate when you arrive. Some readers, unfortunately, try to bargain by telling desk clerks that, for example, the rate should be $30 because they read it in this book. This is unwise, because it makes hotel clerks and managers reluctant to quote rates, for fear readers might, years later, hold their hotel responsible for such quotes.

To cancel the effect of relatively steep Mexican inflation, rates are reported in U.S. dollars (although, when settling your hotel bill, *you will nearly always save money by insisting on paying in pesos*). To further increase accuracy, estimated low- and high-season rates are quoted whenever possible.

Saving Money

The listed accommodation prices are rack rates, the maximum tariff, exclusive of packages and promotions, that you would pay if you walked in and rented an unreserved room for one day. Savvy travelers seldom pay the maximum. Always inquire if there are any discounts, business

HOTEL TOLL-FREE NUMBERS AND WEBSITES

These hotel chains have outstanding or recommended branches at Guadalajara (GD) and Puerto Vallarta (PV):

Blue Bay (PV); tel. 800/BLUEBAY (800/258-3229); website: www.bluebayresort.com

Camino Real(GD, PV); tel. 800/7CAMINO (800/722-6466); website: www.caminoreal.com

Club Maeva, (PV;); tel. 800/GOMAEVA (800/466-2382)

Crowne Plaza, (GD); tel. 800/2CROWNE; website: www.crownegd.com.mx

Fiesta Americana (GD, PV); tel. 800/FIESTA1 (800/343-7821); website: www.fiestaamericana.com.mx

Fiesta Inn, (GD); tel. 800/FIESTA1 (800/343-7821); website: www.fiestainn.com.mx

Guadalajara Plaza, (GD); tel. 800/445-8667; website: www.hotelesgdlplaza.com.mx

Hilton, (GD); tel. 800/445-8667; website: www.hilton.com

Holiday Inn, (GD, PV); tel. 800/465-4329; website: www.basshotels.com

Howard Johnson (GD); tel. 800/IGOHOJO (800/446-4656)

Krystal, (PV); tel. 800/231-9860; website: www.krystal.com.mx

Marriott, (PV); tel. 800/228-9290; website: www.marriot.com

Hotel Presidente Intercontinental, (GD); tel. 800/327-0200; website: www.guadalajara.interconti.com

Sheraton, (PV); tel. 800/325-3535; website: www.sheraton.com

Westin, (PV); tel. 800/228-3000; website: www.westin.com

rates, or packages *(descuentos o paquetes)* (dees-koo-AYN-tohs OH pah-KAY-tays).

For stays of more than two weeks, you'll usually save money and add comfort with an apartment, condominium, or house rental.

Airlines regularly offer air/hotel packages that may save you pesos. These deals often require that you depart for Guadalajara through certain gateway cities (see Getting There, above), which depend on the airline. Accommodations are usually (but not exclusively) in luxury hotels. If you live near one of the Guadalajara gateways, it may pay to contact the airlines for more information.

LUXURY HOTELS

Guadalajara has many attractive, well-managed, international-class hotels, mostly in the upscale western suburbs, around the Plaza del Sol–Expo Guadalajara shopping mall/convention center complex. A number of these hotels, while fine for any visitor who can afford them, cater especially to **businesspersons and convention goers.** Their business guests enjoy lots of special treatment, including entire executive floors, with separate check-in, plush private lounges, and elaborate business centers with meeting rooms, Internet access, and secretarial services.

Their plush amenities, moreover, need not be overly expensive. During the right time of year you can sometimes lodge at many of the big-name spots for surprisingly little. While rack rates ordinarily run $150–300, packages, promotions, and business rates can cut these prices significantly. Shop around for savings via your Sunday newspaper travel section, through travel agents, by logging on either to hotel websites or general websites, such as www.mexconnect.com and www.go2mexico.com, or by dialing the hotels directly in Guadalajara or via their toll-free U.S. and Canada 800 numbers.

MODERATE TO INEXPENSIVE HOTELS

Such lodgings vary from scruffy to spick-and-span, from humble to distinguished. Many such hostelries are the once-grand first-class hotels established long before their luxurious international-class cousins mushroomed on Guadalajara's west side. You can generally expect a clean, large (but not necessarily deluxe) room with bath and toilet and even sometimes a private balcony and a pool. Although guests at many of these hotels enjoy close-in city-center locations convenient for shopping and sight-seeing, such hotels usually lack the costly international-standard amenities—air conditioning, cable TV, direct-dial phones, tennis courts, gyms, and golf access—of the big luxury resorts. Their guests, however, usually enjoy surprisingly good service, good food, and a local ambience more charming and personal than that of many of their five-star competitors.

Booking these hotels is straightforward. All of them may be dialed direct and, like the big resorts, may even have websites, email, and U.S. and Canada toll-free information and reservation numbers.

© BRUCE WHIPPERMAN

Hotel Casa de Cortijo in Mazamitla opens to a tranquil inner garden.

BED-AND-BREAKFASTS AND GUESTHOUSES

North American–style bed-and-breakfasts are new in Mexico; local-style *casas de huéspedes* (guesthouses) are not. **Bed-and-breakfasts** have sprouted in west-side Guadalajaran neighborhoods (mainly Chapalita) and on the Lake Chapala north shore where Americans and Canadians have been relocating.

Casas de huéspedes, not as common in Guadalajara, are family houses where rooms, usually around an interior patio, are offered to guests. While the facilities, such as baths, are usually shared, the ambience is often friendly and the prices, typically around $15 per day, are right.

APARTMENTS, CONDOMINIUMS, AND HOUSES

For longer stays, many Guadalajara visitors prefer the convenience and economy of an apartment or condominium, or the space and comfort of a house rental. Choices vary, from spartan studios to deluxe suites and rambling homes big enough for entire extended families. Prices depend strongly upon neighborhood and amenities, ranging from about $300 per month for the cheapest, to at least 10 times that for the most luxurious.

At the low end, visitors can expect a clean, furnished apartment, convenient to public transportation, in a quiet, middle-class neighborhood. Condominiums—often colloquially named *suites* (soo-EE-tays), such as Suites Bernini—are generally more luxurious and rent for about $1,000 per month. Typically the condos are high-rises with desk services and resort amenities such as pool, hot tub, and sundeck.

House rentals can range from modest suburban bungalows for about $700 per month to rambling villas with pool, garden, a cook, a maid, and gardener for $3,000 per month.

Finding a Long-Term Rental

In Guadalajara as everywhere, location is the key to finding a good rental. In the city, best concentrate your search in the middle- to upper-class westside neighborhoods: Minerva-Chapultepec, Providencia, Chapalita, Ciudad del Sol, and Las Fuentes. Also, take a look at the Lake Chapala north-shore communities, beginning with Chapala town and moving west, through San Antonio, La Floresta, Ajijic, to San Juan Cosala (see the Lake Chapala and Vicinity chapter.)

A number of rental information sources are available. Perhaps the best is the classified section of the weekly *Guadalajara Colony Reporter,* available by subscription in the United States. Send a letter—including your name, address, telephone, and, if applicable, email address—and a check or money order for US$40 (for three months), to: Nuevas Publicaciones en Ingles de Mexico, S.A. de C.V., *Guadalajara Colony Reporter,* 1605-B Pacific Rim Court, PMB 005-42, San Diego, CA 92154. You can also subscribe by calling or faxing 33/3766-6338; or by logging on to their website: www.guadalajarareporter.com.

A load of local information, plus several agency rental listings, usually appear in the monthly Lake Chapala English-language newspaper, *El Ojo del Lago (Eye of the Lake)*. Subscribe by sending a letter—including your name, address, telephone—with a check or money order payable to "David Tingen" for US$25 (for six months) to: El Ojo del Lago, P.O. Box 279, Chapala, Jalisco, Mexico 45900; tel. 33/3765-3676, fax 33/3765-3528; email: ojodellago@laguna.com.mx; website: www.chapala.com.

Some English-speaking **real estate–rental agencies** also maintain (mostly Lake Chapala) rental listings. Currently very active is the Ojo del Lago's parent, **Coldwell Banker–Chapala Realty,** in downtown Chapala, at Hidalgo 223, Chapala, Jalisco 45900; tel. 33/3765-2877, fax 33/3765-3528; email: chapala@infosel.net.mx; website: www.chapala.com. Also active with rentals is **Ajijic Real Estate,** at Colon 1, Ajijic; tel. 33/3766-2077, fax 33/3766-2331; email: email@ajijic.com.; website: www.ajijic.com. Additionally, you might try **Century 21–Vistas Realty,** P.O. Box 281, Chapala, Jalisco 45915; tel./fax 33/3766-2612; email: c21vistas@laguna.com.mx;

website: www.lagunanet.net.mx/c21vistas. Or try **Ajijic Developments** (Jorge Torres), tel. 376/630-30, or 376/637-37; email: ajijicdevsrentas@laguna.com.mx.

You might also consider **exchanging your home** with a Guadalajara or Lake Chapala homeowner for a set period. Log into (or telephone) the home-exchange websites: www.homelink.org (tel. 800/638-3841), www.homeexchange.com, or www.intervacus.com (tel. 800/756-4663).

A number of English-speaking folks in Guadalajara make it their business to help visitors get oriented and find housing. Sandy Brown and Mark Kunce (see By Locally Arranged Tour, later in this chapter) strongly recommend the services of George Enriquez (tel. 33/3811-2862 or 33/3810-0556; email: georgeky@compaq.net.mx), Beatriz de la Garza (tel. 33/3615-2030; email: beatriz dlg@yahoo.com), or José Amezcua (tel. 33/3121-2385; email: joseamlo@hotmail.com).

Other potentially useful rental information sources are the bulletin boards at the **American Society of Jalisco** headquarters and **Sandi Bookstore** (see the Chapalita section of the City: West and North of Downtown chapter), and the **Lake Chapala Society** (see the Ajijic section of the Lake Chapala and Vicinity chapter.)

CAMPING

Few, if any, official public campgrounds are available in the Guadalajara region. However, unofficial camping areas (with no facilities whatsoever—bring everything) exist on some communally owned forest lands. One of the most accessible and pristine is the **Bosque de Primavera,** off old Hwy. 15, at La Venta, about 15 minutes by car or bus west of the *periférico* peripheral boulevard. Here, you have a choice of tenting beneath the pines or beside the bathtub-warm Río Caliente (see the Bosque de Primavera section of the Guadalajara Getaways chapter for more details.)

Other areas ripe for camping are around **Tapalpa.** Weekenders customarily set up tents in the forest along Tapalpa's highway approaches (especially around the pine-clad summit between Atemajac de Brizuela and Tapalpa). Another popular Tapalpa camping spot is the scenic **Las Piedrotas** meadowland preserve a few miles outside of town. Here, a fence limits access to foot traffic, so be prepared to carry your gear in for about a quarter-mile. Furthermore, if the water level (late summer–early fall) is high enough, camping, fishing, and boating opportunities might be available at the **Presa Nogal** reservoir and dam about four miles (seven km) south of town. (See the Guadalajara Getaways chapter for more access details.)

A third possible camping zone, similar to Las Piedrotas in Tapalpa is **Los Dientes** (The Teeth) preserve in the foothill country a few miles northwest of Zapopan town. Here, rock climbers—who spend the day scaling the ponderous, tooth-shaped "Los Dientes" rock outcroppings—often stay on overnight. For more details, contact the Zapopan tourist information office, Av. Vallarta 6503, Zapopan, Jalisco 45010; tel. 33/3110-0754, ext. 118, fax 33/3110-0383; email: turismo@zapopan.gob.mx or rolega@hotmail .com (see the Zapopan section of the City: North and West of Downtown chapter for a complete listing).

Some private *balnearios* (bathing springs) offer good camping possibilities. Although I didn't personally check it out, Jalisco tourism recommends *balneario* **Las Alberquitas,** tel. 377/200-65, with extensive facilities within a 50-acre tree-shaded site, including a campground, spring-fed pools, cafeteria, vegetarian bar, showers, dressing rooms and much more. It's located just outside of Acatlán. From the city center, follow Av. López Mateos about 20 miles (32 km) past the southwest city limits to the Hwy. 80–Barra de Navidad right turnoff; continue another 3 miles (5 km) to the Acatlán junction, where you turn left and follow old Hwy. 54 south a few more miles. Ask for local directions to the *balneario.*

On the other hand, authentically rustic **Balneario El Paraíso,** with basic facilities, offers tropical tranquility and a cool bathing pool, and a bit of space for camping in the shade of a tropical hillside mango grove (with all the free mangos you can eat in May and June, bring insect repellent.) For a change of scene, walk a quarter mile uphill to El Paraíso's big brother **Balneario La Toma** for snack restaurants, big pools, panoramic tropical canyon views, but no space for camping except a bare parking lot. (Near Tequila, an hour west of the city. See the Guadalajara Getaways chapter.)

TRAILER PARKS

Campers who prefer company to isolation stay in trailer parks. Three trailer parks, all in the suburbs, serve Guadalajara region visitors. The best, but smallest, is **PAL Trailer Park** near Lake Chapala (For details, see the Lake Chapala and Vicinity chapter). The other choices are the venerable standbys, the Hacienda Trailer Park, off Av. Vallarta (Hwy. 15), near the western city limits, and the San José El Tajo Trailer Park, on the south prolongation of Av. López Mateos (watch for the green-and-white sign) about three miles (five km) southwest of the *periférico* (peripheral boulevard) overpass. (For details, see the City: West and North of Downtown chapter.)

Food

Many travelers flock to Guadalajara for the food, and for good reason: A fleet of excellent Guadalajara restaurants offer a feast of Italian, French, and Chinese cuisine and a banquet of fresh seafood. Nevertheless, Guadalajara's Mexican-style cooking remains the main attraction. True Mexican food is old-fashioned, home-style fare requiring many hours of loving prepara-

© BRUCE WHIPPERMAN

A good restaurant makes its tortillas in-house.

tion. Such food is short on meat and long on corn, beans, rice, tomatoes, onions, chilies, eggs, and cheese.

Mexican food is the unique product of thousands of years of native tradition. It is based on corn—*teocentli,* the Aztec "holy food"—called *maíz* (mah-EES) by present-day Mexicans. In the past, a Mexican woman spent much of her time grinding and preparing corn: soaking the grain in lime water, which swells the kernels and removes the tough seed-coat, and grinding the bloated seeds into meal on a stone *metate.* Finally, she patted the meal into tortillas and cooked them on a hot, baked-mud *comal* (griddle).

Sages (men, no doubt) wistfully imagined that gentle pat-pat-pat of women all over Mexico to be the heartbeat of Mexico, which they feared would cease when women stopped making tortillas.

Fewer women these days make tortillas by hand. The gentle pat-pat-pat has been replaced by the whir and rattle of the automatic tortilla-making machine in myriad *tortillerías,* where women and girls line up for their family's daily kilo-stack of tortillas.

Tortillas are to the Mexicans as rice is to the Chinese and bread to the French. Mexican food is invariably some mixture of sauce, meat, beans, cheese, and vegetables wrapped in a tortilla, which becomes the culinary be-all: the food, the dish, and the utensil wrapped into one.

If a Mexican man has nothing to wrap in his

CATCH OF THE DAY

Ceviche (say-VEE-chay): A chopped raw fish appetizer as popular in the Guadalajara region as sushi is on Tokyo side streets. Although it can contain anything from conch to octopus, the best ceviche consists of diced young shark *(tiburón)* or mackerel *(sierra)* fillet and plenty of fresh tomatoes, onions, garlic, and chilies, all doused with lime juice.

Filete de pescado (fish fillet): sautéed *al mojo* (ahl-MOH-hoh)—with butter and garlic.

Pescado frito (pays-KAH-doh FREE-toh): Fish, pan-fried whole; if you don't specify that it be cooked lightly *(a medio),* the fish may arrive well done, like a big, crunchy French fry.

Pescado veracruzana: A favorite everywhere. Best with red snapper *(huachinango),* smothered in a savory tomato, onion, chili, and garlic sauce. *Pargo* (snapper), *mero* (grouper), and *cabrilla* (sea bass) are also popularly used in this and other specialties. Shellfish abound: *ostiones* (oysters) and *almejas* (clams) by the dozen; *langosta* (lobster) and *langostina* (crayfish) *asado* (broiled), *al vapor* (steamed), or fried. Pots of fresh-boiled *camarones* (shrimp) are sold on the street by the kilo; cafes will make them into *cóctel,* or prepare them *en gabardinas* (breaded) at your request.

lunchtime tortilla, he will content himself by rolling a thin filling of salsa in it.

Hot or Not?

Much food served in Mexico is not "Mexican." Eating habits, as most other customs, depend upon social class. Upwardly mobile Mexicans typically shun the corn-based *indígena* fare in favor of the European-style food of the Spanish colonial elite: chops, steaks, cutlets, fish, clams, omelettes, soups, pasta, rice, and potatoes.

Such fare is often as bland as Des Moines on a summer Sunday afternoon. *No picante*—not spicy—is how the Mexicans describe bland food. *Picante,* then, means spicy. *Caliente,* the Spanish adjective for "hot" (as in "hot water"), never implies spicy, in contrast to English usage.

Strictly vegetarian cooking is the exception in Mexico, as are macrobiotic restaurants, health-food stores, and organic produce. Meat is such a delicacy for most Mexicans that they can't understand why people would give it up voluntarily. If vegetarians can temporarily tolerate a bit of pork fat *(manteca de cerdo)* commonly used in preparing many typically vegetarian foods, such as beans, eggs, and even *legumbres* (vegetables), then Mexican cooking will suit you fine.

Seafood

Early chroniclers wrote that Moctezuma employed

a platoon of runners to bring fresh fish 300 miles from the sea every day to his court. Around Guadalajara nowadays, fresh seafood is (fortunately) much more available: You'll find it in dozens of establishments, from humble downtown fish taco stalls to sophisticated suburban restaurants.

Fruits and Juices

Squeezed vegetable and fruit juices called *jugos* (HOO-gohs) are among the widely available delights of Guadalajara. Among the many establishments—restaurants, cafes, and *loncherías*—willing to supply you with your favorite *jugo,* the juice bars *(jugerías)* are the most fun. Colorful fruit piles mark *jugerías.* If you don't immediately spot your favorite fruit, ask; it might be hidden in the refrigerator.

Besides your choice of pure juice, a *jugería* will often serve *licuados.* Into the juice, they whip powdered milk, your favorite flavoring, and sugar to taste, for a creamy afternoon pick-me-up or evening dessert. One big favorite is a cool banana-chocolate *licuado,* which comes out tasting like a milkshake (minus the calories).

Alcoholic Drinks

The Aztecs sacrificed anyone caught drinking alcohol without permission. The more lenient, Spanish attitude toward getting *borracho* (soused) has led to a thriving Mexican renaissance of tra-

MEXICAN FOOD

On most Mexican-style menus, diners will find variations on a number of basic themes:

Chiles rellenos: Fresh roasted green chilies, stuffed usually with cheese but sometimes with fish or meat, coated with batter, and fried. They provide a piquant, tantalizing contrast to tortillas.

Enchiladas and **tostadas:** variations on the filled-tortilla theme. Enchiladas are stuffed with meat, cheese, olives, or beans and covered with sauce and baked, while tostadas consist of toppings served on crisp, open-faced tortillas.

Guacamole: This luscious avocado, onion, tomato, lime, and salsa mixture remains the delight it must have seemed to its Aztec inventors centuries ago. In non-tourist Mexico, it's served sparingly as a garnish, rather than in appetizer bowls as is common in the U.S. Southwest (and Mexican resorts catering to North Americans). (Similarly, in non-tourist Mexico, burritos and fajitas, both stateside inventions, seldom, if ever appear on menus.)

Carnes (meats): **Carne asada** grilled beef, usually chewy and well-done. Something similar you might see on a menu is *cecina* (say-SEE-nah), dried salted beef, grilled to a shoeleather-like consistency. Much more appetizing is **birria**, a Guadalajara specialty. Traditional *birrias* are of lamb or goat, often wrapped and pit-roasted in maguey leaves, with which it is served, for authenticity. In addition to *asada,* meat cooking styles are manifold, including *guisado* (stewed), *al pastor* (spit barbecue), and *barbacoa* (grill barbecued). Cuts include *lomo,* (loin), *chuleta* (chop), *milanesa* (cutlet), and *albóndigas* (meatballs.)

Moles (MOH-lays): uniquely Mexican specialties. *Mole poblano,* a spicy-sweet mixture of chocolate, chilies, and a dozen other ingredients, is cooked to a smooth sauce, then baked with chicken (or turkey, a combination called *mole de pavo*). So *típica,* it's widely regarded as the national dish.

Quesadillas: made from soft flour tortillas, rather than corn, quesadillas resemble tostadas and always contain melted cheese.

Sopas: Soups consist of vegetables in a savory chicken broth, and are an important part of both *comida* (afternoon) and *cena* (evening) Mexican meals. *Pozole,* a rich steaming stew of

ditional alcoholic beverages: tequila, mescal, Kahlúa, pulque, and *aguardiente.* Tequila and mescal, distilled from the fermented juice of the maguey, originated in Oaxaca, where the best is still made. Quality tequila (named after the Guadalajara-region distillery town) and mescal come 76 proof (38 percent alcohol) and up. A small white worm, endemic to the maguey, is customarily added to each bottle of factory mescal for authenticity.

Pulque, although also made from the sap of the maguey, is locally brewed to a small alcohol content between that of beer and wine. The brewing houses are sacrosanct preserves, circumscribed by traditions that exclude women and outsiders. The brew, said to be full of nutrients, is sold to

local *pulquerías* and drank immediately. If you are ever invited into a *pulgería,* it is an honor you cannot refuse.

Aguardiente, by contrast, is the notorious fiery Mexican "white lightning," a sugar cane–distilled, dirt-cheap ticket to oblivion for poor Mexican men.

While pulque comes from age-old Indian tradition, beer is the beverage of modern mestizo Mexico. Full-bodied and tastier than "light" U.S. counterparts, Mexican beer enjoys an enviable reputation.

Those visitors who indulge usually know their favorite among the many brands, from light to dark: Superior, Corona, Pacífico, Tecate (served with lime), Carta Blanca, Modelo, Dos Equis,

hominy, vegetables, and pork or chicken, often constitutes the prime evening offering of small side street shops. *Sopa de taco,* an ever-popular country favorite, is a medium-spicy cheese-topped thick chili broth served with crisp corn tortillas.

Tacos or **taquitos:** tortillas served open or wrapped around any ingredient.

Tamales: as Mexican as apple pie is American. This savory mixture of meat and sauce imbedded in a shell of corn dough and baked in a wrapping of corn husks is rarely known by the singular, however. They're so yummy that one tamale invariably leads to more tamales.

Tortas: the Mexican sandwich, usually hot meat with fresh tomato and avocado, stuffed between two halves of a crisp *bolillo* (boh-LEE-yoh) or Mexican bun.

Tortillas y frijoles refritos: cooked brown or black beans, mashed and fried in pork fat, and rolled into tortillas with a dash of vitamin-C-rich salsa to form a near-complete combination of carbohydrate, fat, and balanced protein

Beyond the Basics

Mexican food combinations seem endless. Mexican corn itself has more that 500 recognized culinary variations, all from indigenous tradition. This has led to a myriad of permutations on the taco, such as *sopes* (with small and thick tortillas), *garnacho* (flat taco), *chilequile* (shredded taco), *chalupa* (like a tostada) and *memela.*

Taking a lesson from California *nouvelle cuisine,* avant-garde Mexican chefs are returning to traditional ingredients. They're beginning to use more and more chilies—Habañero, poblano, jalapeño and more—prepared with many variations, such as *chipotle, ancho, piquín,* and *mulato.* Squash flowers *(flor de calabaza)* and cactus *(nopal)* leaves are increasingly finding their way into soups and salads.

More often chefs are serving the wild game—*venado* (venison) *conejo* (rabbit), *guajalote* (turkey), *codorniz* (quail), armadillo and iguana—that country Mexicans have always depended upon. As part of the same trend, *cuitlacoche,* (corn mushroom fungus), *chapulines* (French-fried small grasshoppers), and *gusanos de maguey* (maguey worms) are being increasingly added as ingredients in fancy restaurants.

Bohemia, Indio, Tres Equis, and Negro Modelo. Nochebuena, a hearty dark brew, becomes available only around Christmas.

Mexicans have yet to develop much of a taste for *vino tinto* or *vino blanco* (red or white table wine), although some domestic vintages (especially of the Baja California labels Cetto, Domecq, and Monte Xanic) are often excellent.

Bread and Pastries

Excellent locally baked bread is a delightful surprise to many first-time Guadalajara visitors. Small bakeries everywhere put out trays of hot, crispy-crusted *bolillos* (rolls) and *panes dulces* (pastries). The pastries range from simple cakes, muffins, cookies, and donuts to fancy fruit-filled turnovers and puffs. Half the fun occurs before the eating: perusing the goodies, tongs in hand, and picking out the most scrumptious. With your favorite dozen or two finally selected, you take your tray to the cashier, who deftly bags everything up and collects a few pesos (two or three dollars) for your entire mouthwatering selection.

Restaurant Price Key

In the destination chapters, restaurants that serve dinner are described as budget, moderate, expensive, or a combination thereof, at the end of some restaurant descriptions. **Budget** means that the entrées cost under $7; **moderate,** $7–14; **expensive,** over $14.

Getting Around

BY BUS

The passenger bus is the king of the Mexican road. Dozens of lines, with thousands of buses, from luxury Mercedes-Benz leviathans to humble converted school buses, connect virtually every Guadalajara destination, both in the city and its surrounding region (For many more route and departure details, see the destination chapters).

Intercity Bus Travel

Three distinct levels of intercity service—luxury-class, first-class, and second-class—are generally available. **Luxury-class** (called something like "Primera Plus," depending upon the line) riders enjoy coaches speeding between the major destinations. In exchange for relatively high fares (about $50 for Puerto Vallarta–Guadalajara, for example), passengers enjoy rapid passage and airline-style amenities: plush reclining seats, a (usually) clean toilet, air-conditioning, onboard video, and an aisle attendant.

Although less luxurious, for about two-thirds the price, **first-class** service is frequent and always includes reserved seating. Additionally, passengers enjoy soft reclining cushions and air-conditioning (if it is working). Besides their regular stops at or near most towns and villages en route, first-class bus drivers, if requested, will usually stop and let you off anywhere along the road.

Second-class bus seating is unreserved. In outlying parts of the Guadalajara region, there is even a class of bus beneath second-class, but given the condition of many second-class buses, it seems as if third-class buses wouldn't run at all. Such buses are the stuff of travelers' legends: the recycled old GMC, Ford, and Dodge school buses that stop everywhere and carry everyone and everything to even the smallest villages tucked away in the far mountains. As long as there is any kind of a road, the bus will most likely go there.

Second-class buses are not for travelers with weak knees or stomachs. On long trips, carry food, beverages, and toilet paper. Station food may be dubious, and the toilet facilities may be ill-maintained.

If you are waiting for a first-class bus at an intermediate *salida de paso* (passing station), you have to trust luck that there will be an empty seat. If not, your best option may be to ride a more frequent second-class bus.

Often, you will initially have to stand, cramped in the aisle, in a crowd of campesinos. They are warmhearted but poor people, so don't tempt them with open, dangling purses or wallets bulging in back pockets. Stow your money safely away. After a while, you will be able to sit down. Such privilege, however, comes with obligation, such as holding an old woman's bulging bag of carrots or a toddler on your lap. But if you accept your burden with humor and equanimity, who knows what favors and blessings may flow to you in return.

Guadalajara Bus Stations

Guadalajara has two long-distance bus stations. Most Guadalajara regional towns and villages are accessible from the second-class **Camionera Central Vieja** (Old Central Bus Terminal), dating from around 1960, in the southeast quarter of the downtown district, a few blocks north of Parque Agua Azul. The complex sprawls over about two square city blocks, bounded by Calles Los Angeles and 5 de Febrero on the north and south, and Calles Michel and Analco on the west and east. Here, a flurry of second-class buses heads out daily, from 6 A.M. until about 9 P.M., to destinations up to about 100 miles (160 km) from downtown. These include all listings in the Guadalajara Getaways and Lake Chapala and Vicinity chapters, plus virtually everything in between.

Longer-distance and luxury- and first-class connections are available at Guadalajara's other major bus terminal, the **Camionera Central Nueva** (New Central Bus Terminal), built around 1990 at Guadalajara's southeast edge, about seven miles (11 km, 20 minutes by taxi), from the city center. From this grand airport-

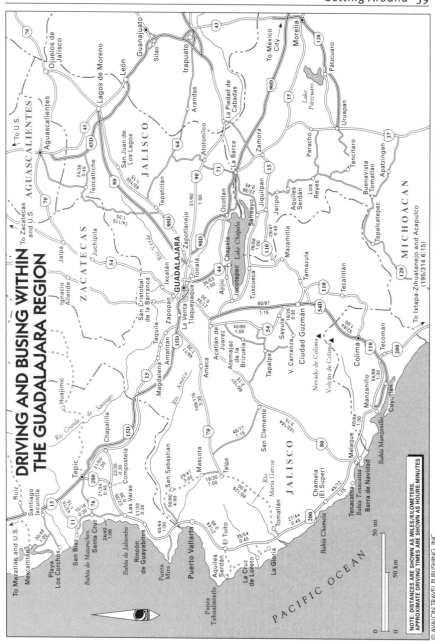

DRIVING AND BUSING WITHIN THE GUADALAJARA REGION

© AVALON TRAVEL PUBLISHING, INC.

NOTE: DISTANCES ARE SHOWN AS MILES/KILOMETERS
APPROXIMATE DRIVING TIMES ARE SHOWN AS HOURS:MINUTES

ON THE ROAD

WHICH BUSES GO WHERE

Destinations

Amatitán, Jal.	RA
Barra de Navidad–Melaque, Jal.	AC, ACP, EL, ETN, PP, TCN
Colima, Col.	AO, ETN, OM, PP, EL
Chapala, Jal.	AGC
Guadalajara	ACP, ATM, AO, EL, ETN, FU, OM, PP, TC, TN, TP
La Venta, Jal. (Bosque de Primavera)	RA
Magdalena, Jal.	RA, TP
Manzanillo, Col.	AC, AO, ACP, EL, ETN, FA, GA, PP, TNS
Mazamitla, Jal.	AM
Mazatlán, Sin.	EL, TC, TN, TNS, TP
Puerto Vallarta, Jal.	AC, EL, ETN, PP, TCN, TNS, TP
San Blas, Nay.	TNS
San Juan de los Lagos, Jal.	OM, TN
Tapalpa, Jal.	ATS
Tepic, Nay.	EL, FU, OM, TC, TNS, TNN, TP
Tequila, Jal.	RA, TP
Villa Corona, Jal. (Chimulco Spa)	FA, ACP

Bus Key:

AC	Autobuses Costa Alegre (subsidiary of FA)
ACP	Autocamiones del Pacífico
AGC	Autotransportes Guadalajara-Chapala
AM	Autotransportes Mazamitla
ATM	Autotransportes Mascota-Guadalajara
ATS	Autotransportes Sur de Jalisco
AO	Autobuses del Occidente
EB	Estrella Blanca
EL	Elite (subsidiary of EB)
ETN	Enlaces Transportes Nacionales
FA	Flecha Amarilla
FU	Futura (subsidiary of EB)
GA	Galeana (subsidiary of FA)
OM	Omnibus de Mexico
PP	Primera Plus (subsidiary of FA)
RA	Rojo de los Altos
TC	Transportes Chihuahuenses (subsidiary of EB)
TCN	Transportes Cihuatlán
TN	Transportes del Norte (subsidiary of EB)
TNS	Transportes Norte de Sonora (subsidiary of EB)
TP	Transportes del Pacífico

style seven-building complex, hundreds of sleek buses roar away daily to national and regional destinations, as far away as Mexico City and the U.S. border, and as close as the more important Guadalajara regional destinations in the Guadalajara Getaways chapter.

For many more details, both on Guadalajara's central bus stations and specific bus lines and departures, see Getting There and Away in the Heart of the City chapter.

Tickets, Seating, and Baggage

Most Guadalajara bus lines do not publish schedules or fares. You have to ask someone who knows (such as your hotel desk clerk), or call the bus station. Few travel agents handle bus tickets. If you don't want to spend the time to get a reserved ticket yourself, hire someone trustworthy to do it for you. Another option is to get to the bus station early enough on your traveling day to ensure that you'll get a bus to your destination.

Although (at the Camionera Central Nueva only) some major lines accept credit cards and issue computer-printed tickets, most reserved bus tickets are still sold for cash and handwritten, with a specific seat number (*número de asiento*), on the back. If you miss the bus, you lose your money. Furthermore, although some bus lines offer airline-style automated reservations systems, most do not. Consequently, you can generally buy reserved tickets only at the local departure *(salida local)* station. (An agent in Guadalajara, for example, cannot ordinarily reserve you a ticket on a bus that originates in Tepic, 100 miles up the road.)

City Buses

Within the metropolitan area, a welter of privately operated city buses, from shiny air-conditioned models to smoky rattletraps, connect Guadalajara's city neighborhoods. Usually their route destinations will be scrawled on their window. Fares run from about $.30 up. Although by far the most economical mode of transport, city buses are often crowded. When possible, pay the extra $.10 and ride one of the air-conditioned buses, which you can recognize because

their windows are all closed and they are less likely to be crowded. For route descriptions and a map of the more useful city bus lines, see the maps, *Guadalajara Bus Routes* and *Bus Routes Downtown,* and the Getting Around sections of the destination chapters.

BY CAR

Driving a car in Mexico may or may not be for you. Be sure to read the pros and cons in By Car or RV under Getting There, earlier in this chapter.

Rental Car

Car and jeep rentals are an increasingly popular transportation option in Guadalajara. They offer mobility and independence for local excursions. At the Guadalajara airport, the gang's all there, including Alamo, Avis, Budget, Dollar, Hertz, and National, plus several local outfits. (For car rental contact specifics, see the By Air section, under Getting There and Away in the Heart of the City chapter.)

Before renting a car, Guadalajara agencies require you to present a valid driver's license, passport, a major credit card, and additionally may require you to be at least 25 years old. Some local companies do not accept credit cards as payment, but do offer lower rates in return.

Base prices of international agencies such as Hertz, National, and Avis are not cheap. With a 17 percent value-added tax and mandatory insurance, rentals run more than in the United States. The cheapest possible rental car, usually a Japanese- or U.S.–brand, Mexican-made compact, runs $40–60 per day or $250–450 per week, depending on the season. Prices are highest during Christmas and pre-Easter weeks. Before departure, use the international agencies' toll-free numbers and websites (see chart, later on) for availability, prices, and reservations. During nonpeak seasons, you may save lots of pesos by waiting until arrival and renting a car in a local in-town (as opposed to the airport) agency. Shop around, starting with the agent in your hotel lobby or with the local Yellow Pages (under *"Automóviles, renta de"*). Also refer to the Down-

CAR RENTAL AGENCY TOLL-FREE NUMBERS AND WEBSITES

Avis	U.S. 800/831-2847	Canada 800/831-2847	www.avis.com
Alamo	U.S. 800/522-9696	Canada 800/522-9696	www.alamo.com
Budget	U.S. 800/472-3325	Canada 800/472-3325	www.drivebudget.com
Dollar	U.S. 800/800-4000	Canada 800/800-4000	www.dollar.com
Hertz	U.S. 800/654-3001	Canada 476/620-9620	www.hertz.com
National	U.S. 800/227-3876	Canada 800/227-3876	www.national.com
Thrifty	U.S. 800/367-2277	Canada 800/367-2277	www.thrifty.com

town Car Rentals section in the Heart of the City chapter.

Car insurance that covers property damage and public liability is a government requirement in Mexico and is therefore an absolute "must" with your rental car. If you get into an accident without such insurance, you will be in deep trouble—probably jail. Some of your credit cards, such as American Express, Mastercard, and VISA, may offer **free rental car insurance** as a benefit for renting your car with their card. If so, this allows you to waive the expensive insurance offered by the rental agency and thereby save yourself $15–20 per day. Check carefully for your car insurance coverage details with your credit card company. For other important car safety and insurance information, read By Car or RV under Getting There, earlier in this chapter.

Driving in Guadalajara

Driving in Guadalajara is similar to driving in a large U.S. city, except you must drive more defensively. Potholes, pedestrians crossing at random points, and reckless drivers dictate more watchful driving than back home.

If you're going to be doing a lot of Guadalajara driving, get a copy (always available at Sanborn's gift shop–restaurant; see destination chapters) of the very reliable **Guia Roji Red Vial Cuidad de Guadalajara** city map.

A number of boulevards, such as east-west expressways Av. Lázaro Cárdenas–Av. Vallarta and north-south Av. Patria–Av. López Mateos, have **laterals** (streets running parallel to the main boulevard) for slower traffic or for turnoffs accessing overpasses and underpasses. Be prepared. Watch for signs indicating the turnoffs to the laterals ahead. If you miss the desired turnoff, look for a *retorno* where you can make a U-turn and correct your mistake.

Be aware also that **left turns,** especially on four- or six-lane expressways with laterals, must often be made from the right lateral, and only in response to a green left-turn signal arrow. Without a lateral, left turn rules are similar to those in the United States.

BY TAXI OR TOUR

Taxis

The high prices of rental cars make taxis a viable option for local excursions. Cars are luxuries, not necessities, for many Guadalajara families. Travelers might profit from the Mexican money-saving practice of piling everyone in a taxi for a Sunday outing. You may find that not only will an all-day taxi and driver cost less than a rental car and relieve you of driving, your driver also may become your impromptu guide.

The magic word for saving money by taxi is *colectivo:* a taxi you share with other travelers. The first place in Guadalajara where you'll practice getting a taxi will be at the airport, where *colectivo* tickets are routinely sold from booths at the terminal door.

If, however, you want your own private taxi, ask for a *taxi especial,* which will run about 3–4 times the individual tariff for a *colectivo.*

Your airport experience will prepare you for in-town taxis, nearly all of which have meters, but

© BRUCE WHIPPERMAN

A very leisurely way of getting around in down-town Guadalajara is to rent a *calandria* (horse-drawn carriage) just north of the cathedral.

which many drivers don't like to use. Best insist— *"Metro, por favor"* ("Metro, please")—on using the meter. If the driver refuses, you have the usually easy option of getting another taxi or establishing the price before the ride starts. Bargaining comes with the territory in Mexico, so don't shrink from it, even though it seems a hassle. If you get into a taxi without an agreed-upon price, you are allowing for a more serious and potentially nasty hassle later. If your driver's price is too high, he'll probably come to his senses as soon as you get out to hail another taxi.

After a few days, getting taxis around town will be a cinch. You'll find that you don't have to take the more expensive taxis lined up in your hotel driveway. If the price isn't right, walk toward the street and hail a regular taxi.

In town, if you can't find a taxi, it may be because they are waiting for riders at the local stand, called a taxi *sitio*. Ask someone to direct you to it: *"Excúseme. ¿Dónde está el sitio taxi, por favor?"* ("Excuse me. Where is the taxi stand, please?")

By Locally Arranged Tour

For many Guadalajara visitors, locally arranged tours offer a hassle-free alternative to sightseeing by car or taxi. Hotels and travel agencies, many of whom maintain lobby-front travel and tour desks, offer a bounty of sight-seeing options.

Alternatively, contact the earnest and friendly operators of **R&R in Mexico,** Mark Kunce and Sandy Brown, whose mission is to help visitors enjoy, appreciate, and get acquainted with Guadalajara. They offer consultations and services, including reasonably priced, all-inclusive tour itineraries. For more information, log on to their website: www.rr-mexico.com or contact them by telephone directly in Guadalajara, at tel. 33/3121-2348, or from the United States by adding the prefix 011-52 to the above number. Alternatively, email them at either info@rr-mexico.hypermart.net or tours@rr-mexico.hypermart.net., or write Mark Kunce, at P.O. Box 437090, San Ysidro, CA 92143-7090.

Mark and Sandy also recommend tour guides. Contact either George Enriquez (tel. 33/3811-2862 or 33/3810-0556; email: georgeky@compaq.net.mx), Beatriz de la Garza (tel. 33/3615-2030; email: beatrizdlg@yahoo.com), or José Amezcua (tel. 33/3121-2385; email: joseamlo@hotmail.com).

In addition, I recommend the services of intelligent, earnest **Lino Gabriel Gonzalez Nuño.** Contact him at A. Obregón 127, Tlaquepaque, Jalisco 45500; tel. 33/3635-4049; email: lino-gabriel@hotmail.com.

If you prefer the services of a reliable, conventional tour agency, contact 32-years-in-the-business **Panoramex,** main office at west-side Federalismo Sur 944, tel./fax 33/3810-5057 or 33/3810-5005. They specialize in very reasonably priced bilingual tourist-route Guadalajara-Tlaquepaque ($15), Lake Chapala ($20), and Tequila ($23) tours.

FESTIVALS AND EVENTS

Mexicans love a party. Urban families watch the calendar for midweek national holidays that create a *puente* or "bridge" to the weekend and allow them to squeeze in a three- to five-day

FIESTAS

The following calendar lists national and notable Guadalajara region holidays and festivals. If you happen to be where one of these is going on, get out of your car or bus and join in!

January 1: **¡Feliz Año Nuevo!** Happy New Year! (national holiday)

January 6: **Día de los Reyes** Day of the Kings; traditional gift exchange

January 15–20: **Fiesta Charro-Tuarina:** in Tapalpa, with rodeos, bullfights, popular dance, and fireworks

January 17: **Día de San Antonio Abad** (decorating and blessing animals)

January 20–February 2: **Fiesta de la Virgen de Candelaria:** Especially in San Juan de los Lagos, Jalisco. Millions, from all over Mexico, honor the Virgin with parades, dances depicting Christians vs. Moors, and rodeos, cockfights, fireworks, and much more.

February 2: **Día de Candelaria:** (plants, seeds, and candles blessed; procession and bullfights, especially in San Juan de los Lagos.)

February 17–27: **Fiestas Taurinas:** in Mazamitla, with *charreadas* (rodeos), *jaripeo* (bull-roping), livestock auctions, judging and prizes, fireworks, and plenty of country food.

February 5: **Constitution Day** (national holiday commemorating the constitutions of 1857 and 1917)

February 24: **Flag Day** (national holiday)

February: The week before Ash Wednesday, usually in late February, many towns, such as Tonalá, stage **Carnaval**—Mardi Gras—extravaganzas.

March 11–19: Week before the **Día de San José** in Talpa, Jalisco (food, edible crafts made of colored *chicle* (chewing gum), dancing, bands, and mariachi serenades to the Virgin)

March 27–30: **Foundation of Mazamitla:** festival, centering around the plaza, with speeches, band concerts, dance, dramatic and athletic performances, crafts fair, and fireworks.

March 18– April 4: **Ceramics and handicrafts fair** in Tonalá (Guadalajara), Jalisco

March 19: **Día de San José** (Day of St. Joseph)

March 21: **Birthday of Benito Juárez** the revered "Lincoln of Mexico" (national holiday)

April 1–19: **Fiesta de Ramos** in Sayula, Jalisco (on Hwy. 54 southwest of Guadalajara; local area crafts fair, food, dancing, mariachis)

April 18–30: Big **country fair** in Tepatitlán, Jalisco (on Hwy. 80 east of Guadalajara; many livestock and agricultural displays and competitions; regional food, rodeos, and traditional dances)

The two weeks before Easter: in Tonalá, the combined **Fiesta del Sol** (Festival of the Sun) and the **National Handicrafts Fair**

The week before Easter: **Fería de Domingo de Ramos** (Palm Sunday) in Tapalpa, when the *jardín* and the surrounding streets are decked out with for-sale ceramics

April: **Semana Santa:** pre-Easter Holy Week, culminating in Domingo Gloria, Easter Sunday (national holiday)

May 1: **Labor Day** (national holiday)

May: (first and third Wednesday) **Fiesta of the Virgin of Ocotlán,** in Ocotlán, Jalisco (on Lake Chapala, religious processions, dancing, fireworks, regional food)

May 3: **Día de la Santa Cruz:** (Day of the Holy Cross, especially in Mascota, Jalisco, and Tequila)

May 3–15: **Fiesta of St. Isador the Farmer:** (blessing of seeds, animals, and water; agricultural displays, competitions, and dancing)

May 5: **Cinco de Mayo:** (defeat of the French at Puebla in 1862; national holiday)

May 10: **Mothers' Day** (national holiday)

May 10–12: **Fiesta of the Coronation of the Virgin of the Rosary** in Tapalpa, Jalisco (processions, fireworks, regional food, crafts, and dances

May 10– 24: **Book fair:** in Guadalajara (readings, concerts, and international book exposition)

June 24: **communal smashing of traditional clay *cantaritos*** (tequila jugs) in Tequila.

June 24: **Día de San Juan Bautista** (Day of St. John the Baptist, fairs and religious festivals, playful dunking of people in water)

June 15–July 2: **National Ceramics Fair** in Tlaquepaque (huge crafts fair; exhibits, competitions, and market of crafts from all over the country)

June 29: **Día de San Pablo y San Pedro** (Day of St. Peter and St. Paul)

First Saturday of July, **Fiesta de la Virgen de la Defensa** in Tapalpa, when townsfolk carry the Virgin home to Tapalpa all the way from the town of Juanacatlán.

July 17–22: **Fiesta de Santa María Magdalena** in Magdalena

July 25–31: **Fiesta de San Cristóbal** in Mazamitla, with special masses, processions, carnival, food, and fireworks.

July 20–25: **Fiesta de Santiago** (St. James) especially in Tonalá, sometimes known as the **Fiesta Pagana** (Pagan Festival), featuring the wild "Dance of the Tastoanes".

August 1–15: **Fiesta de la Asunción,** especially in San Juan de los Lagos and Tequila.

September 14: **Charro Day:** (Cowboy Day, all over Mexico; rodeos)

September 16: **Independence Day** (national holiday; mayors everywhere reenact Father Hidalgo's 1810 Grito de Dolores from city hall balconies on the night of 15 September)

September 15–28: **National Opal Fair** and **Fiesta del Señor de los Milagros** in Magdalena, with parade, mariachis, *mojigangos* (dancing effigies), and an opal exposition.

October 4: **Fiesta de San Francisco:** in Tequila

October 4: **Día de San Francisco** (Day of St. Francis)

October 12: **Día de la Raza** (Columbus Day, national holiday that commemorates the union of the races)

October 12: **Fiesta de la Virgen de Zapopan** in Guadalajara (procession carries the Virgin home to the **Zapopan** cathedral; regional food, crafts fair, mariachis, and dancing)

October (last Sunday): **Día de Cristo Rey** in Ixtlán del Río, Nayarit (Day of Christ the King, with "Quetzal y Azteca" and "La Pluma" *indígena* dances, horse races, processions, and food)

FIESTAS (cont'd)

November 1: Día de Todos Santos (All Souls' Day, in honor of the souls of children. The departed descend from heaven to eat sugar skeletons, skulls, and treats on family altars.)

November 2: Día de los Muertos (Day of the Dead; in honor of ancestors. Families visit cemeteries and decorate graves with flowers and favorite food of the deceased.)

November 20: Revolution Day (anniversary of the revolution of 1910–17; national holiday)

November 30–December 12: National Tequila Fair in Tequila, with commercial liquor fair, rodeos, parade and floats, cockfights, mariachis, carnival, and fireworks.

December 1: Inauguration Day (national government changes hands every six years: 1994, 2000, 2006)

December 8: Día de la Purísima Concepción (Day of the Immaculate Conception), especially in San Juan de los Lagos.

December 12: Día de Nuestra Señora de Guadalupe (Festival of the Virgin of Guadalupe, patroness of Mexico, especially in San Juan de los Lagos

December 16–4: Christmas Week (week of *posadas* and piñatas; midnight mass on Christmas Eve)

December 25: Christmas Day *¡Feliz Navidad!* Christmas trees and gift exchange; national holiday)

December 31: New Year's Eve

mini-vacation. Visitors should likewise watch the calendar. Such holidays (especially Christmas and Semana Santa/pre-Easter week) can mean packed buses, roads, and hotels, especially in town and around beach resorts.

Campesinos, on the other hand, await their local saint's day (or holy day). The name of the locality often provides the clue: in Santa Cruz de las Flores, just west of Hwy. 15/54/80, a few miles south of the city limits, expect a celebration on May 3, El Día de la Santa Cruz (Day of the Holy Cross). People dress up in their traditional best, sell their wares and produce in a street fair, join a procession, get tipsy, and dance in the plaza.

Handicrafts

Mexico is so stuffed with lovely, reasonably priced handicrafts or *artesanías* (pronounced "ar-tay-sah-NEE-ahs") that many crafts devotees, if given the option, might choose Mexico over heaven. A sizable number of Mexican (and Guadalajaran) families depend upon the sale of homespun items—clothing, utensils, furniture, forest herbs, religious offerings, adornments, toys, musical instruments—that either they or their neighbors make at home. Many craft traditions reach back thousands of years to the beginnings of Mexican civilization. The work of generations of artisans has, in many instances, resulted in finery

so prized that whole villages devote themselves to the manufacture of a single class of goods. (For specific stores and sources, see the shopping sections in the Heart of the City, City: South and East of Downtown, and Guadalajara Getaways chapters.)

BASKETRY AND WOVEN CRAFTS

Weaving straw, palm fronds, and reeds is among the oldest of Mexican handicraft traditions. Five-thousand-year-old mat- and basket-weaving methods and designs survive to the present day. All over Mexico, people weave *petates* (palm-frond mats) that vacationers use to stretch out on the beach and that locals use for everything, from keeping tortillas warm to shielding babies from the sun. Along the coast, you might see a woman or child waiting for a bus or even walking down the street weaving white palm leaf strands into a coiled basket. Later, you may see a similar basket, embellished with a bright animal—parrot, burro, or even Snoopy—for sale in the market.

Like the origami paper-folders of Japan, folks who live around Lake Pátzcuaro have taken basket-weaving to its ultimate form by crafting virtually everything—from toy turtles and Christmas bells to butterfly mobiles and serving spoons—from the reeds they gather along the lakeshore.

Hatmaking has likewise attained high refinement in Mexico. Workers in Sahuayo, Michoacán, near the southeast shore of Lake Chapala, make especially fine sombreros. Due east across Mexico, in Becal, Campeche, workers fashion Panama hats or *jipis* (pronounced HEE-pees), so fine, soft, and flexible you can stuff one into your pants pocket without damage.

Although Huichol men (from the Guadalajara region and the neighboring state of Nayarit) do not actually manufacture their headwear, they do decorate them. They take ordinary sombreros and embellish them into Mexico's most flamboyant hats, flowing with bright ribbons, feathers, and fringes of colorful wool balls.

CLOTHING AND EMBROIDERY

Although **traje** (ancestral tribal dress) has nearly vanished in large cities such as Guadalajara, significant numbers of Mexican country women make and wear *traje*. Such traditional styles are still common in remote districts of the Guadalajara region and in the states of Michoacán, Guerrero, Oaxaca, Chiapas, and Yucatán. Most favored is the **huipil**, a long, square-shouldered, short- to mid-sleeved full dress, often hand-embroidered with animal and floral designs. Some of the most beautiful *huipiles* are from Oaxaca, especially from San Pedro de Amusgos (Amusgo tribe;

white cotton, embroidered with abstract colored animal and floral motifs), San Andrés Chicahuatxtla (Trique tribe; white cotton, richly embroidered red stripes, interwoven with greens, blues, and yellows, and hung with colored ribbons), and Yalalag (Zapotec tribe; white cotton, with bright flowers embroidered along two or four vertical seams and distinctive colored tassels hanging down the back). Beyond Oaxaca, Maya *huipiles* are also highly desired. They are usually made of white cotton and embellished with brilliant machine-embroidered flowers around the neck and shoulders, front and back.

Shoppers sometimes can buy other, less-common types of *traje* accessories, such as a **quechquémitl** (shoulder cape), often made of wool and worn as an overgarment in winter. The **enredo** (literally, "tangled") wraparound skirt, by contrast, enfolds the waist and legs, like a Hawaiian sarong. Mixtec women in Oaxaca's warm south coastal region around Pinotepa Nacional (west of Puerto Escondido) commonly wear the *enredo,* known locally as the **pozahuanco** (poh-sah-oo-AHN-koh), below the waist, and when at home, go bare-breasted. When wearing her *pozahuanco* in public, a Mixtec woman usually ties a **mandil,** a wide calico apron, around her front side. Women weave the best *pozahuancos* at home, using cotton thread dyed a light purple with secretions of tidepool-harvested snails, *(Purpura patula pansa),* and silk dyed deep red with cochineal, extracted from the dried bodies of a locally cultivated beetle *(Dactylopius coccus).*

Colonial Spanish styles have blended with native *traje* to produce a wider class of dress, known generally as **ropa típica.** Fetching embroidered blouses *(blusas),* shawls *(rebozos),* and dresses *(vestidos)* fill boutique racks and market stalls throughout the Mexican Pacific. Among the most handsome is the so-called **Oaxaca wedding dress,** in white cotton with a crochet-trimmed riot of diminutive flowers, hand-stitched about the neck and yoke. Some of the finest examples are made in Antonino Castillo Velasco village, in the Valley of Oaxaca.

In contrast to women, only a very small population of Mexican men—members of remote groups, such as Huichol and Cora in the Guadalajara region—wear *traje*. Nevertheless, shops offer some fine men's *ropa típica,* such as serapes, decorated wool blankets with a hole or slit for the head, worn during northern or highland winters, or *guayaberas,* hip-length, pleated tropical dress shirts.

Fine embroidery *(bordado)* embellishes much traditional Mexican clothing, tablecloths *(manteles),* and napkins *(servilletas).* As everywhere, women define the art of embroidery. Although some still work by hand at home, cheaper machine-made factory lace needlework is more commonly available in shops. (Some shops in Tlaquepaque carry embroidery, *traje,* and *ropa típica.* See the City: South and East of Downtown chapter.)

LEATHER

The Guadalajara region abounds in for-sale leather goods, most of which is manufactured locally, or in and León and Guanajuato (shoes, boots, and saddles). For unique and custom-designed articles you'll probably have to confine your shopping to the pricier stores; for more usual though still attractive leather items such as purses, wallets, belts, coats, and boots, veteran shoppers find bargains at individual stores in Tlaquepaque and at Guadalajara's downtown Libertad Mercado, where an acre of stalls offers the broadest selection at the most reasonable prices (after bargaining) in Mexico.

FURNITURE

Although furniture is usually too bulky to carry back home with your airline luggage, low prices make it possible for you to ship your purchases home and enjoy beautiful, unusual pieces for half the price you would pay—even if you could find them—outside Mexico (including transport).

A number of classes of furniture *(muebles,* MWAY-blehs) are crafted in villages near the sources of raw materials, notably wood, rattan, bamboo, or wrought iron.

Sometimes it seems as if every house in Mexico is furnished with **colonial-style furniture,** the basic design for much of it dating back at least to the Middle Ages. Although many variations exist, colonial-style furniture is usually heavily built. Table and chair legs are massive, usually lathe-turned; chair backs are customarily arrow-straight and often uncomfortably vertical. Although usually brown-varnished, colonial-style tables, chairs, and chests sometimes shine with inlaid wood or tile, or animal and flower designs. Family shops turn out good furniture, usually in the country highlands, where suitable wood is available. Shops in Tonalá and Tlaquepaque (see the City: South and East of Downtown chapter), and Mazamitla and Tapalpa (see the Guadalajara Getaways chapter), offer many good examples.

Equipal, a very distinctive and widespread class of Mexican furniture, is made of leather, usually brownish pigskin or cowhide, stretched over wood frames. Factories are centered mostly in Guadalajara and nearby villages.

It is interesting that **lacquered furniture,** in both process and design, has much in common with lacquerware produced half a world away in China. The origin of Mexican lacquerware tradition presents an intriguing mystery. What is certain, however, is that it predated the Conquest and was originally produced only in the Pacific states of Guerrero and Michoacán. Persistent legends of pre-Columbian coastal contact with Chinese traders give weight to the speculation, shared by a number of experts, that the Chinese may have taught the lacquerware art to the Mexicans many centuries before the Conquest.

Today, artisan families in and around Pátzcuaro, Michoacán, and Olinalá, Guerrero, carry on the tradition. The process, which at its finest resembles cloisonné manufacture, involves carving and painting intricate floral and animal designs, followed by repeated layering of lacquer, clay, and sometimes gold and silver to produce satiny, jewel-like surfaces.

A sprinkling of villages produce furniture made of plant fiber, such as reeds, raffia, and bamboo. In some cases, entire communities, such as Ihuatzio (near Pátzcuaro) and Villa Victoria (west of Toluca) have long harvested the bounty of local lakes and marshes as the basis for their products.

© BRUCE WHIPPERMAN

Traditional Huichol yarn paintings depict the host of gods and spirits of the Huichol pantheon.

Wrought iron, produced and worked according to Spanish tradition, is used to produce tables, chairs, and benches. Ruggedly fashioned in a riot of baroque scrollwork, they often decorate garden and patio settings. Several colonial cities, notably Tonalá and Tlaquepaque in Guadalajara, and San Miguel de Allende, Toluca, and Guanajuato, are wrought iron–manufacturing centers.

GLASS AND STONEWORK

Glass manufacture, unknown in pre-Columbian times, was introduced by the Spanish. Today, the tradition continues in factories throughout Mexico that turn out mountains of *burbuja* (boor-BOO-hah), bubbled glass tumblers, goblets, plates, and pitchers, usually in blue or green. Finer glass is manufactured around Guadalajara, mostly in Tlaquepaque and Tonalá, where you can watch artisans blow glass into a number of shapes—often paper-thin balls—in red, green, and blue.

Mexican artisans work stone, usually near sources of supply. Puebla, Mexico's major onyx *(onix)* source, is the manufacturing center for the galaxy of mostly rough-hewn, cream-colored items, from animal charms and chess pieces to beads and desk sets, which crowd curio shop shelves all over the country. *Cantera,* a pinkish stone, quarried near Pátzcuaro, is used similarly.

For a keepsake from a truly ancient Mexican tradition, don't forget the hollowed-out stone *metate* (meh-TAH-teh; corn-grinding basin), or the three-legged *molcajete* (mohl-kah-HAY-teh; mortar for grinding chilies).

HUICHOL ART

Huichol art evolved from the charms that Huichol shamans (see special topic, Huichol) crafted to empower them during their hazardous pilgrimages to their peyote-rich sacred land of Wirikuta. Although the Huichol's original commercial outlets in Tepic, Nayarit, still market their goods, several Guadalajara-area shops, especially in Tlaquepaque and the Huichol museum in Zapopan (and even commercial Christmas catalogs in the United States) now offer Huichol goods. To the original items—mostly devotional arrows, yarn *cicuri* (God's eyes), and decorated gourds for collecting peyote—have been added colorful *cuadras* (yarn paintings) and bead masks.

Cuadras, made of synthetic yarns pressed into beeswax on a plywood backing, traditionally depict plant and animal spirits, the main actors of the Huichol cosmos. Bead masks likewise blend the major elements of the Huichol worldview into an eerie human likeness, usually of Grandmother Earth (Tatei Nakawe).

JEWELRY

Gold and silver were once the basis for Mexico's wealth. Her Spanish conquerors plundered a mountain of gold—religious offerings, necklaces, pendants, rings, bracelets—masterfully crafted by a legion of local blacksmiths and jewelers. Unfortunately, much of that indigenous tradition was lost because the Spanish denied Mexicans access to precious metals for generations while they introduced Spanish methods instead. Nevertheless, a small goldworking tradition survived the dislocations of the 1810–21 War of Independence and the 1910–17 revolution. Silvercrafting, moribund during the 1800s, was revived in Taxco, Guerrero, principally through the efforts of architect-artist William Spratling and the local community.

Today, spurred by the tourist boom, jewelry-making thrives in Guadalajara and other Mexican towns. Taxco, Guerrero, where dozens of enterprises—guilds, families, cooperatives—produce sparkling silver and gold adornments, is the acknowledged center. Many Guadalajara regional shops (notably in Tlaquepaque) sell fine Taxco products—shimmering butterflies, birds, jaguars, serpents, turtles, fish—reflecting pre-Columbian tradition. Taxco-made pieces, mostly in silver, vary from humble but good-looking trinkets to candelabras and place settings for a dozen, sometimes embellished with turquoise, garnet, coral, lapis, jade, and, in exceptional cases, emeralds, rubies, and diamonds.

WOODCARVING AND MUSICAL INSTRUMENTS

Masks

Spanish and native Mexican traditions have blended to produce a multitude of masks—some strange, some lovely, some scary, some endearing, and all interesting. The tradition flourishes in the strongly indigenous southern Pacific states of Michoacán, Guerrero, Oaxaca, and Chiapas, where campesinos gear up all year for the village festivals—especially Semana Santa (Easter week), early December (Virgin of Guadalupe), and the festival of the local patron, whether it be San José, San Pedro, San Pablo, Santa María, Santa Barbara, or one of a host of others. Every local fair has its favored dances, such as the Dance of the Conquest, the Christians and Moors, the Old Men, or the Tiger, in which masked villagers act out age-old allegories of fidelity, sacrifice, faith, struggle, sin, and redemption.

Although masks are made of many materials—from stone and ebony to coconut husks and paper—wood, where available, is the medium of choice. For the entire year, carvers cut, carve, sand, and paint to ensure that each participant will be properly disguised for the festival.

The popularity of masks has led to an entire made-for-tourist mask industry of mass-produced duplicates, many cleverly antiqued. Examine the goods carefully; if the price is high, don't buy it unless you're convinced it's a real antique.

Alebrijes

Tourist demand has made zany wooden animals (*alebrijes,* ah-lay-BREE-hays) a Oaxaca growth industry. Virtually every family in the Valley of Oaxaca villages of Arrazola and San Martín Tilcajete runs a factory studio. There, piles of soft *copal* wood, which men carve and women finish and intricately paint, become whimsical giraffes, dogs, cats, iguanas, gargoyles, dragons, and many permutations in between. The farther from the source you get, the higher the *alebrije* price becomes; what costs $5 in Arrazola will probably run about $10 in Guadalajara and $30 in the United States or Canada.

Other commonly available wooden items are the charming, colorfully painted fish carved mainly in the Pacific coastal state of Guerrero, and the burnished, dark hardwood animal and fish sculptures of desert ironwood from the state of Sonora.

Musical Instruments

Virtually all of Mexico's guitars are made in Paracho, Michoacán (southeast of Lake Chapala, 50 miles north of Uruapan). There, scores of cottage factories turn out guitars, violins, mandolins, *viruelas,* ukuleles, and a dozen more variations every day. They vary widely in quality, so look carefully before you buy. Make sure that the wood is well cured and dry; damp, unripe wood instruments are more susceptible to warping and cracking.

METALWORK

Bright copper, brass, pewter, and tinware; sturdy ironwork; and razor-sharp knives and machetes are made in a number of regional centers. **Copperware,** from jugs, cups, and plates to candlesticks—and even the town lampposts and bandstand—all come from Santa Clara del Cobre, a few miles south of Pátzcuaro, Michoacán.

Although not the source of brass itself, **Tonalá,** in the Guadalajara eastern suburb, is the place where brass is most abundant and beautiful, appearing as menageries of brilliant, fetching birds and animals, sometimes embellished with shiny nickel highlights.

© BRUCE WHIPPERMAN

decorative ironwork, Tlaquepaque

A few Guadalajara factories craft fine **pewter** (now of aluminum instead of the traditionally European copper-tin alloy) plates, trays, candlesticks, bowls and much more, that they sell at regional outlets, notably in Tlaquepaque.

Be sure not to miss the tiny *milagros,* one of Mexico's most charming forms of metalwork. Usually of brass, they are of homely shapes—a horse, dog, or baby, or an arm, head, or foot—which, accompanied by a prayer, the faithful pin to the garment of their favorite saint whom they hope will intercede to cure an ailment or fulfill a wish. Vendors in front of the Guadalajara-region pilgrimage basilicas of Zapopan and San Juan de los Lagos offer swarms of *milagros.*

PAPER AND PAPIER-MÂCHÉ

Papier-mâché has become a high art in Tonalá, where a swarm of birds, cats, frogs, giraffes, and other animal figurines are meticulously crafted by building up repeated layers of glued paper. The result—sanded, brilliantly varnished, and polished—resemble fine sculptures rather than the humble newspaper from which they were fashioned.

Other paper goods you shouldn't overlook include **piñatas** (durable, inexpensive, and as Mexican as you can get), available in every town market; also-colorful, decorative, cutout banners (string overhead at your home fiesta) from San Salvador Huixcolotla, Puebla; and *amate,* wild fig tree bark paintings in animal and flower motifs, from Xalitla and Ameyaltepec, Guerrero.

POTTERY AND CERAMICS

Although the Mexican pottery tradition is as diverse as the country itself, some varieties stand out. Among the most prized is the so-called Talavera (or Majolica), the best of which is made in a few family-run shops in Puebla. The names Talavera and Majolica derive from Talavera, the Spanish town from where the tradition migrated to Mexico; prior to that it originated on the Spanish Mediterranean island of Mayorca, from a combination of still older Arabic, Chinese, and African ceramic styles. Shapes include plates, bowls, jugs, and pitchers, hand-painted and hard-fired in intricate bright yellow, orange, blue, and green floral designs. So few shops make true Talavera these days that other, cheaper, look-alike grades made around Guanajuato are more common, selling for one-half to one-third the price of the genuine article.

More practical and nearly as prized is hand-painted **stoneware** from Tlaquepaque and Tonalá in Guadalajara's eastern suburbs. Although made in many shapes and sizes, such stoneware is often sold as complete dinner place settings. Decorations are usually in abstract floral and animal designs, hand-painted over a reddish clay base.

From the same tradition come the famous *bruñido* pottery animals of Tonalá. Round, smooth, and cuddly as ceramic can be, the Tonalá animals—very commonly doves and ducks, but also cats and dogs and sometimes even armadillos, frogs, and snakes—each seem to embody the essence of its species.

Some of the most charming Mexican pottery, made from a ruddy low-fired clay and crafted following pre-Columbian traditions, comes from western Mexico, especially Colima. Charming figurines in timeless human poses—flute-playing musicians, dozing grandmothers, fidgeting babies, loving couples—and animals, especially Colima's famous playful dogs, decorate the shelves of a sprinkling of shops.

Although most latter-day Mexican potters have become aware of the health dangers of lead pigments, some for-sale pottery may still contain lead. The hazard comes from low-fired pottery in which the lead has not been firmly melted into the glaze. Acids in foods such as lemons, vinegar, and tomatoes dissolve the lead pigments, which, when ingested, can eventually result in lead poisoning. In general, the hardest, shiniest pottery, which has been twice fired—such as the high-quality Tlaquepaque stoneware used for dishes—is the safest.

WOOLEN WOVEN GOODS

Mexico's finest wool weavings come from Teotitlán del Valle, in the Valley of Oaxaca, less than an hour's drive east of Oaxaca City. The weaving tradition (originally of cotton) carried on by Teotitlán's Zapotec-speaking families, dates back at least 2,000 years. Most families still carry on the arduous process, making everything from scratch. They gather the dyes from wild plants and the bodies of insects and sea snails. They hand-wash, card, spin, and dye the wool and even travel to remote mountain springs to gather water. The results, they say, *"vale la pena,"* ("are worth the pain"): intensely colored, tightly woven carpets, rugs, and wall-hangings that retain their brilliance for generations.

Rougher, more loosely woven, blankets, jackets, and serapes come from other parts, notably mountain regions, especially around San Cristóbal de las Casas, in Chiapas, and Lake Pátzcuaro in Michoacán, and Tapalpa in the Guadalajara region.

Sports and Recreation

Guadalajara's balmy year-round climate and the region's plethora of sites—gyms, parks, bike and running paths, forest preserves, bathing springs, reservoirs, rivers, lakes, and more—provide just the right setting for athletic and outdoor diversions.

SWIMMING, RUNNING, AND EXERCISING

Although swimming pools are generally for the use of guests only, less exclusive hotels often allow swimming by nonguests who pay a fee at the desk or buy lunch or a drink at the poolside restaurant. Besides Guadalajara's swarm of hotel swimming pools, dozens of modest-fee *balnearios* (bathing springs) provide ample opportunities for splashing, paddling, and swimming. Popular *balnearios* include **Lindo Michoacán** downtown, **Tobolandia** and **Motel Balneario San Juan de Cosala** near Lake Chapala, **Chimulco** near Acatlán, southwest of town, **La Toma** near Tequila, and **Los Camachos,** near Zapopan, north of town. (See the destination chapters for details.) Furthermore, Lake Chapala visitors

ON THE ROAD

Both swimming and water games are popular in the region's many springs and *balnearios*.

can enjoy some tranquil swimming pools (as opposed to *balnearios*) at the **Hotel Villa Montecarlo** in Chapala and the **Joya del Lago Resort** in Ajijic. Lap swimmers can largely avoid *balneario* crowds by confining their swimming to weekdays and Saturday and Sunday mornings.

Runners, on the other hand, needn't limit their hours. Although they may run in many of Guadalajara's parks, especially favored jogging locations are in Colomos Park and the special jogging track atop the **Hotel Guadalajara Plaza Expo** (See the City: North and West of Downtown chapter) and the highway-side path between Chapala and Ajijic and the Ajijic lakeshore park at the foot of Av. Colón. (See the Lake Chapala and Vicinity chapter.)

As for exercising and weight-lifting, use your hotel exercise room or go to one of the dozens of private exercise gyms scattered around town. (See the destination chapters for details.)

TENNIS AND GOLF

Guadalajara visitors can enjoy a number of excellent private courts and 18-hole courses. Golfers have their pick of at least five good courses: the **Atlas Country Club,** off the airport highway (entrance, northbound side of the freeway, by the big SCI electronics plant, 1.1 miles, 1.8 kilometers) south of the *periférico* (peripheral) highway, tel. 33/3689-2620; the **Chapala Country Club,** Lake Chapala, at San Nicolas, about five miles east of Chapala town, tel. 33/3763-5136; the **Santa Anita Golf Club,** tel. 33/3686-0321, and the **Palomar Golf Club,** tel. 33/3684-4436, both southwest of town, off the prolongation of Blv. López Mateos, and **Las Cañadas Country Club,** tel. 33/3685-0363, north of town, off of Hwy. 54 north.

As for tennis, some of Guadalajara's plush hotels, including the **Crowne Plaza, Fiesta Americana, Camino Real,** and El Tapatío, have tennis courts for guest use. For the general public, the Atlas Country Club and the Santa Anita Golf Club (see above) rent their tennis courts to outsiders. Near Lake Chapala, rental tennis courts are also available at the Chula Vista Country Club, Hotel Villa Montecarlo, the Hotel Real de Chapala, and at lakefront Cristiania Park (see the Lake Chapala and Vicinity chapter for details.)

BALNEARIOS

Except for Balneario Lindo Michoacán downtown (see the Heart of the City chapter), most of Guadalajara region *balnearios* (bathing springs) are located in scenic country spots, located between half an hour and an hour's drive from the city-center, all easily accessible by car, second-class bus (from the old bus station, Camionera Central Vieja), or taxi. These spots are locally very popular and likely to be more relaxing and tranquil on weekdays and crowded and noisy on Sundays and holidays.

Moving clockwise around the region, start with **Tobolandia** artificial water toboggan park, 45 minutes south, near Lake Chapala, on the Chapala-Ajijic highway, tel. 376/621-20, open daily 10 A.M.–6 P.M. About 10 miles (16 km) west along the lakeside highway, droves of families enjoy **Motel-Balneario San Juan Cosala,** tel. 376/621-20, east end of San Juan Cosala town, a complex of several natural warm spring swimming pools and sports facilities at lakeside, one hour south, open daily 9 A.M.–6 P.M.

Another 10 miles (16 km) farther west, near Acatlán town, check out Las Alberquitas, ("Little Swimming Pools") tel. 377/200-65 a big shady natural spring park, 1 hour southwest of the city, off of old Colima Hwy. 54 near Acatlán town. A few miles to the northwest, in Villa Corona village, natural warm spring **Chimulco,** tel. 377/800-14, offers lavish, shaded facilities, open daily 10 A.M.–6 P.M. on Hwy. 80, Barra de Navidad direction. The nearby **Agua Caliente,** tel. 377/800-22, open daily 8 A.M.–6 P.M., offers about the same, one hour southwest of the city.

Moving due west of town, at La Venta, in the Bosque de Primavera forest reserve, three country *balnearios* offer relaxation in the naturally warm waters of the Río Caliente. Although the best developed is the **Balneario Canon de las Flores,** tel. 3/151-0160, open daily 10 A.M.–6 P.M., farther along the dirt access road, **Balneario Las Tinajitas,** and another, even more rustic farther on, are more tranquil; 45 minutes west of the city, off of Hwy. 15, about seven miles (11 km) west of the *periférico* (peripheral) boulevard.

Farther west, a couple of miles west of Tequila town, a pair of *balnearios* offer relaxing water diversions at the tropical edge of the Barranca (canyon of the Río Santiago) about an hour and 15 minutes west of the city. Guests at the very popular **Balneario La Toma** enjoy a pair of big shaded pools (one of which is fed from a cliffside cave) and snack restaurants, all perched on the airy canyon rim. By contrast, the nearby **Balneario Paraíso** offers a small shaded swimming and wading pool, a bit of space for camping and all the mangoes you can eat in season; about an hour west.

For more details and access directions, see the relevant sections of the Lake Chapala and Vicinity (for Tobolandia and San Juan Cosala) and Guadalajara Getaways (for Alberquitas, Chimulco, Aguas Calientes, Canon de las Flores, Las Tinajitas, La Toma, and El Paraíso chapter.)

THE GREAT OUTDOORS

Wildlife Viewing

The Guadalajara region's most easily accessible wildlife habitats are the **Bosque de Primavera,** west of town, off of Hwy. 15; the **Barranca** north of town around Ixcatán, off of Hwy. 54, or west of town; near **Tequila** (around Balneario La Toma); or near **Tapalpa** (around the Las Piedrotas preserve). (See the Guadalajara Getaways chapter and the Zapopan section of the City: West and North of Downtown for access details.)

Look for wildlife by following a quiet side road or path away from the highway, and keep quiet and alert. Animal survival depends on them seeing you before you see them. Occasional spectacular sights, such as a big chickenlike **chacalaca** hiding in a tree, or the bright flash of a red, white, and green **flag bird** *(Trogon mexicanus),* or the radiant green of a big iguana, are the rewards of those prepared to recognize them.

Don't forget your binoculars and your Peterson's *Field Guide to Mexican Birds.* Also be prepared with a copy of John and Susy Pint's excellent *Outdoors in Western Mexico,* a book of weekend hiking adventures.

A local English-speaking naturalist guide, Jeremy Lusch leads visitors on Guadalajara-area nature walks and safaris. He especially recommends a trip to view the little-known colony of seawater crocodiles (some huge, up to a half a ton and 20 feet long) that nest in remote coastal mangrove lagoons. For more information, call tel. 33/3766-1829, or visit Jeremy's website: www.hummingbirdmex.com.

Hunting and Freshwater Fishing

Considerable game, especially winter-season waterfowl and doves, is customarily hunted in freshwater reservoirs and coastal marshes in the neighboring state of Sinaloa northwest of the Guadalajara region. Visitors driving or flying south to Guadalajara can arrange to hunt or fish for freshwater bass along the way. Some of the most popular hunting and fishing reservoirs are Domínguez and Hidalgo, near colonial El Fuerte town (an hour northeast of Los Mochis). Farther south, just north of Culiacán, is the López Mateos reservoir, while farther south still, Lago de Comedero lies two road hours north of Mazatlán or six hours north of Tepic.

On the Jalisco coast, near Puerto Vallarta, anglers report rewarding catches of freshwater bass at the **Cajon de Peñas reservoir,** about an hour's drive south of Puerto Vallarta town.)

Bag limits and seasons for game are carefully controlled by the government's Secretary of Social Development (Secretaría de Desarrollo Social), SEDESOL. It and the Mexican consular service jointly issue the required permits through a time-consuming and costly procedure which, at minimum, runs for months and costs hundreds of dollars.

Private fee agencies are a must to complete the mountain of required paperwork. Among the most experienced is the **Wildlife Advisory Service,** P.O. Box 76132, Los Angeles, CA 90076; tel. 2133/3385-9311, fax 2133/3385-0782.

For many useful hunting and fishing details, including many sites and lodges throughout Northern Mexico, get a copy of Sanborn's *Mexico Recreational Guide to Mexico,* published by Sanborn's insurance agency. Order with credit card ($15.95, plus postage and handling) by phoning 800/222-0158 or by writing Sanborn's, P.O. Box 310, McAllen, TX 78502.

BULLFIGHTING

It is said there are two occasions for which Mexicans arrive on time: funerals and bullfights.

Bullfighting is a recreation, not a sport. The bull is outnumbered seven to one, and the outcome is never in doubt. Even if the matador (literally, "killer") fails in his duty, his assistants will entice the bull away and slaughter it in private beneath the stands.

La Corrida de Toros

Moreover, Mexicans don't call it a "bullfight;" it's the *corrida de toros,* during which six bulls are customarily slaughtered, beginning at 5 P.M. (4 P.M. in the winter). After the beginning parade, featuring the matador and his helpers, the *picadores* and the *bandilleras,* the first bull rushes into the ring in a cloud of dust. Clockwork *tercios* (thirds) define the ritual: the first, the *puyazos,* or "stabs," requires that two *picadores* on horseback thrust lances into the bull's shoulders, weakening it. During the second *tercio,* the *bandilleras* dodge the bull's horns to stick three long, streamer-laden darts into its shoulders.

Trumpets announce the third *tercio* and the appearance of the matador. The bull—weak, confused, and angry—is ready for the finish. The matador struts, holding the red cape, daring the bull to charge. Form now becomes everything. The expert matador takes complete control of the bull, which rushes at the cape, past its ramrod-erect opponent. For charge after charge, the matador works the bull to exactly the right spot in the ring—in front of the judges, a lovely señorita, or perhaps the governor—where the matador mercifully delivers the precision *estocada* (killing sword thrust) deep into the drooping neck of the defeated bull.

ENTERTAINMENT AND EVENTS

Guadalajarans love to party; so much so that parties *(fiestas)* are institutionalized. There seems to be a celebration—saint's day, country agricultural fair, old-fashioned small-town circus and carnival, pilgrimage, rodeolike *charreada*—occurring somewhere in and around Guadalajara every day.

Guadalajara's biggest party is the October 12 **Fiesta de la Virgin de Zapopan,** when a million Guadalajarans fill the streets to accompany their beloved "La Generala" (as the image is popularly known) from the downtown cathedral to her home in the basilica in Zapopan.

In addition to the annual fiestas, Guadalajarans enjoy a steady menu of artistic and cultural events—folkloric and modern dance, symphonic concerts, art expositions, art films, lectures—at locations such as the celebrated **Teatro Degollado** and the **Instituto Cultural Cabañas** on downtown Plaza Tapatío. For details, see the Arts and Entertainment section of the *Guadalajara Colony Reporter* newspaper.

Moreover, Guadalajara is brimming with less formal entertainments, such as mariachi shows, jazz and rock 'n' roll concerts, and oldies-but-goodies dance clubs. For details, pick up a copy of the *Guadalajara Colony Reporter,* and refer to the restaurant and entertainment sections of this book.

SHOPPING
What to Buy

Although bargains abound in Guadalajara, savvy shoppers are selective. Steep import and luxury taxes drive up the prices of foreign-made goods such as professional-grade cameras, computers, sports equipment, and English-language books. Instead, concentrate your shopping on locally made items: leather, jewelry, cotton resort wear, Mexican-made designer clothes, and the galaxy of handicrafts for which Mexico is renowned.

Guadalajara is a magnet for buyers of handicrafts. The major sources, the suburban villages of Tlaquepaque and Tonalá, each nurture vibrant traditions with roots in the pre-Columbian past. This rich cornucopia, the product of hundreds of family workshops and factories, fills dozens of shops, not only in Tlaquepaque and Tonalá, but also in the city at large, including the grand Mercado Libertad in downtown Guadalajara and a number of stores and weekly outdoor markets. (For more details, see Weekly Outdoor Markets, later in this chapter, Handicrafts, earlier, and the Shopping sections throughout this book.)

How to Buy

Credit cards, such as VISA, MasterCard, and, to a lesser extent, American Express, are widely honored in the hotels and boutiques that cater to well-heeled customers. Although convenient, such shops' offerings will be generally higher-priced than those of stores in the older downtown districts that depend more on local trade. Local shops sometimes offer discounts for cash purchases.

Bargaining will stretch your money even farther. It comes with the territory in Mexico and needn't be a hassle. On the contrary, if done with humor and moderation, bargaining can be an enjoyable way to meet (and even befriend) people.

The handicrafts market stalls are where bargaining is most intense. For starters, try offering half the asking price. From there on, it's all psychology: You have to content yourself with not having to have the item. Otherwise, you're sunk; the vendor will sense your need and stand fast. After a few minutes of good-humored bantering, ask for *el último precio* (the final price), which, if it's close, just may be a bargain.

Buying Silver and Gold Jewelry

Silver and gold jewelry, the finest of which is crafted in Taxco, Guerrero, and Guadalajara, fills a number of Guadalajara regional (especially Tlaquepaque) shops. One hundred percent pure silver is rarely sold because it's too soft. Silver (sent from processing mills in the north of Mexico to be worked in Taxco shops) is nearly always alloyed with 7.5 percent copper to increase its durability. Such pieces, identical in composition to sterling silver, should bear the mark ".925," together with the initials of the manufacturer, stamped on their back sides. Other, less common grades, such as "800 fine" (80 percent silver), should also be stamped.

If silver is not stamped with the degree of purity, it probably contains no silver at all and is an alloy of copper, zinc, and nickel, known by the generic label "alpaca" or "German" silver. Once, after haggling over the purity and prices of his offerings, a street vendor handed me a shiny handful and said, "Go to a jeweler and have them tested. If they're not real, keep them." Calling his bluff, I took them to a jeweler, who applied a dab of hydrochloric acid to each piece. Tiny, telltale bubbles of hydrogen revealed the cheapness of the merchandise, which I returned the next day to the vendor.

Some shops price sterling silver jewelry simply by weighing, which typically translates to about $1.25 per gram. If you want to find out if the price is fair, ask the shopkeeper to weigh it for you.

People prize pure **gold** partly because, unlike silver, it does not tarnish. Gold, nevertheless, is rarely sold pure (24 karat); for durability, it is alloyed with copper. Typical purities, such as 18 karat (75 percent) or 14 karat (58 percent), should be stamped on the pieces. If not, chances are they contain no gold at all.

Weekly Outdoor Markets

Guadalajarans' irrepressible commercial urge blossoms forth with *tianguis* (Aztec for "awning") weekly markets in certain neighborhoods of town. They're sure to be set up and running by at least 10 A.M., rain or shine: The **Antique Market,** Sundays, spreads along Av. Mexico, just west of Av. Chapultepec; a few blocks north of that, around Av. Angulo, the **Santa Teresita Market,** also on Sunday, offers a little bit of everything except food.

Also operating on Sunday is the **Artist's Market,** at Chapalita Circle, intersection of Avenidas Guadalupe and de las Rosas; furthermore, in the same southwest quarter of town, is the big Friday **Clothes Market** on Av. Copernicus, between Avenidas Tepeyac and Moctezuma. Even farther southwest, is the country-style Thursday **Santa Anita Market,** in Santa Anita village, west of

Av. López Mateos, about four miles (seven km) south of the *periférico* (peripheral) boulevard.

Supermarkets and Department Stores

Several branches of big Mexican chains—**Gigante, Aurrera,** and **Comercial Mexicana**—serve Guadalajara shoppers with everything from groceries and meats and produce to auto tires and baby clothes.

Guadalajaras' department stores of choice are **Sears-Roebuck, Fábricas de Francia,** and **Suburbia.** A walk along their calm, air-conditioned aisles seems like a journey back to the 1950s, complete with elevator music and plenty of counter clerks. Find them mostly in the shopping malls.

Shopping Malls and Warehouse Stores

Several American-style shopping malls have sprouted in Guadalajara's west-side suburbs since the 1970s. **Plaza del Sol,** on Av. López Mateos, in the southwest suburb, was the first and remains very successful, anchored by Fábricas de Francia and Suburbia and an eclectic swarm of smaller stores.

Although showing its age, **Plaza Patria,** on Guadalajara's northwest side, at the corner of Avenidas Patria and de las Americas, is still popular, with Fábricas de Francia and Suburbia branches and a brigade of smaller shops.

Guadalajara's hottest new malls are **Centro Magno,** between Avenidas Vallarta and Cotilla in the closer-in Minerva-Chapultepec district, and **Centro Pabellón** on the far northwest side, corner of Avenidas Patria and Acueducto. With no department store anchors, these enclosed single-building complexes abound with designer boutiques on the lower floors and a big youth entertainment complexes—video game arcade, food court, and cinemaplex—on the top floors.

Shoppers can enjoy the best of both worlds at the huge, newish, multistory enclosed **Gran Plaza** mall, farther west, on Av. Vallarta, about halfway between the Minerva Fountain and the *periférico* boulevard. Here, both Sears-Roebuck and Fábricas de Francia, and a big multiscreen movie complex, video game arcade, and fast-food court, plus a swarm of upscale boutiques, divert a legion of young customers.

Gran Plaza has attracted U.S. warehouse chains to locate nearby. Just east of Gran Plaza, on Av. Vallarta's south side, are **Wal-Mart** (tel. 33/3673-2451 and 33/3673-2067) and **Sam's Club,** while west of Gran Plaza, on Av. Vallarta's opposite side, is **Price Club,** tel. 33/3629-8700 and 33/3629-8703.(For many more details of shopping malls, see the shopping sections of the City: West and North of Downtown chapter.)

Other Practicalities

TOURIST PERMITS AND VISAS

For U.S. and Canadian citizens, entry by air into Mexico for a few weeks could hardly be easier. Airline attendants hand out tourist permits *(permisos turísticos)* en route and officers make them official by glancing at passports and stamping the cards at the immigration gate. Business travel permits for 30 days or less are handled by the same simple procedures.

Entry is not entirely painless, however. The Mexican government currently charges an approximate $20 fee per person for a tourist permit. For air and bus travelers, this is no problem, since the fee is automatically included in the fare. The fee can be a bit of a hassle for drivers, however. At this writing the government does not allow collection of the fee by border immigration officers. Instead, the officers issue a form that you must take to a bank, where you pay the fee. For multiple entries this can get complicated and time-consuming.

In addition to the entry fee, Mexican immigration states that all entering U.S. citizens must present proof of citizenship—either a valid U.S. passport, an official copy of an original birth certificate, or military ID—while naturalized citizens must show naturalization papers or a valid U.S. passport.

Canadian citizens must show a valid passport or original birth certificate. Nationals of other countries (especially those such as Hong Kong, which issue more than one type of passport) may be subject to different or additional regulations. For advice, consult your regional Mexico Tourism Board office or consulate. For more Mexico-entry details, visit the Mexico Tourism Board's website: www.visitmexico.com, or better yet, call toll-free 800/44MEXICO.

More Options

For more complicated cases, get your tourist permit early enough to allow you to consider the options. Tourist permits can be issued for multiple entries and a maximum validity of 180 days; photos are often required. If you don't request multiple entry or the maximum time, your card will probably be stamped single entry, valid for some shorter period, such as 90 days. If you are not sure how long you'll stay in Mexico, request the maximum. (One hundred eighty days is the absolute maximum for a tourist permit; long-term foreign residents routinely make semiannual "border runs" for new tourist permits.)

Student and Business Visas

A visa is a notation stamped and signed on your passport showing the number of days and entries allowable for your trip. Apply for a student visa at the consulate nearest your home well in advance of your departure; the same is true if you require a business visa of longer than 30 days. Longer-term renewable business and student visas are available (sometimes with considerable red tape). In most cases, the easiest business or student option is to obtain an ordinary 180-day tourist permit and, if you need more time, make a quick round-trip border run for a new 180-day permit.

Your Passport

Your passport (or birth or naturalization certificate) is your positive proof of national identity; without it, your status in any foreign country is in doubt. Don't leave home without one. U.S. citizens may obtain passports (allow four to six weeks) at local post offices.

MEXICO TOURISM BOARD OFFICES

M ore than a dozen Mexico Tourism Board offices and scores of Mexican government consulates operate in the United States. Consulates generally handle questions of Mexican nationals in the United States, while Mexico Tourism Boards serve travelers heading for Mexico. For simple questions and Mexico regional information brochures, dial 800/44MEXICO (800/446-3942) from the United States or Canada or visit their website: www.visitmexico.com.

Otherwise, contact one of the North American regional or European Mexico Tourism Boards for guidance:

In North America

From Arizona, California, Colorado, Hawaii, Idaho, Montana, Nevada, New Mexico, and Utah, contact **Los Angeles:** 2401 W. 6th St., Fifth Floor, Los Angeles, CA 90057; tel. 213/351-2069, fax 213/351-2074.

From Alaska, Washington, Oregon, Idaho, Wyoming, Montana, and the Canadian Provinces of British Columbia, Alberta, Yukon, Northwest Territories, and Saskatchewan, contact **Vancouver:** 999 W. Hastings St., Suite 1110, Vancouver, B.C. V6C 2W2, tel. 604/669-2845, fax 604/669-3498.

From Texas, Oklahoma, and Louisiana, contact **Houston:** 4507 San Jacinto, Suite 308, Houston TX 77004; tel. 713/772-2581, fax 713/772-6058

From Alabama, Arkansas, Florida, Georgia, Mississippi, Tennessee, North Carolina, and South Carolina, contact **Miami:** 1200 NW 78th Ave. #203, Miami FL 33126-1817; tel. 305/718-4091, fax 305/718-4098.

From Illinois, Indiana, Iowa, Kansas, Michigan, Minnesota, Missouri, Nebraska, North Dakota, Ohio, South Dakota, and Wisconsin, contact **Chicago:** 300 North Michigan Ave., 4th Floor, Chicago, IL 60601; tel. 312/606-9252, fax 312/606-9012.

From Connecticut, Delaware, Kentucky, Maine, Maryland, Massachusetts, New Hampshire, New Jersey, New York, Pennsylvania, Rhode Island, and Vermont, Virginia, Washington D.C., and West Virginia, contact **New York:** 21 E. 63rd St., 3rd Floor, New York, NY 10021; tel. 212/821-0313 or 212/821-0314, fax 212/821-3067.

From Ontario and Manitoba, contact **Toronto:** 2 Bloor St. West, Suite 1502, Toronto, Ontario M4W 3E2, tel. 416/925-2753, fax 416/925-6061.

From New Brunswick, Newfoundland, Nova Scotia, Prince Edward Island, and Quebec, contact **Montreal:** 1 Place Ville Marie, Suite 1931, Montreal, Quebec H3B2C3, tel. 514/871-1052 or 514/871-1103, fax 514/871-3825.

In Europe

Mexico also maintains Mexico Tourism Boards throughout Western Europe:

London: Wakefield House, 41 Trinity Square, London EC3N 4DT, England, UK, tel. 207/488-9392, fax 207/265-0704.

Frankfurt: Weisenhuttenplatz 26, 60329 Frankfurt-am-Main, Deutschland, tel. (69) 25-3509, fax (69) 25-3755.

Paris: 4, Rue Notre-Dame des Victoires, 75002 Paris, France, tel. (1) 426-15180, fax (1) 428-60580.

Madrid: Calle Velzquez 126, 28006 Madrid, España, tel. (91) 561-1827, fax (91) 411-0759.

Rome: Via Barbarini 3-piso 7, 00187 Roma, Italia, tel. (6) 487-2182, fax (6) 487-3630.

ON THE ROAD

Entry for Children

Children under 18 may be included on their parents' tourist permits, but complications occur if the children (by reason of illness, for example) cannot leave Mexico with both parents. Parents should avoid such red tape by getting a passport and a Mexican tourist permit for each of their children.

In addition to passport or birth certificate, minors (under age 18) entering Mexico without parents or legal guardians must present a notarized letter of permission signed by both parents or legal guardians. Even if accompanied by one parent, a notarized permission letter from the other must be presented. Divorce or death certificates must also be presented, when applicable.

Guadalajara-bound travelers should hurdle all such possible delays far ahead of time in the cool calm of their local Mexican consulate rather than the hot, hurried atmosphere of a border or airport immigration station.

Bringing Belongings to Mexico

A person may bring a reasonable quantity of articles for personal use into Mexico. Rules include the following: one video, movie, or still camera and 12 rolls of film or videocassettes, books and magazines, medicines, and a portable computer.

If you are **not** a resident of Mexico, you can add a pair of binoculars, a small portable TV, a portable radio or tape recorder, two laser disks, 20 CDs or music tapes, a typewriter, a musical instrument, a tent and camping equipment, a set of fishing gear, a pair of water skis, five toys, scuba equipment, and a VCR. Guns for hunting purposes may be brought into Mexico, but only with the required difficult-to-obtain permits.

Entry for Pets

Pets may be brought into Mexico, if accompanied by an up-to-date certificate of good health (an official U.S. Deptartment of Agriculture form; veterinarians have them) and (for mammals) a current rabies vaccination certificate. For exact details, best consult the Mexico Tourism Board, tel. 800/44MEXICO, or visit their website: www.visitmexico.com.

Don't Lose Your Tourist Permit

If you do, go to **Migración** (the federal immigration office) at the Guadalajara airport at least

---

ROAD SAFETY

Hundreds of thousands of visitors enjoy safe Mexican auto vacations every year. Their success is due in large part to their frame of mind: Drive defensively, anticipate and adjust to danger before it happens, and watch everything—side roads, shoulders, the car in front, and cars far down the road. The following tips will help ensure a safe and enjoyable trip:

Don't drive at night. Range animals, unmarked sand piles, pedestrians, one-lane bridges, cars without lights, and drunk drivers are doubly hazardous at night.

Although **speed limits** are rarely enforced, *don't break them*. Mexican roads are often narrow and shoulder-less. Poor markings and macho drivers who pass on curves are best faced at a speed of 40 mph (64 kph) rather than 75 mph.

Don't drive on sand. Even with four-wheel-drive, you'll eventually get stuck if you drive either often or casually on beaches. When the tide comes in, who'll pull your car out?

Slow down at the *topes* (speed bumps) at the edges of towns and for *vados* (dips), which can be dangerously bumpy and full of water.

Extending the **courtesy of the road** goes hand-in-hand with safe driving. Both courtesy and machismo are more infectious in Mexico; on the highway, it's much safer to spread the former than the latter.

3–4 hours (or, to be sure, a day or two) before your departure and ask for a duplicate tourist permit. Be prepared to show proof of your arrival date, such as an airline ticket stub, your stamped passport, or a copy of your original tourist permit. Savvy travelers carry copies of their passports, tourist permits, car permits, and Mexican auto insurance policies, while leaving the originals in a hotel safe-deposit box.

Car Permits

If you drive to Mexico, you will need a permit for your car. Upon entry into Mexico, be ready with originals and copies of your proof-of-ownership or registration papers (state title certificate, registration, or notarized bill of sale), current license plates, and current driver's license. The auto permit fee runs about $15, payable only by non-Mexican bank MasterCard, VISA, or American Express credit cards. (The credit-card-only requirement discourages those who sell or abandon U.S.-registered cars in Mexico without paying customs duties.) Credit cards must bear the same name as the vehicle proof-of-ownership papers.

The resulting car permit becomes part of the owner's tourist permit and receives the same length of validity. Vehicles registered in the name of an organization or person other than the driver must be accompanied by a notarized affidavit authorizing the driver to use the car in Mexico for a specific time.

Border officials generally allow you to carry or tow additional motorized vehicles (motorcycle, another car, large boat) into Mexico but will require separate documentation and fee for each vehicle. If a Mexican official desires to inspect your trailer or RV, go through it with him.

Accessories, such as a small trailer, a boat shorter than six feet, CB radio, or outboard motor, may be noted on the car permit and must leave Mexico with the car.

For updates and details on documentation required for taking your car into Mexico, call the toll-free Mexican Tourism Board number in the U.S. and Canada, 800/44MEXICO. For many more details on motor vehicle entry and what you may bring in your baggage to Mexico, consult the AAA (American Automobile Associa-

tion) *Mexico TravelBook*. (See Suggested Reading at the end of this book.)

Since Mexico does not recognize foreign automobile insurance, you must purchase Mexican automobile insurance. (For more information on this and other details of driving in Mexico, see Getting There earlier in this chapter.)

Crossing the Border and Returning Home

Squeezing through border bottlenecks during peak holidays and rush hours can be time-consuming. Avoid crossing at 7–9 A.M. or 4:30–6:30 P.M.

Just before returning across the border with your car, park and have a customs *aduana* (official) remove and cancel the holographic identity sticker which you received on entry. If possible, get a receipt *(recibo)* or some kind of verification that it's been canceled *(cancelado)*. Tourists have been fined hundreds of dollars for inadvertently carrying uncanceled car entry stickers on their windshields.

At the same time, return all other Mexican permits, such as tourist permits and hunting and fishing licenses. Also, be prepared for Mexico exit inspection, especially for cultural artifacts and works of art, which may require exit permits. Certain religious and pre-Columbian artifacts, legally the property of the Mexican government, cannot be taken from the country.

If you entered Mexico with your car, you cannot legally leave without it except by permission from local customs authorities, usually the Aduana (Customs House) or the Oficina Federal de Hacienda (Federal Treasury Office). For local details, refer to the Services and Information sections throughout this book.

All returnees are subject to **U.S. customs inspection.** United States law allows a fixed value (presently $400) of duty-free goods per returnee. This may include no more than one liter of alcoholic spirits, 200 cigarettes, and 100 cigars. A flat 10 percent duty will be applied to the first $1,000 (fair retail value, save your receipts) in excess of your $400 exemption. You may, however, mail packages (up to $50 value each) of gifts duty-free to friends and relatives in the United States. Make sure to clearly write "unsolicited gift" and a list of the value and contents on the outside of the package. Perfumes (over $5), alcoholic beverages, and tobacco may not be included in such packages.

Improve the security of such mailed packages by sending them by **Mexpost** class, similar to U.S. Express Mail service. Even better (but much more expensive), send them by **Federal Express** or **DHL** international couriers, which maintain offices in Guadalajara.

For more information on customs regulations important to travelers abroad, write for a copy of the useful pamphlet *Know Before You Go,* from the U.S. Customs Service, P.O. Box 7047, Washington, D.C. 20044; tel. 877/287-8667.

Additional U.S. rules prohibit importation of certain fruits, vegetables, and domestic animal and endangered wildlife products. Certain live animal species, such as parrots, may be brought in, subject to a 30-day agricultural quarantine upon arrival, at the owner's expense. For more details on agricultural product and live animal importation, write for the free booklet *Travelers' Tips,* by the U.S. Department of Agriculture, Washington, D.C. 20250; tel. 202/720-2791. For more information on the importation of endangered wildlife products, contact the Wildlife Permit Office, U.S. Department of the Interior, Washington, D.C. 20240; tel. 202/208-4662.

MONEY
The Peso: Down and Up

Overnight in early 1993, the Mexican government shifted its monetary decimal point three places and created the "new" peso, which subsequently has deflated to about one-third of its initial value of three per dollar, to about nine or 10 per dollar. Since the peso value sometimes changes rapidly, U.S. dollars have become a much more stable indicator of Mexican prices; for this reason they are used in this book to report prices. Regardless, you should always use pesos to pay in Mexico—you'll usually end up paying a little less.

Since the introduction of the new peso, the centavo (one-hundredth of a new peso) has reappeared in coins of 10, 20, and 50 centavos.

Incidentally, the dollar sign, "$," also marks Mexican pesos. Peso coins, in denominations of 1, 2, 5, 10, and 20 and peso bills of 10, 20, 50, 100, and 200 pesos, are common. Since banks like to exchange your traveler's checks for a few crisp large bills rather than the often-tattered smaller denominations, ask for some of your change in 50-peso notes. A 200-peso note, while common at the bank, looks awfully big to a small shopkeeper, who might be hard-pressed to change it.

Banks, ATMs, and Money Exchange Offices

Mexican banks, like their North American counterparts, have lengthened their business hours. Banco Internacional (BITAL) maintains the longest hours: Mon.–Sat. 8 A.M.–7 P.M. Banamex (Banco Nacional de Mexico), generally the most popular with local people, usually posts the best in-town dollar exchange rate in its lobbies; for example, *"Tipo de cambio: venta 9.615, compra 9.720"* means they will sell pesos to you at the rate of 9.615 per dollar and buy them back for 9.720 per dollar.

ATMs (Automated Teller Machines) or *Cajeros Automáticos,* (kah-HEH-rohs out-toh-MAH-tee-kohs) are rapidly becoming the money source of choice in Mexico. Virtually every bank has a 24-hour ATM, accessible (with proper PIN identification code) by a swarm of U.S. and Canadian credit and ATM cards. All ATMs dispense pesos, while only some dispense U.S. dollars.

Since one-time bank charges for ATM cash are hardly negligible (typically about $3 per transaction), get as much the money you can (usually about $300 per day) from a single transaction.

Even without an ATM card, you don't have to go to the trouble of waiting in long bank service lines. Opt for a less-crowded bank, such as BBV–Bancomer, Banco Serfín, Banco Santander–Mexicano, Scotiabank Inverlat, Banco Internacional, or a private money-exchange office *(casa de cambio).* Often most convenient, such offices often offer long hours and faster service than the banks for a fee (as little as $.50 or as much as $3 per $100).

Keeping Your Money Safe

Traveler's checks, the universal prescription for safe money abroad, are widely accepted in the Guadalajara region. Even if you plan to use your ATM card, purchase some U.S. dollar traveler's checks (a well-known brand such as American Express or VISA) at least as an emergency reserve. Canadian traveler's checks and currency are not as widely accepted as U.S. traveler's checks. European and Asian checks are even less acceptable. Unless you like signing your name or paying lots of per-check commissions, buy denominations of $50 or more.

In Guadalajara, as everywhere, **thieves** circulate among the tourists. Keep valuables in your hotel *caja de seguridad* (security box). If you don't particularly trust the desk clerk, carry what you can't afford to lose in a money belt attached to your front side; pickpockets love crowded markets, buses, and airport terminals where they can slip a wallet out of a back pocket or dangling purse in a blink. In the absence of a money belt or waist pouch, guard against this by carrying your wallet in your front pocket, and your purse or daypack (which clever crooks can sometimes slit open) on your front side.

Don't attract thieves by displaying wads of money or flashy jewelry. Don't get sloppy drunk; if so, you may become a pushover for a determined thief.

Don't leave valuables unattended at the beach. Share security duties with trustworthy-looking neighbors, or leave a bag with a shopkeeper nearby.

Tipping

Without their droves of visitors, Mexican people would be even poorer. Deflation of the peso, while it makes prices low for outsiders, makes it rough for Mexican families to get by. The workers at your hotel typically get paid only a few dollars a day. They depend on tips to make the difference between dire and bearable poverty. Give the *camarista* (chambermaid) and floor attendant a couple of dollars (or 20 pesos) every day or two. And whenever uncertain of what to tip, it will probably mean a lot to someone—maybe a whole family—if you err on the generous side.

In restaurants and bars, Mexican tipping customs are similar to those in the United States and Europe: tip waiters, waitresses, and bartenders about 15 percent for satisfactory service.

Investing Your Money Locally

A loyal cadre of satisfied local investors recommend the services of **Lloyd Investment Funds,** Guadalajara main branch, near Plaza del Sol, tel. 33/3880-2000. Other local branches are at Lake Chapala, tel. 376/521-49 (in Chapala) and 376/631-10 (in Ajijic). For more details, see the Plaza del Sol section of City: West and South of Downtown chapter, and the Chapala and Ajijic sections of the Lake Chapala and Vicinity chapter.

DOING BUSINESS IN GUADALAJARA

As a growing legion of foreign companies have discovered, Guadalajara is a good place to do business. Although Jalisco is a Mexican leader in jewelry (50 percent of national sales), footwear (25 percent), clothing and textiles (US$600 million yearly), foreign tourism (12 percent of air arrivals), and handicrafts, Guadalajara's mushrooming **electronics** industry (US$8 billion exported in 2000) is attracting the most attention. The list of firms operating plants—Hewlitt-Packard, Texas Instruments, Intel, Fairchild, Logistix, Tektronics, Motorola, Panasonic, Redwood Systems, IBM, NEC, SCI, Pentex—reads like a who's who of high tech.

Meeting Facilities

Guadalajara is ready with world-class resources for business and professional visitors. The ace in the pack is the one-million-square-foot **Expo Guadalajara,** a superb place to meet, sell, and buy, built in 1987 and continuously updated since. Features include a 280,000-square-foot main exposition hall, a smaller 22,000-square-foot special events hall, a fully equipped business center, a swarm of private negotiating rooms, a 75,000 square-foot multiple-use auditorium—accommodating meetings from 200 to 3,000 persons—exterior patios, lobbies, a seeming mile of loading docks, a pair of fine restaurants, and a swarm of coffee shops and snack bars.

Expo Guadalajara hosts a continuous menu of meetings and exhibitions. Last year's schedule included about 150 events, with themes varying from ice cream and furniture to jewelry and books. (See special topic Expo Guadalajara in the City: West and North of Downtown chapter.)

Additionally, Guadalajara offers a host of fine hotel and other smaller meeting venues, ranging from the planetarium and art museums to the Degollado opera house and lovely old haciendas. For more information on all meeting facilities, visit the website: www.convenciones gdl.com.mx, of the **Guadalajara Convention and Visitors' Bureau** (Oficina de Convenciones y Visitantes). Ask for a copy of their excellent bilingual meeting planner's handbook, *Guadalajara Guide to Congresses, Expositions, and Conventions* ("La Guia Guadalajara de Congresos, Exposiciones, y Convenciones"). You can get more information several ways: in person at Av. Vallarta 4095, upstairs floor (in the Chamber of Commerce Building, past Gran Plaza shopping center, south side of the boulevard); tel. 33/3122-8711 or 33/3122-7544, fax 33/3122-8707; email: gdlovc@convencionesgdl.com.mx.

Business-Oriented Hotels

A number of Guadalajara luxury hotels that cater especially to business travelers deserve special mention. For their super-comfortable accommodations, private executive floors, extensive in-house business centers, and sizeable convention facilities, all for discounted commercial rates, consider the following: Right next to Expo Guadalajara is the down-to-business American-style **Hilton Guadalajara,** and the refined but more relaxed Mexican-style **Guadalajara Plaza Expo.** Within a five-minute taxi ride stand the equally down-to-business **Presidente Inter-Continental,** the charmingly intimate 16-room **Mansión del Sol,** and the regal but restful **Crowne Plaza Guadalajara** garden resort. Farther afield, but still within a 10-minute taxi ride, are the more spartan but still comfortable, mid-size **Holiday Inn Select;**

the high-rise commercial, at-your-service, **Fiesta Americana;** the relaxed, garden hotel **Camino Real,** queen of Guadalajara hostelries; and the class-act, luxury bed-and-breakfast **Casa Madonna.** (For details on all of these good choices, see Accommodations in the Plaza del Sol and Minerva-Chapultepec sections of the City: West and North of Downtown chapter.)

SETTLING IN GUADALAJARA

If you're considering pulling up stakes and moving to Guadalajara, help and advice will be easy to find among the many folks who've already done it. First of all, most folks who've moved to Guadalajara (nearly all American and Canadian retirees) will tell you to do it gradually. Try living in Guadalajara for a spell in a rented house or apartment to see if you like it. Get to know people, listen to their stories, and after six months (or preferably a year to experience all seasons) you'll be ready to make your choice.

In any case, Guadalajara's housing prices are certainly right. Rents for well-located apartments, suites, and houses run about half stateside city prices, for similar amenities. For example, expect to pay about $250 for a studio apartment in a middle-class Guadalajara neighborhood, or about $500 for a semi-deluxe two-bedroom apartment, $600–800 for a large unfurnished house, and $1000–1500 for a large luxurious apartment or house in an upper-class neighborhood.

As soon as (or even before) you arrive in Guadalajara, get copies of the excellent local English-language newspapers, the *Guadalajara Colony Reporter,* and the Lake Chapala area *El Ojo del Lago (Eye of the Lake.)* Both are chock-full of informative articles, event and organization listings, service advertisements, and real estate and rental listings. They're widely available. (For details on how to get a copy, see Finding a Long-Term Rental, in the Accommodations section, earlier.)

Helpful Local Organizations

Both of the newspapers above list local organizations of friendly folks, most of whom have experienced settling into Guadalajara. One of the

© BRUCE WHIPPERMAN

The Guadalajara Zoo is a great location for a family outing.

best organized is the **American Society of Jalisco** (AMSOC), which furnishes new members with a useful information packet and maintains a library, small cafe, community information board, and a busy schedule of educational and social events for members. Visit them at their center, tel. 33/3121-2395, at Av. San Francisco 3332, in the Chapalita neighborhood in the Guadalajara western suburb. (For more details, see the Chapalita section in the City: West and North of Downtown chapter.)

A similarly helpful Lake Chapala organization is the **Lake Chapala Society,** which can be contacted at its activities center, at 16 de Septiembre, in Ajijic, tel. 376/611-40.(For more details, see the Information section in the Lake Chapala and Vicinity chapter.)

Moreover, the **International Friendship Club of Guadalajara** has compiled a handy *Survival Guide to Guadalajara,* packed with useful recommendations, including emergency numbers, doctors, hospitals, services (such as TV repair, plumbing, and carpet cleaning), restaurants, hotels, and much more. Get your copy, customarily on sale for about $3, at the American Society of Jalisco's headquarters. For information on activities and membership in the International Friendship Club, contact former president Adele Vogt, tel. 33/3685-0423 or 33/3685-0445.

Many Guadalajara long-timers swear by the **American Legion,** which functions mostly as a social club, and a place to make friends. Both Lake Chapala and Guadalajara have active branches. For example, try the Guadalajara Alvarez Castillo Post 3, which maintains headquarters at San Antonio 143, in the Colonia Las Fuentes (turn right off Av. López Mateos at Av. de las Fuentes, about two miles, three km south of Plaza del Sol). You don't have to be a war veteran to be an active member. They hold monthly general meetings and regular dinner-dances, breakfasts, and other events. Contact them via tel. 33/3631-1208 or visit their website: www.americanlegion.com.

A raft of other organizations, such as the **Hash House Harriers, Amigos del Lago** (Friends of the Lake), **Grupo Amigos, Rotary Club, Gamblers Anonymous, Masons,** and **Navy League** cordially invite participation by newcomers. See the community calendar events pages of the *Guadalajara Colony Reporter* and *El Ojo del Lago* for specifics.

Relocation Services

Personable Guadalajara relocation specialists **Sandy Brown and Mark Kunce** have teamed up to help people settle into Guadalajara or Lake Chapala. They inherited the relocation service of now-deceased long-timers Fran and Judy Furton, and christened it **R&R in Mexico** during the mid-1990s. Many satisfied customers have since used their services, including tours of sights and neighborhoods and reasonably priced consultations and advice on rentals, real estate, hotels, restaurants, organizations, medical care, investments, and much more. Sandy and Mark's consultations always include a copy of *R&R in Mexico,* their excellent relocation guide.

For more information, log on to their website: www.rr-mexico.com or contact them by telephone directly in Guadalajara, tel. 33/3121-2348. You can also email them at either info@rr-mexico.hypermart.net or tours@rr-mexico.hypermart.net., or write Mark Kunce, P.O. Box 437090, San Ysidro, CA 92143-7090.

Buying a Home in Guadalajara

Thousands of former U.S. and Canadian residents have happily settled and bought homes in the Guadalajara region. Once you decide to take that step, best get a recommendation of a good real estate agent from your local friends. An agent will explain the details that, while generally similar, do differ in important aspects with the rules for buying a U.S. or Canadian home.

BRINGING THE KIDS TO GUADALAJARA

Children in Mexico are treasured like gifts from heaven. Traveling with kids will ensure your welcome most everywhere. On the beach, take extra precautions to make sure they are protected from the sun.

Of course, a sick child is no fun for anyone. Fortunately, clinics and good doctors are available even in small towns. When in need, ask a storekeeper or a pharmacist, *"¿Dónde hay un doctor, por favor?"* ("Where is there a doctor, please?"). In most cases, you'll be in the waiting room of the local physician or hospital in no time.

Children who do not favor typical Mexican fare can easily be fed with always available eggs, cheese, *hamburguesas,* milk, oatmeal, corn flakes, bananas, cakes, and cookies.

Your children will generally have more fun if they have a little previous knowledge of Mexico and a stake in the trip. For example, help them select some library picture books and magazines so they'll know where they're going and what to expect; or give them responsibility for packing and carrying their own small travel bag.

Be sure to mention your children's ages when making air reservations; child discounts of 50 percent or more are often available. Also, if you can arrange to go on an uncrowded flight, you can stretch out and rest on the empty seats.

Family Outings

Guadalajara has plenty of fun places where adults and kids can share a good time. In general, family entertainment spots are more tranquil and relaxing in midweek, in contrast to the crowded weekends and holidays.

Some sunny day, take the kids to a **balneario,** often (but not always) a natural spring beneath great old trees where people have sought the healing waters for centuries (see special topic Balnearios in this chapter).

Guadalajara's kids enjoy a world-class **zoo and amusement park** (the "Magic Jungle"—Selva Mágica, at the north edge of town, end of Calzado Independencia). Bring a picnic and spend the day tripping along the winding paths, past the yawning crocodiles and snoozing turtles in the reptile house, through the leafy aviary and into the "Heart of Africa." Be sure to make your way to the zoo's airy downhill end, and take a break at a picnic table overlooking the vast green panorama of the canyon of the Río Santiago (here, called the "Barranca de Huentitán.")

Later, exit the zoo's west gate to the adjacent Selva Mágica and enjoy the roller coaster and dozens of other rides, plus slides, hot dogs, and video games. The zoo (tel. 33/3674-4488, 33/3674-1162) is open Wed.–Sun. 10 A.M.–6 P.M.; the Selva Mágica (tel. 33/3674-0138, 33/3674-1418), Mon.–Fri. 10 A.M.–6 P.M.; Sat., Sun., and school holidays 10 A.M.–8 P.M. (Unfortunately, the nearby planetarium and science center is sorely in need of renovation; tel. 33/3673-4106. Open Tues.–Sun. 9 A.M.–7 P.M.)

A number of **Guadalajara's several parks,** most in the affluent west-side districts, are fine spots to turn the kids loose. Closest in is **Parque Agua Azul,** corner of González Gallo and Independencia on the south side of downtown, where visitors enjoy plenty of shaded strollable green grassy spaces, plus an orchid house, bird house, butterfly house, and a tropical plant nursery. Open Tues.–Sun. 10 A.M.–6 P.M.

Families find plenty of space for wandering in northwest-side **Parque Colomos** forest reserve, replete with acres of shade, lawns, creeks, a "Lake of the Birds," a Japanese garden, horseback riding, a cactus garden, and a number of picnic areas. Find it on Av. de la Patria, entrance between Avenidas Acueducto and Americas.

Teenagers, on the other hand, might enjoy the genteel and clean **Disco Roller** roller rink (with play area for little ones), plus video games and snacks. Find it at the corner of López Mateos Sur 4537, across from the Office Depot. Open Tues.–Sat. 2:30-9 P.M., Sun. 11 A.M.–9 P.M.; tel. 33/3631-5981.

On another day make an excursion to the very pleasant **Iceland** ice-skating rink at Av. Mexico 2582, just east of Av. López Mateos Norte. Besides skating, one admission gets you skate rental and free video games. Skating sessions are in one-hour time blocks, beginning daily at 9:40 and 11:00 A.M., and 12:20, 1:40, 4:20, 5:40, 7, and 9 P.M. respectively; tel. 33/3615-7818 or 33/3615-4438 for confirmation.

For more details on traveling with children, check out *Adventuring with Children* by Nan Jeffries (see Suggested Reading at the end of this book).

SPECIALTY TRAVEL
Travel for the Handicapped
Mexican airlines and hotels are becoming increasingly aware of the needs of travelers with disabilities. Open, street-level lobbies and large, wheelchair-accessible elevators and rooms are available in most Guadalajara resort hotels.

U.S. law forbids travel discrimination against otherwise qualified persons with disabilities. As long as your health is stable and not liable to deteriorate during passage, you can expect to be treated like any passenger with special needs.

Make reservations far ahead of departure and ask your agent to inform your airline of your needs, such as a boarding wheelchair or in-flight oxygen. Be early at the gate in order to take advantage of the pre-boarding call.

For many helpful details to smooth your trip, get a copy of *Traveling Like Everyone Else: A Practical Guide for Disabled Travelers* by Jacqueline Freedman and Susan Gersten. It's presently out of print but hopefully will soon be available at bookstores or from the publisher (see Suggested Reading at the end of this book). Also useful is *The Wheelchair Traveler,* by Douglas R. Annand. Yet another helpful publication is the *The Air Carrier Access Act: Make it Work For You,* by the Paralyzed Veterans of America; call toll-free 888/860-7244.

Certain organizations both encourage and provide information about disabled travel. One with many Mexican connections is **Mobility International USA** (P.O. Box 10767, Eugene, OR 97440; tel. 541/343-1284 voice/TDD, fax 541/343-6812; website: www.miusa.org). A $35 membership gets you a semiannual newsletter and referrals for international exchanges and homestays.

Similarly, **Partners of the Americas** (1424 K St. NW, Suite 700, Washington, D.C. 20005; tel. 800/322-7844 and 202/628-3300), with chapters in 45 U.S. states, works to increase understanding of people with disabilities, and consequently improve facilities in Mexico and Latin America. They maintain lists of local organizations and individuals whom travelers may contact at their destinations.

Travel for Senior Citizens
Age, according to Mark Twain, is a question of mind over matter: If you don't mind, it doesn't matter. Mexico is a country where entire extended families, from babies to great-grandparents, live together. Elderly travelers will benefit from the respect and understanding Mexicans

accord to older people. Besides these encouragements, consider the number of retirees already happily settled in havens in and around Guadalajara and Lake Chapala.

Certain organizations support senior travel. Leading the field is **Elderhostel** (75 Federal St., 3rd Fl., Boston, MA 02110-1941, tel. 877/426-8056. website: www.elderhostel.org), which publishes extensive U.S. and international catalogs of special tours, study, homestays, and people-to-people travel programs (see also Copper Canyon Tours and Special Tours and Study Options, earlier in this chapter).

A number of newsletters publicize Guadalajara region vacation and retirement opportunities. Among the best is *Adventures in Mexico,* published six times yearly and filled with pithy hotel, restaurant, touring, and real estate information for independent travelers and retirees seeking the "real" Mexico. For information and subscriptions, address Adventures in Mexico, c/o Lloyd Guadalajara (Mark Kunce), P.O. Box 437090, San Ysidro, CA, 92143-7090; in Mexico, write P.O. Box 31-70, Guadalajara, Jalisco 45050, Mexico. Back issues are $2; one-year subscription runs US $18.

Several books and newsletters publicize senior travel opportunities in general. *Mature Traveler* is a lively, professional-quality newsletter featuring money-saving tips, discounts, and tours for over-50 active senior and disabled travelers. Individual copies are $3, a one-year subscription $31.95. Editor Adele Mallot has compiled years of past newsletters and experience into the *Book of Deals,* a 150-page travel tip and opportunity book, which sells for $7.95, plus postage and handling. Order with a credit card by calling 800/460-6676, U.S. number 916/923-6346, or writing John Stickler Publishing Group, P.O. Box 15791, Sacramento, CA 95852. Another good buy is the pamphlet *Complete Guide to Discounts for Travelers 50 and Beyond* and the book *Special Report for Discount Travelers,* which list a plethora of hotel, travel club, cruise, air, credit card, single, and off-season discounts. (Order them for $6 and $17 respectively, from Vacation Publications, Inc., 1502 Augusta, Suite 415, Houston, TX 77057; tel. 7133/3974-6903; website: www .vacationsmagazine.com).

COMMUNICATIONS

Using Mexican Telephones

Although Mexican phone service is improving, it's still sometimes hit-or-miss. If a number doesn't get through, you may have to redial it more than once. When someone answers (usually *"Bueno,"* not *"Hola")* be especially courteous. If your Spanish is rusty, say, *"¿Por favor, habla inglés?"* ("Please, do you speak English?"). If you want to speak to a particular person (such as María), ask, *"¿María se encuentra?"* ("Is María there?"—literally, "Have you encountered María?").

Mexican phones operate more or less the same as in the United States and Canada. Mexican phone numbers have changed frequently in recent years because the Mexican telephone system is growing rapidly. A complete telephone number (in Guadalajara, for example) is generally written like this: 33/3817-2822. As in the United States, the "33" denotes the telephone *lada* (area code), and the "3817-2822" is the number that you dial locally. If you want to **dial this number within Mexico long-distance** first dial "01" (like dialing "1" before the area code in the United States), then "33/3817-2822."

Nearly all *ladas* in Mexico have three numbers (such as 322/ for Puerto Vallarta or 328/ for San Blas). Three large cities only—Guadalajara (*lada* 33/), Mexico City (*lada* 55/) and Monterrey—have two-number *ladas.* Local phone numbers of Guadalajara, Mexico City, and Monterrey contain eight digits; all other local phone numbers contain seven. In this book, the *lada* is included with each phone number listed.

Calling Mexico from the United States

To call Mexico direct from the United States, first dial 011 (for international access), then 52 (for Mexico), followed by the *lada* (area code) and local number. Some Guadalajara regional *ladas* are: Guadalajara, Zapopan, Tlaquepaque, and Tonalá 33/; San Juan de los Lagos 378/; Mazamitla 353/; Tapalpa 343/; Chapala and Aji-

CALLING MEXICO AND CALLING HOME

1. Call Mexico from the United States by first dialing "011-52" (the international access and country codes), then the Mexican area code ("33" for Guadalajara), then the local number (eight digits for Guadalajara, such as 3653-4552).

2. Call the United States from Mexico by first dialing "001," then the area code and local number.

3. The cheapest and often the most convenient way of telephoning in Mexico is by using the economical Ladatel public telephone cards, widely purchasable and usable in town public telephones.

4. Call long-distance numbers in Mexico by first dialing "01," then the *"lada"* (area code), then the local number.

ON THE ROAD

jic 376/; Tequila and Magdalena 374/; and Puerto Vallarta 322/.

Dialing in Guadalajara

In Guadalajara region towns and cities, direct long-distance *(larga distancia)* dialing is the rule—from hotels, public phone booths, and efficient private Computel telephone offices. The **cheapest and often most convenient way to call** is by purchasing and using a **public telephone ("Ladatel") card.** Buy them in 20-, 30-, 50-, and 100-peso denominations at the many outlets—mini-markets, pharmacies, liquor stores—that display the blue and yellow Ladatel sign.

For station-to-station calls to the United States, dial 001 plus the area code and the local number. For calls to other countries, ask your hotel desk clerk or see the easy-to-follow directions in the front of the local Mexican telephone directory.

Another convenient way (although a more expensive one) to call home is via your personal telephone credit card. Contact your U.S. long-distance operator by dialing 800/462-4240 for AT&T; 800/674-6000 for MCI; or 800/877-8000 for Sprint.

Another convenient, but also expensive, way of calling home is collect. You can do this in one of two ways. Simply dial 09 for the local English-speaking international operator; or dial the AT&T, MCI, and Sprint numbers listed in the previous paragraph.

Beware of certain private "call the U.S. with your VISA or MasterCard" telephones installed prominently in airports, tourist hotels, and shops. Tariffs on these phones can run as high as $10 a minute. If you do use such a phone, always ask the operator for the rate, and if it's too high, take your business elsewhere.

In smaller towns, you must often do your long-distance phoning in the *larga distancia* (local phone office). Typically staffed by a young woman and often connected to a cafe, the *larga distancia* becomes an informal community social center as people pass the time waiting for their phone connections. (See the special topic Calling Mexico and Calling Home.)

Post and Telegraph

Mexican *correos* (post offices) operate similarly, but more slowly and less securely than their counterparts in most parts of the world. Mail services usually include *lista de correo* (general delivery, address letters *"a/c lista de correo,"*), *servicios filatelicas* (philatelic services), *por avión* (airmail), *giros* (postal money orders), and Mexpost secure and fast delivery service, usually from separate Mexpost offices.

Mexican ordinary mail is sadly unreliable and

pathetically slow. If, for mailings within Mexico, you must have security, use the efficient, reformed government **Mexpost** (like U.S.P.S. Express Mail) service. For international mailings, check the local Yellow Pages for widely available **DHL** or **Federal Express** courier service.

Telégrafos (telegraph offices), usually near the post office, send and receive *telegramas* (telegrams) and *giros*. *Telecomunicaciones* (Telecom), the new high-tech telegraph offices, add telephone and public fax to the available services.

Electricity and Time

Mexican electric power is supplied at U.S.-standard 110 volts, 60 cycles. Plugs and sockets are generally two-pronged, nonpolar (like the pre-1970s U.S. ones). Bring adapters if you're going to use appliances with polar two-pronged or three-pronged plugs. A two-pronged polar plug has different-sized prongs, one of which is too large to plug into an old-fashioned nonpolar socket.

The Guadalajara region and all of the state of Jalisco operates on central time (although the bordering state of Nayarit, west of Jalisco, operates on mountain time). When traveling by highway east from Nayarit into Jalisco toward Guadalajara, set your watch ahead one hour.

Mexican businesses and government offices sometimes use the 24-hour system to tell time. Thus, a business that posts its hours as 0800–1700 is open 8 A.M.–5 P.M. When speaking, however, people customarily use the 12-hour system.

STAYING HEALTHY

In Guadalajara, as everywhere, prevention is the best remedy for illness. For visitors who confine their travel to the beaten path, a few common sense precautions will ensure vacation enjoyment.

Resist the temptation to dive headlong into Mexico. It's no wonder that people get sick—broiling in the sun, gobbling peppery food, guzzling beer and margaritas, then discoing half the night—all in their first 24 hours. An alternative is to give your body time to adjust. Travelers often arrive tired and dehydrated from travel and heat. During the first few days, drink plenty of bottled water and juice, and take siestas.

Traveler's Diarrhea

Traveler's diarrhea (known in Southeast Asia as "Bali Belly" and in Mexico as "turista" or "Montezuma's Revenge") sometimes persists, even among prudent vacationers. You can suffer turista for a week after simply traveling between California and Philadelphia or New York. Doctors say the familiar symptoms of runny bowels, nausea, and sour stomach result from normal local bacterial strains to which newcomers' systems need time to adjust. Unfortunately, the dehydration and fatigue from heat and travel reduce your body's natural defenses and sometimes lead to a persistent cycle of sickness at a time when you least want it.

Time-tested protective measures can help your body either prevent or break this cycle. Many doctors and veteran travelers swear by Pepto-Bismol for soothing sore stomachs and stopping diarrhea. Acidophilus, the bacteria found in yogurt, aids digestion and is widely available in the United States in tablets. Warm *manzanilla* (chamomile) tea, used widely in Mexico (and by Peter Rabbit's mother), provides liquid and calms upset stomachs. Temporarily avoid coffee and alcohol, drink plenty of *manzanilla* tea, and eat bananas and rice for a few meals until your tummy can take regular food.

Although powerful antibiotics and antidiarrhea medications such as Lomotil and Imodium are readily available over *farmacia* counters, they may involve serious side effects and should not be taken in the absence of medical advice. If in doubt, consult a doctor. (See Guadalajara Doctors and Hospitals, later in this chapter.)

Safe Water and Food

Although municipalities have made great strides in sanitation, food and water are still potential sources of germs in the Guadalajara region. Do not drink local tap water. Drink bottled water only. Hotels, whose success depends vitally on their customers' health, generally provide *agua purificada* (purified bottled water). If, for any reason, the water quality is doubtful, add a water

MEDICAL TAGS AND AIR EVACUATION

Travelers with special medical problems might consider wearing a medical identification tag. For a reasonable fee, **Medic Alert** (P.O. Box 1009, Turlock, CA 95381; tel. 800/344-3226) provides such tags, as well as an information hotline that will provide doctors with your vital medical background information.

For life-threatening emergencies, **Critical Air Medicine** (Montgomery Field, 4141 Kearny Villa Rd., San Diego, CA 92123; tel. 619/571-0482; from the U.S. toll-free 800/247-8326, from Mexico 24 hours toll-free 800/010-0268) provides high-tech jet ambulance service from any Mexican locale to the United States. For a fee averaging about $10,000, they promise to fly you to the right U.S. hospital in a hurry.

ON THE ROAD

purifier, such as Potable Aqua brand (get it at a camping goods stores before departure) or a few drops per quart of water of *blanqueador* (household chlorine bleach) or *yodo* (tincture of iodine) from the pharmacy.

Pure bottled water, soft drinks, beer, and fresh fruit juices are so widely available it is easy to avoid tap water, especially in restaurants. Washing hands before eating in a restaurant is a time-honored Mexican ritual that visitors should religiously follow. The humblest Mexican eatery will generally provide a basin to *lavar los manos* (wash the hands). If it doesn't, don't eat there.

Hot, cooked food is generally safe, as are peeled fruits and vegetables. Milk and cheese these days in Mexico are generally processed under sanitary conditions and sold pasteurized (ask, "*¿Pasteurizado?*") and are typically safe. Mexican ice cream used to be both bad-tasting and of dubious safety, but national brands available in supermarkets are so much improved that it's no longer necessary to resist Mexican ice cream.

In recent years, much cleaner public water and increased hygiene awareness has made salads—once shunned by Mexico travelers—generally safe to eat in cafés and restaurants in Guadalajara. Nevertheless, lettuce and cabbage, particularly in country villages, is more likely to be contaminated than tomatoes, carrots, cucumbers, onions, and green peppers. In any case, whenever in doubt, douse your salad in vinegar *(vinagre)* or plenty of sliced lime *(limón)* juice, the acidity of which kills bacteria.

Afflictions, Medications, and Immunizations

A good physician can recommend the proper **preventatives** for your Guadalajara trip. If you are going to stay in town, your doctor may suggest little more than updating your basic typhoid, diphtheria-tetanus, and polio shots.

For **sunburn protection,** use a good sunscreen with a sun protection factor (SPF) of 15 or more, which will reduce burning rays to one-fifteenth or less of direct sunlight. Better still, take a shady siesta-break from the sun during the most hazardous midday hours. If you do get burned, applying your sunburn lotion (or one of the "caine" creams) after the fact usually decreases the pain and speeds healing.

Tropical Backcountry Precautions

Although most of the Guadalajara region lies within the temperate 5,000-foot (1600-meter) elevation zone, in some lower-elevation areas, notably in the **Barranca** north and west of town and the southwest coastal slope, campers and trekkers should exercise precautions. Doctors usually recommend a gamma-globulin shot against hepatitis A and a schedule of chloroquine pills against malaria. While in backcountry areas, use other measures to discourage mosquitoes—and fleas, flies, ticks, no-see-ums, "kissing bugs" (see below), and other tropical pests—from biting you. Common precautions include sleeping under mosquito netting, burning *espirales mosquito* (mosquito coils), and rubbing on plenty of pure DEET (dimethyl-meta-toluamide) "jungle juice" mixed in equal parts with rubbing (70 percent isopropyl) alcohol. Although super-effective, 100 percent DEET dries and irritates the skin.

Chagas' disease, spread by the "kissing" (or, more appropriately, "assassin") bug, is a potential hazard in the Mexican tropics. Known locally as a *vinchuca,* the triangular-headed, three-quarter-inch (two centimeter) brown insect, identifiable by its yellow-striped abdomen, often drops upon its sleeping victims from the thatched ceiling of a rural house at night. Its bite is followed by swelling, fever, and weakness and can lead to heart failure if left untreated. Application of drugs at an early stage can, however, clear the patient of the trypanosome parasites that infect victims' bloodstreams and vital organs. See a doctor immediately if you believe you're infected.

Also while camping or staying in a *palapa* or other rustic accommodation, watch for scorpions, especially in your shoes, which you should shake out every morning. Scorpion stings and snakebites are rarely fatal to an adult but are potentially very serious for a child. Get the victim to a doctor calmly but quickly. For more snakebite details, see Reptiles and Amphibians under Flora and Fauna in the Introduction chapter.

First-Aid Kit

At tropical elevations, ordinary cuts and insect bites are more prone to infection and should receive immediate first aid. A first-aid kit with aspirin, rubbing alcohol, hydrogen peroxide, water-purifying tablets, household chlorine bleach or iodine for water purifying, swabs, Band-Aids, gauze, adhesive tape, Ace bandage, chamomile *(manzanilla)* tea bags for upset stomachs, Pepto-Bismol, acidophilus tablets, antibiotic ointment, hydrocortisone cream, mosquito repellent, knife, and good tweezers is a good precaution for any traveler and mandatory for campers.

Guadalajara Doctors and Hospitals

For medical advice and treatment, let your hotel, or if you're camping, the closest *farmacia,* refer you to a good doctor, clinic, or hospital. Many Guadalajara doctors practice like private doctors in the United States and Canada once did be-

fore the onset of HMOs, liability, and group practice. They will often come to you if you request; they often keep their doors open even after regular hours and charge reasonable fees. And remember: *cita* means an "appointment," and *nota* means "receipt."

You will generally receive good treatment at the local hospitals in the Guadalajara region. If, however, you must have an English-speaking doctor, **IAMAT** (International Association for Medical Assistance to Travelers, 417 Center St., Lewiston, NY 14092; tel. 716/754-4883; email: iamat@sentex.net; website:www.sentex.net/~iamat) maintains a worldwide network of English-speaking doctors. Some IAMAT medical groups practice in Guadalajara. Contact J. Jaime Rodríguez Parra, M.D., Tarascos 3514-14, Rinconada Santa Rita, tel. 33/3813-0440, 33/813-0700, or 33/813-1025; or Robert A. Dumois, M.D., Francisco Zarco 2345, Colonia Ladron de Guevara, tel. 33/3616-9616, fax 33/615-9542; email: rdumois@infosel.net.mx.

Moreover, Guadalajara's **International Friendship Club** (See Helpful Local Organizations, earlier) recommends a number of hospitals and English-speaking doctors in its handy *Survival Guide to Guadalajara.* Among doctors, two of the most highly recommended are the internists **Dr. Daniel Gil Sánchez,** at the Torre Médico, Av. Pablo Neruda 3265, tel. 33/3642-0213, and **Dr. Michael Ritota Jr.,** Av. Tarascos 3422, tel. 33/3313-0547 or 33/3813-0540.

Others also recommended are cardiologist Dr. Ricardo Ascencio Ochoa, Lacandones 310, tel. 33/3813-0699; general practicioner Dra. Ira Luisa Ceja Martínez, Tarascos 3363, tel. 33/3813-1162, 33/3813-2061, and 33/3813-2577; ophthalmologist Dr. Jaime Ramírez Macías, Av. López Mateos Norte 328, first floor (corner of Av. Mexico) tel. 33/3616-3402 and 33/3616-7229; orthopedist and traumatologist Dr. Cesar Álvarez, Tarascos 3385, tel. 33/3813-0096 and 33/3813-0342; pediatrician Jr. Jaime Unda Gómez, Tarascos 3832-15, second floor, tel. 33/3813-2026, 33/3813-2019, and 33/3813-2090; dentists Dr. Rene Hernández Acevedo, Av. Providencia 2450-202, tel. 33/3642-6300, and Dr. C.D. Alberto Arriola Valdés, Av. Providencia 2450-302, tel.

33/3642-6284 and 33/3642-6283; gynecologist-obstetricians Dr. J. Gabriel Chávez G., Moctezuma 5124, Fracc. Sta. Catalina, tel. 33/3620-3487 and 33/3634-1036, and Dr. Efrain Pérez Pena, Av. Union 163-311 (corner of López Cotilla) tel. 33/3616-8621.

The International Friendship Club also recommends a number of Guadalajara **hospitals.** Probably the most useful for Americans is the **Hospital Americas,** at Av. Americas 932, Guadalajara 44620; tel. 33/3817-3141 and 33/3817-3004. It accepts the coverage of many U.S. HMOs; all staff is U.S.–trained and all hospitalization is in private rooms, with TV, phone, and bathroom.

Additionally recommended are **Hospital Méxicano-Americano,** Av. Colomos 2110, tel. 33/3641-3111, fax 33/3642-6401, ambulance 33/3642-7152, with 24-hour emergency room; **Hospital del Carmen,** Tarascos 3435, tel. 33/3813-0025 and 33/3813-0042, emergencies tel. 33/3813-1224, with 24-hour emergency room; **Hospital San Javier,** Av. Pablo Casals, Col. Providencia, tel. 33/3669-0222, fax 33/3642-6401, ambulance tel. 33/3616-9616, with 24-hour emergency room; and **Hospital Arboledas,** Av. Nicolás Copernico 4000, tel. 33/3631-3051, fax 33/3631-4450, with 24-hour emergency room.

For many more useful details of health and safety in Mexico, consult Dr. William Forgey's *Traveler's Medical Alert, Series 5, Mexico* (Merrillville, IN: ICS Books); or Dirk Schroeder's *Staying Healthy in Asia, Africa, and Latin America* (Emeryville, CA: Moon Publications of Avalon Travel Handbooks, 1999).

Police and Fire Emergencies

Guadalajara and its suburban districts maintain good fire and police infrastructure. Contact the Guadalajara police quickly by dialing 06 for the radio patrol, or the main switchboard: tel. 33/3668-0800; Federal Highway Police: tel. 33/3629-5082; police in Tlaquepaque: tel. 33/3635-8828 or 33/3635-2045; in Tonala: tel. 33/3683-0046, 33/3683-2876 or 33/3683-1656; in Zapopan: tel. 33/3656-5656 or 33/3633-1010.

For **fire** emergencies, call the main switchboard: tel. 33/3619-0510 or headquarters tel. 33/3619-

DISASTER AND RESCUE ON A MEXICAN HIGHWAY

My litany of Mexican driving experiences came to a climax one night when, heading north from Tepic, I hit a cow at 50 mph head on. The cow was knocked about 150 feet down the road, while I and my two friends endured a scary impromptu roller-coaster ride. When the dust settled, we, although in shock, were grateful that we hadn't suffered the fate of the poor cow, who had died instantly from the collision.

From that low point, our fortunes soon began to improve. Two buses stopped and about 40 men got out to move my severely wounded van to the shoulder. The cow's owner, a rancher, arrived to cart off the cow's remains in a jeep. Then the police—a man and his wife in a VW bug—pulled up. *"Pobrecita camioneta,"* "Poor little van," the woman said, gazing at my vehicle, which now resembled an oversized, rumpled accordion. They gave us a ride to Mazatlán, found us a hotel room, and generally made sure we were okay.

If I hadn't had Mexican auto insurance I would have been in deep trouble. Mexican law—based on the Napoleonic Code—presumes guilt and does not bother with juries. It would have kept me in jail until all damages were settled. The insurance agent I saw in the morning took care of everything. He called the police station, where I was excused from paying damages when the cow's owner failed to show. He had my car towed to a repair shop, where the mechanics banged it into good enough shape so I could drive it home a week later. Forced to stay in one place, my friends and I enjoyed the most relaxed time of our entire three months in Mexico. The *pobrecita camioneta,* all fixed up a few months later, lasted 14 more years.

0794 or 33/3619-5241; at the south-side Industrial Zone station: tel. 33/3645-6034 or 33/3645-9593; at the north-side Transito station: tel. 33/3823-0833; in east-side district Gigantes-Manuel Ponce: tel. 33/3644-4555 or 33/3644-4470.

CONDUCT AND CUSTOMS

Safe Conduct

Behind its modern glitz, Mexico is an old-fashioned country where people value traditional ideals of honesty, fidelity, and piety. Violent crime rates are low; visitors are often safer in Mexico than in their home cities.

Even though four generations have elapsed since Pancho Villa raided the U.S. border, the image of a Mexico bristling with *bandidos* persists. And similarly for Mexicans: Despite the century and a half since the *yanquis* invaded Mexico City and took half their country, the communal Mexican psyche still views gringos (and by association all white foreigners) with a combination of revulsion, envy, and awe.

Fortunately, the Mexican love-hate affair with foreigners in general does not necessarily apply to individual visitors. Your friendly *"Buenos días"* or courteous *"por favor"* are always appreciated. The shy smile you receive in return will be your not-insignificant reward.

Women

Your own behavior, despite low crime statistics, largely determines your safety in Mexico. For women traveling solo, it is important to realize that the double standard is alive and well in Mexico. Dress and behave modestly and you will most likely avoid embarrassment. Whenever possible, stay in the company of friends or acquaintances; find companions for beach, sight-seeing, and shopping excursions. Ignore strange men's solicitations and overtures: Mexican man on the prowl will invent the sappiest romantic overtures to snare a "gringa." He will often interpret anything but a firm "no" as a "maybe," and a "maybe" as a yes.

Men

For male visitors, alcohol often leads to trouble. Avoid bars and cantinas; and if, given Mexico's excellent beers, you can't abstain completely, at least maintain soft-spoken self-control in the face of challenges from macho drunks.

The Law and Police

While Mexican authorities are tolerant of alcohol, they are decidedly intolerant of other substances such as marijuana, psychedelics, cocaine, and heroin. Getting caught with such drugs in Mexico usually leads to swift and severe results.

Equally swift is the punishment for nude sunbathing, which is both illegal in public and offensive to Mexicans. Confine your nudist colony to very private locations.

Traffic police around Guadalajara sometimes seem to be watching foreign cars with eagle eyes. If they whistle you over, stop immediately or you will really get into hot water. If guilty, say *"Lo siento"* ("I'm sorry") and be cooperative. Although he probably won't mention it, the officer is usually hoping that you'll cough up a $20 *mordida* (bribe) for the privilege of driving away. Don't do it. Although he may hint at confiscating your car, calmly ask for an official *boleto* (written traffic ticket, if you're guilty) in exchange for your driver's license (have a copy), which the officer will probably keep if he writes a ticket. If after a few minutes no money appears, the officer will most likely give you back your driver's license rather than go to the trouble of writing the ticket. If not, the worst that will usually happen is you will have to go to the *presidencia municipal* (city hall) or *transito* (motor vehicle department) the next morning and pay the $20 to a clerk in exchange for your driver's license.

Pedestrian and Driving Hazards

Although the Guadalajara region's rutted pavements and "holey" sidewalks won't land you in jail, one of them might send you to the hospital if you don't watch your step, especially at night. "Pedestrian beware" is especially good advice on Guadalajara's streets, where it is rumored that some drivers speed up rather than slow down when they spot a tourist stepping off the curb.

Driving regional country roads, where slow trucks and carts block lanes, campesinos stroll

PACKING CHECKLIST

Necessary Items
camera, film (expensive in Mexico)
clothes, hat
comb, brush
guidebook, reading books
inexpensive watch, clock
keys, tickets
mosquito repellent
passport
prescription eyeglasses
prescription medicines and drugs
purse, waist-belt carrying pouch
sunglasses
sunscreen
swimsuit
toothbrush, toothpaste
tourist card, visa
traveler's checks, money
windbreaker

Useful Items
address book
birth control
checkbook, credit cards
contact lenses
dental floss
earplugs
first-aid kit
flashlight, batteries
immersion heater
lightweight binoculars
portable radio/cassette player
razor
travel book light
vaccination certificate

Necessary Items for Campers
collapsible gallon plastic bottle
dish soap
first-aid kit
hammock (buy in Mexico)
insect repellent
lightweight hiking shoes
lightweight tent
matches in waterproof case
nylon cord
plastic bottle, quart
pot scrubber/sponge
sheet or light blanket
Sierra Club cup, fork, and spoon
single-burner stove with fuel
Swiss army knife
tarp
toilet paper
towel, soap
two nesting cooking pots
water-purifying tablets or iodine

Useful Items for Campers
compass
dishcloths
hot pad
instant coffee, tea, sugar, powdered milk
moleskin (Dr. Scholl's)
plastic plate
poncho
short candles
whistle

the shoulders, and horses, burros, and cattle wander at will, is hazardous—doubly so at night.

Socially Responsible Travel

Latter-day jet travel has brought droves of vacationing tourists to developing countries largely unprepared for the consequences. As the visitors' numbers swell, power grids black out, sewers overflow, and roads crack under the strain of accommodating more and larger hotels, restaurants, cars, buses, and airports.

Worse yet, armies of vacationers drive up local prices and begin to change local customs. Visions of tourists as sources of fast money replace traditions of hospitality, television wipes out folk entertainment, Coke and Pepsi substitute for fruit drinks, and prostitution and drugs flourish.

Some travelers have said enough is enough and are forming organizations to encourage visitors to travel with increased sensitivity to Mexico's people and customs. They have developed travelers' codes of ethics and guidelines that encourage visitors to stay at local-style accommodations, use local transportation, and seek alternative vacations and tours, such as language-study and cultural programs and people-to-people work projects. For more information, visit a responsible travel website, such as www.green-travel.com, or www.tourismconcern.org.uk.

WHAT TO TAKE

"Men wear pants, ladies be beautiful," once the dress code of one of western Mexico's classiest hotels, is still good advice. Most men vacationing in casual Guadalajara can get by easily without a jacket, women with simple skirts and blouses. Commercial travelers, however, should probably bring along a light suit for more formal business functions.

Loose-fitting, hand-washable, easy-to-dry clothes make for trouble-free Guadalajara traveling. Synthetic or cotton-synthetic-blend shirts, blouses, pants, socks, and underwear will fit the bill for most every occasion. For breezy or winter nights add a medium-weight jacket.

In all cases, leave showy, expensive clothes and jewelry at home. Stow items that you cannot lose in your hotel safe or carry them with you in a sturdy zipped purse or a waist pouch on your front side.

Packing

What you pack depends on how mobile you want to be. If you're staying the whole time at a self-contained resort, you can take the two suitcases and one carry-on allowed by airlines. If, on the other hand, you're going to be moving around a lot, best condense everything down to one easily carried bag with wheels that doubles as luggage and soft backpack. Experienced travelers accomplish this by packing prudently and tightly, choosing items that will do double or triple duty (such as a Swiss army knife with scissors).

Campers will have to be super-careful to accomplish this. Although camping in lower elevation tropical zones requires no sleeping bag, mountain and winter camping in most of the Guadalajara region does. A compact tent that you and your partner can share is a must against bugs, as is mosquito repellent. A first-aid kit is absolutely necessary (see Staying Healthy, earlier in the chapter).

The Heart of the City

Downtown Guadalajara

People flock to Guadalajara (pop. 3.5 million, elev. 5,214 feet, 1,589 meters) for the same reason that Californians frequently go to Los Angeles: to shop and choose from big selections at correspondingly small prices.

But that's only part of the fascination. Although Guadalajarans like to think of themselves as different (calling themselves, uniquely, "Tapatíos"), their city is renowned as the "most Mexican" of cities. A host of visitors, both foreign and

Mexican, come to Guadalajara to bask in its mild, springlike sunshine, savor its music, and admire its grand monuments.

HISTORY

Before Columbus

The broad Atemajac Valley, where the Guadalajara metropolis now spreads, has nurtured humans for hundreds of generations. Discovered remains date back at least 10,000 years. The Río Lerma-Santiago—Mexico's longest river, which meanders

Plaza de la Liberación is a favorite city-center ground for strolling or early-morning jogging.

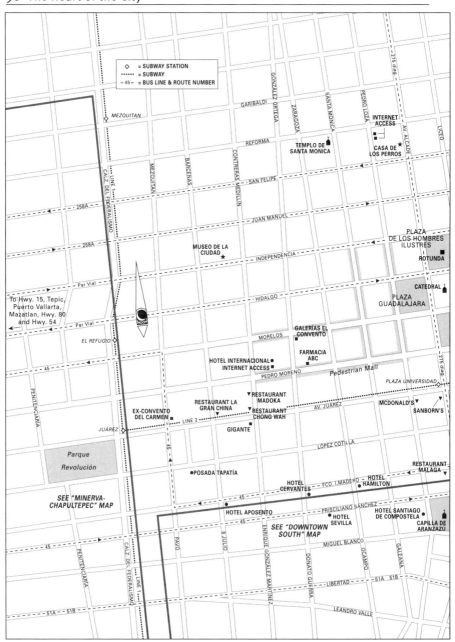

THE HEART OF THE CITY

= SUBWAY STATION
= SUBWAY
– 45 – = BUS LINE & ROUTE NUMBER

GONZALEZ ORTEGA
ZARAGOZA
SANTA MONICA
PEDRO LOZA
275 diag.
AV. ALCALDE
LICEO

GARIBALDI

MEZQUITAN

REFORMA

INTERNET ACCESS

TEMPLO DE SANTA MONICA

CASA DE LOS PERROS

LINE 1
CALZ. DEL FEDERALISMO
MEZQUITAN
BARCENAS
CONTRERAS MEDELLIN

SAN FELIPE

– 258A –

JUAN MANUEL

– 258A –

PLAZA DE LOS HOMBRES ILUSTRES

ROTUNDA

MUSEO DE LA CIUDAD

INDEPENDENCIA

CATEDRAL

– Par Vial –

To Hwy. 15, Tepic, Puerto Vallarta, Mazatlan, Hwy. 80 and Hwy. 54

HIDALGO

PLAZA GUADALAJARA

– Par Vial –

EL REFUGIO

MORELOS

GALERÍAS EL CONVENTO

FARMACIA ABC

HOTEL INTERNACIONAL INTERNET ACCESS

PEDRO MORENO

Pedestrian Mall

PLAZA UNIVERSIDAD

– 45 –

PENITENCIARIA

RESTAURANT MADOKA

RESTAURANT LA GRAN CHINA

RESTAURANT CHONG WAH

MCDONALD'S

SANBORN'S

EX-CONVENTO DEL CARMEN

Line 2

AV. JUÁREZ

JUÁREZ

GIGANTE

– 45 –

LÓPEZ COTILLA

Parque Revolución

RESTAURANT MALAGA

POSADA TAPATÍA

HOTEL CERVANTES

FCO. I. MADERO

HOTEL HAMILTON

SEE "MINERVA-CHAPULTEPEC" MAP

– 45 –

HOTEL APOSENTO

PRISCILIANO SÁNCHEZ

HOTEL SEVILLA

HOTEL SANTIAGO DE COMPOSTELA

CAPILLA DE ARANZAZÚ

– 45 –

PAVO

8 JULIO

ENRIQUE GONZÁLEZ MARTÍNEZ

SEE "DOWNTOWN SOUTH" MAP

MIGUEL BLANCO

OCAMPO

GALEANA

CALZ. DEL FEDERALISMO

DONATO GUERRA

LIBERTAD

51A   51B

– 45 –

PENITENCIARIA

LINE 1

LEANDRO VALLE

– 51A – – 51B –

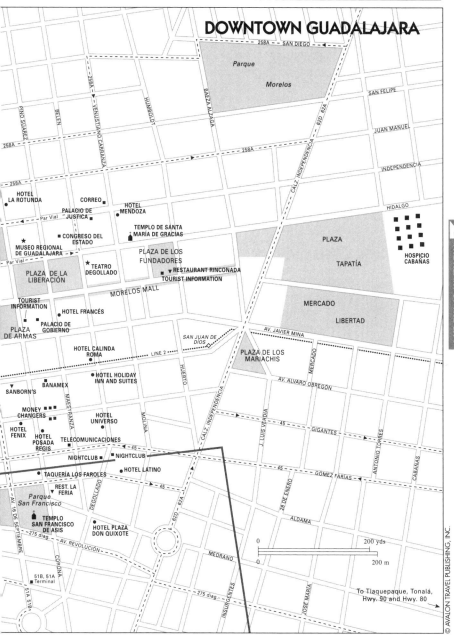

DOWNTOWN GUADALAJARA

THE HEART OF THE CITY

© AVALON TRAVEL PUBLISHING, INC.

across six states—has nourished Atemajac Valley cornfields for at least three millennia.

Although they built no grand pyramids, high cultures were occupying western Mexico by 100 B.C. They left sophisticated animal- and human-motif pottery in myriad bottle-shaped underground tombs of a style found in Jalisco, Nayarit, and Colima. Intriguingly, similar tombs are also found in Colombia and Ecuador.

Guadalajara's early residents' major monumental construction, 2,000 year-old **Iztepete**, now a collection of largely unexplored ceremonial mounds, stands open for visitors at the city's southwest edge. (See the City: West and North of Downtown chapter.)

During the next thousand years after Iztepete, waves of migrants swept across the Valley of Atemajac: Toltecs from the northeast; the Aztecs much later from the west. As Toltec power declined during the 13th century, the Tarascan civilization took root in Michoacán to the southeast and filled the power vacuum left by the Toltecs. On the eve of the Spanish conquest, semiautonomous local chiefdoms, tributaries of the Tarascan Emperor, shared the Atemajac Valley.

Conquest and Colonization

The fall of the Aztecs in 1521 and the Tarascans a few years later made the Atemajac Valley a plum ripe for the picking. In the late 1520s, while Cortés was absent in Spain, the opportunistic Nuño de Guzmán vaulted himself to power in Mexico City on the backs of the native peoples and at the expense of Cortés' friends and relatives. Suspecting correctly that his glory days in Mexico City were numbered, Guzmán cleared out just before Christmas 1529, at the head of a small army of adventurers seeking new conquests in western Mexico. They raped, ravaged, and burned their way west for half a dozen years, inciting dozens of previously peaceful tribes to rebellion.

Hostile Mexican attacks repeatedly foiled Guzmán's attempts to establish his western Mexico capital, which he wanted to name after his Spanish hometown, Guadalajara (from the Arabic *wad al hadjarah,* "river of stones"). Ironically, it wasn't until the year of Guzmán's death in

Spain, 1542, six years after his arrest by royal authorities, that the present Guadalajara was founded. At the downtown Plaza de Los Fundadores, a panoramic bronze frieze shows co-founders Doña Beátriz de Hernández and governor Cristóbal de Oñate christening the soon-to-become-capital of the "Kingdom of Nueva Galicia."

The city grew; its now-venerable public buildings rose at the edges of sweeping plazas, from which expeditions set out to explore far-flung lands. In 1563, Legazpi and Urdaneta sailed west to conquer the Philippines; the year 1602 saw Vizcaíno sail for the Californias and the Pacific Northwest. In 1687 Father Kino left for 27 years of mission-building in Sonora and what would be Arizona and New Mexico; finally, during the 1760s, Father Junípero Serra and Captain Gaspar de Portola began their arduous trek to discover San Francisco Bay and found a string of California missions.

During Spain's Mexican twilight, Guadalajara was a virtual imperial city, the capital of **Nueva Galicia,** a western domain that encompassed the present-day states of Jalisco, Nayarit, Colima, Aguascalientes, and parts of Zacatecas, San Luis Potosí, Sinaloa, and Durango, a realm comparable in size to Old Spain itself.

Independence

The cry, "Death to the *gachupines,* viva México" by insurgent priest Miguel Hidalgo ignited rebellion on September 16, 1810. Buoyed by a series of quick victories, Hidalgo advanced on Mexico City in command of a huge ragtag army. But, facing the punishing fusillades of a small but disciplined Spanish force, Hidalgo lost his nerve and decided to occupy Guadalajara instead. Loyalist General Felix Calleja pursued and routed Hidalgo's forces on the bank of the Río Lerma-Santiago, not far east of Guadalajara. Although Hidalgo and Allende escaped, they were captured in the north a few months later. It wasn't for another dozen bloody years that others—Iturbide, Guerrero, Morelos—from other parts of Mexico realized Hidalgo's dream of independence.

Guadalajara, its domain reduced by the republican federal government to the new state of

Jalisco, settled down to the production of corn, cattle, and tequila. The railroad came, branched north to the United States and south to the Pacific, and by 1900, Guadalajara's place as a commercial hub and Mexico's second city was secure.

Modern Guadalajara

After the bloodbath of the 1910-17 revolution, Guadalajara's growth far outpaced the country in general. From a population of around 100,000 in 1900, Guadalajara ballooned to more than three million by 2000. People were drawn from the countryside by jobs in a thousand new factories, making everything from textiles and shoes to silicon chips and soda pop.

Handicraft manufacture, always important in Guadalajara, zoomed during the 1960s when waves of jet-riding tourists came, saw, and bought mountains of blown glass, leather, pottery, and metal finery.

During the 1980s, Guadalajara put on a new

Baroque spiral Solomonic columns decorate the facade of the 17th-century Aranzazú chapel on Plaza San Francisco.

face while at the same time preserving the best part of its old downtown. An urban-renewal plan of visionary proportions created Plaza Tapatía— acres of shops, restaurants, and offices beside fountain-studded malls—incorporating Guadalajara's venerable theaters, churches, museums, and government buildings into a single grand open space.

SIGHTS

Getting Oriented

Although the Guadalajara metropolis sprawls over a hundred square miles, the treasured mile-square heart of the city is easily explored on foot. The cathedral corner of north-south Av. 16 de Septiembre and Av. Morelos marks the center of town. A few blocks south, another important artery, east-west Av. Juárez, runs above the metro subway line through the main business district, while a few blocks east, Av. Independencia runs beneath Plaza Tapatía and past the main market to the Museo Arqueológico and the green, grassy, Parque Agua Azul a mile south.

Getting Around

The historical heart of Guadalajara is accessible by most folks on foot. If you don't feel like walking, hail a taxi. Short taxi trips within a mile of the city center shouldn't cost more than $2. For longer trips outside of the city center, you can opt for the **subway** (see the special topic Subway—Guadalajara-Style) or one of the oft-crowded city buses.

If you're going to be doing a lot of independent traveling by car or bus in Guadalajara, get a copy of the very reliable ***Guia Roji Red Vial Cuidad de Guadalajara*** city map. It's available at Sanborn's gift shop–restaurant (see the Food section later in this chapter).

City buses are an experience not for the faint of heart. They are plentiful but often packed with commuters. People are generally courteous despite the crowding. Nevertheless, keep your purse buttoned and your wallet secure in a deep front pocket or secure waist pack.

Buses stop at regular marked bus *paradas* (pah-RAH-dahs) or stops. If you want the bus to stop, stand on the curb, face traffic and hold your arm straight out, parallel to the ground.

For trips into the suburbs, a number of useful **city bus** routes diverge from the city center. Go conveniently to the **inner western suburb** (restaurants and upscale Centro Magno shopping center) via the quiet **Par Vial** electric bus, from the corner of Independencia and Alcalde, one block north of the cathedral. For both the inner or the **far western suburbs** (Gran Plaza shopping center) ride a west-bound **bus #45,** from the corner of 16 de Septiembre and Prisciliano Sanchez, bordering the Parque San Francisco, five blocks south of the cathedral.

For the **southwestern** suburbs (luxury hotels, Plaza del Sol shopping center) ride either the **west-bound bus #258A** (corner of Alcalde and San Felipe, three blocks north of the cathedral) or **west-bound bus #51A or #51B** (from the corner of 16 de Septiembre and Av. La Paz) four blocks south of Parque San Francisco.

For the southeastern suburban **handicrafts villages of Tlaquepaque and Tonalá,** ride a **south-bound bus #275 diagonal,** accessible at a sprinkling of city-center stops along 16 de Septiembre. (If, on the other hand, you catch a **north-bound bus #275 diagonal,** it will take you to the colorful pilgrimage town of **Zapopan** at Guadalajara's northwest edge.)

Finally, for the northern suburban **Guadalajara Zoo, Magic Jungle Amusement Park (Selva Mágica),** and **planetarium** complex, ride **east-bound bus 258A** from the corner of Alcalde and Juan Manuel, two blocks north of the cathedral. (Alternatively, you can access the same destinations, via buses #62A and #62D, which run north-south along big thoroughfare Calz. Independencia, beneath Plaza Tapatía).

For a country ride north into the **Barranca,** the tropical canyon of the Río Santiago (Los Camachos *balneario* bathing spring), ride the **Los Camachos Bus** from its terminal at the **Glorieta Normal** (Normal Circle) on Alcalde about a mile north of the city center.

For more city bus hints and details, see the Getting Around sections in the City: West and North of Downtown chapter. Furthermore, if you're going to be riding lots of Guadalajara buses, stop by a downtown newsstand and buy a copy of the handy bus route guide *Guia de*

Rutas de Camiones y Midbuses, published by the bus drivers alliance, Alianza de Camioneros de Jalisco, tel. 33/3637-9815, 33/3810-0178.

Rental Cars, Guides, and Tours

For longer trips in the suburbs and the Guadalajara region's outer reaches, a **rental car** is a convenient, but relatively expensive, option. Car rentals are available at the airport (see the By Air section near the end of this chapter), or from one of several downtown car rental offices, many of which are clustered at the corner of **Niños Héroes** and **Manzano,** near the Hotel Misión Carlton, at the south edge of downtown. There, bargain and shop around among several agencies, including National (tel. 33/3614-7175, 33/3614-7994), Quick (tel. 33/3614-2247, 33/3614-6006), Renta Tu Auto (tel. 33/3614-2020), Marticar (tel. 33/3613-0914), and Alaniz (tel. 33/3614-6353).

If you'd like to hire a guide, or go by conventional tour bus, see By Locally Arranged Tour under Getting Around in the On the Road chapter.

A Walk Around Old Guadalajara

The twin steeples of the **cathedral** serve as an excellent starting point to explore the city-center plazas and monuments. The cathedral, dedicated to the Virgin of the Assumption when it was begun in 1561, was finished about 30 years later. A potpourri of styles—Moorish, Gothic, Renaissance, and Classic—make up its spires, arches, and facades. Although an earthquake demolished its steeples in 1818, they were rebuilt and resurfaced with cheery canary yellow tiles in 1854.

Inside, side altars and white facades climax at the principal altar, built over a tomb containing the remains of several former clergy, including the mummified heart of renowned Bishop Cabañas. One of the main attractions is the **Virgin of Innocence,** in the small chapel just to the left of the entrance. The glass-enclosed figure contains the bones of a 12-year-old girl who was martyred in the 3rd century and forgotten, then rediscovered in the Vatican catacombs in 1786 and shipped to Guadalajara in 1788. The legend claims she died protecting her virginity; it is equally likely that she was martyred for refusing to recant her Christian faith.

Somewhere near the main altar you'll find either a copy of, or the authentic **Virgén de Zapopan.** Sometime between June and October 12, the tiny, adored figure will be the authentic "La Generala," as she's affectionately known; on October 12, a tumultuous crowd of worshippers escorts her back to the cathedral in Zapopan, where she remains until brought back to Guadalajara the next June.

Outside, broad plazas surround the cathedral: the **Plaza Guadalajara** (formerly Plaza Laureles), in front (west) of the cathedral, then moving counterclockwise, the **Plaza de Armas** to the south, **Plaza Liberación** to the east (behind), and the **Plaza de los Hombres Ilustres** to the north of the cathedral.

Across Av. Morelos, the block-square Plaza de los Hombres Ilustres is bordered by 15 sculptures of Jalisco's eminent sons. Their remains lie beneath the stone rotunda in the center; their bronze statues line the sidewalk. Right at the corner you'll find the figure of revered Jalisco Governor Ignacio Vallarta; a few steps farther north stands the statue of José Clemente Orozco, legally blind when he executed his great works of art (see the special topic Josá Clemente Orozco)

Adjacent to and east of the Plaza de los Hombres Ilustres, the colonial building behind the lineup of horse-drawn *calandrias* housed the Seminario de San José for the six generations following its construction in 1696. During the 1800s it served variously as a barracks and a public lecture hall, and, since 1918, it has housed the **Museo Regional de Guadalajara,** 60 Liceo; tel. 33/3614-9957; open Tues.–Sun. 9 A.M.–5:30 P.M.

Inside, tiers of rooms surrounding a tree-shaded interior patio illustrate local history. Exhibits begin with a hulking mastodon skeleton and a small garden of petrified trees and continue through a collection of whimsical animal and human figurines recovered from the bottle-shaped tombs of Jalisco, Nayarit, and Colima. Upstairs, find galleries of Jalisco history and colonial religious art, and life-size displays of contemporary but traditional fishing methods at nearby Lake Chapala

and the costumes and culture of regional Cora, Huichol, Tepehuan, and Méxica peoples.

Back outside, head east two blocks down Av. Hidalgo, paralleling the expansive Plaza Liberación behind the cathedral. On your left you will pass the baroque facades of the *congreso del estado* (state legislature) and the *palacio de justicia* (state supreme court) buildings. Step inside the latter (open Mon.–Fri. 9 A.M.–7 P.M., Sat. 9 A.M.–1 p.m.) for a look at the mural above the staircase, off the patio to the right.

Finished in 1965 by Guillermo Chavez Vega, (see his signature in the top right corner) the mural dramatically interprets 19th century Mexican and Jalisco history. The mural, although obviously Orozco-influenced, is not as arrestingly graphic as those of the master. A bilingual explanation, atop the staircase, identifies the main actors. In the center, Gómez Farías, Father of the Reform, Benito Juárez ("Respect for the Rights of All Is Peace"), and Melchor Ocampo, author of the Laws of Reform, stride down the path of Mexico's nationhood. On the left, archvillain López de Santa Anna holds the chains of slavery. On the right, white-bearded Jalisco governor Ignacio Vallarta lionizes Miguel Hidalgo: "The Reform Revolution Would Not Have Occurred Without the Push That Hidalgo Initiated at Dolores."

Outside, at the eastern end of the plaza, rises the timeless silhouette of the **Teatro Degollado.** The theater's classic, column facade climaxes in an epic marble frieze, depicting the allegory of Apollo and the nine muses. Inside, the Degollado's resplendent grand salon is said to rival the gilded refinement of Milan's renowned La Scala. Overhead, its ceiling glows with Gerardo Suárez's panorama of canto IV of Dante's *Divine Comedy,* complete with its immortal cast—Julius Caesar, Homer, Virgil, Saladin—and the robed and wreathed author himself in the middle. Named for the millionaire Governor Degollado who financed its construction, the theater opened with appropriate fanfare on September 13, 1866, with a production of *Lucia de Lammermoor,* starring Angela Peralta, the renowned "Mexican Nightingale." An ever-changing menu of artists still graces the Degollado's stage. These include an excellent local folkloric ballet troupe every Sunday morning; tel. 33/3614-4773 for information or see Entertainment and Events, later in this chapter.

Just to the north of (on the left as you face) the Teatro Degollado, stands the austere silhouette of the **Templo de Santa María de Gracia,** Guadalajara's original (1549–1618) cathedral. The present building, initiated in 1661, was completed about a century later.

Walk behind the Degollado, where a modern bronze frieze, the *Frisa de Los Fundadores,* decorates its back side. Appropriately, a mere two blocks from the spot where the city was founded, the 68-foot sculpture shows Guadalajara's co-founders facing each other on opposite sides of a big tree. Governor Cristóbal de Oñate strikes the tree with his sword, while Doña Beátriz de Hernández holds a fighting cock, symbolizing her gritty determination (and that of dozens of fellow settlers) that Guadalajara's location should remain put.

Plaza Tapatía

Turn around and face east. The 17 acres of the Plaza Tapatía complex extend ahead for several blocks across sub-plazas, fountains, and malls. Initially wide in the foreground of Plaza de los Fundadores, the Tapatía narrows between a double row of shiny shops and offices, then widens into a broad esplanade and continues beside a long pool/fountain that leads to the monumental, domed Hospicio Cabañas a third of a mile away. Along the Tapatía's lateral flanks, a pair of long malls—continuations of Avenidas Hidalgo and Morelos—parallel the central Paseo Degollado mall for two blocks.

The eastern end of the Morelos mall climaxes with the striking bronze *escudo* (coat of arms) of Guadalajara. Embodying the essence of the original 16th-century coat of arms authorized by Emperor Charles V, the *escudo* shows a pair of lions protecting a pine tree (with leaves, rather than needles). The lions represent the warrior's determination and discipline, and the solitary pine symbolizes noble ideals.

Continue east, to where the Plaza Tapatía widens, giving berth for the sculpture-fountain **Imolación de Quetzalcoatl,** designed and exe-

Mercado Libertad, on the southeast side of Plaza Tapatía, is the modern incarnation of the original centuries-old indigenous market.

© BRUCE WHIPPERMAN

cuted by Víctor Manuel Contreras in 1982. Four bronze serpent-birds, representing knowledge and the spirit of humankind, stretch toward heaven at the ends of a giant cross. In the center, a towering bronze spiral represents the unquenchable flame of Quetzalcoatl, transforming all that it touches. Locals call the sculpture the "big corkscrew," however.

At this point, Av. Independencia runs directly beneath Plaza Tapatía, past the adjacent sprawling **Mercado Libertad,** built in 1958 on the site of the traditional Guadalajara *tianguis* (open-air market), known since pre-Columbian times. Follow the elevated pedestrian walkway south to explore the Libertad's produce, meat, fish, herbs, food, and handicrafts stalls.

On Independencia, just south of the market, musicians at the **Plaza de los Mariachis** continue the second century of a tradition born when mariachi (cowboy troubadour) groups first appeared during the 1860s in Guadalajara. The musical hubbub climaxes Saturday nights and Sunday afternoons, as musicians gather, singing while they wait to be hired for serenades and parties.

The Hospicio Cabañas

Behind the long pool/fountain at the east end of Plaza Tapatía stands the domed neoclassic **Hospicio Cabañas,** the largest and one of the most remarkable colonial buildings in the Americas, designed and financed by Bishop Juan Ruiz de Cabañas; construction was complete in 1810. The purpose of the "Guadalajara House of Charity and Mercy," as the good bishop originally named it, a home for the sick, helpless, and homeless, was fulfilled for 170 years. Although still successfully serving as an orphanage during the 1970s, time had taken its toll on the Hospicio Cabañas. The city and state governments built a new orphanage in the suburbs, restored the old building, and changed its purpose. It now houses the **Instituto Cultural Cabañas,** a center for the arts at Cabañas 8; tel. 33/3654-0008 or 33/3654-0129; open Tues.–Sat. 9 A.M.–8 P.M., Sunday 9 A.M.–2 P.M. Public programs include classes and films, and instrumental, chorale, and dance concerts.

Inside, seemingly endless ranks of corridors pass a host of sculpture-decorated patios. Practice rooms resound with the clatter of dancing feet and the halting strains of apprentice violins, horns, and pianos. Exhibition halls and studios of the **José Clemente Orozco Art Museum** occupy a large fraction of the rooms, while the great muralist's brooding work spreads over a corresponding fraction of the walls. Words such as dark, fiery, nihilistic, even apocalyptic, would not be too strong to describe the panoramas that Orozco executed (1938–39) in the soaring chapel beneath the central dome. On one wall, an Aztec goddess wears a necklace of human hearts; on another, armored, automaton-soldiers menace Indian captives; while in the cupola overhead, Orozco's *Man of Fire,* wreathed in flame, appears to soar into a hellishly red-hot sky.

Sights North of the Cathedral

Return to the cathedral-front street (which continues, changing from 16 de Septiembre to Alcalde, north of the cathedral) and walk north three and a half blocks. On the west side of Alcalde, between San Felipe and Reforma, rises the neoclassic facade of the Museum of Journalism

and Graphic Arts, popularly known as the **Casa de los Perros** (House of the Dogs.)

The present building occupies the site of Guadalajara's first printing press, founded at at the same time as Guadalajara's first university, in 1792. Later, in December 1810, under the orders of rebel priest Miguel Hidalgo, Mexico's first insurgent newspaper, *El Despertador Americano,* was edited and printed by Francisco Severo Maldonado.

The building's popular name originates from the dog shelter maintained by an animal-lover who operated a tailor shop on the site during the mid-1800s. Although subsequent fighting destroyed the building during the 1858–1861 War of the Reform, new owners—tequila distiller Jesùs Flores and his socially prominent wife, Ana González Rubio—replaced it with the present structure in 1896. In recognition of tradition, they topped the new building's French-style facade with a pair of cast-iron pointer terriers, prominently visible from the street.

Inside, the museum maintains a schedule of temporary photography and other graphics arts exhibitions, film screenings, and a library. The permanent exhibits on the bottom floor display a copy of the front page of the original *El Despertador Americano,* an original linotype (automatic typesetting) machine, and a 1950s-vintage television studio mockup. Open Tues.–Sat. 10 A.M.–6 P.M., Sun. 10:30 A.M.–3 P.M.; tel. 33/3613-9285, 33/3613-9286.

Walk two blocks west to the beloved old **Templo de Santa Monica,** built by Guadalajara's Jesuits between 1720 and 1733 (but subsequently destroyed and rebuilt), on the block of Santa Monica between Reforma and San Felipe. Here, admire the resplendent original rococo *portada* (door portal), flanked by two pair of gloriously carved Solomonic columns, clad with stone vines, leaves, and grapes, spiraling upward toward heaven. Walk half a block north, to the corner of Flores, where, above the southwest street corner a kindly St. Christopher carries the child Jesus on his giant shoulder.

For another treat, walk two blocks south and five blocks west, to the **Museo de la Ciudad** (Museum of the City) on Independencia, north

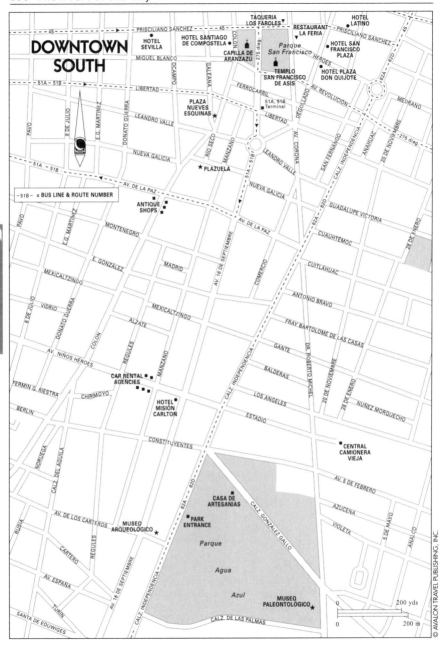

DOWNTOWN SOUTH

-51B- = BUS LINE & ROUTE NUMBER

HOTEL LATINO
TAQUERIA LOS FAROLES
RESTAURANT LA FERIA
HOTEL SEVILLA
HOTEL SANTIAGO DE COMPOSTELA
CAPILLA DE ARANZAZÚ
Parque San Francisco
HOTEL SAN FRANCISCO PLAZA
HOTEL PLAZA DON QUIJOTE
TEMPLO SAN FRANCISCO DE ASIS
PLAZA NUEVES ESQUINAS
51A, 51B Terminal
PLAZUELA
ANTIQUE SHOPS
CAR RENTAL AGENCIES
HOTEL MISIÓN CARLTON
CENTRAL CAMIONERA VIEJA
CASA DE ARTESANIAS
PARK ENTRANCE
MUSEO ARQUEOLÓGICO
Parque
Agua
Azul
MUSEO PALEONTOLÓGICO

PRISCILIANO SANCHEZ
MIGUEL BLANCO
LIBERTAD
NUEVA GALICIA
AV. DE LA PAZ
MONTENEGRO
MADRID
MEXICALTZINGO
ALZATE
AV. NIÑOS HÉROES
CHIRIMOYO
CONSTITUYENTES
AV. DE LOS CARTEROS
AV. ESPAÑA
SANTA DE EDUWIGES
TURIN
CARTERO
RUSIA
BERLIN
NORUEGA
FERMIN G. RIESTRA
MEXICALTZINGO
E. GONZÁLEZ
PAVO
8 DE JULIO
DONATO GUERRA
E.G. MARTINEZ
VIDRIO
COLON
REGULES
MANZANO
CALZ. DEL AGUILA
OCAMPO
GALEANA
LEANDRO VALLE
FERROCARRIL
RIO SECO
MANZANO
AV. 16 DE SEPTIEMBRE
COMERCIO
CALZ. INDEPENDENCIA
62A
62D
275 diag
HÉROES
DEGOLLADO
AV. REVOLUCIÓN
AV. CORONA
SAN FERNANDO
CALZ. INDEPENDENCIA
GUADALUPE VICTORIA
CUAUHTÉMOC
CUITLÁHUAC
ANTONIO BRAVO
FRAY BARTOLOME DE LAS CASAS
GANTE
BALDERAS
LOS ANGELES
ESTADIO
AV. 5 DE FEBRERO
AZUCENA
VIOLETA
5 DE MAYO
ANALCO
CALZ. DE LAS PALMAS
CALZ. GONZÁLEZ GALLO
DR. ROBERTO MICHEL
20 DE NOVIEMBRE
28 DE ENERO
NUÑEZ MORQUECHO
MEDRANO
ANAHUAC
20 DE NOVIEMBRE
275 diag
28 DE ENERO
LEANDRO VALLE
LIBERTAD
NUEVA GALICIA
NUEVA GALICIA
LIBERTAD
PRISCILIANO SANCHEZ
45
51A - 51B

0   200 yds
0   200 m

© AVALON TRAVEL PUBLISHING, INC.

side, between Medellin and Barcenas. Inside, you'll find an excellent exposition of photos, drawings, paintings, papers, and artifacts, depicting 500 years of Guadalajara history, from the Conquest to the present. Don't miss the display, showing the widening of Av. Juárez during the 1950s, when engineers and workers, seemingly miraculously moved the entire city telephone building 50 feet without a single service interruption. Open Wed.–Sat. 10 A.M.–5 P.M., Sun. 10 A.M.–2:30 P.M.; tel. 33/3658-3706.

Sights South of the Cathedral

Just a block east and half a block south of the cathedral front, let the **Palacio de Gobierno,** on Armas' east side, be the first stop of your southside walking tour; open daily 9:30 A.M.–8:30 P.M.) At the **city tourism information booth** *(módulo de información)* just inside

© BRUCE WHIPPERMAN

An arrestingly graphic 1937 mural by José Clemente Orozco adorns the staircase at the Palacio de Gobierno.

the entrance, ask for a copy of their superb all-color *Points of Interest* bilingual foldout map and guide. Open Mon.–Fri. 9 A.M.–3 P.M. and 4–7 P.M., Sat. and Sun. 10 A.M.–12:30 P.M.

The Palacio de Gobierno's main attraction is the epic 1937 **Orozco mural** in the stairwell, right side of the inner patio. (See the special topic José Clemente Orozco.) Here, Father Miguel Hidalgo, with torch in hand, like an avenging angel, leads Mexico's struggle against the evil stooges of Communism, Capitalism, Fascism, and Catholicism. Don't miss the villians, such as General Porfirio Díaz, and the idiotic Benito Mussolini (middle right panel); or the heroes, such as mustachioed Emiliano Zapata (in campesino white cotton).

Plaza San Francisco

Walk four blocks south along 16 de Septiembre to the busy corner of Prisciliano Sánchez. A beloved pair of old churches, the Capilla de Nuestra Señora de Aranzazù, ahead of you on the right side of 16 de Septiembre, and the dignified Templo San Francisco de Asis on the left side, occupy the tree-shaded Parque San Francisco. The **Templo San Francisco de Asis,** built through the initiative of Franciscan padres between 1668 and 1692, stands on the site of a earlier (1552) Franciscan church and convent. Its exterior climaxes in its facade of Solomonic columns spiraling upward like giant barber poles. Inside, the airy, towering nave shines with a glittering baroque *retablo* above and behind the altar.

West, across 16 de September, the **Capilla de Nuestra Señora de Aranzazù,** built between 1749 and 1752, complements the majesty of San Francisco de Asis with its austere simplicity. Inside, visit the Virgén de Aranzazù, who presides above the altar in a regal glass case, beneath a divine golden *retablo*. Beneath nearly as fine a *retablo,* on the western (right) side wall, you can pay your respects to the Lord of the Afflicted; and on the opposite, east wall, you can do the same with a duplicate of the celebrated Virgén de Zapopan. Before leaving the nave, pass a duplicate of the equally beloved Virgén de Talpa, near the door; and on the way, be sure not to miss the little glass case with a swarm of children's toys nearly covering the **Santo Niño de Atocha** (Holy Child of Atocha.)

The tale of the Virgén de Aranzazù deserves retelling. Once upon a time in the remote Basque country of northern Spain, a shepherd stumbled upon an image of the Virgin and Child, caught in a thorn thicket. The amazed shepherd exclaimed to the image: "¡Aranzazù!" ("You are in the thorns!"). After hearing the shepherd's story, the Basque country people adopted his Virgin as their own and subsequently carried the tradition to the New World. In Guadalajara, Franciscan padre Francisco Iñigo Vallejo, with the patronage of rich Basque *hacendados,* got the chapel built in her honor.

Nueve Esquinas

Continue south along Colón, the street that borders the west side of the Aranzazù church. Within a block you enter the colorful working-class **Nueve Esquinas** ("Nine Corners") district. Here, a rainbow assortment of spruced-up 19th-century townhouse facades and hole-in-the-wall local workshops—printers, machine shops, electrical repair—decorate the narrow lanes.

After three short blocks you come to the neighborhood-center **Plaza Nueve Esquinas,** bordered by a squad of *birria* **restaurants** *(birrerias),* so-named for the savory, traditional Guadalajaran meat (goat, pork, or beef) stew that they all serve. Make sure that you have an appetite when you arrive, because a bowl of *birria* here is an opportunity you won't want to miss. Of the several popular restaurants, the best seems to be **Birrias Nueve Esquinas** on Colón, at the plaza-front. (For menu choices and other details, see Downtown Restaurants, in the Food section, later.)

Continue south from the plaza, along Colón one block, passing the shady, intimate little **Plazuela** on the left, at the corner of Nueva Galicia. One more long block brings you to busy Av. La Paz, where a cluster of intriguing **antique shops** occupies the corner of Colón and La Paz across the street. At this writing four stores offer items, ranging from fine restored furniture to dusty bric-a-brac. The most upscale of the four are **Antiguidades Don Porfirio,** on the southeast corner, at Colón 539, and **Antiguidades Padilla,**

two doors south. Both are open Mon.–Sat. 11 A.M.–2 P.M. and 4–7 P.M.

Archaeology and Paleontology Museums and Parque Agua Azul

To explore the worthwhile sights farther south, keep walking south, or hail a taxi (no more than $1.50) to carry you the ten blocks (one mile, 1.6 km) to the **Museo Arqueológico** (say Moo-SAY-oh Ar-kay-oh-LOH-hee-koh), directly across Independencia from the Parque Agua Azul entrance (between 16 de Septiembre and Calz. Independencia)

The museum, officially the Archaeological Museum of Western Mexico, displays an interesting collection of pre-Columbian artifacts from Jalisco, Colima, and Nayarit. The exhibits climax in the delightfully lifelike Colima figurines. Old men snooze, women gossip, children romp, while parrots squawk, dogs frolic, and armadillos scurry—all bringing, to the visitor's mindseye, a long-dead civilization back to vibrant life. Also, notice the explanation of the uniquely intriguing "bottle tombs" *(tumbas de tiro),* of a style found nowhere else but Colombia and Ecuador, as well as the exhibit (if they have one by the time you arrive—ask if they have a brochure or other written material) of the Iztepete archaeological site at the southwest edge of town. (See Sights in the City: West and South of Downtown chapter.) Open Tues.–Sun. 10 A.M.–2 P.M. and 5–7 P.M.; Nucleo Agua Azul 889; tel. 33/3619-0104.

Directly across Calz. Independencia, east of the museum, spend some time at **Parque Agua Azul.** Here, you could enjoy a whole day taking in a concert, strolling through a butterfly or bird house, snoozing on the grass, and more. For more details, see, Entertainment and Events, later in this chapter.

Next, visit the excellent, up-to-date **Paleontology Museum,** on González Gallo, corner of Michel, about half a mile east, at the far corner of Parque Agua Azul. Through a series of innovative permanent exhibits, the visitor explores the methods, tools, and content of paleontology. The grand finale is a transparent walkway over a life-sized model of one of Guadalajara's prime paleontological sites—a lake-bed, rich in remains of

Ice Age animals—saber-toothed tiger, giant sloth, mammoth—which visitors view and identify beneath their very feet. For more information, including a listing of the museum's classes, activities, and temporary exhibitions, visit their website: www.guadalajara.gob.mx/dependencias/museo paleontologico/index.html/. Also email: pale onto01@hotmail.com; tel. 33/3619-7043, 33/3610-6576, 33/3610-5548. Open Tues.–Sat. 10 A.M.–6 P.M., Sun. 11 A.M.–6 P.M.

ACCOMMODATIONS

Downtown Hotels: West Side

Many good hotels, ranging from budget to plush, dot Guadalajara's downtown, within walking distance of museums, monuments, theaters, and shopping. Many have parking garages, a desirable downtown option for auto travelers. Hotels farthest from the city-center cathedral plazas are generally the most economical.

By location (see also special topic Downtown Accommodations by Price), moving east toward the city center, the **Posada Tapatía,** one block off Juárez near the corner of Calle 8 Julio, is about 10 blocks from the cathedral. Its simple but gaily decorated rooms with bath are spread around a light, colorfully restored central patio. Tightly managed by the friendly on-site owner and his mother, the Tapatía offers good prices. Try for a room in the back, away from the noisy street. The 12 rooms rent for about $16 s, $21 d, with fans. López Cotilla 619, Guadalajara, Jalisco 44100; tel. 33/3614-9146; email: agalmaraz @hotmail.com.

A block closer in and one block south, the **Hotel El Aposento** (The Lodging), offers a bit of Porfirian charm at a moderate price. Several years ago, the enterprising owner of this bed-and-breakfast–style hostelry renovated this 19th-century-style hospital to a modern standard hotel. Now, the 19 rooms surround an airy fountain-patio, where guests enjoy a full American-style breakfast, included with their lodging. The rooms, although air-conditioned, high-ceilinged, and clean enough, are less than immaculate, with occasional rug spots and scratched paint. Many of the beds are spacious queen- and king-sized;

lamps are handy for reading, and cabinets and dressers are of polished wood. All rooms include attractively tiled baths with sink and shower, laundry, phones, parking, breakfast, and cable TV. Rates run about $55 s or d in standard double bed, $60 s or d for queen, $65 s or d for king, $75 d with two queen-sized beds. Fco. Madero 545, Guadalajara, Jalisco 44100; tel. 33/3614-1612, 33/3614-2609; (reservations or information) email: mansion1@prodigy.net.mx or info@elaposento.com; website: www.elapo sento.com.

Three blocks closer in, at the northeast corner of Prisciliano Sánchez and Donato Guerra, step up from the sidewalk and enter the cool, contemporary-classic interior of the **Hotel Cervantes.** Here, everything, from the marble-and-brass lobby, the modern restaurant and bar, rooftop-view pool, and exercise room downstairs to the big beds, plush carpets, and shiny marble baths of the rooms upstairs, seems perfect for the enjoyment of its predominately business clientele. For such refinement, rates, at about $48 s, $51 d, are surprisingly moderate; with TV, phones, parking, and air-conditioning; credit cards are accepted. Prisciliano Sánchez 442; tel./fax 33/3613-6686 and 33/3613-6846.

Across the street, on Prisciliano Sánchez between Ocampo and Donato Guerra, the old standby **Hotel Sevilla** offers basic accommodations at budget prices. Its 80 rooms, furnished in dark brown wood and rugs to match, are plain but comfortable. For more light and quiet, get an upper-story room away from the street. Amenities include a lobby with TV, parking, a hotel safe for storing valuables, and a restaurant open daily except Sunday. Rates run $14 s, $15 d, $21 t; fans and telephones included. Prisciliano Sánchez 413, Guadalajara, Jalisco 44100; tel. 33/3614-9354 or 33/3614-9037, fax 33/3614-9172.

One block away, on Madero, the even plainer **Hotel Hamilton** offers a rock-bottom alternative. The 32 bare-bulb, not-so-clean rooms border on dingy; their steel doors seem to enhance the drabness more than increasing security. Store your valuables in the hotel safe. For less noise and more light, get a room in back, away from the street. Rooms rent for $8 s or d, $13 t, with fans but no parking. Madero 381, Guadalajara, Jalisco 44100; tel. 33/3614-6726,

Cheerier and closer in, where the pedestrian strolling mall begins on Moreno, stands the big, 110-room **Hotel Internacional.** Downstairs, a small lobby with comfortable chairs adjoins the reception area. In the tower upstairs, the 1960s-style rooms, most with city views, are clean and comfortable but varied. Look at more than one before moving in. Try for a discount below the asking prices of $55 s or d, which are high compared to the competition. (The hotel does, however, offer a 15 percent discount for a one-week rental). Amenities include fans, some a/c, phones, TV, a cafe, and parking; credit cards are accepted. Pedro Moreno 570, Guadalajara, Jalisco 44100; tel. 33/3613-0330, fax 33/3613-2866.

Downtown Hotels: City Center

Right in the middle of the downtown bustle, the shiny **Hotel Fénix** offers deluxe, moderately priced accommodations. The owners have managed to upgrade this rather basic small-lobby hotel into something more elaborate. The somewhat cramped result, while not unattractive, is sometimes noisy and crowded. During the day, tour groups traipse in and out past the reception desk, while at night guests crowd the adjacent lobby bar for drinks and live combo music. Upstairs the 200 air-conditioned rooms are spacious and comfortably furnished with American-standard motel amenities. Walk-in rates, which run about $76 s or d, are high for a hotel with neither pool nor parking. You might try for a better deal in advance by booking a package through a travel agent. Corona 160, Guadalajara, Jalisco 44100; tel. 33/3614-5714, fax 33/3613-4005.

With the same prime location right across the street, the second-floor **Hotel Posada Regis** offers both economy and a bit of old-world charm. Its clean and comfortable high-ceiling rooms enclose a gracious Porfirian-era indoor lobby/atrium. Evening videos, friendly atmosphere, and a good homey breakfast/lunch cafe provide opportunities for relaxed exchanges with other travelers. The 19 rooms cost $20 s and $25 d, with phones, fans, and optional TV, but no parking;

Guests enjoy tranquil, moderately-priced lodging at city-center Hotel La Rotonda.

credit cards are accepted. Corona 171, Guadalajara, Jalisco 44100; tel. 33/3614-8633; or tel./fax 33/3613-3026.

Central location, comfortable rooms (although some a bit worn), and modest prices explain the popularity of the nearby **Hotel Universo,** two blocks east at López Cotilla, corner of Degollado. Guests enjoy many renovated, carpeted, and draped air-conditioned rooms with wood furniture and ceiling-to-floor tiled bathrooms. The 137 rooms and suites rent for $33 s, $35 d, suites from about $41, with TV, phones, and parking; credit cards are accepted. López Cotilla 161, Guadalajara, Jalisco 44100; tel. 33/3613-2815, fax 33/3613-4734; website: www.trekkersnet .com/universo.

One block north, guests at the **Hotel Calinda Roma** enjoy luxurious amenities—plush lobby, shiny restaurant/bar, rooftop rose garden with pool—usually available only at pricier hostelries. The owners, however, have upped the tariffs; whether they can make them stick is another question. Try bargaining for discounts below the $78 s, $84 d asking rates; with TV, phones, a/c, parking, and **limited wheelchair access;** credit cards are accepted. Some rooms, although clean and comfortable, are small. Look before moving in. Av. Juárez 170, Guadalajara, Jalisco 44100; tel. 33/3614-8650, fax 33/3613-0557.

Across the street, the **Holiday Inn Hotel and Suites** offers a host of luxuries. Upstairs, rooms are luxuriously appointed in soothing pastels, marble baths, plush carpets, and large beds. For all this and more, you'll pay from about $100 d, with cable TV, phones, a/c, parking, classy restaurant, but no pool; credit cards are accepted. Juárez 211; tel. 33/3613-1763, fax 33/3614-9766; (reservations and information) email: holidaycentro@infosel.net.mx; website: www.basshotels.com.

The three-story, authentically baroque **Hotel Frances** rises among its fellow monuments on a quiet side street within sight of the Teatro Degollado. Guadalajara's first hotel, built in 1610, the Frances was restored to its original splendor in the late 1980s. The 40-odd rooms, all with bath, glow with polished wood, bright tile, and fancy frosted cut-glass windows. Downstairs, an elegant chandelier illuminates the dignified, plant-decorated interior patio and adjacent restaurant. However, in order to increase business, **owners have installed nightly live music downstairs,** which for some may not fit with the hotel's otherwise old-world ambience. Rates, however, run a very reasonable $50 s, $53 d; credit cards are accepted; fans only, and there's no parking. Maestranza 35, Guadalajara, Jalisco 44100; tel. 33/3613-1190 or 33/3613-0936, fax 33/3658-2831.

The big colonial-facade **Hotel de Mendoza,** only a couple of blocks north of the Teatro Degollado, is a longtime favorite of Guadalajara repeat visitors. Refined traditional embellishments— neo-Renaissance murals and wall portraits, rich dark paneling, glittering candelabras—grace the lobby, while upstairs, carpeted halls lead to spacious, comfortable rooms furnished with tasteful dark decor, including large baths, thick towels, and many other extras. The 100 rooms and suites rent from $80 s, $90 d, with American cable TV,

phones, a/c, a small pool, refined restaurant, parking, and **limited wheelchair access;** credit cards are accepted. V. Carranza 16, Guadalajara, Jalisco 44100; tel. 33/3613-4646, fax 33/3613-7310; (information and reservations) email: hotel@demendoza.com.mx; website: www.demendoza.com.mx.

A choice location, on a quiet side street just north of the Museo Regional, explains part of the success of the 33-room **Hotel La Rotonda.** Past the small reception of this former mansion, you enter a light courtyard, decorated by old-world stone arches, where guests linger over breakfast. Farther on, corridors lead past a number of intimate rear patios. Most rooms open onto the upstairs courtyard-view balcony, bordered by potted plants and a gilded iron railing. Inside, rooms vary in size, but all are floored with attractive ruddy tiles and appointed with immaculate, up-to-date bathrooms and solid, polished hardwood furniture. Asking rates are about $55 s, $60 d, with phones, cable TV, restaurant, bar, small events salon, fans, parking, and credit cards accepted. Liceo 130, Guadalajara, Jalisco 44100; tel./fax 33/3614-1017, toll-free in Mexico, tel. 01-800/964-78; (information and reservations) email: hotel esucasa@yahoo.com; website: www.sucasa-hoteles.com.mx.

Downtown Hotels: South Side

A number of good-value smaller hotels dot the south-side downtown neighborhood, close to the colorful Parque San Francisco and its pair of beloved old churches. The competent owners of the Hotel Universo (described in an earlier section) also run a pair of recommended budget hotels a block east of the *parque.* Their graceful, authentically colonial **Hotel San Francisco Plaza** is replete with traditional charm. The reception area opens to an airy and tranquil inner patio, where big soft chairs invite you to relax amid a leafy garden of potted plants. In the evenings, the venerable arched stone corridors gleam with antique, cut-crystal lanterns. Upstairs, although the rooms vary, most have high ceilings, with plenty of polished wood, handmade furniture, rustic brass lamps by the bed, and sentimental

DOWNTOWN ACCOMMODATIONS BY PRICE

Accommodations are listed in increasing order of double-room (two people in one bed) rates. Telephone *lada* (area code) is 33; 800 numbers are for toll-free reservations from the U.S. and Canada. 01-800 numbers are for the same from within Mexico; postal code is 44100.

City Center

Hotel Posada Regis Corona 171; tel. 3614-8633; tel./fax 3613-3026; $25

Hotel Universo, López Cotilla 161; tel. 3613-2815, fax 3613-4734; website: www.trekkers net.com/universo; $35

Hotel Frances, Maestranza 35; tel. 3613-1190 or 3613-0936, fax 3658-2831; $53

Hotel La Rotonda, Liceo 130; tel./fax 3614-1017, 01-800/964-78; email: hotelesucasa@ yahoo.com; website: www.sucasa-hoteles.com.mx; $60

Hotel Fénix, Corona 160; tel. 3614-5714, fax 3613-4005; $76

Hotel Calinda Roma, Av. Juárez 170; tel. 3614-8650, fax 3613-0557; $84

Hotel de Mendoza, V. Carranza 16; tel. 3613-4646, fax 3613-7310; email: hotel@demendoza .com.mx; website: www.demendoza.com.mx; $90

Holiday Inn Hotel and Suites, 211 Juárez; tel. 3613-1763, fax 3614-9766 or 800/465-4329; email: holidaycentro@infosel.net.mx; website: www.basshotels.com; $100

Westside

Hotel Hamilton, Madero 381; tel. 3614-6726; $8

Hotel Sevilla, Prisciliano Sánchez 413; tel. 3614-9354, fax 3614-9172; $15

Posada Tapatía, López Cotilla 619; tel. 3614-9146; email: agalmaraz@hotmail.com; $21

Hotel Cervantes, 442 Prisciliano Sánchez; tel./fax 3613-6686 and 3613-6846; $51

Hotel Internacional, Pedro Moreno 570; tel. 3613-0330, fax 3613-2866; $55

Hotel El Aposento, Fco. Madero 545; tel. 3614-1612 or 3614-2609; email: mansion1@ prodigy.net.mx or info@elaposento.com; website: www.elaposento.com; $65

South Side

Hotel Latino, Prisciliano Sánchez 74; tel. 3614-4484 or 3614-6214; website: www.trekkers net.com/universo; $16

Hotel San Francisco Plaza, Degollado 267; tel. 3613-8954, fax 3613-3257; website: www.trekkersnet.com/universo; $40

Hotel Don Quijote Plaza, Héroes 91; tel. 3658-1299 or 3614-2845; $55

Hotel Misión Carlton, Av. Niños Héroes 125; tel. 3614-7272, fax 3613-5539 or 800/ 44UTELL; email: fm981008@prodigy.net.mx; website: www.hotelsmision.com.mx; $85

Hotel Santiago de Compostela, Colón 272; tel. 3613-8880, fax 3658-1925, 800/365-5300; email: hotelsantiagocom@megared.net.mx; $90

old-Mexico paintings on the walls. Each room has a phone, TV, fan, and a large, modern-standard bathroom with marble sink. You'll find a pleasant restaurant with high ceilings and chandeliers downstairs in front and plenty of parking.

All this for $37 s, $40 d; credit cards are accepted. Degollado 267, Guadalajara, Jalisco 44100; tel. 33/3613-8954, fax 33/3613-3257.

The San Francisco Plaza's owners also run the **Hotel Latino,** one of Guadalajara's better cheap hotels, just around the corner at Prisciliano Sánchez. Although it's a plain hotel with a small lobby, the Latino's guests nevertheless enjoy a modicum of amenities. The 57 rooms in four stories (no elevator) are clean, carpeted, and thoughtfully furnished, albeit a bit worn around the edges. Baths are modern-standard, with shiny-tile showers and marble sinks. Rates are certainly right, at about $12 s, $16 d, including a/c, TV, parking, and phones; credit cards are not accepted. Prisciliano Sánchez 74, Guadalajara, Jalisco 44100; tel. 33/3614-4484 or 33/3614-6214.

If the Hotel San Francisco Plaza is full, you might try the less charming but recommended **Hotel Don Quijote Plaza,** half a block south at Héroes. The three tiers of 33 rooms at this renovated 19th-century-vintage hotel surround an inviting inner restaurant patio. The simply but comfortably furnished rooms run about $55 s or d with one double bed, $60 for d or t with two double beds, $80 with spa tub, bath, telephone, TV, air-conditioning, and parking. Héroes 91, Guadalajara, Jalisco 44100; tel. 33/3658-1299, 33/3614-2845.

If, however, you can pay a bit for more refinements, go three blocks west to the **Hotel Santiago de Compostela.** Here, you'll find a graceful, old-world-style hotel tucked to one side of the lively Parque San Francisco. Past the small desk at the foyer, enter a light and elegant patio-bar-lobby, furnished with invitingly soft sofas. Here, a pianist spins soothing semiclassical melodies afternoons after around 4:30 P.M.

Upstairs, the five floors of 95 rooms, all opening onto the airy central atrium, are immaculate and comfortably appointed with carpets and furnishings invitingly decorated in earth tones. Four of the rooms have built-in spa tubs. Baths are deluxe, shiny, and spacious. A rooftop view pool-patio completes the attractive picture. Rates run about $90 d, but ask for a promotional price (which could run as low as $50); with phone, air-conditioning, cable TV, gym, business center, meeting rooms, garage parking, and credit cards accepted. Colón 272, Guadalajara, Jalisco 44100; tel. 33/3613-8880, fax 33/3658-1925; tel. toll-free in Mexico 800/365-5300; email: hotel santiagocom@megared.net.mx.

About a mile south, at the downtown's far southern edge, business travelers might consider the **Hotel Misión Carlton** (formerly the Hilton). During the 1970s, investors wagered a pile of cash, based on a planned new south-end financial center that never really panned out. The result was the present hotel, with a load of deluxe business facilities, including a convention center accommodating 4,000 people, a business and negotiating center, two restaurants, two bars, and 191 deluxe view rooms. Rates, nominally around $150, but usually discounted to about $85 s or d, run about half the rates of comparable hotels around the westside Guadalajara Expo convention center. If the Misión Carlton has a drawback, it's the small pool-patio, noisy from traffic on the adjacent Avenidas 16 de Septiembre and Niños Héroes. Av. Niños Héroes 125, Guadalajara, Jalisco 44100; toll-free in United States and Canada, tel. 800/44UTELL, or 33/3614-7272, 33/3613-5779, fax 33/3613-5539; email: fm981008@prodigy.net.mx; website: www.hotelsmision.com.mx.

Bus Station and Airport Hotels

The suburban Hotels El Serena and Casa Grande offer interesting bus- and air-travel-related options, respectively. For bus travelers, the big long-distance Central Nueva bus station is at Guadalajara's far southeast edge, at least 20 minutes by taxi (figure $8) from the center—for this reason, many find it convenient to stay at the adjacent sprawling, two-pool, moderately priced modern **Hotel El Serena,** with restaurant. Bus and truck noise, however, may be a problem. Ask for a quiet *(tranquilo)* room. The 600 tidy and comfortable rooms, all with bath, rent for about $30 s or d. Rooms vary; look at more than one before moving in. Carretera Zapotlanejo 1500, Guadalajara, Jalisco 45625; tel. 33/3600-0910, fax 33/3600-0015.

For air travelers, try the luxuriously spacious and airy **Hotel Casa Grande,** immediately accessible on foot, just outside the airport terminal exit door. Rates for this business-friendly hotel, with meeting rooms and business center, run about $150 (when reserving, ask for a promotional or business rate) for a comfortable, deluxe double room with TV, phone, big bed, air-conditioning, and a pool, restaurant, bar downstairs, and credit cards accepted. Calle Interior, Aeropuerto Internacional Miguel Hidalgo s/n, Guadalajara, Jalisco 45640; tel./fax 33/3678-9000 or 33/3678-9099; (information and reservations) email: cchica@mail.udg.mx.

FOOD
Breakfast and Snacks
Local folks flock to the acres of *fondas* (permanent food stalls) on the second floor of the **Mercado Libertad** at the east end of Plaza Tapatía. Hearty home-style fare, including Guadalajara's specialty, *birria*—pork, goat, or lamb in savory, spiced tomato-chicken broth—is at its safest and best here. It's hard to go wrong if you make sure your choices are hot and steaming. Market stalls, furthermore, depend on repeat customers and are generally very careful that their offerings are wholesome. Be sure to douse fresh vegetables with plenty of lime *(lima)* juice, however. Open daily about 7 A.M.–6 P.M.

Downtown Guadalajara is not overloaded with

A TROVE OF FRUITS AND NUTS

Besides carrying the usual temperate fruits, *jugerías* and markets are seasonal sources for a number of exotic varieties:

avocado *(aguacate,* ah-gwah-KAH-tay): Aztec aphrodisiac

banana *(platano):* many kinds—big and small, red and yellow

chirimoya *(chirimoya):* green scales, white pulp; sometimes called an *anona*

coconut *(coco):* coconut "milk" is called *agua coco*

grapes *(uvas):* August–November season

guanabana *(guanabana):* looks, but doesn't taste, like a green mango

guava *(guava):* delicious juice, widely available canned

lemon *(limón,* pronounced "lee-MOHN"): uncommon and expensive; use lime instead

lime *(lima* pronounced "LEE-mah"): douse salads with it

mamey *(mamey,* pronounced "mah-MAY"): yellow, juicy fruit; excellent for jellies and preserves

mango *(mango):* king of fruit, in a hundred varieties June–November

orange *(naranja,* pronounced "nah-RAHN-ha"): greenish skin but sweet and juicy

papaya *(papaya):* said to aid digestion and healing

peach *(durazno,* pronounced "doo-RAHS-noh"): delicious and widely available as canned juice

peanut *(cacahuate,* pronounced "kah-kah-WAH-tay"): home roasted and cheap

pear *(pera):* fall season

pecan *(nuez/nueces):* for a treat, try freshly ground pecan butter

piña anona *(piña anona):* looks like a thin ear of corn without the husk; tastes like pineapple

pineapple *(piña):* huge, luscious, and cheap

strawberry *(fresa,* pronounced "FRAY-sah"): local favorite

tangerine *(mandarina):* common around Christmas

watermelon *(sandía,* pronounced "sahn-DEE-ah"): perfect on a hot day

zapote *(zapote,* pronounced "sah-POH-tay"): yellow, fleshy fruit; said to induce sleep

zapote colorado *(zapote colorado):* brown skin, red, puckery fruit, like persimmon; incorrectly called *mamey*

restaurants, and many of them close early. (For much more variety and super-fine dining prospects, see the Food sections in the Minerva-Chapultepec and Plaza del Sol–Chapalita sections of the City: West and North of Downtown chapter.)

Nevertheless, for breakfast, lunch, or supper, you can always rely on **Sanborn's,** which retains the 1950s' ambience and menu of its former Denny's owners. Find it right in the middle of town, at the corner of Juárez and 16 de Septiembre. Open daily 7:30 A.M.–10 P.M.

For a local variation, head directly upstairs to **Restaurant Esquina** on the same corner, open 7 A.M.–10:30 P.M., or to the original **Sanborn's** across the street, open daily 7:30 A.M.–11 P.M. Besides a tranquil, refined North American–style coffee shop, it has a big gift shop upstairs and a bookstore, offering English-language paperbacks and magazines, downstairs.

Local coffee and conversation hangout **Madoka,** a few blocks west on Medillin, between Juárez and Moreno, is as much a cultural experience as is an eatery. Here, a drove of loyal devotees enjoy many coffees plus a broad menu, from omelets to *carne asada.* Open daily 8 A.M.–11 P.M.

For a light breakfast or a break during a hard afternoon of sight-seeing, stop in at **Croissants Alfredo** bakery, north side of Plaza Liberación (in front and east of the Teatro Degollado.) Here, a trove of luscious goodies—flaky croissants, crisp cookies, tasty tarts, and good coffee—can keep you going for hours. Open daily 8 A.M.–9:30 P.M.

If, on the other hand, you need a little break from Mexican cuisine, there's a **McDonald's** for breakfast (at Juárez and Colón, one short block west of Sanborn's). An Egg McMuffin with ham, hashbrowns and coffee, is about $4 until noon, daily.

Downtown Restaurants: City Center

Moving west and south from the Plaza Tapatía, first comes the airy, restored Porfirian **Restaurant Rinconada,** on the Morelos strolling mall behind the Teatro Degollado. The mostly tourist and upper-class local customers enjoy Rinconada for its good meat, fish, and fowl entrées, plus

the mariachis who wander in from the Plaza Mariachi nearby. By 4 P.M. many afternoons, two or three groups are filling the place with their melodies. Morelos 86; tel. 33/3613-9914. Open Mon.–Sat. 8 A.M.–9 P.M., Sun. 1–6 P.M. Moderate–expensive.

Nearby, a few blocks southwest, a pair of clean, well-lighted places for good local food stand out. Try **La Chata** on Corona, between Cotilla and Juárez, next to Bancomer. Although plenty good for breakfast, *cena* (supper) is when the cadre of female cooks come into their own. Here you can have it all: tacos, *chiles rellenos,* tostadas, enchiladas, *pozole, moles,* and a dozen other delights you've probably never heard of, all cooked the way *mamacita* used to. Open daily 8 A.M.–11 P.M. Budget–moderate.

One block south and one block west is the no-nonsense but worthy **Restaurant Málaga,** 16 de Septiembre 210, where the sometimes taciturn but hardworking owner really does come

A chef prepares *birria* at restaurant Birrias Nueve Esquinas.

from Málaga, Spain. The food shows it: an eclectic feast of hearty breakfasts, which include a fruit plate and good French bread; a bountiful four-course *comida corrida* for around $5; many salads, sandwiches, and desserts; and savory espresso coffee. Besides the food, customers enjoy live semiclassical piano solos, daily 2–4:30 P.M. Open Mon.–Sat. 7 A.M.–9 P.M., Sun. 8 A.M.–9 P.M. Budget–moderate.

Downtown Restaurants: West Side

Return a few blocks north, just a block west of the cathedral, to **Sandy's,** at mezzanine level, above the plaza, northeast corner of Colón and P. Moreno, tel. 33/3614-5871. Here, snappy management, service with a flourish, and weekend evening live music make the typical, but tasty, coffee shop menu of soups, salads, meat, pasta, Mexican plates, sandwiches, and desserts seem like an occasion. Open daily 8 A.M.–10:30 P.M. Moderate.

If you're in the mood for a restful lunch or dinner, head west a few blocks to the airy interior patio of **Restaurant San Miguel,** at the northwest corner of Morelos and Donato Guerra. Here, you can enjoy salad, soup, or a full meal. (Warning: They put too much salt in my soup, so best order *"sin sal, por favor"*—"without salt, please.") Open Wed.–Sat. 8:30 A.M.–11 P.M., Sun.–Tues, 8:30 A.M.–6 P.M.; tel. 33/3613-0809. Moderate–expensive.

Enjoy your meal while soaking in the tranquil, traditional ambience beneath the venerable arches and walls of Guadalajara's oldest convent for women, founded by the sisters of Santa Teresa de Jesús, in 1694. The old institution's topsy-turvy history mirrors that of Mexico itself. After its founding, it became the home for the Virgén de Zapopan until her present sanctuary was built decades later. In the 1860s the nuns were expelled by the liberal forces during the War of the Reforms. They were allowed to return by President Díaz in 1895, only to be pushed out by revolutionary general Venustiano Carranza in 1914. The sisters bounced back, returning after the revolution subsided in 1919, but were again expelled by President Calles during the Cristero rebellion

in 1925. Liberal but conciliatory President Lázaro Cárdenas allowed their return in 1939. Finally, the mostly aged sisters vacated their old home, this time voluntarily and for the last time, in 1977.

Continue a few blocks west along Juárez to **Restaurant La Gran China,** between Martinez and 8 Julio, where the Cantonese owner/chef puts out an authentic and tasty array of dishes. Despite the reality of La Gran China's crisp bok choy, succulent spareribs, and smooth savory noodles, they nevertheless seem a small miracle here, half a world away from Hong Kong. Open daily noon–10 P.M. Juárez 590; tel. 33/3613-1447. Budget–moderate.

For a variation, try Gran China's simpler but equally authentic neighbor, **Restaurant Chong Wah,** half a block east, at the corner of E.G. Martinez. Juárez 558; tel. 33/3613-9950. Open noon–8 P.M. Budget–moderate.

Continue several blocks farther, to the far west end of downtown, about a mile from the cathedral, to **Restaurant Copenhagen 77,** one of Guadalajara's classiest institutions. Its brand of unpretentious elegance—polished 1940s decor, subdued live jazz, correct attentive service, tasty entrées—will never go out of style. It's upstairs, at 140 Z. Castellanos; follow Juárez nine blocks west of Av. 16 de Septiembre to the west end of Parque Revolución. Open Mon.–Sat. noon–midnight, Sun. noon–6 P.M.; live jazz afternoons 3–4:30 P.M. and nights 8 P.M.–midnight. Moderate–expensive.

Downtown Restaurants: South Side

Dining prospects are also good around the Parque San Francisco, about five blocks south of the cathedral. At Corona 250, corner of Prisciliano Sánchez, north side of Parque San Francisco, stands the local favorite, **Taquería Las Faroles.** Here, Mexican traditional food lovers can have it all: six kinds of tacos, plus quesadillas, *gringas, torta ahogada* (Mexican dipped sandwich), and much more. Budget–moderate.

One evening, for plenty of food and fun, go nearby, to **La Feria** (The Fair). True to its name, La Feria is a party ready to happen: ceilings hung with a rainbow of piñatas and tassels flowing in the breeze of overhead fans, and tables piled high with goodies.

Here, vegetarian pretensions must be suspended, if only to sample the enough-in-themselves barbecued appetizers—spicy *chorizo* sausage, tacos, *torta ahogada* (hot dipped sandwich), ribs, and much more. Actually, vegetarians needn't go hungry—try the mixed salads, guacamole, or soups, for example. Go for it all and share a big *parrillada* specialty of the house appetizer plate with some friends. By the time the food has gone down, the next course—a mariachi concert, complete with rope tricks and singers, with maybe a juggler or magic act thrown in for good measure, will keep you entertained for hours. Corona 291; tel. 33/3613-7150 or 33/3613-1812. Open daily 1:30 P.M.–midnight. The complete show starts around 9 P.M. Moderate–expensive.

Yet another must-go spot for food is the **Plaza Nueve Esquinas,** on Colón, just two blocks south of the Parque San Francisco. Guadalajara families flock here afternoons and early evenings to feast on traditional Jalisco *birria* meat stew, served up by half a dozen surrounding restaurants. Among the best is restaurant **Birrias Nueve Esquinas.** Among their specialties are *Birria de Chivo Tatemada a Fuego Lento* (*birria* of goat roasted over a low fire) and *Barbacoa de Borrego en Pencos de Maguey* (barbecued lamb in maguey leaf). Alternatively, they offer plenty of more familiar goodies, such as lamb and chicken consommé, cheeseburgers with french fries, guacamole con *totopos* (chips), salad, tacos, and quesadillas. Tel. 33/3613-6260. Open daily 8 A.M.–7:30 P.M. Moderate.

ENTERTAINMENT AND EVENTS
Just Wandering Around
Afternoons any day, and Sunday in particular, are good for people-watching around Guadalajara's many downtown plazas. Favorite strolling grounds are the broad fountain and Plaza Guadalajara in front of the cathedral and the even broader Plaza Liberación behind of the cathedral and, especial-

ly in the evening, the pedestrian mall-streets, such as Colón, Galeana, Morelos, and Moreno, which meander south and west from cathedral-front Plaza Guadalajara.

In your wanderings, don't forget to walk east to the **Plaza de Los Mariachis,** just east of the Plaza Tapatía, adjacent to the Mercado Libertad and the big boulevard, Independencia, that runs beneath the Plaza Tapatía. Take a sidewalk table, have a drink or snack, and enjoy the mariachis' sometimes soulful, sometimes bright, but always enjoyable, offerings.

If you time it right, you can enjoy the concert, which the Jalisco State Band has provided since 1898, in the adjacent Plaza de Armas, south of the cathedral (Thursday and Sunday at 6:30 P.M.), or take in an art film at the Hospicio Cabañas (Mon.–Sat. 4, 6, and 8 P.M.). If you miss these, climb into a *calandria* (horse-drawn carriage) for a ride around town; carriages are available on Liceo between the rotunda and the history museum, just north of the cathedral, for about $15/hour.

Parque Agua Azul
Some sunny afternoon, hire a taxi (about $2 from the city center) and find out why Guadalajara families love Parque Agua Azul. The entrance is on Independencia, about a mile south of Plaza Tapatía. It's a green, shaded place where you can walk, roll, sleep, or lie on the grass. When weary of that, head for the bird park, admire the banana-beaked toucans and squawking macaws, and continue into the aviary where free-flying birds flutter overhead. Nearby, duck into the *mariposario* and enjoy the flickering rainbow hues of a host of *mariposas (butterflies)*. Continue to the orchids in a towering hothouse, festooned with growing blossoms and misted continuously by a rainbow of spray from the center. Before other temptations draw you away, stop for a while at the open-air band or symphony concert in the amphitheater. The park, tel. 33/3619-0328, is open Tues.–Sun. 10 A.M.–6 P.M. Entrance fee is less than a dollar.

For a big list of kid-friendly entertainment, including parks, the zoo, amusement parks, roller- and ice-skating, and more, see Family

Outings in the Bringing the Kids to Guadalajara section of the On the Road chapter.

Music and Dance Performances

The **Teatro Degollado** hosts world-class opera, symphony, and ballet events. While you're in the Plaza Liberación, drop by the theater box office and ask for a *lista de eventos.* You can also call (or ask your hotel desk clerk to call) the theater box office at 33/3614-4773 or 33/3616-4991, for reservations and information. Pick up tickets 4–7 P.M. on the day of the performance. For a very typical Mexican treat, attend one of the regular 10 A.M. Sunday University of Guadalajara folkloric ballet performances. They're immensely popular; get tickets in advance.

You can also sample the offerings of the **Instituto Cultural Cabañas.** It sponsors many events, both experimental and traditional, including folkloric ballet performances every Wednesday. For more information, ask at the Hospicio Cabañas admission desk, or tel.

33/3618-8135 or 33/3618-8132. Open Tues.–Sun. 10 A.M.–5 P.M.

Local jazz mecca **Restaurant Copenhagen 77,** at 140 Z. Castellanos, presents Maestro Carlos de la Torre and his group nightly Mon.–Sat. 8 A.M. to midnight and afternoons 3–4:30 P.M. At the west end of Parque Revolución, about a mile west of the cathedral.

Restaurant/club **Peña Cuicalli** (House of Song) offers rock music Tuesday evenings and romantic Latin Thursday–Sunday evenings. It's at west-side Av. Niños Héroes 1988, next to the Niños Héroes monument; tel. 33/3825-4690.

For some very typically Mexican fun, plan a night out for the dinner and mariachi show at **La Fería** restaurant, at Corona 291, across from Parque San Francisco. (See Downtown Restaurants: South Side, above.)

Fiestas

Although Guadalajarans always seem to be celebrating, the town really heats up during its three major annual festivals. Starting the second week in

The timeless silhouette of the Teatro Degollado, host to a world-class procession of operatic, dance, and symphonic events, graces the Plaza Liberación's south side.

MARIACHIS

Mariachis, those thoroughly Mexican troubadour bands, have spread from their birthplace in Jalisco throughout Mexico and into much of the United States. The name itself reveals their origin. "Mariachi" originated with the French *mariage*, or marriage. When French influence peaked during the 1864–1867 reign of Maximilian, Jaliscans transposed *mariage* to "mariachi," a label they began to identify with the five-piece folk bands that played for weddings.

The original ensembles, consisting of a pair of violins, *vihuela* (large eight-stringed guitar), *jarana* (small guitar), and harp, played exclusively traditional melodies. Song titles such as "Las Moscas" (The Flies), "El Venado" (The Stag), and "La Papaya," thinly disguised their universal themes, mostly concerning love.

Although such all-string folk bands still play in Jalisco, notably in Tecalitlán and other rural areas, they've largely been replaced by droves of trumpet-driven commercial mariachis. The man who sparked the shift was probably Emilio Azcárraga Vidaurreta, the director of radio station XEW, which began broadcasting in Mexico City in 1930. In those low-fidelity days, the subdued sound of the harp didn't broadcast well, so Azcárraga suggested the trumpet as a replacement. It was so successful the trumpet has become the signature sound of present-day mariachis.

Still, mariachis mostly do what they've always done—serenade sweethearts, play for weddings and parties, even accompany church masses. They seem to be forever strolling around town plazas on Saturday nights and Sunday afternoons, looking for jobs. Their fees, which should be agreed upon before they start, often depend on union scale per song, per serenade, or per hour.

Sometimes mariachis serve as a kind of live jukebox which, for a coin, will play your old favorite. And even if it's a slightly tired but sentimental "Mañanitas" or "Cielito Lindo," you can't help but be moved by the singing violins, bright trumpets, and soothing guitars.

June, the southeast neighborhood, formerly the separate village of Tlaquepaque, hosts the **National Ceramics Fair.** Besides celebrated stoneware, Tlaquepaque shops and stalls are stuffed with a riot of ceramics and folk crafts from all over Mexico, while cockfights, regional food, folk dances, fireworks, and mariachis fill the streets.

A few months later, the entire city, Mexican states, and foreign countries get into the **Fiesta de Octobre.** For a month, everyone contributes something, from ballet performances, plays, and soccer games to selling papier-mâché parrots and *elote* (corn on the cob) in the plazas. Concurrently, Guadalajarans celebrate the traditional **Fiesta de la Virgén de Zapopan.** Church plazas are awash with merrymakers enjoying food, mariachis, dances (don't miss the Dance of the Conquest), and fireworks. The merrymaking peaks on October 12, when a huge crowd conducts the Virgin from the downtown cathedral to Zapopan. The merrymakers' numbers often swell to a million faithful who escort the Vir-

gin, accompanied by ranks of costumed saints, devils, Spanish conquistadors, and Aztec chiefs. (For a list of national and Guadalajara region fiestas, see the special topic Fiestas in the On the Road chapter.)

Dancing and Nightclubbing

The big west-side hotels are among the most reliable spots in town for dancing. Moving west from the city center, first comes the **Hotel Fiesta Americana,** about four miles along Avenidas Juárez and Vallarta, on the left side of the Minerva traffic circle. Patrons enjoy dancing both in the lobby bar nightly from about 7 P.M. and in the nightclub **Caballo Negro** from about 9:30 P.M. Call 33/3825-3434 to verify the times.

The **Hotel Crowne Plaza,** a quarter-mile past the Minerva traffic circle, features a live trio for dancing afternoons and evenings in the lobby bar, **La Cantera** (happy hour 5–8 P.M.), and another trio Thurs.–Sat. from about 9 P.M. at the **Bar La Fiesta.** Additionally, its **Da Vinci disco** booms away seasonally from about 9 P.M. Call 33/3634-1034 for confirmation.

On the same boulevard, about a mile farther west, the relaxed tropical garden ambience of the **Hotel Camino Real** offers a luxuriously romantic setting for dancing and dining. Call 33/ 3134-2424 to verify live music programs and times.

Unwind at the downtown **nightclubs** (crowded with twenty- and thirty-somethings most Friday and Saturday nights) on Maestranza, between Sánchez and Madero. **Meridiana 60,** the more genteel of the two, is decorated inside with colored lights flashing on jungly vine-hung walls offers no-cover live salsa-rock music Wed., Fri., and Sat. beginning at 10 P.M.; tel. 33/3613-8489; open 10 A.M.–2 A.M. A few doors south and across the street, **Bar-Discoteca Maskaras** operates a downstairs bar and a no-cover upstairs discoteque (with the door shut so neighbors can sleep and customers can hear each other talk downstairs.); tel. 33/3614-8103; open daily 2 P.M.– 2 A.M.

Besides celebrated stoneware, Tlaquepaque shops and stalls are stuffed with a riot of ceramics and folk crafts from all over Mexico, while cockfights, regional food, folk dances, fireworks, and mariachis fill the streets.

Bullfights and Rodeos

Winter is the main season for *corridas de toros,* or bullfights. The bulls charge and the crowds roar *"¡Olé!"* (oh-LAY) Sunday afternoons at the Guadalajara Plaza de Toros (bullring), on Calz. Independencia about two miles north of the Mercado Libertad.

Local associations of *charros* (gentleman cowboys) stage rodeolike Sunday **charreadas** at Guadalajara *lienzos charro* (rodeo rings). Oft-used Guadalajara rodeo rings include **Lienzo Charro de Jalisco,** just beyond the southeast side of Parque Agua Azul; Calz. Las Palmas 477; tel. 33/3619-3232. Also watch for posters, or ask at your hotel desk or the tourist information office, tel. 33/3688-1600, for *corrida de toros* and *charreada* details and dates.

The Tequila Express

Ride the tourist train to the historic **ex-Hacienda San José,** now preserved as both museum and liquor distillery of the Herradura tequila firm, in the town of Amatitán, a few miles east of

CHARREADAS

The many Jalisco lovers of *charrería,* the sport of horsemanship, enjoy a long-venerated tradition. Boys and girls, coached by their parents, practice riding skills from the time they learn to mount a horse. Privileged young people become noble *charros* or *charras* or *(coronelas)*—gentleman cowboys and cowgirls—whose equestrian habits follow old aristocratic Spanish fashion, complete with broad sombrero, brocaded suit or dress, and silver spurs.

The years of long preparation culminate in the *charreada,* which entire communities anticipate with relish. Although superficially similar to an Arizona rodeo, a Jalisco *charreada* differs substantially. The festivities take place in a *lienzo charro,* literally, the passageway through which the bulls, horses, and other animals run from the corral to the ring. First comes the *cala de caballo,* a test of the horse and rider. The *charros* or *charras* must gallop full speed across the ring and make the horse stop on a dime. Next is the *piales de lienzo,* a roping exhibition during which an untamed horse must be halted and held by having its feet roped. Other bold performances include *jineteo de toro* (bull riding and throwing) and the super-hazardous *paso de la muerte,* in which a rider tries to jump upon an untamed bronco from his or her own galloping mount. *Charreadas* often end in a flourish with the *escaramuza charra,* a spectacular show of riding skill by *charras* in full, colorful dress.

the famed liquor town of Tequila. Included in the tour are viewing of the blue *agave* harvesting process, hacienda and factory tour, Mexican buffet, and a folkloric show, typically including folkloric dances, mariachis, a roping exhibition, and handicrafts. Buy tickets for the 10 A.M.–6 P.M. Saturday-only tour at the Guadalajara Chamber of Commerce at the corner of Vallarta and Niño Obrero, several miles west of downtown. The all-inclusive tariff runs $52 per adult; kids $32, children under six free; tel. 33/3880-9015 or 33/3122-7020. (You can also visit the ex-Hacienda San José Mon.–Fri. on your own. For details, see the Tequila section of the Great Getaways chapter.)

Entertainment and Events Listings

For many more entertainment ideas, pick up the **events schedule** at the Hospicio Cabañas, beyond the long pool/fountain at the east end of Plaza Tapatía, or the tourist information office in Plaza Tapatía, on Paseo Morelos, the mall-extension of Av. Morelos, behind the Teatro Degollado at Morelos 102. Another good source of entertaining events is the weekly English-language *Guadalajara Reporter,* always available at Sandi Bookstore, Tepeyac 718, Colonia Chapalita, tel. 33/3121-0863. (For more details and location, see the local map and the information section in the Plaza del Sol–Chapalita section of the City: West and North of Downtown chapter.) If you still can't find a newsstand copy, contact the newspaper office, at west-of-downtown Duque de Rivas 254, Guadalajara; tel. 33/3615-2177; email: editor@guadalajarareporter.com; website: www.guadalajarareporter.com.

SPORTS

Walking, Jogging, and Exercise Gyms

Walkers and joggers enjoy several spots around Guadalajara. Close in, the **Plaza Liberación** behind the cathedral provides a traffic-free (although concrete) jogging and walking space. Avoid the crowds with morning workouts. If you prefer grass underfoot, try **Parque Agua Azul** (entrance $2) on Calz. Independencia about a mile south of the Mercado Libertad. An even better jogging-

walking space is the **Parque de los Colomos**—hundreds of acres of greenery, laced with special jogging trails—four miles northwest from the city center, before Zapopan; take a taxi or bus #51C, which begins at the old bus terminal, near Parque Agua Azul, and continues north along Av. 16 de Septiembre, through downtown Guadalajara.

Guadalajara has a number of exercise gyms with the usual machines, plus hot tubs and steam rooms. For example, try the big **World Gym** fitness center, with a battery of weight machines, indoor pool, squash courts, mixed aerobics area, 250-meter jogging track, and women-only weights area. It's at Jesús Garcia 804, corner of Miguel Ángel de Quevedo, tel. 33/3640-0576, beside the Cinema Charlie Chaplin. (For details of more gyms in the Minerva-Chapultepec, Plaza del Sol–Chapalita, Lake Chapala, and Tlaquepaque districts, see the Sports sections of City: West and North of Downtown, City: East and South of Downtown, and Lake Chapala and Vicinity chapters.)

Tennis, Golf, and Swimming

Although Guadalajara has few, if any, public tennis courts, the **Hotel Camino Real** rents its courts to the public for about $10 an hour; Av. Vallarta 5005; tel. 33/3134-2424. Also, the **Hotels Fiesta Americana** (Aurelio Aceves 225, Glorieta Minerva; tel. 33/3825-3434) and the **Crowne Plaza** (Av. López Mateos Sur 2500; tel. 33/3634-1034) both have courts for guests.

Guadalajara and the Lake Chapala region have several good golf courses, three of which rent their tennis courts to the public. For details, see Golf and Tennis in the On the Road chapter.

Nearly all the luxury hotels have swimming pools. Three of the most convenient **downtown hotel pools** perch atop the moderately priced Hotels Calinda Roma, Santiago de Compostela, and Cervantes (see Accommodations, earlier).

If your hotel doesn't have a pool, try the World Gym (above), or go to the very popular **public pool and picnic ground** at Balneario Lindo Michoacán. Find it about two miles along Gallo southeast of Parque Agua Azul, corner Calz. J. González Gallo. Río Barco 1614; tel. 33/3635-

9399. Open daily 10 A.M.–5 P.M.; entrance about $4 adults, $2 kids.

For many more **out-of-town swimming sites,** see the special topic Balnearios in the On the Road chapter.

SHOPPING

The sprawling **Mercado Libertad,** at the east end of Plaza Tapatía, has several specialty areas distributed through two main sections. Most of the handicrafts are in the eastern, upper half. While some stalls carry guitars and sombreros, leather predominates—with jackets, belts, saddles, and the most *huaraches* (sandals) you'll ever see under one roof. Here, bargaining *es la costumbre* (the custom). Competition, furthermore, gives buyers the advantage. If the seller refuses your reasonable offer, simply turning in the direction of another stall will often bring him to his senses. The upper floor also houses an acre of food stalls, many of them excellent.

A central courtyard leads past a lineup of bird-sellers and their caged charges to the Mercado Libertad's lower half, where produce, meat, and spice stalls fill the floor. (Photographers, note the photogenic view of the produce floor from the balcony above.) Downstairs, don't miss browsing intriguing spice and *yerba* (herb) stalls, which feature mounds of curious dried plants gathered from the wild, often by village *curanderos* (traditional healers). Before you leave, be sure to look over the piñatas, which make colorful, unusual gifts.

When shopping for handicrafts, it's always best to go to the source, if possible. **Tlaquepaque** and **Tonalá** villages, southeast of the city center, are Guadalajara's most bountiful handicrafts sources. Access them either with an easy taxi ride, or a doable-with-difficulty bus (#275 diagonal) ride from Av. 16 de Septiembre downtown. (See the loads of details under Shopping in the Tlaquepaque and Tonalá sections of the City: East and South of Downtown chapter.)

> *When shopping for handicrafts, it's always best to go to the source, if possible.* **Tlaquepaque** *and* **Tonalá** *villages, southeast of the city center, are Guadalajara's most bountiful handicrafts sources.*

Of the sprinkling of downtown handicrafts shops, the most notable is the big government **Casa de Artesanías Agua Azul,** by Parque Agua Azul, north-side corner of Independencia and González Gallo. Here, you can choose from virtually everything—brilliant stoneware, handsome gold and silver jewelry, and endearing ceramic, brass, and papier-mâché animals—short of actually going to Tonalá, Tlaquepaque, and Taxco. Find it at Calz. Gonsáles Gallo 20, northwest corner of Parque Agua Azul (intersection of Independencia and González Gallo). Open Mon.–Fri. 10 A.M.–6 P.M., Sat. 10 A.M.–5 P.M., Sun. 10 A.M.–3 P.M.; tel./fax 33/3619-4664, 33/3619-5179; email: insarte@prodigy.net.mx; website: www.mexplaza.com.mx/artesania.

Two other better-located, but much less extensive, handicrafts sources in the Plaza Tapatía vicinity are at the **tourist information office** at Morelos 102, and the native vendors in the adjacent alley, called Rincón del Diablo.

If you happen to be near the city center, west of the cathedral, you might drop in at the **Galerias El Convento** complex, in a big restored mansion, on Donato Guerra, corner of Morelos, four blocks west of the cathedral front, between Morelos and Pedro Moreno. Inside, a sprinkling of shops offer fine arts and handicrafts, from leather furniture and Tlaquepaque glass to baroque religious antiques and fine silver. Stop for a restful drink or meal at the Restaurant San Miguel (see Downtown Restaurants: West Side, earlier).

Antique enthusiasts might enjoy visiting Guadalajara's small cluster of *antiguidades* (ahn-tee-gwee-DAH-days) stores in the downtown south-side Nueve Esquinas district. (See Nueve Esquinas in the Sights section, earlier.) At this writing, four stores offer items, ranging from fine restored furniture to dusty bric-a-brac. The most upscale of the four are **Antiguidades Don Porfirio,** at Colón 539, and **Antiguidades Padilla** two doors south. Both are open Mon.–Sat. 11 A.M.–2 P.M. and 4–7 P.M.

Photo, Grocery, and Department Stores

The several branches of the **Laboratorios Julio** chain offer quick photofinishing and a big stock of photo supplies and film, including professional 120 transparency and negative rolls. Its big downtown branch is at Colón 125 between Juárez and Cotilla, tel. 33/3614-2850; open Mon.–Sat. 10 A.M.–8 P.M., Sun. 10 A.M.–6 P.M. One of its westside stores, for example, at Av. Americas 425, corner of Manuel Acuña, tel. 33/3616-8286, is open daily 8 A.M.–9 P.M.

For convenient, all-in-one shopping, including groceries, try **Gigante,** downtown on Juárez, corner of Martínez, tel. 33/3613-8638. Open daily 8 A.M.–10 P.M. For even more under one air-conditioned roof, try the big **Comercial Mexicana** at Plaza del Sol, Av. López Mateos Sur 2077. Open daily 9 A.M.–9 P.M.

For a load of shopping information, including bargaining hints, department stores, shopping malls, warehouse stores, and outdoor produce, antique, clothes, and art markets, see the Shopping section in the On the Road chapter.

SERVICES AND INFORMATION

Money Exchange

Change more types of money (U.S., Canadian, German, Japanese, French, Italian, and Swiss) for the best rates at the downtown street-front **Banamex** office and ATM (Juárez, corner of Corona. Open Mon.–Fri. 9 A.M.–5 P.M.).

If Banamex is closed or its lines are too long, opt for a more convenient bank. Downtown Guadalajara has a squad of bank branches, such as Banco Internacional (Bital, open the longest hours), BBV–Bancomer, Banco Serfín, Banco Santander–Mexicano, and Scotiabank Inverlat, all with ATMs. For example, Bital maintains a close-in office, just two blocks north and across the street from the cathedral front, at the northwest corner of Alcalde and Juan Manuel. Open Mon.–Fri. 8 A.M.–7 P.M., Sat. 8 A.M.– 3 p.m.

After bank hours, go to one of the dozens of *casas de cambio* (money changers) nearby, a block

east of Banamex, on Cotilla between Maestranza and Corona.

Guadalajara's only **American Express** branch is on the west side of town, about three miles west of the city center. It provides both travel-agency and member financial services, including personal-check and traveler's-check cashing. Plaza Los Arcos, Av. Vallarta 2440; tel. 33/3818-2323, fax 33/3616-7665. Open Mon.–Fri. 9 A.M.–6 P.M., Sat. 9 A.M.–1 P.M.

For details of many suburban branch banks, consult the services sections of the City: West and North of Downtown and City: East and South of Downtown chapters.

Consulates

Many countries maintain Guadalajara consular offices. The **U.S. consulate** is at Progreso 175 (between Cotillo and Libertad) about a mile and a half west of the city center. Service hours for American citizens are Mon.–Fri. 8 A.M.–11 P.M.; tel. 33/3825-2700 and 33/3825-2998.

The **Canadian consulate** is in the Hotel Fiesta Americana at Aurelio Aceves 225, local 31, near the intersection of Avenidas López Mateos and Vallarta, about three miles west of the city center. Open Mon.–Fri. 8:30 A.M.–2 P.M. and 3–5 P.M.; tel. 33/3616-5642. In emergencies, after business hours, call the Canadian consulate in Mexico City, toll-free tel. 800/706-2900.

Contact the **British consulate** either through the Canadians, or visit the British Consulate's Guadalajara website: www.embajadabritanica.tradegdl.com.mx

Contact the **German consulate** at Ramón Corona 202, corner Madero, tel. 33/3613-9623, fax 33/3613-2609; the **French consulate** at López Mateos 484, tel. 33/3616-5516; and the **Italian consulate** at López Mateos 790, corner E. Parra. Open Tues.–Fri. 11 A.M.– 2 P.M.; tel. 33/3616-1700, fax 33/3616-2092.

Consular agents from a number of other countries customarily hold Guadalajara office hours, and might be reachable through the **Consular Association of Guadalajara,** tel. 33/3616-0620 or 33/3615-0197. If all else fails, consult the local Yellow Pages under *"Embajadas, Legaciones y Consulados."*

Health, Police, and Emergencies

If you need a doctor or hospital, ask your hotel desk, or, in an emergency, go to the **Hospital Americas**, at Av. Americas 932, Guadalajara 44620, tel. 33/3817-3141 and 33/3817-3004, with many specialists on call. The hospital accepts the coverage of many U.S. HMOs; all staff is U.S.–trained and all hospitalization is in private rooms, with TV, phone, and private bathroom.

For routine medications, one of the best sources is the Guadalajara chain, **Farmacia ABC,** with many branches. For example, you'll find one downtown at 518 P. Moreno between M. Ocampo and D. Guerra, tel. 33/3614-2950. Open daily 8 A.M.–9 P.M.

For many more doctor and hospital recommendations, see Guadalajara Doctors and Hospitals in the Staying Healthy section of the On the Road chapter.

For downtown **police** emergencies, call the radio patrol (dial 060) or the police headquarters at 33/3668-0800 or 33/3617-6060. In case of **fire,** call the *servicio bomberos* fire station at 33/3619-5241 or 33/3619-0794. For suburban emergency numbers, see Police and Fire Emergencies in the On the Road chapter.

Post Office, Telephone, Public Fax, and Internet

The downtown **Guadalajara post office** is two blocks west of the Teatro Degollado, just past the Hotel Mendoza, at Independencia and V. Carranza. Telecomunicaciones offers **public telephone and fax** in the city center, at Degollado and Madero, below the city *juzgado* (jail); open Mon.–Fri. 8 A.M.–6 P.M., Sat. 9 A.M.–2 P.M.

Connect with the **Internet** downtown at travel agency–Internet store Ramos Ramírez (at the street entrance of Hotel Internacional), at Pedro Moreno 570, five blocks west of the cathedral, tel. 33/3613-7318. Or make your connections at one of a pair of small **Internet stores** at nos. 212 and 250 (both open Mon.–Sat. 9 A.M.– 9 P.M.) on Pedro Loza (from the cathedral front, walk two blocks north, one block west) between San Felipe and Reforma.

Tourist Information Office

The main Guadalajara tourist information office is in the Plaza Tapatía, on Paseo Morelos, the mall-extension of Av. Morelos, behind the Teatro Degollado. Morelos 102; tel. 33/3668-1600 or 33/3668-1601, fax 33/3668-1686; website: www.visita.jalisco.gob.mx. Open Mon.–Fri. 9 A.M.–7:30 P.M. and Sat. and Sun. 9 A.M.–1 P.M.

Or go to the **city and state tourism information booth** *(módulo de información)* in the foyer of the Palacio de Gobierno, on Corona, a block southeast from the cathedral front. Ask for a copy of city tourism's superb all-color "Points of Interest" bilingual foldout map and guide. Open Mon.–Fri. 9 A.M.–3 P.M. and 4–7 P.M., Sat. and Sun. 10 A.M. –12:30 P.M.

Publications

Among the best Guadalajara sources of English-language magazines is **Sanborn's,** a North American–style gift, book, and coffee shop chain. There's one located downtown at the corner of Juárez and 16 de Septiembre. Open 7:30 A.M.–11 P.M. Two others are at: **Plaza Vallarta,** Av. Vallarta 1600, open 7–1 A.M.; and **Plaza del Sol,** 2718 López Mateos Sur. Open 7–1 A.M.

You can usually get the excellent *News* from Mexico City at one of the newsstands edging the Plaza Guadalajara (formerly Plaza Laureles), across from the cathedral.

While you're downtown, if you see a copy of the informative local weekly, the ***Colony Reporter,*** buy it. Its pages will be stuffed with valuable items for visitors, including local events calendars, restaurant and performance reviews, meaty feature articles on local customs and excursions, and entertainment, restaurant, hotel, and rental listings. (If you can't find one, call the *Reporter,* tel. 33/3615-2177, to find out where you can get a copy.)

Additionally, suburban southwest-side **Librería Sandi,** always has the *Reporter* plus the best selection of English-language books in the Guadalajara region. Tepeyac 718, Colonia Chapalita, Guadalajara; tel. 33/3121-0863. Open 9:30 A.M.–2:30 P.M. and 3:30–7 P.M.

Language and Cultural Courses

The University of Guadalajara's **Centro de Estudios Para Extranjeros** (Study Center for Foreigners) conducts an ongoing program of cultural studies for visitors. Besides formal language, history, and art instruction, students may also opt for live-in arrangements with local families. Write them at Tomás S. V. Gómez 125, P.O. Box 1-2130, Guadalajara, Jalisco 44100; tel. 33/3616-4399 or 33/3616-4382, fax 33/3616-4013; email: cepe@corp.udg.mx; website: www.cepe.udg.mx. You can also visit their **west-side center,** three blocks north of the Los Arcos monumental arch, on Gómez between Avenidas Mexico and Justo Sierra—telephone first for a *cita* (appointment).

For alternatives, see the special topic Spanish Language Instruction and the Elderhostel programs under Special Tours and Study Options in the On the Road chapter.

GETTING THERE AND AWAY
By Air

Several air carriers connect the **Guadalajara airport** (officially, Aeropuerto Internacíonal Miguel Hidalgo, code-designated GDL) with many U.S. and Mexican destinations.

Mexicana Airlines flights, reservations tel. 33/3678-7676, arrivals and departures tel. 33/3688-5775, connect frequently with the U.S. destinations of Los Angeles, Sacramento, San Francisco, San Jose, Oakland, Las Vegas, and Chicago; and the Mexican destinations of Puerto Vallarta, Tijuana, Mexicali, Hermosillo, Mexico City, and Cancún.

Aeroméxico flights connect frequently with the U.S. destinations of Los Angeles, Phoenix, Atlanta, and New York; and the Mexican destinations of Puerto Vallarta, Acapulco, Culiacán, Torreón, Monterrey, Tijuana, and Mexico City. For reservations, arrivals, and departures: tel. 01-800/021-4010.

Aerocalifornia connects with the U.S. destinations of Los Angeles and Tucson; and the Mexican destinations of Tijuana, Mazatlán, La Paz, Los Cabos, Culiacán, Los Mochis, Durango, Monterrey, Puebla, and Mexico City.

For reservations and flight information: tel. 33/3616-2525.

Up-and-coming **Aviacsa** connects Guadalajara directly with the U.S. destination of Las Vegas, Nevada and the Mexican destinations of Mexicali, Tijuana, Monterrey, Cancún, Oaxaca, and Mexico City. For reservations and flight information: tel. 33/3123-1751 and 33/3123-5253; website: www.aviacsa.com.mx.

Other carriers include: **American Airlines,** which connects daily with Los Angeles and Dallas (reservations toll-free in Mexico: tel. 800/362-70, or local 33/3616-4090); **Delta,** which connects several times daily with Los Angeles and Atlanta (reservations toll-free in Mexico: tel. 800/902-2100); **Continental Airlines,** which connects twice daily with Houston (reservations toll-free in Mexico: tel. 800/900-5000); and **America West Airlines,** which connects with Phoenix (reservations and flight information direct toll-free to U.S. tel. 800/235-9292).

If you're unable to contact the above numbers, you can always go through a travel agent. For example, try American Express, tel. 33/3818-2323 or 33/3818-2325.

Airport arrival is simplified by the many services available inside the terminal. You'll find a money exchange counter (daytime hours only), and banks with **ATMs** inside (Serfín) and just outside the terminal door (Bital). Many **car rental agencies** maintain booths: Avis, tel. 33/3678-0502; Alamo, tel. 33/3613-5551 or 33/3613-5560 (email: alamogdl@ibm.net); Arrasa, tel. 33/3615-0522; Budget, tel. 33/3613-0027 or 33/3613-0286; Dollar, 33/3688-6319; Hertz, tel. 33/3688-5633 or 33/3688-6080; National, tel. 33/3614-7175 or 33/3614-7994 (email:nationalcar@1cabonet.com.mx); Ohama, tel. 33/3614-6902; Optima, tel. 33/3688-5532 or 33/3812-0437; and Thrifty, 33/3825-5080, ext. 121.

Ground transportation is likewise well organized for shuttling travelers the 12 miles (19 km) along Chapala Hwy. 44 into town. Tickets for *colectivos* (shared van taxis) are about $10 for one, $12 for two persons; and *taxis especiales* (individual taxis) are about $13 for one to four persons—purchase them at a booth just outside the terminal door. Few, if any, public buses serve the Guadalajara airport.

Many simple and economical card-operated public telephones are also available; buy telephone cards at the snack bar by the far right-hand terminal exit or the lottery ticket booth in mid-terminal, near the exit door. Also you'll find a newsstand (lobby floor), bookstore (upstairs), and many crafts and gift shops convenient for last-minute business and purchases.

Airport departure is equally simple, as long as you save enough for your international departure tax of $19 ($12 federal tax plus $7 local tax), unless it's already included in your ticket. A **post office** and (secure mail) Mexpost office are upstairs, and a *telecomunicaciones* office (telegraph, fax, long-distance phone) is inside the terminal, to the right as you enter. A **public telephone and fax** office operates in mid-terminal, by the car rental counters.

For arrival and departure convenience, you might consider staying at the adjacent, luxurious **Hotel Casa Grande.** (For details, see Bus Station and Airport Hotels at the end of the Accommodations section earlier in this chapter)

By Car or RV

Four major routes connect the Guadalajara region to the rest of Mexico. To or from **Tepic–Compostela–Puerto Vallarta,** federal Hwy. 15 winds about 141 miles (227 km) over the Sierra Madre Occidental crest. The new *cuota* (toll) expressway, although expensive ($30 for a car, RVs more), greatly increases safety, decreases wear and tear, and cuts the Guadalajara–Tepic driving time from five to three hours. The *libre* (free) route, by contrast, has two oft-congested lanes that twist steeply up and down the high pass and bump through towns. For safety, allow around five hours via the *libre* route to and from Tepic.

To and from Puerto Vallarta, bypass Tepic via the toll *corta* (cutoff) that connects Hwy. 15 (at Chapalilla) with Hwy. 200 (at Compostela). Figure on four and a half hours total if you use the entire toll expressway (about $20), six and a half hours if you don't.

To and from Barra de Navidad in the south-

west, traffic winds smoothly along two-lane Hwy. 80 for the 190 miles (306 km) to and from Guadalajara. Allow around five hours.

An easier road connection to and from Barra de Navidad runs through Manzanillo and Colima along *autopistas* (superhighways) 200, 110, and 54D. Easy grades allow a leisurely 55 mph (90 km/hour) most of the way for this 192-mile (311-km) trip. Allow about four hours to or from Manzanillo; add another hour for the additional smooth 38 miles (61 km) of Hwy. 200 to or from Barra de Navidad (follow the Manzanillo town toll bypass).

To or from Lake Chapala in the south, the four level, straight lanes of Hwy. 44 whisk traffic safely the 33 miles (53 km) to or from Guadalajara in about 45 minutes.

The "Old" Bus Terminal: Camionera Central Vieja

Guadalajara has two bus terminals, one new, one old. The new terminal in the southeast suburb offers mostly first- and luxury-class long-distance direct connections to outlying Jalisco destinations and most other parts of Mexico.

The old terminal, Camionera Central Vieja, occupies about two square city blocks on the southeast edge of downtown, two blocks east of Calz. Independencia and a block north of Parque Agua Azul. From here, a swarm of second-class buses heads out for hundreds of Guadalajara region towns, villages, and crossroads, mostly west, south, and east of the city.

The buses occupy a large interior lot sandwiched between ticketing halls: *sala A* on the northside (Calle Los Angeles) and *sala B* on the southside (Calle 5 de Febrero).

Sala B, which services **west and southwest destinations,** handles most of the traffic. It has a modicum of services, including a Computel (tel. 33/3650-3812, open Mon.–Sat. 7 A.M.–8 P.M., Sun. 8 A.M.–4 P.M.); public telephone, fax, and copy service; left luggage (east end); and food counters. The following are listed in order from east to west:

Transportes Ceocuitatlán (tel. 33/3619-3989, 33/3619-8891) serves west and north-west destinations, including the *periférico* (end of

SUBWAY, GUADALAJARA-STYLE

Since the early 1990s, Guadalajarans have enjoyed a new underground train system, which they call simply the **Tren Ligero,** or "Light Train." It's nothing fancy, a kind of Motel 6 of subway lines—inexpensive, efficient, and reliable. A pair of intersecting lines, Linea 1 and Linea 2, carry passengers in approximately north-south and east-west directions, along a total of 15 miles (25 km) of track. The station most visitors see first is the Plaza Universidad (on Lineas 2), accessible by staircases that descend near the city-center corner of Juárez and Colón. Look for the Denny's restaurant nearby.

Downstairs, if you want to take a ride, deposit the specified number of pesos in the machines, which will give you in exchange a brass *ficha* token, good for one ride and one transfer. If you opt to transfer, you have to do it at Juárez station, the next stop west of Plaza Universidad, where Lineas 1 and 2 intersect. (Hint: Best begin your Guadalajara subway adventure before 9 P.M.; the Tren Ligero goes to sleep by about 11 P.M.)

Av. Vallarta) west; La Venta and the Bosque de Primavera; Amatitán; Tequila; and Tala.

Transportes Tlajomulco (no phone) connects with the southern outskirts destinations of Cuexcomitatán, San Miguel Cuyutlán, Tlajomulco, Cuescomititlán, Las Cuatas, and along Chapala Hwy. 44 south past the airport.

"Blue" *(Azul)* **Autobuses Guadalajara–Talpa–Mascota** (tel. 33/3619-7079, 33/3124-1902) connects, via Hwy. 70 and Ameca, with far southwestern Jalisco destinations of Talpa and Mascota.

Autobuses Sur (no phone), connects with southern destinations of charmingly picturesque Tapalpa mountain town, plus Atemajac de Brizuela, Amacueca, Santa Ana, and Ciudad Guzmán.

"Servicios Coordinados" **Flecha Amarilla** (tel. 33/3619-4533) connects with southwestern destinations of Ameca, Cocula, Villa Corona *(balnearios* Chimulco and Aguascalientes), Navajas, La Villita, and Cruz Vieja.

Rojo de los Altos (tel. 33/3619-2309) connects west via the *periférico,* along Hwy. 15, with La Venta (Bosque de Primavera bathing springs), Ameca, Amatitán (ex-Hacienda San José tequila factory), Tequila, and Magdalena.

Transportes Guadalajara Bella Vista (tel. 33/3619-2619, 33/3650-2858), connects with southwest destinations past the *periférico* (end of López Mateos), Acatlán, and Villa Corona *(balnearios* Chimulco and Aguascalientes).

Transportes Guadalajara–La Vega–Ameca–

Cocula (tel. 33/3650-3033) connects, via Hwy. 15 and Tala, with southwest destinations of Etzatlán, Ameca, La Vega (reservoir fishing), Villa Corona, and Cocula.

Transportes Tenamaxtlenses (tel. 33/3619-0853) connects via Hwy. 80 and Villa Corona, with far southwest destinations of Soyatlán, Tenamaxtlán, Atengo, Juanacatlán, and Tecolotlán.

Autocamiones del Pacífico (tel. 33/3619-9654) connects via Hwy. 80, with the far southwest villages of El Limón, Tolimán, La Villa, Los Guajes, Chiquilistán, and Tuxcacuesco.

Omnibus de la Ribera (tel. 33/3650-0605) connects south via Av. López Mateos, with the Lake Chapala northwest shore towns of Zapotitán, Las Cuatas, Buena Vista, Jocotepec, and warm-spring resort San Juan Cosala.

Sala A, on the opposite, northside of the bus lot, services **southern to eastern destinations.** Moving from the building's east to west end:

Autotransportes Guadalajara–Chapala (tel. 33/3619-5675), the major Lake Chapala line, connects with north-shore destinations of Chapala, Ajijic, and Jocotepec. Luxury- and first-class tickets are available.

Transportes Ciénega (tel. 33/3619-3337) connects southeast with El Salto, Rancho, Pta. Muerto, Rodeo, Atequiza, and Atotonilco.

"Servicios Coordinados" **Flecha Amarilla** (tel. 33/3619-4533) connects with southeast destinations of El Salto, El Verde, IBM, El Muey, La Alameda, and the Hwy. 44 Corredor Industrial.

© BRUCE WHIPPERMAN

The plaza Nueve Esquinas is tucked in a picturesque corner of Guadalajara's colorful downtown southside neighborhood.

ADO (Autobuses del Occidente) (tel. 33/3679-0453) connects with southern and eastern destinations of El Salto, La Laja, La Punta, La Jauja, and Zapotlanejo.

The New Central Bus Terminal: Camionera Central Nueva

The long-distance Guadalajara Camionera Central Nueva is about 20 minutes by taxi (about $8) southeast from the city center. The huge modern complex sprawls past the intersection of the old Tonalá Hwy. (Carretera Antigua Tonalá) and the new Zaplotanejo Autopista (Freeway) Hwy. 90. The Camionera Central Nueva is sandwiched between the two highways. Tell your taxi driver which bus line you want or where you want to go, and he'll drop you at one of the terminal's seven *módulos* (buildings).

For arrival and departure convenience, you might consider staying at the adjacent, moderately priced **Hotel La Serena.** (Look under Bus Station and Airport Hotels at the end of the Accommodations section earlier in this chapter.)

Each of the bus station *módulos* is self-contained, with rest rooms, cafeteria or snack bar,

stores offering snack foods (but few fruits or veggies), bottled drinks, common medicines and drugs, and handicrafts. Additionally, *módulos* #1, #3, and #7 have **public long-distance telephone and fax service.**

Dozens of competing bus lines offer departures. The current king of the heap is **Estrella Blanca,** a holding company that operates a host of subsidiaries, notably Elite, Turistar, Futura, Transportes del Norte, Transportes Norte de Sonora, and Transportes Chihuahenses. Second-largest and trying harder is **Flecha Amarilla,** which offers "Servicios Coordinados" through several subsidiaries. Trying even harder are the biggest independents: Omnibus de Mexico, Enlaces Terrestres Nacionals (National Ground Network), Transportes Pacífico, and Autobuses del Occidente, all of whom would very much like to be your bus company.

To northwest **Pacific Coast** destinations, go to either *módulo* #3 or #4. Take first-class **Elite,** tel. 33/3600-0601, via Tepic and Mazatlán, to the U.S. border at Nogales, Mexicali, and Tijuana. Alternatively, ride first-class Transportes Pacífico, tel. 33/3600-0211, for the same northwest

Pacific destinations as Elite. For western Jalisco and Nayarit Pacific Coast destinations, go by **Transportes Pacífico,** either first-class, tel. 33/3600-0601, *módulo* #3, or second-class, tel. 33/3600-0450, *módulo* #4, for the small southwest Nayarit coastal towns and villages, such as Las Varas, La Peñita, and Rincón de Guayabitos, en route to Puerto Vallarta. Moreover, you can ride second-class **Transportes Norte de Sonora** west and northwest, tel. 33/3679-0463, *módulo* #4, to smaller northern Nayarit and Sinaloa towns, such as Tepic, San Blas, Santiago Ixcuintla–Mexcaltitán, Acaponeta-Novillero, and Escuinapa-Teacapan.

Additionally, in *módulo* #3, second-class **Autotransportes Guadalajara–Talpa–Mascota,** tel. 33/3600-0098, offers connections to the non-touristed western Jalisco mountain towns of **Talpa** and **Mascota,** where you can connect on to Puerto Vallarta by the rugged super-scenic backcountry route via the antique mining village of San Sebastián.

For far southern Pacific destinations of **Zihuatanejo, Acapulco,** and **the Oaxaca coast** you can go one of two ways: Direct to Acapulco by **Futura** (*módulo* #3) east, then south, all in one day, bypassing Mexico City (one or two buses per day). Alternatively, go less directly via Elite (*módulo* #3) west to Tepic or Puerto Vallarta (or by a **Flecha Amarilla** affiliate, *módulo* #1, south

to Tecomán), where you must transfer to a Zihuatanejo-Acapulco southbound Elite bus. This may require an overnight in either Tepic, Puerto Vallarta, or Tecomán and at least two days traveling (along the super-scenic, rarely visited Pacific route), depending upon connections. Finally, in Acapulco, connections will be available southeast to the Oaxaca coast.

If you're bound southeast directly to the city of **Oaxaca,** go conveniently by Futura (*módulo* #3) to Mexico City Norte (North) station, where you transfer, via ADO (Autobuses del Oriente), southeast direct to Oaxaca City.

Also at *módulo* #4 allied lines Autocamiones del Pacífico and Transportes Cihuatlán, tel. 33/3600-0076 (second-class), tel. 33/3600-0598 (first-class), together offer service south along scenic mountain Hwy. 80 to the Pacific via Autlán to **Melaque, Barra de Navidad,** and **Manzanillo.**

For eastern to southern destinations in **Jalisco, Guanajuato, Aguascalietes, Michoacán,** and **Colima,** go to either *módulos* #1 or #2. In *módulo* #2, ride first-class **ETN,** tel. 33/3600-0501, east to Celaya, León, and Aguascalientes, or east to Uruapan and Morelia and southwest and west to Colima, Manzanillo, and Puerto Vallarta. Also in *módulo* #1, Flecha Amarilla subsidiary lines, tel. 33/3600-0052, offer service to a swarm of northeast destinations, in-

THE HEART OF THE CITY

ONE DAY . . .

If you have only one day in Guadalajara, spend it downtown walking around: Visit the cathedral, see the Orozco mural in the Palacio de Gobierno, browse around the Museo Regional, stroll the Plaza Tapatía, and finally, don't miss the Hospicio Cabañas. Have lunch or early supper at La Rinconada restaurant.

If you have two days, add Tlaquepaque, browsing the shops, the Regional Ceramics Museum and the historic house along Independencia. Leave some time for some of the factory shops. Have lunch at Restaurant El Adobe or Restaurant Casa Fuerte.

If three days, add a morning visit to ex-Hacienda San José del Refugio in Amatitán and continue for lunch at Restaurant El Marinero or the Cuervo Restaurant on the plaza in Tequila. Either take the tour through the Cuervo tequila factory, or continue on for a relaxing couple of hours at Balneario La Toma.

If four days, add a day trip, or perhaps an overnight in Tapalpa

On your next trip, come and stay longer, preferably much longer. Be warned: You may find it hard to leave.

cluding León, Guanajuato, and San Miguel de Allende, and southeast and south to Uruapan, Morelia, Puerto Vallarta, Manzanillo, Barra de Navidad, and rarely visited villages—El Super, Tomatlán, and El Tuito—on the Jalisco coast. Also, from *módulo* #2, **Autobuses del Occidente,** tel. 33/3600-0055, offers departures southeast to Michoacán destinations of Zamora, Zitácuaro, Quiroga, Pátzcuaro, and Uruapan. Additionally, **Autotransportes Sur de Jalisco** first- and second-class buses offer southern departures, via old Hwy. 54 or *autopista* 54D, via Sayula, Ciudad Guzmán, Colima, Tecomán, and Cuyutlán, to Manzanillo.

In *módulo* #5, small independent **Linea Azul** tel. 33/3679-0453, offers departures northeast, via Tampico, to the U.S. border, at Matamoros and Reynosa.

Omnibus de Mexico, tel. 33/3600-0184 or 33/3600-0469, dominates *módulo* #6, offering broad service in mostly north and northeast directions: to the U.S. border at Juárez via Zacate-cas, Saltillo, Durango, Torreón, Fresnillo, and Chihuahua; and northeast, via Tampico, to the U.S. border at Reynosa and Matamoros.

The Estrella Blanca subsidiary lines operating out of *módulo* #7 also mostly offer connections north. Ride first-class **Transportes Chihuahuenses,** tel. 33/3679-0404, via San Juan de los Lagos, Zacatecas, Torreon, Chihuahua, and Juárez; luxury-class Turistar, tel. 33/3679-0404, along the same routes as Transportes Chihuahuenses; or first-class **Transportes del Norte,** tel. 33/3679-0404, via San Juan de los Lagos, Zacatecas, Saltillo, Monterrey, and Matamoros, at the U.S. border.

By Train

Passenger rail service to and from Guadalajara has been stopped by the privatization of the Mexican Railways' Pacific route. Unless future government subsidies offset private losses, Pacific passenger trains will have gone the way of buggy whips and Stanley Steamers.

City: West and North of Downtown

For longer than anyone can remember, the march of Guadalajara's history has always pointed west. Nuño de Guzmán, Guadalajara's *conquistador,* hurried west after pacifying the Valle de Atemajac where the city now spreads. Later, explorers, mission fathers, governors, and the crowd of settlers that followed them did the same. To most Guadalajarans the east represented the old and the settled. The west represented opportunity.

That's still true. Guadalajara's 20th-century history has been largely marked by waves of westward development. A glance at a map of metropolitan Guadalajara reveals successive rings of peripheral thoroughfares—Av. López Mateos and the northern and southern *circunvalación* boulevards built during the 1950s, Av. Patria during the 1970s, and now the ***periférico*** that marked the border between city and country at the beginning of the second millennium.

Within those expanding western boundaries, new-style tree-shaded neighborhoods were founded, beginning

Goddess Minerva, beside her fountain and circle, stands guard at Guadalajara's western gateway.

around 1900, when moneyed merchant and professional families began building stylish, landscaped mansions along broad boulevards beyond the old colonial town's western edge.

Most of those mansions still line the streets of the earliest western district, known as the *colonias antiguas,* now part of the **Minerva-Chapultepec** district that spreads west from old city boundary, marked by Av. Federalismo. Here, in the Minerva-Chapultepec district, many of those old houses are still occupied by descendants of the first families—some as residences, but many as smart restaurants and shops that decorate the east-west thoroughfares.

Later, during the 1960s and 1970s, a checkerboard of development spread west, south and north, notably in the southwest-side **Plaza del Sol–Chapalita** neighborhood. Here, the Plaza del Sol shopping-convention–luxury hotel complex achieved phenomenal success, side by side with the charming tree-shaded Chapalita residential village-within-a-city.

Minerva-Chapultepec

GETTING ORIENTED AND GETTING AROUND

Getting Oriented

A number of main boulevards anchor the Minerva-Chapultepec district, from its eastern boundary at **Av. Federalismo** on the downtown side, to the **Minerva Fountain and Traffic Circle** on the west side. **Av. Vallarta,** the district's backbone artery, runs (motor traffic one-way west) past the **University of Guadalajara,** continuing past dozens of upscale businesses, restaurants, and banks, and the **Centro Magno** shopping center before passing under the **Los Arcos** monument and around the Minerva Circle.

North and south of Av. Vallarta run east-bound Avenidas Pedro Moreno and López Cotilla, similarly decorated by stately residences, tony shops, and stylish restaurants. Major arteries **Av. Mexico** and Av. Niños Héroes, respectively define the district's northern and southern edges.

The Minerva-Chapultepec's major north-south business-restaurant avenues, moving west are **Av. Chapultepec, Av. Americas** (which switches to Av. Unión south of Av. Vallarta), and **Av. López Mateos,** which circles the Minerva Fountain, forming the district's western boundary.

Getting Around

Taxis present a convenient option for navigating Guadalajara's western suburbs. Tariffs customarily run between $2 and $8, depending on the length of trip. **Rental cars** are also a convenient,

but more expensive option, best for savvy independent travelers who want to cover lots of ground quickly. **Tours and guides** offer yet more choices. For information on all the above, see the Getting Around sections of the On the Road and Heart of the City chapters.

If you're going to be doing a lot of independent traveling by car or bus in Guadalajara, get a copy of the very reliable *Guia Roji Red Vial Cuidad de Guadalajara* city map. They are available at bookstores and Sanborn's gift shop–restaurant; see the Food section later in this chapter.

A number of useful **bus lines** connect Minerva-Chapultepec district points. All of the Minerva-Chapultepec sights described in the following section are accessible on foot via the quiet diesel-free **Par Vial** east-west electric trolley bus line. It traces a westward route, from the north-side downtown corner of Alcalde, west along Calles Independencia, Justo Sierra, and finally Hidalgo, returning east via Hidalgo all the way to Alcalde.

Access both Minerva-Chapultepec and the far western suburb along Av. Vallarta past the Minerva Circle, via east-west **line 45.** (From the downtown south-side corner of 16 de Septiembre and Madero, ride west along Madero; at Pavo, north to Morelos, continue; at Ramírez, north to Justo Sierra, continue west to López Mateos, passing the Minerva Circle, then west along Vallarta, passing the Gran Plaza shopping center (and Price Club, Wal-Mart, and Sam's Club) continuing to the line's far western terminal. Return east via Av.

Vallarta, continuing east past the Los Arcos monument, along López Cotilla, passing the Centro Magno shopping center, and continuing east, crossing 16 de Septiembre at Prisciliano Sánchez and Plaza San Francisco.

Access the Minerva-Chapultepec south side via east-west **lines 51A and 51B,** whose routes are identical in both the downtown and Minerva-Chapultepec districts. Begin at the downtown southwest corner of Libertad and 16 de Septiembre. Ride south a few blocks, turning west at La Paz, continuing to A. Yañez, two blocks south of the Minerva Circle. Here the bus continues southwest to the Chapalita neighborhood. Return from A. Jañez, at the corner of Lerdo de Tejada, continuing west, turning north at Chapultepec, turning east at Libertad, and continuing downtown to 16 de Septiembre. (For the Chapalita route variations, see the Plaza del Sol–Chapalita section, later in this chapter.)

SIGHTS

Around the University of Guadalajara

Let the brilliant white marble **Rectoría de la Universidad de Guadalajara** (Rectory of the University of Guadalajara) on Av. Vallarta, south side, a few blocks west of Federalismo, be your starting point. The grand neoclassic edifice was designed in large part by noted architect Rafael Urzúa and erected in 1918. Originally intended as the Jalisco state legislature, it became part of the university during the mid-1930s.

Inside, in the lecture hall (open Mon.–Sat. 9 A.M.–8 P.M.), known curiously as the Paraninfo ("Seance Room"), celebrated muralist José Clemente Orozco crafted a pair of monumental works between 1936 and 1939. Spreading across the cupola overhead, *Man*—as creator, thinker, questioner, investigator, and celebrator—displays the master's contemplative side. In contrast, above the stage, spreads *The People and Their Leaders* in which a long fire-ringed procession confronts the evils of militarism, brutality, and false science.

Continue inside around behind the lecture hall (or outside to the Av. López Cotilla southside entrance) to the **Museo de Arte.** Here, six

galleries (two with temporary exhibits, four with permanent) display paintings, sculptures, and graphic arts, both traditional and modern. (At López Cotilla 930, open Tues.–Thurs. and Sat. 10:30 A.M.–6 P.M., Fri. 10:30 A.M.–8 P.M., Sun. noon–6 P.M.; tel. 33/3825-8888, 33/3825-7553.)

Continue out the museum's south entrance, across Cotilla, to the monumental **Templo Expiatorio** (Temple of Atonement), begun in 1897, by Italian architect Adamo Boari, celebrated for the Palace of Fine Arts in Mexico City. Although the soaring neo-Gothic facade and its towering 25-bell carillon is impressive enough, the radiant contemporary French stained-glass windows inside are the main attraction. Besides Biblical themes, one of the glass panes is, interestingly, of architect Díaz Morales, who finished the interior construction in 1972 (and who is buried in the Grand Crypt beneath the sacristy behind the altar). The bells, accompanied by a mechanical procession of the Twelve Apostles, toll daily, at 9 A.M., noon, and 6 P.M. Open daily 7 A.M.–9 P.M.

Around Los Arcos Monument

For more worthwhile sights, walk, take a taxi, or ride the Par Vial bus (four short blocks north on Independencia) west two miles to **Centro Magno** shopping center, corner of Vallarta and Lope de Vega. If nothing else, take a table in the ground-floor cafe, order a refreshment, and relax and enjoy the soaring indoor space around you.

The Centro Magno is one of three recent complexes (including Gran Plaza, on Vallarta farther west, and Centro Pabellón, on Av. Patria, northwest) built within a multifloored roofed structure, around a single towering atrium. These are *the* places to be seen, especially among working- and middle-class youth. (For many more details on all three of these centers, see Shopping, later in this chapter.)

Exit on the north, Av. Vallarta side, where a few blocks west, in the direction of traffic flow, rises the Los Arcos arch. A block before Los Arcos, the astronomical observatory dome atop the white neoclassic building complex on the north side of Av. Vallarta marks the **Institute of Astronomy and Meteorology** (open Mon.– Fri. 9 A.M.–

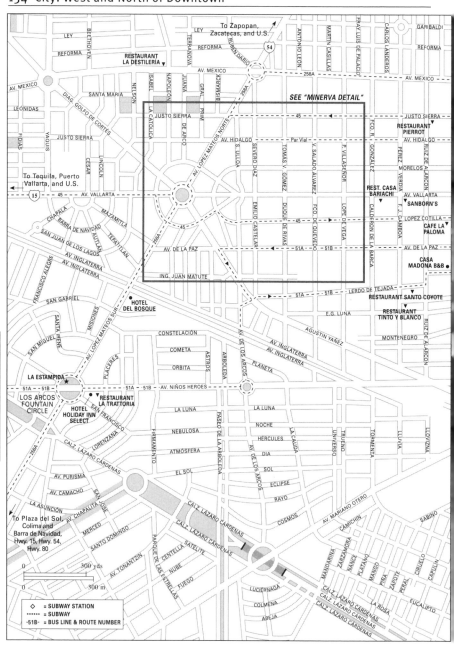

CITY: WEST AND NORTH

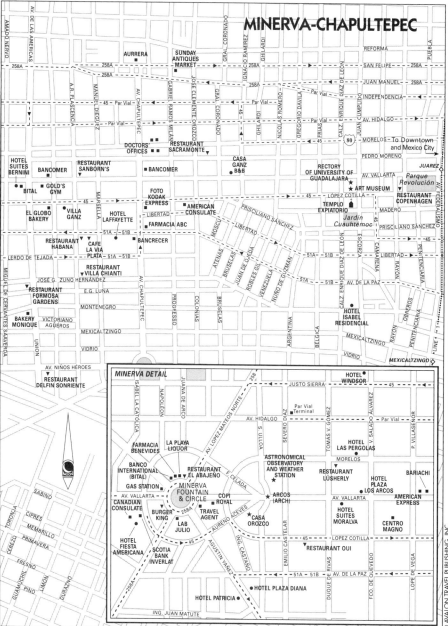

MINERVA-CHAPULTEPEC

6 P.M., at Av. Vallarta 2602, corner of Emilio Castelar, tel. 33/3616-4937, fax 33/3615-9829.)

The Institute conducts both research programs and an educational schedule. It offers tours in English Mon.–Fri. 10 A.M.–2 P.M. Be sure to request that your tour includes an inspection of their antique eight-inch refracting (but currently in need of repair) telescope in the observatory dome. Furthermore, the Institute invites the public to attend their evening "Astronomical Friday" public lecture series, at 7 P.M. on the last Friday of each month. If weather conditions permit, staff customarily bring out telescopes for public viewing of the moon, planets, and stars.

Continue west to the **Los Arcos** neo-Roman triumphal arch, erected 1939-41, on what was, at the time, the country edge of Guadalajara. Inside the south pedestal entry door, find the bilingual information office of **City Tourism.** Open Mon.–Fri. 9 A.M.–7 P.M., Sat. 10 A.M.–6 P.M. and Sun. 10 A.M.–5 P.M. Be sure to pick up a copy of their excellent *"Points of Interest"* fold-out brochure, which describes a number of Guadalajara walking tours.

Los Arcos is more than a monument. In addition to the tourism office, it houses temporary art exhibits and an unusually frank mural, illustrating the best and worst of Guadalajara, halfway up the south-side staircase. Climb the three flights to the rooftop floor and enjoy the sweeping views, both east and west along Av. Vallarta. On the east side, Centro Magno rises before the far-off downtown skyline, while on the opposite side, traffic circles around the Minerva Fountain in front of the shining glass tower of the Hotel Fiesta Americana.

The Orozco House and the Minerva Fountain

Visit the **Casa Museo José Clemente Orozco,** half a block southwest of Los Arcos, at 27 Aurelio Aceves, adjacent to the intimate neighborhood plaza, decorated with a statue of the great muralist.

After Orozco's death in 1949, his wife, Margarita Valladares, modified the house that they had bought a few years earlier and established the present museum, in the memory of her husband, in 1951. Inside, in the soaring studio, the

A single large painting—*The Good Life*— graces the soaring studio that José Clemente Orozco built in his Minerva district house (now the Casa Orozco museum) in the late 1940s.

major work displayed, a giant 1945 painting, *The Good Life,* uses flying chickens to poke fun at decadent devotion to wine, sex, and food.

A small gallery upstairs displays Orozco memorabilia, old photos (notice the 1940 photo of Los Arcos in its then-rural setting), and an interesting palette of Orozco works, a number of which appear in Guadalajara's main Orozco museum in the Centro Cultural Cabañas downtown. A small research library, open to interested visitors, completes the upstairs layout. The museum, tel. 33/3616-8329, is open Mon–Fri. 10 A.M.–4 P.M.

Back outside, and ahead, west, traffic flows around the grand **Minerva Circle,** constructed in the mid-1950s during the term of governor Agustín Yañez. If you prefer safety to chance, best hire a taxi to deposit you on the inner circle curbside, where you can appreciate the helmeted Roman goddess Minerva (equivalent to Greek goddess Athena) close up. Minerva, the goddess of wisdom, with spear and shield ready, guards the city's

JOSÉ CLEMENTE OROZCO

Born into middle-class comfort in Zapotlán, Jalisco, in 1883, Orozco was taken to Mexico City with his family when they resettled in 1888. Soon after José began studying architecture and art in 1908, he was strongly influenced by the work of noted political cartoonist José Guadalupe Posada. One of Orozco's biographers wrote that on his way to college classes, he would stop at Posada's workshop, where the master worked in view of everyone. Orozco later wrote, "This was the first stimulus that awoke my imagination and impulse to put those first figures down on paper."

And he did. After his formal education, Orozco started drawing bordello scenes and political cartoons, which he exhibited in 1916. Around the same time, Orozco, influenced by the apocalyptic early 19th-century work of Goya, completed and exhibited his famous drawing portfolio, *Mexico in Revolution.* This marked the beginning of Orozco's lifelong vocation of jolting the world awake to the suffering and futility of war.

Orozco's first public murals, completed in 1923, were judged too severe and were later altered or destroyed. Seeking more fertile ground, he moved to the United States in 1927 and completed a trio of important murals: at Pomona College, the New School for Social Research, and Dartmouth College. Riding a crest of accomplishment, Orozco returned to Mexico in late 1934.

Now, with nothing to stop him, Orozco was free to create: "I favored black and the province forbidden by the impressionists. Instead of red and yellow sunsets I painted pestilential shadows . . . and instead of nude Indians, drunk women and men."

As he matured, Orozco's work became grander and even more starkly arresting. Between 1934 and 1940 he completed his Guadalajara masterpieces, the *Man of Fire* and *Hidalgo and the Liberation,* respectively, at the Hospicio Cabañas and the Palacio de Gobierno downtown, and the *The People and Their Leaders,* at the University of Guadalajara Rectory.

In the aftermath of his great Guadalajara triumphs, Orozco and his wife, Margarita Valladares, bought a property, part of a farm, on Guadalajara's west-side suburb, in 1946. The Orozcos rebuilt the original house in 1948, including a large studio where José planned to create " . . . works totally different than I've done until now." Unfortunately, time caught up with him. José Clemente Orozco passed away a year later, on September 7, 1949, at the age of 66.

western gate. In the front (west) side, at the statue's feet, the inscription translates as "Justice, Wisdom, Strength, the Custodian of this Loyal City."

Not nearly so well known, but equally monumental, is the nearby dramatic **Estampida** sculpture, of a herd of stampeding wild bronze horses. Find it by following Av. López Mateos about half a mile southwest to the Los Arcos traffic circle, at the intersection of Circunvalación A. Yañez (see the Hotel Holiday Inn high-rise on the east side). The sculpture is on the circle's west-side.

ACCOMMODATIONS

The Minerva-Chapultepec district offers a wide variety of comfortable lodgings to suit many tastes and budgets. They vary from luxury high-rises and budget one-nighters to condo suites and deluxe bed-and-breakfasts. What they all have in common are safe, established neighborhoods, close to shops, restaurants and transportation.

Accommodations Around Av. Chapultepec and Av. Americas

By location (for a listing by price, see chart "Minerva-Chapultepec Accommodations By Price"), moving west from the edge of downtown, start at the very reliable **Hotel Isabel Residencial.** The hotel offers a relaxing garden setting at reasonable prices. The Isabel's 1960s-era amenities—comfortably furnished semi-deluxe rooms with phones, small blue pool, popular coffee shop, and parking—have long attracted a loyal following of Guadalajara return visitors and businesspeople. Its coffee shop usually bustles with residents and merchants during breakfast, lunch, and supper hours. If the hotel has a drawback, it's the general atmosphere, which, although not unfriendly, borders on YMCA-like institutional coolness. On the other hand, the 51A and 51B buses (less than 10 minutes to the city center) run along Libertad, two blocks north of the hotel. The Isabel's 50 rooms rent for $48 s, $53 d, with ceiling fans and **limited wheelchair access.** Ask for a discount for a long-term rental. J. Guadalupe Montenegro 1572, Guadalajara, Jalisco 44100; tel./fax 33/3826-2630; email: hotelisa@telmex.net.mx.

For something quite different, go about eight blocks north and west, to bed-and-breakfast **Casa Ganz,** across from the Alliance Français. Here, a savvy European expatriate owner has converted a large family house into a comfortable, six-unit lodging, offering clean, spacious rooms, attractively furnished with shiny hardwood furniture and large baths with showers. A friendly American manager, a quiet, garden-patio, usable by all guests, and all king-size beds except one, add desirable plusses. Rents vary, depending mainly on size, from $85 for a room with bath to $100 for suites with either kitchenette, a separate bedroom, or a private patio. Daily maid service, cable TV, phone, private bath, special monthly rates, and continental breakfast is included. 1188 Cotilla, Guadalajara, Jalisco 44160; manager tel. 33/3826-2390; email: casa@villaganz.com; website: www.villaganz.com.

The same owner also offers **Villa Ganz,** a deluxe suite-style garden hotel complex seven blocks west (past Americas). All 11 units are deluxe and attractively furnished with king-size beds, carpets, and attractive lamps and bedspreads. Rates for junior, master, and presidential suite grades begin at about $170, with cable TV, telephone, Internet access, fans, parking, and continental breakfast. Ask for a special weekly, monthly or promotional rate. López Cotilla 1739, Guadalajara, Jalisco 44160; tel. 33/3120-1416, 33/3120-1416; email: reservaciones@villa ganz.com; website: www.villaganz.com.

Visitors who prefer a deluxe full-service (but very competitively priced) hotel choose the **Hotel Laffayette.** The Laffayette offers the advantage of plush amenities, a leafy, semi-residential upscale neighborhood, and close proximity to Av. Chapultepec shops, cafes, restaurants, and transportation.

Inside the front door you enter a cool green interior with a bar and restaurant compactly tucked around an elegant lobby. Doors lead outside to a tranquil, tropical pool-patio. Upstairs, the 189 rooms are luxuriously furnished and decorated in navy blue and white, with blue pastel bedspreads. Rates run around $110 d, with commercial discount to around $90 s or d, with air-conditioning, cable TV, parking, credit cards accepted, live music every night except Sun., and two downstairs event rooms seating 50 and 100 respectively. La Paz 2055, Guadalajara, Jalisco 44160; tel. 33/3615-0252, toll-free in Mexico tel. 01-800/362-2200, fax 33/3630-1112; (reservations) email: lafayete@mpsnet.com.mx; website: www.laffayette.com.mx.

For a luxurious combination of elegance, charm, and intimacy, consider **Casa Madonna,** a few blocks west, at Lerdo de Tejada. Casa Madonna is the labor of love of a savvy longtime Guadalajara resident who has converted a 1920s vintage Mexican-style family house into a graceful bed-and-breakfast. Details are her strong point, from the invitingly plush living room couches and artfully placed antique portraits, to the lacy antique dining room tablecloth. Here, guests start their days with a made-to-order breakfast on the garden veranda, and on cool winter nights, they end it over glasses of cabernet and port around a cozy fireplace.

The five rooms, actually spacious suites, named respectively Bugambilia, Girasol, Obelisco, El Nido, and Tabachines, each with unique decor, are all you would expect, blooming with plants, polished antiques, shiny tile, and sparkling modern-standards bathrooms. Single rates range from $90 with double bed to $110 and $125 with king- or queen-size beds (add $15 for a second person); all with cable TV, ceiling fan, phone, laundry, full breakfast, and credit cards accepted. Lerdo de Tejada 2308, Guadalajara, Jalisco 44150, tel. 33/3615-6554; (reservations and information) email: casamadonna@megared.net .mx: website: www.mexweb.com/casamadonna.

On the other hand, moderately priced, comfortable, and modern one- and two-bedroom apartments are available at high-rise **Hotel Suites Bernini,** on Vallarta at the corner of Unión. The approximately 50 semi-deluxe kitchenette apartments are comfortably furnished with wall-to-wall carpets, drapes, living-dining room, and king-size (or two double) beds. One-bedroom-one-bath rentals run about $60 per night, $1,600 per month; two-bedroom-two-bath, $90 and $1,900. All with air-conditioning, cable TV, and parking, but no pool and minimal desk services. Vallarta 1881, Guadalajara, Jalisco 44150; toll-free in Mexico 800/362-8200, tel./fax 33/3615-2418, 33/3616-7274, 33/3616-0858; email: berniniventas2@ megared.net.mx.

Accommodations Around Los Arcos and the Minerva Circle

If you're interested in an even more economical apartment setting, consider the simpler, but conveniently located **Hotel Plaza Los Arcos,** diagonal from Centro Magno. This self-styled "economical business hotel" offers six floors of about 100 kitchenette semi-deluxe (but some worn) apartments, comfortably furnished with sofas, carpets, drapes, floor-to-ceiling windows, private balconies, modern-standard baths, and king-size (or two double) beds. Tariffs for standard one-bedroom units are about $65/night, $1,000/month; for two bedrooms, $85 and $1,300, with TV, phone, air-conditioning, parking, credit cards accepted, but no pool. Av. Vallarta 2452, Guadalajara, Jalisco 44100; toll-free in Mexico 01-800/368-3200, or tel. 33/3615-2062, 33/3615-4805, fax 33/3616-3817; website: www.hotelarcos.com.mx.

The Plaza Los Arcos owners also operate the well-located nine-story **Suites Moralva** across the street. Check it out; they sometimes advertise kitchenette apartments as low as $900 monthly. Av. Vallarta 2477, Guadalajara, Jalisco 44100; same toll-free number as Plaza Los Arcos 800/368-3200, or tel. 33/3615-1845; website (also the same): www.hotelarcos.com.mx.

Circle around to the quiet block directly behind Hotel Plaza Los Arcos to the lively, popular, and reasonably priced four-star **Gran Hotel Las Pergolas** ("The Arbors"). Downstairs, the open-air polished marble lobby leads past the coffee shop and nightclub-bar to an invitingly intimate tropical inner pool-patio. Upstairs, the 158 deluxe rooms, all with modern-standards baths, are comfortably furnished with pastel-toned king-size (or two double) beds, carpets, and drapes. Rooms vary, especially baths; look at more than one. Tariffs are about $72 s or d, ($45 monthly rate), with satellite TV, air-conditioning, parking, basketball and volleyball court, massage and sauna at additional cost, and credit cards accepted. Morelos 2244, Guadalajara, Jalisco 44100; toll-free in Mexico 01-800/713-9615; or tel. 33/3615-0088, 33/3630-0629, fax 33/3630-0576; email: pergolas@foreigner.class.udg.mx; website: www.pergolas.com.mx.

Surprisingly, this elite neighborhood offers an authentic budget alternative in the **Hotel Windsor,** at Salado Álvarez between Av. Mexico and Justo Sierra. Although the Hotel Windsor has seen better times, and is now plain and a bit tattered around the edges, an elegant marble-floored lobby attests to its former glory. Nevertheless, it offers the basics: a quiet residential street-front, kindly manager, and 18 clean rooms of varying sizes, all with double beds, drapes, a bit of furniture, and bath with hot water. Be prepared for bare-bulb lighting, however. The cheapest, plainest rooms go for about $17 s or d; the biggest, with kitchenette, $30 s or d; with fans and cable TV, but credit cards not accepted. Salado Álvarez 131, Guadalajara, Jalisco 44600; tel. 33/3615-7790, 33/3616-7561.

Switching to the truly grand, cross to the west side of the Minerva Circle to the high-powered business **Hotel Fiesta Americana.** From the reception, a cool, carpeted lobby spreads beneath a lofty, light atrium. Adjacent corridors lead to an entire shopping and service center, including a travel agent, gift shop, bank, Canadian consulate, British Trade Office, and much more.

The hotel's lavish in-house business facilities also include a big deluxe business-negotiation center with private rooms and all communication facilities and secretarial help, and an executive lounge with complimentary snacks and drinks, and an entire convention center accommodating more than a thousand participants.

The 396 plush view rooms and suites are furnished in pastel tones, with soft couches, huge beds, and a host of luxury amenities. Rentals begin at about $150 s or d, with tennis courts, spa, restaurants, pool, and sundeck. Aurelio Aceves 225, Guadalajara, Jalisco 44100; tel. 33/3825-3434, fax 33/3630-3725; from Canada and the U.S., toll-free 800/FIESTA1 (800/343-7821); email: crodriguez@fiestaamericana.com.mx; website: www.fiestaamericana.com.mx.

North of the Minerva Circle

A pair of deluxe accommodations, one apartments and the other cottages, about a mile northwest of the Minerva Circle, offer still more options. Closest in is **Quinta Ganz,** operated by the same owner as Casa Ganz and Villa Ganz, mentioned earlier. Here, you'll find a complex of 10 attractively furnished modern two-story apartments, clustered in a leafy garden compound with a swimming pool common to all units. Inside, downstairs, are living room, dining room, and kitchen; upstairs, two bedrooms and a bath. Rentals run about $150/day, monthly rate about $110/day, with maid service, phone, cable TV, and fans. Laundry service is available but extra. Angulo 3047, Fracc. Monraz, Guadalajara, Jalisco 44670; tel. 33/3120-1416; (reservations) email: reservaciones@villaganz.com; website: www.villaganz.com.

Find Quinta Ganz from the Minerva Circle by following Diagonal Golfo de Cortés, the street that radiates northwest from the Minerva Circle's northwest side. Continue seven blocks to a traffic circle; follow the circle counterclockwise to Av. Juan Aldemar Arias at its north side. Continue along Arias four blocks; turn right at Ángulo and continue one and a half blocks to Quinta Ganz, on the right.

Alternatively, nearby, take a look at **Suites Residenciales Margarita** on Eulogio Parra. Past the gate you'll find 28 ranch-style cottages with carports, set in a luxuriously spacious green, grassy park. Inside, the units are clean, semi-deluxe, and comfortably appointed with ceiling-to-floor drapes, white walls, shiny tile floors, and modern dark-wood furniture. Units include a carpeted living room with fireplace, dining area,

kitchenette with stove and refrigerator, and one bedroom with two double beds and a bathroom with tub shower. Extras include a pool-patio, luxuriously set in a scenic canyon setting, and a clubhouse with a meeting salon and hotel desk service. Rentals cost about $120/day, $1,800/month, with cable TV, phone, and credit cards accepted. Eulogio Parra 3190, P.O. Box 1-1881, Guadalajara, Jalisco 44670; tel. 33/3641-6363, fax 33/3641-6837; (reservations and information) email: louis44@infosel.net.mx.

Get there from the Minerva Circle (see Quinta Ganz directions above) by following Diagonal Golfo de Cortés past the first circle, a total of nine blocks, to an intersection with Av. Aztecas. Follow Av. Aztecas from the intersection's north side three blocks; turn right at Eulogio Parras, and after half a block, turn left at the entrance gate.

Accommodations Farther West

Back at the Minerva Circle, continue west along Av. Vallarta about a mile, where on the south side of the boulevard are the **Hotel Camino Real** grounds at Av. Vallarta, the queen of Guadalajara luxury hotels. In contrast to its high-rise local competitors, the Camino Real spreads through a luxurious park of lawns, pools, and shady tropical verdure. Guests enjoy tastefully appointed bungalow-style units opening onto semiprivate pools and patios.

The hotel offers the "Camino Real Club," a 35-unit super-luxurious executive section, with breakfast included. An adjacent convention complex can accommodate meetings from 50 to 1,000 participants. Rates start at $180 s or d and include cable TV, phone, four pools, tennis court, a nearby golf course, two restaurants, and a lobby bar with nightly live music. Av. Vallarta 5005, Guadalajara, Jalisco 45040; from the U.S. and Canada, you may also reserve via toll-free tel. 800/7CAMINO (800/722-6466), in Mexico, toll-free tel. 01-800/903-2100; tel. 33/3134-2424, fax 33/3134-2404; email: crgdlsh@web celmex.net.mx or gdl@caminoreal.com; website: www.caminoreal.com.

A block west, consider the worthy four-star **Hotel Malibu,** a more economical but still deluxe option (and handy) for folks driving in along

Hwy. 15. The hotel is attractively built around an inviting pool-patio and small grove of magnificent tropical trees. Builders have arranged the 121 rooms in two sections, a low-rise two-story tier and an airy tower section. Rooms in both are deluxe and comfortable, but the dim lighting in the low-rise tier made the rooms appear dark and uninviting when I was there. Take a look for yourself, and if the lighting isn't satisfactory, opt for better illumination, privacy, and the balcony view of a tower section room. They're attractively decorated in whites and soothing creams and comfortably furnished in modern style, with double beds and marble shower baths. Rentals run about $85 s or d for standard grade with two double beds, $110 for junior suite with king-size bed, all with air-conditioning, phone, cable TV, restaurant, parking, lobby bar with live music Thursday–Saturday. There's a travel agent (tel. 33/3121-1069, 33/3121-7782) and car rental (tel. 33/3122-3316, 33/3122-1354) next door, and Gran Plaza shopping center and Wal-Mart, Sam's Club, and Price Club on Av. Vallarta nearby. Av. Vallarta 3993, Zapopan, Jalisco 45040, tel. 33/3121-7782, 33/3122-2556, tel./fax 33/3122-3192; (reservations and information) email: malibu@cybercafe.net.mx; website: www.hotelmalibu.com.mx.

If you're interested in saving even more money, go half a block farther west to **Motel Nuevo Vallarta,** a basic but decent 26-room lodging, stacked in three stories with rooms opening onto motel-style outdoor walkways. Rooms themselves are plainly furnished but clean, with either one king-size or two double beds and hot shower-baths. Expect to pay about $33 s or d, additional adult $10, with cable TV, fans, and phone (local calls $.50). Av. Vallarta 3999, Zapopan, Jalisco 45040, tel. 33/3121-2095, 33/3121-0017.

South of the Minerva Circle

A few blocks southeast of the Minerva Circle, at the corner of La Paz, is the **Hotel Plaza Diana.** The Plaza Diana offers luxurious amenities for lower rates than its competitors towering nearby. Past the reception and plush lobby, restaurant, and bar, elevators rise to five floors of 150 rooms, in standard, deluxe, and jr. suite grades. The smallish standard-grade rooms are comfortably furnished with green carpets, chocolate-brown wood furniture, and dark earth-tone ceiling-to-floor drapes, king-size beds, and shiny marble tub baths. Deluxe rooms have about the same, but with two double beds and a larger bath. One entire floor is reserved for nonsmokers. Rates run from about $110 s or d, with air-conditioning, cable TV, phone (local calls $.10), parking, pool, (but no sauna, exercise rooms, or business center). Credit cards accepted. Circunvalación Agustín Yañez 2760, Guadalajara, Jalisco 44130; toll-free in Mexico (reservations) 01-800/024-8181; tel. 33/3615-6428, 33/3616-3285, fax 33/3630-3685; email: hdiana@prodigy.net.mx; website: www.hoteldiana.com.mx.

Right across the street, budget travelers might consider the bare-bones 16-room **Hotel Patricia.** Here, you get a plain, tattered, but clean bare-bulb room with bath, near shops, good restaurants, and right on the 51A-51B bus line. Rooms cost $34 s, $41 d (one bed), $46 d (two beds), if you don't require a receipt. For more quiet, get a room away from the busy street-front. Circunvalación Agustín Yañez 2745C, Guadalajara, Jalisco 44100; tel./fax 33/3630-0117.

For a low profile, deluxe alternative, shift about half a mile southwest to the **Hotel del Bosque.** The 75 rooms encircle an elegant inner garden, sheltered by magnificent shade trees and adjoining a large blue designer pool-patio. Next to the reception-lobby, diners enjoy the view from a cool, graceful restaurant.

The rooms come in deluxe and standard grades, all spotless and comfortably furnished in light pastels, with reading lamps, soft beds, and marble baths. Standard rooms come with one double bed, tile floors, and ceiling fans; deluxe rooms improve upon this with two double beds, marble floors, and air-conditioning; some rooms have kitchenettes. Standard rooms rent for $66 daily rate, $52 weekly; deluxe $105 daily, $90 weekly, all with cable TV, phones, parking, and credit cards accepted. Av. López Mateos Sur 265, Guadalajara, Jalisco 45000; tel./fax 33/3121-4700; (reservations and information) email: hbosque@vianet.com.mx.

About a quarter mile farther south, business travelers often opt for the American-style high-rise

MINERVA-CHAPULTEPEC ACCOMMODATIONS BY PRICE

Accommodations are listed in increasing order of double-room (two people in one bed) rates. 800 numbers are for toll-free reservations from the United States and Canada. 01-800 numbers are for the same from within Mexico. Postal codes, such as 44150, are listed.

Accommodations around Av. Chapultepec and Av. Americas

Hotel Isabel Residencial, J. Guadalupe Montenegro 1572, 44100; tel./fax 33/3826-2630; email: hotelisa@telmex.net.mx; $53

Hotel Suites Bernini, Av. Vallarta 1881, 44150; tel./fax 33/3615-2418, 33/3616-7274, or 01-800/362-8200; email: berniniventas2@megared.net.mx; $60, $1,600/month

Casa Ganz, 1188 Cotilla, 44160; tel. 33/3826-2390; email: casa@villaganz.com; website: www.villaganz.com; $85

Casa Madonna, Lerdo de Tejada 2308, 44150; tel. 33/3615-6554; email: casamadonna@megared.net.mx; website: www.mexweb.com/casamadonna; $105

Hotel Laffayette, La Paz 2055, 44160; tel. 33/3615-0252 or tel. 01-800/362-2200; fax 33/3630-1112; (reservations) email: lafayete@mpsnet.com.mx; website: www.laffayette.com.mx; $110

Villa Ganz, López Cotilla 1739, 44160; tel. 33/3120-1416; email: reservaciones@villaganz.com; website: www.villaganz.com; $170

Accommodations around Los Arcos and the Minerva Circle

Hotel Windsor, Salado Álvarez 131, 44600; tel. 33/3615-7790 or 33/3616-7561; $17

Hotel Plaza Los Arcos, Av. Vallarta 2452, 44100; tel. 33/3615-2062, fax 33/93616-3817; toll-free 01-800/368-3200; website: www.hotelarcos.com.mx; $65, $1,000/month

Gran Hotel Las Pergolas, Morelos 2244, 44100; tel. 33/3615-0088, fax 33/3630-0576; toll-free 01-800/713-9615; email: pergolas@foreigner.class.udg.mx; website: www.pergolas.com.mx; $72, $1,400/month

---

Holiday Inn Select at Av. Niños Héroes. The approximately 225 accommodations come in select, deluxe, and master suite grades. Select rooms are luxurious and comfortable, the deluxe add more space and more extras, including two telephones, one in the bathroom. Master suites have a living room with separate bedroom, two TVs, and two bathrooms, one with a spa tub. Moreover, business travelers can choose a room on one of three executive floors, with complete communication and secretarial services and a relaxing executive lounge with canapes, coffee, cocktails, and wine day.

Rates begin at around $200 d for select grade, $220 d for deluxe, more for suites. Hotel amenities include exercise room, pool, parking, event sa-

lons accommodating up to 800, restaurant, coffee shop, sushi bar, live music evenings in the lobby bar Monday–Saturday, and credit cards accepted. Ask for a commercial or longer-term rate. Av. Niños Héroes 3089, Guadalajara, Jalisco 44520; from the U.S. and Canada, toll-free 800/465-4329; in Mexico, toll-free 01-800/364-77; tel. 33/3122-2020, fax 33/3647-7779; email: selectgd@selectgdl.com.mx; website: www.hola.com or www.selectgdl.com.mx.

Hotels La Serena and Casa Grande

Two hotels, the budget La Serena and the deluxe Casa Grande, on the south outskirts of town offer interesting bus and air travel–related options, respectively. For details, see the end of the

Suites Moralva, Av. Vallarta 2477, Guadalajara, Jalisco 44100; tel. 33/3615-1845; $75, $1,000/month

Hotel Fiesta Americana, Aurelio Aceves 225, 44100; tel. 33/3825-3434, fax 33/3630-3725 or 800/343-7821; email: crodriguez@fiestaamericana.com.mx; website: www.fiestaamericana.com.mx., $150

Accommodations North, South, and West of the Minerva Circle

Motel Nuevo Vallarta, Av. Vallarta 3999, 45040; tel. 33/3121-2095 or 33/3121-0017; $33

Hotel Patricia, Circunvalación Agustín Yañez 2745C, 44100; tel./fax 33/3630-0117; $46

Hotel del Bosque, Av. López Mateos Sur 265, 45000; tel./fax 33/3121-4700; email: hbosque@vianet.com.mx; $66, $360/week

Hotel Malibu, Av. Vallarta 3993, 45040; tel. 3121-7782; tel./fax 33/3122-3192; website: www.hotelmalibu.com.mx; $85

Hotel Plaza Diana, Circunvalación Agustín Yañez 2760, 44130; tel. 33/3615-6428, fax 33/3630-3685, toll-free 01-800/024-8181; email: hdiana@prodigy.net.mx; website: www.hoteldiana.com.mx; $110

Suites Residenciales Margarita, Eulogio Parra 3190, P.O. Box 1-1881, 44670; tel. 33/3641-6363, fax 33/3641-6837; email: louis44@infosel.net.mx; $120, $1,800/month

Quinta Ganz, Angulo 3047, Fracc. Monraz, 44670; tel. 3120-1416; email: reservaciones@villaganz.com; website: www.villaganz.com; $150, $3,000/month

Hotel Camino Real, Av. Vallarta 5005, 45040; tel. 33/3134-2424, fax 33/3134-2404; toll-free 800/722-6466, or 01-800/903-2100; email: crgdlsh@webcelmex.net.mx or gdl@caminoreal.com; website: www.caminoreal.com; $180

Holiday Inn Select, Av. Niños Héroes 3089, 44520; tel. 33/3122-2020, fax 33/3647-7779; toll-free 800/465-4329 or 01-800/364-77; email: selectgd@selectgdl.com.mx; website: www.hola.com or www.selectgdl.com.mx; $200

CITY: WEST AND NORTH

Accommodations section in the Heart of the City chapter.

Trailer Parks

RVers can choose from a pair of Guadalajara metropolitan area trailer parks. At the west end of Av. Vallarta, long-time **Hacienda Trailer Park** remains as ever. About half of the 96 spaces are occupied permanently by the rigs of Canadian and American regulars who return for their annual winter of sunny relaxation. And anyone can see why: In addition to the sparklingly healthful Guadalajara weather, the Hacienda's extensive facilities include concrete pad, all hookups, separate men's and women's toilets and showers, a big blue pool, patio, large clubroom with fireplace, paperback library, billiards room, and enough power for air-conditioning. You can even throw in a golf course and Sam's Club shopping center nearby. For all this, rates run $17/day (one free day per week), $330/month, or $300/month on a yearly basis. While summers at La Hacienda are pretty quiet, winter reservations are mandatory.

Get there from divided Hwy. 15 (Av. Vallarta) about five miles (eight kilometers) west of the Guadalajara city center. If heading eastbound, from the Tepic–Puerto Vallarta direction, pull into the far right lateral lane just after crossing the *periférico* (peripheral highway). After about a mile and a half (two km) from the *periférico,* turn right at the Hacienda Trailer Park sign and follow more signs another few hundred yards to the towering entrance gate. In the reverse, west-bound direction, turn left from Av. Vallarta, at the Hacienda Trailer Park sign about a mile (1.5 km) past Sam's Club. Write to P.O. Box 5-494, Guadalajara, Mexico, 45042; tel. 33/3627-1724 or 33/3627-1843, fax 33/3627-2832 (ask for fax tone).

San José del Tajo Trailer Park, about a mile from the Santa Anita Country Club and Golf Course, remains equally popular. Its very adequate facilities include many shady spaces with all hookups, toilets, showers, pool, clubroom, and tennis court. Rentals run about $18/day, $125/week, $360/month, $11 per day (for a three month stay). Find it on the southern extension of Av. López Mateos Sur (Hwys. 15, 54, and 80), about three miles (five kilometers) south of the *periférico.* Turn right (southbound) at the green-and-white "San José del Tajo" sign. North-bound, it's about a half a mile (one km) north of the Santa Anita village exit; tel. 33/3686-1738.

FOOD

The Minerva-Chapultepec district is famous for food, a legacy of its legion of fine restaurants. Visitors can furthermore choose between dozens of more humble but worthy coffee shops, espresso cafes, bakeries, and over-the-counter fast-food eateries tucked behind and between the showplaces.

Breakfast, Cafes, Bakeries, and Fast-Food

What many satisfied customers like about **Sanborn's** coffee shop is that they know exactly what to expect: long hours, shiny plates and silver-ware, and a moderately priced selection of soups, salads, and hearty breakfast, lunch, and dinner plates.

Choose from two Minerva-Chapultepec Sanborn's locations. The first, at 1600 Vallarta, northeast corner of General San Martín, also includes a large magazine and gift shop that carries everything from paperback novels and perfume to handicrafts and handkerchiefs. Hours are Mon.–Sat. 7–1 A.M. and Sun. 7 A.M.–midnight, tel. 33/3615-5894 and 33/3615-1034.

Or go just a few blocks farther west to **Sanborn's 24-Hour Restaurant,** for good breakfasts around-the-clock, at the southeast corner of Av. Vallarta and Gamboa, tel. 33/3615-5894. (No gift shop here; small magazine stand only.) Another Sanborn's at **Gran Plaza** on Av. Vallarta farther west, is open daily 7:30 A.M.–1 A.M.

The Minerva-Chapultepec district abounds in cafes and coffeehouses, especially along Avenidas Union-Americas and Chapultepec and the neighboring side streets.

Just adjacent (west) of the Laffayette Hotel, try **La Via Plata** (The Silver Way) deli-cafe. Balmy afternoons and evenings are especially enjoyable here over conversation, alongside your cappuccino, sandwich, or salad. Open Sun.–Thurs. 5–11 P.M., Fri. and Sat. 5 P.M.–midnight. La Paz 2121; tel. 33/3616-5102.

Also very popular, especially evenings, is **La Paloma** (The Dove), at López Cotilla on the southwest corner of Cervantes. Pick a table and join the mostly 20- and 30-ish crowd on the open-air veranda while enjoying your pick of a short but tasty menu of breakfasts, soups, salads, sandwiches, and dinner plates. Open daily 8 A.M.–1 A.M. López Cotilla 1855; tel. 33/3630-0091.

A good place for refreshment while shopping or sightseeing is **La Letra Zero** cafe, tucked at street level inside the Centro Magno shopping center (Av. Vallarta 2425, about four blocks east of the Los Arcos arch). For a more substantial offering, go to the adjacent **El Arca** restaurant and take a seat within their menagerie of shiny papier-mâché animals—gorillas, giraffes, hippos—and choose from a professionally prepared menu of international specialties. Open Mon.–Sat. 1:30 A.M.–midnight, Sun. 1:30 P.M.–10 P.M.; tel. 33/3630-0860.

You needn't do without your heart's delight of delectable **pastries** in the Minerva-Chapultepec district. Most renowned are **El Globo,** López Cotilla 1749, a block east of Unión, tel. 33/3616-6408 (takeout only) and **Monique,** at Unión 410, four blocks south of La Paz. Open daily 9 A.M.–10 P.M.; tel. 33/3615-6851.

American-style fast-food has gained a foothold in Minerva-Chapultepec. **McDonald's** maintains a least one close-in outlet: Av. Vallarta 1402, corner of Progreso (one block north of the U.S. consulate, tel. 33/3826-5902). You can also find McDonald's farther west on Av. Vallarta, in Gran Plaza, street level, tel. 33/3122-3436. Both outlets are open Mon.–Thurs. 7 A.M.–10 P.M., Fri.–Sun. 7 A.M.– 11:30 P.M.

Take the kids for a break at the full-fledged (with elaborate kiddie playground) **Burger King,** west side of the Minerva Circle, intersection of López Mateos and Vallarta. Open daily 9 A.M.–10 P.M.; tel. 33/3616-4676. Additionally, you'll find a smaller, but nevertheless popular, Burger King on the top floor of the Centro Magno shopping center, about four blocks east of the Los Arcos arch.

You might enjoy the offerings of the home-grown Italian fast-food outlet **Italianissimo,** with outlets on the upper floors of both Centro Magno and Gran Plaza. If not, choose from several more in the same shopping plazas, including **Kentucky Fried Chicken, Teriyaki, Paris Crepes,** and **Dunkin Donuts.**

Restaurants Around Av. Chapultepec and Av. Americas

Moving from east to west, start at **Restaurant Sacramonte,** where a billowing ceiling and soothing old-fashioned trumpet-free afternoon mariachi serenades set the tone for this gourmet party in progress. The festive ambience notwithstanding, the continuously innovative *mexicana vieja* (old Mexican) menu is what draws the faithful mid- to upper-class crowd of Tapatíos here. The mariachis play Tues.–Sun. 1:30–5:00 P.M. Live piano solos continue afterwards; relaxed atmosphere, fine for kids. At Av. Pedro Moreno 1398, northeast corner of Colonias, a block north of Vallarta. Open daily 1:30 P.M.–12:30 A.M., reservations recommended, tel. 33/3825-5447. Credit cards accepted. Expensive.

Some Guadalajara long-timers swear by **Restaurant Villa Chianti,** at the northwest corner of General San Martín. Here, a mostly elite local and foreign business clientele enjoys a surprisingly innovative menu within the white-columned elegance of a restored *bella época* mansion. Here, customers choose from a surprisingly short but intriguing list of Italian delicacies, ranging from *antipasti* (tuna *carpaccio,* and portobello mushroom slices in prune pesto basil sauce) pastas *(linguine con frutti del mare),* fish (shrimp in saffron and dill cream) and fowl (roasted duck breast in prune sauce with shallots). The wine list, twice as long as the food menu, offers hard-to-get selections from Mexico's premier boutique Monte Xanic (sha-NEEK) winery. Among the whites, try the late harvest chenin blanc; for reds the cabernet franc. (Unfortunately, service on my last visit was less than ideal; and, in an oversight, they brought Coffeemate for creamer. Tut-tut.) Open Mon.–Sat. 1 P.M.–midnight. 2152 José Guadalupe Zuño; tel. 33/3630-2250; email: reservaciones@villachianti.com. Credit cards accepted. Expensive.

Graceful Islamic arches add a touch of Arabian Nights to the refined ambience of **Restaurant Formosa Gardens,** at Unión 322, southwest corner of José Guadalupe Zuño. In this slice of Asia-in-Guadalajara, competent chefs work from a very recognizable menu of Chinese specialties, from pot stickers and egg rolls to sweet-and-sour pork to broccoli beef. Friday and Saturday nights, the friendly Chinese family owners bring in a dinner-time "Chinese Jazz" combo. Open Mon.–Fri. 1:30–10:30 P.M., Sun. 1–5 P.M.; tel. 33/3615-7415, 33/3124-0023, 33/3615-2326. Credit cards accepted. Moderate–expensive.

A few blocks south, at the edge of the Minerva-Chapultepec district, the **Restaurant Delfín Sonriente** (Smiling Dolphin) offers fresh seafood in an unpretentious setting at Niños Héroes, southwest corner of Unión. Although deep in the heart of Guadalajara, signs of its kindly Japanese-Mexican owners surface subtly here. While the appearance of frog's legs, tempura, and sashimi on the menu sharpens the suspicion, a rear addition, with white stucco walls, hand-finished blond wood, and sloping beamed ceilings appears to have been imported straight from the quiet country seacoast of Japan. The rest of the menu—many styles and combinations of shrimp, fish, octopus, with some chicken and beef plates for variety—all including salad bar, is bound to please. Open daily 1–6 P.M. only. Niños Héroes 2239; tel. 33/3616-0216, 33/3616-3441. Moderate.

A trio of northside restaurants (actually outside the northern boundary of the Minerva-Chapultepec district) deserve mention. First, **Restaurant Ma Come No**, at Av. Americas, corner of Manuel Acuña, about a mile north of Av. Vallarta, arguably serves the best Italian food in Guadalajara. The dining room, with open air section in front, rises from a handsomely rustic tiled floor, past whitewashed brick walls to wide *cantera* stone arches supporting a massive beamed ceiling, all leaving the impression of a Tuscan country inn. Decor notwithstanding, the simply excellent food, served with a minimum of pretension, is the main event here. First, try the salad bar which, for a mere $2.50 gets you *antipasti* such as duck roll, frittata, and mushrooms marinated with bean sprouts. Next, choose from the menu of pastas (*ravioli al salmone*), pizzas (thick-crusted and yummy), grilled meats (*fileto al funghi,*) and seafood (*linguini al vongole*). Open Mon.–Sat. 1:30 P.M.–12:30 A.M., Sun. 1:30–8 P.M. Av. Americas 302; tel. 33/3615-4952. Credit cards accepted. Moderate–expensive.

Just a block farther north, vegetarians can regain their equilibrium at **Restaurant Zanahoria** (Carrot), at Americas 332. Eat healthy with your fill of good salads, soups, and hearty vegetable entrées such as spicy baked eggplant, squash-stuffed tamales, and avocado-tomato tacos. Open daily except Tues. 8 A.M.–7 P.M.; tel. 33/3124-6000, 33/3616-6161. Budget–moderate.

A mile farther north, **Restaurant Las Palomas**, at Av. Americas 1491, southwest corner of Sao Paulo, is Guadalajara's clean, poorly lighted place for Mexican food and socializing. A brother-branch of the well-known Las Palomas restaurant in Puerto Vallarta, this place has caught on with the young Guadalajara party crowd. Waiters bustle, carrying huge portions of tasty Northern *(Norteño)* Mexico–style salads, soups, and entrées. Put your dietary pretensions aside with such choices as cheesy *chiles rellenos, enchiladas rancheras,* stuffed chicken breast, *arrachera* (steak cooked in its juice), *costillas* (spareribs), and fish fillets. Open daily, 7 A.M.–midnight, tel. 33/3817-2798. Credit cards accepted. Moderate–expensive.

Restaurants Around Los Arcos and the Minerva Circle

Back a few blocks south of Av. Vallarta, find **Restaurant Vinería Tinto y Blanco**, at Av. Francisco Javier Gamboa, southwest corner of Guadalupe Zuño, whose owner's mission is to introduce wine to Guadalajara. Furthermore, he seems to be getting it right, with a custom wine bar that dispenses any one of a dozen fine varietals while at the same time keeping them out of contact with air. Get a copy of his wine-tasting schedule before you leave.

Next, take a look at the menu. Start, for example, with arugula, betabel, and grapefruit salad with a honey-mustard dressing, continue with *pasta fusilli* in tomato sauce, accompanied with a glass of Chilean Santa Carolina merlot. Finish up with a slice of apple strudel that will melt in your mouth. Open Mon.–Sat. 1 P.M.–midnight. Av. Francisco Javier Gamboa 255; tel. 33/3615-9535. Credit cards accepted. Expensive.

One block north, all roads seem, these days, to lead to **Restaurant Santo Coyote,** Guadalajara's little bit of Hollywood in the suburbs on Lerdo de Tejada at the southeast corner of Gamboa. Although the food is good enough, the atmosphere—a galaxy of hanging lanterns glimmering from beneath a village of luxurious thatched *palapas,* all enclosing an idyllic pond and garden—keeps the crowds coming.

The food, an added plus, is Mexican nouveau at its best. Some entrées, such as *panela a la vinagretta* and *arrachera* you might find exotic, while others, such as a big plate of luscious baby back ribs, you won't. But there are lots of choices, all good. Open Mon.–Sat. 1 P.M.–1 A.M., Sun. 1–11 P.M., reservations recommended. Lerdo de Tejada 2379; tel. 33/3616-6978. Credit cards accepted. Expensive.

At **Restaurant Pierrot,** Justo Sierra 2355, southeast corner of Aurelio L. Gallardo, three blocks north of Vallarta, diners rediscover why French cooking is world-renowned. For example, I started out with *salade de berro* (watercress), continued with their *supe a la oignon gratinee,* and finished off with *filet d' porc normandie* (all washed down with their good Spanish house wine, and accompanied by the lilting piano strains of "La Vie en Rosé"). C'est Magnifique! Open Mon.–Sat. 1:30 P.M.– 12:30 A.M.; tel. 33/3630-2087, 33/3615-4758. Credit cards accepted. Expensive.

At **Casa Bariachi** at Av. Vallarta, corner of Calderón de la Barca, you can enjoy *mucho* mariachi entertainment (starting at 3:30 P.M.), with your salad bar, barbecued beef and chicken, and dessert. Very popular and good place to rub shoulders with American and Canadian resident expatriates. Open Mon.–Sat. 1 P.M.–3 A.M. Av. Vallarta 2221; tel. 33/3616-9900, 33/3615-0029; website: www.bariachi.com. Moderate.

Despite its name, **Restaurant Oui,** at López Cotilla (across Cotilla and a block west from Centro Magno shopping center), does not feature French food, but rather refined Mexican-international. Enter the dark, elegantly masculine shiny brass and glass dining room; overhead glows an artful stained-glass cupola, while all around, floor-to-ceiling windows look out upon an invitingly green and tropical exterior garden-patio. Subdued live music (classical quartet mornings, piano afternoons, jazz quintet evenings) completes the elegant picture.

The service and food are no less than you would expect. Enjoy breakfast choices from waffles and omelets to steak and *huevos rancheros.* For lunch, try a tasty fishburger, or a rich vegetable soup and tuna salad. For dinner, pick from many fish, fowl, and meat entrées—especially beef filets—that round out the menu. Open Mon.–Sat. 8 A.M.–midnight, Sun. 8 A.M.–2 P.M. López Cotilla 2171; tel. 33/3615-0614, 33/3614-3641. Credit cards accepted. Moderate–expensive.

Walk into the front door at **Restaurant Lusherly,** at Duque de Rivas on the southeast corner of Morelos (two blocks north of Av. Vallarta, two blocks east of Los Arcos arch) and let the checkered tablecloths, flower boxes, half-timbered walls, and carved wooden balconies transport you to Switzerland. The menu only enhances the impression. Here you can escape Mexico completely, with delicious choices such as onion soup, *salade mimosa* (hard-boiled egg and lettuce in vinaigrette), and *bratwurst mit rosti nach Berner* (Bern-style veal sausage with hash browns).

If those won't suffice, read through their long list of beef, shrimp, fish, crepes, and more. Open Mon.–Sat. (closed Tues.) 1 P.M.–midnight. Open Sun. 1–7 P.M. Duque de Rivas 5; tel. 33/3615-0509, 33/3616-2988. Moderate–expensive.

Dive back into Mexico at **Restaurant La Destilería,** easily ranking among Guadalajara's best Mexican-style restaurants, at Av. Mexico 2916, corner of Nelson, about five blocks west of López Mateos Norte. With all of the faux overhead piping and steel beams (to resemble a tequila distillery), La Destilería may look like a Chili's or a Señor Frog's, but La Destilería is the real thing. A look at the menu reveals a glossary of traditional Mexican cooking, including house specialties such as *cuitlacoche* (cooked corn fungus), *barbacoa de hoyo* ("pit" barbecued goat wrapped in *agave* leaves), *molcajete,* (lava rock bowl of steaming fowl or meat, *chorizo* sausage, shallots, *nopal* cactus leaves, cheese, and avocado, all in broth); all orders served with the traditional hot, covered *tortillero* platter of corn tortillas. Open Mon.–Sat. 1 P.M.–2 A.M., Sun. 1–6 P.M.; tel. 33/3640-3440, 33/3640-3110. Credit cards accepted. Moderate–expensive.

In second place but trying harder, is **Restaurant El Abajeño,** a credibly authentic branch of the long-time Guadalajara institution at the corner of Av. López Mateos and Av. Vallarta (at the north side of the Minerva Circle). Here, temporarily abandon your diet and pick from *antojitos* (try garlic mushrooms in butter or *enchiladas verdes,* soups (try *sopa de tortilla*), fondues (with bacon), pork loin (*lomo* with guacamole), or chicken (with *mole poblano*). Who needs dessert?

An additional plus here are the mariachis (with trumpets) who play afternoons 2–4 P.M. and the more restful trumpet-free guitar and violin quintet, evenings after 7 P.M. Open daily 1–11 P.M.; tel. 33/3630-2113 and 33/3630-2113. Credit cards accepted. Moderate–expensive.

For a moderately priced Italian option, go to **Restaurant La Trattoria di Pomodoro,** about a mile southwest of the Minerva Circle, at Av. Niños Héroes 3051, a block east of the Holiday Inn Select. "La Trattoria," as it's popularly known, remains popular with its largely middle- and upper-class patrons for its cool, refined atmosphere, crisp service, and reliable menu. A good way to proceed is to skip their so-so complimentary salad bar and go for the **antipasto bar,** a scrumptious selection that often includes eggplant parmesan, roasted zucchini, pickled artichokes, and spinach *torta.*

As for entrées, pasta is their specialty: spaghetti, linguini, fettuccini, fusilli, lasagna, ravioli in many styles, such as *arrabiata, pomodoro,* and primavera. Other choices include chicken in white wine sauce; beef brochette; *scallopini a la Marsala;* shrimp in garlic; and fish filet. Wines include an excellent all-Italian selection, plus some solid Domecq and Cetto Baja California reds and whites. Open daily 1 P.M.–midnight, tel. 33/3122-1817, 33/3122-4428. Credit cards accepted. Moderate.

ENTERTAINMENT AND EVENTS

An evening's excitement isn't hard to find in Guadalajara. Besides the ongoing diversions (refer to the Entertainment and Events sections throughout this book; Family Outings in the On the Road chapter; and the *Colony Reporter* advertisements and entertainment pages) in the town as a whole, you can also enjoy a number of local Minerva-Chapultepec options.

The owners of Restaurant Casa Bariachi (see Restaurants Around Los Arcos and the Minerva Circle, earlier), also operates **Bariachi** ("Here we pay for the mariachis") entertainment bar. Lately they've been setting aside Wednesday nights for sing-alongs, and "Mexican Nights" on Tuesdays and Thursdays (all the tequila you can drink, women $3, men $6). Open nightly from 6 P.M.–3 A.M. Av. Vallarta 2308; tel. 33/3616-9180; website: www.bariachi.com.

Similarly popular, but with a younger crowd, is **Habana** Cuban *tapas* and entertainment bar, a block east of Unión on Av. La Paz. Open Tues.–Sat. 5 P.M.–1:30 A.M. Here, the food is as important as the diversions. Owners are proud of their long list of *tapas,* from asparagus and English roast beef, to crab and Serrano ham. Arrive for *tapas* by 9 P.M. The show (entrance cover $5) begins at 10. Av.

La Paz 2199; tel. 33/3696-0096; reservations are necessary Friday and Saturday nights.

La Vida Leve at López Cotilla 1580, half a block west of Chapultepec, is popular with the twentysomething crowd that prefers high-volume rock (bring earplugs) with their *botanas* (snacks), spaghetti, and baguette sandwiches. Afternoons (coffees, teas, pastries, beer and wine served) are also potentially pleasant here, beneath the big front-yard umbrellas (if you don't mind the street noise from busy Av. Cotilla.) Open Sun.–Thurs. 4–11 P.M., Fri. and Sat. 5 P.M.–1 A.M.

If all else fails, you can opt for a **movie.** Minerva-Chapultepec has plenty of theaters, starting with the baker's dozen screens at **Cinepolis,** at Centro Magno shopping center. Find it at Av. Vallarta 2445, about four blocks east of the Los Arcos arch; tel. 33/3630-3940 for screening programs (or see the Arts and Entertainment section of the *Colony Reporter).* Other popular cinema complexes are at Plaza del Sol (southwest on López Mateos, tel. 33/3630-3940); and Gran Plaza (west of the Minerva Circle, south side of Av. Vallarta, tel. 33/3122-5657).

SPORTS AND RECREATION
Walking and Jogging

Open walker- and jogger-friendly spaces are scarce in the Minerva-Chapultepec district. Nevertheless, if you're in need of a jogging workout you might consider the two-mile-long grassy strip that divides southside Calz. Lázaro Cárdenas west of its intersection with Av. Niños Héroes.

Otherwise, take a taxi (or walk or jog) about two miles north to **Parque Colomos,** Guadalajara's prime walking, jogging, and horseback-riding zone. (From the Minerva Circle, follow diagonal Av. Mar de Cortés northwest; at a circle, diagonal right, north, to Av. Yaquis, continuing as it changes to Arias, then Aqueducto. Then turn right at Neruda and continue half a mile to the Parque Colomos on the left.

Gyms and Swimming

Workout gyms are relatively plentiful in Guadalajara's affluent west-side neighborhoods. In Min-

JORGE NEGRETE AND THE GOLDEN ERA OF MEXICAN FILM

Late at night, in the lobbies of small Mexican hotels, the TV often keeps flickering after everyone has retired to their rooms. The audience is usually only the lobby clerk and maybe a friend or a night-owl guest. They sit, transfixed by an old film of the 1940s or 1950s, frequently of handsome, resolute men in *sombreros* and lovely, brave señoritas. The reason is clear: These old films' crisp dialogues, rapid-fire action, and fine, often-artful photography are irresistible. Not unlike the fans of the American Movie Classics TV channel, Mexicans remain drawn to these old films, from an epoch known as the Golden Era of Mexican film.

Although Mexican filmmaking got started around 1900, it didn't really flower until after World War II, with a new generation of actors and directors, inspired by Russian director Sergei Eisenstein and American John Ford. Perhaps the most prominent of Mexican Golden Era directors was "Indio" Fernández who, collaborating with cinematographer Gabriel Figueroa, made such classics as *La Perla, (The Pearl), La Malquerida (The Unloved Woman), Flor Silvestre, (Wildflower),* and the *Rebelión de los Colgados (Rebellion of the Hanged.)*

Directors notwithstanding, it is the actors whom the public remembers: such unforgettables as María Félix, Dolores del Río, Silvia Pinal, Pedro Armendáriz, Pedro Infante, and Jorge Negrete. Of them all, none was more loved than Jorge Negrete, the "Charro Cantante" ("Singing Cowboy"). Although directors loved to place him in Jalisco *rancho* dramas and romances, such as *Ay Jalisco, No Te Rajes (Jalisco, Do Not Destroy Yourself),* and *Hasta Que Perdió Jalisco, (Until He Loses Jalisco),* Negrete sometimes broke out of the cowboy mold for other roles, such as the historical *En Tiempos de la Inquisición (In the Times of the Inquisition).*

A mold he never broke out of, however, was of the leading man. And as he did on the celluloid, he often fell in love with his leading lady in private. Between 1937 and 1953 Negrete made 45 films and repeatedly dashed the hopes of his millions of Mexican female fans by marrying three of his leading ladies: Elisa Christy in 1938, Gloria Marín in 1941, and María Félix in 1952.

Although Negrete was capable of singing operatic arias and invariably sang in all of his films, he is remembered as much for his dramatic performances and his droll, mildly self-deprecating film persona as his vocal renditions. His mild pathos on screen was more than matched by the sadness of his personal life. Negrete will nevertheless long be remembered for the heartfelt verses that he sang of his love for his homeland: " . . . Dear beautiful Mexico . . . If I die far away . . . let them say that I am sleeping . . . that they may return me to you."

Jorge Negrete, the man for whom everything was not enough, died in Los Angeles, California, of cirrhosis of the liver, on December 5, 1953, at the age of 41.

erva-Chapultepec, you have your choice of a pair of **Gold's Gyms** on Av. Vallarta; one of them at Av. Vallarta 1791, south side of the street, three blocks west of Chapultepec, and another several blocks farther west, on the north side of Vallarta, across from Centro Magno shopping center.

For a gym with a **swimming pool,** walk or take a taxi to the big **World Gym** fitness center, at Jesús Garcia 804, corner of Miguel Ángel de Quevedo, tel. 33/3640-0576, near the Cinema Charlie Chaplin. (Follow López Mateos north from the Miner-

va Circle; after about a mile, turn left at Garcia; continue two blocks to the corner of Quevedo.)

If your hotel doesn't have a pool, you can always take a taxi to the popular **Balneario Lindo Michoacán,** southeast of downtown, at Río Barco 1614, corner of González Gallo, tel. 33/3635-9399. Open daily 10 A.M.–5 P.M.

Tennis and Golf

Guadalajara has many tennis courts and golf courses, all of them private and none of them are in the Minerva-Chapultepec district. For lots of other choices in other parts of town, see Tennis, Golf, and Swimming in the Heart of the City chapter, and Tennis and Golf in the On the Road chapter.

SHOPPING AND SERVICES
Outdoor Markets and Handicrafts

Shopping is one of the Minerva-Chapultepec's residents' prime diversions. Among the most colorful shopping venues are the **outdoor markets** that bloom locally on weekends. Two of them, the **antiques** and the **Santa Teresita** markets occur in the Minerva-Chapultepec vicinity. For more details on these and other outdoor markets, see Outdoor Markets in the Shopping section of the On the Road chapter.

Handicrafts, a Guadalajara specialty, although marginally available at a few Minerva-Chapultepec shops, are best bought at the **Mercado Libertad** near Plaza Tapatía downtown and in **Tlaquepaque** and **Tonalá.** For details, see the Shopping sections of the Heart of the City and City: East and South of Downtown chapters.

Shopping Plazas and Warehouse Stores

Three shopping plazas—one mid-scale and two upscale—provide convenient Minerva-Chapultepec shopping opportunities. The mid-scale option is **Plaza Mexico,** on Av. Mexico, at the north end of Av. Chapultepec. Here, giant **Aurrera** K-mart–style general store–supermarket sells everything, including produce, meat, and groceries.

Farther west, multistory **Centro Magno** rises prominently between east-west Avenidas Vallarta and López Cotilla, midway between Av. Americas and the Minerva Circle. However, lacking a department store anchor, a bank, or even a drugstore, the Centro Magno's success seems to rest on the plethora of youth-oriented designer shoe, clothes, sports, and jewelry boutiques that fill its four (basement, ground, first, and second) floors. The second, highest floor is given over nearly completely to the youthful crowds that flock to the 15-screen cinema complex, the score of fast-food stalls, and the big video game arcade.

In contrast, the larger **Gran Plaza,** on the south side of Av. Vallarta, about a mile west of the Minerva Circle (accessible by bus #45), provides more diverse shopping opportunities. Like the Centro Magno, Gran Plaza has four floors, with the upper level devoted mainly to a cinema multiplex, fast-food stores, and a big video game parlor.

Multistory shop-lined arcades radiate from the central atrium, to department stores **Sears** (open daily 10 A.M.–8:30 P.M.; tel. 33/3669-0210) on one side and **Fábricas de Francia** on the other. At the bottom-floor end of a third arcade is **Sanborn's** coffee shop–restaurant, book and magazine store, and upscale gift emporium (open daily 7:30 A.M.–midnight, tel. 33/3647-2026).

Banks, both with ATMs, are represented by **Bancomer** facing Av. Vallarta, ground floor, open Mon.–Fri. 8:30 A.M.–4 P.M.; and **Citibank,** open Mon.–Fri. 9 A.M.–4 P.M. Other useful ground floor outlets are **Radio Shack,** open daily 10 A.M.–9 P.M., tel. 33/3122-3715; and **Laboratorios Julio,** photo and camera, open Mon.–Sat. 10 A.M.–8:30 P.M., Sun. 11:30 A.M.– 8 P.M., tel. 33/3587-5266; **McDonald's** fast-food, open Mon.–Thurs. 7 A.M.–10 P.M., Fri.–Sun. 7 A.M.–11:30 P.M.

Bottom-floor **information kiosks** list a legion of mostly upscale outlets: about 60 shoe stores, 60 women's clothes boutiques, seven men's clothing stores, four perfume stores, four sporting goods *(deportes)* stores, three women's undergarments *(ropa íntima)* stores, three jewelry *(joyerías)* stores, three opticians *(opticas),* a drugstore, a travel agency, natural foods *(tienda naturista),* Internet access, and more.

Gran Plaza has attracted American **warehouse chains** to locate nearby. Just east of Gran Plaza, on Av. Vallarta's south side, are **Wal-Mart** (tel. 33/3673-2451 and 33/3673-2067) and **Sam's Club** while west of Gran Plaza, on Av. Vallarta's opposite side, is **Price Club,** tel. 33/3629-8700 and 33/3629-8703.

Shopping and Services by Neighborhood

Start in the Av. Chapultepec neighborhood, near the corner of Av. Vallarta, where **banks,** all with

ATMs, are plentiful. Moving from the north, you'll first find Bancomer, at the southeast corner of Chapultepec and Moreno, open Mon.–Fri. 8:30 A.M.–4 P.M., Sat. 10 A.M.–2 P.M. Nearby is long-hours BITAL, at Chapultepec 65, open Mon.–Sat. 9 A.M.–7 P.M.; tel. 33/3616-5833. A few blocks farther south, is Scotiabank Inverlat, at Chapultepec 324 Sur, open Mon.–Fri. 9 A.M.–4 P.M., Sat. 10 A.M.–2 P.M.; tel. 33/3616-6951, 33/3616-6961, 33/3615-1110.

Also along Chapultepec, you'll find some **drugstores,** stocked with everything from bandages and soda pop to stationery and basic groceries. Try **Farmacia ABC,** at the northeast corner of La Paz and Chapultepec, open Mon.–Sat. 7:30 A.M.–11 P.M., Sun. 8 A.M.–10 P.M.; tel. 33/3826-4742.

For quick film development service, some popular film stocks, and point-and-shoot and video cameras, go to **Kodak Express,** at the northeast corner of Chapultepec and Libertad (one block north of La Paz). They're open Mon.–Fri. 9 A.M.–8 P.M., Sat. 10 A.M.–2 P.M., 4–8 P.M.; tel. 33/3825-2080.

For more banks, all with ATMs, move **west** from Chapultepec three blocks to Bancomer, at 1710 Av. Vallarta, northwest corner of Bolivar, open Mon.–Fri. 8:30 A.M.–4 P.M. If they're closed, continue another block and a half west to longer-hours BITAL, Av. Vallarta 1835, south side of street, open Mon.–Sat. 9 A.M.–7 P.M.; tel. 33/3616-0164 and 33/3616-0191.

Continue west to **American Express,** at Av. Vallarta 2440, northeast corner of Lope de Vega, open Mon.–Fri. 9 A.M.–6 P.M., Sat. 9 A.M.–1 P.M.; tel. 33/3818-2325, fax 33/3616-7665. Staff offer full American Express services, including all AmEx credit card services, traveler's checks sales and exchange, cash advances, and check cashing with AmEx card, and all travel agency services.

Minerva Circle Shopping and Services

A few blocks farther west, the Minerva Circle, at the intersection of Av. Vallarta and Av. López Mateos, offers a mini-village of handy shops and services. The streets that radiate from the circle,

moving counterclockwise, beginning with Av. Vallarta on the east side, are: Av. López Mateos Norte, Diagonal Golfo de Cortés, Av. Vallarta west, Av. López Mateos Sur, and Circunvalación A. Yañez. On the circle's east side, start on Av. Vallarta's north side, and move counterclockwise around the circle's outer perimeter. Pass Restaurant Abajeño (see earlier Food section) to **La Playa mini-mart and liquor store,** at the circle's north side, open Mon.–Sat. 9 A.M.–10 P.M., Sun. 9 A.M.–5 P.M.; tel. 33/3615-0636. The modest offering include lots of **good wines,** both room temperature *(templada)* and chilled, liquors, and mixers. Next door, at the corner of Diagonal Mar de Cortés, find **Farmacia Benevides,** open daily 8 A.M.–midnight, tel. 33/3615-1191, with a little bit of everything, including film and development, plenty of over-the-counter remedies, a pharmacist, toiletries, and some snacks.

Continue counterclockwise, across Diagonal Mar de Cortés, to BITAL, **a bank with ATM** but with short hours, Mon.–Fri. 9 A.M.–5 P.M.; tel. 33/3615-1628. Continue next door, to the **Pemex *gasolinera*** (gas station), at the northwest corner of Av. Vallarta. Carefully cross Av. Vallarta southward to the big **Burger King,** complete with elaborate kiddie land.

Behind Burger King towers the **Hotel Fiesta Americana,** itself an entire business service and shopping center. On the bottom floor, find an ATM-equipped branch of **Scotiabank Inverlat,** open Mon.–Fri. 9 A.M.–5 P.M., Sat. 9 A.M.–1 P.M.; tel. 33/3615-1805. Inside, also on the ground floor, you'll find a number of shops and services, including a **newsstand** *(tabaquería),* with a modest selection of English-language newspapers, magazines, and books; a travel agent **Viajes Internacional del Camino,** open Mon.–Sat. 9 A.M.–7 P.M.; tel. 33/3825-3434, ext. 3089; tel./fax 33/3615-1066; the **Canadian consul,** and the local British Commercial Office (for details of the last two, see Health and Emergencies, later in this chapter.)

Continue counterclockwise around the Minerva Circle, carefully crossing Av. López Mateos Sur, to **Laboratorios Julio** photo and camera store, open Mon–Fri. 9 A.M.–2 P.M. and 4–7 P.M., Sat. 10 A.M.–6 P.M.; tel. 33/3124-9666.

Being a branch of the big Guadalajara chain, they offer virtually all photography services, including in-store one-hour development, together with some supplies, still and video cameras, and popular film.

Continuing clockwise, across A. Yañez, find travel agent **Turiservicios,** open Mon.–Fri. 9 A.M.–7 P.M., Sat. 9 A.M.–1 P.M.; tel.33/3615-7800, 33/3616-4694, fax 33/3616-6524; email: turiservicios@infosel.net.mx. Full-service offerings include bus and air tickets, tours, and car rentals. Finally, returning counterclockwise back to Av. Vallarta, west side, find **Copiroyal** full copy services, open Mon.–Fri. 8:30 A.M.–9 P.M., Sat. 9 A.M.–7 P.M.; tel. 33/3616-6058.

COMMUNICATIONS AND INFORMATION

Post, Telephone, and Internet

Although the Minerva-Chapultepec district does have one branch federal post office *(correo),* you'll get much more rapid and secure service at the Mailboxes Etc. branch at López Cotilla 1880, tel. 33/3616-1976, south side of street, between Alarcón and Cervantes. Besides private mailbox rentals with a San Diego, California address (from which mail customarily arrives within a few days), they offer fax, duplicating services, and various mailing services. Business hours are Mon.–Fri. 9 A.M.–8 P.M., Sat. 10 A.M.–2 P.M.

If you must go to a regular government post office, best visit the small, relatively efficient branch in the Chapalita district, tel. 33/3121-4004, on Av. Tepeyac, near the corner of Av. de las Rosas, about a mile southwest of the Minerva Circle. (For more details see the Chapalita section of this chapter, earlier.)

For telephones, use your hotel room phone, or save money by buying a widely available yellow-and-blue telephone (Ladatel) card and use a public telephone.

Check your email or connect to the Internet at one of the various local Internet stores, such as Internet Puro ("Pure Internet") on the top floor at Centro Magno; tel. 33/3630-2210, 33/3616-5900, 33/3630-2666, 33/3630-2101.

American and Canadian Consulates

Two Minerva-Chapultepec consulates serve U.S. and Canadian citizens, respectively. The **U.S. consulate** is at Progreso 175 (between Cotillo and Libertad) a block east of Av. Chapultepec. Service hours for American citizens are Mon.–Fri. 8 A.M.–11 A.M.; tel. 33/3825-2700 and 33/3825-2998.

The **Canadian consulate** is in the Hotel Fiesta Americana at Aurelio Aceves 225, local 31, west side of the Minerva Circle. They are open Mon.–Fri. 8:30 A.M.–2 P.M. and 3–5 P.M.; tel. 33/3616-5642. In emergencies, after business hours, call the Canadian consulate in Mexico City, toll-free tel. 800/706-2900.

A number of other countries maintain Guadalajara consular offices. For more information, see Consulates in the information section of the Heart of the City chapter.

Additionally, the **British Commercial Office** maintains a local headquarters, open Mon.–Fri. 8:30 A.M.–3:30 P.M.; tel. 33/3630-4357, 33/3630-4358, at the Hotel Fiesta Americana, ground floor, on the west side of the Minerva Circle.

Community Organizations

At least three community organizations, the **American Society of Jalisco,** the **International Friendship Club,** and the **American Legion Post 3,** welcome participation by Guadalajara newcomers. For specifics, see Community Organizations in the Information section of the Plaza del Sol–Chapalita section, later in this chapter.

Spanish Language Instruction

Berlitz Language School, at Av. Vallarta 1550, offers language instruction. Call tel. 33/3615-8503 or 33/3630-3987 for more information.

A small business-oriented school, the **Vancouver Language Center,** at Av. Vallarta 1151, also offers intensive or part-time instruction. For more information, telephone 33/3826-0944 or 33/3825-4271.

HEALTH AND EMERGENCIES

Medicines and Doctors

For routine medications, consult the on-duty pharmacist at one of the many Minerva-

Chapultepec drugstores, especially on Av. Chapultepec, Av. Americas, Av. Vallarta, and around the Minerva Circle. For specific locations, see the previous Shopping and Services section.

If you need a doctor, follow your hotel's recommendation, or choose from the list of highly recommended doctors and hospitals in the Guadalajara Doctors and Hospitals section of the On the Road chapter.

Alternatively, you can pick a doctor from the several who maintain Minerva-Chapultepec offices, on Av. Morelos, half a block east of Av. Chapultepec. At Morelos 1558, tel./fax 33/3826-0101, choose from **cardiologist** Dr. Marallino Arrañaga Pazarin; **gynecologist-obstetrician** Dr. Salvador Cerda Guzmán; **proctologist** Dr. Luis F. Enciso Gómez; **neurologist** Dr. Nícolas Huerta Cisneros; **orthopedist-traumatologist** Dr. Eduardo Robles Contreras; **oral surgeon** Doctora María Dolores Flores Pérez; **general surgeon** Dr. Antonio Ruelas Rodríguez, and **urologist** Dr. Guillermo Sierra Martínez. Also at Morelos 1561, across the street, consider **family medicine** practicioner Doctora Bertha Ramos, tel./fax 33/3825-5514.

> *Guadalajara and its suburban districts maintain good fire and police infrastructure. Contact the Guadalajara police quickly by dialing 06 for the radio patrol, or the main switchboard, tel. 33/3668-0800; or Federal Highway Police, tel. 33/3629-5082.*

Additionally, the owner of the Casa Madonna bed-and-breakfast highly recommends the services of her daughter-in-law, **ear-nose-throat and allergy specialist** Doctora Yolanda Sahagùn Muñoz, at Reforma 1758, tel. 33/3615-4452, 33/3616-4706, consultation hours Mon.–Fri. 5–8 P.M.

Police, Fire, and Medical Emergencies

Guadalajara and its suburban districts maintain good fire and police infrastructure. Contact the Guadalajara police quickly by dialing 06 for the radio patrol, or the main switchboard, tel. 33/3668-0800; or Federal Highway Police, tel. 33/3629-5082.

For **fire** emergencies, call the main fire department switchboard at tel. 33/3619-0510 or headquarters at tel. 33/3619-0794 or 33/3619-5241.

For a medical **ambulance,** call your hotel desk, or one of the hospitals that offer ambulance services, such as **Hospital Méxicano-Americano,** Av. Colomos 2110, ambulance tel. 33/3642-7152, with 24-hour emergency room; or **Hospital San Javier,** Av. Pablo Casals, Col. Providencia, ambulance tel. 33/3616-9616, with 24-hour emergency room.

CITY: WEST AND NORTH

Plaza del Sol–Chapalita

Western Guadalajara's development really picked up steam when workers laid out **Plaza del Sol,** Latin America's first U.S.–style shopping mall, in 1969. A decade later, city leaders parlayed Plaza del Sol's phenomenal popularity with another big new project next door—Expo Guadalajara, Latin America's largest convention and exposition center. Expo Guadalajara's subsequent phenomenal success echoed that of Plaza del Sol. By the year 2000, modernized and enlarged, Expo Guadalajara was hosting a growing legion of more than 150 big commercial events—books, jewelry, furniture, electronics, fashion, and textiles shows—that attracted millions of buyers and sellers from all over the world.

As part and parcel of Plaza del Sol–Expo Guadalajara, investors built a diadem of fine hotels and restaurants to accommodate the steady stream of Plaza del Sol–Expo Guadalajara visitors.

Despite their proximity, the tree-shaded neighborhoods—Cuidad del Sol, Rinconada del Sol, Jardines del Bosque, and Chapalita—neighboring Plaza del Sol have remained as planned: quiet refuges, apart from the busy boulevards that bring the shoppers and business visitors.

One of the most charming of these petite business-residential neighborhoods is **Chapalita,** centered scarcely a mile from Plaza del Sol. Over the years, Chapalita has grown quietly and gracefully, into a suburban village that's home for middle-class Guadalajaran families and a generation of Canadian and Americans retirees who came, saw, and decided to stay.

GETTING ORIENTED AND GETTING AROUND
Getting Oriented
Compass directions are only marginally useful around the Plaza del Sol–Chapalita neighborhood, since the main streets run like a spider's web of diagonally intersecting threads. See the map "Plaza del Sol–Chapalita." The district's major traffic artery is **Av. López Mateos,** a divided boulevard that runs diagonally (and main-

ly underground) southeast-northwest across most of the entire metropolitan area. It continues southwest, passing the Minerva Circle, and, within two miles, bisects the Plaza del Sol–Chapalita district, leaving quiet Chapalita on its northwest flank and bustling Plaza del Sol and Expo Guadalajara on its southeast side. Expo Guadalajara, bordering another southwest diagonal boulevard, **Av. Mariano Otero,** lies half a mile to the northeast of Plaza del Sol.

The Plaza del Sol–Chapalita district's southern boundary is marked by the **intersection of Av. López Mateos and Mariano Otero,** while its northern extremity is marked by northwest-southeast expressway **Calzado Lázaro Cárdenas.** Additionally, a pair of roughly parallel east-west business streets, Avenidas Tepeyac and Guadalupe, respectively begin where they cross Calz. Lázaro Cárdenas and run west through the Chapalita neighborhood.

Getting Around
Of course, taxis are always convenient, but if you need to save money, handy buses run frequently through the Plaza del Sol–Chapalita district. See the maps *Guadalajara Bus Routes* and *Bus Routes Downtown.* Very useful is **line 258A,** which connects downtown with the Plaza del Sol and beyond. From the downtown corner of Alcalde and San Felipe, two blocks north of the cathedral, the 258A runs west along San Felipe and its western extension, Av. Mexico. At Av. López Mateos, the bus turns left, southwest, and runs past Plaza del Sol, continuing past Av. Patria, where it returns by virtually the same route.

For the Chapalita-downtown connection, ride either bus 51A or 51B. Both buses start at the downtown corner of Libertad and 16 de Septembre and continue west along La Paz, to A. Yañez. They turn left, south, at Yañez, to Niños Héroes. There, they turn right, west, and continue west along Guadalupe to the Chapalita Circle, at the intersection of Avenidas de las Rosas and Guadalupe. At the Chapalita Circle, they trace different routes. The 51A continues west on Guadalupe all the way to its terminal at the west *periférico*. The 51B heads south a block to Tepeyac, where it turns right, west, and continues west along Tepeyac, turning left at Av. Patria and right at Av. El Colli, continuing all way to its terminal at Colonia El Colli past the *periférico*. Both buses return by the same routes, except at A. Yañez eastbound, they continue east along Lerdo de Tejada to Chapultepec, where they turn left, north, for two blocks to Libertad, where they turn right, east, and continue downtown to 16 de Septiembre.

SIGHTS: A WALK AROUND PLAZA DEL SOL–CHAPALITA

Around Plaza del Sol

Let the Plaza del Sol, on Av. López Mateos Sur, a bit more than a mile (or two kilometers) southwest of the Minerva Circle, be your first sightseeing stop. A visionary idea for Mexico at the time it was conceived during the late 1960s, Plaza del Sol became (and still remains) immensely popular. The reason is clear. In contrast to the high-end youth-oriented plazas that have mushroomed during the 1990s, Plaza del Sol is full of locally-owned stores—department, drug, book, clothing, sports, and much more—useful to a big cross section of Guadalajarans. (For Plaza del Sol shopping details, see the Shopping and Services section, later in this chapter).

Walk northeast along Av. Mariano Otero, the street that borders the "back" (east) side of Plaza del Sol. After about six long blocks, after Hotel Expo Guadalajara, you'll reach **Expo Guadalajara,** at the corner of Avenidas de las Rosas and Mariano Otero. Turn right and enter Expo Guadalajara via the plaza on the immediate right.

Designed to international standards, **Expo Guadalajara** was built on a single level, and spreads over an area about a fifth of a mile (300 meters) on a side. Inside, you'll find an information booth where you can get a handy descriptive brochure.

Nearly daily, a huge squadron of booths buzz with activity in the main exhibition ("convention and multiple use") hall. If you're lucky, maybe you'll catch one of the big fairs, such as fashion (January and July), ice cream (February), computers (March), handicrafts (June), furniture (September), jewelry (October), and books (November). Stop by the convenient food court *(zona gastronómica)* in the middle of the complex for a light meal or refreshment. Av. Mariano Otero 1499; tel. 33/3343-3003, fax 33/3343-

EXPO GUADALAJARA

Since it opened in 1987 as the largest exposition center in Latin America, Expo Guadalajara has maintained leadership among both its national and international counterparts, in both attendance and occupancy rates. It hosts more than 120 events annually, including some of the most important industrywide exhibitions in Mexico.

Expo Guadalajara has kept pace with international design standards, instituting an award-winning quality control system in 1992 and enlarging and modernizing its facilities. Presently about 500,000 square feet (45,000 square meters) in nine flexible modules can handle 50,000 visitors a day and accommodate expositions from small to gigantic. Furthermore, Expo Guadalajara goes a long way toward minimizing the planning and organizing hassles with its convenient one-level design, with 15 loading gates (that can accommodate 65 tractor-trailers simultaneously) that open directly to the exhibition floor.

Expo Guadalajara's latest addition was a 75,000-square-foot (7,000-square-meter) auditorium in 2002. To that, include a plethora of telecommunications and office services and private negotiating facilities, plus a dozen coffee shops, snack bars, and a pair of fine restaurants, all of which contribute to making Expo Guadalajara an excellent setting for seeing, exhibiting, buying, and selling.

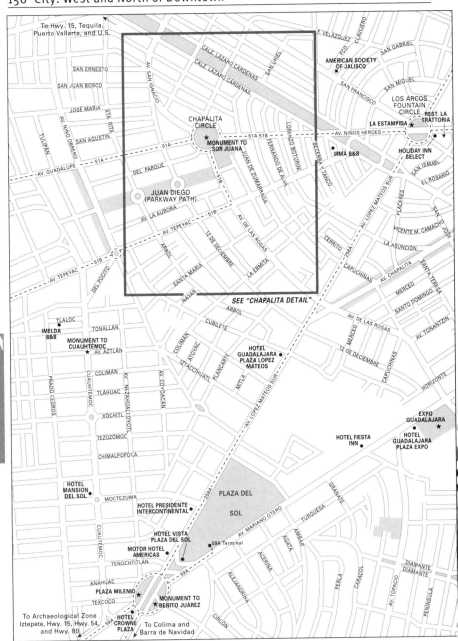

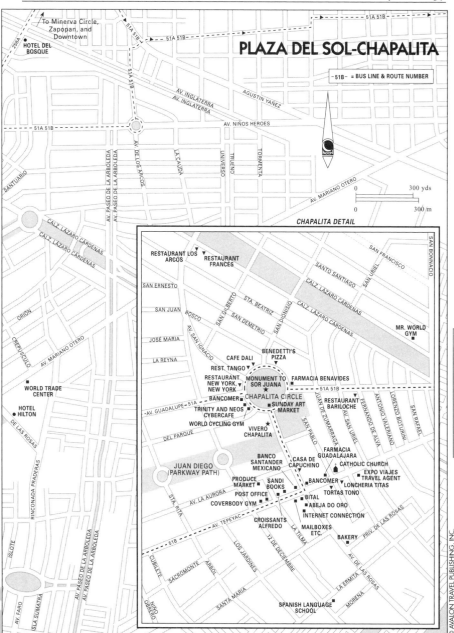

PLAZA DEL SOL-CHAPALITA

-51B- = BUS LINE & ROUTE NUMBER

To Minerva Circle,
Zapopan, and
Downtown

HOTEL DEL
BOSQUE

AV. INGLATERRA
AV. INGLATERRA

AGUSTIN YAÑEZ

AV. NIÑOS HEROES

AV. MARIANO OTERO

0   300 yds

0   300 m

CHAPALITA DETAIL

RESTAURANT LOS
ARCOS

RESTAURANT
FRANCES

SAN ERNESTO

SAN JUAN

JOSÉ MARIA

LA REYNA

CAFE DALI

REST. TANGO

RESTAURANT
NEW YORK,
NEW YORK

BANCOMER

TRINITY AND NEOS
CYBERCAFE

WORLD CYCLING GYM

BENEDETTI'S
PIZZA

MONUMENT TO
SOR JUANA

FARMACIA BENAVIDES

CHAPALITA CIRCLE

SUNDAY ART
MARKET

RESTAURANT
BARILOCHE

VIVERO
CHAPALITA

JUAN DIEGO
(PARKWAY PATH)

BANCO
SANTANDER
MEXICANO

CASA DE
CAPUCHINO

FARMACIA
GUADALAJARA

CATHOLIC CHURCH

EXPO VIAJES
TRAVEL AGENT

PRODUCE
MARKET

SANDI
BOOKS

BANCOMER

LONCHERIA TITAS

TORTAS TONO

POST OFFICE

COVERBODY GYM

BITAL

ABEJA DO ORO

INTERNET CONNECTION

CROISSANTS
ALFREDO

MAILBOXES
ETC.

BAKERY

SPANISH LANGUAGE
SCHOOL

WORLD TRADE
CENTER

HOTEL
HILTON

MR. WORLD
GYM

CITY: WEST AND NORTH

© AVALON TRAVEL PUBLISHING, INC.

3030; website: www.expoguadalajara.com.mx.
Open daily 9 A.M.–8 P.M.

Around the Chapalita Circle

From Expo Guadalajara, walk or taxi about seven
blocks northwest along Av. de las Rosas (passing the Chapalita district's petite commercial
hub, at the corner of Av. Tepeyac) to the Chapalita Circle, at the intersection of Av. Guadalupe
and Av. de las Rosas. The Chapalita Circle, scenic
focus of the Chapalita neighborhood, is a shady,
grassy island park, from which radiate a number of jacaranda-, palm-, and mango-shaded
neighborhood streets.

The circular park itself, perfect for a picnic,
centers around an abstract, gilded sculpture representing the celebrated 18th-century poet-nun
Sor Juana Inés de la Cruz, an early Latin American feminist. A collection of organizations and
individuals (which have awarded a prize in Sor
Juana's honor since 1993) erected the sculpture in
1996. The Chapalita Circle is the site of regular
community activities: Thursdays at 7 P.M., the
Zapopan Municipal Band performs, and Sundays all day, from around 10 A.M., local artists exhibit and sell their works.

Carefully cross back over busy Av. Guadalupe
to Av. de las Rosas, at the south side of Guadalupe
Circle. There, you'll find **Vivero Chapalita** (Chapalita Nursery), at Av. de las Rosas 825. Here
you can see why Guadalajara is such a gardener's
delight. The plants seem to like the weather as
much as the people do. Whether temperate or
tropical, all the favorites—azaleas, ferns, rubber
plants, oranges, lemons, petunias, banana, cactus,
bamboo, bromeliads—and dozens more, thrive
here. Open Mon.–Sat. 9:30 A.M.–7 P.M., Sun.
11 A.M.–3 P.M., no phone.

From the nursery, see the results of all this
gardening ferment by strolling along the tree-
lined garden parkway lane **Juan Diego,** which
heads from the south side of the nursery. Walk
west, past the houses set back behind sweeping
(luxurious for Mexico) green lawns, swathed with
regally tall shade trees. For about a mile (to the
end, marked by busy Av. Niño Obrero and back),
stroll and enjoy the calm, the cooling breeze, the
birdsong, and flash of butterfly wings in the

Tranquil Chapalita Circle centers around the
monument of Sor Juana Inéz de la Cruz.

shade beneath the great rubber *(hule),* mango,
pine, and eucalyptus trees.

El Iztépete Archaeological Zone

Although not actually within the Plaza del
Sol–Chapalita district, the important El Iztépete
Archaeological Zone is easily accessible from it.
By taxi or car, simply drive southwest along Av.
Mariano Otero, about two miles (three kilometers) past the *periférico* (peripheral boulevard),
to the Ixtépete parking lot on the right. Alternatively, ride the 59A bus, southbound, from the
stop on Av. Mariano Otero, on the east ("back")
side of Plaza del Sol shopping center, to the
Iztépete stop just past the *periférico.*

Walk through the entrance gate (open daily 9
A.M.–5 P.M., no facilities) and begin looking along
the path for some of the trove of glistening, jet-
black volcanic glass shards, the source of the label
"El Iztépete" ("Hill of Obsidian").

Most archaeologists who excavated this site, beginning with José Corona Nùñez, in 1954, now

SOR JUANA INÉS DE LA CRUZ

Sor (Sister) Juana Inés de la Cruz was baptized Juana Inés Ramírez de Abaje, in Mexico City, on December 2, 1648. Her remarkable talents began to surface early as she taught herself to read at the age of three. Soon she learned Latin in order to access its broad literature. A natural poet, Sor Juana began writing lyrics of life and love during her latter teenage years as lady-in-waiting to the Mexican viceroy's wife, the Marquesa de Mancera.

Rejecting the option of a life of court intrigue, marriage, and child-rearing, Sor Juana instead chose to follow her intellectual passion by entering the cloister. She first joined the ultra-austere Barefoot Carmelites, but soon quit in favor of the less strict Sisters of San Jerónimo in 1669, at the age of 21.

She was an unusual nun from the outset. Into her cell she eventually packed a 4,000-volume library and a small orchestra of violins, guitars, and lutes. She received a continuous stream of Mexico City *intelligencia* and literary collaborators. During her most productive years, the 1670s and 1680s, Sor Juana wrote extensively, in many styles, from 65 sonnets (many of love) and plays (both alone and in collaboration), to a lengthy poem, *Primero Sueño (First Dream),* outlining her social and political ideas. The wit and charisma of her work earned her the unofficial title of "Mexico's Tenth Muse."

Eventually, however, church authorities couldn't tolerate such a free spirit under their ecclesiastical roof. In her famous defense, *Reply to Sister Philotea of the Cross* Sor Juana argues for a woman's right to pursue intellectual freedom.

Nevertheless, she heeded the authorities' admonitions and, around 1690, sadly sold her library and musical instruments and gave the proceeds to charity. Returning to a strictly cloistered life, Sor Juana volunteered to nurse victims of an epidemic. Tragically contracting the disease herself, she died in Mexico City, on April 17, 1695, at the age of 46.

A considerable body of Sor Juana literature is available in English. Check out *Women in Hispanic Literature: Icons and Fallen Idols,* Beth Miller, editor, 1983; *A Sor Juana Anthology,* Alan Trueblood, 1988; *Sor Juana: Or, the Traps of Faith,* Octavio Paz, 1988; *Plotting Women: Gender and Representation in Mexico,* Jean Franco, 1989; and *Coded Encounters: Writing, Gender, and Ethnicity in Colonial Latin America,* Francisco J. Cevallos-Candau, editor, 1994.

CITY, WEST AND NORTH

believe that El Iztépete was probably both a ceremonial-pilgrimage center and commercial meeting ground for both working and bartering for obsidian. Here, people probably gathered from all over Western Mexico to both pay homage to the gods and obtain obsidian, prized for decorative and practical purposes—cutting tools, knives, hunting implements, and weapons.

Climb the reconstructed ceremonial stairway to the summit of the main (and only excavated) mound, a height of about 20 feet (six meters) above the surrounding fields. Look toward the horizon, opposite the *periférico,* for the hulking, truncated silhouette of the active **Cerro Colli** volcano several miles to the southwest.

In the foreground, the approximately 15-acre brushy field occupies the core of a much larger ar-chaeolgical zone that extends over a 10-square-mile (25-square-kilometer) irregular area to the south, southeast, and northwest. Also in the foreground, look for the three other brush-covered mounds, including a suspected ball court about 150 yards south, all yet to be excavated.

Back at the main mound, excavations have revealed that the present construction, dating from around A.D. 900, represents the third and final construction that overlays, like the peels of an onion, two earlier lower platforms, dating from around A.D. 0 and A.D 400, respectively. The earliest two constructions, especially their stairways and rectangular substructures, show strong Teotihuacán influences. (See Teotihuacán, in the History section of the Introduction chapter.)

© BRUCE WHIPPERMAN

Many archaeologists believe that El Iztépete (The Hill of Obsidian), at Guadalajara's far southwestern edge, was once an important ceremonial and trade center.

ACCOMMODATIONS

Hotels Around Expo Guadalajara and Plaza del Sol

With only a few exceptions, the hotels around Expo Guadalajara and Plaza del Sol are high-rise deluxe lodgings, catering to Guadalajara business travelers. As a group, they're strong on business services, meeting facilities, and the luxury amenities that their high tariffs reflect.

By location (for a listing by price, see the chart Plaza del Sol–Chapalita Accommodations, by Price), from Expo Guadalajara, and moving southwest, first find the high-powered **Hotel Hilton,** right across the street. In its third Guadalajara incarnation, the Hilton chain seems to have gotten it right.

Here, business travelers can have everything under one roof. The big downstairs **business center** has a reception and services area, leading to eight meeting rooms, accommodating 5–40 persons, and three interviewing rooms for 2–4 persons. On-site bilingual secretarial service and all communications services are readily available. Furthermore, the in-hotel **convention center** can accommodate 20–1200 in a total of 12 various rooms and an auditorium for 300 for events, projections, and promotions.

Upstairs, the 422 rooms and suites include an exclusive, self-contained executive floor, with 20 spacious master suites and 11 super-deluxe rooms, free morning continental breakfast and afternoon canapés and cocktails.

All accommodations are super-deluxe, with a computer and fax outlet, satellite TV, safety deposit box, magnetic door card, telephones, cable TV, and much more. For all this, tariffs begin at a north-of-the-border style $300 s or d rack rate, $227 s or d commercial rate, $244 commercial rate for the executive floor, add $27 per extra person. This includes two good restaurants and lobby bar with live music nightly and credit cards accepted. Kids under 10 stay free with parents. All rooms include use of the pool, exercise gym, sauna, and aerobics room. Av. de las Rosas 2933, Guadalajara, Jalisco 44540; tel. 33/3678-0510, fax 33/3678-0521; from the U.S. or Canada, toll-free 800/HILTONS (800/445-8667); or from Mexico toll-free, 01-800/003-1400; email: reservas@hiltonguadala jara.com.mx; website: www.hilton.com.

Around the corner of de las Rosas, consider the very worthy **Hotel Guadalajara Plaza Expo,** which offers a plethora of super-deluxe amenities for easier south-of-the-border prices. Enter and continue past the reception to the elegantly carpeted and flower-decorated lobby.

Elevators rise to about seven floors of 204 plush rooms, adorned with soft quilted floral bedspreads, and carpeted and draped in dark earth tones. On the top floor, guests enjoy a panoramic-view pool sundeck, an exercise gym, and a unique jogging track.

Furthermore, guests have use of a business center, with secretarial services and computer, fax, copier, and negotiating and conference rooms for 10–120 people.

Prices begin at about $130 s or d, commercial rate, $150 rack rate, with phone, cable TV, two kids free with parents, safety deposit boxes at desk, restaurant, lobby sports bar, live music nightly, credit cards accepted, and special rooms for the handicapped. Mariano Otero 3261, Guadalajara, Jalisco 45050; toll-free from the U.S. and Canada 888/223-7646, from Mexico, toll-free tel. 800/719-6033; tel. 33/3669-0215, fax 33/3122-2850; email: hotelguadplza@infosel.net.mx; website: www.hotelesgdlplaza.com.mx.

Two blocks farther south, consider the more economical but still deluxe four-star **Hotel Fiesta Inn.** This efficient branch of the well-managed Fiesta Americana chain combines a business- and family-friendly atmosphere with downstairs coffee shop, modest business center and meeting rooms, gym, pool, and comfortable deluxe rooms and suites upstairs. Rates begin at around $120 s or d, including parking. Av. Mariano Otero 1550, Guadalajara, Jalisco 45055; toll-free 800/FIES-TA-1 from the U.S. and Canada; toll-free 800/504-5000 from Mexico; tel. 33/3669-3200, fax 33/3669-3247; email: resfigdl@fiestainn.com.mx; website: www.fiestainn.com.mx.

Move west several blocks to the Hotel Guadalajara Plaza Expo's sister **Hotel Guadalajara Plaza López Mateos.** An attractive but smallish lobby area welcomes guests; the adjacent lobby bar provides live (but loud in the lobby because of the proximity) entertainment nightly, and a deluxe restaurant offers good breakfasts, lunches, and dinners.

Outside, beyond the entrance driveway, the hotel's 142 rooms and suites gracefully enclose a tranquil, tropical pool-garden. In a pair of two-story neocolonial wings, the 30 "royal" suites, all with living rooms, are elegantly adorned in soft greens and reds.

The 112 standard rooms, in a seven-story view high-rise wing, are tastefully decorated in earth-toned pastels with splashes of blue and black. Standard room prices begin at $110 s or d (business rate), $120 s or d (rack rate), and $140 s or d for suites. All accommodations include deluxe bathroom with shower, cable TV, phones, and parking included; credit cards are accepted.

Back in the lobby area, guests have the use of a modest business center, with meeting rooms, bilingual secretarial services, fax, copier, and Internet connection ($.05/minute, bring your own laptop.) For events and business conferences, a pair of salons, accommodating up to 400 persons, are available. López Mateos Sur 2128, Guadalajara, Jalisco 45050; from U.S or Canada, toll-free 888/223-7646; from Mexico, toll-free 01-800/719-6033; tel. 33/3647-5300, fax 33/3122-1842; email: hotelguadplza@infosel.net.mx; website: www.hotelesgdlplaza.com.mx.

Plaza del Sol Hotels

A few blocks south rises the landmark golden glass tower of the **Hotel Presidente Intercontinental.** Situated right across López Mateos (via pedestrian bridge) from the Plaza del Sol and a five-minute taxi ride to Expo Guadalajara, this vast hostelry appeals to both general and business travelers.

Downstairs, guests enter a high, light lobby-atrium, decorated by a big flowing fountain. Nearby, guests enjoy a pair of good restaurants and relax to live music in the lobby bar early evenings and a nightclub until the wee hours. Furthermore, business clients have the use of a well-equipped business center, with bilingual secretarial services, all communication services, and negotiating rooms. A big in-house conference-exhibition center accommodates up to 1,600 participants.

Upstairs, 414 luxuriously furnished rooms and suites, including an exclusive "Club International" business floor, provide a host of amenities. The business floor is the plushest, with its own private lounge with complimentary canapés and drinks, in-room printer, Internet connection, VCR, newspaper, and shoe-shine service.

Rates begin at about $170 s or d and go up to about $350 for the most luxurious suites, with pool, spa, gym, and credit cards accepted. López Mateos Sur and Moctezuma, Guadalajara, Jalisco 45050; from the U.S. and Canada, toll-free 800/327-0200; in Mexico, 01-800/90-444; tel. 33/3678-1234, fax 33/3678-1222; website: www.guadalajara.interconti.com.

Just four blocks away, you might seriously consider a much different, but equally luxurious alternative—the boutique **Hotel Mansión del Sol.** A quick look downstairs—polished oak paneling, plush Persian carpets, antique Chinese tapestries, elegant guest-only restaurant—begins to reveal the gracious amenities of this distinguished small hotel.

The 15 spacious rooms expand the impression, with handsomely masculine hardwood paneling, king-size beds, soft carpets, and roomy, deluxe shower baths. Designed with the business client in mind, the rooms additionally provide a big work desk with 24-hour in-room Internet access.

Back by the lobby, guests have the use of a business center, including bilingual secretarial service and all communication and copy services at no extra charge. Furthermore, after a hard day of shopping or negotiating, you can work out in the small but deluxe gym, soak in the spa, steam in the sauna, or simply relax in the sun in the lush, tropical exterior patio garden.

Get all this from only about $150 s or d (business rate), $175 s or d (rack rate), with big continental breakfast, afternoon snack, parking, credit cards accepted, valet parking, but no pool. Av. Moctezuma 1596, Guadalajara, Jalisco 45050; U.S. and Canada, dial toll-free 800/537-8483; in Mexico, toll-free 01-800/715-9339; tel. 33/3647-4762, fax 33/3647-9447; email: lamansiondelsol@usa.net; website: www.lexres.com.

On the other hand, budget-conscious travelers have a solid option nearby, at the old standby **Motor Hotel Americas,** at López Mateos Sur.

Dating from the early 1970s, at the very beginning of the Plaza del Sol, the Motor Hotel Americas plugs along, remaining popular by keeping standards up and prices down.

The 100 rooms are distributed in two wings: the original garden wing, built around an inner pool-patio, and the newer tower wing, with private balcony views. The garden rooms are smaller and older, but nevertheless clean and comfortable. Natural light is limited, however. For privacy, drapes must be drawn, since the room windows face outside walkway corridors. In the tower section, rooms are newer, larger, and more private. Guests in the upper-level (especially the third and fourth story) rooms enjoy their own balconies with airy views overlooking the surrounding neighborhood and the billowing clouds above the serrated, southwest mountain horizon.

The prices are certainly right. Garden section rates run $48 s or d, tower section $62, $80 with kitchenette; all with air-conditioning, cable TV, coffee shop, two pools, three meeting rooms, and parking. López Mateos Sur 2400, Guadalajara, Jalisco 45050; in Mexico, toll-free 01-800/849-2178; tel. 33/3631-4048, 33/3631-4206, tel./fax 33/3631-4415.

Directly across López Mateos, the **Hotel Vista Plaza del Sol** seems to be trying harder, especially for family and business travelers. Don't let the cramped downstairs lobby-restaurant-bar area put you off. Business travelers should instead go upstairs and take a look at the 37-room, two-suite executive floor, with staffed business center, providing phones, printer, fax, and computers with Internet access, plus continental breakfast, free afternoon drinks, and free shuttle transportation to Expo Guadalajara. Family travelers have access to a pool and coffee shop downstairs, special events for families, and a five-minute walk to the movie theaters, fast-food restaurants, and stores at Plaza del Sol.

Room rates begin at about $110 s or d, two kids free with parents, with cable TV, air-conditioning, and parking. Av. López Mateos Sur 2375, Guadalajara, Jalisco 45050; in Mexico, toll-free 01-800/368-8000; tel. 33/3647-8890; email: ventasplazadelsol@vistahotel.com; website: www.vistahotel.com.

For an outstanding luxury option, go to the **Hotel Crowne Plaza,** formerly Holiday Inn. Walk into the lobby and feast your eyes on the immaculate, polished interior, where nothing, not even a single bit of dust, seems to mar the gracious, old world–style ambience. Farther on, in the interior garden, the impression continues, next to the broad green lawn and manicured flower beds, beneath the great shady trees and beside the gracefully curving blue swimming pool.

The 289 accommodations—suites at the garden level, rooms in a high-rise wing—are as deluxe as you would expect, tastefully adorned in soothing earth tones, with marble baths, tub showers, and garden-view windows or private city-vista balconies, and including many luxury extras.

Business accommodations are equally lavish, including a special "Plaza Club" executive floor, with continental breakfast, afternoon hors d'oeuvres, shoe shine, and private check-in and check-out.

The list goes on. Business conference options include 13 possible meeting-exhibition rooms, accommodating 10–800 people. Entertainment and recreation facilities feature an excellent deluxe restaurant, coffee shop, lobby bar with nightly live music, a nightclub, billiard room, a full gymnasium, big pool, and tennis court.

For all this, rates begin at about $175 s or d; ask for a commercial or weekend package discount. Av. López Mateos Sur 2500, Guadalajara, Jalisco 45050; toll-free tel. 800/2CROWNE in the U.S. and Canada; tel. 33/3634-1034, fax 33/3631-9393; email: crownegd@crownegdl .com.mx; website: www.crownegd.com.mx.

Although not in the Chapalita–Plaza del Sol district, the **Hotel Howard Johnson** caters especially to business clients in the southside industrial section about two miles southwest of the Plaza del Sol. Here, you get about what you get back home, nine floors of 125 comfortable standard-grade semi-deluxe air-conditioning rooms, a step or two above Motel 6 (for more quiet, get a room facing away from the noisy expressway). Rooms on the more deluxe executive floor have plusher carpets and soft easy chairs.

Back downstairs, guests enjoy the use of a modest business center (check first to see if it's up and running), and a compact but attractive lobby with a sports bar in the middle and a coffee shop tucked at the far end. Conference facilities, in the basement, consist of five meeting rooms, accommodating 40–200 participants. Room rates run a high $120 s or d for standard (ask for a discount—if you don't get it, shop around); executive floor rooms go for about $118 s or d, including commercial discount. Calz. Lázaro Cárdenas 1060; toll-free tel. 800/IGOHOJO (800/446-4656) from the U.S. and Canada; toll-free 01-800/366-6900 in Guadalajara; 01-800/505-4900 in the rest of Mexico; tel. 33/3810-3535, fax 33/3810-4686.

Chapalita Bed-and-Breakfasts

A growing number of householders, especially in and around the Chapalita district, rent rooms in their homes for modest rates. Although information about these comes largely by word-of-mouth, a few public information sources are accessible. Easiest of all is the classified section of the ***Colony Reporter*** newspaper, generally available at bookstore Librería Sandi at Tepeyac 718, three doors from the southwest corner of Av. de las Rosas, open Mon.–Fri. 9:30 A.M.–2:30 P.M. and 3:30–7 P.M., Sat. 9:30–2 P.M.; tel. 33/3121-0863. Another good rental information source is the **bulletin boards** at Librería Sandi and the **American Society of Jalisco** headquarters, at San Francisco 3392, open Mon.–Fri. 9:30 A.M.–2 P.M.; tel. 33/3121-2395. (From the north side of Calz. Lázaro Cárdenas, two blocks west of its intersection with Av. Guadalupe, follow Av. San Bonifacio one long block north and turn right on San Francisco. Continue one short block to the headquarters, at the next corner, of Fco. Javier, on the north side, opposite the Colegio Guadalupe.)

Below are three acceptable bed-and-breakfast lodgings whose owners kindly agreed to be listed. Kindly make a courtesy telephone call before you arrive. All are within walking distance of either Av. Tepeyac or Plaza del Sol buses and shopping.

Moving west along Av. Tepeyac (four short blocks west of Lázaro Cardénas and half a block north, right), find **Bed-and-Breakfast Irma,** the

PLAZA DEL SOL–CHAPALITA ACCOMMODATIONS BY PRICE

Accommodations, with telephone *lada* (area code) 33/, are listed in increasing order of double rates (two people in one bed). The 800 or 888 numbers are for toll-free reservations from the United States and Canada. The 01-800 numbers are for the same from within Mexico. Postal codes, such as 44540, are also listed.

Hotels Around Guadalajara Expo

Hotel Guadalajara Plaza López Mateos, Av. López Mateos Sur 2128, 45050; tel. 3647-5300, fax 3122-1842, 888/223-7646, or 01-800/719-6033; email: hotelguadplza@info sel.net.mx; website: www.hotelesgdlplaza.com.mx; $110

Hotel Fiesta Inn, Av. Mariano Otero 1550, 45055; tel. 3669-3200, fax 3669-3247, 800/ FIESTA-1, or 01-800/504-5000; email: resfigdl@fiestainn.com.mx; website: www.fiesta inn.com.mx; $120

Hotel Guadalajara Plaza Expo, Mariano Otero 3261, 45050; tel. 3669-0215, fax 3122-2850, 888/223-7646, 01-800/719-6033; email: hotelguadplza@infosel.net.mx; website: www.hotelesgdlplaza.com.mx; $130

Hotel Hilton, Av. de las Rosas 2933, 44540; tel. 3678-0510 or 800/HILTONS (800/445-8667), 01-800/003-1400, fax 3678-0521; email: reservas@hiltonguadalajara.com.mx; website: www.hilton.com; $227

Hotels Around Plaza del Sol

Motor Hotel Americas, Av. López Mateos Sur 2400, 45050; tel. 3631-4048 or 3631-4206; tel./fax 3631-4415, 01-800/849-2178; $48

Hotel Vista Plaza del Sol, Av. López Mateos Sur 2375, 45050; tel. 3647-8890, 01-800/368-8000; email: ventasplazadelsol@vistahotel.com; website: www.vistahotel.com; $110

Hotel Mansion del Sol, Av. Moctezuma 1596, 45050; tel. 3647-4762, fax 3647-9447, 800/537-8483, or 01-800/715-9339; email: lamansion-delsol@usa.net; website: www.lexres.com; $150

Hotel Presidente Intercontinental, Av. López Mateos Sur and Moctezuma, 45050; tel. 3678-1234, fax 3678-1222, 800/327-0200, or 01-800/90-444; website: www.guadala jara.interconti.com; $170

Hotel Crowne Plaza, Av. López Mateos Sur 2500, 45050, tel. 3634-1034 or 800/2CROWNE, fax 3631-9393; email: crownegd@crownegdl.com.mx; website: www.crownegd.com.mx; $175

Chapalita Bed-and-Breakfasts

Bed-and-Breakfast Imelda, Tlaloc 499, Colonia Chapalita, 45040; tel. 3121-8674; $30

Bed-and-Breakfast Irma, San Rafael 485, Colonia Chapalita, 45040; tel. 3122-9372; $30

Bed-and-Breakfast Gloria, Axayacatl 476, Colonia Chaplita, 45040; tel. 3631-9531, fax 3632-4185; $35 enterprise of personable, English-speaking Irma Yepson López. Behind a small jungle of front-yard verdure, you'll enter a rather dark but homey living room. Four comfortably furnished, but less than immaculate rooms, one downstairs, three upstairs, one with its own bath, three with shared bath, are available. Irma, friendly in her own quirky bohemian way, is a source of entertainment all by herself. Her prices, $20 for one, $30 for two, in double bed, including full, made-to-order breakfast, are certainly right. Av. San Rafael 485, Colonia Chapalita, Guadalajara, Jalisco 45040; tel. 33/3122-9372.

About a mile (14 blocks) farther west along Tepeyac (to Cuauhtémoc, then two blocks south to Tlaloc), find **Bed-and-Breakfast Imelda.** Charming, refined Imelda Baldini rents four rooms in her immaculate, comfortable family home on a quiet residential street. One room, on the ground floor, has a king-size bed; other rooms, upstairs have two beds and one bed. All rooms have TV and private bathrooms. A small but inviting interior patio is available for guest relaxation. Made-to-order breakfast (juice, coffee, bread, hot cakes, eggs) is served in the kitchen. All this for about $20 for one, $30 for two. Tlaloc 499, Colonia Chapalita, Guadalajara, Jalisco 45040; tel. 33/3121-8674; email: baldini@ guadalajara.net.

Continue southwest (south along Cuauhtémoc 10 blocks, west along Axayacatl five blocks) to **Bed-and-Breakfast Gloria.** Semiretired former Texas resident Gloria Meija offers three spacious, comfortable upstairs rooms, each with private bath, in a quiet, residential suburban neighborhood convenient to Plaza del Sol. The immaculate, comfortably furnished rooms, are all upstairs, where they share a homey sitting room with soft couches and a TV. Two of the rooms open to a sunny deck overlooking the verdant backyard garden. In the kitchen downstairs, Señora Meija serves breakfast to order (fruit, coffee, toast, jam, and eggs) for guests. Prices start at a modest $30 s, $35 d in a double bed; $50 per person for the biggest room with two beds. Axayacatl 476, Colonia Chapalita, Guadalajara, Jalisco 45040; tel. 33/3631-9531, fax 33/3632-4185.

Trailer Parks and Camping

Folks who prefer lodging in their own RV or tent have the choice of two Guadalajara-area trailer parks. See Trailer Parks in the Minerva-Chapultepec Accommodations, earlier.

FOOD
Breakfast, Cafes, Bakeries, and Fast-Food

Around the **Plaza del Sol,** coffee shop–style **Sanborn's Restaurant** (in the Plaza del Sol, open daily about 7:30 A.M.–11 P.M.) is one of the best bets for breakfast or a light meal. Also in Plaza del Sol, you can try **VIPs,** open about the same hours as Sanborn's, also in Plaza del Sol, for a variation on the same coffee shop theme. For faster food, also in Plaza del Sol, try Pizza Hut, Dunkin Donuts, Dairy Queen, or Burger King.

Hotel coffee shops also offer good options. Best bets for breakfast or lunch are, at mid-scale: Motel Americas, Hotel Vista del Sol, and Hotel Fiesta Inn; or upscale: Hotel Crowne Plaza, Hotel Guadalajara Plaza López Mateos, or Expo Guadalajara Plaza Expo (see Accommodations, above).

Chapulita, on the other hand, offers good, more local-style options, many of them right near the village-center corner of Tepeyac and Av. del las Rosas. For bakeries, choose from **Croissants Alfredo,** open daily 8 A.M.–9:30 P.M.; tel. 33/3121-4979, or the friendly **Varas Pan Integral** whole wheat bakery, open Mon.–Sat 8 A.M.–9 P.M., Sun. 9 A.M.–4 P.M.; tel. 33/3122-2518. (From Av. Tepeyac, find it a long block south along de las Rosas, corner of Privado las Rosas. Besides a swarm of scrumptious, cookies, pastries, and donuts, try their tasty **macrobiotic meals** to go.)

Two blocks north, for a good sit-down breakfast, many locals swear by coffee shop–style **Restaurant New York, New York** (see Chapalita Restaurants later), west side of the Chapalita Circle.

For plenty of veggie options, try the relaxing, outdoor **Lonchería Tita's,** at Tepeyac 591, one block east of the de las Rosas corner, across the street from the church. Pick from a bunch of salads, fruit drinks, and sandwiches, graded according to nutrition: "naturista," with fresh avocado, nuts, lettuce, and tomato, being the healthiest, and "dinosaur," with lots of meat, the least healthy. Other choices include omelettes, quesadillas, *tortas,* and much more; open Mon.–Sat. 7:30 A.M.–4:30 P.M., Sun. 7:30 A.M.– 3 P.M.; tel. 33/3122-9970.

On the other hand, walk across the adjacent lane to **Tortas Tono** for a *torta,* the Mexican sandwich: typically chicken or pork loin, with tomato, lettuce, avocado, and jalapeño pepper (remove it, if you prefer) in a hot, crispy *bolillo* (bun).

Restaurants

Like the breakfast and lunch options, serious supper dining around the Plaza del Sol is mostly confined to the hotels, with good gourmet options available at the **Hotel Crowne Plaza,** the **Hotel Mansión del Sol** (only hotel guests and their guests admitted), and the **Hotel Guadalajara Plaza Expo.**

One hotel restaurant, however, the super-plush **Restaurant Belvedere,** at the Hotel Hilton (see Accommodations, earlier) is outstanding. One look at the Belvedere menu, with French, Italian, and Mexican food rolled into one menu, gives the clue that you're in for something unusual

I was initially dubious that they could pull it off, but was forced by the sheer excellence of everything to change my mind. I'll simply mention some of the choices and leave the rest to you: For Mexican, try either quesadillas with mushroom, *cuitlacoche,* and *flor de calabaza,* or *sopes estilo Guadalajara.* (Or, if you're a truly adventurous eater, go for the deep-fried *gusanos de maguey*—maguey worms). People tell me they're excellent.

For Italian, choose from Serrano ham with melon, or *carpaccio di salmone;* for French, go for tricolor soup, or seafood soup *al pernado.* Actually, it's probably best to let the waiter order for you; it seems especially difficult to go wrong at the Belvedere. Expensive.

Chapalita Restaurants

Chapalita residents enjoy a sprinkling of good, close-in restaurants. By location, moving south-

west, start at class-act seafood **Restaurant Los Arcos,** at Av. Lázaro Cárdenas 3549, corner of San Ignacio. It is one of a chain of 10 that started humbly in Culiacán in Sinaloa and spread all over northwest Mexico. The label "Los Arcos" comes from the 19th-century brick aqueduct (now in ruins) near the original restaurant.

Times change, however, and now a flood of local middle- and upper-class customers return to enjoy dozens of impeccably prepared and served fresh choices, from oysters on the half shell and clam chowder *(crema de almeja),* to stuffed *corbina* fillet and fresh trout *(trucha).* Open Mon.–Sat. 11 A.M.–10:30 P.M., Sun. 11 A.M.–8 P.M., reservations recommended, tel. 33/3122-3719, credit cards accepted; family atmosphere. Moderate–expensive.

If Restaurant Los Arcos is full and you arrive without a reservation, don't despair; go next door, on Calz. Lázaro Cárdenas, to **Restaurant Frances,** open about the same hours. Here, contrary to the restaurant's name, the food is country-style Mexican barbecue, with all the trimmings, including mariachis. Moderate–expensive.

Move south, along San Ignacio, to the vicinity of the Chapalita Circle, where a number of restaurants offer good choices. For a little bit of everything in an informal family atmosphere, try **Restaurant New York, New York,** at Av. San Ignacio 1197, right on the Chapalita Circle's west quadrant. Here, you can enjoy professional service and a long list of familiar options, such as hot cakes, waffles, eggs any style for breakfast, or soup (try *tlalpeño*) and a hamburger for lunch; or starve up for supper and splurge with the salad bar and a T-bone steak. Stay late enough to enjoy the live music Wed.–Sat. 10 P.M.–midnight. Open daily 8 A.M.–midnight, tel. 33/3121-2606, 33/3121-8657. Credit cards accepted. Moderate.

In the adjacent quadrant, north across San Ignacio, try the **Café Dalí,** at Av. Guadalupe 1144, where, beneath a surreal faux Salvador Dalí ceiling and wall mural, you can select from a list of fondues, crepes, salads, baguette sandwiches, meats, and chicken. Their many tasty coffees also make this a good spot for breakfast. Open Mon.–Sat. 8 A.M.–midnight, Sun. 8 A.M.–11 P.M.; tel. 33/3439-9038. Moderate.

For upscale elegance, go four blocks east (toward Calz. Lázaro Cárdenas) to Argentine **Restaurant Bariloche,** at Av. Guadalupe 721, corner of Fernando Alvo de Ixtlilxochitl (eekstleel-soh-CHEE-tl). Here, the emphasis is on meat, wine, and entertainment, specializing in gaucho-style barbecue (with other choices for lighter eaters), plenty of good Argentine red wines, and a tango show. Open Thurs.–Sat from 10 P.M. Show Mon.–Sat 1:30 P.M.–1:30 A.M., Sun. 1:30 P.M.–7:30 P.M. Reservations recommended, especially for late supper before the show; tel. 33/3122-4270, 33/3122-3270. Credit cards accepted. Expensive.

For many more good restaurant choices, consult the Food section in the earlier Minerva-Chapultepec section.

ENTERTAINMENT AND EVENTS

Around the Plaza del Sol, the hotels are the most reliable entertainment sources. Nearly all of them recommended in Accommodations above have nightly live music at their lobby bars; at least two—the **Hotel Crowne Plaza** and the **Hotel Presidente Intercontinental** have full-blown nightclubs. Telephone the individual hotels for program details.

Plaza del Sol has a pair of **movie theater** options. Try either the five-screen **Multicinema** at Plaza del Sol (tel. 33/3630-3940) or the 12-screen **Cinemark** complex at the underground Milenio shopping plaza, a few blocks south, at Av. López Mateos 3333B, corner of Mariano Otero, tel. 33/3634-0509.

Chapalita offers some regularly scheduled community entertainment. Start at the Chapalita Circle and enjoy the **band concert** Thursday evenings at 7 P.M. Sundays, bring a picnic lunch and stroll around the Chapalita Circle and enjoy perusing the **artists' market** offerings 10 A.M.–5 P.M.

Enjoy a similar, but more extensive diversion on Sundays, from around 10 A.M., at the **antique market** two miles northwest, on Av. Mexico, along the blocks east of its Av. Chapultepec intersection.

The Chapalita Circle also offers nighttime diversions. Enjoy the live music at **Restaurant**

New York, New York Wed.–Sat. 10 P.M.–midnight. Alternatively, Argentine **Restaurant Bariloche,** four blocks east of the Chapalita Circle, offers a nightclub-style tango show, Thurs.–Sat, from 10 P.M. Call the restaurants to confirm programs. (See Chapalita Restaurants above).

For many more Guadalajara entertainment suggestions, see the Entertainment and Events sections of the Minerva-Chapultepec section of this chapter, and the Entertainment and Events section of the Heart of the City and City: East and South of Downtown chapters.

SPORTS AND RECREATION
Gyms and Swimming

If you're staying in one of the super-luxurious Expo Guadalajara–Plaza del Sol hotels—namely, the Hilton, Guadalajara Plaza Expo, Presidente Intercontinental, and Mansión del Sol—simply go to their exercise gym for a workout. If you're content with swimming for exercise, all of the Expo Guadalajara–Plaza del Sol hotels recommended in the earlier Accommodations section (except the Mansión del Sol) have pools.

Alternatively, Chapalita has a number of gyms. One of the better ones is **Coverbody Gym,** at 990 Tepeyac, by the post office, a block and a half west of the Av. de las Rosas corner. Here, for a mere $25 a month you can have the use of many fitness machines, a sauna, aerobics classes, and more. Open Mon.–Fri. 7 A.M.–9 P.M., Sat. 8 A.M.–1 P.M.; tel. 33/3121-4177.

Also very promising is the newly remodeled rehabilitation center, **Mundo Físico,** no telephone yet, strongly recommended by the American Society of Jalisco (see Communication and Information later in this chapter), at San Francisco 3376 in the block just west of the American Society's headquarters. Mundo Físico offers a plethora of facilities, including two heated swimming pools, (one outdoor, one indoor), paddle tennis, squash, handball, a fitness gym with professional trainers, sports medicine, steam room, sauna, spa, water aerobics, and natural food cafe and more. Fees start at about $100 per month for all-inclusive programs. Call the American Society of

Jalisco to find out if Mundo Físico accepts day-fee guests.

Walking and Jogging

Among the airiest Expo Guadalajara–Plaza del Sol walking and jogging locations is the unique panoramic-view **jogging track** atop the Hotel Guadalajara Plaza Expo (see Accommodations earlier).

Otherwise, the shady Chapalita neighborhood affords some walking and jogging opportunities. The grassy fields at the **Ciudad de Niños** (between Avenidas Guadalalupe and Tepeyac, two blocks west of Av. Niño Obrero) and the **Club de Leones** (a few blocks farther west, at the corner of Tepeyac and Prado Tabachines) appear ideal for jogging.

Another pleasant close-in walking and jogging space is the shady three-block **Av. Juan Diego** parkway lane (see Around the Chapalita Circle, in the earlier Sights section.)

Tennis and Golf

Except for the tennis court at the Hotel Crowne Plaza, the Plaza del Sol–Chapalita neighborhood has no publicly available tennis courts or golf courses. Greater Guadalajara, however, has many. For options, see Tennis, Golf, and Swimming in the Heart of the City chapter, and Tennis and Golf in the On the Road chapter.

SHOPPING AND SERVICES
Plaza del Sol Shopping

The perennially popular Plaza del Sol is one of Guadalajara's prime shopping grounds. Variety, the secret to Plaza del Sol's success, is immediately visible at the main Av. López Mateos busstop (buses 258A from downtown, plus numbers 359, 59, 640, and 24) entrance, across from the big golden glass landmark Hotel Presidente Intercontinental. Directory kiosks (also at the eastside Mariano Otero, bus 59A, entrance) list the possibilities: shoe and women's clothing boutiques, about two dozen each; plus many jewelry, baby, ice cream, and gift boutiques. Finally, you'll find some banks, all with ATMs, travel agencies, pharmacies, electronics, a copy shop,

bookstore, stationers *(papelerías)*, and swimsuit *(traje de baño)* shops.

Specific locales include **department stores** Suburbia, Zaragoza, and El Nuevo Mundo, Gigante supermarket, Tennis World, G.D. Computer, Levis, Oshkosh B'Gosh, Laboratorios Julio photo store, Federal Express, Jantzen, and Sony. Fast-food options include Burger King, Dairy Queen, and Dunkin Donuts. For restaurants, choose among Pizza Hut and coffee shops Sanborn's and VIPs.

Some stores are especially useful, such as the excellent book and magazine store **Librería Mexico,** with *Time, Newsweek, USA Today,* and the excellent Mexico City *News* newspaper. Find them open daily 8:30 A.M.–9:30 P.M.; tel. 33/3123-1847, just inside the López Mateos entrance.

For **email and Internet access,** go to Hazard Net, open Mon.–Sat 11 A.M.–7 P.M., Sun. 11 A.M.–3 P.M.

For more convenient shopping plaza choices, see Shopping Plazas and Warehouse Stores in the Minerva-Chapultepec section, earlier.

Outdoor Markets and Handicrafts

Sunday is the big day at the **Artists' Market,** at Chapalita Circle, intersection of Avenidas Guadalupe and de las Rosas. On Friday, continue (via bus 51B) about two miles farther west along Tepeyac and visit the big **Clothes Market** on Av. Copernicus, between Avenidas Tepeyac and Moctezuma. Dedicated lovers of outdoor markets venture even farther, to the country-style Thursday **Santa Anita Market,** in Santa Anita village, west of Av. López Mateos, about four miles (seven km) south of the *periférico* (peripheral boulevard).

Handicrafts are scarce around Plaza del Sol and Chapalita. Best head to the Guadalajara's best handicrafts sources, at **Tlaquepaque and Tonalá.** (See the Tlaquepaque and Tonalá shopping sections in the City: East and South of Downtown, and also see the shopping section of the Heart of the City chapter.)

Natural Food and Bakery

If **natural food** is your thing, go to **La Panza Es Primera** store and restaurant, in the Plaza del Sol shopping center, open Mon.–Sat.

10 A.M.–8:30 P.M. and Sun. 11 A.M.–8 P.M.; tel. 33/3123-1847.

In Chapalita, get your fill of plenty of good juice drinks, yogurt, whole wheat bread and cookies, vitamins, supplements, and more at the **Abeja de Oro** (Golden Bee), at Av. de las Rosas 591, two doors south of Tepeyac, open Mon.–Fri. 8:30 A.M.–8 P.M., Sat. 8:30 A.M.–4 P.M., Sun. 8:30 A.M.–2 P.M.

One of the local best is **Varas Pan Integral,** whole wheat bakery, with a scrumptious assortment of in-house cookies, pastries, bread, donuts, dietetic bread, and macrobiotic food to go. Find them at Av. de las Rosas 420, a long block south of Tepeyac, open Mon.–Sat. 8–9 P.M., Sun. 9 A.M.–4 P.M.

Services

A plethora of services is available locally. Around Plaza del Sol, simply study the kiosk at the Av. López Mateos entrance and follow the map to the source inside. (See Plaza del Sol Shopping, earlier.)

A similar abundance of services is available around the Chapalita village corner of Av. Tepeyac and Av. de las Rosas. Within a block in any of the four directions, you have three banks with ATMs, Internet access, beauty shop, barber, bakery, locksmith, bookstore, laundry and dry cleaners, TV repair, natural food, car repair, pharmacy, and shoe repair.

For example, right at the corner of Avenidas Tepeyac and de las Rosas, you have banks **Bancomer,** open Mon.–Fri. 8:30 A.M.–4 P.M., on the northeast corner, **Banco Santander Mexicano,** open Mon.–Fri. 9 A.M.–4 P.M., on the northwest corner; and, with the longest hours of all, **Bital** open Mon–Fri. 8 A.M.–7 P.M., Sat. 8 A.M.–3 P.M.

For laundry, go to **Laundromat Aguamatic** on the southeast corner of Av. de las Rosas and Tepeyac, open daily 8 A.M.–9 P.M.

Get your film developed and your camera repaired at the **Laboratorios Julio** branch, at Guadalupe 1162, local 7, tel. 33/3587-5272, on the Chapalita Circle, open Mon.–Sat. 10 A.M.–8 P.M., Sun. 11 A.M.–5 P.M. As a branch of the big citywide chain, they offer virtually all photo services, plus in-house quick development, popular

films, and some SLR and point-and-shoot cameras and supplies.

Get English-speaking travel services at highly recommended **Expoviajes,** Tepeyac 487, tel. 33/3121-9524, about three blocks east of Av. de las Rosas, past and across Tepeyac from the church.

COMMUNICATIONS AND INFORMATION
Post and Internet

Chapalita residents enjoy an up-to-date **post office,** with a stamp-dispensing machine (exceptional for Mexico), lots of P.O. boxes, and reliable Mexpost mail service. Find them on Tepeyac, in the second block (past Librería Sandi), west of the Av. de las Rosas corner.

Trying harder, **Mailboxes, Etc.,** at Tepeyac 701A, near the corner of Av. de las Rosas, offers photocopies, Internet access ($3.50/hr), fax (33/3122-3089), efficient Federal Express and Mexpost mailing services, and P.O. boxes ($300/year). Open Mon.–Fri. 9 A.M.–8 P.M., Sat. 10 A.M.–2 P.M.; tel. 33/3121-2939; email: mbe030@megared.net.mx.

Longer-hour Internet access ($2/hr) is available at **Trinity and Neos Cyber Café** since 2000, at Av. Guadalupe 1162, local 4, on the Chapalita Circle's southwest quadrant, between Av. Guadalupe and Av. del Parque. Also available are printer, fax, and computer classes; open Mon.–Sat. 10 A.M.–9 P.M., Sun. 11 A.M.–8 P.M.; tel. 33/3344-3074.

Internet connections are also available at the Plaza del Sol, at **Hazard Net,** open Mon.–Sat. 11 A.M.–7 P.M., Sun. 11 A.M.–3 P.M., on the south side, just before the department store.

Bookstores

A pair of excellent bookstores serve local residents. In the Plaza del Sol, go to **Librería Mexico.** (For details, see Plaza del Sol Shopping above.)

In Chapalita, all roads seem to lead to **Librería Sandi,** both community information center and bookstore. First, be sure to pick up a copy of the very useful *Colony Reporter* newspaper. Then browse around and appreciate the best English-language book selection in Western Mexico, with a book and magazine selection as complete as your neighborhood bookstore back home. Before you leave, be sure to glance at the community bulletin board. Open Mon.–Fri. 9:30 A.M.–2:30 P.M. and 3:30–7 P.M., Sat. 9:30 A.M.–2 P.M. Find Sandi, at Tepeyac 718, two doors west (past Banco Santander Mexicano) of the Av. de las Rosas corner, tel. 33/3121-0863, 33/3647-4600; email: sandibooks@vinet.com.mx.

Community Organizations

At least three local organizations offer assistance to and encourage participation by Guadalajara newcomers. Very helpful is the **American Society of Jalisco** with headquarters at San Francisco 3332 (directions below), open Mon.–Fri. 9:30 A.M.–2 P.M.; tel. 33/3121-2395, tel./fax 33/3121-0887.

Besides a very respectable library, they maintain a small cafe, clubroom, and always try to have an information volunteer on duty. Watch the Community Calendar pages of the *Colony Reporter* (available at Librería Sandi, see above) for announcements of their social events. For more information, visit their website: www.american society.org; email: info@amsoc.hypermart.net. (Get to their headquarters from the north side of Calz. Lázaro Cárdenas, two blocks west of its intersection with Av. Guadalupe, where you follow Av. San Bonifacio one long block north to San Francisco, then turn right, east, and continue one short block to the headquarters, at the corner of Fco. Javier, on the north side, opposite the Colegio Guadalupe).

The American Legion Post 3 offers many activities for the English-speaking community. You need not be a veteran or legionnaire to participate. Their social events (see the Community Calendar pages of the *Colony Reporter*) are good occasions to meet and exchange laughs, ideas, and information with local residents. Find them at San Antonio 143, Colonia Las Fuentes (from Plaza del Sol continue south, via car or taxi along Av. López Mateos about three miles to Av. Las Fuentes; turn right and continue two very long blocks to the Las Fuentes traffic circle. Follow San Antonio, one of the streets that radiate, like the spokes of a wheel, from the circle.); tel. 33/3621-1208, website: www.go.to/americanlegion.

Still another helpful local organization is the **International Friendship Club of Guadalajara,** which promotes social, philanthropic, and cultural activities. Monthly meetings, usually for breakfast, are conducted in English, and include a speaker. One of their accomplishments is an extensive "Survival Guide to Guadalajara," chockfull of hard-to-get information. For-sale copies are routinely available at the American Society of Jalisco headquarters. For more information about the International Friendship Club, contact friendly former president Adele Vogt, tel. 33/3685-0423 or 33/3685-0445.

Libraries

Both the **American Society of Jalisco** and the **American Legion Post 3** (see above), maintain general English-language libraries. Collections, although heavy on paperback novels, also have plenty more, including guidebooks, cookbooks, histories, and travel literature of Mexico.

Spanish Language Instruction

Guadalajara community organizations, schools, and individuals offer Spanish classes and tutoring. The American Society of Jalisco (see above) volunteers conduct small Spanish classes.

A neighborhood **Spanish Language School** offers classes, at Ermita 1443. (From the Av. de las Rosas–Tepeyac corner, walk three blocks south along Av. de las Rosas to Ermita, then one block west.) For more information, call or fax the director, Julia Barra, tel. 33/3121-4774; email: spanscho@representative.com.

Instructor **Barbara Wallace** regularly conducts Spanish-language classes and offers tutorial service. For more information, contact her at tel. 33/3673-2140.

For more options, see the special topic Spanish Language Instruction and Instruction classified advertisements in the *Colony Reporter* newspaper.

HEALTH AND EMERGENCIES

Medicines and Doctors

For simple remedies, consult the on-duty pharmacist at one of the several local pharmacies. For example, in Plaza del Sol, try **Farmacia ABC,** open daily 8 A.M.–10 P.M., in Zone B, local 13, tel. 33/3647-4839.

In Chapalita, on Av. Tepeyac, one block east of Av. de las Rosas, next to the church, go to the **24-hour Farmacia Guadalajara,** with an on-duty pharmacist, an extensive selection of over-the-counter medications, and some grocery and deli items to boot, tel. 33/3121-2580, 33/3121-2581. Alternatively, on the Chapalita Circle, try the **Farmacia Benevides,** Av. Guadalupe 1130, east

side of the circle, open daily 8 A.M.–midnight, tel. 33/3122-7149.

For a doctor, follow your hotel's recommendation, or consult one of the several highly recommended doctors listed in Guadalajara Doctors and Hospitals under Staying Healthy in the On the Road chapter.

Police, Fire, and Medical Emergencies

See "Police, Fire, and Medical Emergencies" at the end of the earlier Minerva-Chapultepec section of this chapter.

Zapopan

The midsize provincial town of Zapopan (sah-POH-pahn) is one of Guadalajara's best-kept secrets. It is the *cabercera* (headquarters) of a spreading 345-square-mile, fabulously productive *municipio* (township, municipality) with a population well over one million and more than six-fold the land area of the *municipio* of Guadalajara.

A glance at a detailed map of the Guadalajara metropolitan zone reveals that much of Guadalajara's upscale western suburb is actually part of the Zapopan *municipio.* Within its jurisdiction, Zapopan encompasses the metropolitan area's three top shopping plazas, the Plaza del Sol, Gran Plaza, and Plaza Patria, and a big fraction of Guadalajara's super-deluxe hotels, including three of the top four: the Crowne Plaza, Presidente Intercontinental, and Camino Real. Add to that the burgeoning new Zapopan industrial parks, from Av. López Mateos Sur (Motorola, Kodak) to Belén in the north (Interlub, Bardahl Oil) and the hundreds of thousands of acres of fertile corn and cattle hinterland and you have the fifth-richest *municipio* in Mexico, producing a larger peso gross product than any one of several entire Mexican states.

HISTORY

It requires a look at history to understand how all this came about. Once upon a time, Zapopan was a small rural town, with miles of country separating it from the center of power and wealth

in Guadalajara. At that time, Zapopan people were much more concerned with corn and cattle than politics and power. Zapopan's municipal leaders looked to their western hinterland, home of their patrons, the rich *hacendados* who tended cattle on huge swaths of valley and mountain territory.

Meanwhile, Guadalajara's prosperous investors gradually pushed development westward; they bought great tracts of land, which they filled with the streets, homes, and businesses that inexorably overflowed the west side, from south to north, engulfing the small town of Zapopan.

Nevertheless, old Zapopan lives on, home to those who quietly adhere to the old-Mexico values that are reflected by their credo that Zapopan is the "Land of Friendship, Work, and Respect." And as part and parcel of their traditions, Zapopan people proudly continue to welcome the multitudes of faithful who arrive to pay their respects to the miraculous Virgen de Zapopan.

The Virgin of Zapopan

Although the early history of Zapopan, "place of the zapote trees," as a settlement of the mystery-draped "Chicomoztoc" people, is uncertain, the origin of Zapopan's miraculous Virgin is not. The Virgin, considered to be the very founder of the town, was first known as the "Virgin of the Pacification" because, probably more than anyone or anything else, she was responsible for extinguishing the fiery rebellion

CITY: WEST AND NORTH

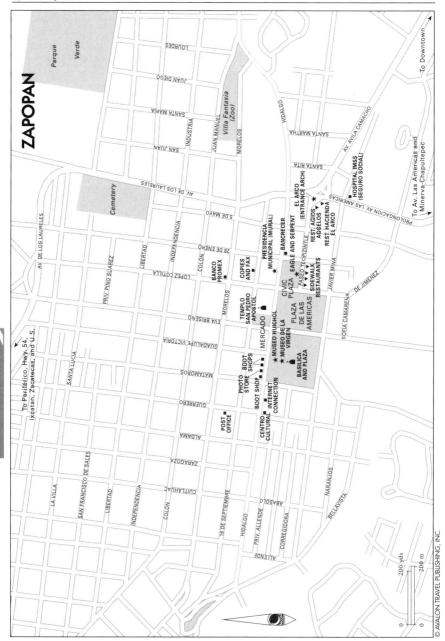

ZAPOPAN

Parque Verde

Cemetery

Villa Fantasia (Zoo)

LOURDES

JUAN DIEGO

SANTA MARIA

SAN JUAN

JUAN MANUEL

INDUSTRIA

MORELOS

AV. DE LOS LAURELES

5 DE MAYO

28 DE ENERO

INDEPENDENCIA

LIBERTAD

PRIV. PINO SUAREZ

COLON

LOPEZ COTILLA

MORELOS

EVA BRISEÑO

GUADALUPE VICTORIA

MATAMOROS

GUERRERO

ALDAMA

ZARAGOZA

CUITLAHUAC

16 DE SEPTIEMBRE

HIDALGO

PRIV. ALLENDE

CORREGIDORA

ABASOLO

COLON

INDEPENDENCIA

LIBERTAD

SAN FRANCISCO DE SALES

LA VILLA

SANTA LUCIA

AV. DE LOS LAURELES

ALLENDE

NARANJOS

BELLAVISTA

SOFIA CAMARENA

JAVIER MINA

DE JIMENEZ

SANTA RITA

SANTA MARTHA

AV. AVILA CAMACHO

HIDALGO

PROLONGACION AV. LAS AMERICAS

HOSPITAL IMSS
SEGURO SOCIAL

EL ARCO
(ENTRANCE ARCH)

REST. AGIOS
AGGELOS
REST. HACIENDA
EL ARCO

PASEO TEOPZINTLE

SIDEWALK
RESTAURANTS

PLAZA DE LAS
AMERICAS

CIVIC
PLAZA

EAGLE AND SERPENT

BANCRECER

PRESIDENCIA
MUNICIPAL (MURAL)

BANCO
PROMEX

COPIES
AND FAX

TEMPLO
SAN PEDRO
APOSTOL

MERCADO

★ MUSEO DE LA
VIRGEN

★ MUSEO HUICHOL

BASILICA
AND PLAZA

PLAZA DE LA
VIRGEN

PHOTO
STORE   BOOT
         SHOPS

BOOT SHOP

INTERNET
CONNECTION

CENTRO
CULTURAL

POST
OFFICE

To Periférico, Hwy. 54,
Ixcatán, Zacatecas, and U.S.

To Downtown

To Av. Las Américas and
Minerva-Chapultepec

AV. LAS AMERICAS

200 yds
200 m
0

© AVALON TRAVEL PUBLISHING, INC.

Stalls displaying religious goods surround the Basílica de Zapopan.

known as the Mixtón War. (See the History section of the Introduction chapter.)

In 1541, alarmed and saddened by the rebellion's carnage and destruction, Jesuit missionary friar Antonio de Segovia brought the humble but already revered corn-paste figure on a mercy pilgrimage from Michocán, hoping to put a stop to the bloodshed. With nothing more than the frail figure tied to the front of his robe, Segovia confronted a hostile band of natives near the town of Apozol, in the mountains about 50 miles (80 kilometers) north of Zapopan. Segovia's sermon must have been powerful, for soon the natives began seeing a mysterious, brilliantly overpowering light radiating from the figure. Eventually captivated by the Virgin's power, the natives fell to their knees and surrendered their arms. The word spread and within weeks the Mixtón War was over.

Father Segovia brought the miraculous Virgin south to the nearest settlement, at Zapopan, where the local townspeople accepted her as their own on December 8, 1542. The very same miraculous figure, now called the "Virgin of Zapopan" is

feted in a grand procession of many hundreds of thousands of Guadalajarans every October 12.

GETTING THERE AND GETTING ORIENTED

Getting There

Get to Zapopan from downtown Guadalajara, via local bus 275 diagonal (which runs northwest, all the way from Tonalá through Tlaquepaque to downtown Guadalajara), running north along 16 de Septiembre to the Normal Circle. From there, it continues northwest along Av. Ávila Camacho, past the Zapopan entrance arch, then up west along Hidalgo. It returns southeast along virtually the same route.

By taxi or car, follow Av. Manuel Ávila Camacho, which diagonals northwest at the Normal Circle about a mile north along Av. Alcalde, from the Guadalajara downtown cathedral. Continue about three miles from the Normal Circle to Zapopan, marked by the monumental entrance arch on the left.

Getting Oriented

The heart of Zapopan is small, easy to know, and accessible on foot. The town's axis runs east-west, from the welcoming **Arco** entrance arch on the east side. Uphill, west, past the arch, visitors stroll beside the sidewalk restaurants of the **Paseo Teopizintle** and the flag-decorated **Plaza de las Américas,** finally arriving at the towering **Basílica de Zapopan** that shelters Zapopan's beloved patron.

The commercial heart of town concentrates along a single street, Av. Hidalgo, that similarly runs east-west, a block north of the basilica. Besides the usual commercial establishments, along Hidalgo you'll also find the **municipal plaza,** the *presidencia municipal* (town hall), the parish church of **Paroquia San Pedro Apóstol** and the town **market.**

SIGHTS

Around the Basilica

Let Zapopan's neo-baroque entry **arch** be your first stop. Erected generations ago in memory

THE HUICHOL

Because the Huichol have retained more of their traditional religion than perhaps any other group of indigenous Mexicans, they offer a glimpse into the lives and beliefs of dozens of now-vanished Mesoamerican peoples.

The Huichol's natural wariness, plus their isolation in rugged mountain canyons and valleys, has saved them from the ravages of modern Mexico. Despite increased tourist, government, and mestizo contact, prosperity and better health swelled the Huichol population to around 20,000 by the late 1990s.

Although many have migrated to coastal farming towns and cities such as Tepic and Guadalajara, several thousand Huichol remain in their ancestral heartland—roughly 50 miles (80 km) northeast of Tepic as the crow flies. They cultivate corn and raise cattle on 400 *rancherías* in five municipalities not far from the winding Río Altengo valley: Guadalupe Ocotán in Nayarit, Tuxpan de Bolanos, San Sebastián Teponahuaxtlán, Santa Catarina, and San Andrés Cohami ata in Jalisco.

Although studied by a procession of researchers since Carl Lumholtz's seminal work in the 1890s, the remote Huichol and their religion remain enigmatic. As Lumholtz said, "Religion to them is a personal matter, not an institution and therefore their life is religion—from the cradle to the grave, wrapped up in symbolism."

Hints of what it means to be Huichol come from their art. Huichol art contains representations of the prototype deities—Grandfather Sun, Grandmother Earth, Brother Deer, Mother Maize—that once guided the destinies of many North American peoples. It blooms with tangible religious symbols, from green-faced Grandmother Earth (Tatei Urianaka) and the dripping Rain Goddess (Tatei Matiniera), to the ray-festooned Grandfather Sun (Tayau) and the antlered folk hero Brother Kauyumari, forever battling the evil sorcerer Kieri.

The Huichol are famous for their use of the hallucinogen peyote, their bridge to the divine. The humble cactus—from which the peyote "buttons" are gathered and eaten—grows in the Huichol's Elysian land of Wirikuta, in the San Luis Potosí desert 300 miles east of their homeland, near the town of Real de Catorce.

To the Huichol, a journey to Wirikuta is a dangerous trip to heaven. Preparations go on for weeks, and include innumerable prayers and ceremonies, as well as the crafting of feathered arrows, bowls, gourds, and paintings for the gods who live along the way. Only the chosen—village shamans, temple elders, those fulfilling vows or seeking visions—may make the journey. Each participant in effect becomes a god, whose identity and very life are divined and protected by the shaman en route to Wirikuta.

of the city's indigenous founders, the arch abounds with symbolism: the god and goddess of corn in the side niches; at the top center, Diana the Huntress, and above her, at the summit, an eagle, guardian of all. The arch was the work of architect Guillermo González Ibarra and his wife, María del Carmen Rabago, who sculpted the reliefs and statues that adorn the arch's sides and facade.

Walk uphill, west, past the gushing, monumental fountain, supported by a squad of kneeling, naked cherubs. Pass the restaurants and

shops and you continue along **Paseo Teopizintle** (named for the Aztec god of corn) and the Plaza de las Américas, bordered on the south side by the 28 flags of all the American republics.

Arrive at the soaring baroque **basilica** (begun in 1690, finished in 1730), home of the beloved Virgin of Zapopan. The volcanic stone facade's richly ornate style is called "plateresque," because it resembles the scroll designs first found on elaborate 17th-century silver-plated tableware.

Inside the basilica, the legendary image, one of the beloved "three sister" virgins (see the special topic, The Three Sisters of Mexico) has enjoyed generations of popularity so enormous that it must be seen to be believed. Local folks, whenever they happen by, often stop to say a prayer (or at least make the sign of the cross as they pass) in front of the cathedral gate. Inside, some faithful crawl the length of the sanctuary to pay their respects to the diminutive blue-and-white figure. The adoration climaxes on October 12, when a rollicking crowd of hundreds of thousands accompanies the Virgin of Zapopan (affectionately known as "La Generala," from the downtown Guadalajara cathedral home to Zapopan, where she stays October 13–May 20.

Huichol Museum

After the basilica, have a look inside the excellent adjacent **Museo Huichol Wirrarica,** founded in 1961 by Franciscan friar Ernesto Loera, who wanted to increase public understanding of the Huichol culture. The Huichol, who call themselves the Wirraritari ("people who inhabit places of thorny plants") are among the most resistant to modernization of Mexico's indigenous peoples. For centuries they have retired to their high homeland strongholds in mountainous Nayarit and Jalisco and fought off conversion and Mexicanization. As a result, their traditions remain strong. (See special topic, The Huichol).

Before you leave, don't miss the fine examples of Huichol Indian handicrafts in the adjacent museum-shop. Sale items include eerie beaded masks, intriguing yarn paintings, and *ojos de dios* (God's eyes) yarn sculptures.

For more information on Huichol history and traditions, purchase the excellent English language pamphlet "Wirraritari," at the shop counter. Find the museum on your left as you exit the basilica; open Mon.–Sat. 10 A.M.–2 P.M. and 4– 6 P.M., Sun. 10 A.M.–2 P.M.; tel. 33/3636-4430.

Also don't miss the very interesting **Museo de la Virgen** next to the Huichol Museum, open approximately the same hours. Inside, you'll find

> *The Huichol, who call themselves the Wirraritari ("people who inhabit places of thorny plants") are among the most resistant to modernization of Mexico's indigenous peoples.*

mementos and excellent, detailed exhibits of the Virgin of Zapopan's miraculous history.

Plaza, Town Hall, Church, and Market

If you have more time for strolling, from the basilica, walk downhill, east, two blocks along Hidalgo to the broad **civic plaza,** on the north side of the street, flanked by dignified Old world–style municipal offices and banks. Just above street level, contemplate the dramatic **eagle and the serpent** bronze sculpture. It represents the story, preserved in ancient records, of the founding of the Aztec capital of Tenochtitlán in the Valley of Mexico in 1325. After wandering over Western Mexico for generations, the Aztecs came upon what soothsayers had predicted: an eagle with a serpent in its beak, at the very spot where they should build their capital.

Continue north across Hidalgo to the ***presidencia municipal*** (town hall) and take a look at the 1970 mural, *The Universal Revolution,* in three panels, by muralist Guillermo Chávez Vega.

The center panel depicts a young woman in red pointing toward the future, while around her, giant hands reach out for goals not yet realized. In the background, independence and revolution heroes Hidalgo, Madero, Villa, Zapata, Carranza, Obregón, Calles, and Cárdenas stand guard.

In the left panel a nude woman, surrounded by doves of peace and the muralist's heroes Ho Chi Minh, Fidel Castro, V. Lenin, and Karl Marx all preside in triumph, next to an astronaut who appears to float listlessly in space.

Finally, on the mural's right side another nude woman, with the wings of an angel, representing the spirit of freedom, triumphing over capitalist villains, including Napoleon, who ruthlessly substitute machines for man.

Continue uphill along Hidalgo, across Emiliano Zapata, one block to the parish church **Parroquia San Pedro Apóstol,** finished in 1819. Inside, find the notable painting, the *Baptism of Jesus,* by the renowned 17th-century painter Juan Correa.

Finally, uphill behind the church, visit the colorful local **market,** corner of Pino Suárez and Hidalgo, festooned with fruit stalls and *fondas* brimming with steaming pots of *guisados* (stews), piles of hot tamales, and *cazuelas* (clay pots) of savory *chiles rellenos.*

Sights Outside of Town

Good roads lead from Zapopan town to its spreading rancho and mountain hinterland, famous for the **Barranca,** the 2,000-foot-deep canyon of the Río Santiago. At the viewpoint **Mirador Dr. Atl,** past San Isidro, around Km 15, Saltillo Hwy. 54, motorists stop to admire the canyon vista and the waterfall **Cola del Caballo** (Horse's Tail) as it plummets hundreds of feet to the river below.

Past that, a small paradise of springs decorates the lush canyonland. First, at Km 17, comes **Los Camachos,** a forest and mountain-framed *balneario* (bathing park) with pools and restaurants; a few miles farther along is the hot spring bathing complex **Balneario Nuevo Paraíso,** at Km 24.

About a half mile farther (follow the left side road from the highway) stop at **Ixcatan,** ancient village of *arrieros* (mule-drivers), whose animals for centuries carried charcoal here for sale.

Admire the picturesque old town **church,** graced by a quaint, triple-arched belfry, with a trio of old bronze bells, respectively inscribed with the dates of 1834, 1791, and the third, illegible, but probably dating from around 1700. The lintel over the entrance bears inscriptions of 1691 and 20th of November 1726, presumably marking the beginning and end of construction. Before leaving, examine the stones in the church's front yard, which bear map-like inscriptions, speculated to be directions to safe havens during the Mixtón War that blazed around these parts in 1541–42.

Nearby, about three miles (five kilometers) farther along the road north though town, you may be able to see the spectacular **Geiseres de Ixcatan** (Ixcatan Geysers). (Unfortunately, due to wanton vandalism, the owners of the property have not been allowing unaccompanied outsiders. Zapopan Tourism is trying to remedy this—see Get There, later in this chapter, for advice).

Get to the Barranca from the Guadalajara city center by car or taxi via Hwy. 54, the Saltillo-Zacatecas highway, which heads northward along Av. Alcalde from the city-center cathedral. Bus riders can go via the "Los Camachos" bus #S-165 (which continues to Ixcatan and which leaves the Normal Circle, on Av. Alcalde about a mile north of the downtown cathedral, about every hour from 5 A.M. until the early afternoon).

Alternatively, from the Zapopan basilica, take a taxi, or ride a "Ixcatan"-labled bus from Av. Hidalgo, or drive north, easiest along Av. Laureles main boulevard, nine blocks north of the basilica, to the *periférico.* Turn right, east, and continue about a mile to the signaled road to San Isidro, the northerly extension of Av. José María Pino Suárez. Turn left and continue straight ahead, about five miles (eight kilometers), through the lush green San Isidro canyon country home development and golf course, to Saltillo Hwy. 54, where you should turn left.

Hacienda Santa Lucia and Huaxtla Warm Springs

Zapopan offers a host of rarely visited country delights. West of town, consider visiting venerable **Hacienda Santa Lucia,** the most accessible of Zapopan's several old country haciendas. At its largest extent during the 1800s, it encompassed around 60,000 acres of wheat, corn, and cattle. Now, it still encloses a very respectable 10,000 acres; and moreover its Zaragoza family owners welcome visitors (on specified weekdays or by appointment) and are renting out its beautiful garden for weddings and parties.

The hacienda's features include a crumbling former company store, the "Taberna" former mescal factory, and an elaborate family chapel, with baroque Spanish *retablo* and saint, Santa Lucia, brought from Italy. For more information, contact the Hacienda directly, in Spanish, at tel./fax 33/3897-0788; email: hdaluci@attglobal.net; website: www.haciendasantalucia.com.mx.

Get there from Zapopan downtown by private tour or taxi, via the road to Tesistán, Av. Hidalgo's western extension, past the *periférico* eight miles (about 12 kilometers) to Tesistán. After passing the Tesistán plaza and church (on the left and right,

© BRUCE WHIPPERMAN

Residents of semitropical Huaxtla village, one hour northwest of Zapopan, invite visitors to enjoy their curative warm spring pools and tranquil, tree-shaded former sacred site, now a park.

respectively), turn left on (another) Av. Hidalgo and continue another half mile (one kilometer) to the hacienda, at Calle Juan M. Ruvalcaba 139, at the Santa Lucia village plaza. By bus similarly go from Av. Hidalgo via bus S-160 to Nextipac, which passes through Tesistán and Santa Lucia.

If you start early enough, on the same day, you can continue to **Huaxtla,** the tropical canyon-slope village, famous for its curative *aguas termales* (warm springs), open daily 9 A.M.–5 P.M. The all-paved but narrow and steep access road affords magnificent views of the lush tropical **Barranca** (canyon of the Río Santiago.)

At Huaxtla village itself, great old *higuera* (wild fig) trees shade a big bathing pool of blue-tinted (from natural sulfur) warm spring water. The people are friendly and welcoming. Bring a picnic and enjoy the afternoon.

Get there from downtown Zapopan also via the road to Tesistán (as described above). But, about six miles (10 kilometers) past the *periférico,* turn right (or left, if doubling back from Hacienda Santa Lucia) on to the road to Colotlán, Hwy. 23. After approximately another 10 miles (16 kilometers), follow a narrow paved side road right. Continue, enjoying the airy canyon vistas, another approximately five miles (eight kilometers) to Huaxtla village and the springs.

For more information on Zapopan sights and possible tours (which they customarily offer; just say what you want to visit), contact the **Zapopan tourist information office** at Plaza Centro, Av. Vallarta 6503, Zapopan, Jalisco 45010; at the periférico, tel. 33/3110-0754, ext. 118, fax 33/3110-0383; email: turismo @zapopan.gob.mx or rolega@hotmail.com. Open Mon.–Sat. 9 A.M.–7:30 P.M.

HOTELS AND RESTAURANTS
Hotels

Good hotels are scarce around Zapopan town. By far the best is four-star **Hotel Country Plaza,** about five blocks south of the Zapopan entrance arch. Guests enjoy refined upscale amenities, including a good restaurant up front and, beyond the reception, an airy atrium with a blue pool, spa, and exercise room tucked at the far end. Business visitors have available four meeting rooms accommodating up to 300 and three negotiating rooms accommodating about 10 persons each.

As for accommodations, three storys of about 100 rooms in increasing order of luxury—standard, superior, jr. suite, and "country" suite—enclose the atrium. All are deluxe, comfortable, and decorated in soothing pastels, with modern-standard bathrooms. Rates begin at about $80 s or d for standard, running up to about $180 for the super-deluxe "country" suites, all with air-conditioning, phones, cable TV, travel agent, shop, and parking. Credit cards accepted. Prolongación Av. Américas 1170, Zapopan, Jalisco 45160; tel. 33/3633-4633, fax 33/3656-2522; email: hcountry@infosel.net.mx; website: www.countryplaza.com.mx.

CITY: WEST AND NORTH

Budget-conscious travelers might check out the nearby three-star **Suites Jacarandas Plaza,** about three blocks southeast of the Zapopan entrance arch. Although I didn't actually inspect this place, it appears to offer acceptable accommodation, especially for families, with a dozen two- and three-bedroom kitchenette apartments. Prices are right, at about $50 for two, $65 for three, $75 for four, with fans and TV. Call ahead for availability. Av. Ávila Camacho 880, Zapopan, Jalisco 45160; tel. 33/3656-3840, 33/3656-3968.

Restaurants

Zapopan's better restaurants line the Paseo Teopizintli, between the entrance arch and the basilica. First, at #356, find old-Mexico-style **Restaurant Hacienda El Arco** on the left, just uphill from the arch. Here, enjoy breakfast, lunch, or dinner in the airy patio beneath the rustic red-tiled eaves. The friendly husband-wife team puts out a hearty Mexican country menu of *carnes asadas* (roasted meats), chicken, and *antojitos* such as tacos, tamales, quesadillas, and *chiles rellenos.* Mariachi troubadours regularly perform here afternoons and evenings; open daily approximately 8 A.M.–9 P.M. Moderate.

Next door, at #342, be sure to visit the Greek-owned and operated **Restaurant Zorba Agios Aggelos,** the popular *taverna* meeting ground of Guadalajara's Greek community. Take a seat beneath one of the shady umbrellas out front and let the impression grow that you've been transported to some Greek island halfway around the world. The menu—gyros and falafel, moussaka, kabobs, *dolmas* (stuffed grape leaves), *retsina* wine—completes the fantasy. Join in the Greek circle and line dancing Friday and Saturday evenings, approximately 8–11 P.M. Open daily approximately 8 A.M.–11 P.M. Credit cards accepted. Moderate–expensive.

For good local-style seafood, go uphill about a block to the cluster of sidewalk eateries, the most highly recommended of which is **Restaurant Manzanillo,** at Paseo Teopizintli 124, open daily approximately 8 A.M.–9 P.M. Here, pick from a long menu of many styles of seafood—*almejas* (clams), *ostiones* (oysters),

© BRUCE WHIPPERMAN

Sidewalk restaurants cluster near the foot of the Zapopan entrance arch.

pulpo (octopus), *camarones* (shrimp), *cangrejo* (crab), *calamare* (squid) and fish prepared many ways. Budget–moderate.

ENTERTAINMENT, EVENTS, SPORTS, AND RECREATION
Entertainment and Events

Zapopan people stick close to home, relying upon friends and family for most entertainment. Families, especially on Friday and Saturday evenings, enjoy strolling along the **Paseo Teopizintle,** Zapopan's favorite people-watching ground, and listening to the strolling mariachi bands.

Excitement peaks at Zapopan's yearly country **religious festivals.** Church-linked neighborhood clubs, called *mayordomias,* organize a list of events—processions, *mañanintas* (early masses), barbecues, dances, carnival rides and games, food stalls—that highlight each religious festival.

If you're in the Zapopan vicinity at certain times, join the festivities at the local church: January 18, fireworks at the Zapopan basilica; May 20, departure of the Virgin from the Zapopan basilica; July 25, Santiago (St. James) festival in Nextipac, Santa Ana Tepatitlán, and San Juan de Ocotán; July (last Sunday), Virgen del Refugio festival, in El Batán; August 15, fair of the Virgen de la Asunción, in La Experiencia; September 8, festival of the Señora de Loreto, in Santa Ana Tepatitlán; October (third Sunday), festival of Santo Domingo, in Tesistán; November 22, festival of Santa Cecilia, in Tesistán; December 1–8, festival of the foundation of Zapopan, in Zapopan; December 12, festival of the Virgin of Guadalupe, everywhere.

The one festival that you won't be able to avoid noticing if you're present on October 12— **La Romería de la Virgen de Zapopan**—is a grand stroll of a million Guadalajara merrymakers and dozens of dance troupes who accompany the Virgin from the Guadalajara cathedral to the Zapopan basilica.

Sports and Recreation

Parque Colomos, greater Guadalajara's prime **walking, hiking, jogging, and horseback-riding** ground, is only a mile and a half due south from Zapopan. Bring a picnic and romp, ride, run, or relax to your heart's content. Park extras include a Japanese garden, bird lake, and big cactus garden. Open daily from 9 A.M.–6 P.M.

Get there by car or taxi via Av. Américas south, passing Av. Patria about half mile, turning left at Montevideo; after four blocks, diagonal right on La Rioja to the dead-end; turn right one block to another dead-end at El Charco. Turn left to the park entrance.

Zapopan **golf** enthusiasts enjoy the 18-hole **Las Cañadas Country Club** course, tel. 33/3685-0363, 33/3685-0412. Get there by car or taxi, via the *periférico* northwest of Zapopan. At the intersection of the *periférico* and the highway to Tesistán, turn right, east, and continue about a mile to the signaled **road to San Isidro,** the northerly extension of Zapopan Av. José María Pino Suárez. Turn left, north, and continue straight ahead, winding about five miles

(eight kilometers), through the lush green San Isidro country home development and golf course. The driveway is on the left.

Plenty of sports and recreation opportunities are available outside of Zapopan. See Tennis, Golf, and Swimming in the Heart of the City chapter, and Tennis and Golf in the On the Road chapter.

SHOPPING AND SERVICES
Downtown Zapopan

For general shopping, you can get much of what you need on Av. Hidalgo downtown. For fruit, vegetables, and groceries, go to the municipal **market** a block downhill and north of from the basilica, corner of Hidalgo and Eva Briseño; in the block adjacent to the basilica are pharmacies and a photography shop. In the same block, you'll also find a number of good **boot shops** that cater to visitors, continuing the Zapopan rural *vaquero* (cowboy) tradition. Moreover, a block north of Hidalgo, behind the **presidencia municipal** is a small photocopy shop.

Banks, all with ATMs, are well represented, with Bancrecer, at Av. Hidalgo 229, between Cotilla Zapata and 28 de Enero, tel. 33/3636-4606, 33/3636-7372, and Promex, a block north, at López Cotilla 8, corner of Morelos, tel. 33/3656-8385 and 33/333/3656-0673.

Plaza Patria

For lots more general shopping opportunities, go to **Plaza Patria,** about a mile southwest of downtown Zapopan along Av. Ávila Camacho, at the boulevard intersection of Av. Patria. Built in the 1970s and now aging, Plaza Patria nevertheless still rivals Plaza del Sol in popularity, with a swarm of stores—many women's clothes, shoes and jewelry, department stores Fábricas de Francia and Suburbia, banks Promex (tel. 33/3633-2806), Banamex (tel. 33/3673-0406, 33/3673-0579), travel agent Van Gogh (tel. 33/3642-2070, 33/36422071, 33/3642-2072), pharmacy Farmacia Guadalajara, tel. 33/3641-2617 and 33/3641-2670 and much more.

INFORMATION, COMMUNICATIONS, HEALTH, AND EMERGENCIES

Tourist Information Office

Lots of Zapopan information is available at the municipal tourism office, at Plaza Concentro, at Av. Vallarta 6503, just inside (east of) the *periférico*. Find them at upstairs offices G13 and G14, tel. 33/3110-0755, ext. 118, fax 33/3110-0383; email: turismo@zapopan.gob.mx or role ga@hotmail.com. Open Mon.–Sat. 9 A.M.–7:30 P.M. Telephone or email ahead to verify office hours. Be sure to get a copy of their handy, detailed bilingual "Guide to Tourist Attractions and Services."

Post and Internet

Get stamps and mail letters at the local post office, on Moctezuma near the corner of 16 de Septiembre, a block north of Hidalgo. For Internet connections, try the small store on the south side of Hidalgo, a block north of the basilica, just before the Cultural Center, corner of Guerrero.

Health and Emergencies

For routine medications, consult the on-duty pharmacist at one of the downtown Zapopan pharmacies. If you need a doctor, follow your hotel's recommendation, or choose from the list of highly recommended doctors and hospitals with ambulance services in the Guadalajara Doctors and Hospitals section of the On the Road chapter.

For **police** emergencies, dial 06 for the radio patrol, or telephone the Zapopan police station, at tel. 33/3818-2200, ext. 1500, 1504, or 1114. In case of Zapopan **fire emergencies,** dial the fire station *(bomberos),* tel. 33/3656-8577.

City: East and South of Downtown

Guadalajara visitors flock to the southeast-side towns of **Tlaquepaque and Tonalá** to buy the renowned handicrafts that these towns' many hundreds of family factories produce. Although Tlaquepaque and Tonalá are each headquarters of their respective sprawling *municipio* (township or municipality), the core village-centers, arguably Mexico's most important handicrafts sources, are the main attractions.

About five miles southeast of downtown, Tlaquepaque ("tlah-kay-PAH-kay") town, although completely surrounded by the Guadalajara metropolis, is nevertheless separate, with its own church, town hall, accommodations, restaurants, and locally owned shops and businesses close by the old village *jardín* (garden).

Although replete with village charm, Tlaquepaque is not sleepy. Visitors swarm in, by day to stroll and shop, and by night to savor the delicious snacks and delight in the bright mariachi entertainment for which Tlaquepaque is famous.

On the other hand, **Tonalá,** another five miles farther east, at Guadalajara's country edge, retains a measure of its drowsy rural past.

The arches fronting the Tonalá *presidencia municipal* form a cool vantage to take a break from the plaza-front.

Nevertheless, an initial glance inside a few of its multitude of handicrafts shops reveals Tonalá's mission. Behind the street-side adobe and brick walls, thousands of Tonalá people are hard at work. Their labor and know-how is the source of Tonalá's celebrated ceramics and its renowned papier-mâché and brass, in a plethora of human, animal, and floral designs.

History

With only five miles separating them, Tlaquepaque and Tonalá share virtually the same history. Most historians agree that the early tribes of the eastern Atemajac Valley, the **Cocas and Tecuexes** (tay-KWAY-shays), whose traditions reflected much of the ancient Toltec heritage, were ruled by monarchs whose seat was located at present-day Tonalá. The original name, Tonallan (toh-NAH-yahn, "Place of the Rising Sun") reflected its preeminence. The sun, long a popular Tonalá decorative theme, was at the center of the pre-Conquest religion, a faith probably similar to that of the present-day Huichol people. (See special topic, The Huichol.)

Tonallan's dominance, as source of local military, political (and consequently, religious) authority, probably also led to its strong ceramics tradition. Early Spanish missionaries labeled Tonalá as a "factory of paganism," because every house seemed to be a workshop where family members spent their working hours crafting pottery images of their gods.

Just prior to the Spanish Conquest, an underage child-heir named Xuchitzín (Precious Flower) became Tonalá's ruler. Consequently, a distinguished relative, Lady Tzapotzingo (Fruit of the Zapote), was chosen to temporarily take charge as **Cihualpilli** (queen). According to tradition, Cihualpilli (see-wal-PEE-yee) was a benign and wise ruler, who encouraged the arts and crafts, including a renowned metalworking factory, famous for gold jewelry.

Tlaquepaque

Tlaquepaque was once a sleepy village of potters miles from the old Guadalajara town center. Attracted by the quiet of the country, rich families built Tlaquepaque mansions during the 19th century. Now, entrepreneurs have moved in and converted them into restaurants, art galleries, and showrooms, stuffed with quality Tonalá and Tlaquepaque ceramics, glass, metalwork, and papier-mâché.

SIGHTS

Getting Oriented

Tlaquepaque's primary axes are east-west **Av. Independencia** and north-south **Av. Madero,** which intersect beneath a grand rectangular white arch that stretches diagonally between the pink, portaled **El Parián** restaurant–mariachi center on the southeast and the *jardín* plaza with a bandstand on the northwest. Stand (or imagine standing) under the arch and diagonally face the *jardín*. Av. Madero runs north, on your right, and on your left, pedestrian shopping mall Av. Independencia heads west. On the *jardín's* far left (west) side, past the bandstand, rises the old **Santuario de la Soledad,** while on the *jardín's* north side rises the popular **Parroquia San Pedro** parish church.

A Walk around Old Tlaquepaque

Much of Tlaquepaque's charm flows from its village ambience, which allows most everything to be easily reached on foot. Start at the town center, beneath the arch at the intersection of Avenidas Madero and Independencia. Since you can't avoid them, you might as well check out the offerings of the regiment of **handicrafts stalls** up and down the streets.

After that, head to the westside of the *jardín* (named in honor of *insurgente* Miguel Hidalgo),

© BRUCE WHIPPERMAN

The Tlaquepaque coat of arms dates from the founding of the town in the early colonial era.

to the beloved old **Santuario de Nuestra Señora de la Soledad.** The Augustinian monastic order, who began construction in 1742 and finished in 1813, dedicated it to the Virgin of Solitude.

Inside, around the crucifix-shaped nave, see the graphic prints of all the stations of the cross. Up front, in the left transept, pay your respects to **La Imaculada,** the Virgin of the Immaculate Conception, and in the right transept, the **Virgin of Guadalupe.** In the center, above the altar, on an austere Gothic stone *retablo,* the Virgin of Solitude reigns from beneath her gilded cupola, while at the tip-top of the *retablo,* the omnipresent Eye of God surveys all.

If you have time, see if the *sacristan* (keeper of the church) is around. Ask him to show you inside the sacristy (*sacristía,* behind the altar, offer a donation). Inside you'll find the more precious paintings, including the noted *Jesus Visiting the Home of Mary and Martha in Bethany,* dating from 1685.

Walk to the *jardín's* adjacent north side, to the **Parroquia San Pedro,** Tlaquepaque's popular parish church, modified extensively since

its construction around 1700. After a few minutes wandering through its beautifully restored interior, head into the courtyard, through the door at the nave's north (left) side. Here, enjoy the preciously detailed miniature pageant of dozens of Bible stories, from Noah and his Ark and Rachel at the well to Jesus on the Mount and Paul on the road to Damascus.

Sights West and North of the Jardín

Cross the *jardín* to the Independencia pedestrian mall and head right, west, a block to the **Casa Histórica,** at Independencia 208, northwest corner of Contreras Medellín. This late colonial mansion is typical of the manor houses built by rich Guadalajarans in Tlaquepaque during the 19th century. This one is especially notable, for here, on June 13, 1821, Guadalajara municipal and royal authorities signed on to the revolutionary Plan de Iguala of national independence leader General Agustín Iturbide. Seeing the writing on the wall, royalist Governor-General José Cruz quickly withdrew, thus making Guadalajara independent of Spain months before the rest of Mexico.

The kindly present owner bids the public welcome. Stroll the spacious inner patio, shaded by what appears to be the majestic grandfather of all *hule* (rubber) trees. Around the patio's periphery a few potters craft the ceramic vases, jars, and bowls for sale back by the entrance door.

Before you leave, don't miss the owner's shop (on the left before you head out the front door), which exhibits a miniature throng of charming nativity figurines *(nacimientos)* and fine porcelain statuettes. Open Mon.–Sat. 10 A.M.–7 P.M., Sun. 10 A.M.–5 P.M.; tel./fax 33/3635-9350.

For a further treat, cross the street to the **Museo Regional de Cerámica y Arte Popular,** open Tues.–Sat. 10 A.M.–6 P.M., Sun. 10 A.M.–3 P.M.; tel. 33/3635-5404. The building itself is historically significant, being the former home of infamous *hacendado* Francisco Velarde, who was both a close associate of the notorious ex-President Santa Anna and later collaborated with the French imperialists, a crime for which he was executed by republican authorities during the 1860s.

Times change, however, and now his former house brims with super-fine examples of Jalisco ceramics and other handicrafts. Examination of all the outstanding examples in the eight galleries constitutes a mini-education in fine Jalisco handicrafts, from *bruñido* and blown glass to *petatillo* and papier-mâché. A ninth for-sale gallery sells fine examples of all the above and much more.

Continue one block north of Independencia to the **Casa de los Artesanos,** at Morelos 288, between Cruz Verde and Medellín. Inside, a dozen rooms bloom with the handiwork of the more than 100 members of the Tlaquepaque artisans guild. Here, you can see nearly the entire range of possible handicrafts—furniture, both in wood and iron, intricate basketry, shining blown glass, fetching papier-mâché animals, baroque angels, handsome stonework, oil paintings, and colorful stoneware. Moreover, all of it is for sale, and if you don't see exactly what you want, you can go to the source, using their address-telephone list of all the contributing artisans. Find them open Mon.–Fri. 9 A.M.–7 P.M., Sat. 9 A.M.–6 P.M., Sun. 10 A.M.–2 P.M.; tel. 33/3657-3846, 33/3635-5756.

Continue north on Medellín two blocks to Tlaquepaque's gem, the **Centro Cultural del Refugio** (open daily 9 A.M.–8 P.M.; tel. 33/3635-1089), at Donato Guerra 164, which occupies the entire square block between Medellín and P. Sánchez. One hint that you're in for something special is the line of majestic, ancient *higuera* (wild fig) trees along the same block.

The graceful old building's history reflects the last century and a half of Mexico's history. Built in 1859, it was a hospital run by the Hermanas de Caridad (Sisters of Charity), who were exiled by the republican government in 1874. The Josephine Sisters took over and continued it as a hospital until 1935. Later, renamed the Hospital Refugio, it was operated privately by the brothers Castiello Fernández del Valle until 1979. The city inaugurated it as the Casa de la Cultura in 1985 and has since used it for a busy schedule of artistic and cultural education, exhibitions, events, and performances.

The theater is past the east entrance, at Donato Guerra 160, where the line of trees ends. See the

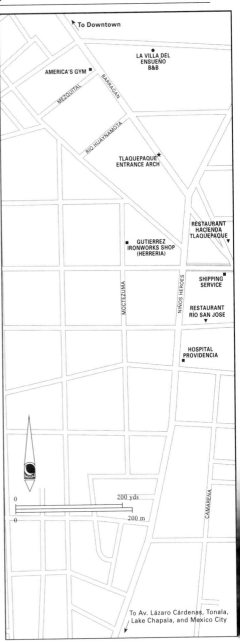

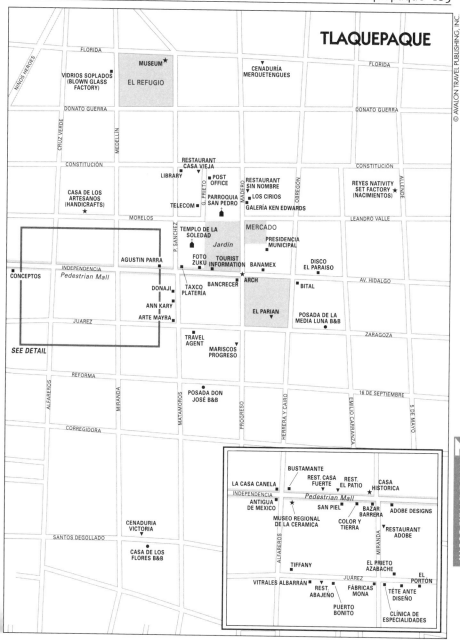

TLAQUEPAQUE

FLORIDA

NIÑOS HÉROES

MUSEUM ★

VIDRIOS SOPLADOS
(BLOWN GLASS
FACTORY)

EL REFUGIO

CENADURÍA
MERQUETENGUES

FLORIDA

CRUZ VERDE

DONATO GUERRA

DONATO GUERRA

MEDELLIN

CONSTITUCIÓN

CONSTITUCIÓN

RESTAURANT
CASA VIEJA

LIBRARY

POST
OFFICE

RESTAURANT
SIN NOMBRE

REYES NATIVITY
SET FACTORY ★
(NACIMIENTOS)

OBREGÓN

ALLENDE

CASA DE LOS
ARTESANOS
(HANDICRAFTS)
★

G. PRIETO

MADERO

LOS CIRIOS

PARROQUIA
SAN PEDRO

GALERÍA KEN EDWARDS

TELECOM

MORELOS

LEANDRO VALLE

P. SÁNCHEZ

TEMPLO DE LA
SOLEDAD

MERCADO

Jardín

PRESIDENCIA
MUNICIPAL

AGUSTIN PARRA

FOTO
ZUKU

TOURIST
INFORMATION

BANAMEX

DISCO
EL PARAISO

CONCEPTOS

INDEPENDENCIA
Pedestrian Mall

DONAJI

TAXCO
PLATERÍA

BANCRECER

ARCH

BITAL

AV. HIDALGO

ANN KARY

ARTE MAYRA

EL PARIAN

POSADA DE LA
MEDIA LUNA B&B

JUAREZ

ZARAGOZA

SEE DETAIL

TRAVEL
AGENT

MARISCOS
PROGRESO

ALFAREROS

REFORMA

MIRANDA

MATAMOROS

POSADA DON
JOSÉ B&B

PROGRESO

HERRERA Y CAIRO

16 DE SEPTIEMBRE

EMILIO CARRANZA

5 DE MAYO

CORREGIDORA

CENADURIA
VICTORIA

SANTOS DEGOLLADO

CASA DE LOS
FLORES B&B

BUSTAMANTE

LA CASA CANELA

REST. CASA
FUERTE

REST.
EL PATIO

CASA
HISTORICA

INDEPENDENCIA
Pedestrian Mall

ANTIGUA
DE MEXICO

SAN PIEL

BAZAR
BARRERA

ADOBE DESIGNS

MUSEO REGIONAL
DE LA CERAMICA

COLOR Y
TIERRA

RESTAURANT
ADOBE

MIRANDA

TIFFANY

EL PRIETO
AZABACHE

EL
PORTÓN

VITRALES ALBARRÁN

REST.
ABAJEÑO

FÁBRICAS
MONA

TÉTE ANTE
DISEÑO

JUÁREZ

PUERTO
BONITO

CLÍNICA DE
ESPECIALIDADES

ALFAREROS

BUILDING CHURCHES

Although European architects designed most of Mexico's colonial-era churches, embellishing them with old-world Gothic, Renaissance, baroque, and Moorish decorations, native artists added their own geometric, floral, and animal motifs. The result was a blend that manifested in intriguing variations all over Mexico.

Sometimes the native influence led to poor ("provincial") versions of European designs; other times (notably, the Templo de Nuestra Señora de Aranzazú and the Templo de Santa Monica in downtown Guadalajara), artists merged brilliant native decorations with the best of European-style vaults, arches, and columns.

The Layout

Mexican church design followed the Egypto-Greco-Roman tradition of its European models. Basically, architects designed their churches beginning with the main space of the **nave,** in the shape of a box, lined with high lateral windows. Depending on their origin and function, builders constructed three basic types of churches—the monk's **monastery or convent** (*convento*), the bishop's **cathedral** (*catedral*), and the priest's parish church (*templo, parroquia*).

With only masonry to work with, and often faced with the constant threat of earthquake, colonial-era builders raised massively thick walls, supported on the exterior with ponderous buttresses. Key elements were naves, with or without **transepts** (*cruceros*), cross spaces separating the nave from the altar, making the church plan resemble a Christian cross. They placed the **choir** (*coro*) above and just inside the entrance arch.

At the opposite, usually the east, or sunrise end of the church, builders sometimes extended the nave beyond the transept to include a **presbytery** (*presbiterio*), which was often lined with seats where church officials presided. Past that the building ended at the **apse** (*ábside*), the space behind the altar, frequently in semicircular or half-octagonal form. Within the apse rises the gilded **retable** (*retablo*) adorned with sacred images, attended by choirs of angels and cherubs.

---

bulletin board just inside. The ticket office is on the right. For more information, ask at the ticket office for a copy of *Refugiarte,* the center's small monthly magazine (*revista mensual*), which contains a list of events (*lista de eventos*) and classes.

If you have more time, wander around inside the gracefully restored interior. Pause in the lovely portaled lime-tree garden, and take a look at the temporary exhibitions.

If interested in enrolling in classes (guitar, accordion, painting, ceramics, papier-mâché, dance, photography, and much more), walk around the corner to Medellín 194, tel. 33/3635-1089, ext. 21) for more information.

ACCOMMODATIONS

Tlaquepaque visitors enjoy a sprinkling of comfortable lodgings. City visitors, attracted by Tlaquepaque's rewarding shopping, its good restaurants, and its quietly picturesque neighborhood lanes are increasingly choosing Tlaquepaque as a deserving destination by itself.

Bed-and-Breakfasts

A few Tlaquepaque innkeepers have merged the North American bed-and-breakfast tradition with the Mexican *posada* style of accommodation for those visitors who appreciate the best of both worlds.

Beginning in the northwest corner of town and moving diagonally southeast, start with **La Villa del Ensueño** (The Villa of the Dream).

This graceful lodging is just about evenly split between similar branches on opposite sides of its quiet neighborhood side street. Guests at the approximately 30-unit complex, formerly a pair of 19th-century villas, enjoy rooms

Larger churches usually incorporated side altars, presided over by images of locally popular saints, nearly always including the Virgin of Guadalupe.

The Facade

Outside, in front, rises the facade *(fachada)*, sometimes in a uniform style, but just as often a mixture of Renaissance, Gothic, and baroque, with some Moorish *(mujedar)* worked into the mix. A proliferation of columns nearly always decorates Guadalajara church facades, from the classic Etruscan, Doric, Ionic, and Corinthian *(Toscano, Dórico, Jónico, Corintio)* pillars to spiraled Solomonic *(Salomónico)* barber's poles and bizarre *estipites. Estipite* columns, a baroque feature of plateresque facades (so-named for their resemblance to elaborate silverware designs), usually begin with a classical capital (base) but rise, curiously, like an inverted obelisk, widening to a pair or trio of elaborately carved prismatic blocks and narrowing quickly again to an identical capital at the top.

Convents

The monastery (or convent) style churches, besides all of the above, included living and working quarters for the members of the order, typically built around a columned patio called the **cloister** *(claustro)*. A corridor through an arched porch *(portería)* adjacent to the nave usually led to the cloister, from which monks and nuns could quickly reach the dining hall, or **refectory** *(refectorio)*, and their private rooms, or cells *(celdas)*.

The missionary fathers designed their churches with an eye to handling the masses of natives whom they hoped to convert. For them, padres included an **atrium** *(atrio)*, a large exterior courtyard in front of the facade. For the partly initiated natives, they often built an open chapel *(capilla abierta)* on one side of the atrium. Conversions also occurred at smaller open chapels *(pozas)*, built at the corners of the atrium.

artfully nested along sunny bougainvillea-draped balcony walkways and intimate fountain patios. Two heated pools, an old but usable tennis court, breakfast room adjoining a sunny veranda, and an intimate bar with soft couches, are all available for guest relaxation.

Staff gladly offer advice regarding sights, restaurants, and tours. After-hours, a knowledgeable hotel desk manager is available 24 hours for help and advice. An in-house driver with a Chevrolet Suburban is available for transportation and tours for up to seven people at $10 per hour.

All rooms and suites are both immaculate and attractively neocolonial, with rustic red-tiled floors, wall art, bed lamps, floor-to-ceiling drapes, and shiny tiled baths. Rates begin at about $75 s or d for standard, $100 for deluxe, $120 for two-bedroom deluxe, and $140 for suites, all with fans, continental breakfast, and

parking. Florida 305, San Pedro Tlaquepaque, Jalisco 45500; tel. 33/3635-8792, fax 33/3659-6152. For reservations and more information, from the U.S. and Canada, write Aldez Enterprises P.O. Box 1080, Agoura Hills, CA 91376; toll-free 800/220-8689, fax 818/597-0637; email: aldez@pacbell.net; website: www.mexonline.com/ensueno.htm.

Shift east and south several blocks to the south central part of town, four blocks south of Independencia, to **Casa de las Flores**, at Santos Degollado. Enter from a quiet neighborhood street and pass through a flowery garden of bright bougainvillea, fragrant roses, and jacaranda to a trellis-shaded patio. Here, guests enjoy continental breakfast in the morning and coffee and conversation around a log fire on cool winter nights. An added plus is the friendly knowledgeable hosts, American Stan Singleton (from

Old world palm-fringed patios and sunny arched corridors decorate the Refugio, Tlaquepaque's graceful old former convent, now a cultural center.

Davis, CA), and José Gutiérrez, who enjoy volunteering their services as guides ($10/hr.)

A few steps past the patio, arrive at the modern stucco two-story, seven-room lodging complex. Guests enjoy spotless, comfortable, marble-floored rooms, attractively decorated with crafts and polished handmade wooden furniture. Rates run about $70 s, $90 d, with fans, modern-standard baths, and generous continental breakfast included. Santos Degollado 175, San Pedro Tlaquepaque, Jalisco 45500; tel./fax 33/3659-3186, cellular 33/3102-9345.

Return two blocks north and one block east to Reforma, between Matamoros and Progreso, to **Hotel Mesón Don José.** Here, architect-owner Soledad Ríos has converted a big space into a charmingly intimate leafy garden lodging with four deluxe suites tucked behind a beautiful blue lap (with lanes) swimming pool.

All suites are beautifully decorated with plenty of gorgeous tile, fetching handicrafts, colorful, heirloom-quality hand-sewn bedspreads and polished rustic wooden furniture. Two smaller and less deluxe (but still comfortable) rooms are also available up front. The suites run $105 s, $125 d with two large beds; the smaller rooms $75 with one bed, $90 for two beds. All with cable TV, fans, parking, and credit cards accepted. Reforma 139, San Pedro Tlaquepaque, Jalisco 45500; tel. 33/3635-7522, 33/3639-3085, fax 33/3659-9315; email: meson_don jose@hotmail.com; website:www.members .tripod.com/mdonjose.

Budget travelers will appreciate the **Posada de la Media Luna** (Inn of the Half Moon), centrally located just a block east of El Parián and the plaza. The owners, with bright paint and lots of savvy, have turned something potentially humdrum into an attractive lodging, elevated away from the noise and bustle on busy Calle Juárez downstairs. About 20 rooms line both sides of a long, sunny upstairs patio, invitingly decorated with potted plants and umbrella-shaded tables for breakfast and relaxation. The rooms themselves are clean, and simply but comfortably furnished with pastel bedspreads, rustic wooden furniture, and some reading lamps. Baths are likewise clean and well-maintained, with hot-water showers. Prices run about $34 s or d, $44 t or q, with fans, TV, and continental breakfast, but no parking. Juárez 36, San Pedro Tlaquepaque 45500; tel./fax 33/ 3635-6059, 33/3657-7631; email: pinaluna @jal1.telmex.net.mx; website: www.geocities .com/thetropics/paradise/1501/index.html.

Hotels La Serena and El Tapatío.

A pair of Tlaquepaque area hotels cater to particular needs. **Hotel La Serena,** about three miles (five minutes by taxi) south of the Tlaquepaque center, near the new bus station, is especially convenient for bus passengers. For details, look at the end of Accommodations in the Heart of the City chapter.

Five-star landmark **Hotel Tapatío,** reigning

over its own airy hilltop estate, about five minutes by taxi south of Tlaquepaque, seems perfect for visitors who crave luxury. Here, guests can have it all, including two restaurants, bars, live music nightly, nine clay tennis courts, exercise gym, running track, disco, and heated outdoor swimming pool with kiddie pool. Rooms are spacious, clean, and comfortable, running from semi-deluxe standard-grade rooms for about $110 s or d, through fancier deluxe for about $150, to suites for $200, all with private view balcony, air-conditioning, phone, satellite TV, babysitting (at extra charge), shops, travel agent, extensive business and meeting facilities, and more.

For reservations and more information, write Hotel Tapatío at Carretera a Chapala, Km 6.5, Tlaquepaque, Jalisco 45588, or dial tel. 33/3635-6050 or fax 33/3635-6664. You may also telephone toll-free, from Mexico tel. 01-800/361-8000, from the U.S. and Canada, 800/858-8471, or from the U.S. only, tel. 888/844-1524; email: htapatio@prodigy.net.mx; website: www.htapatio.com.

FOOD

Food Stalls and Market *Fondas*

You could enjoy a week of delicious, inexpensive food right around the Tlaquepaque *jardín.* Food stalls begin opening daily around noon, are most active around 5–8 P.M., and close around 10 P.M. Saturdays and Sunday are busiest.

Many of the food-stall options are rich and fatty, but understandably popular. Best-liked seem to be heaping bowls of french fries smothered in chopped hot dogs. If that's not enough, go for *chicarones* (deep fried pork rinds), fried bananas, hamburgers, and deep-fried-on-the-spot potato chips.

As for drinks, the fresh fruit *aguas* are yummy, such as sweet dark red *jamaica* (hah-MAI-kah), *horchata* (rice milk, sugar, and spices), and *fresa* (strawberry—red and fruity.) If you prefer, two or three juice (*jugo:* HOO-goh) stands supply fresh orange, apple, watermelon (*sandía),* carrot (*zanahoria*), pineapple, and many more fresh juices. For dessert, pick up two or three of the yummy cakes, pies,

Carts deliver dessert to restaurants along Tlaquepaque's busy but auto-free Av. Independencia.

custards, and cheesecakes for sale on tables around the *jardín's* northwest side.

For healthier (and more typically Mexican) budget-priced meals, go to the ***fondas*** (permanent food stalls) inside the market, across the street from the *jardín's* northeast corner (of Madero and Leandro Valle). Inside, choose from dozens of offerings, including savory stews (*guisados* and *birrias*), tamales, *chiles rellenos,* chicken in *mole,* and loads more. Remember: If it's steaming, it's safe. Although rarely necessary anymore, douse salads in plenty of lime *(limón)* juice as a precaution.

Probably the busiest food stall in Tlaquepaque (if not in all of Guadalajara) is **Taquería Paco,** on Progreso (Av. Madero's southern continuation), a block south of the *jardín.* Here, a dedicated team puts out about a two dozen meat and fish tacos a minute to a throng of enthusiastic customers.

Continue south three blocks and turn right a block and a half to the local favorite, **Cenaduría Victoria,** at Santos Degollado 182, north side of street, between Miranda and Matamoros. Victoria (open daily 6–9 P.M., in front of the house), who started out by serving whatever she would

have fixed for her family, is getting so popular that she may have to open a restaurant.

Macrobiotic food fanciers need not go without in Tlaquepaque. **Cafe Biomega,** at P. Sánchez 176, two blocks north of the *jardín's* west side, offers a yummy selection of soy hamburgers and tacos, fish tacos, salad, soy coffee, juices, yogurt, natural cereals, honey, wheat bread, and more. Find them open Mon.–Fri. 9 A.M.–6 P.M., Sat. 9 A.M.–5 P.M.; tel. 33/3344-1266, 33/3635-7833.

El Parián

Several independent cafe-restaurants serve the multitude of tables that surround the interior patio of El Parián, diagonally (southeast) across the Madero-Independencia intersection from the *jardín.* Every evening, families crowd in for the free mariachi entertainment; food is just a sideshow.

Nevertheless, competition keeps standards up and prices down. Among the better options seems to be **Salon Monterrey,** on the west (Av. Progreso) side. Here, a long menu of Mexican favorites—shrimp *al gusto,* chicken in *mole* sauce, *pozole,* hamburgers, spaghetti—and much more satisfies

MEXICAN HAT DANCE *(JARABE TAPATÍO)*

Mexican folk celebrations usually blend indigenous and Spanish tradition. In dance, the Spaniards' contribution was the *jarabe* (for "sweet" as in syrup) courtship dance of ancient, perhaps even pre-Christian European origin.

Of the many regional Mexican *jarabes,* the most celebrated is the *Jarabe Tapatío* (*Tapatío* referring to its Jalisco origin), popularly known in the United States as the "Mexican Hat Dance." It is traditionally performed to the captivating rhythms of nine consecutive *sones* (melodies). The dancers, men, often in fancy *charro* braid and sombreros, and women in peasant blouses and colorfully full *poblana* skirts, tap with heel and toe, around each other, while never touching, and always keeping proper distance.

After several minutes, the performance climaxes, accompanied by *La Paloma (The Dove),* melody, with the man, his back straight, hands clasped behind, following his partner as she eludes him, prancing gingerly around his sombrero's ample brim.

In the anticlimactic finale, the dancers turn toward the audience and dance to and fro, accompanied by the saucy melody of the *Diana,* to the shouts and whistles of the audience.

Such traditional staged performances are invariably tame compared to the spontaneous *rancho* celebrations. Away from city constraints, people kick back and join sizzling, hours-long *jarabe* fiestas, accompanied by mariachis and singing by the excited participants and onlookers.

Folkloric dancers at Tlaquepaque's prime entertainment venue, El Parián, nearly always perform the Jarabe Tapatío on Friday, Saturday, and Sunday evenings.

the customers. Open daily from around 11–1 A.M. Strolling mariachis weeknights, show Fri., Sat., and Sun. about 9–11 P.M.

Restaurants

Several good restaurants sprinkle the Tlaquepaque downtown blocks. Most of them lie on or near the Av. Independencia pedestrian mall. Since many restaurants depend on street traffic, most open around noon and close by around 8 P.M. A few do serve breakfast, from around 9 A.M., and suppers until around 11 P.M.

Starting on the westside and moving east, first find **Restaurant Hacienda Tlaquepaque,** on the short diagonal street that runs northwest from Independencia, a block east of Niños Héroes. Inside, patrons enjoy airy old-Mexico patio ambience, live mariachi music Fri.–Sun 3–6:30 P.M., and a familiar menu of salad and soup appetizers and pasta, fish, fowl, and meat entrées. Open daily 12:30–8 P.M.; tel. 33/3344-5092, 33/3344-50982. Credit cards accepted. Moderate–expensive.

Half a block east, just past the corner of Alfareros, step into the patio of **Restaurant Casa Fuerte,** at Independencia 224. Afternoons, a trio plays, while ceiling fans whir softly and water trickles musically into the courtyard fountain. For me, the only blot on this inviting picture was the spotty service. (I had to send cold food back twice and had to ask three times before I got a bottle of soda water.) Nevertheless, its relaxing, refined atmosphere and hearty, innovative Mexican menu makes Casa Fuerte a place worth a second try. Find it open daily noon–8 P.M., with live music 3–6 P.M. except Monday; tel. 33/3657-8499, 33/3639-6481. Credit cards accepted. Moderate–expensive.

A few doors farther, at Independencia 186, consider the tourist shopper's long-time favorite **Restaurant El Patio.** The Mexican-international menu of soups, salads, beef, chicken, and fish, and the shaded, relaxing courtyard atmosphere are good enough to keep the customers coming. For a splurge, order one of their huge platters, enough for five. Open daily, beginning with breakfast 9 A.M.–8 P.M.; tel. 33/3635-1108. Credit cards accepted. Moderate–expensive.

Just past the next corner, enter the Adobe Designs handicrafts store, at Independencia 195 and continue through the spacious interior to Tlaquepaque's class-act **Restaurant El Adobe** in the rear. The restaurant's light, lively atmosphere creates a relaxing counterpoint to a hard morning of Tlaquepaque bargaining.

Here, Mexican nouveau cuisine reigns. For starters, try Mexican stuffed wontons, continue with mushroom soup or passion salad, and climax with macaroni in mescal sauce or cheese-stuffed chicken breast. Finish with one of their excellent espresso coffees. They're open daily noon–7 P.M. (with flute, guitar, and base trio 2:30–6 P.M.), tel. 33/3657-2792. Credit cards accepted. Expensive.

Half a block south and west, at Juárez 231, between Miranda and Alfareros, **Restaurant El Abajeño** continues a Guadalajara tradition. This worthy local representative of the long-time Guadalajara chain brings in the crowds, especially on weekends, with mariachis and an extensive Mexican-style menu. Choices include *antojitos* (such as garlic mushrooms in butter or *enchiladas verdes),* soups (especially *sopa de tortilla*), fondues (with bacon), pork loin (*lomo,* with guacamole), or chicken (with *mole poblano*). Open daily from noon until about 8 P.M.; tel. 33/3635-9097. Credit cards accepted. Moderate–expensive.

Two blocks north of Independencia, on Guillermo Prieto (the one-block street running north from the *jardín's* northwest corner), corner of Constitución, **Restaurant Casa Vieja** seems to be trying harder, with both breakfast and late evening suppers. In the patio of a genuine *casa vieja* (old house), savor the 18th-century rustic garden atmosphere while enjoying a selection of innovative Jalisco dishes. Start out with *ensalada Adam y Eva* (spinach, with sesame, pecan, apple, and cheese), continue with *lomo de Santa Clara* (roast loin of pork smothered in mild red chili sauce, with bits of *nopal* leaves and potatoes), and finish with fried ice cream (no joke) and cappuccino. Open daily 8:30 A.M.–10:30 P.M.; tel. 33/3657-6250. Credit cards accepted. Expensive.

On the same north side of town, one day try the **Restaurant Sin Nombre** (No Name Restaurant),

CITY: EAST AND SOUTH

at Madero 80, half a block north of the *jardín.* Inside, within a shady, rustic tile-roofed patio, a pair of strolling peacocks and a sonorous flute, guitar, and base trio set a relaxing tone. The menu is an added plus, with options including *pollo sin nombre* (no-name chicken), Tlaquepaque fillet, and *chiles en nogada* (two big mild chilies stuffed with chopped meat, pineapple, and pear, and topped with grated nuts.) Hours are 10 A.M.–10 P.M., the trio plays Wed.–Sun. 2:30–4:30 P.M.; tel. 33/3635-4520, 33/3635-3768. Credit cards accepted. Expensive.

For seafood, all local roads seem to lead to **Mariscos Progreso,** at Progreso 80, half a block south of El Parián. Owners bring in the crowds with mariachis, a relaxing patio atmosphere, and simply good shrimp, fish, octopus, squid, clams, and oysters in many styles. Open daily 11 A.M.–8 P.M.; tel. 33/3639-6149. Credit cards accepted. Moderate.

Tasty *cenas* (suppers) are the tradition at **Cenaduría Los Merequetengues** (may-ray-kay-TAYNG-gays) at Florida 83, east of the corner of Madero, three blocks north of the *jardín.* This is the place where you find out if your favorite Mexican restaurant back home cooks Mexican food "the way it's supposed to be." Here, a local family runs a simple, clean establishment, invitingly decorated with sentimental old-Mexico country scenes. (Don't let the old Gepetto—of Pinocchio fame—in the corner scare you; he's simply a wooden, although startlingly realistic, dummy.)

Turn to the wall menu for dozens of tasty choices, from *sopes* (tortillas topped with spiced meat and vegetables), enchiladas and *flautas* (beef, chicken, cheese, or *verdes),* tacos *dorados, pozole,* and much more. Open Mon.–Sat. 7 P.M.–midnight, Sun. 2–10 P.M. Budget–moderate.

ENTERTAINMENT AND EVENTS
Just Wandering Around
Afternoon and evening strolls around Tlaquepaque's central *jardín* yield a bounty of old-Mexico entertainment. First are the food stalls, where, for starters, you can choose from hot dogs, popcorn, sweet corn, sweet fruit *aguas,* and chilled coconut juice.

A walk around Tlaquepaque's quiet back lanes often yields old-fashioned surprises, such as kerosene delivery by horse.

For light exercise, bat an *aeroglobo* (big, plastic, sausage-shaped balloon) around to your heart's content. Cool down with a stroll along the rows of **handicrafts and trinket stalls.** Bargain for good deals, especially in leather wallets, belts, purses, and $3 "silver diamond rings."

For restful, sit-down entertainment, take a seat inside the adjacent block-square, porticoed **El Parián** entertainment garden. Order your favorite *antojitos* (such as tamales, tacos, and enchiladas) and enjoy the evening mariachi and folkloric dance show (usually beginning around 9 P.M., earlier Sundays).

Reinvigorated and inspired by the dancers, try some gyrating on your own to the live or disco music at **El Pórtico** buffet-nightclub, at Independencia 50, a block and a half east of the *jardín.* Although El Pórtico is usually open until after midnight, call tel. 33/3659-3870 to confirm hours and programs.

Festivals

Tlaquepaque overflows with events and entertainment during the annual **Fería San Pedro Tlaquepaque,** for about two and a half weeks, beginning June 15. Concurrently with the Tlaquepaque National Ceramics Fair and the San Pedro *patronal* religious festival, the community puts out a stupendous creative effort, a two-week schedule of daily plays, films, concerts, recitals, art exhibits, poetry readings, and much more. All of this climaxes around the Parroquia San Pedro on the *jardín,* on the day of St. Peter and St. Paul, June 29. A few days later, the excitement peaks again, at the awarding of the national ceramics prizes at the Centro Cultural del Refugio. For more information and a complete schedule, pick up the June issue of *Refugiarte,* the Tlaquepaque city cultural magazine, at the Centro Cultural del Refugio office, at Donato Guerra 160, tel. 33/3635-1089, fax 33/3639-5205 (see Sights earlier).

SPORTS AND RECREATION

Tlaquepaque visitors are usually too busy strolling and shopping, and local people are too busy working, for much formal sports and recreation. Nevertheless, some opportunities do exist.

Gym, Swimming, Tennis, and Golf

America's Gym at 2492 Barragán, has exercise machines and provides aerobics classes for both day guests and members. Call tel. 33/3635-5820, or drop by (on the northwest side, across Barragán, from the end of Av. Florida) for details.

For **swimming,** best stay at either of the bed-and-breakfasts **Casa del Ensueño** or **Mesón Don José,** or the **Hotel Tapatío,** all three of which have pools large enough for lap swimming workouts. (For details, see the Accommodations section, earlier.)

Serious **tennis** enthusiasts stay at the Hotel Tapatío, with nine clay courts, four of which are night-lit. Additionally, the Atlas Country Club (see below) rents courts to the public.

(The hotel Villa del Ensueño does have a playable but cramped tennis court that is okay, at least for volleying. Bring your own racquets and balls, however.)

Greater Guadalajara has a number of excellent **golf courses.** Closest to Tlaquepaque is the **Atlas Country Club,** off the airport-Chapala highway (golf club entrance, northbound side of the freeway, by the big SCI electronics plant) 1.1 miles (1.8 kilometers) south of the *periférico,* tel. 33/3689-2620.

SHOPPING

Nearly all of Tlaquepaque's handicrafts shops lie along the east-west **Av. Independencia** pedestrian mall and the parallel bustling business street Av. Juárez, a block south. Although most Tlaquepaque shops do not manufacture what they sell, a few of them do, and invite visitors into their workshops. For more details, see Tlaquepaque Factory Shops, later in this chapter.

Shops Along Av. Independencia

Av. Independencia's four blocks from Av. Niños Héroes on the west to the *jardín* is arguably Guadalajara's most pleasantly relaxing shopping ground. A tranquil automobile-free ambience allows carefree strolling and unfettered handicrafts browsing opportunities.

Consequently, many (but not all) of the shops are decidedly upscale. Nevertheless, careful looking and sharp bargaining can yield prizes—furniture, jewelry, sculpture, ceramics, glassware, papier-mâché, leather—at a fraction of North American and European prices.

(A number of the more exclusive shops, claiming to have fixed prices, turn up their noses at bargaining. But bargaining is such a strong Mexican tradition that you might nevertheless achieve success by making them an offer they cannot refuse. At least ask them for a discount *(descuento)*. For bargaining tips, see How to Buy in the On the Road chapter shopping section.)

Start your shopping tour at **Ricardo Preciado Conceptos,** on the west side, at Independencia 281, midway between Av. Niños Héroes and Calle Alfareros, tel. 33/3639-4103, fax 33/3635-4469. Inside, you'll find an innovative array of art-for-furniture. One main theme is ironwork, from practical tables and chairs to whimsical motorcycles and animal sculptures, pieced together from discarded machine and electronics parts. Also find lots of innovatively rustic wood furniture, resembling something out of 7th-century Europe. Store hours are Mon.–Sat. 10 A.M.–8 P.M., Sun. noon–4 P.M. For more information, email: disenosycosarp@infosel.net.mx.

Half a block east, just before the intersection of Independencia and Alfareros (Potters), a pair of regally restored former mansions, now fine handicrafts galleries, enjoy a dignified retirement facing each other from opposite sides of the street. On the north side, **La Casa Canela,** Independencia 258, tel. 33/3657-1343, takes pride in its museum-quality religious art, furniture, paper flowers, pottery, blown glass, classic Tlaquepaque and Tonalá stoneware, and much more. Open Mon.–Fri. 10 A.M.–2 P.M. and 3–7 P.M., Sat. 10 A.M.–6 P.M., Sun. 11 A.M.–3 P.M.

Across the street, **Antigua de Mexico,** Independencia 255, tel. 33/3635-3402, specializes in new baroque-style gilt wood reproductions, being one of the few studios in Mexico to manufacture fine 17th century–style furniture. Open Mon.–Fri. 10 A.M.–2 P.M. and 3–7 P.M., Sat. 10 A.M.–6 P.M.

Cross Alfareros a few doors east to the **Sergio Bustamante** store, on Independencia's north side, an upscale outlet for the famous sculptor's arresting, whimsical studies in juxtaposition. Bustamante supervises an entire Guadalajara studio-factory of artists who put out hundreds of one-of-a-kind variations on a few human, animal, and vegetable themes. Prices seem to depend mainly on size; gold rings and silver bracelets may go for as little as $200, while a two-foot humanoid chicken may run $2,000. Don't miss the rest room. Open Mon.–Sat. 10 A.M.–7 P.M., Sun. 10 A.M.–2 P.M., tel. 33/3639-5519.

Half a block farther, leather is seemingly sacred at **San Piel** (Saint Leather), at Independencia 225A, tel. 33/3659-6582. Items, all made at the owner's Guadalajara factory, include supple jackets, stylish purses, luggage large and small, bags and briefcases, belts, and more. Combat the high asking prices by offering half the marked price. If you can't get what you want, try their sister store, half a block east, at Independencia 186C. Store hours are Mon.–Sat. 10 A.M.–7 P.M., Sun. 10:30 A.M.–5 P.M.

Right next door, earth tones set the mood at **Color y Tierra** (Color and Earth), at Independencia 225, tel./fax 33/3635-3505. Here, the exquisite rules, from pastel-hued lampshades to one-of-a-kind handwrought museum-quality cabinets and tables, of wood and rattan *(tule)*. The finest pieces run $2,000 and up; make offers or ask for a *descuento*. Find them open Mon.–Sat. 10:30 A.M.–7 P.M., Sun. 11 A.M.–5 P.M. For more information, email:colorytierra@terracota.com.mx.

Descend a few steps down the economic scale to **Bazar Barrera,** a few doors east, at Independencia 205, tel./fax 33/3635-1961, and pick from a huge selection of all-Mexico handicrafts. Whatever you've always wanted will probably be here: paper flowers, copperware, a bust of your favorite Mexican president, pewter, papier-mâché parrots, onyx eggs, nativity sets, tile country scenes, Talavera-style ceramics—and on and on. Hours are Mon.–Sat. 10 A.M.–7 P.M., Sun. 10 A.M.–2 P.M.; email: jave79@starmedia.com.

Continue east, across the street, and step into the airy, mid-scale **Adobe Designs,** chic warehouse, at Independencia 195, corner of Miranda, tel. 33/3639-8954, 33/3657-2405. Browse their eclectic, carefully selected array, including shiny rustic furniture, art-to-wear, designer candles-as-furniture, fine ironwork, and earth-toned lamps from all over Mexico and the world. Find them open Mon.–Fri. 10 A.M.–7 P.M., Sat. and Sun. 11 A.M.–7 P.M.; email: zanate72@yahoo.com. (Don't miss the exquisite **Restaurant El Adobe,** perfect for a mid-shopping lunch break; find it at the rear of the store. For details, see the Food section, earlier.)

Just next door, east, stand a pair of interesting small glassware-ceramics stores. First comes **Lamparas y Detalles,** at Independencia 181, tel. 33/3635-7415, outlet of Tiffany-style lamps, Talavera-style ceramics, paintings in baroque-style art, gilded picture frames, and much more.

Next door, enter **Arte en Vidrio** (Art in Glass), at Independencia 177, tel./fax 33/3635-1212; email: aartenvidrio@hotmail.com, for all the glass tableware—tumblers, pitchers, vases, and more—that you're ever likely to want. Both stores are open Mon.–Sat. 10 A.M.–7 P.M., Sun. 11 A.M.–3 P.M.

Guadalajara's king of baroque reproductions is **Agustín Parra,** at Independencia 154 and 158, on the north side of the street, near the corner of P. Sáchez. Open Mon.–Sat. 10 A.M.–7 P.M., Sun. 10 A.M.–4 P.M. Inside, find a treasury of new baroque-style art, including rococo-framed religious paintings and scroll-like gilded chairs and tables, all climaxing in a magnificent 15-foot $500,000 *retablo* (altarpiece) for your family chapel. (Delivery is extra.) Contact them at tel. 33/3657-8530, tel./fax 33/3657-0316; email: barroco@infosel.com.mx; website: agustinparra.com.mx.

Although not made locally, silver jewelry is well-represented at **Platería Taxco** at Independencia 148, northeast corner of P. Sánchez, tel./fax 33/3639-6894. Here you can have reasonably priced silver without having to travel all the way to the source. The source, the savvy Torres family, of Taxco, Guerrero, has come to Tlaquepaque instead.

Choose from their grand (Sterling .925 pure) array, which sells by weight, at the very reasonable rate of about $1.20 per gram. If they don't have exactly what you want they'll make it to order for you. (For hints, see Buying Silver and Gold Jewelry in the shopping section of the On the Road

chapter. Find them open Mon.–Sat. 10 A.M.–7:30 P.M., Sun. 11 A.M.–4 P.M.

For a treat, head south on Sánchez (which becomes Matamoros) half a block to the **Donaji** textiles shop, a little corner of Oaxaca in Tlaquepaque, at Matamoros 12. Open Mon.–Sat. noon–8 P.M., Sun. noon–4 P.M. Get your heart's desire of Oaxaca textiles, including fine wool *tapetes* (serape-rugs) from Teotitlán del Valle, fetching *huipiles* from San Pedro Amusgos, richly embroidered "wedding dresses" from San Antonio Castillo Velasco, intricate embroidery *(bordado)* from all over, blankets *(mantas),* baby clothes, and tablecloths *(manteles).*

A few doors farther south on Matamoros, don't miss the **Anne Kary** shop, detailed in Tlaquepaque Factory Shops, later in this chapter.

Shops Along Av. Juárez

Although none of the Av. Juárez shops are as spectacularly upscale as some of the shops on Independencia, many excellent handicrafts, at negotiable to very reasonable prices, can be the reward of concentrated effort here. Begin a few doors east of Av. Matamoros and work your way west.

For starters, try leather store **El Prieto de Azabache,** at 138 Juárez. Open Mon.–Sat. 10 A.M.–8 P.M., Sun. 10 A.M.–5 P.M.; tel. 33/3639-7997. They offer loads of fine leather jackets, coats, boots, purses, and women's sandals, at relatively high asking prices. If you find something you want, make offers or ask for a discount. For more information, fax 33/3639-5281 or email: lesterpiel@hotmail.mail.com.

Walk back west toward to the west corner of Matamoros to high-profile **Artesanías Mayra,** at 154 Juárez. Open Mon.–Sat. 10 A.M.–6 P.M., Sun. 10 A.M.–3 P.M.; tel./fax 33/3635-787. Accessories—brass and glass lamps and chandeliers, mirrors, pictures and picture frames—and leather *equipal* furniture are plentiful here.

Walk across to the south side of the street, to **El Portón,** at Juárez 159, an invitingly airy furniture warehouse. Open Mon.–Sat. 10:30 A.M.–7 P.M., Sun. 11 A.M.–3 P.M. Browse among their handsome offerings, including rustic desks, chairs, tables, beds, sideboards, stunning wool rugs from San Miguel de Allende, frames and framed pictures, and much more. For more information call tel. 33/3635-7665, fax 33/3657-9636; email: aldanaerica@yahoo.com.

A few doors west, check out the attractively quirky **Teté Ante Diseno,** at Juárez 173. Open Mon.–Sat. 10 A.M.–7:30 P.M.; tel. 33/3635-7341, 33/3635-7965. Walk past a huge, rusted iron cauldron, weathered stone statues, and a giant copper vat, to showrooms inside, filled with mostly new (but appealing) antique reproduction sideboards, dressers, china cabinets, and chandeliers. Some pieces, such as an astronomical armillary sphere, sundial, baroque cherubs, and madonnas with child, appear to be genuine antiques *(antiguidades).* But, if you're seriously interested, bring an antiques expert if you're not one yourself.

On the next corner, at Miranda, treat yourself to **Fábricas Mona's** big fabric shop, at Juárez 205. Open Mon.–Sat. 10 A.M.–6:30 P.M., Sun. 11 A.M.–3 P.M.; tel. 33/3635-6681, 33/3659-1715, fax 33/3659-3112. Wander through this wonderland of textiles, mostly hand-woven and hand-embroidered, from all over Mexico, with much from Oaxaca. You'll find shelf after shelf of tablecloths, napkins *(servilletas),* throw rugs *(tapetes),* serapes, vests, *huipiles,* skirts *(faldas),* shirts *(camisas),* blouses *(blusas),* pillowcases *(fundas),* curtains *(cortinas),* and a mini-warehouse of fabric by the roll. For more information, email: monas@prodigy.net.mx.

A few doors farther west, check out **Puerto Bonito,** at Juárez 223. Open Mon.–Sat. 10 A.M.–7 P.M., Sun. 11 A.M.–3 P.M.; tel. 33/3639-4110. Inside, find a treasury of baroque reproductions, from fine table settings from Tlaxcala and genuine Talavera pottery, to candelabras and chandeliers to gilded wooden angels and horses.

Tiffany glass fanciers will appreciate a pair of nearby shops. First find **Vitrales Albarran,** south side of Juárez, midway between Miranda and Alfareros. Open Mon.–Sat. 9 A.M.–7 P.M., Sun. 11 A.M.–3 P.M.; tel./fax 33/3635-7037. Although they do have some items on display, they specialize in fine lampshades and other stained-glass

pieces to order. For more information, email: vitralesalbarran@hotmail.com.

By contrast, **Tiffany,** across the street and half a block west, at Juárez 248, open Mon.–Sat. 10 A.M.–6 P.M., Sun. 11 A.M.–3 P.M., carries a lovely, extensive inventory and will also make to order. Pick from a whole ceiling of gorgeous chandeliers and lamps and shelves of glittering fine table lamps (the antiqued brass bases for which are imported from the United States). For more information, call tel./fax 33/3639-0464.

Tlaquepaque Factory Shops

The following describe the five Tlaquepaque factory shops that I visited, among the several that welcome visitors. For more possibilities, inquire at the Casa de los Artesanos, at 288 Morelos, between Cruz Verde and Medellín, a block north of Independencia, tel. 33/3657-3846, 33/3635-5756; email: artecal@hotmail.com. (Even more factories are open to visitors in Tonalá; see the Tonalá section, later in this chapter.)

Nacimientos (nativity figures) are the specialty of a number of Tlaquepaque home factories, notably that of José Cruz Reyes (shown).

Begin your factory tour on the west side and continue generally east. Start one block west of Niños Héroes, at the backyard ironwork shop of the father-son team of **Roman Gutierréz Muro and Baulio Gutierréz Pérez,** at Moctezuma 2657, half a block north of Independencia. Within their ramshackle but well-equipped compound, personable Roman and Baulio can fashion a remarkably clever and diverse range of ironwork, from scroll-like tables and chairs to ingenious animals and flowers. See their samples and their photo catalog.

Show them a sketch of what you want and they'll probably be able to make it readily, for a reasonable price. Call (in Spanish) 33/3659-0526, for an appointment.

One of Tlaquepaque's most renowned handicrafts producers is **Vidrios Soplados** (Blown Glass), in the north-central town quarter, at Medellín 179, between Florida and D. Guerra. Enter their small street-front store, decorated with clutches of lustrous glass *esferas* (glass spheres), tableware, vases, figurines, and much more. Continue to the fascinating workshop in the big rear yard, where workers bend, twist, blow, and mold white-hot globs of glass into gleaming works of art. They're open for non-appointment visitors Mon.–Fri. 7–10 A.M. and Sat. 11 A.M.–3 P.M.; tel./fax 33/3659-1790; email: earturperez@hotmail.com.

Return south four blocks to pewter *(peltre)* showroom and factory **Ann Kary,** at Matamoros 28, half a block south of Independencia. Traditional European pewter is made of tin, alloyed with other metals, such as nickel, but Ann Kary's ware, a vast collection of decorative metal bowls, plates, crucifixes, picture frames, and much more, is of aluminum. Ask to visit the shop in the rear, where workers put the finishing touches on the pieces. Find them open Mon.–Fri. 9 A.M.–6 P.M., Sat. 9 A.M.–5 P.M.; tel./fax 33/3659-7739, 33/3659-6292, website: www.annkary.com.

Candles are the theme at the small **Los Cirios** store-workshop, a block north of the *jardín,* at Madero 70. Continue through the Galería Ken Edwards up front, to the Los Cirios part of the store at the left rear. Here, you find a garden of candles, many huge, in innovative shapes—cones,

cubes, cylinders, and more—and in a rainbow of bright colors. Watch the fascinating ongoing work of creation in the workshop, adjacent to the displays. Open daily 10 A.M.–6:30 P.M.; tel. 33/3635-2426, fax 33/3635-5456, website: www.loscirios.com. (Don't miss the adjacent **Ken Edwards** stoneware store while you're there. Better still, if you have time, visit the Ken Edwards factory in Tonalá, details in the Tonalá section, later in this chapter.)

In the same neighborhood, three blocks farther east, find the homey (because it *is* a home) factory of kindly *maestro* **José Cruz Reyes,** at Allende 66. See his workers meticulously mold, fire, and decorate ceramic nativity figurines *(nacimientos),* most of which are sold in fetching for-sale miniature nativity sets. Call him (in Spanish), tel. 33/3458-4654, for an appointment, Mon–Sat. only.

SERVICES
Banks
At least three banks, all with ATMs, serve the Tlaquepaque town center. Most are along Hidalgo-Independencia, near the *jardín.* For longest banking hours, go to **Banco Internacional** (BITAL), corner of Hidalgo, just east of El Parián. Open Mon.–Sat. 8 A.M.–7 P.M. On the other side of the street, half a block west, at Hidalgo 88, you'll find popular **Banamex** open Mon.–Fri. 9 A.M.–5 P.M., Sat. 10 A.M.–1:30 P.M.; tel. 33/3636-1701. Another half block west, at Independencia 115A, corner of Progreso (across from El Parián) is **Bancrecer.** Open Mon.–Sat. 9 A.M.–5 P.M., Sat. 10 A.M.–2 P.M.; tel. 33/3635-3515.

COMMUNICATIONS AND INFORMATION
Post and Telecommunications
The Tlaquepaque **post office** *(correo)* and **telecom** are on Guillermo Prieto, the short street that runs north from the *jardín's* northwest corner. First find Telecom, on the left, west side of the street, at #29. Open Mon.–Fri. 8 A.M.–7 P.M., Sat. 9 A.M.–noon. Services provided are telephone, with public fax 33/3635-0980, money

orders, and Internet access $2/hr. Half a block farther north, find the *correo* at G. Prieto 88. Open Mon.–Fri. 8 A.M.–7 P.M., Sat. 9 A.M.–1 P.M.; tel 33/3635-0503.

Tourist Information and Library

The most accessible city **tourist information** source is at the booth *(módulo)*, open Mon.–Fri. 9 A.M.–3 P.M., Sat. and Sun. 10 A.M.–2 P.M., on Independencia, south side of the *jardín*. The official city tourism office, **Sub-dirección de Turismo y Artesanías,** is at Juárez 283, westside, between Alfareros and Niños Héroes; tel./fax 33/3635-1532, 33/3635-1554, 33/3635-1599; email: turismo@tlaquepaque.gob.mx, website: www.tlaquepaque.gob.mx.

Tlaquepaque's modest municipal **library** *(biblioteca)* is at the southeast corner of P. Sánchez and Constitución. Open Mon.–Fri. 8 A.M.–7:30 P.M.; tel. 33/3635-1089, 33/3639-4363. A highlight of its (nearly all Spanish) collection is the hard-to-get *Los Indios de Mexico* five-volume set, by Fernando Benítez, cat. 972.0098 B43. Get there by walking west from the *jardín* along Independencia one block to Sánchez, then right (north) two blocks to the corner of Constitución.

Guide, Transportation, Travel Agent, Shipping Service, and Photography

Well-informed, English-speaking, licensed **Lino Gabriel González Nuño** is available for local and greater Guadalajara tours. He would probably be very helpful in bargaining for the best prices. Contact him at Obregón 127, Tlaquepaque, Jalisco 45500; tel. 33/3195-6315 (cellular) and 33/3635-4049.

For safe, reliable transportation, hire **Oscar "Willy" Klauditz,** who offers his Chevrolet Suburban ($10 per hour, up to seven persons) for local and greater Guadalajara trips (such as the destinations in the Great Getaways chapter). Moreover, Willy, a German immigrant, is a Tonalá specialist, who can guide you to the right shops and factories to suit your shopping needs and help you get your purchases packed and sent. Contact him at his taxi site downtown, tel. 33/3683-2194, or message tel. 33/3615-3363, 33/3613-1228, or through bed-and-breakfast

hotel La Villa del Ensueño; see Accommodations, earlier. (Although highly experienced, Willy is a driver first and a guide second, while Lino, above, is primarily a guide. A good combination might be to bring Lino along as your guide and let Willy do the driving.)

(For more guide and tour suggestions, see By Locally Arranged Tour in the Getting Around section of the On the Road chapter.)

A number of **travel agents** have Tlaquepaque offices. For example, try **Framsaworld** travel, in the small shopping plaza de los Artesanías, at Juárez 145, just east of Matamoros. Open Mon.–Fri. 9 A.M.–2:30 P.M. and 3:30–7 P.M., Sat. and Sun. 11 A.M.–3 P.M. Here, get your car rental, and airline and bus tickets, including Greyhound, ETN and Estrella Blanca, and Tequila train tour tickets. For more information, email: framsaworld@telmex.net.mx., or dial tel. 33/3635-3314 or fax 33/3635-7983.

Tlaquepaque's town-center photo shop is the professionally owned and operated **Photo Studio Kolor Zuku,** at Independencia 136, half a block west of the *jardín*. Open Mon.–Sat. 10 A.M.–8 P.M., Sun. 10 A.M.–2 P.M.; tel./fax 33/3657-2048, 33/3859-4087. Services include one-hour color development, black-and-white development and printing, transparencies, camera repair, enlargements, and some for-sale film and equipment, including point-and-shoot and SLR cameras.

A number of local **shipping agencies** package and send your purchases safely home. A good example is **Sebastián Exports,** at Independencia 299A, west end, half a block before Niños Heroes; tel. /fax 33/3657-7282.

HEALTH, EMERGENCIES, AND GETTING THERE

Medicines and Doctors

Tlaquepaque residents enjoy the services of a number of pharmacies, a hospital with an emergency room, a medical specialty clinic, and individual doctor's offices. For routine remedies, consult the on-duty pharmacist at **Farmacia Benavides** at Independencia 70, right in the middle of the town; tel. 33/3635-2137.

For nonemergency medical consultations, **Hospital Providencia** doctors hold regular office hours Mon.–Sat. 10 A.M.–2 P.M. and 4–8 P.M. Find them at the hospital, at Niños Heroes 29, east side of street, between Juárez and Reforma, tel. 33/3639-5155 and 33/3637-8735.

Alternatively, try the **Clínica de Especialidades** specialty clinic, Dr. Roberto Rodríguez in charge. Available here are the on-call services of many specialists, at Juárez 199, corner of Miranda; tel. 33/3635-5842.

(For more Guadalajara doctor and hospital information and recommendations, see Guadalajara Doctors and Hospitals in the Staying Healthy section of the On the Road chapter.)

Police, Fire, and Medical Emergencies

For police and fire emergencies, call the Tlaquepaque police at 33/3635-2045 or 33/3635-8828. In a medical emergency, ask your hotel desk to get you a taxi or ambulance (Red Cross 33/3613-1550, 33/3614-5600) to the 24-hour emergency room at Tlaquepaque Hospital Providencia, or alternatively, to the **Hospital Méxicano-Americano** (20-minute drive in emergency) at north-side Av. Colomos 2110.

Getting There

Get to Tlaquepaque from downtown Guadalajara by taxi (about $8) or ride the oft-crowded city bus 275 diagonal (look for "Tlaquepaque" scrawled on the front window), from stops along downtown north-south Av. 16 de Septiembre. The bus continues southwest for about three miles (five kilometers) to the big **Puente Artesanal** Tlaquepaque entrance arch over Av. Barragán, just before the Av. Niños Héroes traffic circle. The Av. Independencia pedestrian shopping mall

is on the left (east) side, one block past (south of) the traffic circle.

By car, from the center of town, the key is to get to the entrance to Tlaquepaque from Guadalajara, marked by a soaring arch over the southeast end of Boulevard General Marcelino Garcia Barragán. Driving south along downtown Av. 16 de Septiembre, at Plaza San Francisco, turn left at Calz. Revolución, the street that runs just behind the San Francisco church. Mark your odometer.

Continue 1.1 miles (1.8 kilometers) to where you turn right at main thoroughfare Calz. del Ejército. After two short blocks, turn left at Barragán, and continue another 1.7 miles (2.8 kilometers) to the entrance arch. Park and walk straight ahead (careful crossing the Av. Niños Héroes traffic circle) about 100 yards to the Av. Independencia pedestrian mall.

(Although local buses or your own wheels can get you to Tlaquepaque, crowds of bus commuters and congested city streets increase the desirability of a **local guide or tour.** Contact your hotel travel desk, a travel agent, or a well-equipped agency such as Panoramex, at Federalismo Sur 944, tel. 33/3810-5057 or 33/3810-5005; or Gray Line, at Calz. del Ejército 1336, tel. 33/3619-1347, fax 33/3619-1348, which conduct reasonably priced bilingual tours daily from the city center. For individual **guide** recommendations, see the Guide, Transportation, Travel Agent, Shipping Service, and Photography section, earlier.

If you're going to be doing lots of independent or car traveling around Guadalajara, best get a copy of the very reliable *Guia Roji Red Vial Ciudad de Guadalajara* city street map. It's available at Sanborn's gift shop–restaurants. For locations, see the previous two destination chapter Food sections.

Tonalá

About five miles farther southeast past Tlaquepaque, Tonalá reigns over its sprawling *municipio* (pop. 350,000) of towns, factories, farms, and ranches. When the Spanish arrived in 1530, Tonalá was dominant among the small chiefdoms of the Atemajac Valley. Tonalá's queen and her royal court were adorned by the glittering handiwork of an honored class of silver and gold crafters. Although the Spaniards carted off the valuables, the dominance of Tonalá craftsmanship remains today. Most handicrafts sold in Tlaquepaque are actually made in Tonalá.

To the visitor, nearly everyone in Tonalá seems to be making something. Tonalá family patios are piled with their specialties, whether it be pottery, stoneware, brass, or papier-mâché.

Besides the daily host of visitors shopping for souvenirs, gifts, and home decorations, a resolute platoon of professional buyers frequent Tonalá's multitude of small handicrafts factories, negotiating for wholesale lots of merchandise for shipment all over Mexico and the rest of world.

SIGHTS
Getting Oriented

Tonalá's easy-to-follow street grid and small size makes it simple to explore. The center of town is the **Plaza Principal,** at the intersection of east-west **Calle Benito Juárez** and north-south **Calle Francisco Madero** (which becomes Calle Hidalgo north of Juárez).

Stand (or imagine standing) at the corner of Juárez and Madero and face north. Straight ahead is Calle Hidalgo, usually decorated with the *tianguis* (awnings) of handicrafts sellers. To the right (east) is the Plaza Principal and central **kiosco** (bandstand). In the building farther to the right, bordering the plaza, is the town **market.**

Across Juárez, on your left, rises the white, spired facade of the venerable **Santuario del Sagrado Corazón de Jesús.** Half a block farther north, on the left side of Hidalgo, stands the dignified, colonnaded **Palacio Municipal** town hall.

A Walk Around Tonalá

Start at the **Santuario del Sagrado Corazón de Jesús,** an 1899 reconstruction of an earlier church. Inside, dramatic paintings of all the stations of the cross decorate the nave walls. Up front, a lovely modern *retablo* rises behind the altar, with an image of Jesus on a throne of billowing clouds, draped in a cape of gold. Above him, his words, *"Venid todos a mi"* ("All come to me") summon the faithful. Finally, before you leave, pay your respects to the Virgen de la Misericordia (Virgin of the Merciful) in the chapel to the right of the nave.

Let Tonalá's **Palacio Municipal** be your next stop. A number of notable art works decorate its interior corridors. (The tourism office is inside, open Mon.–Fri. 9 A.M.–3 P.M.) Call for an appointment, tel. 33/3683-0047, 33/3683-0048,

In Tonalá's central plaza, an athletic Queen Cihualpilli dramatically wields a long lance.

THE CONQUEST OF TONALLAN

The arrival of the Spanish, in the person of Nuño de Guzmán and his small army, on March 25, 1530, changed Tonallan forever. Tonallan Queen Cihualpilli, after consultation with her ruling council, decided to receive the Spaniards on friendly terms. Nevertheless, a rebellious group of her subjects attacked Guzmán's forces, who retaliated, forcing Cihualpilli, her court, and bodyguards to retreat to their fortified hilltop, north of town, now named *Cerro de la Reina* (Queen's Hill), but in those days called "Bellybutton Hill" because of its shape.

After a fierce siege, Spanish steel and cannon finally slashed a bloody path to the hilltop, and Guzmán's forces captured Cihualpilli. She and her people, however, remained unrepentant.

Tonalá's official history recounts, that, at a mass gathering, Cihuallpili's subjects angrily screamed at the Spanish conquistadors: "To arms! To arms! Enemy! Betrayer!" Guzmán, exasperated, grabbed the captive Cihualpilli by the hand and withdrew his sword, declaring, "Here you will die, woman." With innocence and heroism she answered, "You are a warrior and should not hesitate, since I am only a woman, with no fear, standing by your side."

Spaniards who later narrated the conquest of Tonallan wrote that theTonallan people were "faithful as lambs in peace, and ferocious as lions in war."

While the passage of time has softened the memory of their battle against Spanish arms, storytellers have mythologized the war to a struggle between an apparition of Santiago (Apostle St. James) as a warrior upholding the Spanish (and therefore God's) cause against the idolaters. Still, today the sick and lame make the most of the myth, begging alms in the name of Santiago.

Local folks breathe new life into the legend every July 25, Santiago's feast day, in Tonalá's traditional dance, *La Danza de Los Tastoanes.* Excitement peaks as ferociously masqueraded participants reenact the part of the indigenous defenders (Los Tastoanes), evading the sword swipes of a horseback-mounted Santiago.

33/3683-0049, ext. 221, and they may offer to take you on a tour of at least the interior of the Palacio Municipal, if not of the entire town.

To the left after you enter, at the right foot of the stairway, admire the large *bruñido*-technique ceramic tile plaque, commemorating the arrival of the Spanish, on March 25, 1530. The plaque's lower portion illustrates the **Cerro de la Reina** (see below) and the **sun god, Tonatiu.**

Climb the stairs, passing the rogue's gallery of grotesque, but authentic, masks on the left, before the upper floor landing. See the shiny copper floor doors, emblazoned with the sun god, in the upstairs balcony corridor.

Back downstairs, continue straight ahead from the foot of the stairs, just past the patio corner, on the right, and admire another *bruñido* plaque, by noted ceramist Jorge Wilmot, of a copy of the ancient Aztec document **Lienzo de Tlaxcala.**

Outside, cross Hidalgo east and enter the Plaza Principal. To the right of the Porfirian-era 1890 bandstand, stands a dramatically Olympian bronze of Cihualpilli, Tonalá's legendary queen, hurling a spear as if it were a javelin. (The statue depicts a Tarzanesque woman of about age 20, while Cihualpilli was a widow of about 40 at the time of her people's battle with *conquistador* Nuño de Guzmán in 1530.)

Continue east half a block along the plaza's south side, to the landmark parish church and ex-convent **Parroquia de Santiago.** The present building, started by the Augustinian friars around 1625, was their home until 1799, when the local "secular" (as opposed to monastic) clergy replaced them and finished rebuilding the original church in 1813.

The interior is replete with religious symbolism. Moving clockwise around the nave, first find a painted stucco image of Santiago (St. James), looking like Jesus, with sword in hand, mounted atop his traditional white horse. Next to him, San Rafael, following Jesus' charge to become "a fisher of men" sits with a fish in his left hand. Above

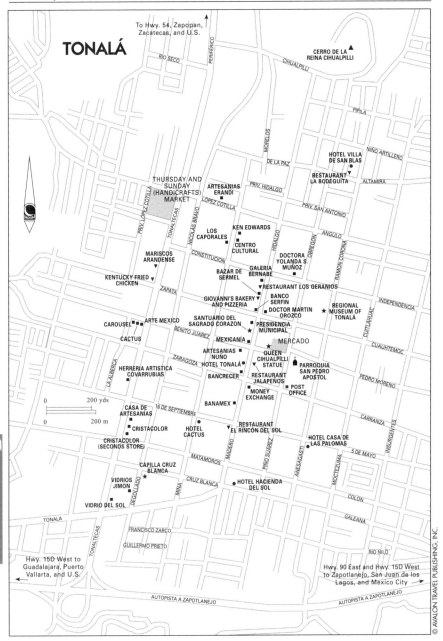

TONALÁ

To Hwy. 54, Zapopan, Zacatecas, and U.S.

PERIFÉRICO

RIO SECO

CIHUALPILLI

CERRO DE LA
REINA CIHUALPILLI

PIPILA

MORELOS

DE LA PAZ

NIÑO ARTILLERO

HOTEL VILLA
DE SAN BLAS

RESTAURANT
LA BODEGUITA

ALTAMIRA

THURSDAY AND
SUNDAY
(HANDICRAFTS)
MARKET

ARTESANIAS
ERANDI

PRIV. HIDALGO

LOPEZ COTILLA

PRIV. LOPEZ COTILLA

TONALTECAS

NICOLAS BRAVO

PRIV. SAN ANTONIO

LOS
CAPORALES

KEN EDWARDS

CENTRO
CULTURAL

HIDALGO

OBREGON

ANGULO

RAMON CORONA

CONSTITUCION

DOCTORA
YOLANDA S.
MUÑOZ

MARISCOS
ARANDENSE

BAZAR DE
SERMEL

GALERIA
BERNABÉ

RESTAURANT LOS GERANIOS

KENTUCKY FRIED
CHICKEN

ZAPATA

GIOVANNI'S BAKERY
AND PIZZERIA

BANCO
SERFIN

INDEPENDENCIA

DOCTOR MARTIN
OROZCO

REGIONAL
MUSEUM OF
TONALÁ

CUITLAHUAC

CAROUSEL

ARTE MEXICO

SANTUARIO DEL
SAGRADO CORAZON

CACTUS

BENITO JUAREZ

PRESIDENCIA
MUNICIPAL

MEXICANÍA

MERCADO

CUAUHTEMOC

LA ALBERCA

HERRERIA ARTISTICA
COVARRUBIAS

ARTESANIAS
NUÑO

ZARAGOZA

HOTEL TONALÁ

QUEEN
CHIHUALPILLI
STATUE

PARROQUIA
SAN PEDRO
APOSTOL

PEDRO MORENO

BANCRECER

RESTAURANT
JALAPEÑOS

MONEY
EXCHANGE

POST
OFFICE

BANAMEX

0   200 yds

0   200 m

18 DE SEPTIEMBRE

CASA DE
ARTESANIAS

CRISTACOLOR

HOTEL
CACTUS

RESTAURANT
EL RINCON DEL SOL

CARRANZA

INSURGENTES

HOTEL CASA DE
LAS PALOMAS

CRISTACOLOR
(SECONDS STORE)

MATAMOROS

MADERO

PINO SUAREZ

ANESAGASTI

MOCTEZUMA

5 DE MAYO

CAPILLA CRUZ
BLANCA

VIDRIOS
JIMON

CRUZ BLANCA

HOTEL HACIENDA
DEL SOL

DEGOLLADO

MINA

COLON

VIDRIO DEL SOL

GALEANA

TONALA

TONALTECAS

FRANCISCO ZARCO

GUILLERMO PRIETO

RIO NILO

Hwy. 15D West to
Guadalajara, Puerto
Vallarta, and U.S.

Hwy. 90 East and Hwy. 15D West
to Zapotlanejo, San Juan de los
Lagos, and Mexico City

AUTOPISTA A ZAPOTLANEJO

AUTOPISTA A ZAPOTLANEJO

© BRUCE WHIPPERMAN

Many Guadalajara restaurants have in-house musicians.

the altar is the Sacred Heart of Jesus, and below that, elevated just a step above the nave floor, is the original 1630 *cantera* stone baptismal fount.

On the *retablo* behind the altar stand replicas of the Virgin of San Juan de los Lagos, on the left, and the Virgin of Talpa on the right. (See the special topic Three Sisters of Mexico.) Finally, step through the nave's right-hand side door (with keystone dated 1744) and take a turn around the cloister of the Augustinian ex-convent.

Sights North of the Plaza Principal

Make the **Museo Regional Tonallan** your first north-side stop, at Ramón Corona 170, near the corner of Constitución, one block east and two blocks north of the Santiago parish church. Appropriately housed in a rustic old-Tonalá adobe, the museum's mission is to interpret the history and demonstrate the practice of Tonalá crafts. Artisans exhibit their technique, displays illustrate historical events, masters exhibit their finished work, and local people stage drama and productions on a stage beneath the traditional sun symbol of Tonalá. Find it open Mon.–Fri. 10 A.M.–5 P.M.

Next, walk a fraction of a block north and turn left, west, at Independencia and continue three blocks to the **Museo Regional de la Cerámica,** north side of Independencia, between Hidalgo and Morelos. Ten exhibition rooms on two floors exhibit super-fine examples of ceramics from all over Mexico. After feasting your eyes on the many luscious examples, from Oaxaca's lustrous San Bartolo blacks and brilliant Atzompa reds to Michocán's rich Uruapan green and Tonalá's gorgeous *petalillo,* pick out your favorites for sale in their shop. Open Tues.–Fri. 10 A.M.–5 P.M., Sat. 10 A.M.–3 P.M., Sun. 10 A.M.–2 P.M.

Finally, make a pilgrimage (six blocks north along Hidalgo) to the **Cerro de la Reina** (Queen's Hill), originally known as "Cerro del Ombligio" ("Bellybutton Hill"). Stroll to the summit and enjoy the airy panorama of the surrounding Valle de Atemajac.

This hilltop was the setting for the final bloody battle between the Spaniards and Queen Cihualpilli and her people in 1530. Nearby, a statue depicts the queen embracing the True Cross. Other statues dramatize the Queen's fierce, spear-brandishing guardian warriors. If it's open, take a

CITY: EAST AND SOUTH

TAKING PEOPLES' PICTURES

Like most folks everywhere, typical Guadalajara people on the street rarely appreciate strangers taking their pictures. The easiest route to overcoming this is a local friend, guide, or even a willing interpreter-bystander who can provide an introduction. Lacking that, you'll need to be at least semifluent in Spanish in order to introduce yourself or say something funny to break the ice.

A sometimes useful way to go is to offer to send them a copy of their picture. If they accept, make sure that you follow through. If somehow the picture doesn't come out, at least send them a picture of you, explaining why.

Although it's becoming less common, some people still believe that they might lose their soul if they let you take their picture. In such a case, humor again might help (or perhaps offering to let them take a picture of you first).

Markets are wonderful picture-taking places but pose challenges. Vendors are often resistant, to the point of hostility, if you try to take their picture behind their sumptuous pile of tomatoes or stack of baskets. The reasons aren't hard to understand. They're grumpy partly because sales are probably disappointing, and, since they have to stay put, they probably feel used. Buying something from them might go a long way toward soothing their feelings.

Under all circumstances, please do not offer to pay people for the privilege of taking a person's picture. It will be a shame if you do, because they're going to be thinking money whenever they see tourists. Much better, turn the photo session into a person-to-person exchange by offering to send them a copy of their picture.

As for church picture-taking, remember churches are places of worship and not museums. Don't be rude and try to take pictures of people at the altar. Moreover, churches are usually dark inside, and, unless you have a flash-suppress option or unusually high speed film, your flash will disturb worshippers.

A Tonalá artisan turns mute clay into gorgeous handicrafts.

look around inside the hilltop chapel, built in honor of the Virgin of Guadalupe, of locally quarried volcanic stone.

Although ordinarily quiet, this hilltop bustles with activity on Holy Saturday, the day before Easter Sunday. As part of the combined National Handicrafts Fair and the Tonalá Festival of the Sun, dancers reenact the battle, in the *Dance of the Tastoanes* and pilgrims trace the stations of the cross. (See Entertainment and Events, later in this chapter.)

Later, if you have time during your Tonalá shopping tour, visit the **Capilla de la Cruz Blanca** (Chapel of the White Cross), the spot where the Spaniards celebrated Guadalajara's first mass, on March 25, 1530. Find it at the corner of Calles Cruz Blanco and Degollado, four blocks south and two blocks east of the main town plaza.

ACCOMMODATIONS
Hotels
Tonalá's several recommendable hotels, although fine for the general traveler, were initially built to accommodate the platoons of professional buyers that visit Tonalá year-round. Make advance reservations, especially for the Saturday and Wednesday nights before the big Sunday and Thursday outdoor *tianguis* markets.

By location, starting at the south end and moving north, first find the especially business-friendly **Hotel Hacienda del Sol,** whose savvy owner is trying harder to make it *the* Tonalá destination of choice. When I arrived, the job was mostly complete, with a spacious courtyard leading upstairs to about 30 new, clean, comfortable rooms, furnished with either one king-size or two single or two double beds and attractively tiled, modern-standard bathrooms with shower. Extras include handcrafted furniture, designer bed lamps, rustic wall art, fax and Internet access, free transportation to and from Guadalajara Expo, and a truck to move merchandise. Rates run about $35 s or d, $40 t, and $45 q, with fans, telephone, cable TV, and credit cards accepted. By the time you arrive, the owner says, he will have a pool, exercise gym, and a sauna. For more information and reservations, email: hdelsol@tonala.org or visit the website: www.tonala.gob.mx/hdelsol.

Two blocks east and two blocks north, the **Hotel Casa de las Palomas,** at Anesagasti 125, Tonalá, Jalisco 45400, corner of Cinco de Mayo, tel./fax 33/3683-5542, and 33/3683-5542, also caters to business clientele. Past the small front lobby area, the hotel's two upper floors of 22 rooms overlook an inner parking courtyard.

Little has been spared to make the rooms attractive and comfortable, including creamy pastel bedspreads, rustic-chic tile floors, designer reading lamps, and modern standard bathrooms. The hotel's only apparent drawback is the noise and exhaust from the cars in the parking courtyard. Alleviate this problem by getting a third-floor room. Expect to pay about $30 s, $35 d, with satellite TV, fans, and parking.

Three blocks due west and a step downscale, the **Hotel Cactus,** near the corner of 16 de Septiembre, may interest budget-conscious travelers. Owned by the blown-glass artisan-owners of nearby Tienda Cactus, the hotel's two stories of 25 rooms line opposite sides of a dim interior corridor. Rooms, plain but clean and acceptable for a night or two, rent for about $22 s, $28 d, $33 t, with shaded reading lamps, cable TV, fans, and parking. Javier Mina 153, Tonalá, Jalisco 45400; tel. 33/3683-2176, 33/3683-2914.

Still basic but cheerier than the Cactus is longtime **Hotel Galería Tonalá,** with its entry doubling as a cut-rate art gallery, just half a block south of the main plaza. The 22 plain but clean rooms run about $22 s or d with a double bed, or $27 d with two beds, with fans, TV, and hot water bath. Madero 22, Tonalá, Jalisco 45400; tel./fax 33/3683-0595.

Tonalá's most picturesque lodging, the **Hotel Villas Don Blas,** is tucked on a quiet, north-end lane. A labor of love for its on-site owners Rafael Ángel and his American wife Diana Romo, Villas Don Blas is named in honor of Rafael's late father.

After several years of building, Rafael's monument has blossomed. He's a stonemason and

The making of the high-fired pottery *Petalillo* is a tradition carried on by a few long-time Tonalá families. The pottery is laboriously hand-painted before the second and final firing.

it shows. The easily worked local volcanic stone, called *cantera,* decorates the facade in a feast of Renaissance columns, arches, window sills, and downspouts.

The elegantly quirky decorations extend to the rooms. The most attractive are upstairs, above a pair of garden corridor-patios. Most rooms are spacious, with at least two double beds, reading lamps, and rustic handmade wooden furniture. Baths, with sinks (some of which are mounted on classic stone pedestals of Rafael's design) are uniquely attractive. Rates run from $22 s or d, $27 with kitchenette, to $55 for the most roomy upstairs suite. Cerrada Altamira 10, Tonalá, Jalisco 45400; tel./fax 33/3683-2588; email: villas donblas@tonala.org; website: www.tonala.gob .mx/donblas/index.htm.

(Get there, from the main plaza, corner of Juárez, by walking north along Hidalgo five blocks; turn right at de la Paz and continue three short blocks and turn left at uphill lane Cerrada Altamira and continue half a block to the hotel on the right.)

FOOD

Breakfast, Bakery, Snacks, and Market *Fondas*

One of Tonalá's best spots for breakfast and baked offerings is the combined **Giovanni's Bakery and Pizzeria,** side-by-side, at 61A-61B Hidalgo, tel. 33/3683-0303, half a block north of the Palacio Municipal. Start in the morning with breakfast at the pizzeria, with favorites such as eggs *al gusto,* pancakes, French toast, and much more. For lunch and supper, enjoy sandwiches (hamburger, tuna, cheese), spaghettis, raviolis, and many pizzas, including a vegetarian option. The pizzeria is open daily 8 A.M.–10 P.M.

For dessert, cross over to the bakery side and select from their mounds of scrumptious cookies, cakes, muffins, tarts, and more. (Bakery open daily 7 A.M.–9 P.M.) For other breakfast options, go to Restaurant El Rincón del Sol or Restaurant Bodeguita—see Restaurants, below.

Take a comforting food retreat from Mexico at the **Kentucky Fried Chicken,** on west-side thoroughfare Av. Tonaltecas, corner of Emiliano Zapata (three blocks west of the main plaza). You won't be able to miss it, on Av. Tonaltecas, site of the grand Thursday and Sunday open-air handicrafts market.

On the other hand, dive into Mexico by savoring the steaming offerings of the **fondas** (permanent food stalls) in the market, on the main plaza, just east of the bandstand. Inside, select from many choices, from flavorful *pozoles* (hominy and pork or chicken soup) and *guisados* and *birrias* (beef, lamb, and goat stews), to rich *chiles rellenos,* quesadillas, tamales, *moles,* and loads more. Remember: Hot (preferably steaming) food is invariably safe. As a precaution, best drench uncooked vegetable salads in plenty of *limón* (lime) juice.

Restaurants

A sprinkling of recommended Mexican country-style restaurants provide relaxing respites for visitors after hard mornings or afternoons selecting from Tonalá's seemingly endless displays of pottery, *petalillo,* and papier-mâché.

Moving across town from south to north, first check out **Restaurant El Rincón del Sol** at 16 de Septiembre 61, southwest corner of Madero, two blocks south of the main plaza, tel. 33/3683-1989. In a relaxing hacienda-style patio setting, kick back and savor Tonalá food at its most typical, along with live troubadour music Thur.–Sun. 3–6 P.M. House specialties include a number of styles of beef fillets, fondue with *chorizo* sausage, quesadillas with *cuitlacoche* (cooked black corn mushroom), cream of carrot soup, and salad (green or chef). Afterwards, continue to their long list of cocktails, wines, tequilas, brandies, and rums; open daily 8:30 A.M.–8 P.M. Credit cards accepted. Moderate.

One block north, at Madero 23, step inside shoppers' standby, **Restaurant Jalapeños,** open daily 10 A.M.–8 P.M.; tel. 33/3683-0344, a block south of the main plaza. Unfortunately, lack of fans (check to see if they've installed some) may make this place uncomfortably warm on a hot, or even warm, day. Otherwise, pick from their long menu of *típica* Mexican specialties, heavy on beef, light on salads and chicken. For a simple

meal, go for their tortilla soup, followed by tuna salad *(ensalada de atùn).* On the other hand, for something more typical, try their hearty *platón tonalteca,* a big plate of quesadillas, fish tacos, guacamole, chips, and refried beans. Credit cards accepted. Moderate.

By contrast, **Restaurant Los Geranios,** at Hidalgo 69, half a block north of the plaza, offers a short menu and a cool, refined atmosphere. Operated by the artisan-proprietors of Bazar Sermel next door, Los Geranios specializes in light, innovative, Mexican-style lunch and early supper specialties, daily except Sat. 11 A.M.–5 P.M. For example, start with onion soup or green salad, continue with a plate of enchiladas or maybe chicken *en mole,* and finish with *flan* custard for dessert. Credit cards accepted; tel. 33/3383-0486. Moderate.

Large seafood **Restaurant Arandense,** three blocks west, at Tonaltecas 69 (between Independencia and Zapata), is a locally popular spot to relax for lunch, especially during the Thursday and Sunday open markets. Airy, family atmosphere, strolling mariachis, and good fresh seafood—oysters, clams, octopus, shrimp, and fish: whole, filleted, and stuffed—and *típica* favorites, such as *arrachera* (marinated grilled beef strips) keep the customers streaming in. Open daily 11 A.M.–6 P.M.; tel. 33/3683-5349. Moderate.

Several blocks farther north and east, **Restaurant Bodeguita,** at the Hotel Villa de San Blas (see Hotels earlier), offers a varied menu, home-cooked in the kitchen of friendly American co-owner Diana Romo. Most of the year (July–February, Tues.–Sat. 8 A.M.–10 P.M.), Diana serves American breakfasts to order, and lunches and suppers, including international and Mexican favorites. These include hamburgers, french fries, bacon and tomato sandwiches, fish tacos, enchiladas, and *arrachera* (marinated grilled beef strips). The remainder of the year (March–June, Tues.–Sat. 3–10 P.M.), Diana serves late lunch and supper only. Sometimes she and her also personable husband, Rafael, bring in a jazz combo for evening entertainment. Call ahead, tel. 33/3683-2588. Credit cards accepted. Moderate.

Diana and Rafael recommend two other

restaurants that I didn't have time to check out: **Restaurant El Amigo,** at Av. Tonalteca 135, three blocks west and three blocks north of the main plaza, and **Restaurant El Trópico de Tonalá,** at Madero 15, just a few doors south of the main plaza.

ENTERTAINMENT AND EVENTS
Festivals
Tonalá's hardworking people take time out to whoop it up during three big local yearly festivals. For more information and event schedules, watch for street posters and contact Tonalá's **Turismo.** (See Communications and Information, later in this chapter.)

The Tonalá year heats up early, with the Mardi Gras–like **Carnaval,** which climaxes on Shrove Tuesday (six weeks and five days before Easter Sunday and the day before Ash Wednesday). Besides plenty of music, street dancing, floats, and carnival rides and games, dancers delight the crowd as they poke fun at the former Spanish colonials in the **Los Viejitos** (Little Old Ones) traditional dance.

Tonalá's year climaxes again in the joint municipal **Fiesta del Sol** (Festival of the Sun) and the **National Handicrafts Fair** (Fería Nacional Artesanal), during the two weeks preceding Easter Sunday. The town overflows with events, including a daily handicrafts street market, expositions of Jalisco and national handicrafts, all-Jalisco handicrafts competitions, demonstrations of technique by master craftspersons, float parade, bands, literary and artistic performances, sports events, carnival games, fireworks, cockfights, and finally, a pilgrimage of the stations of the cross on the Saturday before Easter Sunday.

Tonalá's other big annual blowout, the **Fiesta de Santiago** (St. James), sometimes known as the **Fiesta Pagana** or Pagan Festival, peaks on July 25, with the not-to-be-missed ***Dance of the Tastoanes.*** In Tonalá's unique reenactment of the Conquest, a mounted Santiago swings his sword against a troupe of fearsomely masked "Tastoanes," indigenous warriors. The local crowd of onlookers, whipped to excitement by drum-beats and the staccato rhythm of indigenous flutelike *chirimias,* roars with delight as the defending Tastoanes fiercely persist, beneath Santiago's punishing charges and blows.

SPORTS AND RECREATION
Walking and Jogging
Tonalás quiet back streets (away from the crowded main plaza area) are excellent for walking. For example, start at the southeast-side corner of Anesagasti and Matamoros, and walk north gradually uphill, a total of one mile (1.6 kilometer) to the top of the 200-foot (60-meter) **Cerro de la Reina.** Return for a total of two miles and repeat for a total of four miles.

If that's not enough, **jog** some laps around the Cerro de la Reina's breezy summit park. Each full circuit will amount to approximately a quarter mile.

Gyms, Swimming, Tennis, and Golf
Tonalá has no nearby gyms or swimming pools. However, check with the Hotel Hacienda del Sol (see Hotels, earlier), whose owner may very well have fulfilled his assurance that he'd soon install a pool and an exercise gym.

Moreover, Tonalá has neither golf course nor tennis courts. For good options elsewhere, see Gyms, Swimming, Tennis, and Golf in the Tlaquepaque section of this chapter, earlier.

SHOPPING
Right at the source, Tonalá is an unexcelled shopping ground. For super bargains and *mucho* holiday excitement and color, visit the **Thursday and Sunday** *tianguis* (market), which spreads over half the town, from the west-side Av. Tonaltecas four blocks east, past the Tonalá main plaza.

During any day of the week, a small mountain of attractive handicrafts are available in the dozens of shops that dot the blocks around Tonalá's central plaza corner of north-south Av. Hidalgo-Madero and east-west Av. Juárez.

Below are a pair of contiguous shopping tours that can be done singly or continuously. The shortest requires a couple of hours around the plaza. It continues for an approximately four-hour loop that takes in several of the renowned factory stores that welcome visitors.

Near the Plaza

Many interesting handicrafts shops dot **Av. Francisco Madero,** from a couple blocks south of the main plaza, to a couple of blocks north (where Av. Madero has become Av. Hidalgo.) As you browse the shops, wandering gradually north, there are some shops that you should be sure to visit.

One of these is **Carousel,** at Madero 88, west side of the street. Open Mon.–Sat. 9 A.M.–6 P.M., Sun. 9 A.M.–3 P.M. Here owners specialize in the rustic but decorative, such as merry-go-round horses, quixotic Don Quijotes, and bright chandeliers.

Continue north half a block to **La Antigua Tonalá,** at Madero 50, tel. 33/3683-0200, about a block south of the Plaza, westside of the street. Here, you'll find a store full of hand-hewn tables, chairs, and chests, with a number of Tonalá

© BRUCE WHIPPERMAN

Elderly Tonalá vendors prepare to call it a day.

stoneware place settings to go with them. Open Mon.–Sat. 10 A.M.–7 P.M., Sun. 10 A.M.–3 P.M.; they ship.

Moving north, turn the corner of Juárez west a few steps to **Artisanías Nuño,** Juárez 59, tel. 33/3683-0011. Here, pick from a fetching menagerie, including parrots, monkeys, flamingos, and toucans, in papier-mâché, brass, and ceramics. Open Mon.–Sat. 10 A.M.–7 P.M., Sun. 10 A.M.–5 P.M.; bargain for very reasonable buys.

Continue another few doors and across the street, to **La Flor de Yahuac** paper flower store, at Juárez 80. Open Mon.–Sat. 10 A.M.–7 P.M., Sun. 10 A.M.–5 P.M.; tel. 33/3683-0017. Inside, select your hearts content from the festoons of realistically lovely lilies, sunflowers, roses, and more.

Walk back to the plaza corner, to **La Mexicanía,** at Hidalgo 13, tel. 33/3683-0152, north corner of Juárez. In the 10 years that I've been coming to Tonalá, La Mexicanía has prospered and expanded, by virtue of its diverse, all-Mexico collection. This is heaven for Mexico handicrafts lovers. If you've wanted a particular item—a weaving or a *huipil* from Oaxaca, a jaguar mask from Guerrero, a guitar from Michoacán, an ironwood sailfish from Sonora, a Huichol indigenous yarn painting, or a Guanajuato papier-mâché clown, they've got it. Open Mon.–Sat. 10 A.M.–7 P.M.

A block and half farther north, don't miss **El Bazar de Sermel,** at Hidalgo 67, tel. 33/3683-0010. Here, master craftspersons have stretched the Tonalá papier-mâché tradition to the ultimate. Stop in and pick out the life-size flamingo, pony, giraffe, or zebra you've always wanted for your living room. Open Mon.–Fri. 9 A.M.–6:30 P.M., Sat. 9 A.M.–2 P.M., Sun. 10 A.M.–3 P.M.

Continue a few doors north to **Galería Bernabe** factory store, at Hidalgo 83. Open Mon.–Fri. 10 A.M.–6 P.M., Sat. and Sun. 10 A.M.–3 P.M.; tel. 33/3683-0040, tel./fax 33/3683-0877. Celebrated founders of the 200-year *petalillo* (little petal) double-fired technique, Bernabe specializes in intricate, fetching animal and plant designs in black, green, and white. Some of the best pieces are reminiscent of fine ancient Chinese ceramics. Offerings vary, from glistening vases, pitchers, and bowls, to gorgeous table settings for a dozen or more. If you can't find exactly what you want, they'll create your own design to order.

Tour of Factory Stores

With your handicrafts appetite whetted by the excellent **Galería Bernabe,** above, continue (north half a block, turn left at Cotilla, then right at Morelos) to **Los Caporales** big factory store, at Morelos 155B. Los Caporales specializes in glistening, high-fired *corcho*-technique ware, from decorative animal figurines to utilitarian plates, bowls, and vases. Past the rear of the showroom, tour the factory, where workers begin with humble clay that they mix, mold, smooth, paint, glaze, and finally fire into handsome works of art. Open Mon.–Fri. 9 A.M.–6 P.M., Sat. 10 A.M.–2 P.M. For more information, email: caporales@info sel.net.mx and/or visit the website: www .ceramica-caporales.com.mx.

Continue north, across the street to **Ken Edwards** store and factory, at Morelos 184. Founder Ken Edwards, elaborating on the intricate high-fired *petalillo* stoneware, gained international renown during the 1970s and 1980s. He turned his operation over to present owner Pedro Velasco and moved to Guatemala. But his tradition lives on, in the irresistible heirloom animal and floral design table settings that the factory produces. Open Mon.–Fri. 8:30 A.M.–4 P.M., Sat. 8 A.M.–1 P.M.; tel. 33/3683-0313, fax 33/3683-0716. For more information, email: kenedwards@infosel.com.mx; website: kenedwards.com.mx.

No Tonalá factory tour would be complete without a visit to **Artesanías Erandi** (half a block north, turn left on Cotilla), at López Cotilla 118. Here, you're at the source of the much-imitated high-fired Erandi style, well-known all over Mexico. Step into the rear factory and view craftspersons putting life into the fetching motifs—curled up cats, preening ducks, bearded men-in-the-moon. Open Mon.–Fri. 9 A.M.–6 P.M., Sat. 9 A.M.–2 P.M.; tel. 33/3683-0253, fax 33/3683-0871. For more information email: erandi@att.net.mx; website: www.erandi.com.

Next, head west a block to divided Av. Tonaltecas, turn left (south) and continue three blocks to the woodcrafts and furniture stores, at the southwest corner of Av. Juárez.

First comes **Arte Mexicano** at Juárez 235. The all-rustic selection, made at their factory, nearby at Av. Tonalá 482, includes chairs, tables, sideboards, chandeliers, and rocking horses. If you don't find what you want, they'll make it for you. Open Mon.–Sat. 10 A.M.–7 P.M., Sun. 10 A.M.–5 P.M.; tel./fax 33/3683-1479.

Next, enter **Cactus** furniture and handicrafts, at Juárez 237. Select from a big array of much rustic, but also finer china cabinets, dining room sets, sofas, bedsteads, chairs, and stools, at both retail and wholesale prices. Open Mon.–Sat. 10 A.M.–7 P.M., Sun. 10 A.M.–6 P.M.; tel/fax 33/3683-1772.

Finally, next door, find **Carousel,** at Juárez 239. Browse through their appealing selection of big horses, facsimiles of famous Diego Rivera paintings, baroque religious carvings, candelabras, and Don Quixote figures. (A similar offering is available at their main shop, at Madero 88, see earlier shopping Near the Plaza) Open Mon.–Sat. 9 A.M.–6 P.M.; tel. 33/3683-2915.

A block and a half farther south, fine ironwork is king at **Herrería Artistica Covarrubias,** at Tonaltecas 106. The showroom (be sure to see the factory in back) gleams with a host of nearly everything that can be crafted from iron—tables, chairs, cabinets, shelves, benches, chandeliers—and also brass and copper. If you don't see it here, take a look at their catalog and special order what you've always wanted. Open daily 9 A.M.–6 P.M.; tel./fax 33/3683-2420.

Half a block farther south and across the street, the **Casa de los Artesanos,** at Av. Tonaltecas 140, displays the handiwork of more than 50 artisan families. Inside, everything you see is for sale. Pick from a seeming myriad of attractive glass, ceramics, furniture, metalwork, papier-mâché, and much more, all of which testifies to the popular appeal of Tonalá handicrafts. Open Mon.–Sat. 9 A.M.–7 P.M.

Continue another half block south to what appears to be the glass capital of Tonalá, **Crista-**

color **Export,** with a huge (public-inaccessible) factory looming behind the store up-front. Although they produce a small mountain of glassware daily, they do sell directly to the public, with discounts of up to 20 percent for purchases of $500 or more. The showroom displays a multitude of fetching blue, green, and colorless glassware—tumblers, goblets, pitchers, bowls, wine glasses. Open Mon.–Fri. 10 A.M.–6 P.M., Sat. and Sun. 10 A.M.–4 P.M.

For super 50-percent-off bargains, go to their **seconds store** next door south. (If the seconds had defects, I couldn't recognize them.) For more information, call tel. 33/3683-0661, 33/3683-0665, fax 33/3683-0668; email: cristacolor@ iserve.net.mx.

Continue to another pair of glass factories. Two blocks farther south, find **Vidrios del Sol,** at Av. Tonaltecas 281. Step inside and pick from a rainbow flock of decorative glass, from whales to cocktail stirrers to silver glass spheres and hurricane lampshades. Don't be put off by the dust that covers everything; they're too busy selling to clean it off. Open daily 10 A.M.– 6 P.M.; tel. 33/3683-1015, fax 33/3683-2832; email: vidriosdelsol@hot mail.com; website: www.vidriosdelsol.com.mx.

Circle the block (south half a block, left at Av. Tonalá, and left again at Santo Degollado, to **Vidrios Jimón,** in the middle of the block. Out front, the factory, which you shouldn't miss, sounds like a volcano, from the roar of the gas-fired ovens inside. Enter through the store, which displays a shiny, multicolored—yellow, blue, silver, red—array of mirrored glass balls. Open Mon.–Fri. 8 A.M.–5 P.M., Sat. 8 A.M.–2 P.M., Sun. 10 A.M.–2 P.M.

SERVICES
Banks and Money Exchange
Three downtown banks, all with ATMs, serve Tonalá customers. Moving from south to north on Madero-Hidalgo, start at **Banamex,** at Madero 83, open Mon.–Fri. 9 A.M.–5 P.M.; next comes **Bancrecer,** at the adjacent corner (at Zaragoza). Across the street from that, find **Bancomer,** open Mon.–Fri. 8:30 A.M.–4 P.M. Finally, three blocks farther north, is **Banco**

Serfín, corner of Zapata, open Mon.–Fri. 9 A.M.–4 P.M.

After bank hours, go to the *casa de cambio* (money exchange) **Dinero Internacional,** at Madero 51, southeast corner of Zaragoza, tel. 33/3683-3788 and 33/3683-1632.

Travel Agent, Packing Services, and Guides
For your air and bus tickets, car rental, hotel reservations, and more, go to **Agencia de Viajes Alfa,** at Zapata 80, half a block north and a block west of the Palacio Municipal, tel. 33/3603-0853.

Several Tonalá agencies pack and ship purchases. For example, on the north side, try **Promart,** at Privada del Cajón 69, tel. 33/3683-1434, fax 33/3683-2380; email: promart@prodigy.net.mx. (From the Palacio Municipal, walk north on Hidalgo two blocks to López Cotilla. Walk one more short block and turn right on Privada San Antonio, then left on Privada del Cajón.

Alternatively, on the south side, go to **Exportonalá,** at Av. Tonalá 271. Walk south from the main Plaza four blocks to the Madero-Cruz Blanca corner, from which Av. Tonalá angles southwest. Continue a few blocks on Av. Tonalá; tel./fax 33/3683-3314, 33/3683-1025; email: exportonala@infosel.net.mx.

A number of **guides** are available for Tonalá sight-seeing and shopping. English-speaking German immigrant **Willy Klauditz** is especially well-recommended. For details, see under Communications and Information in the Tlaquepaque section, earlier.

COMMUNICATIONS AND INFORMATION
Post, Telephone, and Internet
The Tonalá **post office** *(correo)* is at Pino Suárez 39, half a block south of the Parroquia Santiago parish church, a block east of the plaza. They're open for business Mon.–Fri. 9 A.M.–3 P.M., Sat. 9 A.M.–1 P.M.

Email, Internet, telephone, and fax service is available at **Instituto MG,** at Hidalgo 39, tel. 33/3683-1765, north side of the Palacio Municipal. Find them open Mon.–Sat. 10 A.M.–8 P.M.

Tourism Office and Local Newspaper

Tonalá's generally helpful **Turismo,** tel. 33/3683-0047, 33/3683-0048, 33/3683-0049, ext. 221, is open Mon.–Fri. 9 A.M.–3 P.M. For more information, email: communicacionsocial@tonala .gob.mx or visit the Tonalá website: www .tonala.gob.mx.

Pick up a copy of the information-packed *Guía Tonalá* newspaper for a load of informative hotel, restaurant, shopping, and service advertisements and interesting historical articles. Free copies are generally available in stores, restaurants, and hotels around town. Alternatively, get a copy at their editorial office, Pedro Moreno 39A, tel. 33/3683-2752. (Find it on the block that runs along the north side of the Parroquia Santiago Apóstol parish church, a block east of the plaza.)

HEALTH, EMERGENCIES, AND GETTING THERE

Medicines and Doctors

For routine medications, consult with the pharmacist on duty or family medicine practitioner Dr. Mario Martín Orozco, at his **Farmacia Homeopático** (Homeopathic Pharmacy) at Hidalgo 39, half a block north of the plaza. Dr. Orozco's office hours at the pharmacy are Mon.–Fri. 4–8 P.M., Sat. 11 A.M.–2 P.M.; tel. 33/3681-4594, 33/3683-1364.

For ear, nose, and throat consultations, go to highly recommended Dra. Yolanda Sahagùn Muñoz, at Independencia 44, tel. 33/3683-2780. Her office hours are Wed. 12:30–2 P.M. and Sat. 5:30–8 P.M.

Also, follow your hotel's recommendation, or consult one of the several other physicians that advertise in the *Guía Tonalá* newspaper, such as: Dr. Luis Medrano Solis, general medicine, Madero 160, tel. 33/3683-0164, long office hours; Dr. José Luis Maestro Oceguera, general medicine, Zaragoza 115A, tel. 33/3683-4044, emergency cellular tel. 04433/3453-6569; Dr. Juan de la Cruz Regín Chavez, general medicine and birthing, Independencia 44, tel. 33/3683-2780; and Dr. J. Fernando Salazar Inclán, gynecologist, Constitución 69, tel. 33/3683-0944.

For more Guadalajara-area doctor and hospital information and recommendations, see Guadalajara Doctors and Hospitals in the Staying Healthy section of the On the Road chapter.

Police, Fire, and Medical Emergencies

For the Tonalá **police,** dial tel. 33/3683-0046 or 33/3683-2876; for the **firefighters** *(bomberos),* dial tel. 33/3619-5241, 33/3619-0794, or 33/3823-3561.

In a medical emergency, ask your hotel to get a taxi or ambulance (Red Cross tel. 33/3613-1550, 33/3614-5600) to either their closest recommended hospital or the 24-hour emergency room at Tlaquepaque Hospital Providencia in Tlaquepaque (tel. 33/3639-5155 and 33/3637-8735). Or have the ambulance take you to the highly recommended **Hospital Méxicano-Americano** (in Guadalajara, 25-minute drive in emergency) at north-side Av. Colomos 2110.

Getting There

Get to Tonalá from downtown Guadalajara by taxi (about $15) or ride the oft-crowded **city bus 275 diagonal** (look for "Tlaquepaque" or "Tonalá" scrawled on the front window), from stops along downtown north-south Av. 16 de Septiembre. The bus continues southeast along boulevards Revolución, then Barragán about three miles (five kilometers), passing under the big "Puente Artesanal" Tlaquepaque entrance arch, and continuing along Av. Corregidora in Tlaquepaque, past the new Central Bus Station, continuing another two miles, to Tonalá. Get off at north-south main street Av. Francisco Madero and walk a few blocks north to the Tonalá central plaza, at the corner of east-west Av. Benito Juárez.

By car, from either Guadalajara's westside or the city center, get to Tonalá via cross-town expressway Calz. Lázaro Cárdenas. From the westside, connect to Lázaro Cárdenas via Av. López Mateos south; likewise, from downtown, connect via Calz. Gobernador Curiel, the southern prolongation of Calz. Independencia.

Traveling east on Calz. Lázaro Cárdenas, follow the Tonalá (and Zapotlanejo and Mexico City) signs to **Hwy. 90 Autopista Zapotlanejo–Mexico City** and turn off right at the Tonalá exit.

Turn left (north), crossing over the freeway. After one long block, turn right, east, onto four-lane Av. Tonalá. After three more blocks you'll be at north-south Av. Francisco Madero, where you should park somewhere and walk the three or four blocks north to the Tonalá town plaza, at the corner of Madero and Benito Juárez.

Although local buses or your own wheels can get you to Tonalá, crowds of bus commuters and congested city streets increase the desirability of a **tour or local guide.** For details, con-tact your hotel travel desk, a travel agent, or a reliable, well-equipped agency such as Panoramex, at Federalismo Sur 944, tel. 33/3810-5057 or 33/3810-5005; or Gray Line, at Calz. del Ejército 1336, tel. 33/3619-1347, fax 33/3619-1348, who conduct reasonably priced bilingual tours daily from the city center. For **individual guide** recommendations, see the Tlaquepaque Services section, earlier, and the By Locally Arranged Tour section under Get-ting Around in the On the Road chapter.

Lake Chapala and Vicinity

The folks who live around shallow Lake Chapala, Mexico's largest lake, pride themselves on their lake's brilliant sunsets, its quiet country ambience, and its famously temperate weather. Formed by gigantic earth movements millions of years ago, the lake originally spread far beyond its present cucumber-shaped 50- by 12-mile (80- by 20-km) basin south of Guadalajara.

Now, rounded, gentle mountains shelter the sprinkling of small towns and villages that decorate the shoreline. Chapala's sleepy, rural southern lakeside contrasts with the northern shore, which has become both a favored holiday retreat for well-to-do Guadalajara families and home to a sizable colony

of American and Canadian retirees. The 10-mile procession of petite, picturesque towns—Chapala, Chula Vista, San Antonio, La Floresta, Ajijic, San Juan Cosala, and others—scattered along the northern shore have collectively become known as the "Chapala Riviera." Here, a stream of visitors and an abundance of resident talent and resources sustain good restaurants and hotels as well as fine shops that offer the works of an accomplished community of artisans and artists.

Lake Chapala

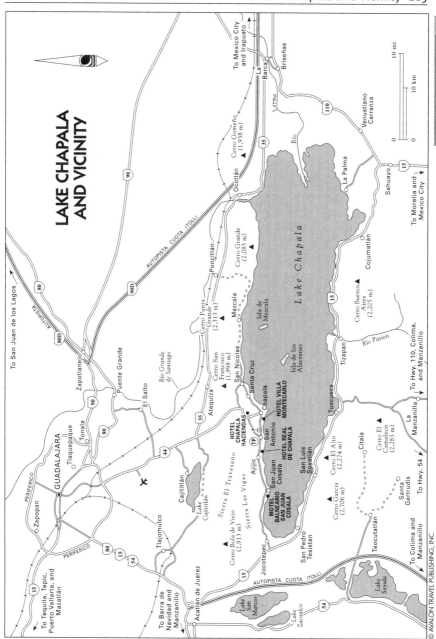

LAKE CHAPALA AND VICINITY

Lake Chapala

HISTORY

Bands of hunter-gatherers, attracted by the lake basin's trove of fish, game, and wild fruits and grains, may have occupied Lake Chapala's shores as early as 10,000 B.C. Interestingly, they probably used the strategy of driving wild animals into the lake, where they could be subdued more easily. The Paleontology Museum in Guadalajara (see Sights in the Heart of the City chapter) displays remains of a number of species, such as antelope, camel, horse, and a very complete mammoth, all unearthed at likely hunting grounds near the prehistoric lakeshore.

OF WHITEFISH AND WATER HYACINTHS

On the scale of geologic time, lakes are momentary features of the landscape. Mother Nature, having created lakes in the first place, immediately sets out to drain them, evaporate them, or pack them with silt. Plants encroach on their shores until, finally, they're filled and forgotten. Such natural forces are particularly consequential for a shallow lake, such as Lake Chapala, which, although large in area, averages only about 15 feet deep.

In recent years nature has not intruded upon Lake Chapala nearly as much as people have. Factories, towns, and farms are demanding an ever-greater share of the lake's most significant source, the Río Lerma, which trickles through four states before entering Lake Chapala's eastern end. Without care, it may simply dry up.

Most of the same upstream culprits who demand more water are also major polluters. The resulting contamination does double harm, both shrinking the fish population and increasing the plague of water hyacinth plants.

The delicious whitefish *(pescado blanco)*, which comprises a number of species of the genus *Chirostoma*, once flourished in both Lake Chapala and Lake Pátzcuaro in Michoacán. But, as at Pátzcuaro, the Chapala whitefish catch has declined steadily since the 1960s, when yearly hauls in excess of 2,000 tons were routine.

The water hyacinth, *Eichornia crassipes,* a native of South America, was introduced into Lake Chapala long ago for the beauty of its purple blossoms and brilliant green leaves. It has since burgeoned into a three-pronged menace. Besides blocking the navigation of fishing boats, canoes, and tourist launches on great swaths of the lake's surface, the hyacinth kills fish by decreasing water oxygen and encourages mosquitoes and other disease carriers to breed beneath its floating mass.

The water hyacinth, or *lirio* as it's known locally, has defied attempts at eradication. Authorities gave up trying to kill it with chemicals; a more benign solution involved the introduction of manatees, which officials hoped would make quick work of the hyacinth. Unfortunately, hungry local fishermen made quicker work of the manatees. In recent years a few mechanical harvesters have operated on the lake, pathetically scratching away at the nightmarishly swelling vegetable expanse.

Huge floating hyacinth beds, which appear as solid green fields when viewed near the shore, cover areas varying from as little as a few percent to as much as a fifth of the lake's surface. For a few weeks, as westerly winds prevail, the *lirio* beds drift and clog the western shore, only to reverse direction after the winds change, a few weeks or months later.

While whitefish fingerlings from a government lakeshore hatchery are repopulating the lake, whitefish from commercial ponds reduce the pressure on the lake fishery. Meanwhile, government eco-scientists are studying both the *lirio* and the whitefish at a local laboratory. And if the Consortio Nacional de Agua, a four-state Lake Chapala blue-ribbon commission, continues to move effectively to manage water use and curb pollution, Lake Chapala may yet find its way back to health.

Recorded history began for Lake Chapala during the 1400s, when a tribe known as the Cocas, after victorious campaigns against Purépecha (Tarascans) of Michoacán, established themselves at Cutzatlán (now San Juan Cosala) on Chapala's northwest shore. Under King Xitomatl, Cutzatlán flourished. A flurry of new towns, such as Axixic (now Ajijic), Xilotepec (now Jocotepec), and later Chapala (around 1500), was established.

> *It seems that warriors of the Coca tribe used to sanctify themselves by ritually splattering the blood of their vanquished battlefield victims on themselves.*

An Intriguing Mystery

In contrast to Ajijic, the origin of the name Chapala remains an unsolved puzzle. Every scholar seems to have a different explanation. It's tempting to believe that the name has something to do with grasshoppers, which the Aztecs called *chapulín.* Another possibility stems from the name Chapa, a local chief at the time of the conquest. The name also might originate with *chapalac,* which translates as "wet place." On the other hand, the word *chapaltlán* (place of many pots) provides the most intriguing explanation of all. It seems that warriors of the Coca tribe used to sanctify themselves by ritually splattering the blood of their vanquished battlefield victims on themselves. Later, as a ceremonial substitute for their own bodies, they sprinkled the victims' blood on small clay jars and figurines, which they tossed into the water at the Chapala lakefront as offerings to their lake god. Fishing nets still bring in little ceramic human forms or animals from the lake-bottom.

Conquest, Colonization, and Modern Times

The Spanish, in the person of Captain Alonso de Ávalos and a platoon of soldiers, arrived in the

atlatl (throwing spear); a potent weapon

THE BATTLE OF MEZCALA

Lake Chapala was the stage of a renowned heroic drama played out during the Mexican War of Independence (1810–21). The struggle centered on the small, half-mile-long island of Mezcala, located mid-lake about six miles east of Chapala town. There, for four continuous years (1812-16), a determined battalion of *insurgente* guerrillas held off the best the royal Spanish army and navy could throw at them.

The rebels' principal players were Marcos Castellanos, a fiery local priest; and José Santana, an indigenous village leader who by heroic example eventually became the rebel commander. On the Spanish side, General José de la Cruz directed the several thousand royalist soldiers deployed around the lakeshore; his subordinate officer, José Navarro, led the day-to-day campaign against the insurgents.

The rebels—a thousand armed men, plus women and children—retreated to the island in late 1812. There they fortified their island with walls, ditches, and sharp underwater stakes. By day, they grew fruits and vegetables and manufactured their own shot; by night, they resupplied themselves at friendly shoreline farms and raided lakeshore garrisons.

In June 1813, both sides were ready for battle. Royalist commanders, having accumulated a small army of troops, acres of supplies, and boats carried over the mountains all the way from San Blas, demanded the Mezcala rebels surrender. "Let blood run first!" the rebels answered.

Blood did run, freely, for three years. Hundreds on both sides fell, as the tide of battle swept from island to shore and back again. In late 1816, many rebels, suffering from a two-year blockade, were sick and starving. General de la Cruz was meanwhile weary of wasting lives and resources in a futile attempt to dislodge the rebels. Santana, negotiating for the rebels, bargained for a full pardon, including repaired farms, supplies, and seeds for his men, and a good church position for Castellanos. To his surprise, de la Cruz accepted.

In November 1816 the rebels left the island, inspiring others to fight on for the *independencia* they finally achieved five years later.

early 1520s. Impressed by the Spanish armor, guns, and horses, the Cocas offered little resistance. Franciscan padres arrived soon afterwards, baptized the Cocas' chief Andrés Carlos and, not insignificantly, named their new Ajijic church San Andrés.

It was not long before Ajijic and Chapala, the Lake Chapala Riviera's best-known towns, began to assume their present characters. The curative springs around Ajijic (in Nahuatl "the place where water overflows") have long attracted travelers and settlers to the lakeshore. Spanish colonists arrived early, in 1530, when the Saenz family was awarded rights of *encomienda* to the labor of the local people. Their establishment, the Hacienda de Cuije, prospered, manufacturing *mescal* liquor for generations. During the 1910 revolution, the local campesinos divided its holdings into a number of small *ejidos* that tried several schemes, including coffee production and gold re-

fining, with mixed results. In 1938, new managers converted the old main house into a hotel, the Posada Ajijic, which now lives on as a picturesquely elegant lakeshore restaurant.

During the twilight decade of President Porfirio Díaz's 34-year rule, Lake Chapala began to surge as a tourist destination. Many rich foreigners, encouraged by government laissez-faire policies, were living in Mexico. One of them, Septimus Crow, came and developed hot springs and lakeshore land around Chapala town. He raved about Chapala to his wealthy friends, who came and also built sumptuous homes. President Díaz, who visited in 1904 and for some years thereafter, opened the floodgates. Dozens of millionaire families soon moved to Chapala. One such was Alberto Braniff, of the famous airline family. In 1906 he bought a fancy lakeshore Victorian mansion, which remains gracefully preserved as the El Cazador restaurant.

The fame of Lake Chapala spread. Improved transportation—first trains, then cars and airplanes—brought droves of visitors from the United States, Canada, and Europe by the 1940s. Soon, Ajijic—with its picturesque cobbled lanes, quiet lakeshore ambience, and bargain prices—enticed a steady stream of American and Canadian retirees to stay. Their lovely restored colonial homes and bougainvillea-adorned gardens still grace Ajijic and its surroundings today.

SIGHTS

Getting Oriented

Chapala and Ajijic are the Chapala Riviera's most-visited towns. Chapala (pop. about 10,000), at the Hwy. 44 freeway terminus from Guadalajara, is both the main business center and a weekend picnic spot for Guadalajara families. Ajijic (ah-HEE-heek, pop. about 5,000), by contrast, is the scenic, artistic, and tourism center, retaining the best of both worlds—picturesque rustic ambience *and* good, reasonably priced restaurants and hotels.

The paved lakeshore highway runs about five miles west from Chapala to Ajijic, through the tranquil retirement communities of Chula Vista (marked by the golf course on the uphill side), San Antonio, and La Floresta. From Ajijic, the route continues another five miles past lakeshore vineyards and gardens to San Juan Cosala village and hot springs resort. About five miles farther on, you reach Jocotepec, the lake's west-end commercial center, just before arriving at the Morelia-Guadalajara Hwy. 15 junction.

On the opposite, eastern side of Chapala town, the lakeshore is much less developed. The road, which runs east as Paseo Corona from the Chapala lakefront, is paved for about five miles to San Nicolas (pop. about 1,000). After that, it changes to gravel, passing small inlets and tiny isolated cliff-bottom beaches en route to sleepy Mezcala (12 miles, 19 km, 30 minutes from Chapala).

Chapala Town Bypass

Drivers headed for Ajijic, La Floresta, and San Antonio who want to avoid Chapala town traffic do so via the *libramiento* (bypass road) that forks from Hwy. 44 two miles uphill from Chapala. The *libramiento* continues for four miles, joining the lakeshore highway about a mile east of the center of Ajijic.

Getting Around

Generally light traffic makes an **automobile** the most convenient way to explore Lake Chapala. Car rentals are available either directly at the Guadalajara airport (see the By Air section, under Getting There and Away, in the Heart of the City chapter) or through a Chapala travel agent such as Viajes Vikingo, tel. 376/765-3292, fax 376/765-3494.

Or catch one of the red-and-white local **minibuses** that run frequently from curbside across from the Chapala bus station (about six blocks uphill from the lake, along main street Francisco I. Madero). Most frequent is the westbound bus, which heads along the lakeshore to San Juan Cosala and back via Ajijic, and which will stop anywhere along the road. Other lakeshore destinations (departing from inside the terminal) include Jocotepec every half hour 5 A.M.–8:30 P.M., and San Nicolas eastbound every half hour 7 A.M.–7 P.M.

A Walk Around Chapala Town

Start your Chapala walk beneath the great shady trees in the old town **plaza,** three blocks from the lakefront, on main street Av. Francisco I. Madero. Stroll toward the lake a block and a half, to the town **church.** Although dedicated to St. Francis of Assisi when founded in 1538, the church wasn't completed for more than 200 years. Inside rest the venerated remains of Padre Miguel de Bolonia, one of the pioneer local Franciscan missionaries. He was probably instrumental in building the 16th-century former hermitage (now merely a crumbling foundation) on Cerro San Miguel, the hill that rises just west of town. A white summit cross marks the spot.

Continue across lakefront boulevard Paseo Corona, past the curio stands, to the municipal **pier.** In good times, the adjacent anchorage is free of *lirio* (water hyacinths). Otherwise, boaters must frequently chop a navigation path through the

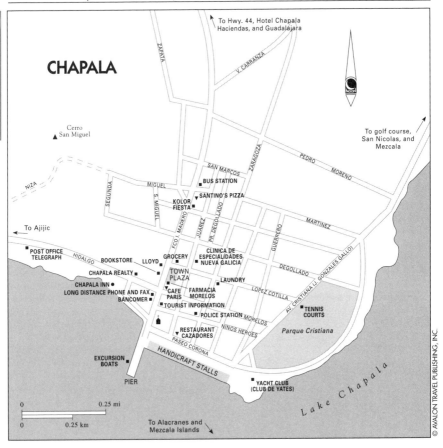

CHAPALA

To Hwy. 44, Hotel Chapala
Haciendas, and Guadalajara

Cerro
San Miguel ▲

To golf course,
San Nicolas, and
Mezcala

To Ajijic ←

ZAPATA

V. CARRANZA

ZARAGOZA

PEDRO MORENO

MARTINEZ

SAN MARCOS

NIZA

SEGUNDA

MIGUEL

S. MIGUEL

FCO. MADERO

JUAREZ

PR. DEGOLLADO

GUERRERO

AV. CRISTIANIA (J. GONZALES GALLO)

BUS STATION

SANTINO'S PIZZA

KOLOR
FIESTA

POST OFFICE
TELEGRAPH

HIDALGO

BOOKSTORE

LLOYD

GROCERY

CLINICA DE
ESPECIALIDADES
NUEVA GALICIA

DEGOLLADO

CHAPALA REALTY

TOWN
PLAZA

LAUNDRY

LOPEZ COTILLA

CHAPALA INN
LONG DISTANCE PHONE AND FAX
BANCOMER

CAFE
PARIS

FARMACIA
MORELOS

TOURIST INFORMATION

POLICE STATION

MORELOS

NINOS HEROES

TENNIS
COURTS

Parque Cristiana

RESTAURANT
CAZADORES

PASEO CORONA

EXCURSION
BOATS

HANDICRAFT STALLS

PIER

YACHT CLUB
(CLUB DE YATES)

Lake Chapala

0   0.25 mi
0   0.25 km

To Alacranes and
Mezcala Islands

© AVALON TRAVEL PUBLISHING, INC.

thick green vegetable carpet. (In the worst of times, the lake recedes, leaving the pier high and dry.)

From the pier, a number of excursions are possible, from a one-hour ride along the lakeshore to extended lake and island tours. These could include a two-hour visit to Scorpion Island (Isla Alacranes), with its regional food restaurants and bird-watching; or four hours round-trip to Mezcala Island (Isla Presidio) with its ruins and bird-watching. Rental rates run about $15 hourly per boat while running, $10 hourly while waiting. For Mezcala Island (see the special topic The Battle of Mezcala), bring food and drinks; none may be available on the island, which is a national monument.

If you continue east a quarter mile, past the curio stands lining the lakefront walkway, you'll reach spreading green **Parque Cristiania,** one of Mexico's most complete public parks. Appropriately built for the droves of Sunday visitors, Cristiania has a children's playground, a picnic area, good public tennis courts, and a big swimming pool, all usable for modest fees.

The Braniff Mansion and the "Hump"

Head back west along lakefront boulevard Paseo Corona, where, a block before the church, you'll see the big Victorian **Braniff Mansion,** now the Restaurant Cazaderos, corner of Degollado. Open daily 8 A.M.–5 P.M. Drop in for lunch or a drink and relax and enjoy the passing scene from the mansion veranda. Later, step inside and admire what amounts to an informal museum of Porfiriana, from the original silk wallpaper to patriarch Alberto Braniff's white-bearded portrait (which bears an uncanny resemblance to revolutionary President Venustiano Carranza).

From the downtown traffic intersection and signal on Madero, a block uphill from the church, Av. Hidalgo heads west along the lakeshore toward Ajijic. Follow it about six blocks to view an inextricably connected pair of Chapala fixtures, one as famous as the other is notorious. The famous one is the spreading, parklike **Hotel Villa Montecarlo,** adjacent to the lake. Facilities inside, which the public can enjoy for a fee of about $6 per day, include flowery green lakeview grounds, tennis courts, picnic areas, and pools, one of which is fed by a natural underground hot spring.

The subterranean hot water gathers along an **earthquake fault** that runs from the adjacent hillside, beneath the highway and hotel grounds. Earth movement along the fault causes the notorious 50-yard-long rough "hump" in the highway adjacent to the hotel. The pesky mound defies all attempts to alter its growth, which must be scraped off regularly to keep the road passable. Citizens of Chapala, irritated by hump-caused traffic jams, have long petitioned local government for a solution. Engineers, after many proposals, have widened the road and installed underground drains. Hopefully, this will not upset the natural balance and interfere with the hot spring for which the Hotel Villa Montecarlo was built in the first place.

Exploring Ajijic

Continue west by car or bus, about five miles along the lakeshore highway. Past La Floresta, marked by a shady stretch of great trees overarching the highway, an old church tower poking above the left-side neighborhood identifies Ajijic. Its main street is Colón, which runs downhill toward the lake, on the left from the traffic signal.

A good first stop would be **Ajijic Fine Arts Center** (Centro de Bellas Artes de Ajijic, CABA) at 43 Colón. It's a community center as much as

a gallery, where artists and interested local folks gather for classes (painting, graphics, photography, ceramics, sculpture) and exhibits, coffee, and conversation Tues.–Sun. 10 A.M.–5 P.M.; tel. 376/766-1920. (Try the heavenly rear-garden **Restaurant Santuario** for a tranquil light lunch, supper, or refreshment, open Tues.–Sun. noon–8 P.M.)

Continue downhill a half block to the Ajijic town **plaza** and take a look inside the old (circa 1540) chapel of the Virgin of Santiago on the north (uphill) edge of the plaza. From the opposite side of the plaza, head east one block to the baroque parish **church of San Andrés,** founded during the mid-1500s and completed in 1749. For nine days during Ajijic's late-November **Fiesta de San Andrés,** the church's spreading front courtyard and surrounding streets overflow with food stands, carnival rides, pitch-penny games, fireworks, and folk dancing. Moreover, Ajijic's **Semana Santa** (pre-Easter week) celebration at this same spot is becoming renowned for its elaborately costumed, three-day reenactment of Jesus' trial and crucifixion.

A woman artisan of the Trique people of Oaxaca weaves in front of Restaurant Posada Ajijic, at the Lake Chapala shorefront.

From the church-front, head downhill along Castellanos; after two blocks, turn right at 16 de Septiembre. Not far, on your left, will be the **Neill James Library,** open Mon.–Sat. 10 A.M.–2 P.M., and the lovely garden it shares with the adjacent Spanish-language library. Open Mon.–Sat. 10:30 A.M.–1 P.M. and 4–6 P.M. The garden is a delight for quiet contemplation. Before you leave, look over the notices of local performances, exhibits, and fiestas on the walkway bulletin board between the two buildings.

Continue half a block west along 16 de Septiembre to the corner of Morelos, where you'll enjoy browsing through the excellent **arts and crafts shops** clustered here.

Note: Although Morelos has a different name, it is actually the downhill continuation of Colón. The reason is Ajijic streets change names midtown. Streets that run parallel to the lakeshore change names at the Colón-Morelos line. Streets that run perpendicular to the lakeshore change names at the Constitución-Ocampo line.

Ajijic Lakeshore

Continue another block downhill to the Ajijic lakeshore and pier. Late afternoons, a gentle breeze often cools the lakeshore. Overhead, great white clouds billow above blue mountains bordering the far lakeshore. On the beach by the pier, fishermen mend their nets, while at the beach's uphill edge, a few *indígena* women in native costumes weave their colorful wares beneath the great trees that shelter the **Restaurant Posada Ajijic.**

The restaurant is the present incarnation of the Hacienda de Cuije, founded here by the Saenz family in 1530. In 1938, Englishman Nigel Millet turned the building into a hotel, the Posada Ajijic. By the 1970s, the Posada Ajijic was attracting a loyal clientele, which included a number of artists, writers, and film stars such as Elizabeth Taylor and Charles Bronson. New owners, the Eager family of Vancouver, Canada, took over in 1975 and stayed until 1990, when they moved to another hotel nearby. The current proprietors, who operate it as a restaurant exclusively, remodeled the Posada Ajijic to its present state of rustic elegance.

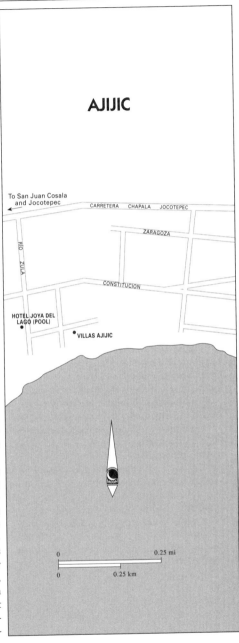

AJIJIC

To San Juan Cosala and Jocotepec

CARRETERA   CHAPALA   JOCOTEPEC

ZARAGOZA

RIO ZULA

CONSTITUCION

HOTEL JOYA DEL LAGO (POOL)

VILLAS AJIJIC

0   0.25 mi

0   0.25 km

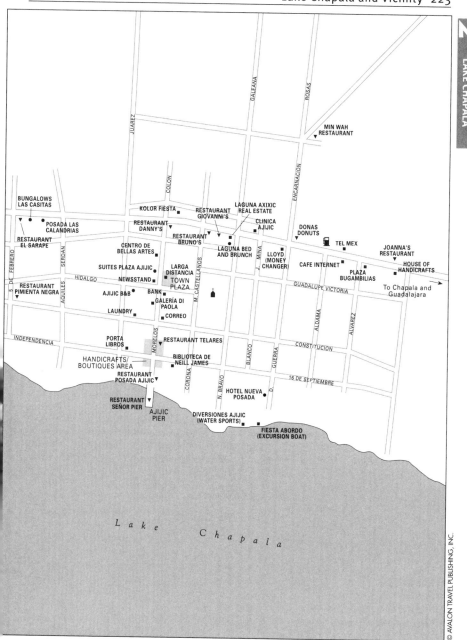

© AVALON TRAVEL PUBLISHING, INC.

spiny bromeliad, relative of the pineapple

For a look at the showplace **Hotel La Nueva Posada,** which the Eager family built in 1990, stroll four blocks east (left as you face the lake). Their gorgeous neocolonial creation at the foot of Donato Guerra spreads from its intimate, art-decorated lobby through an airy, romantic terrace restaurant, climaxing in a verdant, semitropical lake-view garden.

If you time your Ajijic arrival right (winter only), you might be able to join an informative tour of Ajijic's lovely homes and gardens. Local volunteers conduct the programs regularly and give the donations (customarily, about $10 per person) to the Jocotepec School for the Deaf. Call 376/766-0589, 376/766-0652, or 376/766-0376 for information.

ACCOMMODATIONS

The Chapala Riviera offers a wide range of lodgings, from luxury lake-view hotels and friendly motel complexes to intimate bed-and-breakfasts and a good trailer park. Although both Ajijic and Chapala have plenty of colorful old-Mexico atmosphere, Ajijic is quieter and more charming, and consequently has

most of the better lodgings. Rates depend strongly upon availability and season; unless otherwise specified, the lodging figures given below approximate winter high-season rates. Summer low-season (MayOctober) prices will generally be 10–30 percent lower.

Ajijic Hotels

By location, starting on the highway and moving downhill, first comes the **Posada Las Calandrias,** about four blocks west of Danny's restaurant at Carretera Chapala-Jocotepec #8 Poniente. Many folks with cars and RVs like the motel-style setup and the winter reunions with fellow Ajijic long-timers. The 25 clean, comfortable, but not fancy one- and two-bedroom apartments include living room, kitchen, ceiling fans, and plenty of winter-season company around a blue pool and sundeck adjacent to the parking lot. By night, residents relax on their front porches, enjoying the balmy evenings visiting and playing cards; later some might stroll down the street together for dinner at a favorite restaurant. One-bedroom apartments rent, year-round, for about $30 per day, $180 per week, or $450 per month; two-bedrooms (with fireplaces) for $45 per day,

$260 per week, or $600 per month. All rentals include fans, TV, and daily maid service. Get your winter season (November–April) reservations in early. Write to P.O. Box 76, Ajijic, Jalisco 45920; tel. 376/766-1052.

If you can't get in at Las Calandrias, try the neighboring **Bungalows Las Casitas,** one door to the west. Here, as next door, about two dozen simply but comfortably furnished apartments surround a pool and sundeck by the parking lot. The friendly winter residents are mainly North American retirees. One-bedroom units rent for $32 per day, $150 per week, and $430 per month; two-bedrooms run half again as much. Discounts are generally available during May–July and September–November low seasons. All have kitchens, living rooms, ceiling fans, maid service, and satellite TV. Carretera Chapala-Jocotepec 20 Poniente, Ajijic, Jalisco 45920; tel. 376/766-1145.

On the highway, only a couple of blocks from the town center, the Laguna Real Estate office marks the location of its **Laguna Bed and Brunch.** Reserve through Laguna Real Estate. Four comfortable rooms with bath, an adjacent cheery breakfast room/living room/lobby, and a partially shaded outside patio keep a steady stream of satisfied customers returning year-round. Extras are king-size beds, a shelf of thick used paperbacks, and sofas for reading and socializing. Hearty breakfasts are included with lodgings. Rooms rent for $35 s or d high season, about $30 d low season. By day, you can make inquiries or access Laguna Bed and Brunch through the real estate office or by telephone. With your key, you can get in anytime through the residential entrance at Zaragoza 29 Oriente, behind the real estate office, one block downhill from the highway. Carretera Chapala-Ajijic 24 Oriente, Ajijic, Jalisco 45920; tel. 376/766-1174, fax 376/766-1188; email: laguna@laguna.com.mx.

Nearby on Colón by the plaza, close to everything, is **Ajijic Plaza Suites.** The small, sometimes busy lobby leads to a sunny, apartment-lined inner patio. Inside, the new owners have spruced up the 12 one-bedroom units with tasteful, colorful Mexican-style decor. Rentals run about $35 s, $40 d, including breakfast, phone, maid service,

optional satellite TV, and **limited wheelchair access.** Credit cards accepted. Colón 33, P.O. Box 555, Ajijic, Jalisco 45920; tel. 376/766-0383, fax 376/766-2331; email: ajijic@infosel.net.mx.

Around the downhill corner, at Hidalgo 22, the new **Ajijic B&B** attracts a cadre of loyal returnees. The front entry leads you into an inviting fountain courtyard, past breakfast tables set beneath a shady side portico to a manicured tropical garden, with the six rooms set artfully to one side. Inside, they are lovingly decorated in earth tones and pastels, embellished with flowers hand-painted on the walls, and hung with original oils and watercolors. Rooms include ceiling fans, king-size beds, modern-standard decorator bathrooms, telephones, and large-screen TVs. Rates run about $65 s or d, including full breakfast. Make reservations early, especially during the winter; tel. 376/766-2377, fax 376/766-2331; email: ajijic@infosel.net.mx.

Arguably Ajijic's loveliest lodging is **Los Artistas,** on the east side of town. Owners Kent Edwards and Linda Brown's lovingly tended accommodations are arranged around the edge of a flowery rear garden. Rooms, some with king-size beds, all with attractively tiled and fitted baths, are artfully furnished with weavings, paintings, and sculpture. Rooms vary; if possible, take a peek before picking. Rates range $52–70 d, including breakfast, swimming pool, and parking. Reserve early, especially for the winter season. Find it about five blocks east of main street Colón. Constitución 105, Ajijic, Jalisco 45920; tel. 376/766-1027, fax 376/766-1762; email: artistas@laguna.com.mx; website: www.losartistas.com.

Lakeshore Hotels

Nearby, downhill, stands Ajijic's class-act newish **Hotel La Nueva Posada,** on the east-side lakeshore. It's so attractive, prospective winter guests need reservations far in advance. Its Canadian family/owners have spared little in embellishing the hotel's neocolonial decor. Past the lobby, an elegant but comfortable bar provides nightly piano entertainment, and a romantic, airy terrace-restaurant leads to a verdant, lake-view garden. The 17 accommodations vary from poolside rooms to upstairs view suites. All are immaculate and tastefully decorated in colonial style, with original watercolor and native crafts. Rooms rent, year-round, for $55 s, $65 d, $70 t, (add about $5 for view), including full breakfast, ceiling fans, and parking. Bargain for a low-season or long-term discount; credit cards are accepted (although you get a 10 percent discount if you pay cash). Donato Guerra 9, P.O. Box 30, Ajijic, Jalisco 45920; tel. 376/766-1444, fax 376/766-1344; email: posada@laguna.com.mx.

Two more deluxe accommodations occupy lakeshore spots on opposite ends of town. The Universidad Autónoma de Guadalajara owns one, the plush **Hotel Real de Chapala** in the choice La Floresta subdivision just east of Ajijic. Except for Christmas and Easter holidays and weekends, the hotel is minimally occupied, and consequently very quiet. Its lavish facilities—a spreading lakefront park, big blue pool, night-lit tennis courts, volleyball, soccer field, billiard room, Ping-Pong, and bars and restaurants—are often unused. Weekends are more lively; guests, mostly middle- and upper-class Guadalajarans, enjoy seasonal live combo music Friday and Saturday evenings, and mariachis and folkloric dance on Sunday. The 86 spacious, luxurious rooms and suites (40 of which have lake and mountain views) rent from about $85 s or d, with ceiling fans, queen-size beds, satellite TV, parking, and **limited wheelchair access.** Credit cards accepted. Paseo del Prado 20, Ajijic, Jalisco 45920; tel. 376/766-0007 or 376/766-0014, fax 376/766-0025.

The condo-style **Villas Ajijic,** in the quiet lakeshore neighborhood on the opposite side of town, offers an entirely different option. Although owners have allowed the complex to deteriorate, visitors with children might find the space and the kid-friendly environment here desirable.

The two-story, tile-and-stucco apartments cluster around a inner garden leading to an adjoining pool (check to see if it's clear and clean) and kiddie playground in a spacious grassy meadow by the beach (which is, unfortunately, often clogged with water hyacinths.) The units themselves are spacious, Spanish-style apartments with two bedrooms, dining room, living room, bar, view balcony in upstairs units, and modern-standard kitchens.

They rent for $80 per day or $1,000 per month high season, about $55 per day and $850 per month low season, with hotel-style desk manager, maid service, satellite TV, and telephone. Linda Vista 14, Fracc. Tío Domingo, Ajijic, Jalisco 45920; tel./fax 376/766-0983; website: www.guadalajara.net/villas.

Get there via the lakeshore highway, about a mile west of the Ajijic town center. Turn left, downhill, at the Hotel Danza del Sol sign at Río Bravo Street. After two blocks, turn left at the Coronado Resort sign at Ocampo; after one block, turn right at the second Ajijic Resort sign. One block farther, turn left at the Villas Ajijic sign.

Chapala Hotels

Arguably Chapala town's finest most tranquil lodging is the **Chapala Inn,** on the lakeshore promenade, west of the pier. The former mansion, now a bed-and-breakfast, retains a good measure of its gracious old-world ambience. Enter from the lake side and pass through the light, spacious living room, past a well-stocked library, and an elegant dining room. Upstairs, the several rooms are immaculate, spacious, high-ceilinged, and comfortably appointed with polished 1930s-era furniture and large, spotless bathrooms. Guests additionally enjoy an airy, shaded lake-view patio ideal for quiet relaxation. Rates are $47 s, $60 d, including breakfast, lap pool, and parking, but no phones or TV. 23 Paseo Ramón Corona, Chapala, Jalisco 45900; tel. 376/765-4809, fax 376/765-47686; email: chapalainn@laguna.com.mx; website: www.mexonline.com/chapalainn.htm

(At this writing, the venerable former Hotel Nido, at Av. Fco. Madero 202, former favorite of three generations of Lake Chapala visitors, is being renovated by the city for new uses.)

About six blocks west along Chapala's main lakeshore street, **Hotel Villa Montecarlo** basks in palmy, lake-view grounds. The site, originally developed because of its hot spring, is now owned and operated by the University of Guadalajara. The natural setting—lush green lawns overlooking the lake's mountain- and cloud-framed expanse—sets the tone. When not gazing at the view, guests can soak in the natural warm pool, cool off in another, play some tennis, or enjoy a drink at the bar or a meal in the restaurant. The double-story, motel-style lodging tiers occupy only one side of the grounds and consequently avoid cluttering the views. The rooms, furnished in 1960s semi-deluxe style, open to airy balconies, many with lake vistas. They rent for about $35 s or d ($70 weekends), two kids under 10 free with parents, with ceiling fans, TV at extra cost, tennis courts, but no phones. Hidalgo 296, Chapala, Jalisco 45900; tel./fax 376/765-2120 or 376/765-2024, 376/765-3366.

By contrast, guests at the **Hotel Chapala Haciendas** enjoy a high hillside setting, five minutes' drive uphill from the lakeshore. Its lush country lake-view location, inviting pool-patio, friendly

LAKE CHAPALA ACCOMMODATIONS BY PRICE

Accommodations, with telephone *lada* (area code) 376/, are listed in increasing order of double (two people in one bed) rates. 800 numbers are for toll-free reservations from the United States and Canada. 01-800 numbers are for the same from within Mexico. Postal codes are listed.

Ajijic Hotels (Postal Code 45920)

Posada Las Calandrias, No. 8 Poniente, P.O. Box 76; tel. 376/766-1052; $30/day, $180/week, $450/month

Bungalows Las Casitas, Carretera Chapala-Jocotepec 20 Poniente; tel. 376/766-1145; $32/day, $150/week, $430/month

Laguna Bed and Brunch c/o Laguna Real Estate, Carretera Chapala-Ajijic 24 Oriente; tel. 376/766-1174, fax 376/766-1188; email: laguna@laguna.com.mx; $35

Ajijic Plaza Suites Colón 33, P.O. Box 555; tel. 376/766-0383, fax 376/766-2331; email: ajijic@infosel.net.mx; $40

Los Artistas Constitución 105; tel. 376/766-1027, fax 376/766-1762; email: artistas@laguna.com.mx; website: www.losartistas.com; $52

Ajijic B&B Hidalgo 22; tel. 376/766-2377, fax 376/766-2331; email: ajijic@infosel.net.mx; $65

Hotel La Nueva Posada Donato Guerra 9, P.O. Box 30; tel. 376/766-1444, fax 376/766-1344; email: posada@laguna.com.mx; $65

Hotel Real de Chapala Paseo del Prado 20; tel. 376/766-0007 or 376/766-0014, fax 376/766-0025; $85

Villas Ajijic Linda Vista 14, Fracc. Tío Domingo; tel./fax 376/766-0983; website: www.guadalajara.net/villas; $80/day, $1,000/month

Chapala Hotels (Postal Code 45900)

Hotel Chapala Haciendas Km 40, Carretera Guadalajara-Chapala, tel. 376/765-2720; $25

Hotel Villa Montecarlo Hidalgo 296; tel./fax 376/765-2120, 376/765-2024, or 376/765-3366; $35

Chapala Inn 23 Paseo Ramón Corona; tel. 376/765-4809, fax 376/765-47686; email: chapalainn@laguna.com.mx; website: www.mexonline.com/chapalainn.htm; $60

San Juan Cosala

Motel Balneario San Juan Cosala P.O. Box 181, Chapala, Jalisco 45900; tel./fax 376/761-0302 or 376/761-0222; $55

family management, and reasonable prices explain the Chapala Hacienda's past popularity with both North American and Mexican vacationers. Unfortunately, Hotel Chapala Haciendas, exterior appearance has been allowed to deteriorate during the past few years. My last two visits, both during the summer low season, the pool was green and stagnant, although the rooms were still in good shape. Have a look around to see if the place is up to your standards before putting your money down.

Breakfast, sunrise view, piano-bar, and live oldies-but-goodies music Wednesday and Saturday evenings nevertheless remain popular traditions in the hotel's homey restaurant. The 20 rooms, in rows facing a lush garden and panoramic lake views, are simply but attractively furnished, with rustic high-beamed rattan ceilings. Rentals run $20 s, $25 d, with discounts for long-term stays. Km 40, Carretera Guadalajara-Chapala, Chapala, Jalisco 45900; tel. 376/765-2720.

San Juan Cosala Hot Spring Resort

San Juan Cosala, on the lakeshore eight miles (13 km) west of Chapala, has long been famous for its therapeutic hot springs. The major hotel is the **Motel Balneario San Juan Cosala,** whose complex of several big blue pools and a water slide is a weekend and holiday magnet for Mexican families. Although the main pools and facilities are open to the public for a fee of $6 adults and $3 kids, the hotel reserves some pools and gardens for hotel guests only. Other hotel amenities include hot tub, massage, natural vapor sauna, and volleyball, basketball, and tennis courts. The rooms, while not luxurious, are comfortably furnished with two double beds and have airy, private garden patios, which, from the second floor, have lake views. If you prefer peace and quiet, best book your stay during the calm midweek period. The approximately 50 rooms rent for $50 s, $55 d, two kids under 8 free with parents, breakfast included. Contact the motel at P.O. Box 181, Chapala, Jalisco 45900; tel./fax 376/761-0302 or 376/761-0222.

Trailer Park

The long-established **Pal Trailer Park,** on the Chapala lakeshore highway three miles west of Chapala, just past the Chula Vista golf course and tennis courts, amounts to a mini-village, with many year-round residents. Its host of deluxe extras include a heated swimming pool, separate children's pool, satellite TV hookup, recreation room and barbecue area, pure water system, Laundromat, night security guard, and clean, separate toilets and showers for men and women. Its 110 large (40- by 30-foot) spaces, each with terrace, rent for $14 per day, $90 per week, $320 per month, or about $3,000 per year, with all hookups, including 30-amp electric power. Tent camping is permitted, but for 2–3 days only. Write for reservations at P.O. Box 84, Chapala, Jalisco 45900; tel. 376/766-1447, fax 376/766-0040; email: lloyd@lloyd.com.mx, website: www.southmex.com/palresort.html.

Long-Term Rentals and Home Exchanges

A number of agents rent Chapala-area apartments, houses, and condos. Among the busiest is **Coldwell Banker–Chapala Realty,** in downtown Chapala, Hidalgo 223, Chapala, Jalisco 45900; tel. 376/765-2877 or 376/765-3676, fax 376/765-3528; email: chapala@infosel.net.mx, website: www.chapala.com. **Ajijic Real Estate,** at Colón 1, Ajijic, tel. 376/766-1716, fax 376/766-0967; email: rentals@infosel.net.mx does about the same. Also, check the local newspapers—the *Guadalajara Colony Reporter* and *Ojo del Lago*— classifieds and the bulletin board at the Ajijic post office, a block downhill from the town plaza, or the Neill James library, a block downhill and a block east from the post office. (If you can't find a copy of *Ojo del Lago*, drop by their headquarters, at the Coldwell Banker–Chapala Realty office in Chapala, at Av. Hidalgo 223, or telephone 376/765-3676 or 376/756-2877, fax 376/765-3528; email:ojodellago@laguna.com.mx.

FOOD
Breakfast and Snacks

In Ajijic, all roads seem to lead to **Danny's Restaurant** on the lakeshore highway at Colón.

Hot breakfasts (eggs, hash browns, and toast, $4), hamburgers, Mexican specialties, bottomless cups of coffee, and plenty of friendly conversation long ago ensured Danny's local following. Open Mon.–Sat. 8 A.M.–5 P.M., Sun. 8 A.M.–1 P.M.; tel. 376/776-2222.

Alternatively, you can try **Evies,** for good coffee and American breakfast, at 21 Hidalgo, half a block west of the Ajijic plaza. Open daily, except Wed., 8 A.M.–4 P.M.

Two Ajijic bed-and-breakfasts offer both breakfast and a Sunday brunch to the public. The **Laguna Bed and Brunch** offers a country breakfast Mon.–Sat. 8–11 A.M. This includes several entrée choices plus fruit, rolls, apple-bran muffins, and coffee or tea for about $2. On Sunday, local folks crowd in for its even heartier brunch, offered 8 A.M.–noon, for about $4. Goodies include all of the above plus old-fashioned tummy-fillers such as beef pot pies, mashed potatoes, and vegetables; or enchiladas, rice, and refried beans. Get there from the highway, through Laguna Real Estate, or through Laguna Bed and Brunch's front door, a block downhill from the highway, at Zaragoza 29 near the corner of Galeana. Reservations are required, tel. 376/766-1174.

© BRUCE WHIPPERMAN

Cerveza raiz (literally "root beer") is as delicious and popular in Mexico as it is everywhere.

The **Ajijic B&B,** farther down the hill at 22 Hidalgo, half a block west of the town plaza, seasonally offers a similar Sunday brunch 11 A.M.–4 P.M. Be sure to phone or fax ahead, tel. 376/766-2377, fax 376/766-2331, for reservations.

In Chapala, **Cafe Paris,** right in the center of town on Madero, corner of Hidalgo, enjoys similar renown. Good service, tasty offerings—breakfasts, soups, salads, sandwiches, Mexican plates, beer, wine, and cafe espresso—and shady sidewalk tables attract a loyal local and North American clientele. Open daily 9 A.M.–9 P.M.

Another relaxing spot in Chapala is **Restaurant Los Cazadores** in the distinguished old Braniff Mansion on lakeshore Av. R. Corona, a block south of the church. Here you can enjoy the lakefront scene over a leisurely breakfast or lunch on the airy front veranda. Before you leave, step inside for a look at the collection of polished Porfiriana that adorns the mansion's venerable silk-covered walls. Open daily 8 A.M.–5 P.M.

Homier but just as enjoyable is **Che Mary,** where regulars flock for bountiful, very reasonably priced breakfasts, lunches, and dinners in an inviting, airy palapa setting. It's on Madero, across the street and about two blocks uphill from the Chapala town plaza. Open daily 8 A.M.–10 P.M.

The baked offerings of **Santino's Pizza** in Chapala (Madero 467A, two blocks up the street from the plaza) are equally good on location or delivered. Open daily 1–10 P.M.; tel. 376/775-2360.

Ajijic Restaurants

The resident brigade of discriminating diners has led to the unusually high standards of Ajijic's successful restaurants. Starting on the highway, east side, and moving downhill toward the lake, first comes **Joanna's Restaurant,** tel. 376/766-0437, whose bona fide claim of "authentic German cuisine" seems a marvel, a continent and an ocean away from Lüneburg where Joanna was born. But remarkable it is—from the *Gemischechter Fruhling Salat* (with *Hausdressing*) through the *Reibekuche* (potato pancakes) and *Mandel Forelle* rainbow trout, to the finale of scrumptious apple strudel. Find Joanna's at 118A Blv. La Floresta, three blocks east of the gas station, in a

CHOCOLATL

The refreshing drink *chocolatl* enjoyed by Aztec nobility is a remote but distinct relative of the chocolate consumed today by hundreds of millions of people. It was once so precious, chocolate beans were a common medium of exchange in pre-Conquest Mexico. In those days a mere dozen cacao beans could command a present value of upwards of $100 in goods or services. Counterfeiting was rife—entrepreneurs tried to create *chocolatl* from anything, including avocado seeds. Moreover, *chocolatl* was thought to be so potent an aphrodisiac and hallucinogen that its use was denied, under penalty of death, to commoners.

Although intrigued, Europeans were put off by *chocolatl's* bitter taste. Around 1600, a whole shipload of chocolate beans was jettisoned at sea by English privateers who, having captured a Spanish galleon, mistook its cargo for goat dung.

The French soon made *chocolatl* easier to stomach by powdering it; the British added milk; and finally the Swiss, of Nestlé fame, cashed in with chocolate candy. The world hasn't been the same since.

Though *chocolatl* found its way to Europe, it never left Mexico, where hot chocolate, whipped frothy with a wooden-ringed *molinillo* (little mill), is more common now than in Aztec times. In Mexico, chocolate is more than mere dessert—used to spice the tangy *moles* of southern Mexico, it's virtually a national food.

suburban house, set back from the north side of the street. Open Tues.–Thurs. 1–8 P.M., Fri.–Sun. 1–9 P.M. Moderate–expensive.

Two blocks west, plain good food at very reasonable prices draws a flock of local Americans and Canadians to coffee shop–style **Salvador's,** on the highway in front of the Plaza Bugambilias shopping center. Besides a very familiar American-style breakfast, lunch, and dinner menu, owner Salvador also offers a big $5 Sunday brunch and specialties of the day, such as roast beef, lasagna, and stuffed rainbow trout, all for around $5. Open Mon.–Fri. 7 A.M.–8 P.M., Sun. 7 A.M.–5 P.M., (closed Sat.) 88 Carretera Oriente highway; tel. 376/776-2301. Inexpensive.

Next comes **La Trattoria de Giovanni** (or just Giovanni's), a spacious (but dark in the daytime) restaurant/bar, also on the highway, lake-side, at the corner of Galeana. Here, friends and family gather for a good time. The happy mixture of folks—kids, retirees, Mexicans, Americans, Canadians—is both a cause and effect of the amiable atmosphere. The food—pizzas, pastas, salads, fish, chicken, steaks—is crisply served and tasty. Desserts, which include carrot cake and apple, chocolate, or banana cream pie, are a specialty. Open

Mon.–Sat. noon–10 P.M., Sun. noon–8 P.M.; tel. 376/766-1733. Moderate.

Next door, the friendly owner/chef of **Restaurant Bruno's** is so skilled that he has to open only a few hours per day (12:30–3 P.M. and 6–8 P.M.) to be successful. Bruno, who also sometimes waits on tables, puts out an innovative repertoire of mostly Italian- and Chinese-style dishes at lunchtime, and good old reliables such as barbecued ribs or chicken for dinner. He buys his food fresh daily, and in quantities calculated so that nothing will be left over. By 3 P.M. on a busy day, he begins to run out of food. Arrive early for a full choice. Recently, Bruno has been cooking on weekends only. Check when you call for reservations; tel. 376/766-1674. Moderate.

Diners seeking elegance enjoy a number of good Ajijic options. For the food, many Ajijic regulars pick **Los Telares,** downhill about two blocks below the Ajijic town plaza. Patrons have a choice of seating, either in the sunny central patio/garden or in the shady surrounding veranda. Likewise they have plenty of choices in the long menu of tasty appetizers, soups and salads, and expertly prepared continental-style meat, seafood, and pasta entrées. Open Sun.–Thurs.

noon–9 P.M., Fri. and Sat. noon–10:30 P.M. Reservations strongly recommended; tel. 376/766-0428. Expensive.

Soft lighting, live background piano melodies, and an airy stone-arched dining room terrace set the romantic tone of the **Hotel La Nueva Posada** restaurant. The menu of mesquite-broiled fish, chicken, ribs, and steaks garnished with delicious broiled vegetables provides the successful conclusion. The hotel is at Donato Guerra 9, by the east-side lakefront. Open daily 8 A.M.–9 P.M. Reservations recommended; tel. 376/766-1444 or 376/766-1344. Moderate to expensive.

For a relaxing lakeshore lunch or sunset dinner, try the longtime **Restaurant Posada Ajijic** at the foot of Colón. Once a hacienda, later a hotel, the Posada Ajijic restaurant now rests in comfortable old age beneath a grove of venerable, giant eucalyptus trees. Inside the dining room, furnished in colonial-style leather and wood, spreads beneath rustic beamed ceilings to lake-view windows. Service is crisp, and the soups, salads, sandwiches, and entrées (chicken, fish, steak) are tasty and professionally presented. Open Mon.–Thurs. noon–9 P.M., Fri. and Sat. noon–1 A.M., Sun. noon–9 P.M. Recorded dance music Fri.–Sun. evenings; tel. 376/766-1430. Moderate.

Local Ajijic folks recommend a number of other restaurants, too numerous to describe in detail. They include: **Min Wah,** for good Chinese cooking, at Callejon del Tepala 6 (from landmark Lloyd's Financial on the highway, go about three blocks uphill), tel. 376/766-0686, open daily 11 A.M.–9 P.M. Moderate; **Pimienta Negra,** featuring Lebanese–Middle Eastern food, on Ocampo, about three blocks west of the Ajijic Plaza, open Tues.–Thurs. noon–8 P.M., Fri. and Sat. noon–8 P.M., Sun. noon–6 P.M. Moderate-expensive; **El Sarape,** for good Mexican cooking, Tex-Mex, and Arizona-Mex style, with salad bar, west-side Ajijic, on the highway, just west of Bungalows Las Casitas, tel. 376/766-1599, open daily 11 A.M.–8:30 P.M. Moderate; and **Restaurant Diana de Italia,** for perfect *pasta al dente* and a good Sunday brunch (11:30 A.M.–3 P.M.), on the plaza, in San Antonio (midway between Ajijic and Chapala), at Independencia 124, a few blocks downhill from the highway, tel. 376/766-0097. Moderate-expensive.

Groceries

In Ajijic, smart shoppers go to **Super El Torito** for a wide selection of fresh veggies, fruit, meat, groceries, and a small but good English-language newsstand. It's open daily 7:30 A.M.–9 P.M., at Plaza Bugambilias, on the highway, east side, tel. 376/766-2202. **Super Lake,** tel. 376/766-0174, midway between Ajijic and Chapala, enjoys equal popularity. It offers a wide choice of groceries, vegetables, and fruits, plus many frozen foods, a deli, and a soda fountain. Also available are magazines and newspapers, including the Mexico City *News, USA Today,* and the informative local monthly, *El Ojo del Lago.* It's open daily 8 A.M.–8 P.M. in San Antonio, on the lake side of the highway.

In downtown Chapala, the best bet for groceries and fresh fruits and vegetables is the town market, east side of the plaza, open daily until around 6 P.M.

ENTERTAINMENT AND EVENTS
Nightlife

As many locals do, start off your Lake Chapala evening in proper style by enjoying the sunset (5:30–6:30 P.M. in the winter, an hour later in summer). An excellent spot to ensure that you don't miss something spectacular is the Ajijic pier at the foot of Colón. The Chapala pier offers a similarly panoramic prospect.

Evening lake cruises offer another possibility. While at the Chapala pier, ask the boatmen about a *crucero de puesta del sol* (sunset cruise). In Ajijic, seasonal onboard parties *(fiestas a bordo)* leave by lake cruiser from the beach, foot of Donato Guerra by the Hotel La Nueva Posada, on weekends around noon and 4 P.M. Additional special cruises, when passengers can enjoy both the sunset and the full moon shimmering on the lake, depart at around 4 P.M. from the same point on dates when the moon is full.

Furthermore, Chapala romantics sometimes organize horseback *lunadas* (moonlight rides) to a campfire-lit viewpoint in the hills above Ajijic. Dates depend on the full moon. Watch for an announcement in the "Mark Your Calendar" section of the local newspaper, *El Ojo del Lago* (get a copy at its Chapala office, tel. 376/765-3676), or check with the tourist information office in Chapala.

A major exception to the generally quiet nights around Ajijic and Chapala occurs at the Ajijic **Hotel La Nueva Posada** bar La Corona, with live piano happy hour Tues.–Thurs. 7–10 P.M., and music for dancing, Fri. and Sat. 8–11 P.M. Find it at the lakeshore, foot of Donato Guerra, four blocks east, two blocks downhill from the central plaza, tel. 376/766-1444.

Subdued and very appropriate for dinner is the live music that **Las Telares** restaurant, tel. 376/766-0428, two blocks downhill from the Ajijic plaza, customarily offers Saturday and Sunday 7–9 P.M.

Hotel Chapala Haciendas, tel. 376/765-2720, a five-minute drive uphill from downtown Chapala along the highway to Guadalajara, entertains patrons with Armando's piano-guitar-drum combo Wednesdays and Saturdays 7–11 P.M.

For more entertainment suggestions such as concerts, plays, and art exhibitions, see the informative "Lakeside Living" and "Mark Your Calendar" sections in the widely available English-language monthly, *El Ojo del Lago.*

Fiestas

Occasional local festivals quicken the ordinarily drowsy pace of Lake Chapala life. Jocotepec, at the lake's west end, kicks off the year in early January with the two-week fiesta of **El Señor del Monte.** The fiesta's origin is local—an image of Jesus on the Cross, originally carved from the branches of a *guaje* tree, is believed miraculous because it was seen either glowing or burning (depending on which account you believe). Nevertheless, folks make plenty of the legend, with a swirl of events including masses, processions, bullfights, and cockfights, all accompanied by a continuous carnival and fair. The celebration climaxes on the third Sunday of January, when downtown is awash with merrymakers thrilling to the boom, roar, and flash of a grand fireworks display.

The local North American community joins in the party, usually in early February, with a big, for-charity **Chili Cook-off** on the beach by the Ajijic pier. Events include "Las Vegas Lounge" gambling tables; a "Mexican Night" with music, dancing, and a "Miss Chili Cook-off" pageant; and, finally, chili judging and awards, with plenty left over for everyone. For schedule and entry information, contact *El Ojo del Lago* newspaper, P.O. Box 279, Chapala, Jalisco 45900; tel. 376/765-3676 or 376/765-2877, fax 376/765-3528; email: ojodellago@laguna.com.mx.

Merrymaking continues with **Carnaval** (Mardi Gras) dancing and parades before Ash Wednesday, the first day of Lent, usually in late February. On several subsequent Fridays, rockets boom high over town and village streets, as image-bearing processions converge for special masses at local churches. This all culminates in **Semana Santa** festivities, notably in Ajijic, where local people, in full costume, reenact Jesus' ordeal.

The hubbub resumes in Chapala around October 4, with the climax of the fiesta of the town patron, **San Francisco.** Townsfolk dance, join processions, watch fireworks, ride the Ferris wheel, and pitch pesos. Later, party animals can enjoy more of the same during Ajijic's **Fiesta de San Andrés** during the last nine days of November.

SPORTS AND RECREATION
Jogging and Gyms

The breezy Lake Chapala shore is the best spot for a stroll or a jog. Best to get out early or late and avoid the heat of the day. In Ajijic, try the beach by the pier (foot of Colón), where several hundred yards of level, open meadow invite relaxing walking and running. In Chapala, the lakefront boardwalk or the grassy perimeter of Parque Cristiania on lakefront Av. R. Corona, a few hundred yards east of the church, offers similar opportunities. Alternatively, you might join company with the many local folks who bike, jog, and walk along the paved bicycle path *(pista)* that parallels the Chapala-Ajijic highway.

A few Chapala and Ajijic gyms, such as the **Estudio Body Line** gym, tel. 376/766-2260 (on the highway, in the Bugambilias shopping plaza, second floor), offer machines and low-impact aerobics classes.

Swimming

Although Lake Chapala's shallowness (which keeps bottom mud stirred up) and hyacinth-clogged shorelines make it uninviting, hotel pools remain an option. In Chapala, both the lakeshore **Chapala Inn** and uphill **Hotel Chapala Haciendas** have inviting, medium-size, but unheated pools. For access details, see Accommodations, earlier. Most luxurious, however, is the big lake-view pool at the **Hotel Villa Montecarlo,** whose palmy grounds and natural hot spring are open for public day use. Cost is about $6 per adult; call ahead, tel. 376/76521-20, to see if the big pool is open.

In Ajijic, an equally luxurious swimming possibility exists at the beautiful lakefront pool at the **Hotel Real de Chapala,** where, for the price of a poolside lunch, you can enjoy a swim. Although a similar prospect exists at the nearby **Hotel La Nueva Posada,** a better swimming opportunity is available at the **Balneario Motel San Juan Cosala hot spring resort,** where spring-fed lake-view pools are available for public use, $6 per day per adult, $3 children.

Probably the best local lap swimming ($3 per person) spot is at the **Hotel Joya del Lago,** on Calle Río Zula, on the far west side of town. Get there by taxi, car, or foot about one mile west of Ajijic town center. (From the highway, turn toward the lake, at the Hotel Danza del Sol sign and continue about three long blocks downhill, to Hotel Joya del Lago, on the right.)

Tobolandia waterslide park is a favorite with kids, with two big, warm-water swimming pools, waterslides, picnic ground, restaurant, and more. Find it on the Chapala-Ajijic highway, entrance at the Guadalajara cutoff road. Open daily except Monday 10 A.M.–6 P.M.; adults $6, kids $3.

Water Sports and Boat Launching

Although winds and currents often push mats of pesky water hyacinths onto Lake Chapala beaches, lake access is possible at certain times and locations. If so, nothing else will stop you

LAKE CHAPALA UP AND DOWN

Of all the many threats to Lake Chapala, the most serious is that the lake may one day dry up completely. No problem, optimists say. They point out that Lake Chapala nearly dried up in 1955 but recovered in the 1970s, flooding Chapala town street under two feet of water for weeks. Nevertheless, recently, the lake level has dropped even lower than in 1955. In the summer of 2001, Lake Chapala's level dropped ominously, to its lowest in living memory: so low that its shoreline receded a quarter mile from the Chapala town dock and lighthouse.

Although people disagree on the gravity of the problem, virtually everyone agrees that the drying of Lake Chapala would be a manifold tragedy. Besides the demise of the beautiful shimmering lakeshore sunsets, the lake's temporizing effect on weather would be erased, resulting in hotter summers and colder winters. More immediate would be the loss of easy irrigation for lakeshore farms and water for Guadalajara's people and industries.

And therein may lie a major part of the problem. According to government data, since the city of Guadalajara began drawing water from Lake Chapala during the 1970s, the lake level has steadily dropped a total of at about 18 feet (6 meters). From other perspectives, the last quarter-century witnessed a net loss of seven-eighths of the lake's total water volume, a shrinkage of it area by 40 percent, and a reduction of its average depth from about 22 feet (seven meters) in the mid-1970s to a mere four feet (1.4 meter) in the summer of 2001.

Although people can cross their fingers and hope that successive years of abundant rainfall will restore Lake Chapala's level, more is clearly necessary in the long term. Hopefully, resolute regional and federal leadership will soon produce the conservation measures necessary to save this precious resource.

from floating your kayak, or your sailboard, on the lake.

If you want to launch your own boat, ask the Club de Yates (YAH-tays) de Chapala if you can rent its boat ramp (although in recent years, the lake level has been so low that boaters can launch right on the beach in Ajijic). You can find the club on lakefront Paseo Corona, across from Parque Cristiania, about a half-mile east of the Chapala pier, tel. 376/765-2276.

Golf, Tennis, and Horseback Riding

Local enthusiasts enjoy a pair of **nine-hole golf courses.** The Chula Vista Country Club, tel. 376/765-2515, greens carpet the intimate valley that spreads uphill from the highway, midway between Chapala and Ajijic. Play starts daily at 8 A.M.; the last round begins at 3 P.M. The nine-hole greens fee runs $22 weekdays, $32 weekends, plus caddy, $6. A clubhouse bar and restaurant serves food and refreshments. Golfers enjoy similarly good conditions at the nine-hole **Chapala Country Club,** tel. 376/763-5136, overlooking the lake near San Nicolas, about five miles (eight km) east of Chapala.

Private tennis courts are available at the Chula Vista Country Club, tel. 376/765-2515, $3 per hour; the Hotel Villa Montecarlo in Chapala, tel. 376/765-2120, $6 per day; and the Hotel Real de Chapala, tel. 376/766-0007, in Ajijic (night-lit), $8 per hour. Even cheaper, but nevertheless well-maintained **public tennis courts** are available at Parque Cristiania, on the lakefront, about half a mile east of downtown Chapala.

Guided **horseback rides and rental horses** ($5 per hour) are available daily at the corner of Avenidas Camino Real and Camino del Lago, in La Floresta subdivision, a block west of the Hotel Real de Chapala.

SHOPPING
Handicrafts and Clothes

For the more common, but attractive, handicrafts, try the stalls that line the lakefront walkway, beginning at the Chapala pier. Look for good bargains in Oaxaca wool weavings, Jocotepec

a traditional Huichol yarn painting

serapes, Tonalá pottery and papier-mâché, Guadalajara *huaraches,* Paracho (Michoacán) guitars, Santa Clara del Cobre (Michoacán) copperware, and dozens more colorful items brought from all over Mexico.

In Ajijic, you have at least a couple of close-to-the-source handicrafts options: the woven art of a number of indigenous women at lakeshore (in front of the Restaurant Posada Ajijic), foot of Colón-Morelos, and the Jalisco State **Casa de las Artesanías** (House of Handicrafts), tel. 376/766-0548. Open Mon.–Fri. 10 A.M.–6 P.M., Sat. 10 A.M.–4 P.M., Sun. 10 A.M.–2 P.M. Watch for the sign on the highway as you're entering from Chapala, just after the big white roadside sculpture on the left. Inside, a host of Jalisco handicrafts—shiny Tlaquepaque red-and-blue glass and fine painted stoneware, fanciful painted pottery figures, cute papier-mâché and pottery animals from Tonalá, charming nativity sets, bright paper flowers—fill the gallery.

Ajijic's well-to-do resident expatriate community has nurtured local arts and crafts activity. Products of Chapala area artists and artisans, combined with national sources, make up a number of unusually fine selections in several Ajijic shops and boutiques. A good place to start is **Centro de Bellas Artes de Ajijic,** a block and a half downhill from the highway. Colón 43, tel. 376/766-1920. Open Tues.–Sun.

10 A.M.–5 P.M. As much a community art center as a store, it offers many sensitively executed paintings and photographs by local artists. Don't miss the tranquil, verdant sculpture garden and cafe in the rear.

Downhill two blocks, on the east side, just uphill from the post office, don't neglect to step into the **Galería de Paola;** tel. 376/766-1010, fax 376/766-2572, labor of love of owner-photographer María de Paola Blum. Here, you can peruse downstairs and upstairs and be entertained by her eclectic gallery of carefully chosen sculptures, paintings, photos, handicrafts, and artistic odds and ends. Open Mon.–Sat. 10 A.M.–3 P.M. and Sun. 11 A.M.–2 P.M.

Additional interesting Ajijic shops cluster another block downhill, near the corner of Morelos (Colón's downhill continuation) and 16 de Septiembre. Among the best is **Mi México,** the labor of love of its expatriate owners, at Morelos 8, corner of 16 de Septiembre, tel./fax 376/766-0133. Their collection seems to include a little bit of everything handmade—paintings, jewelry, Guadalajara resortwear, block-printed cottons, Balinese batiks—from all over Mexico and the world. Open Mon.–Sat. 10 A.M.–2 P.M. and 3–6 P.M., Sun. 11 A.M.–3 P.M.

Ready-to-wear clothes are a specialty of **Opus Boutique,** across the street, at Morelos 15, tel./fax 376/766-1790; email: loiscugi@laguna.com.mx. The inventory blooms with attractive, comfortable resortwear—dresses, slacks, skirts, blouses—and some Indonesian batiks, jewelry, and small paintings. Open Mon.–Sat. 10 A.M.–6 P.M., Sun. 11 A.M.–3 P.M.

Directly across the street downhill, **La Flor de la Laguna,** Morelos 17, tel. 376/766-1037, offers a bright kaleidoscope of Mexican handicrafts. Its assortment includes glistening papier-mâché parrots, a rogue's gallery of masks, and a fetching menagerie of nativity sets, yarn dolls, and much more in leather, wood, brass, copper, and cotton. Open Mon.–Sat. 10 A.M.–6 P.M., Sun. 10 A.M.–2 P.M.

On the same side of Morelos, a few doors uphill, is **Calipso,** where eclectic, attractively arranged wares fill two intimate, adjacent rooms. You'll find it at Morelos 7 and 7B, open Mon.

and Wed.–Sat. 10:30 A.M.–2 P.M. and 3:30–6:30 P.M., Sun. 11 A.M.–4 P.M. Calipso specializes in unusual resortwear—dresses, skirts, blouses—in striking bright and dark hues, plus some pieces of tie-dyed art-to-wear, bright clay dolls, colorful wooden horses, silver jewelry, leather purses, and more.

Continue next door to **Ángel Cantor** ("Singing Angel"), at Morelos 13, tel. 376/766-0717. Here, a galaxy of selected all-Mexico handicrafts includes ceramic masks, antique photo postcards, fine Tlaquepaque stoneware, shiny Oaxaca metal-framed mirrors, and a pile of attractive baskets. Open Mon.–Sat. 10 A.M.–7 P.M., Sun. 10 A.M.–5 P.M.

Continue west along the prolongation of 16 de Septiembre (which has changed to Independencia) half a block from the Morelos corner, to **Porta Libros,** another labor of love (at Independencia 7). Here, a library of used books, mostly old paperbacks, and new magazines, fills several small rooms.

After a hard day perusing so many shops, you might want to **take a break.** You have at least three good possibilities. Off the town plaza, on Hidalgo, half a block west of the bank, you'll find **Evie's** restaurant, open Mon.–Sat. 8 A.M.–4 P.M., Sun. 8 A.M.–3 P.M., closed Wed., whose friendly owners' specialties are house-roasted coffee, home-baked fruit pies, and gourmet soups and sandwiches. Next, two blocks downhill from the town plaza is **Las Telares** restaurant, right among the shops, at Morelos 6, open from noon daily. Lastly, try the **Restaurant Posada Ajijic,** open daily at noon, at the foot of Colón.

Finally, be sure to take a look at the attractive hand-woven art—wool rugs, serapes, blankets, and more—that a number of indigenous Guerrero, Oaxaca, and Chiapas women make and sell, adjacent to the Restaurant Posada Ajijic.

Photofinishing, Cameras, and Film

The best local photo services are available in downtown Chapala, at **Foto Centro** on Madero, corner of Romero, two blocks uphill from the town plaza, tel. 376/765-4874. Open Mon.–Sat. 9 A.M.–7 P.M., Sun. 9 A.M.–2 P.M. Besides the usual color print films, its relatively broad film stock includes professional 120 Ektacolor and Fujicolor, black-and-white, and both Ektachrome and Fujichrome 35 mm transparency films. Foto Centro additionally offers some point-and-shoot cameras and common photo accessories. Services, besides color negative, transparency, and black-and-white developing and printing, include enlargements, photo identity cards, and camera repairs.

In Ajijic, you'll find a smaller branch of Foto Centro on the uphill side of the highway, across from Danny's Restaurant. Open Mon.–Sat. 9 A.M.–2:30 P.M. and 4:30–7 P.M. It offers developing services and a small stock of popular film, point-and-shoot cameras, and supplies.

SERVICES

Money Exchange

In both Chapala and Ajijic, bank-rate money exchange, traveler's checks, and prompt service in English are available at **Lloyd's.** In Chapala, go to Madero 232, across from the town plaza, tel. 376/765-4750 and 376/765-3598, fax 376/765-4545; in Ajijic, it's on the highway, east side of the town center, across the street and a block west of the gas station, tel. 376/766-3110, fax 376/766-3115. Lloyd's, moreover, offers a number of financial and investment services. Both branches are open Mon.–Fri. 9 A.M.–5 P.M.

Conventional **banks,** all with ATMs, are well represented in Chapala, all located near the corner of Hidalgo (the Ajijic highway) and main street Madero. Moving uphill, first comes long-hours **Banco Internacional,** tel. 376/765-4110, open Mon.–Sat. 8 A.M.–7 P.M. Two doors farther is **Bancomer,** tel. 376/765-4515, open Mon.–Fri. 8:30 A.M.–4 P.M. After bank hours, use the banks' **ATMs,** or the small **Casa de Cambio TLC Divisas** that changes money until about 7 P.M. around the corner from Bancomer.

In Ajijic, change your U.S. or Canadian cash or traveler's checks at plaza-front **Bancomer,** corner of Hidalgo and Colón, tel. 376/766-2300, open Mon.–Fri. 8:30 A.M.–4 P.M., Sat. 10 A.M.–2 P.M. After hours, use the bank's ATM or go to the hole-in-the-wall *casa de cambio* at Colón 28, on the plaza, west side, tel. 376/766-2213, open Mon.–Fri. 8:30 A.M.–5 P.M., Sat. 8:30 A.M.–4 P.M.

Tour Guides

Some local guides offer tours and assistance getting settled. Contact the earnest and friendly operators of **R&R in Mexico,** Mark Kunce and Sandy Brown, whose mission is to help visitors enjoy, appreciate, and get acquainted with the Guadalajara–Lake Chapala region. They offer consultations and services, including reasonably priced, all-inclusive tour itineraries. For more information, contact them by telephone directly in Guadalajara, at tel. 376/121-2348; email: info@rr-mexico.hypermart.net or tours@rr-mexico.hypermart.net; website: www.rr-mexico.com.

You might also check out English-speaking naturalist and guide Jeremy Lusch, who leads visitors on Chapala and Guadalajara area tours, nature walks and safaris. Besides city excursions to Guadalajara, Tonalá, and Tlaquepaque, he leads visitors on nature walks and safaris to view the seawater crocodiles (some huge, up to a half a ton and 20 feet long) that nest in remote coastal mangrove lagoons. For more information, dial tel. 376/766-1829; email: j_lusch@hotmail.com; website: www.hummingbirdmex.com.

Post, Telecommunications, and Internet

Both the Chapala town *correo* and *telecomunicaciones* are on lakeshore Av. Hidalgo, about three blocks west of Madero. The *correo* (downstairs, in back) is open Mon.–Fri. 9 A.M.–3 P.M., while the *telecomunicaciones* (upstairs, in front) is open Mon.–Fri. 9 A.M.–2 P.M.

In Ajijic, the small *correo* is at Colón and Constitución, one block downhill from the plaza; it's open Mon.–Fri. 8 A.M.–2 P.M., and (sometimes) Sat. 9 A.M.–1 P.M.

Computel, at the Chapala town plaza, tel. 376/765-4951, provides long distance and fax service daily 7 A.M.–10 P.M. Long-distance phone, fax, photocopies, and Internet connection ($3 per hour) are available at **Centro de Copiado de Chapala,** at the center of town, corner of Madero and Hidalgo; fax 376/765-3311. Open Mon.–Fri. 9 A.M.–6 P.M., Sat. 9 A.M.–2 P.M.

In Ajijic, Internet access ($4 per hour) is available at **Cafe Internet,** on the highway, east side of town, across from Telmex telephone office.

At **Mailboxes, Etc.,** you can have everything—express mail, fax, long-distance phone, message center, mailbox, copies, office services, and even a San Diego, California, P.O. box. Find them on the highway in San Antonio, halfway between Ajijic and Chapala at Carretera Chapala-Jocotepec 144, San Antonio Tlayacapan, Jalisco; tel. 376/766-0647, fax 376/766-0775. Open Mon.–Fri. 9 A.M.–6 P.M., Sat. 9 A.M.–3 P.M.

Health, Police, and Emergencies

Ajijic has a well-equipped small private hospital, the **Clínica Ajijic** on the highway, No. 33 Oriente, four blocks east of Colón, tel. 376/766-0662 or 376/766-0500. They offer 24-hour ambulance service and English-speaking specialists available for both regular and emergency consultations.

If you get sick in Chapala, contact your hotel desk or the **Clínica de Especialidades Nueva Galicia,** at Juárez 563A, tel. 376/765-2400, 376/765-4549, a few steps north of the northeast plaza corner. Here, general practitioner Dra. Adela Macias Vengas and gynecologist Dr. Felipe de Jesús Ochoa, and a number of others, offer services, on-call 24 hours.

If you prefer homeopathic treatment, go to **Farmacia Abejita** (Little Bee), next to the above doctors' office, at Juárez 559, corner of L. Cotilla, tel. 376/765-2266. They're open Mon.–Wed. and Fri. and Sat. 10 A.M.–2 P.M. and 4:30–8 P.M., Sun. and Thurs. 10 A.M.–2 P.M.

For medicines and routine advice, the best-supplied Chapala town pharmacy is **Hector's** at 435A Madero, half a block north of the plaza, tel. 376/765-4002. Find them open Mon.–Wed. and Fri. and Sat. 9 A.M.–9 P.M. and 3–8 P.M., and Sun. and Thur. 9 A.M.–3 P.M. In Ajijic, get your medicines and drugs from **Farmacia Cristina,** at Plaza Bugambilias, on the highway, about six blocks west of the town center, tel. 376/766-1501. Open daily 8 A.M.–9 P.M.

For **police emergencies** in Chapala, call tel. 376/765-2851, or go to the police station on Niños Héroes, corner of Zaragoza. (From the Hidalgo-Madero town center, go one block

south, two blocks east.) In Ajijic, contact the police at the *presidencia municipal* (town hall), on Colón, west side of the plaza, tel. 376/766-1760.

Consulates

The U.S. consul in Guadalajara, at Progreso 175, about a mile west of the city center, a block south of Av. Vallarta and a block east of Av. Chapultepec, maintains service hours for American citizens, Mon.–Fri. 8 A.M.–11 P.M.; tel. 376/825-2700 or 376/825-2998. **The consul also periodically visits the Lake Chapala area.** The visitation schedule is customarily listed in the Lake Chapala Society's section of *El Ojo del Lago* newspaper, and posted on one of the bulletin boards at the Neil James Library (on Av. 16 de Septiembre) in Ajijic.

The **Canadian consulate** is also in Guadalajara, at the Hotel Fiesta Americana at Aurelio Aceves 225, local 31, west side of the Minerva Circle. They are open Mon.–Fri. 8:30 A.M.–2 P.M. and 3–5 P.M.; tel. 376/616-5642. In emergencies, after business hours, call the Canadian consulate in Mexico City, toll-free tel. 800/706-2900.

A number of other countries maintain Guadalajara consulates. For details, see Consulates in the Heart of the City chapter.

Travel and Real Estate Agents

Travel and real estate agents can provide many services and are also often willing sources of information. One of the most successful local travel agencies is **Viajes Vikingo,** in San Antonio, on the Chapala-Ajijic highway, at 133A, tel. 376/766-0936, fax 376/766-1058; email: travel@laguna.com.mx.

Also highly recommended are **Coldwell Banker–Chapala Realty,** at Hidalgo 223, tel. 376/765-2877, fax 376/765-3528, and **Laguna Real Estate** in Ajijic, at #24, on the highway, tel. 376/766-1174, fax 376/766-1188; email: laguna@laguna.com.mx.

Handicrafts and Fine Arts Courses

Jalisco State **Casa de las Artesanías** (House of Handicrafts) offers pottery, painting, weaving, and other courses in handicrafts. For more information call 376/766-0548, or drop into its Ajijic gallery, open Mon.–Fri. 10 A.M.–6 P.M.,

Sat. 10 A.M.–4 P.M., Sun. 10 A.M.–2 P.M., on the highway as you're entering from Chapala, just after the big white roadside sculpture on the left.

The **Centro de Bellas Artes de Ajijic** (Fine Arts Center of Ajijic) offers painting, sculpture, ceramics, and photography classes. Ask for details at Colón 43, Ajijic, tel. 376/766-1920, open Tues.–Sun. 10 A.M.–5 P.M., a block and a half downhill from the highway.

INFORMATION
Tourist Information Office
The small Chapala office of Jalisco state tourism is downtown, near the lakefront, at Madero 407, upper level, across the street from the *presidencia municipal* (formerly Hotel Nido). During regular hours, Mon.–Fri. 9 A.M.–6 P.M., Sat. 9 A.M.–1 P.M., the staff will answer questions and give out brochures and maps.

Bookstore, Newspaper, and Library
The best local bookstore, **Libros y Revistas de Chapala,** is across from the Chapala town plaza, at Madero 230; open daily November–May 9 A.M.–7:30 P.M., June–October 9 A.M.–6 P.M., tel. 376/765-2534. Its extensive stock includes racks of English paperback books and dozens of American popular magazines and newspapers, such as *USA Today* and, during the winter, the *Toronto Globe and Mail* and *Los Angeles Times.* It also has many Mexico maps and a number of guidebooks. In Ajijic, the small newsstand by the plaza, at Colón 29, open daily 9 A.M.–2 P.M. and 3–6 P.M., offers a very limited assortment of American newspapers and magazines.

While in Chapala, be sure to pick up a copy of the very informative local monthly *El Ojo del Lago.* Its lively pages are packed with details of local exhibits, performances, and events; pithy articles of Mexican lore and nearby places to visit; and even interesting advertisements. If you can't find a copy, drop by the editorial office at Av.

> *Conservation-minded local citizens have joined together to form Amigos del Lago, "Friends of the Lake." They advise and monitor government efforts to restore Lake Chapala and sponsor educational projects, such as lakeshore trash cleanup and tree-planting.*

Hidalgo 223, at Coldwell Banker–Chapala Realty, tel. 376/765-3676, fax 376/765-3528; email: ojodellago@laguna.com.mx.

The **Neill James Library,** a good work of the charitable Lake Chapala Society, stands in its flowery showplace garden two blocks downhill from the Ajijic town plaza on Calle 16 de Septiembre, a block east of main street Colón; open Mon.–Sat. 10 A.M.–2 P.M. Its broad all-English loan collection includes many shelves of classic and contemporary literature, donated by Ajijic residents. The Society also maintains the adjacent Spanish-language children's library. Open Mon.–Sat. 10:30 A.M.–1 P.M. and 4–6 P.M. In the corridor between the two buildings, an informative bulletin board and community calendar details local cultural, civic, and social events.

The Lake Chapala Society
The Lake Chapala Society, a volunteer civic organization, welcomes visitors at their information desk, open Mon.–Fri. 10 A.M.–1 P.M., at the Society's Neill James Library headquarters on Calle 16 de Septiembre, two blocks above the lakeshore and a block east of Colón, in Ajijic. They invite newcomers to sign up and take part in their extensive schedule of social events and activities, from Great Books and Ham Radio, to Computer Club and eye doctor visits. For more information, see the Lake Chapala Society's section in *El Ojo del Lago* newspaper, or dial tel. 376/766-1582, 376/766-1140, or visit their website:www.mexconnect/mex/lcsindex.html.

Amigos del Lago
Conservation-minded local citizens have joined together to form Amigos del Lago, "Friends of the Lake." They advise and monitor government efforts to restore Lake Chapala and sponsor educational projects, such as lakeshore trash cleanup and tree-planting. Recently their focus has broadened to political protests and lobbying efforts.

For more information, contact articulate and bilingual Aurora Michel, one of the organization's friendly spark plugs (and Chapala manager of Lloyd's Financial) at Fco. Madero 232, tel. 376/765-2149 and 376/765-3598, or at home at 376/766-3111.

GETTING THERE AND AWAY
By Air

Chapala is accessible directly from many U.S. gateways via the Guadalajara airport, just 21 miles (33 km) north of the lake. For flight and airport details, see Getting There and Away, at the end of the Heart of the City chapter.

By Car or RV

The town of Chapala is less than an hour—about 33 miles (53 km) by the federal Hwy. 44—south of the Guadalajara city center. The road connections with major Guadalajara region destinations are the same as those from Guadalajara downtown (see By Car or RV in the Heart of the City chapter), except for minor adjustments. For example, if you're connecting with Lake Chapala directly to or from Tepic or Puerto Vallarta, use the Guadalajara *periférico* (peripheral city-center bypass). This links the

Chapala Hwy. 44 directly with the west-side Tepic–Puerto Vallarta leg of Hwy. 15.

To or from the southern destinations of Barra de Navidad, Colima, and Manzanillo, route yourself south of Guadalajara, along the lake's northwest shore, via Hwy. 15's Jocotepec-Acatlán de Juárez leg. Around Acatlán de Juárez, pay close attention to turnoff signs. They'll guide your connection from Hwy. 54D *cuota autopista* (toll freeway) (Colima and Manzanillo) or two-lane Hwy. 80 (Barra de Navidad).

By Bus

The main Lake Chapala bus station is in Chapala downtown on Madero at M. Martínez, about three blocks uphill from the town plaza. The red-and-white first- and second-class buses of **Autotransportes Guadalajara-Chapala,** tel. 376/765-2212, connect about every half hour with the Guadalajara downtown old terminal (Camionera Vieja) until about 8:30 P.M., and every half hour until about 8:30 P.M. with the new suburban Guadalajara Camionera Central Nueva. Other red-and-white departures connect about every half hour with both Jocotepec and San Nicolas, and every hour with Mezcala.

Guadalajara Getaways

Guadalajara's appeal overflows beyond its metropolitan boundaries. Major pilgrimage shrines, picturesque, pine-shadowed mountain villages, relaxing hot springs resorts and spas, lovely cascades and waterfalls, picturesque old haciendas, Tequila factory tours and tasting, opal mines, and much more await those willing to venture an hour or two beyond Guadalajara's city limits.

The seven getaway destinations described below are reachable in an average drive or bus ride of about an hour and a half, the closest in under an hour, the farthest a little more than two hours. They're all good for an overnight or, even better, a two-night stay that allows a day for getting oriented and a second day for relaxing and lingering. Some places you might want to stay a week or more. The getaways begin with San Juan de los Lagos in the northeast, and work clockwise around the regional map to Magdalena in the west.

Rental horses await riders in the Tapalpa main *jardin*.

© BRUCE WHIPPERMAN

San Juan de los Lagos: A Shrine for All Seasons

The renown of San Juan de los Lagos, (pop. about 50,000), springs from the faith of the many hundreds of thousands of devotees who flock annually to worship the Virgin of San Juan de los Lagos. She is one of a trio of miraculous Virgins (see special topic The Three Sisters of Mexico) who have captured the faith and compassion of tens of millions of Mexicans.

For the discerning visitor, a trip to San Juan de los Lagos can be an eye-opening journey into an old Mexico—of devoted crowds, favorite traditional foods and sweets, festoons of religious trinkets—still vibrant and a wonder to experience despite 100 years of modernization and oft-hostile antireligious federal policies.

HISTORY

The first Spaniards bypassed the village of Mezquititlán (Place of Mesquite), the Tecuexe

DISTANCES/TIMES FROM GUADALAJARA TO:

	mi	km	hrs:min
San Juan de los Lagos	96	155	2:00
Mazamitla	82	132	2:15
Tapalpa	57	92	1:30
Chimulco Spa	43	70	1:00
Río Caliente Spa	15	25	0:45
Tequila	43	70	1:00
Magdalena	50	81	1:15

GUADALAJARA GETAWAYS

indigenous village site of present-day San Juan de los Lagos. A need arose however, after the devastation and suffering of the Mixtón War. Missionaries came to heal and convert the starving and sick.

Fray Miguel de Bolonia built a chapel, refuge, and hospital at the village which, in 1542, he had christened as San Juan Bautista de Mezquititlán. Soon thereafter, the chapel aquired a figurine of the Virgin of the Immaculate Conception, humbly fashioned of native canes.

Three generations later, in 1623, that very image gained fame for restoring the life of a 7-year-old girl, daughter of itinerant circus folk. The figure's fame skyrocketed, attracting hosts of visitors and a pile of offerings. In 1633, authorities decided to establish a local township to handle the crowds of pilgrims and administer the donations. Being in the district of Santa María de los Lagos, the authorities named the town San Juan de los Lagos, after St. John the Baptist.

During the colonial period, the town and municipality, buoyed by the constant pilgrim influx and its rich agricultural hinterland, prospered. In 1810, San Juan de los Lagos leaders were among the first to embrace the insurgency of revolutionary priest Miguel Hidalgo, who was received enthusiastically when he passed through in early 1811.

In the aftermath of the Revolution of 1910, the strong Catholic faith of local people came into conflict with the anticlerical provisions of the revolutionary Constitution of 1917. When President Plutarco Calles (1924-28) attempted to zealously enforce the law, the people of San Juan de los Lagos and the surrounding "Los Altos" upland region mounted a fiercely disciplined guerrilla campaign, killing federal troops and harassing officials.

When federal troops executed their leader, Anacieto González Flores, in April 1927, the guerillas, known as "Cristeros," crying ¡Viva Cristo Rey!, mounted a full-scale war. Federal authorities responded with a brutal, scorched-earth policy, burning farms and crops, killing livestock, and moving all the country people into concentration camps in towns. Deprived of food

© BRUCE WHIPPERMAN

A million pilgrims visit the basilica of the Virgin of San Juan de los Lagos in a typical year.

and support, the guerrilla nevertheless kept fighting, but with diminished vigor, until 1935.

SIGHTS
Getting Oriented
Let San Juan's double-steepled **basilica** be your reference. Standing on the front steps, with the basilica facade behind you, you'll be facing west, with the main plaza (Plaza Principal) in front of you. The east-west street running to your right is Rita Pérez de Moreno, the one to your left is Juárez. Running north-south, on the far side of the plaza, Hidalgo runs to the right past Moreno, while Guerrero, Hidalgo's southward extension, runs left, south, past the plaza. Running east-west, one block north of Moreno, is Independencia, while on the south side, one block south of Juárez, Porvenir runs likewise east-west.

Around the Basilica

Since you're right there, climb the stairs and pass beneath the rose-tinted volcanic stone facade of the basilica, officially, the **Catedral Basilica Santuario de la Virgen de San Juan de los Lagos.** In addition to the approximately ten daily masses, the faithful flock inside continually, resting in the pews, pausing up front to pay their respects, and kneeling to pray for the Virgin to grant a wish.

She reigns above all, in a shiny silver case, flanked by glittering marble and gold, all beneath the all-seeing Eye of God. In a room to the left of the altar, be sure to view the displayed mass of mute testimony—pictures, letters, clothing, bouquets—from the Virgin's followers.

Back outside, wander through the ranks of **stalls,** along Moreno on the basilica's north side, and behind, to the east, along Juárez. The abundance is staggering: embroidery, sombreros, serapes, religious goods—pious angels, baby Jesuses, gilded portraits of Jesus and San Juan—and a small mountain of old-fashioned sweets, from dates and *rollos* (fruit rolls) of tamarind and guava *(guayaba),* to *rompope* (guava eggnog) and coconut candy.

Be sure not to miss the *milagro* stands at the foot of the basilica front steps. The faithful buy the *milagros,* diversely shaped metal charms—dog, cat, horse, leg, hand, baby, man, woman—for making requests (by pinning the token to the robe) of their patron saint.

El Pocito

Despite its petite size, El Pocito (The Little Well) is San Juan's most endearing and not-to-be-missed pilgrimage stop. From the basilica-front, walk west along Moreno three blocks (passing the larger, but less notable Chapel of the Retablo of the Virgin on the right at block two), west to the chapel yard, at the north-side corner of Primavera. Inside, the chapel, officially "La Capilla del Primer Milagro" (The Chapel of the First Miracle), shelters El Pocito, the "Little Well" where the Virgin worked her wonder in 1623.

The story began when the 7-year-old daughter of an itinerant circus master died from a fall from a trapeze. The next day, the people were about to bury her, when Ana Lucía, an indigenous woman who for many years had been the custodian of the chapel and its humble cane figurine of the Virgin of Immaculate Conception, placed the Virgin on the girl's breast, and she amazingly came to life. The girl left with her father and his circus troupe, Ana Lucía lived on for 20 more

M

GETAWAYS

THE THREE SISTERS OF JALISCO

In all of Mexico, only the Virgin of Guadalupe exceeds in adoration the all-Jalisco trio—the "Three Sister" Virgins of Talpa, Zapopan, and San Juan de los Lagos. Yearly they draw millions of humble Mexican pilgrims who bus, walk, hitchhike, or in some cases crawl, to festivals honoring the Virgins. Each Virgin's popularity springs from some persistent, endearing legend. The Virgin of Talpa defied a haughty bishop's efforts to cage her; the Virgin of Zapopan rescued Guadalajara from war and disaster; the Virgin of San Juan de los Lagos restored a dead child to life.

Talpa, Zapopan, and San Juan de los Lagos townsfolk have built towering basilicas to shelter and honor each virgin. Each small and fragile figurine is draped in fine silk and jewels and worshipped by a continuous stream of penitents. During a virgin festival the image is lifted aloft by a platoon of richly costumed bearers and paraded to the clamor, tumult, and cheers of a million or more of the faithful.

Even if you choose to avoid the crowds and visit Talpa, Zapopan, or San Juan de los Lagos on a nonfestival day, you'll soon see the hubbub continues. Pilgrims come and go, bands and mariachis play, and curio stands stuffed with gilded devotional goods crowd the basilica square.

A regiment of religious souvenir stalls fills the streets around the San Juan de los Lagos basilica.

years, finally passing away at age 110, and ever-increasing multitudes of pilgrims came to visit the Virgin year after year.

Be sure to visit the room, the former hospital, outside, to the north of the chapel, where wall pictures dramatize the Virgin's story and the modest belongings—knitted booties, caps, dresses, gloves—of children whose parents asked the Virgin to protect them, decorate the walls.

ACCOMMODATIONS

San Juan de los Lagos has a swarm of hotels, some good, some bad, but most indifferent. Unfortunately, demand has driven prices up and kept quality down. Several are nevertheless recommendable. Prices quoted are the normal, non-fiesta rates; expect increases of 10–30 percent during times of high occupancy. (See Fiestas, later in this chapter.)

Moving from west to east, start at the worthy moderately priced **Hotel Primavera,** three blocks due west of the plaza. Well situated on a quiet back street, the Primavera offers four floors of 50 comfortably furnished clean rooms, with color-coordinated bedspreads, shiny tile floors, drapes, and well-maintained bathrooms. Rooms vary in size, with one to three beds. Rentals run from about $33 s, $44 d, to kitchenette suites sleeping six for $95; all with fans and TV. Other amenities: parking, elevator, and a restaurant. Credit cards accepted. Primavera 13, San Juan de los Lagos, Jalisco 47000; tel. 378/785-1506, fax 378/785-2220.

Move three blocks east to the northwest plaza corner and the big **Hotel Posada Arcos.** The four floors of 130 rooms and suites, arranged in tiers around a central atrium, are not well designed with respect to both privacy and noise. Windows of most rooms (which look out on tiled, and therefore noisy, atrium corridors) must have their drapes drawn for privacy. (Consequently, get one of the quieter, more private rooms with windows facing outward toward the plaza.) Rooms are clean and comfortable, but many are not particularly well-maintained. Make sure that everything works before you move in. Rates begin at $60 s, $65 d, and $70 t, with air-conditioning, TV, and phones. There's also a restaurant. Credit cards accepted. Rita Pérez de Moreno y Hidalgo, San Juan de los Lagos, Jalisco 47000; tel./fax 378/785-1580; email: posada_arcos@sanjuan2.redial.com.mx; website: www.hotelposada-arcos.com.mx.

In exchange for a plaza-front location, you get more for your money at the **Hotel Balha Grande,** two blocks north and two blocks east of the plaza. Past the attractive (but low-ceilinged) lobby and the modern coffee shop–restaurant in the back, an elevator and stairs lead to four floors of about 60 upstairs rooms and suites. Inside, they are simply but comfortably furnished with cool white walls and attractive floral bedspreads, with fixed wall reading lamps, white tile floors, and shiny shower baths. Get a room away from the street for less noise. Expect to pay about $50 s, $55 d, with fans, TV, and parking. Beg-nino Roma 75, San Juan de los Lagos, Jalisco

GETAWAYS

47000; tel. 378/785-4606 or 378/785-4607, fax 378/785-0418; email: hotbalgran@sanjuan2 .redial.com.mx.

On the same street, half a block east, uphill, at the corner of Matamoros, stands the high-rise **Hotel Estancia Real,** queen of local hotels. Builders have taken maximum advantage of the uphill site to provide panoramic westward (sunset) views of the basilica and surrounding downtown. Rooms are arranged in about eight floors, around an airy inner atrium. All are deluxe and attractively decorated with plush carpets, large beds, and luxury bathrooms. Additionally, guests in the suites, on the building's southwest corner, enjoy magnificent views, soft couches, elegantly carved interior stone columns and arches, and large whirlpool bathtubs. Rentals run about $50 s, $70 d for rooms, view suites $110 s or d; all with air-conditioning, cable TV, phone, parking, and a restaurant. Credit cards accepted. Begnino Roma 95, San Juan de los Lagos, Jalisco 47000; toll-free in Mexico tel. 800/714-4496; tel./fax 378/785-2521, 378/785-5100, or 378/785-5101; email: estancia-real@sanjuan2.redial.com.mx; website:www.estancia-real .com.mx.

Nearby, two short blocks south and a block east, find budget alternative **Posada Andrea,** at Plazuela de Romo 4, San Juan de los Lagos, Jalisco 47000; tel. 378/785-0663. Past the small reception and lobby, the 36 rooms, in three floors, are modern, clean, and simply but comfortably furnished. Some rooms are a bit dark, however. Look at more than one before moving in. Rates run about $33 s or d, with shower bath, fan, TV, and parking.

Among the many other local hotels (none of which I checked out personally), the moderately priced, centrally located **Hotel Roma,** at Vicente Guerrero 26, tel. 378/785-2536, toll-free tel. 800/710-9952, was highly recommended. Other centrally located standbys that you might check out in an emergency are Hotel Fanny, Independencia 2, tel. 378/785-4343; Hotel Diana, Diana 6 (south side of the basilica), tel. 378/785-2009; Hotel Frances, Independencia 3, tel. 378/785-2009; and Hotel Quinta Cesar, Juárez 99, tel. 378/785-2610.

FOOD

Market *Fondas, Juguerias,* and Natural Food

The market *fondas* (food stalls) are probably the best food choice for your money around the main plaza. Find them on the upper floor of the market, in the block diagonally northwest of the main plaza. Look around and choose from dozens of savory *guisados* (stews) of chicken, pork, lamb, or beef, as well as, rice, tamales, *chiles rellenos,* and much more. Remember, if *fonda* food is hot, it's wholesome.

Also in the market, stop at one of the *juguerias* (juice bars) for your choice of delicious orange *(naranja),* pineapple *(piña),* strawberry *(fresa),* apple *(manzana),* or banana *(plátano)* juice *(jugo).*

For natural vitamins, minerals, teas, cereals, and more, go to **Rincón Naturista San Juan.** Find them on north-south lane a short block east of the basilica's back side. Open Mon.–Sat. 10 A.M.–3 P.M. and 5–8 P.M., Sun. 10 A.M.–3 P.M. Fortuna 109; tel. 378/785-3249.

Restaurants

Of the acceptable choices around the main plaza, consider low-end open-air **Restaurant Imelda** at the northwest corner of Guerrero and Independencia, a block north of the plaza's northwest corner. Here you have approximately the same options as at the market *fondas*—eggs and pancakes for breakfast, soups, sandwiches, stews, chicken, *chiles rellenos,* and more. Open daily 8 A.M.–7 P.M. You can get about the same at **Restaurant Señorial,** a block and a half south, across the street from the plaza's west side.

For a more refined atmosphere, try the hotels. The **Restaurant Veranda** in the Hotel Posada Arcos, northwest plaza corner, seems to offer the best plaza-front restaurant combination of food, atmosphere, and service. Glistening white plates and blue tablecloths set the stage. The very recognizable menu—hamburgers, hot dogs, onion soup, omelettes, and many entrées, including fish, chicken, and steak—provides many choices.

The restaurants at both the **Hotel Balha Grande** and **Hotel Estancia Real** (see Accommodations, above) provide similarly refined atmospheres and familiar, reliable food choices.

ENTERTAINMENT AND EVENTS

Although the continual crowds and the plaza-front trinket stalls seem to make San Juan's basilica-front blocks appear like a nonstop party, several local fiestas periodically ratchet the excitement up to a near-fever pitch.

Fiestas

Excitement peaks during a pair of winter *ferias.* The entire month of December amounts to a continuous party, beginning December 1–8, when hundreds of thousands of merrymakers crowd in for the *Fiesta de la Inmaculada Concepción de la Santísima Virgen.* (Come if you enjoy crowds, and make your hotel reservations very early.)

Concurrently, December 1–12, the parish church, Parroquia de San Juan Bautista, celebrates the **Virgin of Guadalupe,** with carnival games, traditional dances, processions, floats, masses, food, and fireworks.

During Christmas, *Navidad,* people crowd in to celebrate, December 20–25, with plenty of food, fireworks, and *Las Posadas* processions around the town.

The second *feria* kicks off with the *Fiesta de la Virgen de Candelaria,* January 23–February 2, highlighted by processions and traditional dances. These include *La Presentación del Niño Jesús al Templo* and the *Danza de los Christianos y Moros,* a thinly disguised reenactment of the Conquest of Mexico.

During Passover (Pasqua) and Easter Week (Semana Santa), celebration peaks again with reenactments of the passion, death, and resurrection of Jesus on the days just before Easter Sunday.

The Virgin returns into focus once again, between August 1 and 15, with the *Fiesta de La Asunción,* the celebration of the ascent of the Virgin Mary into heaven.

SERVICES AND INFORMATION

Banks and Communications

A few banks dot the downtown streets. For long hours and an ATM, go to **Banco Internacional,** (BITAL), open Mon.–Sat. 8 A.M.–7 P.M., at Moreno 37, two blocks east of the basilica, tel. 378/785-0010.

To make a local or long-distance **telephone** call, buy a **Ladatel phone card** and use it at the many public street telephones. Answer your **email** or connect to the **Internet** at Café Mundo Virtual, on Independencia, upstairs, a few doors west of Hidalgo.

Tourism Office

Get your questions answered at the local office of Jalisco Turismo, at Segovia 10, south side of street, corner of Fortuna, one short block directly behind the basilica, tel./fax 378/785-0979.

MEDICAL AND EMERGENCIES

Pharmacies, Doctors, and Hospitals

For routine remedies, consult the pharmacist on duty at one of several pharmacies. For example, try the **Farmacia Guadalajara,** open Mon.–Sat. 9 A.M.–9 P.M., Sun. 9 A.M.–7 P.M., on Independencia, between Hidalgo and Zaragoza, one block directly north of the main plaza.

Alternatively, go to the very professional 24-hour pharmacy at the **Clínica San José,** at Plazuela de Romo 2, tel. 378/785-1581 or 378/785-2727. Find it by following Moreno four blocks east of the basilica front, to Plazuela de Romo, the short block that diagonals left from Moreno.

If you need a **doctor,** follow your hotel's recommendation, or call the 24-hour Clínica San José (see the preceding paragraph), with many specialists on call.

For **emergency medical care,** have a taxi take you to the 24-hour emergency room of the Jalisco State Hospital Regional, tel. 378/784-0225, or the Hospital Seguro Social, tel. 378/785-1777, both on the Guadalajara highway, half a mile east of downtown.

Police and Fire Emergencies

Contact the *policía* downtown, at the city hall *(presidencia municipal)* on Segovia, directly behind the basilica, tel. 378/785-0730. In case of fire, call the *bomberos,* at Santa Rosa 12, tel. 378/785-0730.

GETTING THERE

By Car

Get to San Juan de los Lagos by car, via Hwy. 80D. From the center of Guadalajara, follow expressway Calz. Lázaro Cárdenas east. Follow the Hwy. 90 (Tonalá–Zaplotanejo–Mexico City) signs. Continue about 10 miles (16 kilometers) to the Hwy. 80D *cuota* (toll) turnoff to Tepatitlán–San Juan de los Lagos–Lagos de Moreno. Continue north another 72 miles (116 kilometers) an hour and a half to San Juan de los Lagos.

By Bus

First, ride city bus 275 diagonal (or better, use a taxi) to the Central Camionera Nueva (New Central Bus Station), see Getting There and Away in the Heart of the City chapter. Tell the taxi driver that you want to go to San Juan de los Lagos, or ask to be dropped at one of the bus company counters that provide first- or luxury-class service to San Juan de los Lagos. These include: Omnibus de Mexico, in *módulo* 6, tel. 33/3600-0184 or 33/3600-0469; Estrella Blanca (Turistar, Transportes del Norte, Transportes Chihuahuenses), *módulo* 7, tel. 33/3679-0404; Flecha Amarilla (Primera Plus), *módulo* 1, tel. 33/3600-0052, or ETN, *módulo* 2, tel. 33/3600-0501.

Mazamitla: Into the Sierra del Tigre

Mazamitla (elev. 7,280 feet, 2,220 meters) is a village of deep traditions and picturesque back streets that nestle on the side of a lush, pine-tufted mountainside. Lately, Mazamitla has managed to attract the new because of what's old. In the beginning, a few well-to-do Guadalajarans began coming, attracted by Mazamitla's hearty country food, its handicrafts, and its fresh, pine-scented air. Now, the hillsides are dotted with weekend cabins in the woods, a few rustic-chic developments, and some knotty pine *posadas* for the middle- and upper-class city folks who now flock in on holidays and weekends.

HISTORY

Mazamitla (pop. about 12,000) straddles the boundary between the Purépecha (Tarascan) culture of Michoacán and the Nahuatl (Aztec) culture of Jalisco. Although the name "Mazamitla" ("place where arrows for deer-hunting are made") is of Nahuatl origin, Purépecha influence is locally evident. A number of introduced plants, such as avocados, and local street and *barrio* names, such as Charandas, Charácuaro, Coporo, and Huricho are native to Michoacán culture.

The earliest records place Nahuatl-speaking people living in the vicinity by at least 1165.

Later, in 1481, the army of the Purépecha emperor invaded and subdued Mazamitla, en route to the prized salt beds of dry Lago de Sayula.

Purepécha influence was overrun by the Spanish, scarcely a year after their victory over the Aztec empire. In 1522, Spanish Captains Alonso de Ávalos and Cristóbal Juan Rodriguez Villafuerte arrived in Mazamitla with a company of soldiers and cavalry. Local people peaceably accepted the authority of the Spanish king and Catholic baptism, sheltering themselves beneath the fold of the Virgin Mary and Saint Christopher. Legal recognition followed with the founding of the town, officially San Cristóbal de Mazamitla, on March 27, 1537, under the authority of Viceroy Antonio de Mendoza.

SIGHTS

Getting Oriented

The steps of the town parish church, the **Parroquia de San Cristóbal,** built in 1940, is a good spot to get your bearings. With the church facade behind you, you're looking north, toward the main plaza bandstand *(kiosco)*. Behind that is the north plaza-front street, which becomes Allende, west (left, downhill) from the plaza and Reforma, east (right, uphill) from the plaza. Main north-south

Strolling Around Mazamitla

The main plaza is a fine spot for strolling, enjoying the sunshine, and relaxing in general. A choice vantage point for taking it all in is the second-story front porch balcony of the **Posada Alpina,** on the plaza's north side.

It's also fun also to escape the plaza bustle and explore nearby, where a number of antique adobe houses decorate the back lanes. Start directly on the plaza's east side, at **Palacio Yarín,** at Cuauhtémoc 2, corner of Juárez. You can see another interesting old house, north two blocks and west another two blocks, at the corner of Galeana and Mina, by the market and the woodcrafts shops. A third lovely old adobe house, more easily viewable because it's being run as a hotel, is the **Casa Cortijo Azul** (see Accommodations, below), two blocks south of the plaza, at the corner of Guillermo Prieto.

© BRUCE WHIPPERMAN

Mazamitla's handsome Parroquia de San Cristóbal sets the scenic stage at the town plaza.

Beyond the downtown, streets give way to paths that lead to Mazamitla's scenic outdoors. Be sure to include the private park (open daily 9 A.M.–5 P.M.) that surrounds **El Salto** waterfall. Get there by walking south on Juárez a few blocks from the plaza; at the dead-end street, turn right and continue three blocks and turn left at Paseo los Cazos. Continue about three long blocks, past an intersection, to the horse rental station. Past that another long downhill block is the entrance to El Salto park, on the right. Pay the entrance fee and continue past a restaurant and picnic tables. Follow the trail downhill through the pine-shaded grounds, to the scenically precipitious rock-wall waterfall.

Back at the **horse rental** station, if you have more time, rent a horse with guide to lead you on a local excursion. These might include **Los Cazos** private park (canyons, creek, one hour, $5), **El Tabardillo** panoramic viewpoint (two hours, $7), or all the way to the summit of **El Tigre** mountain, elev. 8,990 feet (2,740 meters), an eight-mile, four-hour round-trip, elevation gain 1,710 feet, 520 meters (four hours, $17). (If you, like I, enjoy the exercise, skip the horse and hire a guide only for about half the above prices.)

ACCOMMODATIONS

Mazamitla has about two dozen hotels, mostly knotty pine cabin-style, built to accommodate the many visitors who come on weekends and holidays, when reservations are necessary. Other times you will probably have your pick of the choicest rooms for cut-rate (ask for a *descuento*) prices. Of the seven hotels I inspected, I can recommend five:

Start off at the **Posada Alpina,** on the plaza's north side (opposite the church), at Portal Reforma 8, Mazamitla, Jalisco 49500; tel./fax 353/538-0104. Past the reception and pleasantly airy patio restaurant, stairs rise to the 17 rooms, most arranged around the interior balcony corridor, overlooking the patio. Inside, they are simply but attractively furnished with white walls, wood-beamed ceilings, and polished wooden floors. Rear rooms, away from the busy plaza-front, are quieter and more private. One pleasant extra here is the rustic wooden porch upstairs in front, with seats and tables for relaxing and enjoying the plaza view below. Rates begin at about $30 d, with baths and king-size beds.

Walk two blocks south of the plaza to the antique **Casa Cortijo Azul,** Juárez 10, Mazamitla, Jalisco, 49500, at the corner of Juárez and Guillermo Prieto, tel. 353/538-0068. Enter the tranquil interior garden patio, once the center of family life, now a restful spot for guests to read and relax. The hotel is old and in need of some repairs. Plusses, however, include bright hand-embroidered bedspreads, hand-hewn wood floors, fireplaces, massive beamed ceilings, and a friendly female manager. But unless owners have made improvements since I was there, the rooms will vary in desirability. Lamps may be in need of repair and plumbing might leave something to be desired. Look around and pick the best. Prices, at about $6 per person, are certainly right.

Continue a block east, to the end of Juárez, where a sign and a driveway lead downhill a hundred yards to the rambling, wooded grounds of **Cabañas El Ranero,** rental office at Gómez Farias 30, Mazamitla, Jalisco 49500; tel. 353/538-0223. A quick look around reveals a small village of about 15 wood and stucco cabins scattered on a tree-shaded hillside. Within all this, personable owner-manager Rafael Díaz maintains a forested park, including a small farm of fighting cocks, ducks, and a regiment of frogs in a big pond. To enjoy this place you have to be okay with the roosters crowing and the frogs singing, but it seems a small payment to make for such a charmingly bucolic atmosphere.

The cabins themselves are equally quaint—knotty pine throughout, slightly rickety, but appealing. They appear to be fine for either families or couples who enjoy (and are prepared to put up with) the unusual. Units vary, but are generally spacious and airy, with big living rooms with soft couches, beamed ceilings and fireplaces, but mostly bare-bulb lighting. Stairs and ladders lead to second-floor bedrooms and lofts and at least one bathroom. Kitchens are basic, with utensils, stove, and refrigerator. Some of the cabins have inviting exterior patios with barbecues, picnic tables, and lawn furniture for relaxing. Prices run about $20 per adult, no extra charge for kids.

© BRUCE WHIPPERMAN

Mazamitla visitors enjoy a number of rustic lodgings, from chalets and knotty pine cabins to historic family houses, such as the Casa Cortijo Azul.

HACIENDAS AND COUNTRY HOUSES

A recently established network of historic haciendas and country houses is providing opportunities for visitors to get out into the countryside, breathe the fresh air, and appreciate some of the delights of rural Jalisco. The effort is not unlike similar efforts in Spain, Portugal, and other countries with large numbers of underutilized historic palaces, estates, and castles.

Facilities include comfortably furnished accommodations with baths, often with amenities, such as restaurant, swimming pool, terrace, chapel, and in some cases, a whole working ranch to wander. Activities can include trips to local sites of interest, such as lakes, waterfalls, and pilgrimage shrines. More vigorous activities can include hiking, cycling, kayaking, horseback riding, mountain climbing and rappelling, and volleyball. At least one of the haciendas offer lessons in the arts of *charreria,* such as horseback riding and bull roping and riding (*jaripeo*) for men; and for women, also horseback riding, or *escaramuza,* sidesaddle horseback riding.

The network extends all over the state of Jalisco, presently in nine haciendas and seven *casas rurales.* They are located, moving counterclockwise, from the west, at Ahualulco, Etzatlán, Mascota, and Tapalpa; to the south, at Sayula, Tlajomulco, and Mazamitla; to the east, at Zapotlan del Rey and Lagos de Moreno; and to the far north, at Bolanos.

If you're convinced you want to visit one of these places, some seem especially attractive and well-organized:

In Mascota, try the **Mesón de Santa Elena,** tel. 338/386-0313, 33/3629-0492, or Meson del Refugio, tel. 338/386-0767, 33/3631-5974; email: mesondelrefugion@yahoo.com.gdalajara.

In Tapalpa (see the Guadalajara Getaways chapter), **Hostal la Casona de Manzano,** tel. 343/432-0032 or 343/432-0767.

In Mazamitla (see the Guadalajara Getaways chapter), **Hostal el Ciervo Rojo,** tel. 353/538-0129.

In Lagos de Moreno, **Hacienda Sepulveda** tel. 474/741-8454, fax 474/741-8454; email: jserrano@leon.podernet.com.mx.

In Ahualuco, **Hacienda el Carmen,** tel. 373/733-0110, 33/3633-1771, fax 33/3656-9456; email: sauceda@lasauceda.com; website: www.lasauceda.com

For more information, including the excellent booklet *Haciendas y Casas Rurales de Jalisco* contact the tourist office in downtown Guadalajara, at Morelos 102, Plaza Tapatía, tel. 33/3668-1600, 33/3668-1601; email: dhernand@gobierno.jalisco.gob.mx, or rmorales@gobierno.jalisco.gob.mx; websites: www.jalisco.gob.mx, www.jaliscotour.com, www.visitjalisco.com.

For something fancier, continue southeast and uphill a few blocks to **Cabañas Monteverde,** Chavarría y Constitución, Mazamitla, Jalisco 49500; tel./fax 353/538-0425. Inside the gate and past the reception office, pine-shaded lanes wind through a complex of about 60 cabins sprinkled through inviting, park-like grounds. Tucked beneath the trees are a restaurant, and tennis, volleyball, and basketball courts and a small soccer (*"futbol rápido"*) field for guest use.

Accommodations come in three sizes: small (studio) size, for around two adults and two kids; medium, with bedrooms, for four adults and four kids; and large, with bedrooms, accommodating about six adults and six kids. Most accommodations are single-storied and attractively furnished, with dark, wood-paneled walls, but with light streaming in through large windows that look out on lovely forest vistas. The medium units are more luxurious, with high beamed ceilings, fireplaces, soft couches, and fully furnished kitchenettes. Rates begin at about $47 midweek (Sun.–Thurs.), $55 weekend, for small units; $70 and $95 for medium, and $100 and $140 for large. For more information and reservations, email: montever@prodigy.net.mx; website: www.monteverde.com.mx, or call the Guadalajara reservations line, tel. 33/3616-1060, 33/3616-1826, fax 33/3615-6812.

On the west side of town, about four blocks west of the plaza, you'll find **Hotel Colina de los Ruiseñores** (Hill of the Nightingales), at Allende 50, Mazamitla, Jalisco 49500; tel. 353/538-0484. Personable on-site owners have built a collection of about 20 artfully designed, quaintly rustic accommodations, in a two-floor wing overlooking an inviting patio garden. Although rooms vary in details, they have polished tile floors, shaded reading lamps, attractive hand-loomed bedspreads, fireplaces, and lots of fragrant knotty pine throughout. Rates run about $17 per person, kids under 10 free. For more information, dial their Guadalajara numbers, tel. 33/3615-6475, fax 33/3615-3203; email: ariarce@prodigy.net.mx.

Other lodgings that seem to appear promising from the outside are the Hotel Las Charandas, south side, end of Madero, at Obregón 2, tel. 353/538-0254; Hotel Loma Bonita, on Loma Bonita, two blocks west of Hotel Monteverde, tel. 353/538-0500; Villas Las Glorias, west side, across the street and east of Hotel Colina de los Ruiseñores, at Allende 37, tel. 33/3620-4490; and Cabañas d' Nellys, east side, at Zapata 26, two blocks uphill from the church, tel. 353/538-0093.

FOOD
Local Specialties
Among Mazamitla's prime attractions are its hearty country specialties. At the top of the list is *El Bote,* a bountiful broth of chicken, beef, and pork, with vegetables and condiments, simmered in *pulque; El Sanchocho,* morsels of vinegar-marinated mango, jícama, and carrots; *menguiche,* sour cream seasoned with onion, pepper, green chili sauce, cilantro, and eaten with *totopos* (tortilla chips).

Drinks include yummy a *ponche* (punch) of blackberry, capulín, and the cherry-plum-like *ciruela;* and a wine of quince, *atole,* and honey.

Restaurants
You can get most of the above and more, starting right on the main plaza. For example, try the restaurant in the **Posada Alpina,** at Portal Reforma 8, north side of the plaza, tel. 353/538-0104. Besides local specialties, they additionally offer a very recognizable list of breakfasts, soups, sandwiches, and entrées. Find them open daily 8 A.M.–9 P.M. Moderate.

Equally well located half a block west (near the northwest plaza corner) and trying just as hard is **Posada Mazamitla,** at Hidalgo 2, tel. 353/538-0606, open daily 8:30 A.M.–6:30 P.M. Besides the traditional *El Bote,* all day Sunday, they continue the rest of the week with *pacholas de metate, costillitas con chile* (baby back ribs in chile sauce), and **carne en adobo,** (beef, slow-simmered in a rich, mild *mole* sauce). Moderate.

Probably the most popular restaurant in Mazamitla is **El Troje,** at Galeana 53, five blocks north of the plaza, across from the **gasolinera.** Choose from a long menu of many local specialties, including *filete gaucho* with garlic shrimp; *arrachera* (marinated steak); *chile poblano* with shrimp, bathed in sauce; and stir-fried vegetable *fajitas.* (Unfortunately the crush of weekend crowds lowers the food and service standards at El Troje; go midweek if at all possible.) Open daily 10 A.M.–7 P.M.; tel. 353/538-0070. Moderate–expensive.

Groceries, Baked Goods, and *Conservas*
Abarroteria Chávez, beneath the portal, on the plaza's north side, stocks a supply of basic staples and canned goods. Find them open daily 8 A.M.–10:30 P.M.

A number of **bakeries** serve Mazamitla visitors and residents. Try either (or both): **El Molino,** at 16 de Septiembre 17, tel. 353/538-0131 (a block north of the plaza); or **Pasteleria Gloria,** at Aquiles Serdán 14 (a block south and a block west of the church), tel. 353/538-0542.

Conservas (canned fruits, jellies, and jams) are a Mazamitla old-time specialty. Find them at a number of locations: for example, at **Conservas Elena,** at Reforma 7B (half a block east of the plaza's northeast corner), tel. 353/538-0629; or **Conservas Emma,** at Allende 46, tel. 353/538-

0118, four blocks west of the plaza's northwest corner, a few doors before the Hotel Colina de los Ruiseñores.

ENTERTAINMENT AND EVENTS
Fiestas

Although Mazamitla always seems busy, excitement peaks during annual town festivals, when hotel reservations are especially recommended. Check with the Mazamitla tourism office for details and schedules.

The festival year heats up early, with the **Fiestas Taurinas,** February 17–27, with *charreadas* (rodeos), *jaripeo* (bull-roping), livestock auctions, judging and prizes, fireworks, and plenty of country food.

Enthusiasm climaxes again March 27–30, with the **Foundation of Mazamitla** festival, centering around the plaza, with speeches, band concerts, dance, dramatic and athletic performances, crafts fair, and fireworks.

Processions, special masses, carnival games, food, and fireworks around the church mark the patronal **Fiesta de San Cristóbal** during the last week of July.

The September 13–17 national **Fiestas Patrias** (Patriotic Festivals) culminate with the reenactment of Father Hidalgo's *Grito de Dolores* by the Mazamitla presidente (mayor) at the plazafront *presidencia municipal.*

Mazamitla's festival year comes to a joyful conclusion with the **Fiesta Guadalupana** (Festival of the Virgin of Guadalupe) December 3–12. Mazamitla people celebrate their indigenous and colonial heritage by dressing up and parading in *traje* (ancestral tribal dress) and *ropa típica* (colonial traditional dress), and enjoying lots of old-fashioned food treats, performing traditional dances, and oohhing and aahhing as fireworks paint the sky with showers of red, white, and green over the plaza.

SHOPPING AND SERVICES
Handicrafts

Woodcrafts are a Mazamitla specialty. Local creativity in wood appears nearly boundless, inspiring a host of woodcrafts—fetching wooden clocks, diminutive log houses and flower carts, animals (owls, racoons, bears), picture frames, and much more—decorate the shelves of a number of plaza-

Toy log cabins are a Mazamitla woodcraft specialty.

Horseback riding on the local pine-shadowed trails is a popular and scenic Mazamitla pastime.

front shops. For example, near the plaza's northeast corner of Hidalgo and 16 de Septiembre, try **Artesanías del Bosque** (Forest Handicrafts), at Reforma 2, local 1, tel. 353/538-0132, just uphill from the plaza's northeast corner, open daily 10 A.M.–8 P.M.; **Artesanías Conchita,** at local 3, in the same complex; **Sima Artesanías,** across the street, at Reforma 3B; and Artesanías Julio Emmanuel, around the corner, at 16 de Septiembre 2.

Bank and Travel Agent

Mazamitla's bank, **Banco Serfín,** with ATM, conveniently located beneath the plaza's west-side portal, is open Mon.–Fri. 9 A.M.–4 P.M. Get your air tickets, hotel reservations, cabaña rentals, and more at **Viajes Internacional,** at Galeana 14, tel. 353/538-0580. (Get there from the plaza's northwest corner by walking one block west to Galeana, then one block north.)

INFORMATION AND COMMUNICATIONS

Tourist Information Office

Mazamitla's city tourist information, on the plaza's west side, tel. 353/538-0149, 353/538-0450, or 353/538-0608, next to the police station, answers questions Mon.–Fri. 9 A.M.–3 P.M. Saturdays and Sundays they customarily maintain an information booth on the sidewalk out front, open 9 A.M.–2 P.M.

Mail letters and buy stamps at Mazamitla's *correo* (**post office),** at Gómez Farías 18, across the street from the plaza church's west side.

As for telephones, buy a Ladatel telephone card and use it in one of the several public telephones around the plaza. Alternatively, go to the small *larga distancia* (public long-distance phone office), open daily 8 A.M.–9 P.M., on 16 de Septiembre, half a block north of the plaza's northeast corner.

MEDICAL AND EMERGENCIES

Pharmacy and Doctor

For routine remedies, see the pharmacist or doctor on duty at one of a number of local pharmacies. For example, try kindly **Doctor Lorenzo Nuño Barrios,** at his small pharmacy at 16 de Septiembre 6, half a block north of the plaza's northeast corner, open Mon.–Sat. 8 A.M.–2 P.M. and 4–8 P.M.; tel. 353/538-0127. If he's not

GETAWAYS

available, go to **Farmacia de la Sierra,** at Hidalgo 1, northwest corner of the plaza, tel. 353/538-0034.

Medical, Police, and Fire Emergencies

In a medical emergency, follow your hotel recommendation, or have a taxi to take you to the local **Seguro Social Hospital,** on Xochitl, seven blocks north of the plaza, tel. 353/538-0350.

For both police and fire emergencies, contact the police station, at the *presidencia municipal,* west side of the plaza, tel. 353/538-0202.

GETTING THERE

By Car

From Guadalajara, follow Av. López Mateos Sur to the Hwy. 15 right turnoff (watch for Hwy. 15 Jocotepec/Morelia/Mexico City signs), about 15 miles (25 kilometers), or half an hour south, of the *periférico* (peripheral boulevard). Continue another 33 miles (55 kilometers), passing Jocotepec and Soyatlán, along the Chapala south lakeshore, another hour, to Tuxcueca. At the Mazamitla sign, turn right, and continue another 26 miles (42 kilometers), or 45 minutes, uphill via Manzanilla, to Mazamitla.

By Bus

Mazamitala is conveniently accessible by first-class **Autotransportes Mazamitla** buses, from the Guadalajara's Nueva Central Camionera (New Central Bus Station), *módulo* 2. Buses customarily depart daily, every 30 minutes, from about 7:15 A.M. until about 8:15 P.M. Be sure to call tel. 33/3600-0733 or 33/3635-3723 for schedule confirmation.

From the Mazamitla bus station, on 16 de Septiembre, four blocks north of the plaza, buses return to Guadalajara daily, approximately every 30 minutes, from about 4:30 A.M. until about 6:15 P.M. Call tel. 353/538-0410 for confirmation.

Tapalpa: Gem of the Highlands

Tapalpa (pop. 16,000, elev. 6,780 feet, 2,060 meters) seems to have been able to combine the best of both worlds. From a distance, the entire village—completely of adobe-walled, tile-roofed houses clustering around a proud old church—appears like a vision of colonial Mexico. Move closer, however, and, instead of old-world country folks, you see mostly city people, in shorts and T-shirts, strolling the plaza, sampling homemade sweets and relaxing in plaza-front eateries, enjoying the country cooking for which Tapalpa is famous.

HISTORY

In the Beginning

Although archaeological evidence indicates that Tapalpa's first settlers may have been of Otomi origin, the later, pre-Conquest indigenous residents were Nahuatl (Aztec language) speakers, tributaries to the kingdom of Sayutlán (present-day Sayula). Records show that they paid their tribute mainly with textile dyes taken from local plants, and pottery, exuberantly decorated with the bright mineral colors extracted from nearby deposits. Thereby Tapalpa's original name, "Tlapalpan" or "Land of Colors," was born.

Moreover, archaeologists have uncovered a swarm of treasured remains—jadeite, onyx, terracotta, and stone petroglyphs—that suggest that Tapalpa was once an important ceremonial center.

The Spanish arrived in 1523; quickly the Tapalpa people accepted baptism, and Franciscan missionaries put up the first big church in nearby Atlacco in 1533. They taught the local people to plant and husband groves of peaches and avocados and began building the present Tapalpa Church of San Antonio in 1535.

Colonial and Modern Times

During the colonial era, Tapalpa drew Spanish colonists for its mineral wealth—iron, mercury, silver, and gold. Settlers founded bronze and ironworks in the nearby locality, still known as the "Ferrería de Tula" (Tula Ironworks), although

JUAN RULFO

Juan Rulfo, celebrated leading light of 20th-century Latin American literature, was a child of Jalisco country landholders, made destitute by the ravages of both the 1910–17 revolution and the 1926–29 Cristero rebellion. He was deeply marked by the destruction and terror born of both conflicts. His mother died and his father and a number of relatives were assassinated while he was still a child. Bereft of close family, young Juan grew up in an orphanage and with relatives. He studied law briefly in Guadalajara but moved to Mexico City in 1935 to pursue a writing career.

Bleakness, sadness, and violence pervades his few major works. He began to write short stories during the 1940s and collected them into his first important publication, *El Llano en Llamas (The Burning Plain)*, published in 1953 and translated into English in 1967. Each narrative, typically of seemingly simple country people, is uniquely crafted, but each with the common thread that blends them into Rulfo's view of the universal human condition.

Rulfo's acknowledged masterpiece, *Pedro Páramo,* published in 1955 and repeatedly revised, in 1959, 1964, and 1980, established his renown. The author, thinly disguised as the protagonist, Juan Preciado, fulfills his mother's dying request by returning to his shadowy Jalisco hometown, Comala, in search of this father. Although Preciado discovers that his father, Pedro Páramo (whose surname implies "wasteland"), is long dead, Preciado's search resurrects his father's restless spirit, which recounts its horrific life tale of massacre, rape, and incest.

Although he was achieving literary fame, Rulfo barely scraped by on his early earnings as tire salesman, immigration clerk, and later scriptwriter and television producer. Finally, as the National Institute of Indigenous Affairs editorial director, he achieved a modest level of comfort.

In recognition of his literary accomplishments, Rulfo was asked to become an advisor to the Mexican Writer's Center, during which time he influenced a new generation of writers, such as Carlos Fuentes and Octavio Paz. Recognition rained down upon him: notably, the prestigious Xavier Urrutia prize in 1956, the National Prize of Letters in 1970, and the Spanish Prince of Asturias prize in 1983.

Despite the acclaim, Rulfo remained moody and remote. In a rare interview, in 1966, asked why he didn't bother to teach any writing classes, he answered, " . . . I have no facility with words."

Rulfo's passion for photography remains one of his lesser-known but nevertheless significant legacies. A few exhibitions have revealed his images, captured between 1940 and 1955, of lonely places and marginalized people that he claimed his written works could not describe. The Juan Rulfo Foundation of Guadalajara archives the bulk of his 6,000 mostly unexhibited images.

Born in Barranca de Apulco, in southwest Jalisco, on May 16, 1918, Juan Rulfo died in Mexico City, on January 7, 1986.

products once manufactured, such as iron grillwork and bronze bells, have long ceased being made there.

Paper, another noted local product, was made at the La Constancia paper mill, the ruins of which still stand south of town. Built in 1840, La Constancia was the first paper factory in Latin America; it continued operating until the turbulence of the 1910 revolution shut it down.

The Tapalpa municipality has taken three generations to recover from the devastation and depopulation suffered during the 1910 revolution and the succeeding 1925–30 "Cristero" rebellion. The resulting destruction and anarchy left Tapalpa open to the ravages of guerillas and bandits, such as the notorious Pedro Zamora, whose gang burned the town three separate times, leaving terror and misery in their wake.

But those bad old times have now faded to barely a memory. One glance around the automobile-free, invitingly picturesque main plaza reveals that enterprising Tapalpa residents have entered a new, prosperous era, with a host of businesses—pharmacies, groceries, creameries, hotels, restaurants, and handicrafts shops that serve the influx of visitors.

SIGHTS

Getting Oriented

Savvy planners have transformed the Tapalpa **Jardín Principal** into a relaxing, traffic-free strolling ground. The **Allende steps** on the jardín's west side is a good place to get yourself oriented. Standing on the steps, facing downhill, you're looking east. On your right, south side, stand **Los Arcos** (the Arches) and the venerable Templos San Antonio (in two sections). On your left, Quintero runs east-west uphill from between the *presidencia municipal* and the bank, on the *jardín's* northeast corner. Straight ahead is the *jardín* bandstand, officially the **Foro de Arte y Cultura,** and behind that, the former street, now pedestrian mall **Matamoros** runs north-south along the *jardín's* east-side shop fronts.

Around the *Jardín*

After taking a look into the *jardín's* pair of recently restored old churches, the Templos San Antonio (in two parts, one with a distinguished dome, 1535), and the **Capilla de la Purísima** (behind, dating from 1555), stroll around and sample the goodies for sale beneath the Matamoros portal. Here, a concentration of sweets shops and creameries offers stacks of *conservas* (jam, such as peach, in ceramic jars), sugary bon-bons, rolls of chewy tamarind, *rompope* (guava eggnog), guava-nut cookies, and plenty of white cheese.

Later, take a table on the airy balcony-front of the **Restaurant Paulina,** (west side, by the Allende steps) and order a drink or an *antojito* lunch, and take in the *jardín* scene below.

Sights Out of Town

A number of interesting attractions beckon to visitors with the time to venture a few hours beyond the town limits. Not-to-be-missed is **Las Piedrotas** (The Big Rocks), easily reached by car or on foot, about three miles (five kilome-

Take the scenic entrance to Tapalpa's Jardín Principal via the Allende steps, passing the fountain on your way.

Las Piedrotas, a group of rounded rocks near Tapalpa, are a popular weekend excursion destination.

ters) south of town. Along the way (at mile 1.2, kilometer 2.0) you pass the ruins of the 1840 **La Constancia** paper mill on the right, and a quarter mile farther a private **trout farm,** stocked and ready for fishing.

Las Piedrotas, however, are the main attraction. As you approach from a distance they resemble a family of giant mushrooms in the process of sprouting from the ground. On the top of a mountain, where such rocks would be a dime a dozen, Las Piedrotas wouldn't be worth a mention, but bulging where they are, they present an extraordinary contrast to their bucolic cow pasture surroundings.

Las Piedrotas are a favorite with families, especially with preteens and teenagers who delight in climbing their friendly slopes and exploring their many mysterious niches, overhangs, and passageways. After gazing for a spell at their rounded, tan forms it's not hard to begin imagining animal form—especially seals, whales, and walruses—among the giant, rounded boulders. Bring a picnic and spend the day; add camping gear and stay on overnight. (Get there by car, taxi, or on foot, via a rough but passable road that veers left, Guadalajara direction, from the southern extension of Hidalgo, six blocks from the Allende steps, just before the gas station.)

El Salto del Nogal and Presa del Nogal

Although not easy to access on foot, Jalisco's highest waterfall, El Salto del Nogal, cascading 315 feet (105 meters) in two stages, into a cliff-bottom pool is an impressive sight, especially during the high-water summer season. From Tapalpa, it's about seven miles (12 kilometers), the last half-mile on foot, down a twisting, slippery narrow path. Ask for a guide at the tourist information office (see Information below) and drive your car, hire a taxi, or walk.

An experienced guide will both ensure your safety and point out interesting features along the way. These include the spring and swimming pool (stop for a swim on the way back) at the town of **Atacco** (mile 1.5, kilometer 2.5) and the caves at the village of **Refugio de la Barranca** (mile 6, kilometer 10) where the Cristero fighters hid out during their rebellion.

Another good way to visit the waterfall is via the **Hotel Posada Las Margaritas** (see Accommodations, later). The hotel owner operates the **Restaurant Cascada La Molina** above the waterfall. On weekends, they ferry people by car across their land to the restaurant, which, besides food, offers therapeutic massage and traditional *temascal* hot room treatments.

An easier excursion is to the reservoir **Presa del Nogal,** about five miles (seven kilometers) east of town. If the water is high (most likely during the summer rainy season), the reservoir affords opportunities for fishing, kayaking, canoeing, and camping along its green shoreline. Bring your own equipment.

Get there from the town *jardín,* via east-west Calle Bracamontes (also known as the road to San Gabriel). Follow Matamoros, past Los Arcos, two blocks to Bracamontes, and turn left. Set your odometer. After about three miles (five kilometers), pass the Tapalpa Country Club road. Continue past a couple of signs, the first at about mile 3.5 (kilometer 5.5) and another a fraction of a mile (about a kilometer) farther. Finally, turn left at about mile 4.5 (kilometer 7) at the entrance road to a big fenced-in development. Continue over a bridge, curving gradually left around the lakeshore a few hundred yards to lake access, on the left, just before the dam.

ACCOMMODATIONS
Hotels
Tapalpa has a number of comfortable hotels. Best arrive with a reservation, especially on weekends, holidays, and during fiesta times. (See Entertainment and Events, later.)

Fanciest in town is **Hotel La Casa de Maty,** Matamoros 69, Tapalpa, Jalisco, 49430; tel./fax 343/432-0189. Here, you can have it all: 14 semi-deluxe rooms, with fireplaces, overlooking a leafy rear patio garden that stair-steps down to a rear veranda with a solarium-enclosed spa for guest use. Kids enjoy a recreation room with video games downstairs; adults a billiards room upstairs. Rates run $90 d, with king-sized be; or $105 for two double or four single beds, accommodating four, all with parking, restaurant, and credit cards accepted.

Another good choice is the more spartan **Hotel Posada Las Margaritas,** uphill, at 16 de Septiembre 81, Tapalpa, Jalisco 49430; tel./fax 343/432-0799. Owners offer eight immaculate, rustic-chic accommodations, lovingly decorated with bright wall paintings to match the room themes, such as *colibri* (hummingbird), *palomas,* (doves), or *uvas* (grapes). Three rooms offer king-size beds for two for $45; four larger kitchenette "villas," sleeping four, go for $65, and a huge multi-bedroom kitchenette "villa," sleeping 12, rents for $170, all with parking, but no restaurant.

On the other side of town, the newish **Hotel Posada Real,** offers an attractive neo-rustic-colonial style alternative, at Juárez 229, Tapalpa, Jalisco 49430, tel./fax 343/432-0589 (a block above Hidalgo and about four blocks, south of the *jardín.*). The 21 compactly arranged, clean, comfortably furnished rooms, with up-to-date baths, go for $45 d, with king-size bed, $60 with fireplace, rising to about $90 for a suite sleeping up to seven, with parking and credit cards accepted.

If all the above lodgings are full, Tapalpa has more good hotel choices to check out: El Mesón de Ticuz, privada de Pedro Loza 555, tel. 343/432-0351; Hotel Posada La Loma, Bracamontes 197, tel. 343/432-0168; Posada La Hacienda, Matamoros 7, tel. 343/432-0193; and Villa San José, Ignacio T. López 91, tel. 343/432-0431, fax 343/432-0397.

Tapalpa Country Club
Luxury lodgings with lots of sports extras are available about three miles (follow Calle Bracamontes) south of town, at the **Tapalpa Country Club,** kilometer 5.5, carretera Tapalpa-San Gabriel, Tapalpa, Jalisco 49430; tel. 343/432-0720, fax 343/432-0710. Accommodations start with suites with king-size beds with breakfast for two adults, for about $150, with cable TV, golf course, tennis courts, horseback riding, volleyball, mountain bikes and credit cards accepted. For reservations and more information, call toll-free in Mexico tel. 01-800/713-7030; email: tapalpa country@infosel.net.mx; website: www.tapalpa country.com

Campground

Campamento Gaía offers tent spaces, showers, picnic tables, and electricity at a distant mile 9 (kilometer 15) along the graded gravel road to San Gabriel (southward extension of Calle Bracamontes), south of town. For more details, dial cellular tel. 0443/200-2018 or 0443/402-2744.

FOOD

Traditional Dishes

Tapalpa is famous for *borrego al pastor* (lamb stew, shepherd-style), available at restaurants both along the road into town and in town itself. Another favorite is *tamales de alcelga* (chard), available locally in season.

Favorite local drinks include the yummy *ponche de granada* (pomegranate punch) and *rompopes* (eggnogs) of guava, almond, or pine nuts.

Groceries, Creameries, and Bakeries

Get nearly all the goodies you need right on the *jardín*. Start with the **Cremería La Hacienda** at Matamoros 11, five doors from the corner bank, open daily 8 A.M.–9 P.M. (except 8 A.M.–3 P.M. Sun. and Wed.), tel. 343/432-0194. Pick from a selection of basic groceries and a few deli items, hot dogs, and cheese in a refrigerated case. For what you can't get at the *cremería,* continue next door to **Minisuper Perigrina** (Pilgrim), at Matamoros 13, tel. 343/432-0258.

For dessert, return two doors to the Dulcería del Centro, at Matamoros 9, for a big selection of party goods and traditional sweets, including peanut brittle, and *jericaya* (brown sugar and milk) candy.

Get your fresh baked goods at **Panadería Dona Tere,** on Hidalgo, two and a half blocks south (past Bracamontes) of the Allende steps. The rich selection includes wheat bread *(pan integral),* cookies, donuts, and much more

Restaurants

One of the most relaxing restaurants in town is the airy, tourist favorite **Restaurant Paulina,** overlooking the *jardín,* on the Allende steps, at Allende 69, open daily except Thurs., 9 A.M.–10 P.M.; tel. 343/432-0109. Pick from an all-Mexican menu of eggs, French toast, or pancakes for breakfast, and *antojitos,* such as *chiles rellenos, enchilada al la Tehuacán,* quesadillas, tamales, and smoked pork chops for lunch or dinner. Moderate.

Go upscale at Tapalpa's fanciest restaurant, in the **Hotel La Casa de Maty,** on the *jardín,* at Matamoros 69, open daily 8 A.M.–10 P.M.; tel. 343/432-0189. Within the refined, high-ceilinged, dark wood–paneled dining room, patrons pick from a very recognizable and professionally prepared and served menu of soups, salads, pastas, meats, fish, and fowl. Moderate.

For traditional specialties, a number of restaurants are highly recommended. In town, try refined **Restaurant Los Girasoles** (Sunflowers), at Obregón 110, half a block downhill from the *jardín*-front church. Plainer, but still highly recommended, is **Hostería Antigua,** which claims to have invented *borrego al pastor,* at Hidalgo 283, three and a half blocks south of the Allende steps,

Besides butter, milk, yogurt, and cheese, Tapalpa's several creameries specialize in homemade caramel, bon-bons, custard, fruit preserves, eggnog, and much more.

GETAWAYS

tel. 343/432-0361. On the Guadalajara highway, a mile and a half (two and a half kilometers) out of town, try country-style restaurant **Chepe y Gina** for good *birría* and *borrego al pastor.*

ENTERTAINMENT AND EVENTS

Fiestas

Tapalpa's hardworking residents throw a number of big yearly fiestas. The year starts on a high note with the local **Fiesta de la Virgen de Guadalupe,** which features traditional *mañanitas* masses, dressing up and parading, and folk dancing, and climaxes in a big fireworks blowout on January 13.

Two days later, people have barely had time to catch their breaths when the **Fiesta Charro-Tuarina** begins on January 15 with *charreadas,* (rodeos), *corridas de toros* (bullfights), popular dances in the *jardín,* all climaxing with fireworks on January 20.

A week before Easter, local potters get their big chance to sell their wares in the **Fería de Domingo de Ramos** (Fair of Palm Sunday), when the *jardín* and the surrounding streets are decked out with riots of colorful for-sale ceramics.

The first Saturday of July, seemingly half the town joins a pilgrimage for the **Fiesta de la Virgen de la Defensa,** in which townsfolk take turns in carrying the Virgin home to Tapalpa all the way from the town of Juanacatlán.

In the *Fiestas Patrias,* September 13–16, the whole town seems to fire up, with rodeos, parades of townsfolk on horseback in *charro* (gentleman cowboy) dress, decorated floats, and the reenactment of the *Grito de Dolores* by the mayor at the *presidencia municipal,* all climaxed by fireworks.

SHOPPING AND SERVICES

Handicrafts

Tapalpa continues its ancient handicrafts tradition to the present day. Local products include hand-painted pottery, brightly painted papier mâché, wool, hand woven sarapes, *tapetes* (tapestries and throw rugs), *morrales* (backpacks), *alfombras* (carpets), and *colchas* (bedspreads).

A number of town-center shops sell some or all of the above. Start right on the *jardín,* at **Artesanías La Hacienda,** tel. 343/432-0194, at Morelos 7, upstairs, on the west side of the *jardín* near the tourist information office.

Some hotels and restaurants also sell handicrafts. For example, try **Restaurant Girasoles,** at Obregón 110 (half a block downhill from the church) and **Hotel Posada La Loma,** at Bracamonte 197, tel. 343/432-0168.

Others sell handicrafts right out of their factory shops. Ask for suggestions and access details at the tourist information office. (See Information, later in this chapter.)

Bank and Travel Agent

Change money at **Bancrecer,** with ATM, at the northeast *jardín* corner of Quintero and Matamoros. Banking hours are Mon.–Fri. 9 A.M.–5 P.M., Sat. 10 A.M.–2 P.M.; tel. 343/432-0715 and 343/432-0705.

Get your tickets and flights confirmed at travel agent **Agencia de Viajes Sayula,** at Matamoros 128, a blocks north of the *jardín,* just across the street from the church, tel. 343/432-0089.

INFORMATION AND COMMUNICATIONS

Tourist Information Office

Get your questions answered at the Tapalpa **Turismo** (tourist information office), tel. 343/432-0650, right on the *jardín's,* northwest corner, near Quintero. They're open Mon.–Fri. 9 A.M.–4 P.M., Sat. 10 A.M.–8:30 P.M., Sun. 10 A.M.–5:30 P.M.

Telephones and Post Office

For telephone, use your Ladatel card at one of the several public telephones around the *jardín.* Otherwise, use the public telephone and fax at **Las Ramírez** grocery store, at Morelos 2, just north of the plaza, corner of Quintero and Morelos. Find them open daily 8 A.M.–9:30 P.M.; tel. 343/432-660.

Mail postcards and buy stamps at the Tapalpa *correo* (post office) on Hidalgo, across the street at the top of the Allende steps.

MEDICAL AND EMERGENCIES

Doctors, Pharmacies, and Centro de Salud

If you get sick, consult with **Doctor Ruben Lozana Montes de Oca** at his pharmacy, **Farmacia del Centro** (open daily 8:30 A.M.–9:30 P.M.) on Morelos, half a block north of the **jardín,** tel./fax 343/432-0357.

Alternatively, consult with **Dr. Heliodoro Chavez,** at his **Farmacia Divina Providencia,** at Hidalgo 33A, a block north of the Allende steps, tel./fax 343/432-0473.

A third option is to go to the Tapalpa **Centro de Salud,** on the Guadalajara highway out of town, on the right, about a block past the gas station, tel. 343/432-0363.

Police and Fire Emergencies

In case of either police or fire emergencies, contact the police station, at the *presidencia municipal,* tel. 343/432-0008.

GETTING THERE

By Car

From Guadalajara, follow Av. López Mateos Sur about 16 miles (27 kilometers), or half an hour, south of the *periférico* (peripheral boulevard) to the old Hwy. 54 *(libre)* Acatlan-Sayula-Colima south turnoff. Continue another 31 miles (52 kilometers) south to Amacueca. Turn right and follow the "Tapalpa" signs another 20 miles (32 kilometers) to Tapalpa.

(If you have an extra hour for the return trip, take the scenic route by turning left, at Frontera, about 6 miles (10 kilometers) downhill from Talpa. Continue over a picturesque, pine-shadowed pass to Atemajac de Brizuela, another 15 miles (25 kilometers). Turn right at the "Guadalajara" sign and continue downhill, to Hwy. 54 *(libre)* at Zacoalco, where you turn left, north, toward Guadalajara.

By Bus

Tapalpa-bound **Autotransportes de Jalisco** buses leave from the Guadalajara Camionera Central Vieja (Old Central Bus Terminal), see Getting There and Away in the Heart of the City chapter. At least 10 direct buses depart approximately hourly between about 6 A.M. and 5 P.M.). Call tel. 33/3600-0346 for confirmation.

Return to Guadalajara, from the Tapalpa bus station, at Matamoros 129 (just south of the **jardín** across Matamoros from the church). Guadalajara-bound buses run about every hour between 6 A.M. and 6 P.M. Call the bus station, tel. 343/432-0020, for confirmation.

Chimulco and Río Caliente Spas: At the Source

The Guadalajara region's flock of natural warm springs continues to soothe the tired and sick as they have for countless generations. Warm springs resorts Chimulco and Río Caliente are outstanding, albeit very different examples. Chimulco is a family-friendly mid-scale resort, with bungalows and trailer park, within a private park of swimming pools, water slides, and curative sulfur water baths about an hour south of Guadalajara. In contrast, Río Caliente is an upscale, but low-profile, unpretentious private hot-spring retreat for adults, set in the pristine Bosque Primavera forest about 45 minutes west of Guadalajara.

CHIMULCO

Chimulco ("Place of Vapors") was a sacred healing ground of the indigenous Chimulhucanes people for untold generations before the arrival of the Spanish, who established nearby Villa Corona (pop. 16,000, elev. 4,610 feet, 1,405 meters), around 1550.

Sights and Activities

Inside the entrance gate a quarter mile off Hwy. 80, Chimulco (day-use fee $7 adults, kids half price) offers a wealth of aquatic delights. Naturally healing warm sulfur water feeds half a dozen pools. Children head straight toward the big,

Chimulco Spa and Balneario offers a dozen activities, from water slides and inner-tubing for kids to water massage and lap swimming for their parents.

kids-only pool, complete with bouncy music and Willy the Whale, a pretend lighthouse that spews jets of water, water slides, both straight and super twisty, and a "lazy man" river inner tube run.

Meanwhile, adults enjoy therapeutic jet water massage, smaller private pools, a private night pool, plenty of space, and tennis courts.

Additional facilities for everyone to enjoy include a shady picnic ground with barbecues and benches, and adjacent shallow Lake Atotonilco, which, at high water, becomes a ripe fishing ground from the shoreline or your own boat.

Accommodations and Food

Spend an overnight or a week in one of Chimulco's clean, comfortable kitchenette bungalows, set beneath a shady grove on the quiet side of the complex. They come in two sizes: with one bedroom, with living-dining room, kitchenette, and bath, sleeping two adults and two kids, for about $50 nightly, and larger two-bedroom versions, sleeping four adults and two kids for about $70.

The adjacent shady **trailer park,** with about 20 spaces, with concrete pads and all hookups, runs about $17 nightly, with a 20 percent discount for a one-month stay.

For reservations and more information, dial 377/778-0014 or 377/778-0209, fax 377/778-8016; website: www.chimulco2001@hotmail.com.

As for food, you could either bring your own (shop at the on-site mini-mart or at stores in Villa Corona across the highway), eat in the on-site restaurant-snack bar, or check out the several decent local restaurants.

Neighboring Facilities

Chimulco is just one of a number of Villa Corona water-park complexes. Very worthy of consideration is similarly lavish **Agua Caliente,** in its own large lakeside park, including a campground, on Hwy. 80, kilometer 56, about a quarter mile west of Chimulco. For more information and reservations, dial tel. 377/778-0022.

Getting There

Get to Villa Corona and Chimulco **by bus,** from either the old or new central bus stations. (See Getting There and Away in the Heart of the City chapter.)

At the downtown Guadalajara Camionera Central Vieja, catch one of the several daily "Servicios Coordinados" (Flecha Amarilla) (tel. 33/3619-4533) Villa Corona–bound buses.

Similarly, at the suburban Camionera Central Nueva, go either by Flecha Amarilla subsidiary lines, in *módulo* 1, tel. 33/3600-0052 or by allied lines Autocamiones del Pacífico and Transportes Cihuatlán, tel. 33/3600-0076 (second-class), tel. 33/3600-0598 (first class), in *módulo* 4.

By car, from Guadalajara, follow Av. López Mateos Sur about 16 miles (26 kilometers) south of the *periférico* (peripheral boulevard), where you turn off the expressway right, onto Hwy. 80 (Melaque–Barra de Navidad direction) west. Continue approximately another seven miles (11 kilometers) to Villa Corona, where you turn left, westbound, at the "Chimulco" sign.

RÍO CALIENTE SPA AND THE BOSQUE DE PRIMAVERA

The boiling-hot Río Caliente ("Hot River") gurgles from its subterranean cliffside source and steams downhill through the Bosque de Primavera (Forest of Spring) preserve, sustaining a number of local hot-spring *balnearios* along the way. Closest to the source is Río Caliente Spa, on whose land the spring bubbles forth.

Sights

From the Río Caliente Spa, trails lead out, lacing the Bosque de Primavera. They follow the river from the source downhill, or lead uphill through the lush pine-oak woodlands that coat this still-active volcanic wonderland.

Although frequented by weekend day-trippers, the Bosque de Primavera trails are empty on weekdays, when you'll probably have the Bosque de Primavera pretty much to yourself. Along the paths, if you're quiet and patient, you might glimpse any one of a hundred bird species, from hawks *(halcones)* and vultures *(zopilotes),* to colorful orioles, dainty vermilion flycatchers, and golden vireos. Mammals that you might see along the trail include deer, armadillos, wildcats, and the piglike wild *jabalí.*

Accommodations and Food

The Río Caliente Spa is a tranquil village of brick cottages nestled beside and above the steaming Río Caliente, which gushes, steaming hot, from a nearby cliff-bottom. Inside, the approximately 50 spartan-chic accommodations, each with its own fireplace, are enclosed in attractively rustic brown brick walls, with shiny tile floors, comfortable beds, handmade wooden furniture, and immaculate shower baths.

Rates begin at about $160 per day per person, including taxes and all meals and many activities (see below). Spa treatments are extra. One-week packages, including some treatments, run about $1,000 for two.

Lodging rates include three hearty (but meatless) macrobiotic buffet meals with plenty of choices (for example, cereal, eggs, hash browns, and coffee for breakfast, and split pea soup, tossed salad, and fish tacos for lunch or dinner). No alcoholic beverages or smoking are allowed in common rooms or lodging rooms.

Hotel Activities

Lodging and food are only the beginning at Río Caliente Spa. Guests (who are largely college-educated upper-middle-class Americans and Canadians, usually more women than men) can choose a full schedule at no extra cost. Activities include hikes, yoga, water exercise, steam room, Tai Chi, and professionally led workshops, such as "Journal Writing," or "Relationships, Work, and Self Esteem."

Other services, such as mud wrap, pedicure, massage, facial, dermabrasion, antiaging, medical therapies, horseback riding, shopping and sightseeing trips, are available at extra cost.

Alternatively, guests can opt to simply relax, reading or conversing in the patio by the spa's pair of outdoor swimming pools and the two secluded nude bathing pools.

Some people have described Río Caliente as more a retreat than a spa. If you're planning on bringing a big designer wardrobe and working out half the day on the treadmill or stair-step machine, this place is not for you. Hiking takes the place of machines, noise is kept a minimum,

© RÍO CALIENTE SPA

Day hikes are an included activity at Río Caliente Spa. (Be careful crossing the steaming Río Caliente, however.)

and food is plentiful, but healthfully low in fat, white sugar, and salt.

For reservations (mandatory in winter, recommended all times) and more information, you may contact their North American agent, Spa Vacations, Ltd., P.O. Box 897, Millbrae, CA 94030; tel. 650/615-0601; email: riocal@aol.com; website: www.riocaliente.com. In Mexico, for reservations, contact their Guadalajara agent, Turiservicios (across the Minerva Circle from the Hotel Fiesta Mexicana) at Av. Vallarta 2785, Guadalajara, Jalisco 44600; tel/fax. 33/3615-7800. You may also fax Río Caliente directly for reservations, at fax 33/3151-0887. **Credit cards are *not* accepted** at the spa, although American checks are.

Guadalajara travelers can reach the **Río Caliente Spa** most easily by airport taxi. The spa has a system for guests to get together and share transportation. By car or bus from Guadalajara, or from Hwy. 15 (via Tepic-Tequila) eastbound, see access details in the section below.

The Bosque de Primavera

The Río Caliente Spa is only a small, albeit important part of the Bosque de Primavera. The Bosque de Primavera itself is a communally owned reserve for public use and enjoyment. It stretches over dozens of square miles of forest, river, and mountain, not far west of Guadalajara's metropolitan edge.

Camping is allowed, with your own equipment, for a small fee, and three local-style *balnearios* (bathing resorts) line the warm Río Caliente, all accessible along the entrance road. Use the following access directions to guide your arrival:

By car or bus, follow Hwy. 15 west, exit the four-lane highway by turning left (westbound) at La Venta village, marked on the highway, by "Bosque de Primavera" and "Cañon de las Flores" signs, 7.1 miles (11.5 kilometers) west of the *periférico.* Mark your odometer.

Follow the "Cañon de las Flores" signs through the village, straight ahead, south, about four blocks, then right, west, another four blocks, then left, south again. At mile .8 (kilometer 1.3) you arrive at the Balneario Cañon de las Flores on the left (with warm pools, water toboggan, restaurant, picnic ground, and playground equipment; adults

$3, parking $2). If they have a rope across the road, ask them to let you pass (which they're obligated to do), and continue a fraction of a mile farther to the sign and right-hand dirt road leading to the **Balneario Las Tinajitas** (about the same facilities and prices as Cañon de las Flores).

A glance at the handsome pine grove around you is a clue that you are in the Bosque de Primavera pine-oak forest. Camping is allowed most anywhere. Take care not to start a forest fire and clean up your camp.

Continue ahead; at mile 2.1 you arrive at a gate where, to continue, you have to pay about half a dollar to an attendant. At the same spot, a dirt road heads right, through the pines downhill

to the river and the rustic **Balneario El Bosque** (open Fri., Sat., and Sun. 8 A.M.–6 P.M., $1 per person).

Continue ahead; at mile 2.9, kilometer 4.7, the road splits. Take the left fork for the Río Caliente Spa gate a quarter of a mile farther. The right fork continues to the river, and some lovely riverside camping spots.

By bus get to Bosque de Primavera via second-class **Rojo de los Altos** (tel. 33/3619-2309) buses, which connect west, from the downtown Camionera Central Vieja, *sala* A. (See Getting There and Away, in the Heart of the City chapter.) Ask the driver to let you off at La Venta, then taxi or walk from the highway.

Tequila: Where the Agave is King

The ranks of cactus-like plants that spread over the valleys and hills an hour's drive west of Guadalajara are the source of the tradition that has propelled the name of the country town of Tequila (pop. 35,000) to worldwide renown.

That seemingly humble source, the leathery and spiny **blue agave,** cousin of the so-called "century plant," of Mexico and the southwest United States, is harvested and processed for its sugary *aguamiel* (honey water) juice that is distilled into the fiery liquor, known everywhere as "tequila."

HISTORY
In the Beginning
Although the fermented alcoholic drink, called *pulque,* is part of indigenous Mexican tradition, liquor distillation is not. *Pulque,* like its distant American relatives, Budweiser beer, California wine, and Japanese sake contains only the modest percentage of alcohol (usually 5–15 percent) obtainable directly from fermentation.

> *That seemingly humble source, the leathery and spiny blue agave, cousin of the so-called "century plant," of Mexico and the southwest United States is harvested and processed for its sugary aguamiel (honey water) juice that is distilled into the fiery liquor, known everywhere as "tequila."*

To get stronger stuff, you have to boil (technically, "distill") the alcohol away from the water. And there's where the Spanish came into the picture. Hernán Cortés introduced liquor distillation into Mexico with the Conquest, in 1521.

Colonial Mexican distillers made *ron* (rum) and *aguardiente* (white lightning) from sugar cane, and *mezcal* (in some places, known as *raicilla*) from the juice of agave and agavelike plants. Finished products of all such distilled liquors contain sharply increased alcohol levels, as much as 45–50 percent (90–100 proof). Nowadays, commercial liquors made in Mexico and the United States generally contain a standard 40 percent (80-proof) alcohol level.

Local Developments
The history of the town of Tequila corresponds closely with that of the Cuervo and Sauza families, who were prominent pioneer liquor distillers. It was about a century after the 1656 founding of the town of Tequila that José Antonio de Cuervo settled and began distilling

mezcal locally in 1758. In 1795, his son, José María Guadalupe de Cuervo obtained an exclusive governmental license to distill *"el vino mezcal de tequila,"* the forerunner of present-day tequila.

In 1873, Cenobio Sauza de Madrigal established a local distillery and began competing with the Cuervos. Subsequently, both the Cuervos and Sauzas won international awards for their products, whose purity and uniquely clean taste gained renown among a growing number of liquor afficionados, especially in the United States.

SIGHTS
Getting Oriented

Tequila is not a large town, and most attractions can be reached within a few blocks of the main plaza. Get your bearings by standing (or imagine yourself standing) on the sidewalk adjacent to the west, or plaza, side of the main town church,

Harvested *piñas* (named after pineapples, which they resemble) await processing into tequila liquor.

La Parroquia de la Purísima Concepción. With your back to the church, you'll be looking west. Calle Juárez, immediately in front of you, runs both north and south of the church. On your right, plaza-front street Vicente Albino Rojas, runs east-west along the plaza's north flank, while Av. Sixto Gorjon runs along the plaza's south flank. On the far side of the plaza, Calle Ramón Corona borders the plaza's west flank, while, from the plaza's far west side, Calle José Cuervo runs west, away, from you, between the Cuervo liquor distillery **La Perseverancia** on the left, and the **Cuervo Museum** on the right.

Cuervo Distillery and Museums

Your first Tequila stop should be **Cuervo Distillery "La Rojena,"** on Calle Cuervo, half a block west of the town plaza. Inside, via guided tour, view the operations of the venerable (1873) distillery. The raw material are *piñas,* the pineapple-shaped hearts of the blue agave plants, shorn of their long, blue-green leaves. Pass the big cooker ovens where the *piñas* are digested and then pressed for their sweet *aguamiel* juice. Next, the juice is fermented in big vats, then distilled in gleaming copper kettles, and finally barreled, aged, and bottled.

The tour ends in the long exit hall, decorated with the big Gabriel Flores 1969 mural that dramatizes the role of Tequila in the march of Mexican history. (**Tours** are conducted Monday through Friday. Two daily tours are in English, at 10 A.M. and 1 P.M., and two in Spanish, at noon and 2 P.M. Arrive early and buy your ticket ahead of time. Alternatively, call Guadalajara tel. 33/3134-3372, for schedule and reservations or visit the Cuervo website: www.josecuervo.com)

Afterward, walk across Calle Cuervo and take a look inside the small **La Tienda Gift Shop and Museum,** open Mon.–Sat. 10 A.M.–6 P.M. You might also stop for a drink, snack, or lunch at the new Cuervo restaurant and shopping center, back at the plaza corner of Calle Cuervo.

Next, walk south a block along west plaza-front street Ramón Corona to the city **Museum of Tequila,** corner of Luís Navarro, open Tues.–Sun. 10 A.M.–5 P.M.; tel. 374/742-2410. Inside, rooms of excellent displays illustrate the

TEQUILA

A s local liquor production rocketed upward, reaching millions of cases per year during the 1970s, Sauza, Cuervo, and several other eminent regional liquor manufacturers became concerned that any distilled spirit could be labeled "tequila." In 1977 they cemented international appellation-of-origin agreements that limited the name "tequila" to liquors distilled only from juice made up of at least 60 percent by weight of locally grown blue agave plants.

The 60 percent limit notwithstanding, the finest tequilas continued to be made from 100 percent agave juice. By the 1990s tequila had become so popular that demand was far outstripping the supply of the slow-growing local blue agave. By 2000, despite thousands of newly-planted acres, connoisseur-grade 100 percent blue agave tequila, like many fine California or French varietal wines, was routinely selling for hundreds of dollars a bottle.

All tequila is not the same. Manufacturers produce authentic tequila in three grades: **blanco, reposado,** and **añejo.** Tequila *blanco*, although conforming to the minimum requirements to be labeled "tequila," is not aged. To pass muster, however, it must be double distilled to crystal clarity, have a rich taste that is unmistakably of agave, and consist of 38 percent alcohol (76 proof) by volume.

Further processing begins with good tequila *blanco*, and transforms it through care and aging. Tequila *reposado* ("rested") is aged a minimum of two months in either French or American oak barrels. During the process, the liquor acquires a light straw color that should sparkle with flashes of gold when finished. Additionally, good *reposados* exhibit light floral and fruit aromas, with soft, pleasing hints of toasted wood.

Increased care and longer aging distinguish the finest tequila *añejo*, which must be aged a minimum of 12 months, preferably in French oak barrels. Depending upon barrel time, the liquor takes on a medium to dark amber shade that should sparkle with flashes of red to bright copper. Oxygen penetrating through the barrel during the aging process leads to a fine soft taste and rare, rich aromas, resulting in a liquor excellent for after-dinner consumption. Some manufacturers are pushing the process even farther, producing ultra-fine tequilas aged five years or more, which retail for upwards of $400 a bottle.

© BRUCE WHIPPERMAN

The fermented agave juice is heat-distilled for its liquor content in big, shiny copper distillation kettles.

GETAWAYS

early history of Mexican alcoholic beverages, especially *pulque* (interestingly represented by the rabbit hieroglyph) and *agave* culture.

Make your last museum stop on the plaza's north side, at Albino Rojas 22, a few doors east of Corona, at the interesting private **Sauza Museum.** The museum, tel. 374/742-0247, open Tues.–Sun. 10 A.M.–5 P.M. is housed in the Sauza family *recinto* (reception hall). It's the life project of family head Sylvia Sauza, daughter of tequila patriarch Francisco Javier Sauza. Presently, Sylvia's daughter, personable English-speaking Helena Erickson Sauza, is in charge of the museum and associated shop, La Tiendita.

Inside the museum, wander the rooms of Sauza memoribilia, including oil paintings, historical photographs, antique distillation equipment, charming old promotional posters and calendars, and a handsome silver and braid *charro* outfit, presented by renowned Mexican singing cowboy actor, Pepe Guizar. While you're there, you might ask if and when their venerable family mansion, the **Quinta Sauza** nearby, is open for public tours.

Sights Outside of Town: Ex-Hacienda San José and Balneario La Toma

If you have a second day, Tequila offers at least two worthwhile nearby excursions. Visit the **ex-Hacienda San José,** now preserved as both museum and working distillery of the Herradura tequila firm, in the town of Amatitán, on Hwy. 15, not far east of Tequila. Visits are by guided tour only, and include an introductory video, the hacienda chapel, and the working Herradura tequila factory.

Guides conduct tours Mon.–Fri. hourly, at 9, 10, and 11 A.M., and noon. Entrance fee is $8 per person. For more information, call the hacienda tour office, at tel. 374/745-0011, ext. 248.

Get there, from Tequila, via old Hwy. 15 *(libre),* seven miles (11 kilometers) east of Tequila. At the west (Guadalajara) side of Amatitán, just before the highway climbs the hill, turn left at the side lane that you can see continuing beneath the railroad bridge. Continue to the ex-Hacienda gate within a few hundred yards, on the right. (From Guadalajara, turn right, just after old

Hwy. 15 *(libre)* has finished its winding, downhill descent, just before Amatitán.)

You can also visit the ex-Hacienda San José via the **Tequila Express** Saturday rail excursion from downtown Guadalajara. It's a complete party, including the museum and distillery tour, plus a Mexican buffet and a folkloric show. Get your tickets from the Guadalajara Chamber of Commerce. For more details, see Tequila Express in the Entertainment and Events section of the Heart of the City chapter.

On the other hand, **Balneario La Toma,** 15 minutes by car or taxi west of Tequila, perched on the tropical edge of the **Barranca** (Canyon) of the Río Santiago, affords a chance to enjoy Tequila's great outdoors. The *balneario* (bathing spring), with three big, spring-fed pools, a cave-waterfall, picnic tables, snack restaurants, and panoramic tropical canyon views, is famously popular. For maximum peace and tranquility, avoid crowded Saturday, Sunday, and holiday afternoons.

For a nearby change of scene, drive or stroll the road downhill from La Toma, about a quarter mile, to rustic **Balneario El Paraíso,** which offers basic facilities, tropical tranquility, a cool, spring-fed bathing pool, and a bit of space for camping beneath a shady tropical hillside mango grove (with all the free mangoes you can eat in May and June). Bring insect repellent.

Get there via old Hwy. 15 *(libre),* northwest of the main Tequila old Hwy. 15 crossing (at the monumental statue of the *"agavero"* agave cutter.) Mark your odometer at the statue. At mile 1.9 (kilometer 3.0), at the top of the hill, make a sharp right from Hwy. 15, at the bar "El Texano" sign. Continue along the graded dirt road, past a school at mile 2.7 (kilometer 4.2). Soon, at the next fork, turn right for Balneario La Toma, or left for Balneario El Paraíso, which you'll find, on the right, at mile 3.0 (kilometer 4.9).

ACCOMMODATIONS

Tequila overnighters have their choice of a sprinkling of modest but recommendable hotels. Right next to the plaza church and colorful town market, consider the worthy **Hotel San Fran-**

cisco, at Vallarta 10, Tequila, Jalisco 46400; tel. 374/742-1757. Here you have your basic, clean small-town hotel, with eight upstairs rooms, plainly but comfortably furnished, with bedspreads and drapes and well-maintained hotwater shower bath. Rentals cost $17 s, $22 d, with fans.

A few blocks east, along the main street, check out the new **Posada del Agave,** at Sixto Gorjon 83, Tequila, Jalisco 46400; tel. 374/742-0774. Brand new at this writing, the hotels rooms sparkle with shiny designer tile floors, color-coordinated bedspreads and drapes, shaded reading lamps, and shiny, 1990s-standard baths. Smart designers located the rooms in two floors, away from the busy street-front. For such amenities, prices run a reasonable $20 s or d in one double bed, and $28 d or t in two double beds, with TV, fan, and telephone.

Out on the highway, a few blocks northwest of the main town crossing, stands the **Hotel María Isabel,** at Carretera Internacional 63, Tequila, Jalisco 46400; tel./fax 374/742-1592. The María Isabel offers a selection of about six accommodations, ranging from rooms to three-bedroom suites. The good news is that they're light and immaculate, with attractively rustic bedsteads, dressers, and bedspreads, and hotwater shower baths. Unfortunately, reading lamps are lacking, and the hotel fronts the noisy highway. Bring earplugs. Prices run about $20 s or d, $32 for two-bedroom suites sleeping up to four, and $42 for three-bedroom suites, sleeping up to six.

FOOD
Food Stalls, Bakeries, and Groceries
Get your fill of hearty country cooking at the food stalls *(fondas)* on Albino Rojas, behind the plaza church. Get there early, when food is fresh and hot.

Plenty of fruits, veggies, groceries, and baked goods are available in the town **market,** in the alley off of Vallarta, just north of the Hotel San Francisco and east of the plaza church. Alternatively, you can get about the same at the several bakeries *(panaderías)* and grocery stores *(abarroterias)* on the main ingress street, Sixto Gorjon.

Restaurants
Tequila visitors enjoy a few good restaurants. Starting right on the plaza, go to the local seafood headquarters, **Restaurant Marinero,** at Albino Rojas 16, tel. 374/742-1674. Besides plenty of ceviche options, also choose from shrimp, octopus, oyster, and clam cocktails, plus soups, fish fillets in eight styles, and pizza. Find them open also for breakfast, daily 9 A.M. until 10:30 P.M. Moderate–expensive.

Although construction wasn't yet finished when I was there, the new **Cuervo Restaurant** on the west side of the plaza, corner of Corona and Cuervo, should be up and operating when you read this.

Another good restaurant choice is **Carnes Guadalajara,** at Sixto Gorjon 111, three blocks into town from the Hwy. 15 crossing. Here, a friendly, hardworking proprietor specializes in country specialties, such as *birria de agave* (lamb cooked in agave juice) and *carnes en su jugo,* (meat in its juice), and barbecued steaks. Despite the meat, vegetable eaters can always order a vegetable omelette, *(omelet de verduras),* or a mixed salad *(ensalada mixta)* or pasta smothered in tomato sauce *(salsa de tomate).*

For maximum relaxation with your food, first choice goes to refined open-air **Restaurant Campestre Mariscos El Mar II,** on the highway northwest of town. Here, enjoy the freshest and best from the coast. Extras include playground equipment for kids and a panoramic canyon view. Open Sun.–Thurs. noon–8 P.M., Fri. and Sat. noon–10 P.M. Moderate–expensive. Get there by car or taxi, via Hwy. 15, 1.8 miles (2.8 kilometers) northwest of the main Tequila highway crossing. Find it on the right at the crest of the hill.

ENTERTAINMENT AND EVENTS
Fiestas
Local *barrios* celebrate their respective patron saints often and well, with carnivals, food, processions, masses, and fireworks. If you enjoy ceremony and revelry, arrive for the **Fiesta de Santa**

Cruz, May 1–3; the **Fiesta de la Señora de la Asunción,** August 1–15; the **Fiesta de San Francisco,** September 27–October 4; and the **Fiesta de la Purísima Concepción.**

Patron saints notwithstanding, Tequila people also celebrate a pair of unique nonreligious festivals. First, on June 24, everyone goes overboard in a communal smashing of traditional clay *cantaritos* (tequila jugs).

The festival year climaxes in the **National Tequila Fair,** November 30–December 12. The town becomes awash with celebrations, starting with the crowning of a tequila queen, and then successively, manufacturers' exposition of products, rodeos, parade and floats, cockfights, mariachi serenades, carnival games, all topped off by a fireworks *spectaculo.*

SHOPPING AND SERVICES
Handicrafts Shops
Make your first Tequila shopping stop at **La Tiendita,** the shop of the Sauza Museum, at 22 Albino Rojas, on the north side of the plaza. Choose from shelves and counters full of all-Mexico handicrafts, individually selected by Sauza family head, Sylvia Sauza, and her daughter and store manager, Helena Erickson Sauza. Hours are Tues.–Sun. 10 A.M.–5 P.M.; tel. 374/742-0247.

A few doors to the west, check out the handicrafts offering of **Regalos Palomar,** then go to **Cuervo Restaurant and Shopping Center,** at plaza's west side and see what the new stores there have to offer.

Banks and Travel Agent
Choose among three banks, all with ATMs, around the Tequila plaza. Start at **Bancrecer** at the northwest plaza corner, open Mon.–Fri. 9 A.M.–5 P.M.; tel. 374/742-2314; or go two blocks south and one block east to **Banamex,** at the northwest corner of Juárez and J. Rodríguez de Hilar, open Mon.–Fri. 9 A.M.–3 P.M.; tel. 374/742-1690; or **Bancomer,** across the street, at the southwest corner of the same intersection, open Mon.–Fri. 8:30 A.M.–4 P.M.

Get your air tickets at travel agent **Tequi Tours,**

tel. 374/742-2331, at Sixto Gorjon 35, north side of street, between Degollado and Bravo.

COMMUNICATIONS AND INFORMATION
Post and Telecommunications
The Tequila *correo* (post office) is on the plaza, at Juárez 4, tel. 374/742-0457; the *telecom* (public telephone, fax, and money orders) is next door, at Juárez 4, tel. 374/742-0085. For long-distance telephone after hours, buy a Ladatel card at a drug or grocery store and use it in one of the several plaza-front public telephones, or use the public telephone and fax at the **Super Farmacia del Centro,** on the plaza, north side.

Tourist Information Office
The Tequila **Turismo** tourist information office, tel. 374/742-2411, is in the Museum of Tequila, corner of Corona and Navarro, a block south of the plaza's southwest corner. Find them open Mon.–Sat. 10 A.M.–3 P.M.

MEDICAL AND EMERGENCIES
Pharmacy and Hospital
For simple remedies, consult the physician or pharmacist on duty at one of several local pharmacies, such as **Super Farmacia del Centro,** on the plaza, north side.

For a doctor in a hurry, follow your hotel's advice, or have a taxi take you to the **Hospital Seguro Social,** at Sixto Gorjon 225, tel. 374/742-0266 or 374/742-0138.

Police and Fire
In a police or fire emergency, contact the police headquarters at the ***presidencia municipal,*** tel. 374/742-0012 or 374/742-0313, on the south side of the plaza.

GETTING THERE
By Bus
A number of bus lines serve the town of Tequila, from the suburban Camionera Central Nueva. (See Getting There and Away in the

Heart of the City chapter). For example, lines serving western destinations, such as Transportes Pacífico, tel. 33/3600-0211, in the terminal's *módulo* 4, have second-class departures that stop in Tequila.

Alternatively, go by second-class **Rojo de los Altos** (tel. 33/3619-2309) buses, that connect with Tequila, from the downtown Guadalajara Camionera Central Vieja, *sala* A. (See Getting There and Away in the Heart of the City chapter.)

By Car

From Guadalajara, drive west, along either Av. Vallarta or Calz. Lázaro Cárdenas. Continue west, Tepic direction, along old Hwy. 15 *(libre,* one hour total) or Hwy. 15D *cuota* (toll, 40 minutes) to Tequila, about 37 miles, 60 kilometers west of the Guadalajara *periférico.* A monumental statue, "El Agavero," (The Agave Cutter) on the left, marks the town entrance intersection at Av. Sixto Gorjon.

Magdalena: In the Land of Opals

HISTORY

Before the Spanish

Like most Mexican towns, Magdalena's history stretches back long before the arrival of the Spanish. The present town coincides with the pre-Conquest Tecuexe town of Xuchitepec (Hill of Flowers), undoubtedly referring to the high hill, Cerro Norte, north of town that during the summer rainy season usually sports a coat of colorful wildflowers.

Old Xuchitepec was a tributary of the chiefdom of Etzatlán (a still-important town, 15 miles south). Xuchitepec people once lived on two islands in a now-dry lake (which paradoxically they had to evacuate because of floods), west of the present town.

The Spanish, in the person of Francisco Cortés de Buenaventura, Hernán Cortés' nephew, arrived in 1524. Buenaventura's company of cavalry and foot soldiers caught the Xuchitepec chief,

Although Magdalena's "opal fever" of the 1960s and 1970s has subsided, dozens of local mines still yield treasures.

© BRUCE WHIPPERMAN

Goaxicar, unprepared. Goaxicar fled with his warriors, leaving his daughter behind, with no choice but to accept baptism, taking the name of Magdalena, which became synonymous with the town. Later, Franciscan padres built a convent and a church, which they dedicated, with the name, Santa María Magdalena de Xuchitepec.

The Opal Story

No evidence exists that Magdalena's original inhabitants knew of the riches in opals buried beneath their land. Nevertheless, opals, those prized multihued stones, were known in pre-Conquest Mexico. Historical data indicate that the Aztec nobility treasured opals for ornamentation from at least A.D. 1200. They called them *vitzitziltecpal* (the humming bird stone) for their shimmering colors, akin to the hummingbird's flashing plumage.

Although the Conquest erased the knowledge of the old Aztec mines, opals were rediscovered in Mexico's Querétaro state in 1840 and in Magdalena, by prospector Alfonso Ramírez in 1957. Although the rush that led to Magdalena's 1965–1975 "opal fever" has subsided, plenty of opals are sold locally in town shops and by street sellers who station themselves on the west side of the town plaza.

The excitement that opals arouse is justified. Opals, which come in all colors of the rainbow, plus jet black and milky white, are prized for their uniquely enchanting iridescence. Their colors are due to various trace minerals. If an opal were pure, its color would merely mimic the colorless transparency of glass which, like opal, is composed of nearly pure silicon dioxide, the same as silica sand and quartz.

Opals differ slightly from quartz or glass, however, because they contain a few percent by weight of loosely bound ("hydrated") water. The opal's water content is both a blessing and a curse. The presence of water gives opals their unique shimmer, but at the same time, makes them more fragile than most precious stones. Opals must retain their water content or their beauty will be destroyed. Experts recommend that owners of opals keep them away from flame and store them under water occasionally to preserve their beauty.

SIGHTS

Opals of Magdalena

Go right to the primary source, to **Ópalos de Magdalena,** the museum-store three blocks east of the Magdalena town center. This is the family enterprise of personable Javier López Ávila, whose mission is to promote Magdalena opals. He's doing an effective job of it, judging from his shop's wealth of jewels, in dozens of forms, from jet-black opal turtles and sparkling silver and gold necklaces, to shimmering bracelets and handsome statuettes.

As part of his enterprise, Javier also arranges tours and packages for visiting local **opal mines.** Visits can include lodging, guide, and transportation to view both the opal diggings and the nearby *"tumbas de tiro"* (bottle-shaped tombs) of Huitzizilipan.

Javier's store is the Magdalena arm of the **Ópalos de Mexico** partnership, which also maintains workshops and showrooms in both Guadalajara and Querétaro. Javier's store is open Mon.–Sat. 10 A.M.–2 P.M. and 4–7 P.M., at Independencia 115, on Hwy. 15, three blocks east of the town plaza. For tour arrangements reservations and more information, call or fax tel./fax 374/744-0447; website: www.opalosdemexico.com.

You can also visit the Ópalos de Mexico Guadalajara store, in the World Trade Center (the multifloored building, adjacent to Guadalajara Expo) at Av. Mariano Otero 1329, Local 4A (fourth floor), Guadalajara, Jalisco 44540, tel. 33/3669-0836 (or in Querétaro, at Río Yaqui 300, Colonia Menchaca, tel. 422/220-7446).

ACCOMMODATIONS

Hotels

Magdalena has only a few hotels. First choice goes to the town-center **Hotel El Ópalo,** at Allende 36, Magdalena, Jalisco 46470. The three floors of 28 rooms, around a quiet inner courtyard, are plain but clean and comfortably furnished with large beds and tile and shower baths. Guests in some upper-floor rooms enjoy eastward views of the green silhouettes of the Tequila volcano and Cerro Norte. Rates are right, at about $11 s, $13 d in one double bed, or $20 d in two double beds, with fans and TV. Arrive with a reservation, especially during the opal festival, during the last two weeks of September.

A pair of barely acceptable, emergency-only hotels serve truckers and drop-in guests at the east end of town, on old Hwy. 15 *(libre),* near the entrance from the toll Hwy. 15D.

The best of the pair is probably the loosely managed motel-style Magdalena Inn, at the far eastern edge of town, at kilometer 73, Carretera 15, Magdalena, Jalisco 46470; tel. 374/744-0983. Rooms are clean but plain and may need some basic maintenance, such as light bulbs. Make sure everything's working and in place before moving in. For less truck noise, get one of the rooms at the back of the parking lot, farthest from the highway. Rates are $13 s or d in one double bed, $20 d in two double beds, with TV.

Last choice goes to the Quinta Minas, with 25 rooms, at M. Ávila Camacho 450, west of the toll Hwy. 15D entrance, across from the hospital, tel. 374/744-0560. Rates run $13 s, $15 d in one bed, $22 in two.

FOOD

Fondas and Taco Stands

Hearty, economical meals—especially *guisados* and *birrias* (stews), and tamales, enchiladas, and *chiles rellenos*—are available at the downtown market *fondas* (permanent food stalls) just east of the plaza-front church.

Beginning around 6 P.M., evening action centers around a number of **taco and snack stands** that set up at curbside, on Mina, the street behind the plaza-front church.

Restaurants

A single family seems to have cornered the Magdalena restaurant trade, with a trio of restaurants, all named "Lupita," after the founder. The 1920 original, **Fonda Lupita,** open daily 7 A.M.–11 P.M., is still the best, however, at Independencia 26, on the main highway ingress street, a block northeast of the town plaza, tel. 374/744-0142.

Here, the local protocol is to check inside the kitchen (right up front) and see what's cooking

for the day. You'll often find Magdalena country specialties, such as rich *caldo de res con verderas* (beef-vegetable soup), and *carne con chile* (beef or pork chile stew), or *chicharron con chile* (delicious but fatty deep-fried pork rinds in chile). Also, they'll usually be offering a another local specialty, *jocoque:* a milk product, intermediate between yogurt and cheese. Budget–moderate.

For a variation on the same menu, also try Lupita II, half a mile east on the continuation of the same main street, at Manuel Ávila Camacho 382.

Alternately, try rival **Restaurant Evangelina,** at Ramón Corona 47, across the street from the plaza's northwest corner, open daily 8:30 A.M.–10 P.M. Here, you can enjoy breakfast (omelette, or *huevos al la mexicana* with toast and coffee), or *carne asada* (grilled beef), quesadilla, or *camarones al gusto* (shrimp as you like them).

ENTERTAINMENT AND EVENTS

Fiestas

Although life usually goes on quietly in Magdalena, folks do rev up for a few festivals, when hotel reservations are mandatory. Excitement builds with special masses, carnival rides, procession, and food, during the **Fiesta de Santa María Magdalena,** July 17–22.

The fiesta year peaks during the combined **Fería Nacional de Ópalos** and the **Fiesta del Señor de los Milagros,** September 15–29. Local people go all out, with pilgrimages, cultural and sports events, a popular dance, float parade, mariachi serenades, *mojigangos* (stilt-mounted dancing effigies), grand opal and handicrafts expositions and plenty of food.

SHOPPING AND SERVICES

Buying Opals

Although the September 15–29 National Opal Fair (see above) is the best time to buy local opals, jewelry, and handicrafts, a number of shops are open year-round near the town plaza (excepting Ópalos de Magdalena, three blocks east, see Sights, above). Of the three or four plaza-front shops, one of the best-established seems to be **Ópalos y Artesanías Mexicanas,** open Mon.–Sun. 9 A.M.–2

P.M., tel. 374/744-0708, on the plaza's west side, at Corona 31.

Besides the shops, individuals—the men who usually hang out on the plaza's west side—sell opals. However, in order to deal with them, you must either have a command of Spanish or ask a friend to bargain for you. (Moreover, experts warn that opals, if recently mined, may change colors until they mature long enough for their hydrated water content to stabilize. For this reason, it's safest to buy from an established dealer who can furnish you with a bona fide guarantee of authenticity.)

Bank, Travel Agent, and Photography

Change money at **Bancomer,** with ATM, open Mon.–Fri. 8:30 A.M.–4 P.M.; tel. 374/744-0050, diagonally across from the plaza's northwest corner.

Mina, the street that runs behind the church, has a travel agent **Agencia de Viajes Narsamy,** tel. 374/744-0717, open Mon.–Sat. 9 A.M.–2 P.M. and 4–7 P.M. Next door, at Mina 11, get development service, film, and other photo supplies at **Magdalena Photo Radio,** open Mon.–Sat. 9 A.M.–9 P.M.

COMMUNICATIONS, MEDICAL, AND EMERGENCY

Post Office and Long-Distance Telephone and Fax

Find the Magdalena *correo* (post office) at Ávila Camacho 7 (on the highway, about four blocks west of the town plaza).

The public long-distance telephone (*larga distancia*) and fax (and maybe Internet connection) is at Independencia 45, on the plaza-front north, across the street from the taxi stand. Find them open daily 9 A.M.– 9 P.M.

Doctor and Hospital

For medical consultation, see **Internist Alfonso Islas Rivera, M.D.,** at Independencia 102A, cellular tel. 0443/449-5379, about three blocks

© BRUCE WHIPPERMAN

Finding opals is at least backbreaking, and at most, dangerous work, using dynamite, picks, shovels, and bare hands to split rocks open to see what's inside.

east of the plaza, south side of the street, across from Ópalos de Magdalena.

If Doctor Rivera isn't available at his office, you may find him (or another doctor) at the **Hospital Regional,** with 24-hour emergency room, on the highway, east of downtown, at M. Ávila Camacho 435.

GETTING THERE

Get to Magdalena, by either car or bus, by virtually the same directions as for Tequila (see preceding section), except that by car you drive an additional 10 miles (16 kilometers) farther west from Guadalajara.

Resources

Glossary

Many of the following words have a social-historical meaning; others you will not find in the usual English-Spanish dictionary.

abarrotería—grocery store
alcalde—mayor or municipal judge
alfarería—pottery
andando—walkway or strolling path
antojitos—native Mexican snacks, such as tamales, *chiles rellenos,* tacos, and enchiladas
artesanías—handicrafts, as distinguished from *artesanio,* a person who makes handicrafts
audiencia—one of the royal executive-judicial panels sent to rule Mexico during the 16th century
ayuntamiento—either the town council or the building where it meets
bandidos—bandits or outlaws
bienes raíces—literally "good roots," but popularly, real estate
birria—goat, pork, or lamb stew, in spiced tomato broth, especially typical of Jalisco
boleto—ticket, boarding pass
cabercera—head town of a municipal district, or headquarters in general
cabrón—literally a cuckold, but more commonly, bastard, rat, or S.O.B.; sometimes used affectionately
cacique—chief or boss
calandria—early 1800s-style horse-drawn carriage, common in Guadalajara
camionera—bus station
campesino—country person; farm worker
canasta—basket of woven reeds, with handle
casa de huéspedes—guesthouse, usually operated in a family home
caballero—literally, "horseman," but popularly, gentleman
caudillo—dictator or political chief
charro, charra—gentleman cowboy or cowgirl
chingar—literally, "to rape," but is also the universal Spanish "f" word, the equivalent of "screw" in English

churrigueresque—Spanish baroque architectural style incorporated into many Mexican colonial churches, named after José Churriguera (1665–1725)
científicos—literally, scientists, but applied to President Porfirio Díaz's technocratic advisers
cofradía—Catholic fraternal service association, either male or female, mainly in charge of financing and organizing religious festivals
colectivo—a shared public taxi or minibus that picks up and deposits passengers along a designated route
colegio—preparatory school or junior college
colonia—suburban subdivision-satellite of a larger city
Conasupo—government store that sells basic foods at subsidized prices
correo—post office
criollo—person of all-Spanish descent born in the New World
cuadra—a rectangular work of art, usually a painting. In Guadalajara, often refers to a Huichol yarn painting.
Cuaresma—Lent
curandero(a)—indigenous medicine man or woman
damas—ladies, as in "ladies room"
Domingo de Ramos—Palm Sunday
ejido—a constitutional, government-sponsored form of community, with shared land ownership and cooperative decision making
encomienda—colonial award of tribute from a designated indigenous district
estación ferrocarril—railroad station
farmacia—pharmacy, or drugstore
finca—farm
fonda—food stall or small restaurant, often in a traditional market complex
fraccionamiento—city sector or subdivision
fuero—the former right of clergy to be tried in separate ecclesiastical courts
gachupín—"one who wear spurs"; a derogatory term for a Spanish-born colonial

gasolinera—gasoline station

gente de razón—"people of reason"; whites and mestizos in colonial Mexico

gringo—once-derogatory but now commonly used term for North American whites

grito—impassioned cry, as in Hidalgo's *Grito de Dolores*

hacienda—large-landed estate; also the government treasury

hidalgo—nobleman; called honorifically by "Don" or "Doña"

indígena—indigenous or aboriginal inhabitant of all-native descent who speaks his or her native tongue. Commonly, but incorrectly, an Indian *(indio)*

jejenes—"no-see-um" biting gnats, especially around San Blas, Nayarit

judiciales—the federal or state "judicial," or investigative police, best known to motorists for their highway checkpoint inspections

jugería—stall or small restaurant providing a large array of squeezed vegetable and fruit *jugos* (juices)

juzgado—the "hoosegow," or jail

larga distancia—long-distance telephone service, or the *caseta* (booth) where it's provided

licencado—academic degree (abbr. Lic.) approximately equivalent to a bachelor's degree

lonchería—small lunch counter, usually serving juices, sandwiches, and *antojitos* (Mexican snacks)

machismo; macho—exaggerated sense of maleness; person who holds such a sense of himself

mestizo—person of mixed European/indigenous descent

mescal—alcoholic beverage distilled from the fermented hearts of maguey (century plant)

milpa—native farm plot, usually of corn, squash, and beans.

mordida—slang for bribe; "little bite"

palapa—thatched-roof structure, often open and shading a restaurant

panga—outboard launch *(lancha)*

papier-mâché—the craft of glued, multilayered paper sculpture, especially in Tonalá, Jalisco, where creations resemble fine pottery or lacquerware

Pemex—acronym for Petróleos Mexicanos, Mexico's national oil corporation

peninsulares—the Spanish-born ruling colonial elite

peón—a poor wage-earner, usually a country native

piñata—papier-mâché decoration, usually in animal or human form, filled with treats and broken open during a fiesta

plan—political manifesto, usually by a leader or group consolidating or seeking power

Porfiriato—the 34-year (1876–1910) ruling period of president-dictator Porfirio Díaz

pozole—stew, of hominy in broth, usually topped by shredded pork, cabbage, and diced onion

preventiva—municipal police

presidencia municipal—the headquarters, like a U.S. city or county hall, of a Mexican *municipio,* countylike local governmental unit

pronunciamiento—declaration of rebellion by an insurgent leader

pueblo—town or people

quinta—a villa or country house

quinto—the royal "fifth" tax on treasure and precious metals

retorno—cul-de-sac

rurales—former federal country police force created to fight *bandidos*

Semana Santa—pre-Easter holy week

Tapatío, Tapatía—a label, referring to anyone or anything from Guadalajara or Jalisco

taxi especial—private taxi, as distinguished from *taxi colectivo,* or collective taxi

telégrafo—telegraph office, lately converting to high-tech *telecomunicaciones* or *telecom,* offering telegraph, telephone, and public fax services

vaquero—cowboy

vecindad—neighborhood

yanqui—Yankee

zócalo—town plaza or central square

Pronunciation Guide

Your Guadalajara adventure will be more fun if you use a little Spanish. Mexicans, although they may smile at your funny accent, will appreciate your halting efforts to break the ice and transform yourself from a foreigner to a potential friend.

Spanish commonly uses 30 letters—the familiar English 26, plus four straightforward additions: ch, ll, ñ, and rr, which are explained in "Consonants," below.

Vowels

Once you learn them, Spanish pronunciation rules—in contrast to English—don't change. Spanish vowels generally sound softer than in English. (Note: The capitalized syllables below receive stronger accents.)

Pronounce *a* like ah, as in hah: *agua* AH-gooah (water), *pan* PAHN (bread), and *casa* CAH-sah (house).

Pronounce *e* like ay, as in may: *mesa* MAY-sah (table), *tela* TAY-lah (cloth), and *de* DAY (of, from).

Pronounce *i* like ee, as in need: *diez* dee-AYZ (ten), *comida* ko-MEE-dah (meal), and *fin* FEEN (end).

Pronounce *o* like oh, as in oh: *peso* PAY-soh (weight), *ocho* OH-choh (eight), and *poco* POH-koh (a bit).

Pronounce *u* like oo, as in cool: *uno* OO-noh (one), *cuchara* koo-CHAR-ah (spoon), and *usted* oos-TED (you).

Accent

The rule for accent, the relative stress given to syllables within a given word, is straightforward. If a word ends in a vowel, n, or s, accent the second-to-last syllable; if not, accent the last syllable.

Pronounce *gracias* GRAH-seeahs (thank you), *orden* OHR-dayn (order), and *carretera* kah-rray-TAY-rah (highway).

Otherwise, accent the last syllable: *venir* veh-NEER (to come), *ferrocarril* feh-rroh-cah-RREEL (railroad), and *edad* eh-DAHD (age).

For practice, apply the accent ("vowel, n, or s")

rule for the vowel-pronunciation examples above. Try to accent the words correctly without looking at the "answers" to the right.

Exceptions to the accent rule are always marked with an accent sign: (á, é, í, ó, or ú), such as *teléfono* tel-LAY-foh-noh (telephone), *jabón* hah-BON (soap), and *rápido* RAH-pee-doh (rapid).

Consonants

Seventeen Spanish consonants, *b, d, f, k, l, m, n, p, q, s, t, v, w, x, y, z,* and *ch,* are pronounced almost as in English; *h* is used, but is silent—not pronounced at all.

As for the remaining seven *(c, g, j, ll, ñ, r, and rr)* consonants, pronounce *c* "hard," like k as in keep: *cuarto* KWAR-toh (room), Tepic tay-PEEK (capital of Nayarit state). Exception: Before *e* or *i*, pronounce *c* "soft," like an English s, as in sit: *cerveza* sayr-VAY-sah (beer), *encima* en-SEE-mah (atop).

Before *a, o, u,* or a consonant, pronounce *g* "hard," as in gift: *gato* GAH-toh (cat), *hago* AH-goh (I do, make). Otherwise, pronounce *g* like h as in hat: *giro* HEE-roh (money order), *gente* HEN-tay (people).

Pronounce *j* like an English h, as in has: *jueves* WAY-vays (Thursday), *mejor* may-HOR (better).

Pronounce *ll* like y, as in yes: *toalla* toh-AH-yah (towel), *ellos* AY-yohs (they, them).

Pronounce *ñ* like ny, as in canyon: *año* AH-nyo (year), *señor* seh-NYOR (Mr., sir).

The Spanish *r* is very lightly trilled, with the tongue at the roof of your mouth like the British r in very ("vehdy"). Pronounce *r* like a very light English d, as in ready: *cuatro* KWAH-tdro (four). *Pero* PEH-roh (but) is almost like it sounds, but too much d and you'll have Pedro, or too much trilled r and it becomes *perro* (dog).

Pronounce *rr* like a Spanish *r,* but with much more emphasis and trill. Let your tongue flap. Practice with *burro* BOO-rroh (donkey), *carretera* kah-rray-TAY-rah (highway), and Carrillo cah-RREE-yoh (proper name), then really let go with *ferrocarril* feh-rroh-cah-RREEL (railroad).

Spanish Phrasebook

A profitable route to learning Spanish in Mexico is to refuse to speak English. Prepare yourself (instead of watching the in-flight movie) with a basic word list in a pocket notebook. Use it to speak Spanish wherever you go.

Basic and Courteous

Courtesy is very important to Mexican people. They will appreciate your use of basic expressions. (Note: The upside-down Spanish question mark merely warns the reader of the query in advance.)

Hello—*Hola*
How are you?—*¿Cómo está usted?*
Very well, thank you.—*Muy bien, gracias.*
okay, good—*bueno*
not okay, bad—*malo, feo*
and you?—*¿y usted?*
(Note: Pronounce *"y"* (and) like the English "ee," as in "keep.")
Thank you very much.—*Muchas gracias.*
please—*por favor*
You're welcome.—*De nada.*
Just a moment, please.—*Momentito, por favor.*
How do you say . . . in Spanish?—*¿Cómo se dice . . . en español?*
Excuse me, please (when you're trying to get attention).—*Excúseme, con permiso.*
Excuse me (when you've made a boo-boo).—*Lo siento.*
good morning—*buenos días*
good afternoon—*buenas tardes*
good evening—*buenas noches*
Sir (Mr.), Ma'am (Mrs.), Miss—*Señor, Señora, Señorita*
What is your name?—*¿Cómo se llama usted?*
Pleased to meet you.—*Con mucho gusto.* or simply *Mucho gusto.*
My name is . . . —*Me llamo . . .*
Would you like . . . ?—*¿Quisiera usted . . . ?*
Let's go to . . . —*Vámonos a . . .*
I would like to introduce my . . . —*Quisiera presentar mi . . .*

wife—*esposa*
husband—*esposo*
friend—*amigo* (male), *amiga* (female)
sweetheart—*novio* (male), *novia* (female)
son, daughter—*hijo, hija*
brother, sister—*hermano, hermana*
father, mother—*padre, madre*
See you later (again)—*Hasta luego (la vista).*
goodbye—*adiós*
yes, no—*sí, no*
I, you (showing respect), you (very familiar or a youth) he, she—*yo, usted, tú or ti, él, ella*
we, you (pl.), they—*nosotros, ustedes, ellos*
Do you speak English?—*¿Habla usted inglés?*
Speak more slowly, please—*Habla más despacio, por favor.*

Getting Around

If I could use only two Spanish phrases, I would choose *"Excúseme,"* followed by *"¿Dónde está . . . ?"*

Where is . . . ?—*¿Dónde está . . . ?*
the bus station—*la terminal autobús*
the bus stop—*la parada autobús*
the taxi stand—*el sitio taxi*
the train station—*la terminal ferrocarril*
the airport—*el aeropuerto*
the boat—*la barca*
the bathroom, toilet—*el baño, sanitorio*
men's, women's—*el baño de hombres, de mujeres*
the entrance, exit—*la entrada, la salida*
the pharmacy—*la farmacia*
the bank—*el banco*
the police, police officer—*la policía*
the supermarket—*el supermercado*
the grocery store—*la abarrotería*
the laundry—*la lavandería*
the stationery (book) store—*la papelería (librería)*
the hardware store—*la ferretería*
the (long distance) telephone—*el teléfono (larga distancia)*
the post office—*el correo*

the ticket office—*la oficina boletos*
a hotel—*un hotel*
a cafe, a restaurant—*una café, un restaurante*
Where (Which) is the way to . . . ?—*¿Dónde (Cuál) está el camino a . . . ?*
How far to . . . ?—*¿Qué tan lejos a . . . ?*
How many blocks?—*¿Cuántos cuadras?*
(very) near, far—*(muy) cerca, lejos*
to, toward—*a*
by, through—*por*
from—*de*
the right, the left—*la derecha, la izquierda*
straight ahead—*derecho, directo*
in front—*en frente*
beside—*a lado*
behind—*atrás*
the corner—*la esquina*
the stoplight—*la semáforo*
a turn—*una vuelta*
right here—*aquí*
somewhere around here—*acá*
right there—*allí*
somewhere around there—*allá*
street, boulevard, highway—*calle, bólevar, carretera*
bridge, toll—*puente, cuota*
address—*dirección*
north, south—*norte, sur*
east, west—*oriente (este), poniente (oeste)*

Doing Things

Verbs are the key to getting along in Spanish. They employ mostly predictable forms and come in three classes, which end in ar, er, and ir, respectively:

to buy—*comprar*
I buy, you (he, she, it) buys—*compro, compra*
we buy, you (they) buy—*compramos, compran*

to eat—*comer*
I eat, you (he, she, it) eats—*como, come*
we eat, you (they) eat—*comemos, comen*

to climb—*subir*
I climb, you (he, she, it) climbs—*subo, sube*
we climb, you (they) climb—*subimos, suben*

Got the idea? Here are more (with irregularities marked in bold).

to do or make—*hacer*
I do or make, you (he she, it) does or makes—**hago,** *hace*
we do or make, you (they) do or make—*hacemos, hacen*

to go—*ir*
I go, you (he, she, it) goes: **voy, va**
we go, you (they) go: **vamos, van**

to say, tell—*decir* (regular, except: **digo, dice, dicen** I say, you say, they say)
to talk—*hablar*
to love—*amar*
to swim—*nadar*
to walk—*andar*
to work—*trabajar*
to want—*desear, querer* (irregular: **quiero, quiere,** *queremos,* **quieren)**
to feel—*sentir* (irregular: **siento, siente,** *sentimos,* **sienten)**
to read—*leer*
to write—*escribir*
to repair—*reparar*
to arrive—*llegar*
to stay (remain)—*quedar*
to stay (lodge)—*hospedar*
to look at—*mirar*
to look for—*buscar*
to give—*dar* (regular, except: **doy,** I give)
to have—*tener* (irregular: **tengo, tiene,** *tenemos,* **tienen)**
to come—*venir* (irregular: *vengo, viene, venimos, vienen)*

Spanish has two forms of "to be." Use *estar* when speaking of location: "I am at home." **"Estoy** *en casa."* Use *ser* for state of being: "I am a doctor." **"Soy** *una doctora."* Estar is regular except for **estoy,** I am. Ser is very irregular:

to be—*ser*
I am, you (he, she, it) is—*soy, es*
we are, you (they) are—*somos, son*

At the Station and on the Bus

I'd like a ticket to . . . —*Quisiera un boleto a . . .*
first (second) class—*primera (segunda) clase*
round-trip—*ida y vuelta*
how much?—*¿cuánto?*
reservation—*reservación*
reserved seat—*asiento reservado*
seat number . . . —*número asiento . . .*
baggage—*equipaje*
Where is this bus going?—*¿Dónde va este autobús?*
What's the name of this place?—*¿Cómo se llama este lugar?*
Stop here, please.—*Pare aquí, por favor.*

Eating Out

A *restaurante* (res-tao-RAHN-tay) generally implies a fairly fancy joint, with prices to match. The food and atmosphere, however, may be more to your liking at other types of eateries (in approximate order of price): *comedor, café, fonda, lonchería, jugería, taquería.*

I'm hungry (thirsty).—*Tengo hambre (sed).*
menu—*lista, menú*
order—*orden*
soft drink—*refresco*
coffee, cream—*café, crema*
tea—*té*
sugar—*azúcar*
drinking water—*agua pura, agua potable*
bottled carbonated water (uncarbonated water)—*agua mineral (sin gas)*
glass—*vaso*
beer—*cerveza*
dark—*obscura*
draft—*de barril*
wine—*vino*
white, red—*blanco, tinto*
dry, sweet—*seco, dulce*
cheese—*queso*
snack—*antojo, botana*
daily lunch special—*comida corrida*
fried—*frito*
roasted—*asada*
barbecue, barbecued—*barbacoa, al carbón*
breakfast—*desayuno*

eggs—*huevos*
boiled—*tibios*
scrambled—*revueltos*
bread—*pan*
roll—*bolillo*
sweet roll—*pan dulce*
toast—*pan tostada*
oatmeal—*avena*
bacon, ham—*tocino, jamón*
salad—*ensalada*
lettuce—*lechuga*
carrot—*zanahoria*
tomato—*tomate*
oil—*aceite*
vinegar—*vinagre*
lime—*limón*
mayonnaise—*mayonesa*
fruit—*fruta*
mango—*mango*
watermelon—*sandía*
papaya—*papaya*
banana—*plátano*
apple—*manzana*
orange—*naranja*
fish—*pescado*
shrimp—*camarones*
oysters—*ostiones*
clams—*almejas*
octopus—*pulpo*
squid—*calamare*
with meat (without meat)—*con carne (sin carne)*
chicken—*pollo*
pork—*puerco*
beef, steak—*res, biftec*
the bill (or check)—*la cuenta*

At the Hotel

In the Guadalajara region, finding a reasonably priced hotel room presents no problem except during the high-occupancy weeks after Christmas and before Easter.

Is there . . . ?—*¿Hay . . . ?*
an (inexpensive) hotel—*un hotel (económico)*
an inn—*una posada*
a guesthouse—*una casa de huéspedes*
a single (double) room—*un cuarto sencillo (doble)*

with bath—*con baño*
shower—*ducha*
hot water—*agua caliente*
fan—*abanico, ventilador*
air-conditioning—*aire acondicionado*
double bed—*cama matrimonial*
twin beds—*camas gemelas*
How much for the room?—*¿Cuánto cuesta el cuarto?*
dining room—*comedor*
key—*llave*
towels—*toallas*
manager—*gerente*
soap—*jabón*
toilet paper—*papel higiénico*
swimming pool—*alberca, piscina*
the bill (or check), please—*la cuenta, por favor*

At the Bank

The often-long lines, short hours, and minuscule advantage in exchange rate at the *banco* make a private *casa de cambio* a very handy alternative:

bank—*banco*
money—*dinero*
money-exchange bureau—*casa de cambio*
I would like to exchange traveler's checks.—*Quisiera cambiar cheques de viajero.*
What is the exchange rate?—*¿Cuál es el cambio?*
How much is the commission?—*¿Cuánto cuesta el comisión?*
Do you accept credit cards?—*¿Aceptan tarjetas de crédito?*
money order—*giro*
teller's window—*caja*
signature—*firma*

Shopping

Es la costumbre—it is the custom—in Mexico that the first price is never the last. Bargaining often transforms shopping from a perfunctory chore into an open-ended adventure. Bargain with humor, and be prepared to walk away if the price is not right.

How much does it cost?—*¿Cuánto cuesta?*
too much—*demasiado*

expensive, cheap—*caro, barato (económico)*
too expensive, too cheap—*demasiado caro, demasiado barato*
more, less—*más, menos*
small, big—*chico, grande*
good, bad—*bueno, malo*
smaller, smallest—*más chico, el más chico*
larger, largest—*más grande, el más grande*
cheaper, cheapest—*más barato, el más barato*
What is your final price?—*¿Cuál es su último precio?*
Just right!—*¡Perfecto!*

Telephone, Post Office

In smaller Mexican towns, long-distance connections must be made at a central long-distance office, where people sometimes can sit, have coffee or a *refresco*, and socialize while waiting for their *larga distancia* to come through.

long-distance telephone—*teléfono larga distancia*
I would like to call . . . —*Quisiera llamar a . . .*
station to station—*a quien contesta*
person to person—*persona a persona*
credit card—*tarjeta de crédito*
post office—*correo*
general delivery—*lista de correo*
letter—*carta*
stamp—*estampilla*
postcard—*tarjeta*
aerogram—*aerograma*
air mail—*correo aero*
registered—*registrado*
money order—*giro*
package, box—*paquete, caja*
string, tape—*cuerda, cinta*

Formalities

Although many experienced travelers find Mexico among the most exotic of worldwide destinations, crossing the border remains relatively easy.

border—*frontera*
customs—*aduana*
immigration—*migración*
tourist card—*tarjeta de turista*
inspection—*inspección, revisión*

passport—*pasaporte*
profession—*profesión*
marital status—*estado civil*
single—*soltero*
married, divorced—*casado, divorciado*
widowed—*viudado*
insurance—*seguros*
title—*título*
driver's license—*licencia de manejar*
fishing, hunting, gun license—*licencia de pescar, cazar, armas*

At the Pharmacy, Doctor, Hospital

For a developing country, Mexico provides good health care. Even small Guadalajara regional towns have a basic hospital or clinic.

Help me please.—*Ayúdeme por favor.*
I am ill.—*Estoy enfermo.*
Call a doctor.—*Llame un doctor.*
Take me to . . . —*Lleve me a . . .*
hospital—*hospital, sanatorio*
drugstore—*farmacia*
pain—*dolor*
fever—*fiebre*
headache—*dolor de cabeza*
stomache ache—*dolor de estómago*
burn—*quemadura*
cramp—*calambre*
nausea—*náusea*
vomiting—*vomitar*
blood—*sangre*
medicine—*medicina*
antibiotic—*antibiótico*
pill, tablet—*pastilla*
aspirin—*aspirina*
ointment, cream—*pomada, crema*
bandage—*venda*
cotton—*algodón*
sanitary napkins (use brand name)
birth control pills—*pastillas contraceptivos*
contraceptive foam—*espuma contraceptiva*
diaphragm (best carry an extra)
condoms—*contraceptivas*
toothbrush—*cepilla dental*
dental floss (bring an extra supply)
toothpaste—*crema dental*

dentist—*dentista*
toothache—*dolor demuelas*

At the Gas Station

Some Mexican gas station attendants are experts at shortchanging you in both money and gasoline. If you don't have a locking gas cap, either insist on pumping the gas yourself, or make certain the pump is zeroed before the attendant begins pumping. Furthermore, the kids who hang around gas stations are notoriously light fingered. Stow every loose item—cameras, purses, binoculars—out of sight *before* you pull into the *gasolinera.*

gas station—*gasolinera*
gasoline—*gasolina*
leaded, unleaded—*plomo, sin plomo*
full, please—*lleno, por favor*
gas cap—*tapón*
tire—*llanta*
tire repair shop—*vulcanizadora*
air—*aire*
water—*agua*
oil (change)—*aceite (cambio)*
grease—*grasa*
My . . . doesn't work.—*Mi . . . no sirve.*
car—*automóvil*
battery—*batería*
radiator—*radiador*
alternator, generator—*alternador, generador*
tow truck—*grúa*
repair shop—*taller mecánico*
tune-up—*afinación*
auto parts store—*refaccionería*

Numbers and Time

zero—*cero*
one—*uno*
two—*dos*
three—*tres*
four—*cuatro*
five—*cinco*
six—*seis*
seven—*siete*
eight—*ocho*
nine—*nueve*

10—*diez*
11—*once*
12—*doce*
13—*trece*
14—*catorce*
15—*quince*
16—*dieciseis*
17—*diecisiete*
18—*dieciocho*
19—*diecinueve*
20—*veinte*
21—*veinte y uno,* or *veintiuno*
30—*treinta*
40—*cuarenta*
50—*cincuenta*
60—*sesenta*
70—*setenta*
80—*ochenta*
90—*noventa*
100—*cien*
101—*ciento y uno,* or *cientiuno*
200—*doscientos*
500—*quinientos*
1,000—*mil*
1999—*mil novecientos noventa y nueve*
2000—*dos mil*
2001—*dos mil y uno,* or *dos mil uno*
10,000—*diez mil*
100,000—*cien mil*
1,000,000—*milión*
one-half—*medio*
one-third—*un tercio*
one-fourth—*un quarto*

What time is it?—*¿Qué hora es?*
It's one o'clock.—*Es la una.*
It's three in the afternoon.—*Son las tres de la tarde.*
It's 4 A.M.—*Son las cuatro de la mañana.*

It's 6:30.—*Son las seis y media.*
It's a quarter till 11—*Es un cuarto hasta once.*
It's a quarter past five—*Es un cuarto después cinco.*

Monday—*lunes*
Tuesday—*martes*
Wednesday—*miércoles*
Thursday—*jueves*
Friday—*viernes*
Saturday—*sábado*
Sunday—*domingo*

January—*enero*
February—*febrero*
March—*marzo*
April—*abril*
May—*mayo*
June—*junio*
July—*julio*
August—*agosto*
September—*septiembre*
October—*octubre*
November—*noviembre*
December—*diciembre*

last Sunday—*domingo pasado*
last year—*año pasado*
next December—*diciembre próximo*
yesterday—*ayer*
tomorrow—*mañana*
the day after tomorrow—*pasado mañana*
in the morning—*en la mañana*
an hour—*una hora*
a week—*una semana*
a month—*un mes*
a week ago—*hace una semana*
after—*después*
before—*antes*

Suggested Reading

Some of these books are informative, others are entertaining, and all of them will increase your understanding of Mexico. Some are easier to find in Mexico than at home, and vice versa. Take a few along on your trip. If you find others that are especially noteworthy, let us know. Happy reading.

History

Calderón de la Barca, Fanny. *Life in Mexico, with New Material from the Author's Journals.* New York: Doubleday, 1966. Edited by H. T. and M. H. Fisher. An update of the brilliant, humorous, and celebrated original 1913 book by the Scottish wife of the Spanish ambassador to Mexico.

Casasola, Gustavo. *Seis Siglos de Historia Gráfica de Mexico (Six Centuries of Mexican Graphic History).* Mexico City: Editorial Gustavo Casasola, 1978. Six fascinating volumes of Mexican history in pictures, from 1325 to the present.

Collis, Maurice. *Cortés and Montezuma.* New York: New Directions Publishing Corp., 1999. A reprint of a 1954 classic piece of well-researched storytelling. Collis traces Cortés' conquest of Mexico through the defeat of his chief opponent, Aztec emperor Montezuma. He uses contemporary eyewitnesses—notably Bernal Díaz de Castillo—to revivify one of histories greatest dramas.

Cortés, Hernán. *Letters from Mexico.* Translated by Anthony Pagden. New Haven: Yale University Press, 1986. Cortés' five long letters to his king, in which he describes contemporary Mexico in fascinating detail, including, notably, the remarkably sophisticated life of the Aztecs at the time of the Conquest.

Díaz del Castillo, Bernal. *The True Story of the Conquest of Mexico.* Translated by Albert Idell. Garden City: Doubleday, 1956. A soldier's still-fresh tale of the Conquest from the Spanish viewpoint.

Garfias, Luis. *The Mexican Revolution.* Mexico City: Panorama Editorial, 1985. A concise Mexican version of the 1910–1917 Mexican revolution, the crucible of present-day Mexico.

Gugliotta, Bobette. *Women of Mexico.* Encino CA: Floricanto Press, 1989. Lively legends, tales, and biographies of remarkable Mexican women, from Zapotec princesses to Independence heroines.

León-Portilla, Miguel. *The Broken Spears: The Aztec Account of the Conquest of Mexico.* New York: Beacon Press, 1962. Provides an interesting contrast to Díaz del Castillo's account.

Meyer, Michael, and William Sherman. *The Course of Mexican History.* New York: Oxford University Press, 1991. An insightful, 700-plus-page college textbook in paperback. A bargain, especially if you can get it used.

Novas, Himlice. *Everything You Need to Know About Latino History.* New York: Plume Books (Penguin Group), 1994. Chicanos, Latin rhythm, La Raza, the Treaty of Guadalupe Hidalgo, and much more, interpreted from an authoritative Latino point of view.

Reed, John. *Insurgent Mexico.* New York: International Publisher's Co., 1994. Republication of 1914 original. Fast-moving, but not unbiased, description of the 1910 Mexican revolution by the journalist famed for his reporting of the subsequent 1917 Russian revolution. Reed, memorialized by the Soviets, was resurrected in the 1981 film biography *Reds.*

Ridley, Jasper. *Maximilian and Juárez*. New York: Ticknor and Fields, 1999. This authoritative historical biography breathes new life into one of Mexico's great ironic tragedies, a drama that pitted the native Zapotec "Lincoln of Mexico" against the dreamy, idealistic Archduke Maximilian of Austria-Hungary. Despite their common liberal ideas, they were drawn into a bloody no-quarter struggle that set the Old World against the New, ending in Maximilian's execution and the subsequent insanity of his wife, Carlota. The United States emerged as a power to be reckoned with in world affairs.

Ruíz, Ramon Eduardo. *Triumphs and Tragedy: A History of the Mexican People*. New York: W. W. Norton, Inc., 1992. A pithy, anecdote-filled history of Mexico from an authoritative Mexican-American perspective.

Simpson, Lesley Bird. *Many Mexicos*. Berkeley: The University of California Press, 1962. A much-reprinted, fascinating broad-brush version of Mexican history.

Unique Guide and Tip Books

American Automobile Association. *Mexico TravelBook*. Heathrow, FL: 1995. Published by the American Automobile Association, offices at 1000 AAA Drive, Heathrow, FL 32746-5063. Short sweet summaries of major Mexican tourist destinations and sights. Also includes information on fiestas, accommodations, restaurants, and a wealth of information relevant to car travel in Mexico. Available in bookstores, or free to AAA members at affiliate offices.

Burton, Tony. *Western Mexico, A Traveller's Treasury*. Guadalajara: Editorial Agata (Juan Manuel 316, Guadalajara 44100). A well-researched and lovingly written and illustrated guide to dozens of fascinating places to visit, both well-known and out of the way, in Michoacán, Jalisco, and Nayarit.

Church, Mike and Terry. *Traveler's Guide to Mexican Camping*. Kirkland, WA: Rolling Homes Press, P.O. Box 2099, Kirkland, WA 98083-2099. This is an unusually thorough guide to trailer parks all over Mexico, with much coverage of the Pacific Coast in general and the Puerto Vallarta region in particular. Detailed maps guide you accurately to each trailer park cited and clear descriptions tell you what to expect. The book also provides very helpful information on car travel in Mexico, including details of insurance, border crossing, highway safety, car repairs, and much more.

Franz, Carl. *The People's Guide to Mexico*. Emeryville, CA: Avalon Travel Publishing, 12th edition, 2002. An entertaining and insightful A-to-Z general guide to the joys and pitfalls of independent economy travel in Mexico.

Freedman, Jacqueline, and Susan Gersten. *Traveling like Everybody Else: A Practical Guide for Disabled Travelers*. Brooklyn NY: Lambda Publishing, Inc. It's presently out of print, but hopefully will be available soon at bookstores or from the publisher (3709 13th Ave., Brooklyn, NY 11218; tel. 718/972-5449).

Graham, Scott. *Handle with Care*. Chicago: The Noble Press, 1991. Should you accept a meal from a family who lives in a grass house? This insightful guide answers this and hundreds of other tough questions for persons who want to travel responsibly in the Third World.

Howells, John, and Don Merwin. *Choose Mexico*. Oakland, CA: Gateway Books (distributed by Publishers Group West, Berkeley, CA). A pair of experienced Mexico residents provide a wealth of astute counsel about the important questions—health, finance, home ownership, work, driving, legalities—of long-term travel, residence, and retirement in Mexico. Includes specific sections on Puerto Vallarta, Guadalajara, and Lake Chapala.

Jeffries, Nan. *Adventuring with Children.* San Francisco: Avalon Travel Publishing, 1992. This unusually detailed book starts where most travel-with-children books end. It contains, besides a wealth of information and practical strategies for general travel with children, specific chapters on how you can adventure—trek, kayak, river-raft, camp, bicycle, and much more—successfully with the kids in tow.

Rogers, Steve, and Tina Rosa. *The Shopper's Guide to Mexico.* Santa Fe, NM: John Muir Publications. A well-written guide to shopping in Mexico, with emphasis on handicrafts. Contains inventory details and locations of out-of-the-ordinary shops in towns and cities all over Mexico, including much on the Pacific centers, especially Puerto Vallarta, greater Guadalajara, Mazatlán, Pátzcuaro, and Oaxaca.

Stillman, Alan Eric. *Kwikpoint.* Alexandria VA: GAIA Communications, P.O. Box 238, Alexandria, VA 22313-0238; email: kwik point@his.com. Eight dollars by cash or check gets you a super handy, durable color foldout of pictures to point to when you need something in a foreign country. The pictures, such as a frying pan with fire under it (for "fried"), a compass (for "Which direction?"), a red lobster, and a cauliflower, are imaginative and unmistakable, anywhere between Puerto Vallarta and Pakistan or San Blas and Santander.

Weisbroth, Ericka, and Eric Ellman. *Bicycling Mexico.* New York: Hunter, 1990. These intrepid adventurers describe bike trips from Puerto Vallarta to Acapulco, coastal and highland Oaxaca, and highland Jalisco and Michoacán.

Werner, David. *Where There Is No Doctor.* Palo Alto: Hesperian Foundation (P.O. Box 1692, Palo Alto, CA 94302). How to keep well in the backcountry.

Fiction

Bowen, David, and Ascencio, Juan A. *Pyramids of Glass.* San Antonio: Corona Publishing Co., 1994. Two dozen–odd stories that lead the reader along a month-long journey through the bedrooms, the barracks, the cafes, and streets of present-day Mexico.

Doerr, Harriet. *Consider This, Señor.* New York: Harcourt Brace, 1993. Four expatriates tough it out in a Mexican small town, adapting to the excesses—blazing sun, driving rain, vast, untrammeled landscapes—meanwhile interacting with the local folks while the local folks observe them, with a mixture of fascination and tolerance.

Fuentes, Carlos. *Where the Air Is Clear.* New York: Farrar, Straus, and Giroux, 1971. The seminal work of Mexico's celebrated novelist.

Fuentes, Carlos. *The Years with Laura Díaz.* New York: Farrar, Straus, and Giroux, 2000. A panorama of Mexico from Independence to the 21st century, through the eyes of one woman, Laura Díaz, and her great-grandson, the author. One reviewer said that she " . . . as a Mexican woman, would like to celebrate Carlos Fuentes; it is worthy of applause that a man who has seen, observed, analyzed, and criticized the great occurrences of the century now has a woman, Laura Díaz, speak for him." Translated by Alfred MacAdam.

Jennings, Gary. *Aztec.* New York: Atheneum, 1980. Beautifully researched and written monumental tale of lust, compassion, love, and death in pre-Conquest Mexico.

Peters, Daniel. *The Luck of Huemac.* New York: Random House, 1981. An Aztec noble family's tale of war, famine, sorcery, heroism, treachery, love, and finally disaster and death in the Valley of Mexico.

Porter, Katherine Ann. *The Collected Stories.* New York: Delacorte, 1970.

Rulfo, Juan. *The Burning Plain.* Austin: University of Texas Press, 1967. A celebrated Guadalajara author tells stories of people torn between the old and new in Mexico.

Traven, B. *The Treasure of the Sierra Madre.* New York: Hill and Wang, 1967. Campesinos, *federales,* gringos, and *indígenas* all figure in this modern morality tale set in Mexico's rugged outback. The most famous of the mysterious author's many novels of oppression and justice set in Mexico's jungles.

Villaseñor, Victor. *Rain of Gold.* New York: Delta Books (Bantam, Doubleday, and Dell), 1991. The moving, best-selling epic of the author's family's gritty travails. From humble rural beginnings in the Copper Canyon, they flee revolution and certain death, struggling through parched northern deserts to sprawling border refugee camps. From there they migrate to relative safety and an eventual modicum of happiness in Southern California.

People and Culture

Berrin, Kathleen. *The Art of the Huichol Indians.* Lovely, large photographs and text by a symposium of experts provide a good interpretive introduction to Huichol art and culture.

Castillo, Ana. *Goddess of the Americas.* New York, Riverhead Books, 1996. Here, a noted author has selected from the works of seven interpreters of Mesoamerican female deities, whose visions range as far and wide as Sex Goddess, the Broken-Hearted, the Subversive, and the Warrior Queen.

Lewis, Oscar. *Children of Sánchez.* New York: Random House, 1961. Poverty and strength in the Mexican underclass, sympathetically described and interpreted by renowned sociologist Lewis.

Medina, Sylvia López. *Cantora.* New York: Ballantine Books, 1992. Fascinated by the stories of her grandmother, aunt, and mother, the author seeks her own center by discovering a past that she thought she wanted to forget.

Meyerhoff, Barbara. *Peyote Hunt: The Sacred Journey of the Huichol Indians.* Ithaca: Cornell University Press, 1974. A description and interpretation of the Huichol's religious use of mind-bending natural hallucinogens.

Palmer, Colin A. *Slaves of the White God.* Cambridge: Harvard University Press. A scholarly study of why and how Spanish authorities imported African slaves into America and how they were used afterwards. Replete with poignant details, taken from Spanish and Mexican archives, describing how the Africans struggled from bondage to eventual freedom.

Riding, Alan. *Distant Neighbors: A Portrait of the Mexicans.* New York: Random House Vintage Books. Rare insights into Mexico and Mexicans.

Toor, Frances (1890–1956). *A Treasury of Mexican Folkways.* New York: Crown Books, 1947, reprinted by Bonanza, 1985. An illustrated encyclopedia of vanishing Mexicana—costumes, religion, fiestas, burial practices, customs, legends—compiled during the celebrated author's 35-year residence in Mexico.

Wauchope, Robert, ed. *Handbook of Middle American Indians.* Vols. 7 and 8. Austin: University of Texas Press, 1969. Authoritative surveys of important Indian-speaking groups in northern and central (vol. 8) and southern (vol. 7) Mexico.

Flora and Fauna

Goodson, Gar. *Fishes of the Pacific Coast.* Stanford, California: Stanford University Press, 1988. Over 500 beautifully detailed color drawings highlight this pocket version of all you ever wanted to know about the ocean's fishes (including common Spanish names) from Alaska to Peru.

Leopold, Starker. *Wildlife of Mexico.* Berkeley: University of California Press. Classic, illustrated layperson's survey of common Mexican mammals and birds.

Mason, Jr., Charles T., and Patricia B. Mason. *Handbook of Mexican Roadside Flora.* Tucson: University of Arizona Press, 1987. Authoritative identification guide, with line illustrations, of all the plants you're likely to see in the Puerto Vallarta region.

Morris, Percy A. *A Field Guide to Pacific Coast Shells.* Boston: Houghton Mifflin. The compleat beachcomber's Pacific shell guide.

Novick, Rosalind, and Lan Sing Wu. *Where to Find Birds in San Blas, Nayarit.* Order through the authors at 178 Myrtle Court, Arcata, CA 95521; tel. 707/822-0790.

Pesman, M. Walter. *Meet Flora Mexicana.* Delightful anecdotes and illustrations of hundreds of common Mexican plants. Published around 1960, now out of print.

Peterson, Roger Tory, and Edward L. Chalif. *Field Guide to Mexican Birds.* Boston: Houghton Mifflin. With hundreds of Peterson's crisp color drawings, this is a must for serious birders and vacationers interested in the life that teems in the Puerto Vallarta region's beaches, jungles, lakes, and lagoons.

Wright, N. Pelham. *A Guide to Mexican Mammals and Reptiles.* Mexico City: Minutiae Mexicana, 1989. Pocket-edition lore, history, descriptions, and pictures of commonly seen Mexican animals.

Art, Architecture, and Crafts

Baird, Joseph. *The Churches of Mexico.* Berkeley: University of California Press. Mexican colonial architecture and art, illustrated and interpreted.

Cordrey, Donald, and Dorothy Cordrey. *Mexican Indian Costumes.* Austin: University of Texas Press, 1968. A lovingly photographed, written, and illustrated classic on Mexican Indians and their dress, emphasizing textiles.

Covarrubias, Miguel. *Indian Art of Mexico and Central America.* New York: Knopf, 1957. A timeless work by the renowned interpreter of *indígena* art and design.

Martínez Penaloza, Porfirio. *Popular Arts of Mexico.* Mexico City: Editorial Panorama, 1981. An excellent, authoritative, pocket-sized exposition of Mexican art.

Sayer, Chloë. *Arts and Crafts of Mexico.* San Francisco: Chronicle Books, 1990. All you ever wanted to know about your favorite Mexican crafts, from papier-mâché to pottery and toys and Taxco silver. Beautifully illustrated by traditional etchings and David Lavender's crisp black-and-white and color photographs.

Specialty Travel

Annand, Douglas R. *The Wheelchair Traveler.* Step-by-step guide for planning a vacation. Accessible information on air travel, cruises, ground transportation, selecting the right hotel, what questions to ask, solutions to problems that may arise, and accessibility to many wonderful destinations in the United States and Mexico.

Internet Resources

A number of websites may help you prepare for your Mexico trip:

Travel in General

www.travelocity.com, www.expedia.com
Major sites for airline and hotel bookings

**www.travelinsure.com,
www.worldtravelcenter.com**
Good for travel insurance and other services

Specialty Travel

www.elderhostel.org
Site of Boston-based Elderhostel, Inc., with a huge catalog of ongoing study tours, including three or four in the Guadalajara region.

www.miusa.org
Site of Mobility International, with a number of services for the handicapped, including many connections in Mexico.

Home Exchange

**www.homexchange.com,
www.intervacus.com, www.homelink.org**
Sites for temporarily trading your home with someone else in dozens of places in the world, including Guadalajara and Lake Chapala. tel. 800/756-HOME (for homexchange and intervacus), tel. 800/638-3841 (for homelink)

U.S. Government

www.travel.state.gov
The U.S. State Department information website. Lots of subheadings and links of varying completeness (e.g., the subheading covering medical care available worldwide listed only about a dozen doctors and hospitals). Other links, however had plenty of solid information, especially consular advice, such as travel advisories or information on accessing U.S. citizens arrested overseas. It also has a detailed list of Mexican consulates and offices in the United States, although some of it was out of date.

Destinations

Mexico in General

www.visitmexico.com
The official website of the public-private Mexico Tourism Board; a good general site for official information, such as entry requirements. It has lots of summarily informative subheadings, not unlike an abbreviated guidebook. If you can't find what you want here, call their toll-free information number 800/44-MEXICO.

www.mexconnect.com
A very good work in progress; with dozens upon dozens of subheadings and links, especially helpful for folks thinking of working, living, or retiring in Mexico.

www.amtave.com
This is the website of the Mexican Association of Adventure and Ecotourism. Lists contact addresses, telephones, and emails of dozens of ecotourism operators in nearly all Mexican states. Also links to ecotours and activities in many Mexican states.

www.planeta.com
Extensive ecotourism website with dozens of links to Mexico ecotourism adventures and information.

www.go2mexico.com
An aspiring commercial site that covers the Pacific Mexico destinations of Mazatlán, Puerto Vallarta, Ixtapa-Zihuatanejo, Acapulco,

Huatulco, Oaxaca, Guadalajara, and Manzanillo (including current weather reports.) However, several of these destinations are very incomplete at this writing. A work in progress, potentially good if completed.

www.mexicodesconocido.com.
The site of the excellent magazine *Mexico Desconocido ("Undiscovered Mexico")* that mostly features unusual and off-the-beaten-track destinations. Presently the site covers only a few locations; hopefully it will expand in the future.

Jalisco in General
www.jalisco.com
Fair site, with lots of random information, potentially helpful if it had more detailed subheadings and more links. Some links, such as connections to state government offices, might be useful, however.

www.puertovallarta.net
Wow! All you need to prepare for your Puerto Vallarta trip. Contains a wealth of details in dozens of competently linked subheadings, such as hotels, both humble and grand, car rentals, adventure tours, and on and on. Nearly every tourism service provider in Puerto Vallarta seems to be on board.

www.virtualvallarta.com
The relatively new website of *Vallarta Lifestyles* magazine. May eventually become strong like its parent magazine in things upscale, such as boutiques, expensive restaurants, and condo sales and rentals.

Guadalajara
www.vivegdl.com.mx
Official joint site of Guadalajara-area tourism offices. English translation available. Extensive, but contains only neutral summary information of limited usefulness. For example, they list lots of hotels, according to categories, with phone, fax, email addresses, and services available, but no prices, photos, or links

for reservations as most commercial sites do. The daily current events listing would be handy if you were in Guadalajara at the time you logged on.

www.businessgdl.com.mx
Business-oriented site of the Tourism and Economic Promotion of Guadalajara.

www.convencionesgdl.com.mx
Site of the Guadalajara Convention and Visitors Bureau.

www.tlaquepaque.gob.mx,
www.zapopan.gob.mx
Respective sites of Tlaquepaque and Zapopan municipal governments.

www.americansociety.org
Site of the very helpful and well-organized American Society of Jalisco, with many services for visitors; headquarters in the western Guadalajara district of Chapalita.

www.gotoamericanlegion.com
Site of the very popular local American Legion chapter (all welcome as social members) headquartered in Guadalajara's southwest suburban Las Fuentes district.

www.guadalajarareporter.com
Site of the English-language Guadalajara newspaper.

www.rr-mexico.com
Information on tour, counseling, and resettlement services in the Guadalajara area. Maintained by the friendly and very professional team of Sandy Brown and Mark Kunce, owners-operators of R&R in Mexico.

Chapala and Ajijic
www.chapala.com
The site of the excellent monthly Chapala-area newspaper, *El Ojo del Agua.* Doesn't contain the entire newspaper—only the (good, however) monthly lead articles per edition,

archived back about three years to the beginning of publication. Also the site of parent Coldwell Banker–Chapala Real Estate. Excellent for home rentals and sales.

www.ajijic.com
Site of Ajijic Real Estate; lots of Lake Chapala home rental and purchase information.

Accommodations Index

Restaurant Index

General Index

Acknowledgments

A host of sympathetic people both at home and in Mexico contributed mightily to this book. I first gratefully thank the multitude of unnamed Mexican people—in shops, on the streets, at their front doors, and behind hotel, *turismo,* and bank counters—who tolerantly responded to my queries. At times, their help was vital—such as that unforgettable episode when a dozen-odd campesinos pitched in and helped haul my car 100 feet up from a steep, boulder-strewn cornfield where I had suddenly and unexpectedly driven it one night.

To others I am also deeply indebted. In Guadalajara, a load of thanks to Leo Magaña of Mesón San José for his kindness and help. I owe the same to his son, Arturo, for his generosity and time spent in treating me to fascinating personal tours of Guadalajara neighborhoods. I am similarly grateful to Sandy Brown and Mark Kunce, of R&R in Mexico, for their generosity with their time and expertise.

I owe the same to many others: in Chapalita, to Irma Jepson López of Bed-and-Breakfast Irma; in Tlaquepaque, to guide Lino Gabriel G. Nuño, ironwork master Roman Gutierrez, and Veronica Flores of Casa de Artesanos. In Tonala, I thank my super-conscientious and kind guides from Tonala *turismo,* and Rafael Ángel and his American wife Diana Romo of Villas Don Blas. I owe a similar debt to my excellent tour guides from Zapopan tourism.

Farther afield, I am grateful to friendly and knowledgeable workers of Tapalpa tourism, publicity director Franzi at Río Caliente spa, Helena Elena Sauza, the personable director of the Sauza Museum in Tequila, and Javier López Ávila in Magdalena for generously imparting his knowledge and experience of opals to me. This book is much richer because of them.

Thanks also to the others who have encouraged me since then, especially my fellow members of the Society of American Travel Writers and San Francisco Bay Area Travel Writers. Singular among them was the late Rebecca Bruns, whose excellent guidebook, *Hidden Mexico,* has been a major inspiration for my present work.

Back home in Berkeley, thanks for the sympathetic cooperation of the friendly staff at my office-away-from-home, Cafe Espresso Roma. Special acknowledgement is due to espresso maestro Miguel and his skilled successors, whose delicious, individually decorated, early morning lattes made this book possible.

Thanks also to my friend and business partner, Halcea Valdes, who generously managed without me while I was away in Mexico.

I owe a debt beyond counting to my mother Joan Casebier, my late father and stepmother Bob and Hilda Whipperman, and my sister Doris Davis, for their help in making me who I am.

Finally, I owe a mountain of gratitude to my wife Linda, who cheerfully kept our home together during my absence and lovingly welcomed me back when I returned.

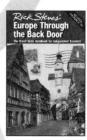